A Political Companion to Herman Melville

A POLITICAL COMPANION TO
Herman Melville

EDITED BY JASON FRANK

Scholarly publisher for the Commonwealth,
serving Bellarmine University, Berea College, Centre College of Kentucky, Eastern Kentucky University, The Filson Historical Society, Georgetown College, Kentucky Historical Society, Kentucky State University, Morehead State University, Murray State University, Northern Kentucky University, Transylvania University, University of Kentucky, University of Louisville, and Western Kentucky University.

Editorial and Sales Offices: The University Press of Kentucky
663 South Limestone Street, Lexington, Kentucky 40508-4008
www.kentuckypress.com

17 16 15 14 13   5 4 3 2 1

Library of Congress Cataloging-in-Publication Data

A Political Companion to Herman Melville / edited by Jason Frank.
pages cm
Includes bibliographical references and index.
ISBN 978-0-8131-4387-3 (hardcover : acid-free paper) —ISBN 978-0-8131-4389-7 (pdf) — ISBN 978-0-8131-4388-0 (epub)
1. Melville, Herman, 1819–1891—Political and social views. 2. Politics and literature—United States—History—19th century. I. Frank, Jason A., editor of compilation.
PS2388.P6P65 2013
813'.3—dc23
2013033109

This book is printed on acid-free paper meeting the requirements of the American National Standard for Permanence in Paper for Printed Library Materials.

Manufactured in the United States of America.

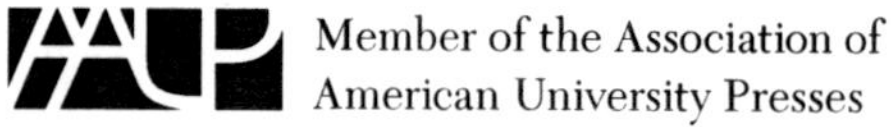

Member of the Association of
American University Presses

For John H. Schaar
1928–2011

Contents

Series Foreword

Those who undertake a study of American political thought must attend to the great theorists, philosophers, and essayists. Such a study is incomplete, however, if it neglects American literature, one of the greatest repositories of the nation's political thought and teachings.

America's literature is distinctive because it is, above all, intended for a democratic citizenry. In contrast to eras when an author would aim to inform or influence a select aristocratic audience, in democratic times public influence and education must resonate with a more expansive, less leisured, and diverse audience to be effective. The great works of America's literary tradition are the natural locus of democratic political teaching. Invoking the interest and attention of citizens through the pleasures afforded by the literary form, many of America's great thinkers sought to forge a democratic public philosophy with subtle and often challenging teachings that unfolded in narrative, plot, and character development. Perhaps more than that of any other nation's literary tradition, American literature is ineluctably political—shaped by democracy as much as it has in turn shaped democracy.

The Political Companions to Great American Authors series highlights the teachings of the great authors in America's literary and belletristic tradition. An astute political interpretation of America's literary tradition requires careful, patient, and attentive readers who approach a text with a view to understanding its underlying messages about citizenship and democracy. Essayists in this series approach the classic texts not with a "hermeneutics of suspicion" but with the curiosity of fellow citizens who believe that the great authors have something of value to teach their readers. The series brings together essays from varied approaches and viewpoints for the common purpose of elucidating the political teachings of the nation's greatest authors for those seeking a better understanding of American democracy.

Patrick J. Deneen
Series Editor

INTRODUCTION

American Tragedy

The Political Thought of Herman Melville

Jason Frank

> "The ship! The hearse!—the second hearse!" cried Ahab from the boat; "its wood could only be American!"
>
> —Herman Melville, *Moby-Dick*

Melville has not received as much attention from political theorists as some other major writers of the American Renaissance—especially Emerson, Whitman, and Thoreau. His work is left out of anthologies of American political thought, overlooked on syllabi, and very rarely engaged in professional research. Various explanations for this neglect come immediately to mind. Unlike the others, for example, Melville was never a political activist; he was not overtly engaged in the momentous political struggles of his time over slavery and white supremacy, industrialization and class conflict, western settlement and Native displacement, national unity and sectional discord, self-governance and imperial expansion. He was also almost exclusively a writer of fiction—short stories, novels, and poems—not of political essays, treatises, and reviews. Melville's work is moreover not easily situated on the ideological spectrum of left to right, liberal to conservative, and not easily placed within the discursive paradigms of liberalism and republicanism that often frame scholarship in the history of American political thought. His writing strikes a note of dissonance in the established harmonies of the American political tradition.

Though there are several outstanding anthologies examining Melville's work, this is the first to be dedicated solely to his political thought. This introduction proceeds from the premise that political theory's general neglect of Melville has impoverished our understanding not only of American political thought in the nineteenth century, but of the American political tradition itself. Melville's collected work—from *Typee* (1846) to *Billy Budd* (posthumously published in 1924)—offers what is arguably nineteenth-century America's most sustained interrogation of the American political imaginary, of the narratives and norms, principles and presuppositions, that animate the American political tradition and give shape to American political identity. Though Melville was not actively engaged in the political struggles mentioned above, the essays in this volume will show that his fiction wrestled with the conflicting values and commitments underwriting these struggles with a philosophical depth and subtlety unsurpassed by his contemporaries. Melville's "provocative, prophetic books," one recent biographer writes, "compose a kind of underground history of America."[1] Michael Rogin—the political theorist whose work on Melville is the most important exception to the field's general neglect of him—has dubbed Melville America's Marx because of Melville's systematic critique of the structures of domination in nineteenth-century America. Following Melville's own invitation in the opening line of *Moby-Dick* (1851), we might instead call him America's Ishmael, the quintessential biblical outcast and prophetic voice of America's dispossessed and disinherited—its "renegades and castaways."[2]

Although Melville was not directly engaged in the partisan politics or reform movements of his time, he demonstrated a preoccupation with political critique across the entire span of his writing career; it is seriously misleading to claim that "politics never engaged him deeply."[3] Melville sometimes evinced his literary preoccupation with politics by overtly espousing positions. His first novel, *Typee,* for example, includes lengthy condemnations of missionary violence and moral hypocrisy in the South Seas, reflections on the "civilized barbarity" of colonialism, and even a concluding vindication of Lord George Paulet's brief governance of the Hawaiian Islands. *Mardi* (1849), Melville's first work of experimental fiction, dwells on the violence of the slave trade and the moral inconsistencies of a slave-owning republic. *White-Jacket* (1850), his report of life aboard a military frigate, admires British naval policy while railing against the practice of flogging in the United States Navy. "The Paradise of Bachelors and the Tartarus of Maids" (1855) is, among other things, an indictment of the economic exploitation and spiritual alienation that characterized the industrial workplace, where workers in a demonic paper mill (in this case young women) "did not so much seem accessory wheels to the general machinery as mere cogs to the wheels," "blank-looking girls with blank, white folders in their blank hands, all blankly folding blank paper."[4]

These were controversial positions in his time, and Melville was criticized by some of his contemporaries for taking them.[5] Melville's political significance, however, goes far beyond his positions on the controversial issues of the day, and it also exceeds the political ideologies that underwrote those positions. More important for contemporary political theory is how Melville's fiction articulates political critique at the level of philosophical principle and deep cultural presupposition. Melville did not merely critically engage the politics of his time—the ideological controversies, conflicts of interest and identity, and personal animosities that define American democratic pluralism, then and now—but, rather, interrogated the very space of the political, the stage on which these controversies appeared and became publicly legible and significant. Melville's best work examines the usually inarticulate conditions that animate and surreptitiously unite competing political positions, claims, and identities. His work is preoccupied with what Toni Morrison has called "the unspeakable unspoken" in American politics, its unifying professions of faith, its hegemonic rites of assent.[6]

Melville's engagement with the unspeakable unspoken of American politics is perhaps most profoundly exemplified in his masterpiece, *Moby-Dick,* but this "little lower layer" of political preoccupation can be traced across the entire span of his work. Consider the following examples: *Typee*'s exposure of the distorting but hegemonic discourses of "savagery" and "civilization," and its investigation of how the arbitrary demarcations of cultural "taboo" work to naturalize relations of domination in everyday life (among both the Marquesas Islanders and European colonizers); Melville's subversive exploration of the artificiality and precariousness of seemingly natural social roles in *Pierre* (1852), especially those roles central to the Victorian cult of domesticity (sister, mother, and wife; son, brother, and husband); the influential philosophical examination of social entrapment and passive resistance in "Bartleby the Scrivener" (1853), with its reflections on the inscrutability of personal identity and the uncanny challenge posed by the "doctrine of preferences" to the "doctrine of assumptions"; *Benito Cereno*'s (1855) dramatization of the mechanisms through which white supremacy and fantasies of American innocence misrecognize violence as legitimate authority, and its demonstration of how the psychological interdependence of master and slave works to perpetuate and contest that violence; the American "Metaphysics of Indian-Hating" examined in *The Confidence-Man* (1857), and the co-implication it establishes between moral certitude and genocidal demonization (just "as the brother is to be loved," Melville writes, so "is the Indian to be hated"); the tightly imbricated discursive relationship between national identity and blood sacrifice, patriotism and death, poetically explored in *Battle-Pieces* (1866); and *Billy Budd*'s probing study of law's dependence on violence, the norm's exposure to the exception, and the tragic vicissitudes of political judgment in times of emergency and crisis.

These literary examinations of the unspeakable unspoken in American politics also demonstrate Melville's profound understanding of the political power of narrative and his subversive commitment to political possibilities opened up by narrative proliferation and reorientation (an understanding and commitment formally enacted in such works as *Moby-Dick,* "Bartleby the Scrivener," *Benito Cereno,* and *Billy Budd,* with their reflexive proliferation of competing stories *about* stories). "Truth uncompromisingly told will always have its ragged edges," Melville wrote in *Billy Budd,* and he employed this raggedness in his work to loosen the grip of authorized cultural narratives and tropes. Melville recognized that the principles and cultural presuppositions that compose the American political imaginary were primarily transmitted not by edict and argument so much as by tales and telling. He was acutely attuned to the stories that Americans tell themselves about themselves, and to the mechanisms through which these stories shaped—and continue to shape—American self-understanding, moral orientation, and identity. As many literary scholars have recognized, Melville had a distinctly biblical appreciation of America's defining "stories of peoplehood."[7] As is true of *Israel Potter*'s (1855) provocative retelling of the revolutionary birth of the nation—the book is ironically dedicated to "His Majesty, the Bunker-Hill Monument"—Melville's work at once mobilizes and subverts dominant cultural narratives, articulating their essential features and then exposing the values, commitments, and lives that these monumental narratives erase and deny. Potter's story, for example, begins heroically in the fight for American independence, but then deviates dramatically from the expected script of individual and political self-making established by such culturally paradigmatic works as Franklin's *Autobiography.* (Franklin is savaged in the novel.) Melville presents Potter as a revolutionary hero, but Potter's postrevolutionary life is defined by exile, loss, and disappointment rather than independence, progress, and triumphant achievement. Many of Melville's greatest stories are populated with such isolated individuals caught up, carried away, and tragically disregarded by the prevailing winds of modernity and progress, not only Israel Potter and that "inscrutable scrivener" Bartleby, but also Pip and Jimmy Rose, Don Benito and all those lost souls aboard the *Fidèle* as it makes its way down the Mississippi River. Melville's literary catalogue of ruined lives reads like the debris piling up at the feet of Walter Benjamin's "Angelus Novus" as he is swept backward by the winds of progress, mournfully wishing he could "stay, awaken the dead, and make whole what has been smashed."[8] Such stories are animated by a concern that America's fantastic narratives of heroic independence and futurity diminish the actual lives of mortal, vulnerable, interdependent human beings, especially those monumental narratives associated with American exceptionalism, the hegemonic discourse of American national experience to which Melville's oeuvre can be read as a sustained counternarrative—a resounding "No! in thunder."

"The United States has solved all the major problems of mankind," declared Melville's contemporary the great American orator and Massachusetts senator Edward Everett in 1853, perfectly exemplifying the exceptionalist hubris of his age.[9] Melville eloquently captured the core elements—and biblical associations—of American exceptionalism in a passage from *White-Jacket:*

> And we Americans are the peculiar, chosen people—the Israel of our time; we bear the ark of the liberties of the world. . . . God has predestined . . . great things from our race. . . . Long enough have we been skeptics with regard to ourselves, and doubted whether, indeed, the Messiah had come. . . . But he has come in *us,* if we but give utterance to his prompting. . . . Let us always remember that with ourselves almost for the first time in the history of the earth, national selfishness is unbounded philanthropy; for we cannot do a good to America but we give alms to the world.[10]

The messianic moral certitude of such exceptionalism not only defined mid-nineteenth-century American political culture, but reverberates across the long course of American political history, sometimes with an abiding sense of obligation and mutual sacrifice—as in Winthrop's "A Model of

Christian Charity" or Lincoln's Gettysburg Address—but often with the vicious triumphalism of armed innocence wronged—from the Pequot War to George W. Bush's wars of freedom. America has long seen itself as what Reinhold Niebuhr called "the darling of divine providence" and "tutor of mankind in its pilgrimage to perfection."[11] The idea that America's singular history is endowed with universal significance—that its "national selfishness" is the same as "unbounded philanthropy," and that doing "good to America" is to "give alms to the world"—has remained a potent concept in American political history. It engenders the sense of moral purity and "innocency" that leads one of Melville's paradigmatic American captains—Amasa Delano aboard the *Bachelor's Delight*—to reprove Don Benito with the chillingly familiar statement that "the past is passed; why moralize upon it? Forget it."[12] Melville's work is an extended response to Delano and the culture of freedom he personifies, an examination of the disavowal of tragedy, the haunting presence of past injustice, and the moral and political cost of such imperatives of independence, futurity, and forgetting.

In Melville's time these exceptionalist ideas were given influential articulation by his friend Evert Duyckinck and the Young America movement, democratic nationalists and literary boosters of American expansion and "Manifest Destiny" (a term coined by John L. Sullivan, one of their most prominent supporters). Melville was associated with Young America in his early career, but he eventually became a searing critic of their core ideals (they are satirized in *Pierre*). His early association with Young America may help explain why so many prominent twentieth-century scholars misunderstood Melville as a *proponent* of American exceptionalism rather than one of its most articulate and thoroughgoing critics. For Progressive admirers like Lewis Mumford and Vernon Parrington, as well as for cold war liberals such as F. O. Matthiessen, Melville was a committed exceptionalist, but one who grew increasingly skeptical of America's ability to live up to its professed ideals. Thus, Mumford could write that Melville "laid open America" and "was a yardstick to measure the shortcomings of its professed civilization," and Matthiessen could identify Melville with his transcendentalist contemporaries on the basis of their shared concern with American consumerism, materialism, and imperialism.[13] Whereas Melville's work was often condemned by his contemporaries as subversive, irreligious, and even mad, his twentieth-century admirers have just as often celebrated his work as a sane and sober literary affirmation of as-yet-unrealized American ideals. The twentieth-century canonization of Melville as a great American writer, and *Moby-Dick* as the great American novel, has been beset from the beginning by a tension, if not paradox: how can the writer said to best encompass and exemplify the "idea of America" in the nineteenth century also be responsible for the most rigorous literary interrogation of the underlying assumptions of that idea?

What many of his twentieth-century admirers failed to recognize was that Melville understood the very ideals invoked by his transcendentalist contemporaries to critique the failings of American society—freedom, independence, self-reliance—as complicit in the political pathologies they were called on to diagnose and critique. One of Melville's central political theoretical insights, dramatized across his work but most brilliantly engaged in *Moby-Dick,* is that, when viewed from "a little lower layer," America's defining ideal of freedom as autonomy engenders the material and spiritual forms of domination that mark American history and mar its democratic futures.[14] Melville's far-reaching literary explorations of the tragic interdependence of freedom and domination and its penetration of human affairs—from the formal policies and legislation of the state to the unconscious motivations of individuals and collectives—help define his continued significance to scholars interested in the complexities of the American political tradition and to present-day citizens critically reflecting on their political condition, so powerfully defined by pervasive border anxieties coupled with feral libertarianism. Melville's insights on these questions are just as relevant to today's "don't tread on me" democracy as they were in the decade leading up to the Civil War.

While most readers agree on the sharply critical thrust of Melville's work—approaching him as "one of early America's frankest commentators on the hopes and failures of democracy"—many also lose sight of the precise conceptual nature of Melville's critique.[15] This is of obvious importance for political theorists turning to Melville's work. The central conceptual difference around the question of critique may be stated as follows: Was Melville engaged in a form of immanent critique? Is he best understood as a "connected critic" who appealed to the highest ideals professed by American society—formal equality, for example, or the rights of "life, liberty, and the pursuit of happiness"—in order to critique its failure to live up to those ideals in practice? Or, on the contrary, was Melville's political critique more radical? Does Melville's work adopt a critical perspective *beyond* those most highly professed ideals, thereby bringing the ideals themselves into critical focus?[16] If the former conceptualization is more accurate, then Melville can be placed alongside such other prominent nineteenth-century critics of American democracy as Emerson, Whitman, and Thoreau. This Melville remains inscribed within the horizon of American exceptionalism and its hegemonic "rites of assent," where even political protest performs the work of cultural authorization through an overarching commitment to the promise of the new, to what Sacvan Bercovitch, the most influential proponent of this view, describes as America's "long-nurtured vision of futurity."[17] If Melville writes from a perspective beyond the horizon of those ideals, however, then his work brings the prospects and the precepts of American democracy into a more skeptical and critical view.

In this latter instance, it might be tempting to situate Melville's work *outside* the tradition of American political thought altogether—as, for example, Louis Hartz famously did with the work of the nineteenth-century conservative sociologist George Fitzhugh.[18] But Melville's work is not so easily bracketed from the tradition. Unlike Fitzhugh, whose *Cannibals All!* (1849) defended southern race slavery from the perspective of a feudal authoritarianism reminiscent of Thomas Carlyle, Melville sustained a conflicted and tragic commitment to the democratic ideals he scrutinized in his work, at once affirming and exposing them. "Stay true to the dreams of thy youth!" was the telling challenge Melville wrote to himself on the box holding his final manuscript of *Billy Budd*. Melville's political thought unfolds primarily in the tragic mode, but his affirmation of tragedy does not merely reflect a "fatalistic attitude toward political change tied to his pessimistic view of mankind."[19] One way to appreciate his distinct contribution to American political thought is to understand how he lodges tragedy at the very heart of a dominant tradition built around its systematic disavowal. Melville was, as Joyce Carol Oates writes, "imbued with a tragic vision as elevated as that of Sophocles and Shakespeare," making him America's "tragic visionary."[20] Like Sophocles's and Shakespeare's, Melville's work chastens and mitigates. In the place of moral self-certitude and messianic providentialism, he expresses skepticism and doubt; in the place of capacious perfectionism he emphasizes finitude and limitation. Melville's work dwells on irresolvable tensions, contradictions, and paradoxes: with every triumph comes a defeat (the "cadaverous triumphs" of "Bartleby"), with every emancipation a new form of entrapment (the "stalled winds" of *Benito Cereno*'s very non-

Hegelian master-slave dialectic), with every moral advance a hidden moral cost (the heroic monumentalization of independence in *Israel Potter* diminishes the actual lives of those who fought for it). Melville's ubiquitous sea metaphor captures this worldview in an all-encompassing symbolism: it is a space of freedom *and* a space of paralysis, a space of joyous exhilaration *and* a space of terror. In *Moby-Dick* only the black cabin boy, Pip, "the most insignificant of the *Pequod*'s crew," caught in the whale line and temporarily abandoned at sea, fully grasps this tragic duality and the basic challenge it poses for political life.

Melville openly declares his affiliation with tragedy in "Hawthorne and His Mosses" (1850), a text that announces Melville's own literary project as much as it describes Hawthorne's. There Melville writes admiringly of Hawthorne: "He says No! in thunder, but the Devil himself cannot make him say yes. For all who say yes lie."[21] Melville's brilliant appreciation of Hawthorne's "blackness, ten times black" reveals the countervailing skepticism and Calvinistic sense of original sin that Melville shared with the older writer, to whom he dedicated *Moby-Dick* (while also suggesting the centrality of race to America's own tragic history). Both were sharply critical of the moral perfectionism of their contemporaries and deeply suspicious of utopian thinking. Though Melville and Hawthorne shared a tragic sense of human limitation at odds with the triumphalism of their age, however, the political ethos that each cultivated from this shared sentiment was remarkably different. Hawthorne's skepticism led him to embrace a politics of acquiescence if not outright indifference—it enabled what one biographer calls "a cowardly protection and freedom from commitment"—whereas Melville's work emphasizes the inescapability of the double binds of tragedy, the dilemmas of human agency in a world of "mortal inter-indebtedness," but then it also continues to wrestle with affirmation and the imperatives of action nonetheless.[22]

Some scholars who have emphasized the tragic dimensions of Melville's thinking have overlooked this important contrast and its political consequences. The emphasis on tragedy among many cold war admirers of Melville, for example, was primarily intended to deflate the hubris of political radicalism—its purported utopianism—and to affirm instead a perseverant human spirit that achieves ethical wisdom—if not political emancipation—through undergoing struggle with "a deluge of calamity." Their association of Melville with a "moral humanism" that transcends the realm of politics, or accepts it only as an unfortunate concession to necessity, might be more accurately characterized as a "mortalist humanism," since it emphasized shared vulnerability, precariousness, and finitude as the ethical basis of a common humanity.[23] C. Wright Mills rightly targeted this politically quiescent conception of tragedy as an abdication of political responsibility and a replacement of social and political action with the solace of individual understanding and ethical satisfaction. Rather than affirming such intellectual and ethical withdrawal from the conflicting imperatives of political life, Melville's dramatization of tragedy is sustained by an energizing struggle against the tragic insights his work continually affirms; indeed, the very thumping vitality of Melville's prose seems stylistically to defy quiescence and resignation. Hawthorne seems to have recognized this very important difference between them in a journal entry written shortly after a despondent Melville had visited him in England (where Hawthorne was serving as the American consul in Liverpool). Melville can "neither believe, nor be comfortable in his unbelief," Hawthorne wrote, "and he is too honest and courageous not to try to do one or the other."[24]

Hawthorne's invocation of Melville's "honest and courageous" struggle with divinity and religious belief applies equally to Melville's fraught commitment to democracy and its core ideals. Melville embraced "a ruthless democracy on all sides," but he did not shrink from confronting the dangers and violence attending that commitment.[25] In placing tragedy at the heart of his political thinking, Melville sought to establish democratic commitment in a chastened recognition of the failure of any unitary and foundational perspective, not to treat it as an expression of Nature or provide it with a new moral foundation. (Unlike most present-day democratic theorists, Melville did not believe in the reconciling power of abstract principles.) As Robert Milder insightfully writes, "Democracy in Melville's writing is not set against a backdrop of universal consonance and seen as its natural expression in society and politics; it is set against the backdrop of blackness, or tragic dissonance, and advanced as a humanly wrought stay against nothingness and common victimhood."[26] Melville hoped to reorient democratic politics through counternarratives that could engender what he described in *Moby-Dick* as an honest and courageous ethos of "mortal inter-indebtedness" that might sustain the hard political work of this "humanly wrought stay against nothingness" and disenthrall readers of their fantasies of "masterlessness," of their cherished delusions of chosenness and "innocency."[27] Melville even cast a critical eye on the defining American value of freedom itself, which he believed, taken as a superordinate ideal, set the course for self-destruction, not to mention the terrible violence it inflicts on those perceived as obstacles to its (impossible) achievement. In the place of the "City upon a Hill" and the "Citadel of Liberty," "Manifest Destiny" and "Nature's Nation," Melville envisioned a more reflexive, chastened, and just democratic politics, one animated by a tragic awareness of its inevitable complicities and exclusions, and one mature enough to confront the basic difficulties of humans living together—the vicissitudes of our political life—rather than disavow these difficulties through escapist fantasies of absolute independence.

The essays collected in this volume do not speak with a single voice or always concur with the broad interpretation of Melville's political thought put forward here. Indeed, some contributors contest this account of Melville as tragic critic of the dominant traditions of American politics and culture (for example, Ferguson, McWilliams, and Berkowitz), whereas others extend and elaborate on this account by examining particular works and themes in closer detail (for example, Mihic, Shulman, Hecht, Mariotti, Balfour, and Dumm). Others focus on a different set of contemporary political and theoretical issues entirely or set Melville in a more international and universalist context (for example, Attell, Jonik, Strong, and Culbert). Without expressing enforced consensus, all of these essays demonstrate how particular works—from Melville's early South Sea adventures to *Billy Budd,* from sprawling and difficult novels like *Moby-Dick* and *Pierre* to lesser-known stories such as "Cock-A-Doodle-Doo!" and "The Encantadas"—insightfully engage with questions of central importance for political theorists and historians of political thought. The result is a richly ragged account of Melville as a political thinker who was preoccupied with political dilemmas from the beginning to the end of his writing career. The chronological organization of the volume aims to provide readers with a sense of this continuity of preoccupation, appreciation for the range and diversity of Melville's work, and the juxtaposition of different essays focused on more widely known and discussed texts (*Typee, Moby-Dick,* "Bartleby the Scrivener," *Benito Cereno,* and *Billy Budd*).

In "Who Eats Whom? Melville's Anthropolitics at the Dawn of Pacific Imperialism," Kennan Ferguson rejects readings of Melville that interpret *Typee* and *Omoo* as unambiguously critical of American empire. Ferguson argues that Melville develops an "anthropolitical imaginary" in these early novels that subverts European colonial scripts of civilization and barbarism but that offers a different and more distinctly American justification for colonialism in their place. These novels develop a "scientific" and "zoological" view of indigeneity that "dislocates Pacific Islanders into the realm of pure nature" and affirms the preservation of cultural difference as a means of conquest and domination. According to Ferguson, *Typee* and *Omoo* establish a distinctive imperial framework that Melville develops in his later work and that influences American understandings of its own imperial prospects in the second half of the nineteenth century. Sophia Mihic's contribution, "'The End Was in the Beginning': Melville, Ellison, and the Democratic Death of Progress in *Typee* and *Omoo*," takes up Ferguson's provocation and offers a sharply contrasting view of Melville's early novels. Mihic argues that Melville refuses, "to force a verb, [to] noble savage [the Marquesan Islanders] out of their humanity" and ascribe to them a "nature" on which a civilizational discourse of progress and modernization might be founded and authorized. In Tommo and Toby's encounter with the Typees, "states of artifice meet states of artifice," Mihic writes, and through them Melville develops an alternative framework for thinking about cross-cultural dialogue and political action "without the operative assumption of a better future and without the guarantee of one's own status." Mihic draws out the political consequences of these insights through a productive comparison with Ralph Ellison's exploration of similar themes in *Invisible Man* (a novel that begins with an epigraph from *Benito Cereno*). On Mihic's reading, both Melville and Ellison force readers to confront the responsibility of political action without the falsifying support of the "world picture of progress," and to "act within a field of present possibility rather than wait for a logic of history."

In "Chasing the Whale: *Moby-Dick* as Political Theory," George Shulman does not enter into debates over Melville as imperialist or anti-imperialist, but he turns instead to examine how *Moby-Dick*'s tragic emplotment of "romances of liberal emancipation and national redemption" refuses the criteria often used to frame those debates. Shulman's complex excavation of tragedy differs from those that reduce "the tragic" to a particular content or worldview. Instead, Shulman shows that Melville's deployment of tragedy dramatizes the conflictive perspectives and experiences undergone in the novel. To read *Moby-Dick* "not as a melodrama, or as a philosophic treatise defending a single (even 'tragic') point of view, but as a tragedy," Shulman writes, "is to experience the mutually constituting tension between 'Ahab' and 'Ishmael' as modalities of democratic life, at once incommensurate and necessary." Shulman, in other words, aims not to extract a political theory from Melville's great novel but to seize on the novel as an exemplary occasion for reevaluating what political theory is, what we should expect from it, and how it might operate within a broader democratic context. In this, according to Shulman, Melville's novel shares much in common with ancient tragedy itself, "a form of mediation by which a political community can reflect on its core axioms, constitutive practices, and fateful decisions."

Susan McWilliams's "Ahab, American" also rejects readings of *Moby-Dick* that reduce the novel to a series of political lessons, particularly those readings that present Ahab as a pathological and even totalitarian Other to American liberalism and affirm Ishmael as the good, tolerant, democratic alternative that Melville endorses. While McWilliams does not portray Melville as gripped by the double binds of tragedy to the same extent as Shulman—her essay is guided by Tocquevillean values of civic association and fraternal interdependence—she does portray Ahab as a representative American whose isolation and desire to dominate are shared by the *Pequod*'s motley crew and, by extension, the American citizenry they represent. As such, *Moby-Dick* dramatizes widespread practices and norms that seriously threaten "democratic flourishing in the United States" in Melville's own time and our own.

In "'Mighty Lordships in the Heart of the Republic': The Anti-Rent Subtext to *Pierre*," Roger W. Hecht examines other obstacles to "democratic flourishing" by situating one of Melville's most difficult and controversial novels in an often-overlooked political context. Hecht argues that Melville's treatment of the Anti-Rent Wars, which pitted tenant farmers against large landed proprietors in New York during the 1840s, serves as the platform for Melville's philosophically rigorous interrogation of the "natural" claims to property rights in the nineteenth century, and how these rights were used to justify the creation of "Mighty Lordships in the Heart of the Republic" that made a mockery of America's celebrated democratic equality. The Glendinning family's hidden illegitimacies expose a gulf between property and propriety, ownership and moral authority, in the novel that challenges central premises of American liberalism and questions its compatibility with democracy. According to Hecht, Melville's novel relentlessly tracks the consequences of this founding contradiction and how it grounds the "larger social and political criticism scholars have found in *Pierre*."

Turning from Melville's novels to his short stories from the 1850s—several of them compiled in *Piazza Tales* (1856)—Shannon Mariotti's "Melville and the Cadaverous Triumphs of Transcendentalism" revisits Melville's uncertain relationship to Emerson and Thoreau. Surveying the inconclusive scholarship on this question, Mariotti develops her own distinctive account of this relationship through a careful reading of what she considers two "companion" stories: "Cock-A-Doodle Doo!" and "Bartleby the Scrivener." Mariotti argues that Melville elaborates a "skeptical critique of transcendental practices of awakening" and their underlying "theory and practice of self-reliance," which terminates not in noble autonomy but in an abstract evasion of socially embedded and embodied life. In "Language and Labor, Silence and Stasis: Bartleby among the Philosophers," Kevin Attell situates "Bartleby the Scrivener" in a very different philosophical context by examining the story's importance for an influential group of modern philosophers: Maurice Blanchot, Gilles Deleuze, Jacques Derrida, Giorgio Agamben, Michael Hardt and Antonio Negri, and Slavoj Žižek. Attell argues that the remarkable uptake of Melville's tale by Continental theorists has mediated the polemics and disagreements between them and can serve as an illuminating prism for understanding their competing political preoccupations, especially at the level of "first principles of the philosophical-political argument." Arguing that the Continental "Bartleby" crystallizes into two dominant themes—the withdrawal of language and meaning, and the productivity of labor and action—Attell demonstrates not only the philosophical complexity of Melville's story, but also the political resources it offers to present-day efforts to think politics beyond the binary organization of our conceptual and institutional life, a politics that points to a "new space outside the hegemonic position *and* its negation."

In "Melville's 'Permanent Riotocracy'" Michael Jonik also turns to contemporary Continental philosophy, and especially to the work of Deleuze, alongside the South American revolutions of 1808–1826, to elaborate and explain a central political theme in Melville's work: the recurrent trope of mutiny, sedition, insurrection, and riot. Referring to many of Melville's works, but focused primarily on his enigmatic "Encantadas," Jonik argues that Melville's "permanent riotocracy" is misunderstood as a conservative's skeptical regard for the possibilities of revolutionary emancipation; rather, it is Melville's effort to diagnose "the structure of the workings of revolt" and envision new forms of egalitarian collectivity. The "outlandish politics" reiterated across Melville's work aims to knock "the ego world off its identity axis," Jonik writes, and conceive a "politics that does not consist in an instituted, consolidated paternal authority or state-controlled system, but multiplies into an 'archipelago of brothers, a community of explorers,' mutually implicated in the struggle for universal emancipation."

Melville's literary reflections on the workings of rebellion and insurrection are also at the heart of the volume's two essays on *Benito Cereno,* Melville's tragic masquerade of racial domination and slave rebellion. In "What Babo Saw: *Benito Cereno* and 'the World We Live In,'" Lawrie Balfour examines the story's "imaginative destabilization of prevailing fictions of race" and its "attention to the rituals that cloaked the viciously inegalitarian racial order" to argue that the story reveals as much about how racial domination operates in the *wake* of slavery as it does about the racist justifications for enslavement itself. According to Balfour, *Benito Cereno* allows readers to see how racial domination persists in slavery's afterlife not in spite of "white goodwill," but, in part, because of it. In the context of radical racial inequality, civic goods like "friendship" and "social trust," much lauded by democratic theorists and political scientists alike, work to obscure the living legacies of slavery and, in doing so, help sustain them. Tracy B. Strong's contribution—"'Follow Your Leader': *Benito Cereno* and the Case of Two Ships"—also centers on the story's examination of the mechanisms of racial domination, but he situates this examination in relation to what he considers broader questions of sovereignty, leadership, and rule: to what there is in all "human relations [that] gives rise to slavery." Strong argues that while focused on the dynamics of racial domination, Melville's story also illuminates troubling continuities between sovereignty and enslavement; it approaches "slavery as a *consequence* of the fact of domination and it is thus about the meaning of how one follows one who is in power." The novel "impresses on the reader the ease with which one accepts one's prejudices as natural, and the difficulty in abandoning them. . . . *This difficulty is made all the greater by virtue of the fact that one is not clear for what one abandons them.*" To "follow your leader," Strong argues, is to ultimately be enthralled by—and driven to—death.

Thomas Dumm's "The Metaphysics of Indian-Hating Revisited" turns to the last novel Melville published in his lifetime—*The Confidence-Man*—

to examine the distinctive form of racial demonization Melville analyzes there, and its solemn echoes in subsequent American political culture, from the novels of Laura Ingalls Wilder to Vice President Dick Cheney's rationalization for the War on Terror. According to Dumm, Melville's "Metaphysics of Indian-Hating" has two prominent characteristics: proclamations of innocence vis-à-vis their enemies, and a related sense of moral superiority over them. Like Strong in his analysis of domination, Dumm argues that Melville attempted to provide a political and existential analysis of the psychosocial dynamics of demonization. Melville, he writes, sought "to understand the origins of a permanent human emotion, that of hatred, and its changing object that becomes fixed, an obsession. In this sense his understanding is as close to Freud's as it may have been to Plato's."

In "Melville's War Poetry and the Human Form"—the only essay in the volume dedicated to Melville's poetry—Roger Berkowitz examines the tragic vision of war developed in *Battle Pieces and Aspects of the War* (1866). According to Berkowitz, Melville's poetic reflections on the Civil War offer a searching examination of the necessity and insufficiency of "forms, measured forms," in political life. Human spirit and vitality surge in times of war, even as humanity is undone; war ravages human association and brings new association to life; it breaks with law and procedure, yet demands a "lawful formality that will straitjacket human passion into an equally human need for order." In the end, Berkowitz considers Melville's Civil War poems as attempts to imbue poetic form with the "compelling power to rebind a broken people." As Berkowitz notes, Melville's troubling vision of war as the occasion for "formal acts of greatness" through which we might "bind ourselves to a grand vision of who we are" also has powerful echoes in his last work of fiction, the posthumously published *Billy Budd*.

The volume's last two chapters offer mutually supporting readings of *Billy Budd* that break from recent interpretations focused on dilemmas of legal form and judgment during "states of exception." Like Berkowitz's, Jason Frank's contribution—"'The Lyre of Orpheus': Aesthetics and Authority in *Billy Budd*"—focuses on the problem of "forms, measured forms," but for Frank this concern leads to an investigation of the mechanisms of aesthetic-affective captivation and the role of these mechanisms in producing, sustaining, and contesting authoritative relations aboard the H.M.S. *Bellipotent* and, by extension, within the American republic during the Gilded Age. On Frank's reading, Melville's preoccupation with the performative maintenance of political authority in the novel is "before the law" in two distinct senses: "it is at once *prior to* law and a question of law's appearance *in front of* its beholden subjects." Jennifer L. Culbert's "Melville's Law" also attends to the appearance or presentation of law through a reading of *Billy Budd* that moves beyond approaches that attempt to grasp the "essence of law" as an object of inquiry (especially prominent in recent "Law and Literature" scholarship) to an appreciation for the strange and paradoxical dilemmas that emerge in the *quest* for such answers. For Culbert these questions are central to the "experience of law" itself, which is obscured by the dominant legal-positivist portrait of law—"being subject to an external or internal will"—and has a surprising resonance with the shattering experience of love. The image of law that emerges from Culbert's essay is not a "willed blow resolving matters" but a "touch exposing and unsettling them," thereby demonstrating the continued vitality of Melville's final work of fiction for provoking us to reflect on our own experience being subjects to—and of—the law.

Melville's admirers have often wondered at his prescience and prophetic power, how he managed to capture a century and a half ago, in the words of C. L. R. James, "the world in which we live."[28] The essays gathered here should only enhance that appreciation and wonder. Taken together, they demonstrate Melville's importance to American political thought—and especially to its dissenting traditions—but also to political theoretical reflection more broadly construed. Melville does not offer us a unifying public philosophy, and we should be skeptical of efforts to translate his work into a clarified and systematic political theory. His stories, novels, and poems, however, provoke us to engage more deeply and reflectively with some of the most pressing issues of our political life—to restate just a few engaged above: empire, freedom, race, progress, memory, violence, individualism, democracy, war, and law—and to do so without the mendacious simplifications of our public discourse and the arid abstractions of much of our political theory. Melville's political thought does not offer up authoritative rules, norms, procedures, or principles that might adjudicate our political conflicts; it does not save us from the difficult work of facing up to—and wrestling with—these difficulties ourselves. Taking Melville's work seriously as political theory can provoke us to think more reflexively about what we expect political theory to provide, and what kind of authority it can claim when it is situated in a purported democracy and addressed to free and equal democratic citizens.

Notes

1. Laurie Robertson-Lorant, *Melville: A Biography* (1996; repr., Amherst: University of Massachusetts Press, 1998), xvi.

2. Michael Paul Rogin, *Subversive Genealogy: The Politics and Art of Herman Melville* (New York: Knopf, 1983). Two other important exceptions to political theory's general neglect of Melville's work are Wilson Carey McWilliams, "Herman Melville: The Pilgrim," in McWilliams, *The Idea of Fraternity in America* (Berkeley: University of California Press, 1973), 328–371; and John H. Schaar, "The Uses of Literature for the Study of Politics: The Case of Melville's *Benito Cereno*," in Schaar, *Legitimacy in the Modern State* (New Brunswick, N. J.: Transaction, 1981), 53–88.

3. Andrew Delbanco, *Melville: His World and Work* (New York: Knopf, 2005), 155. Delbanco's wonderful book provides plenty of evidence to trouble this claim.

4. Herman Melville, "The Paradise of Bachelors and the Tartarus of Maids," in *Billy Budd and Other Stories* (New York: Penguin, 1986), 277.

5. The reception of Melville's work, and the frequent focus of his contemporaries on the controversial political positions taken in them, is documented in Brian Higgins and Hershel Parker, eds., *Herman Melville: The Contemporary Reviews* (New York: Cambridge University Press, 1995).

6. Toni Morrison, "Unspeakable Things Unspoken: The Afro-American Presence in American Literature," *Michigan Quarterly Review* 28, no. 1 (1989): 1–34. Morrison's focus is on white supremacy and the centrality of race to classic American literature. She emphasizes Melville's significance in this regard, describing him as the canonical American writer it "has been almost impossible to keep under lock and key."

7. Ilana Pardes insightfully elaborates this point in relation to Melville's subversive resignification of biblical stories in *Melville's Bibles* (Berkeley: University of California Press, 2008). See also Rogers M. Smith, *Stories of Peoplehood: The Politics and Morals of Political Membership* (New York: Cambridge University Press, 2003).

8. Walter Benjamin, "Theses on the Philosophy of History," in *Illuminations: Essays and Reflections*, ed. Hannah Arendt (New York: Schocken Books, 1968), 257.

9. Quoted in Robertson-Lorant, *Melville: A Biography*, 332.

10. Herman Melville, *White-Jacket; or, The World in a Man-of-War*, ed. Harrison Hayford, Herschel Parker, and G. Thomas Tanselle (Evanston and Chicago: Northwestern University Press and the Newberry Library, 1970), 151; emphasis in original.

11. Reinhold Niebuhr, *The Irony of American History* (1952; repr., Chicago:

University of Chicago Press, 2008), 70. Niebuhr's study, originally published in 1952, remains an insightful study of the moral and political dangers of American exceptionalism. His concerns resonate powerfully with Melville's at points, particularly in the guilt both writers believe emerges ironically from America's overconfidence in its own virtue.

12. Herman Melville, *Benito Cereno*, in *Billy Budd and Other Stories*, 257.

13. Lewis Mumford, *Herman Melville* (New York: Harcourt, Brace, 1929), xvi; F. O. Matthiessen, *American Renaissance: Art and Expression in the Age of Emerson and Whitman* (New York: Oxford University Press, 1941).

14. I develop this reading in "Pathologies of Freedom in Melville's America," in *Radical Future Pasts: Untimely Essays in Political Theory*, ed. Romand Coles, Mark Reinhardt, and George Shulman (Lexington: University Press of Kentucky, forthcoming).

15. Dennis Berthold, "Democracy and Its Discontents," in *A Companion to Melville*, ed. Wyn Kelley (New York: Blackwell, 2006), 149–164, 150.

16. See Michael Walzer, *The Company of Critics: Social Criticism and Political Commitment in the Twentieth Century* (New York: Basic Books, 1988); and Sacvan Bercovitch, *The Rites of Assent: Transformations in the Symbolic Construction of America* (New York: Routledge, 1993). Walzer celebrates connected criticism, whereas Bercovitch argues it "co-opts the energies of radicalism . . . to the ideological premises of modern democratic liberalism" (438).

17. Sacvan Bercovitch, afterword to *Ideology and Classic American Literature*, ed. Bercovitch and Myra Jehlen (New York: Cambridge University Press, 1986), 438.

18. Louis Hartz, *The Liberal Tradition in America* (New York: Harcourt, Brace, 1955), 145–200.

19. Larry J. Reynolds, "*Billy Budd* and American Labor Unrest: The Case for Striking Back," in *New Essays on* Billy Budd, ed. Donald Yannella (New York: Cambridge University Press, 2002), 38. Many twentieth-century Melville scholars—from British Melville revivalists to prominent first-generation Americanists like F. O. Matthiessen and Newton Arvin—also emphasized the tragic elements of Melville's thinking, but they did so to affirm a moderate political conservatism in his work. I want to suggest, in contrast to these interpretations, that Melville's conception of the tragic led him not to a law-and-order centrism but to a democratic realist appreciation for the unavoidable power conflicts that mark social and political life and that cannot be justly contained or fairly adjudicated by appeal to neutral principles, procedures, or law.

20. Joyce Carol Oates, "'Then All Collapsed': Tragic Melville," afterword to Melville, *Billy Budd and Other Stories* (New York: Signet, 2009), 354.

21. Herman Melville, "Hawthorne and His Mosses," in *Pierre, Israel Potter,*

The Piazza Tales, The Confidence-Man, Uncollected Prose, Billy Budd (New York: Library of America, 1984), 1158.

22. Larry Reynolds, *Devils and Rebels: The Making of Hawthorne's Damned Politics* (Ann Arbor: University of Michigan Press, 2008), 8.

23. See Bonnie Honig, "Antigone's Two Laws: Greek Tragedy and the Politics of Humanism," *New Literary History* 41, no. 1 (2010): 1–33.

24. Taken from Delbanco, *Melville,* 253.

25. Herman Melville to Nathaniel Hawthorne, June 1851, in *The Letters of Herman Melville,* ed. Merrell R. Davis and William H. Gilman (New Haven: Yale University Press, 1961), 127.

26. "Far from precluding egalitarian democracy or opposing it in spirit," Milder elaborates, "a tragic view of experience made democracy all the more imperative [for Melville], the very indifference of nature and absence or silence of God obliging human beings to huddle together for mutual protection and support." Robert Milder, *Exiled Royalties: Melville and the Life We Imagine* (New York: Oxford University Press, 2006), 51, 65.

27. The term is taken from D. H. Lawrence, *Studies in Classic American Literature* (1923; repr., New York: Viking, 1972). The centrality of this conception of freedom to nineteenth-century American political culture is explored in Wilfred M. McClay, *The Masterless: Self and Society in Modern America* (Chapel Hill: University of North Carolina Press, 1994).

28. C. L. R. James, *Mariners, Renegades and Castaways: The Story of Herman Melville and the World We Live In* (1953; repr., Hanover, N.H.: Dartmouth College Press, 2001), 1.

1

Who Eats Whom?

Melville's Anthropolitics at the Dawn of Pacific Imperialism

Kennan Ferguson

> In no respect does the author make pretension to philosophic research.
>
> —Herman Melville, *Omoo*

"From where?" asks Melville, in story and novel. What is the source of justice, of desire, of revenge, of human experience? When someone arrives at a new destination, what brought him (for the narrator is always male) there? How do we attempt to escape our pasts and how does their return compromise us? The role of the past in the present and the demand for causation and those resistances to that demand constitute both literature and humanity within Melville's corpus.

But the question should be asked of Melville himself as well. From where did his authorship arise? What dynamics of literature made him the famed writer who by the twentieth century was considered one of the greatest American novelists? Surprisingly to some, the answer lies not in the United States, but in the South Pacific. Long before Melville's posthumous fame as the writer of *Moby-Dick,* before his brief and suggestive novellas and short stories that make Billy Budd and Bartleby familiar names, he came to the literary world's attention as a writer of putatively autobiographical nonfiction. Focusing on sailors and savages, civilization and cannibalism, he emerged not as a literarily canonical figure but as an author of adventure. In his first two works, *Typee* and *Omoo,* Melville operated as an anthropological narrator, a sympathetic captive, and a possible fabulist.

Both books tell of adventures in the South Pacific. The first describes how Tommo, the narrator and stand-in for Melville, jumps ship to escape the drudgery of civilization and finds himself captured by a tribe of Marquesans. These Taipis, called "Typees" by Melville, he first thinks to be cannibals, but after living among them for a while, he ultimately comes to admire their life and culture, even though he still desires escape.[1] The second follows the same narrator (now, revealingly, called "Typee" by his new shipmates) to Tahiti, where he observes the mostly pernicious effects that colonial administration has on the indigenous islanders. The political content, genre trouble, and imperial outlook of these works have drawn the attention of today's critics, but they were far more popular in Melville's day than any of his subsequent posthumously canonized work. These books formed the basis for Melville's fame, and for the tropes that his later writing would draw out and develop.[2] In each case, the narrator comes to doubt his own knowledge: appearances are subverted, assumptions are disproved, surfaces mislead. In his later work, Melville would extend these doubts to much of nineteenth-century American existence.

Melville gave the Anglophone world an imaginary of the South Seas, especially the islands of the Marquesas and of Tahiti, as powerful as that developed a generation later in France by Paul Gauguin. Melville did so in the middle of the nineteenth century, in a time of imperial expansion, when the relationships between the United States, England, and France—among other imperial powers—were being contested on the lands and bodies of Pacific peoples. In the stories narrated in these two tales (many of which depended on—were even plagiarized from—others' works), Melville presented scientific knowledge, cultural study, adventure, and narrative ambiguity in the form of reportage.

His anthropolitical imaginary presents the Pacific Islanders as a beguiling mixture of savagery and wisdom, populating islands of beauty and danger. Unlike his fellow white sailors, Melville sees the indigines as justified in their violence both against one another and against foreign invaders, and he views the intrigues between island chieftains and queens as equivalent to those of their European counterparts. He reports on their clothing, food, toilette, and traditions with a benignant eye, noting that his admiration for their culture opens him to a charge of being sympathetic with cannibals. The admiration he feels for the "native damsels" hints at an erotic freedom, one embodied in the emblematic figure of his lover, the girl Fayaway. But these admiring glances mix with a simultaneous narration of civilization and savagery that dislocates Pacific Islanders into the realm of pure nature, a narration that undermines a simple interpretation of Melville as an anti-imperialist. Telling of his own capture, Melville emphasizes the danger of the warlike tribes. When he discusses his own travels, he highlights the distances involved. And when he explains the practices of "natives," he underscores their strangeness and inhumanities. The Typee and the Tahitians are not peoples to be emulated, even if they are to be admired, for the civilized man should never aspire to such a lack of society.

The Pacific thus became for his readers a manifold and complex place: a location of primitive but beguiling cultures, one threatened by the currents of colonization overwhelming them but also of delights and conquests for the courageous traveler. Melville wrote "the mythopoetic source for a wide variety of literary conventions which have been used to dramatize the culture clash between Western civilization and the primitive world."[3] For many, Melville's experience with and generosity toward Pacific Islanders mark him as a critic of American imperialism, and indeed he strongly criticized the missionary work, consular power, and sailorly ignorance he found. But in its place he introduced an idea of indigenes as people to be visited, experienced, and investigated: a scientific, zoological approach to such cultures. In doing so, Melville created a new template of imperialism for the American imaginary, one that holds itself as protecting cultures from foreign influence while manipulating them to its own ends; as saving peoples from the vagaries of international capital while using them as a touristic destination; as valuing encounters with alterity while ultimately remaining unmarked by the experience. *Typee* and *Omoo* taught America how to be an empire. This would be an empire of cultural zookeepers and armchair anthropologists who mobilized difference for imperial ends rather than the more familiar and more violent European models of English colonization and Belgian work camps, but an empire nonetheless.[4]

The Anthropologist's Eye

The respective narrators of the books, Tommo and Typee, both come across as travelers with a greater-than-average knowledge of history, discernment regarding situation, and sympathy for their island interlocutors. They are not normal sailors, in other words, but interlopers in work in the Pacific that began in earnest before their arrival. Because of the claims to facticity and verity that begin each work, each narrator stands in for Melville more overtly than do most others for their authors.

They thus serve not only as adventurers but also as what we would today call theorists. Melville overtly denied that what he was doing was theory, which his period associated with European decadence, precisely because he did not want to be seen as presenting merely an updated Rousseau. In an intellectual milieu that perceived theory as bloodless, abstract, and divorced from reality, Melville's philosophy, even his political philosophy, would emerge not from a Kantian investigation into first principles but from the lived experience of explorers, natives, and seamen. It would be empirical, descriptive, scientific, and, most of all, adventurous. It was only by actively grappling with the complexities of the world, especially the diversity of its peoples and their cultures, that one could begin to discover one's own self. If philosophy embodied dead thinking, adventure promised embodied living.

These are also books of anthropology and history. In the course of Tommo's and Typee's adventures, they describe not only their own dangers and excitements, but also the practices, living conditions, and language of Marquesans, Tahitians, and sailors. Experiencing these worlds as outsiders and naïfs, they nonetheless quickly become proficient in important procedures of understanding and action. What a sailor sees as savagery they see as justified; what a missionary sees as incomprehensible they see as cultural; what a native sees as a local outrage they see as part of a complex system of emergent colonial power.

This insightfulness comes in part from these narrators' ability to understand native languages with superhuman alacrity, so that they can know a fairly complex lingua (or at least its pidgin version) with an authorial omniscience. It comes also from their location outside the presumed narrative timeline—they speak of access to research materials and documents consulted after the fact of the experience being recounted. Perhaps most tellingly, this discernment also comes from the ability to make connections—between English captains, Maori harpooners, Tahitian chieftains, and American readers. All combine to explore the emergent complexities of the Pacific, to be surprised by its myriad peoples, languages, and events. As creators of these connections, they become anthropologists of cultures: they explain histories and practices with an eye to appreciating their complexities, authors who teach why and how these far-flung islands are intriguing and useful to an emergent American power.

A retelling of a simple encounter with a farmer became, for Melville, an opportunity to generalize for two chapters about all "Farming in Polynesia."[5] The second of those chapters digresses further, explaining the history of cattle raising and hunting in Hawai'i. Critics have read similar excurses in *Moby-Dick* (concerning kinds of whales, for example) as everything from a temporal narrative device designed for slowing the plot to an engagement about nature with contemporary Romantic authors. The similarity of these divagations in *Typee* and *Omoo* shows their roots in Melville's anthropological impulse: the author provides the important social, political, and historical contexts so that the reader understands not just that cows existed in Tahiti, but how and when they came to be there.

Hogs and sailors and cows and whale oil: all are taken from one place and put in another, and the author and reader alike find these changes and juxtapositions worth figuring out. When the Typee take Tommo prisoner, he soon discerns out that they are not the savage, vicious, disorganized warriors of the sailors' nightmares, but instead a complexly organized society dedicated to protecting itself from conquest, both militarily and symbolically. Tommo's realization that their life revolves not around warfare and cannibalism but instead around making tapa cloth, gathering fruits and raising pigs, swimming in shaded pools, and fishing, allows him to question why one tribe has a reputation for friendliness while another is feared. He discovers that reputation serves a purpose, that it could effectively serve to protect a group from the predations of the ships that appear on their shores and make demands on them.

The Europeans, he noted, engaged in "unprovoked atrocities" against natives who originally welcomed them: "The instinctive feeling of love within their breasts is soon converted into the bitterest hate."[6] Both books overflow with stories of captains whose ships require aid (water, food, sex, or shelter) and who presume that their need translates into obligations on the part of native groups. If those demands are not properly met, they turn to vengeance; to teach the savages lessons in propriety, the European sailors kill, burn, rape, poison, and steal.[7] Their lives, lands, and possessions, the narrators note, are constantly at risk from the whites and from other tribes, and part of their reputations and external practices is meant to signal to these outsiders that their ferocity knows no limits, even alongside the pleasures and relaxations of their quotidian lives.[8]

Melville's proto-anthropology, then, looked not only to describe native practices (a classic subject of travelogue), but also to examine these in relation to causes and effects, structures of power and war, which explain external reputations and rumors.[9] Tommo constantly fears the specter of cannibalism; he is almost convinced by his fellow captive, Toby, that a suckling pig he is being fed is actually a human baby, and he repeatedly worries that the Typee's hospitality merely covers a larger desire to fatten him up for a feast. Failing to see evidence of cannibalism over the course of his capture, he begins to suspect that it was merely a rumor the Typee spread to appear fierce to their enemies. (Ultimately, when he sees a member of the Happar tribe captured and presumably killed, Tommo gathers as much evidence as possible to prove that the Happar had been eaten. This serves both to convince him to attempt his ultimately successful escape and to reinforce the idea of the ferocious Typee) (*Typee*, 270–277).

Melville's descriptions of these foreign practices were not entirely his own. In truth, much of his representation of Pacific cultures was literally unoriginal. Not content merely to borrow insights from previous writers, Melville overtly plagiarized throughout both books. At times he recognized his own references, as when he clearly states the histories on which he relies; at others he entirely neglects to mention his sources, as in his unattributed use of Captain David Porter's *Journal of the Cruise of the U.S. Frigate* Essex.[10] He also borrowed their writing styles, their histories, even their personal experiences with islanders.

James Cook's voyages to the South Pacific remained the most popular template in Melville's time.[11] The first version of these, John Hawkesworth's 1774 description of Cook's travels, set a particularly compelling framework for the international conception of the Pacific. Hawkesworth repeatedly interjected Rousseauian declarations that human nature was obviously pure and innocent before being corrupted by societal living.[12] The idea of the Pacific region as free from the corruption of politics became so powerful that by his third voyage, Cook traveled with a special passport in his possession, granted by Benjamin Franklin to protect him from American sailors by representing his project's transcendence of the British-American hostility.[13]

The success of *Typee* depended equally on images of a beautiful, uncorrupted humanity. The central figure of the novel—the persona who though filling only a few pages became famous as the imagined archetypal Pacific Islander to Melville's readers—is the girl Fayaway. Referred to as a "damsel," a "nymph," and a "maiden," Fayaway provides the book with both a recurrent erotic charge and a symbolic referent to the island's beauty. It probably does not damage her attractiveness (to both Tommo and the reader) that she is generally found wearing the "primitive and summer garb of Eden" (*Typee,* 107). She is often found swimming and playing with her many friends and sleeping alongside the narrator.

Her "easy unstudied graces" arise not only from her natural beauty, which the narrator spends a considerable amount of time describing, but also from her nurture, raised as a "child of nature": "breathing from infancy an atmosphere of perpetual summer," "nurtured by the simple fruits of the earth," and "enjoying a perfect freedom from care and anxiety" (*Typee,* 106); this all combined to produce a personality fully dedicated to fun, to pleasure, and to relaxation.

In the most famous (and infamous) scene of the book, Tommo challenges the taboo that females cannot enter canoes and manages to teach the islanders "a little gallantry" (*Typee,* 159). Once in the canoe, Fayaway seems "all at once to be struck with some happy idea," removes her tapa robe, and lifts it as a sail. As her hair flies in the breeze, Tommo recounts, the canoe shoots toward the shore; "a prettier little mast than Fayaway made was never shipped aboard any craft" (ibid., 160–161).

This image of a naked nymph using her tapa tunic as a sail for a primitive canoe proved so appealing and tantalizing to a Western audience that it served as the cover for a number of editions of the book. Combining innocence, sexuality, desire, beauty, and subservience, Fayaway encapsulated and embodied a version of Polynesia as a land of freedom and satiated desire. Both playing on and inflaming the masculinist Western perception that the Pacific was made up of beauteous and fierce humans, Fayaway proved both easily seduced (though the book never overtly mentions her amorous activities, there seems to be little doubt, as she and Tommo are constantly "stealing away" or waking up together) and yet still resistant to the constraints of Western ideals and power (the dress that Tommo makes for her from cloth he has stolen from his ship is easily and often shucked, and Fayaway and her nymph friends can easily dunk Tommo when he swims with them) (*Typee,* 161, 158).

It should be clear that Fayaway is less an actual individual than an idealized version of Melville's Polynesian maiden. Her commitment to Tommo's pleasure, her dewy-eyed emotionalism, even her blue eyes point to her as a fiction. The idea that a girl whose people have known only canoes would spontaneously decide that the craft should be powered by a sail is equally far-fetched. And the success of Melville's rendition led to a common trope in expansionist literature: rare was the subsequent account of Hawai'i or Tahiti that did not contain a rendition of the innocent, sensual, and undressed girls to be found there.[14] Even those seeking the subjugation or elimination of native islanders recognized the power of Melville's imagery; Elizabeth Parker, the white wife of an American living in Hawai'i, wrote only five years after *Typee*'s appearance in the United States that she had "looked in vain for his noble warrior, or graceful Fayaway, in the wide-mouthed, flat-nosed creatures around me."[15]

Even though Parker and other Americans read Melville's idealizations as applying to all Pacific peoples, he actually placed them in a somewhat complex anthropolitical hierarchy. The Typee as a race compare favorably with the "dark-hued Hawaiians and the woolly-headed Feegees" (*Typee,* 217) who show their inferiority through their skin and hair. The Marquesans, in contrast, had a "European cast [to] their features—a peculiarity seldom observable among other uncivilized people" (ibid.). Melville's anthropolitics not only recognized but reinforced the idea that a scientific outlook served to place different peoples in racial relation to one another; he merely argued that the people he spent time with belonged on a higher rung of such a ladder. Once their proper place is determined, it is implied, then those of European descent can properly conceive of their rightful connection to the natural world. Melville would not make savages of his readers; he would, rather, point out the scientific value and anthropological hierarchies of a racialized world. In doing so, he posits the Typee as both the highest of the savages and most convincingly in touch with the Edenic possibilities of human life in nature. This latter skill, the ability to live with one's natural surroundings, is what the missionaries and administrative authorities most challenge.

Missionary Positions

Many theorists have examined Melville's development of nature in its antipathetic relation to culture. The unrepresentable nature of the great white whale at the core of his masterpiece points to a large array of symbolic untamability: the sublime that always resists the capture and control of the rationalized Western world.[16] The behavior of those who hope to capture and constrain the wild represents not only a distrust of natural order, but also a dismissal of other humans' points of view. The organization of civilization opposes both the greatness of nature and the particularity of democratic respect. Melville rightly takes his place among the great critics of modernity, showing how contemporary forms of authority and self-interest undermine the human ability to see one another as equals and the world as a site of wonder and sublimity.

In both these first two works, Melville excoriates missionaries. *Typee* overtly compares the alleged savagery of the islanders with the ostensible civilization of American evangelists, a comparison summarized by an outraged contemporary of Melville's: "Redundant with bitter charges against the missionaries, [he] piles obloquy upon their labor and its results, and broadly accuses them of being the cause of the vice, destitution, and unhappiness of the Polynesians wherever they have penetrated."[17] *Omoo* describes at length a laughable sermon, given by a missionary, in absurd pidgin: "The Island no more yours, but the Wee-Wees' (French). Wicked priests here, too . . . no you speak, or look at them—but I know you won't. . . . Soon these bad men be made to go very quick. Beretanee [British] ships of thunder come, and away they go" (*Omoo,* 498). By Melville's estimation, the only aspect of Christianity the Tahitians come to embrace is the Sabbath, when they refuse to work.

Like most nineteenth-century American authors, Melville often overtly refers to or indirectly alludes to the Bible; indeed, his references and allusions are particularly elaborate and hermeneutically dense. But his religious usages more often than not undercut the solemnity of religion. To note that "the penalty of the Fall presses very lightly upon the valley of Typee" (*Typee,* 229–230) or that a group of islanders are "sunk in religious sloth, and require a religious revival" (ibid., 211) took the mission and language of the Christian faith fairly lightly. To Joseph Firebaugh it showed "the rhetoric of the Bible paraphrased and burlesqued."[18] The narrator makes clear that his own attitude is not particularly pious; upon discovering that the captain, Nathan Coleman, was long ago responsible for introducing mosquitoes to Tahiti, he "found much relief in coupling the word 'Coleman' with another of one syllable, and pronouncing them together energetically" (*Omoo,* 543). Though he does not reprint the particular obscenity he used here, the careful reader can suspect one of a number of sacrilegious interjections.

Unsurprisingly, Melville portrays missionaries unflatteringly. At the end of *Omoo,* he finally reveals how they ultimately triumphed in Tahiti. The machinations of the king, Pomaree II ("a sad debauchee and drunkard, and even charged with unnatural crimes"), who was driven from the throne, led him to raise an army abroad with the help of the missionaries and "slaughter" his countrymen: "Thus, by force of arms, was Christianity finally triumphant in Tahiti" (*Omoo,* 633). Melville presents the missionaries not only as wrecking the traditional Pacific life, but also as introducing evil. "So far as the relative wickedness of the parties is concerned," he surmises, "four or five Marquesan Islanders sent to the United States as Missionaries might be quite as useful as an equal number of Americans dispatched to the Islands in a similar capacity" (*Typee,* 151).

His attacks on U.S. missionaries proved enough to scuttle the American publication of *Typee.* Not until he removed all references to missionaries as well as a critical comment about the dispossession and extirpation of the "Red race" in North America was it printed in the United States.[19] Yet even with these redactions, readers did not miss Melville's attempt to contrast the two civilizations: referring to the Typee as cannibals, a review in the *New York Daily Tribune* recommended "the effect of eating one's neighbors, as a humanizing effect for some of our war-breathing legislators."[20]

Melville ultimately blamed the missionary history for the massive depopulation of the Pacific Islands. He noted that "about the year 1777, Captain Cook estimated the population of Tahiti at about two hundred thousand" (*Omoo,* 517). By the middle of the nineteenth century, this had decreased to nine thousand. "These evils, of course, are solely of foreign origin," he notes. The various evils the missionaries stood against, such as drunkenness, smallpox, wars, and child murder, were precisely the evils they themselves had brought (ibid., 519).

These mistreatments of the natives are echoed in the reprehensible behavior of those entrusted with authority on board the ships of these imperial powers.[21] The authorities (of "Papeetee," Tahiti) obstruct justice in a section of *Omoo* that highlights issues of political legitimacy and democracy (*Omoo,* 401–414). The captain of the ship, already ineffective, takes ill and is brought ashore, leaving his bad-tempered and dictatorial first mate, Jermin, in command. The already mutinous crew are denied access to land or food, as Jermin (properly) fears they will desert. Consequently, Typee and the educated doctor on board convince the crew to petition the English consul for redress.

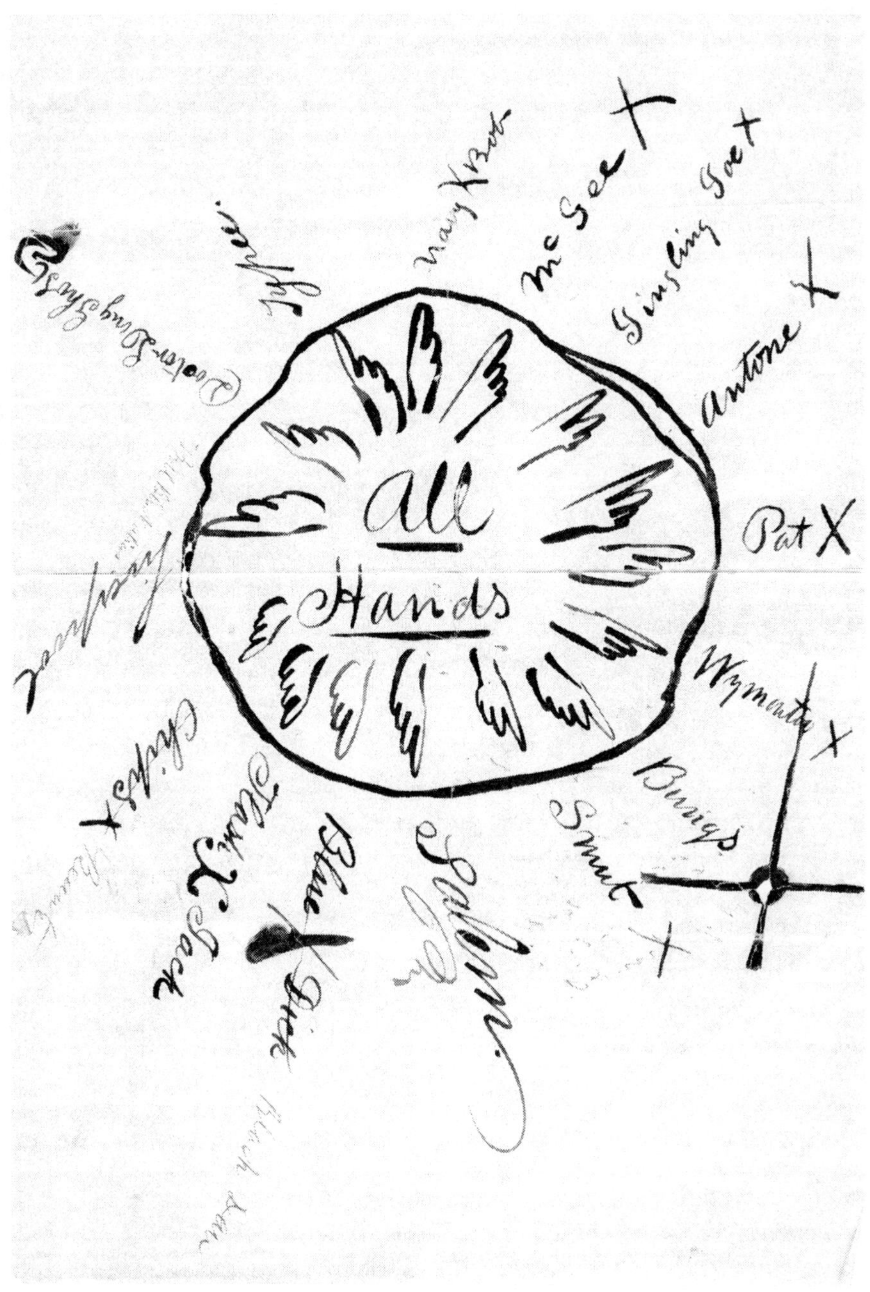

Figure 1. Round robin from Melville's *Omoo* manuscript. (Courtesy of the University of Florida Digital Collections at George A. Smathers Libraries)

It would not do to sign such a document normally, for one name would have to come first. Fearing that one of the crew would be seen as the leader of this incipient rebellion and accused as a mutineer, Typee suggests a "round robin." Under the list of grievances, a circle is drawn, labeled "all Hands," and each crewmember signs or marks his name in a rotating corporate signatory.

How common the round robin was at sea remains unclear, but Melville assumed the process unusual enough not only to explain it in detail to his readers, but also to present it as one of the few images in any of his published works. The round robin, in his telling, collectivizes the crew, showing how a democratic affiliation can arise through opposition to authority. (That the round robin is written on blank pages torn from the book *A History of the Most Atrocious and Bloody Pirates* cannot be accidental.) It is worth noting that the historical document on which this is based—the adjudicated mutiny that involved Melville himself—had a clear ordering of names and no round robin.[22]

Authority proves feckless and self-interested, from the captain to the consul to the missionaries. The consul, representing the order of the islands, sees no reasons to respond to the democratic demands of the crew, and—through a series of events—a number of them end up arrested for mutiny and imprisoned by the consular authorities. These authorities, however, remain dependent on the colonized Tahitians for the effecting of the punishment, and it is in this distance between the colonizer and the colonized that Melville recognizes the generosity and humanity of the latter. The locale of imprisonment proves to be a "beautiful spot" (444) and the jailer, a Tahitian who calls himself "Capin Bob," an exceedingly cheerful and indulgent man. The prisoners are told to remain within earshot and are pinioned in the stocks only at night.

In both *Typee* and *Omoo,* Melville juxtaposes two forms of unjust power—on the one side the lack of recognition of the legitimacy of the islanders who live under missionary and colonial control, and on the other the lack of democratic practices among the Europeans who see themselves as bringing civilization to the Pacific world. It may be true that, in the words of one critic, Melville presented "life on board a ship [a]s a microcosm of the tyranny exercised in most nineteenth-century societies,"[23] but the relationship between the two is not as simple as one merely reflecting the other. Melville showed, instead, how the particularity of individual tyranny had an *outside:* that of the project of empire. Yet this realization on the part of the characters, the author, and—presumably—the reader did not necessarily translate into outrage or political opposition. At the moment of decision, Melville's characters prove to be revenants: they go home and, in doing so, once again recognize their alliance with the powers that they have so recently been criticizing.

Tattoo You

A map of the Marquesan Islands appeared on the page opposite the table of contents of *Typee*'s first edition (in its original British titling, *Narrative of a Four Months' Residence among the Natives of a Valley of the Marquesas Islands; or, A Peep at Polynesian Life*). The American edition contained the same map. Melville had a map of Tahiti specifically engraved for *Omoo.*[24] In both cases the maps added nothing beyond geographical context to the narrative, both because the scale of the maps is too small to see the particular valleys and bays that Melville describes and because the plot and events of the books don't depend as much on geographical space as on cultural relationships. This God's-eye view of the islands geographizes these Pacific peoples just as Melville's anthropological discourse positions them in relation to the civilized world.

This demarcation of land is reinforced by the stories the books tell: they mark each place as particular, special, and insecure. The islands and the people who live there are both endangered and isolated, imperiled in their smallness while protected from the broader forces outside them by the vast distances of the sea. The maps that begin each book mark the inhabitants, positioning them within the missionary-empire nexus that (Melville hinted) would soon come to swallow them up. In writing the books, Melville himself also marked them: as zones of adventure, excitement, and forbidden desires. And it is this second kind of demarcation that enables an imaginary of the Pacific as a location of ur-humanity, where the effects of a corrupt Western civilization have not yet been felt.

A third kind of marking is at work, one that fascinates the authorial stand-ins but that each finally rejects. As Sophia Mihic notes, Tommo engages with and becomes part of the Typee culture (certainly more so than does his companion, Toby), but the partiality of this acceptance ultimately becomes a rejection and a leave-taking: the mark of a tourist rather than a full participant. Although both narrators remain adventurers, they both ultimately refuse the connection to these foreign lands that would forever situate their bodies in relation to the Pacific. They reject the mark that would locate them in the social culture of the islands: the tattoo.

Many of Melville's critics, especially those who notice his imperial sympathies, emphasize this aspect of *Typee* and *Omoo;* conversely, his champions often overlook the role of the tattoo. The complexities of Melville's attitude toward imperial power—as he criticizes consular and missionary remakings of local cultures while simultaneously positioning these indigenes as desiderata for an emergent American anthropolitics—are rivaled by the complexities of Pacific tattoo. Melville expresses fascination with the tattoo, noting how it serves as a mode of physical, material communication between and among the bodily experiences of different natives, sailors, and travelers.

Sometimes he plays this for humor, as when, in the first chapter of his first published work, he describes a formal encounter between French sailors and the king and queen of Nukuheva. The queen, fascinated by the tattoos on an "old salt" among the French, bids him show his ink. In return, she, "eager to display the hieroglyphics on her own sweet form," turns around, bends over, and lifts her skirts, shocking the French into a hasty retreat (*Typee,* 16–17).

Other times he played it for horror, as when the crew of the *Julia* meet up with Lem Hardy, previously an Englishman but now a "renegado from Christendom and humanity" (*Omoo,* 353). Hardy signifies his deserter status by being tattooed with a blue band across his face and a blue shark on his forehead. That he had voluntarily submitted to this mark, "far worse than Cain's," which could never be erased, only increased the crew's horror (ibid.). Melville underscores the evil of tattooing through Tommo's insistence on the minimal nature of the tattoos on even the perfect Fayaway, describing her as not "altogether freed from the hideous blemish": "Three minute dots, no bigger than pinheads, decorated either lip, and at a little distance were not at all discernable. Just upon the fall of the shoulder were drawn two parallel lines half an inch apart" (*Typee,* 107).

And at still other times, the tattoo is represented as the nexus upon which generosity, hierarchy, and art are most fittingly synchronized. In *Omoo* the story of the "Lora Tattoo" tells of the history of La Dominica, where highly skilled tattooists have become more costly than most can afford. The wise

"Noomai, King of Hannamanoo," therefore transforms tattoo into a public good and offers his palace to tattooists, provided they "practice without fee upon the meanest native soliciting their services" (*Omoo,* 356–359).[25] Even a novelist could hardly conceive of a better system of artistic support than such full state patronage.

But Melville's narrators ultimately refuse to participate in this discourse of equality, this recognition that they themselves are embodied in the Pacific. Though Tommo seems content enough in his extended pseudo-captivity, one event stands out as motivating his escape from the Typee. As Samuel Otter asserts, the critical moment in the narrative (though not necessarily in the fictional temporality of the story, which jumps back and forth in time) arrives when Tommo becomes convinced that he will be tattooed as a member of the Typee.[26]

Tommo first encounters the tattooist "Karky the artist" engaged in his work, and the anthropological narrative takes over (*Typee,* 253–257). The narrative explains that Karky's tattoos are painted with a shark's tooth on a stick (among a range of sharp implements for various patterns), a piece of wood wielded as a hammer, and a candlenut-based black fluid. But once Karky notices Tommo, he becomes obsessed with the idea of tattooing his "white skin." His desire transfers quickly to Tommo's previous friends, to the king and the chiefs, and to the larger society. He receives a "choice of patterns. I was at perfect liberty to have my face spanned by three horizontal bars, . . . or to have as many oblique stripes slanting across it; or . . . I might wear a sort of freemason badge upon my countenance in the shape of a mystic triangle" (ibid., 256).

Tommo is happy to participate in Typee culture: "I made a point of doing as the Typee did" (*Typee,* 245). In many cases, he learns their customs and manages to take part in them, even to the point of enjoying them. In one narrative he describes his amazement that anyone could eat raw fish, consuming them "in the same way a civilized being would eat a radish" (ibid., 244). He feels outraged and disgusted at seeing Fayaway eating a fish whole, though "in a more ladylike manner than any other girls of the valley" (ibid., 245). But in time he comes to eat the fish himself, and even "to relish them" (ibid.). Temporary participation in Marquesan life seems fine, even a learning experience.

Permanence, however, proves different. The tattoo would mark him as Typee forever and always. It would signal to those in his homeland that his traveling has exceeded the limit of touristic voyeurism and that he has transformed himself visually in service of a foreign culture. It would mark him, literally, as an outsider in the Bostonian culture to which he will undoubtedly return, to which he had returned by the time of the book's writing. *Typee,* after all, was dedicated to Lemuel Shaw, the chief justice of Massachusetts, Melville's father-in-law at the time of the book's publication.

This inscription highlights one important similarity between Melville the author and Tommo the character. Tattoo, as some critics have noted, writes.[27] Printing on the skin of the subject—or, more properly, printing patterns of meaning subcutaneously—is a mode of marking that stays in the body until death. Like other kinds of writing, it demands a concordance between more than one person. Just as writers need a kind of generosity and forbearance from their readers, tattooists need agreement and cooperation from their canvases. Tommo's fear that he could be forcibly tattooed, as the traditional Hawaiian tattoo artist Keone Nunes has pointed out, was absurd: an unwilling subject can destroy the artistic intent of a tattoo by merely flinching or twitching at any given moment.[28]

So why does Tommo (and, presumably, the armchair traveler) remain convinced that he could be tattooed at any minute? It is possible that the tribe want to preserve their reputation as fierce, in which case his tattooed face will mark him as a previous captive; it is also possible that they ascribe unfortunate events to the presence of an untattooed adult in their midst.[29] Tommo, however, sees it merely as an insult to be potentially forced on him and, other than dismissing it as part of the Typee religion ("they were resolved to make a convert out of me") (*Typee,* 256), does not seem to inquire into the importance of tattoo. He thus resists, and ultimately escapes, the possibility of joining the Typee way of life.

Melville's fear of tattoo bespeaks his distrust of the full flowering of native cultures. Even though both he and his readers saw *Typee* as an embrace of native life, it ends on a breathtakingly imperialist note. In the appendix, Melville (no longer the narrator Tommo, here, in a strange authorial shift) admiringly recounts the British takeover of the Hawaiian kingdom. In doing so, Melville the author belies an underlying attitude toward Pacific peoples: he celebrates their ways of life so long as they stay within the natural world, but when they demand equality and recognition within the civilized realm, they go too far. Melville's anthropolitical imaginary celebrates humans in cultural zoos, but their escape from such enclosures threatens the systems of civilization to which he ultimately returns.

With the restoration of the monarchy, he argues, brought about by the Hawaiian royalty and ill-advised American outrage against the overthrow, civilization faces riotous threat. In Melville's telling, Lord George Paulet generously took over the islands, forcing King Kamehameha III ("the imbecile king") (*Typee,* 293) out of power at gunpoint in order to better regulate the islands.[30] Melville argues that Paulet "endeared himself to nearly all orders of the islanders" (ibid., 294–295) during his rule, but through coordination between the king and the missionaries he was shunted out of power. Since these figures preferred "continually shifting regulations" (ibid., 295), the lawlessness of the post-appropriation period "reveals in their true colors the character of the Sandwich islanders," in that they "had plunged voluntarily into every species of wickedness and excess, and by their utter disregard of all decency plainly showed . . . they were in reality as depraved and vicious as ever" (ibid., 297).

The Hawaiians thus cannot be trusted to rule themselves. In presuming political and cultural equality with the English or American societies, they have set themselves up to be ridiculed. Only an outsider such as Paulet can develop true order. To end his book, Melville falsely claims that "the great body of the Hawaiian people invoke blessings on his head, and look back with gratitude to the time when his liberal and paternal sway diffused peace and happiness among them" (*Typee,* 298). Only through a disinterested and civilized ruler can such a people interact with the rest of the world.

Melville's attitude toward the Hawaiian people and the Hawaiian monarchy showed his distrust of Pacific Islanders who claim autonomy within the modern world. The prelapsarian bliss of the Typee can exist on its own terms, but only in isolation from true civilization. The influences of the Europeans must be resisted, whether in the form of missionaries, consular authorities, or kings; once introduced, such developments make a people ridiculous, laughable, and inferior. The Typee need to remain independent and unaffected, to remain as the anthropological destination where Fayaway and her friends welcome the white male traveler.

Tattoo, conversely, embodies complicity. Connection, shared meaning, the materiality of the body, the coordination of artistic creation and reception: tattoo literalizes these connections of self to others. A tattoo shows a direct association to a moment, to a place, to a people. Ultimately, Tommo, Typee, and Melville reject this recognition, even as their reputations and fame are built on them. One can desert a ship, a captain, a society, but never one's own body.

These connections between narrator and author, between Typee and sailor, between nature and culture—as much as Melville undermines the logic of such divisions (especially in his later works), his narratives still reject the implications of these connections. The older, European modes of colonialism insisted on the full subsumption of the native to the colonial power, whether through military annihilation and genocide or through missionary and political acceptance of the colonial way of life. Melville's pointed criticisms and vicious satires of these systems properly sting. But the American version of anthropolitical imperialism he replaces it with, whereby native peoples are to be protected in their proper place, entails its own exclusions. Their cultures can be celebrated, but not their aspirations to engage the world on their own terms; they can be visited, with great profit, but the visitor should not be lured away from his own kind of life; they can have their own religion and practices, but safely tucked away in a valley or on an island. For Melville, the Typee should continue to live free from interference, so long as their markings do not appear on the skin of Americans. In truth, Hawaiians and Typee and Tahitians alike are already implicated in the American project, and Melville's denial of the mutuality of these interconnections merely points to a new way of imagining empire, not to its end.

Notes

1. Michael Clark notes that Tommo's name echoes that of the fictional Cherokee Tomo, who in Philip Freneau's "The Splenetic Indian" in *The Tomo Cheeki Essays* travels into the heart of the civilized world (in this case, Philadelphia) to learn from and report on white people before returning home. Clark, "A Source for Melville's Tommo," *American Transcendental Quarterly* 44 (1979): 261–264.

2. The fame of *Typee* was such that the sequel was advertised, in "imposing majuscules," with only five words in London newspapers. The advertisement read, in full, "OMOO, by the author of TYPEE." Described in "Pacific Rovings," *Blackwood's Magazine,* June 1847, 754.

3. William Heath, "Melville and Marquesan Eroticism," *Massachusetts Review* 29, no. 1 (Spring 1988): 45.

4. One way to emphasize the continuity of these projects is to note the attitude such empires have toward those who want to be treated as equals on the

international stage. Melville's attitudes toward the Hawaiian kingdom, recounted below, prove telling.

5. Herman Melville, *Omoo,* in *Typee, Omoo, Mardi* (New York: Library of America, 1982), 531–538. Further citations of this work are given parenthetically in the text by title and page number.

6. Herman Melville, *Typee,* in *Typee, Omoo, Mardi,* 37. Further citations of this work are given parenthetically in the text by title and page number.

7. In *Omoo,* for example, Melville explains the military history of Tahiti as being one in which Britain and France ("for once in their brawling lives") cooperate to subjugate the island. It begins when French sailors kidnap and rape "a number of women from the shore" and continues as guerilla attacks by the Tahitians are met with increased assaults by French sailors, who, "infuriated with liquor, gave no quarter" (452–453).

8. Wendy Stallard Flory points out that a concern for publicity explains the strange and contradictory behavior of one of Tommo's Typee friends, Marnoo. In just one paragraph at the end of *Typee,* Marnoo tells Tommo that escape from the valley is impossible, that it is a wonderful place to keep living, that he should never have come originally, that they will eat him, and that he will help Tommo escape (279). Flory argues that this is part of a project of advertising the ferociousness of the Typee to protect them from further incursion. Flory, "Taking the Polynesians to Heart: Melville's *Typee* and Merwin's *Folding Cliffs,*" in "*Whole Oceans Away*": *Melville and the Pacific,* ed. Jill Barnum, Wyn Kelley, and Christopher Sten (Kent, Ohio: Kent State University Press, 2007), 265–278.

9. Roxanne Euben, *Journeys to the Other Shore: Muslim and Western Travelers in Search of Knowledge* (Princeton: Princeton University Press, 2006).

10. For a brutal account of these transgressions, including word-for-word lifting of experiences, see Charles Roberts Anderson, *Melville in the South Seas* (1939; repr., New York: Dover, 1966). Anderson does note (217), however, that Melville acknowledges his debt to Charles Wilkes. See also Bryan Short, "Plagiarizing Polynesia: Decolonization in Melville's *Omoo* Borrowings," in Barnum et al., "*Whole Oceans Away,*" 98–110.

11. Brian Richardson, *Longitude and Empire: How Captain Cook's Voyages Changed the World* (Vancouver: University of British Columbia Press, 2005).

12. See Hoxie Neale Fairchild, *The Noble Savage: A Study in Romantic Naturalism* (New York: Columbia University Press, 1928), esp. 104–112.

13. T. Walter Herbert Jr., *Marquesan Encounter: Melville and the Meaning of Civilization* (Cambridge: Harvard University Press, 1980), 81.

14. Amy S. Greenberg, "Fayaway and Her Sisters: Gender, Popular Literature, and Manifest Destiny in the Pacific, 1848–1860," in Barnum et al., "*Whole Oceans Away,*" 17–30.

15. Elizabeth Parker, *The Sandwich Islands as They Are, Not as They Should Be* (San Francisco: Burgess, Gilbert, and Still, 1852), 7; quoted in Greenberg, "Fayaway and Her Sisters," 24.

16. Christina Fredricks's *Melville's Art of Democracy* (Athens: University of Georgia Press, 1995) develops this theme particularly well, but it can be found in many romantic readings of *Moby-Dick.*

17. "*Typee:* The Traducer of Missions," *Christian Parlor Magazine* 3 (July 1846): 74–83, reprinted in *Herman Melville: The Contemporary Reviews,* ed. Brian Higgins and Hershel Parker (Cambridge: Cambridge University Press, 1995), 55.

18. Joseph J. Firebaugh, "Humorist as Rebel: The Melville of *Typee,*" *Nineteenth-Century Fiction* 9, no. 2 (September 1954): 117.

19. Michael Paul Rogin, *Subversive Genealogy: The Politics and Art of Herman Melville* (New York: Knopf, 1983), 45.

20. *New York Daily Tribune,* April 4, 1846, reprinted in Higgins and Parker, *Herman Melville: The Contemporary Reviews,* 42–43.

21. The connection of the onboard behavior of the sailors to the larger political world explicitly reappears in Melville's later work, most notably in his treatment of the slave trade in *Benito Cereno.*

22. Rogin, *Subversive Genealogy,* 85.

23. John Carlos Rowe, *Literary Culture and U.S. Imperialism: From the Revolution to World War II* (New York: Oxford University Press, 2000), 88.

24. Gordon Roper, "Historical Note," in Herman Melville, *Omoo: A Narrative of Adventure in the South Seas,* ed. Harrison Hayford, Hershel Parker, and G. Thomas Tanselle (Evanston and Chicago: Northwestern University Press and the Newberry Library, 1968), 333–335.

25. Willowdean Chatterson Handy explains that Melville's story was unlikely, on the basis of information he gathered in 1920, and suspects that it was taken from the *Voyages and Travels* of Georg H. Von Langsdorff, dated 1813. See Handy, *Tattooing in the Marquesas* (Honolulu: Bernice P. Bishop Museum, 1922), 5–6, 17.

26. Samuel Otter, "Race in *Typee* and *White-Jacket,*" in *The Cambridge Companion to Herman Melville,* ed. Robert S. Levine (Cambridge: Cambridge University Press, 1998), 12–36.

27. Stanley Orr, Matt Rollins, and Martin Kevorkian, "Lines of Dissent: Oceanic Tattoo and the Colonial Context," in Barnum et al., "*Whole Oceans Away,*" 291–304.

28. Keone Nunes, "K~kau i ka uhi," quoted ibid., 296.

29. Other travelers to the Marquesas told similar stories, including one who was forcibly tattooed and another who agreed to be tattooed everywhere except for his face and hands. See Anderson, *Melville in the South Seas,* 151–153.

30. As Ralph S. Kuykendall notes in *The Hawaiian Kingdom, 1778–*

1854: Foundation and Transformation (Honolulu: University of Hawaii Press, 1938), Paulet was actually demanding British law for British subjects, a 299-year lease on parts of Honolulu, and $100,000. Jean Iwata Cachola argues that Kamehameha temporarily stepped down to avoid bloodshed. Cachola, *Kamehameha III: Kauikeaouli* (Honolulu: Kamehameha Schools Press, 1995).

2

"The End Was in the Beginning"

Melville, Ellison, and the Democratic Death of Progress in Typee *and* Omoo

Sophia Mihic

Drawing a distinction between the savage and civilized in *Typee* and *Omoo,* Herman Melville demonstrates the contrastive nobility of the Marquesan Islanders. He does not, however, to force a verb, noble savage them out of their humanity. They are hospitable but cunning, indulgent, and controlling. Likewise, the critique of progress inaugurated in Melville's first two novels is not a simple reversal. The relationships among past and future, archaic and modern, are too complicated to allow for an easy trade-off between progress and regress. In *Typee* and *Omoo* events and revelations that do not fit the progressive world picture prompt its effacement; and when the assumption of progress is relaxed, problems of moral and epistemic perspective emerge and transfigure the meanings of actions. Melville explores these dilemmas throughout his work and elicits his readers' surprise at strengths and weaknesses, possibilities and refusals, where we do not expect them. This surprise is on display in *Benito Cereno* when the blind stupidity of an American democrat is contrasted to the insightfulness of an aristocratic Spanish captain. And it is on display when the young Yankee adventurer in *Typee* escapes from his native captors in *Omoo.* He was a free man shipped on board an Australian vessel, and his life was suddenly much more austere and degraded. His food was sparse and spoiled, his quarters were cramped and rotted, and the company was meaner upon his return to civilization. He missed the kindness of his Typee companions even though he had struggled to leave them. He moved from an "indulgent captivity" to a constrained freedom and wondered at "how far short of our expectations is oftentimes the fulfillment of our most ardent hopes."[1]

Still, we do go on advancing our plans—even though our hopes and grander assumptions of progress routinely fail us. The young adventurer will join a successful enough mutiny on the ship of his newfound freedom, and the aristocrat will die because he cannot live with his newfound understanding of his slave's superiority. None of the characters is ever really "saved" by these upendings. There are shadows cast upon them all, but they act nonetheless. Melville's texts comprehend what it means to act without direction: without the operative assumption of a better future and without the guarantee of one's own status. What political lessons can we learn from such perseverance when the assumption of progress is thwarted and our faith in it is dissipated? Let us take this dissipation as a gift and explore the possibilities it presents as Melville does.

Pairing Melville's *Typee* with Ralph Ellison's *Invisible Man,* I will argue that democratic maturity requires giving up on progress and being always ready to reframe our perspectives to see the world as it appears before us. This is the lesson Ellison's protagonist learns through a course of misadventures. "I believed in hard work and progress and action," he tells us, "but now after first being 'for' society and then 'against' it, I assign myself no rank or even limit, and such an attitude is very much against the trend of the times." His world, however, "has become one of infinite possibilities."[2] I will argue that the savages Melville's protagonist encounters are quite civilized, because they, like Ellison, comprehend a world of possibility without progress: they understand that to stage a picture of the world is to exercise power and political agency. Can we follow them and accept that the democratic struggle of self-rule is never *the* struggle, progressing toward emancipation, but instead daily struggles to define ourselves? To do so would be to understand politics not as a matter of having to overcome anything—history, the law, man—but instead as entering into, seeing, and effecting where and what we are as a polity. This will always be an incomplete endeavor. But in refusing the world picture of progress, striving to resist it, we see the world provisionally at least in the moment and we can act from this vantage. We can act within a field of present possibility rather than wait for a logic of history to unfold before us and guide our actions. "Life," Ellison writes and Melville understands, "is to be lived, not controlled; and humanity is won by continuing to play in face of certain defeat."[3]

For Melville and Ellison, to see is to see ourselves and others in the myriad of hopes and prospects with which we each and all frame our individual lives and collective existence. This effort is never solipsistic; and resisting the assumption of progress does not mean that we can assume away the past simply to be here now. We may sometimes withdraw and hibernate or otherwise gain our repose, but we must ultimately return to the world that never leaves us even in our seclusion. Melville's protagonist thinks of "home" and "mother" while in the world of the islanders—these are the only English words he taught his host, Marheyo, while captive[4]—and Ellison's protagonist, ruminating alone, finds he must "at least *tell* a few people" what he is thinking about life in the world he has tried to leave.[5] What do these exercises in thinking tell us? Pursuing our hopes and prospects without the assumption of progress may require conservation—the path without progress may sometimes be conservative—and at other times it may even prompt destruction. We may sometimes have to backtrack and begin again. These are lessons learned in *Typee* before the protagonist and his companion, Toby, recover terrain they have just crossed over. Stalling the decision to turn back, they know "there is scarcely anything when a man is in difficulties that he is more disposed to look upon with abhorrence than a right-about retrograde movement—a systematic going over of the already trodden ground" (*Typee,* 70–71). And these are lessons ultimately embraced by Ellison's protagonist, who tells us, "I have come a long way and returned and boomeranged from the point in society toward which I originally aspired."[6] No one and nothing, including the assumption of progress, determines in toto the execution of anyone's plan for living or the facts of any given present.

How are we to grow up and act within this contingency? If the notion of maturity without progress is too paradoxical to bear, let us think not of unhinging the two completely, but instead of resisting by pluralizing progress. Can we celebrate a retrograde, as well as a forward, movement? There are many ways to take direction and to define success. Paganizing and rendering polytheistic the fact that we go on along many winding and even recursive journeys, as Melville pluralizes and effaces the monotheism of the Christian God and as Ellison deconstructs the American dream, will be the approach of this essay. With Melville and Ellison, let us relax the onto-theology of progress, the almighty god progress—its lingering hold, that is, on contemporary self-understanding and political possibility. The pervasive assumption of progress defines a right wing currently pursuing a globally "manifest" American destiny. At the same time those to the left cannot use the words *liberal, leftist,* or *socialist* to name themselves and often present themselves instead as "progressives." The American war machine, the oligarchy, and resistance to these effects of empire are all presented as striving toward some better future. Can we stand still for a moment and attend to the democratic present? Can we step back and separate the twin gods of republic and empire in the American context and save the republic? Probably not, because the two have never really been separate, but let us follow Melville's lead and at least play with the idea that we savages might find a way to help ourselves.[7]

Travel Narratives and the Remove of Thinking

The *Typee* and *Omoo* pair is in many ways the same book as *Invisible Man,* even though their publications are separated by roughly one hundred years. All three novels tell stories of American men on journeys. They are tales of ups and downs and of removal from the world in order to understand it. The misadventures of Ellison's black protagonist as he travels from the South to the North—through his education and into work and participation in "the Brotherhood"—are not as picturesque as the travels of Melville's white protagonist in the South Seas. But the perceived quaintness of *Typee* and *Omoo* obscures the philosophical insights Melville and Ellison share in these works. Ellison adopts and develops temporal structures and narrative devices suggested by nineteenth-century existentialists such as Nietzsche and Dostoyevsky. Melville, however, finds and propagates these structures and devices. He is a nineteenth-century existentialist, as many have recognized interpreting his later work.[8] Yet as an American whose work and thinking begin with reflection on his experiences with the Typee, Melville comprehends dimensions of collectivity and of race and race-thinking in ways that the European existentialists could not.[9] Nietzsche and Dostoyevsky are a bridge between Melville and Ellison. Or perhaps we should think of them as their third whale in the context of this essay. In existential—or what Hannah Arendt would call *existenz*—philosophy, we find cradled the insights regarding progress and regress that Melville and Ellison share and tie expressly to politics.[10] Their critique of progress is not simply saying no to the modern now and its progressive vision. Their critique is, further, an alternative mode of seeing—of descrying—and thus of thinking and acting. Melville and Ellison comprehend the task of world disclosure in concert with self-disclosure. They bring to light for us the always provisional, and often haphazard, tasks of enacting and participating in collective life. And in *Typee* and *Invisible Man* they ponder the joys and trials of striving to flourish despite one's outsider, or minority, status. We can read Ellison through Melville to begin an exploration of these revelations, because he was clearly influenced by Melville. But we can also read Melville through Ellison to demonstrate that the earlier writer's philosophical thinking does not begin with that other whale and the encounter with Hawthorne.

Consider, first, the narrative device of withdrawal from the world. It is very much a device in *Invisible Man*—one borrowed from Dostoyevsky's *Notes from Underground* and Nietzsche's *Thus Spoke Zarathustra.* Ellison's novel begins, and ends, with the protagonist's hiding underground in a basement, "hibernating," in order to reflect on where and who he is after the failure of his various plans. Dostoyevsky's protagonist, too, goes underground, whereas Nietzsche's Zarathustra ascends mountains to think in seclusion. Each of these deployments of withdrawal serves epistemic imperatives: each physically figures the remove of abstraction in a world in which the two-world framework of appearance and reality has collapsed. They serve a horizon of thought in which appearance is reality; all is "socially constructed," to use the phrase of our time; and there is no outside noumenal to provide an Archimedean point and thus God's-eye view on the phenomenal. Despite these foundational realignments, we nonetheless persist in the habit of trying to think. How do we do so? Seclusion and temporary withdrawal provide an approximation of the Archimedean remove.

Before making the decision to withdraw and hibernate, the protagonist of *Invisible Man* tells us: "I realized that I couldn't return to Mary's, or to any part of my old life. I could approach it *only from the outside,* and I had been as invisible to Mary as I had been to the Brotherhood." To continue his life, he would first have to stop and think. "No, I couldn't return to Mary's, or to the campus, or to the Brotherhood, or home. I could only move ahead or stay here, underground. So I would stay here until I was chased out. Here, at least, I could try to think things out in peace, or, if not in peace, in quiet."[11] His reflections underground let him explore the conclusion that he is an invisible man "simply because people refuse to see me."[12] They see instead who they want and presume him to be. "I was never more hated," he concludes, "than when I tried to be honest. . . . On the other hand, I've never been more loved and appreciated than when I tried to justify and affirm someone's mistaken beliefs; or when I tried to give my friends the incorrect, absurd answers they wished to hear."[13] This crisis of affirmation returns the protagonist to his grandfather's deathbed instructions to "agree 'em to death and destruction."[14] His grandfather is sharing a strategy of resistance—one that enters into what is being seen by the hegemonic white gaze and strives to subvert this dominance. What is of interest here, for my argument, is the turn back to the past to understand a present predicament of sight and insight (and of blindness).

Tacking back and forth between the opening chapters and conclusion of the book, the protagonist tells us "the end was in the beginning."[15] Trying to understand his present prompted what Toby and Tommo understood as "a right-about retrograde" in his thinking. He boomeranged. He had to return to and systematically recover and revise the meaning of his grandfather's mysterious words. "On his deathbed," we are told, "he called my father to him and said, 'Son, after I'm gone I want you to keep up the good fight. I never told you, but our life is a war, and I have been a traitor all my born days, a spy in the enemy's country ever since I gave up my gun in Reconstruction. Live with your head in the lion's mouth. I want you to overcome 'em with yeses, undermine 'em with grins, agree 'em to death and destruction, let 'em swoller you till they vomit or bust wide open.'" The family was shocked by his sudden vehemence. "They thought the old man had gone out of his mind. He had been the meekest of men. The younger children were rushed from the room, the shade drawn and the flame of the lamp turned so low that it sputtered on the wick like the old man's breathing. 'Learn it to the younguns,' he whispered fiercely; then he died."[16]

"But my folks," the passage continues, "were more alarmed over his last words than over his dying."[17] They told the children not to speak of it, but the protagonist thought of it as he won awards and praise from whites. He was seemingly following his grandfather's advice; he was being meek and good and hardworking; but "the old man had defined it as *treachery*" and as war and not as goodness.[18] Underground, in his seclusion, he was still uncertain and pondered his grandfather's meaning: "Weren't they their own death and their own destruction except as the principle lived in them and lived in us?" Are whites to be fought for their own good or for the good of the whole? Isn't it for both? "Was it that we of all, we, most of all had to affirm the principle, the plan in whose name we had been brutalized and sacrificed . . . because we were older than they in the sense of what if took to live in the world with others?"[19] How should we understand this effacement of the progressive world picture: this recognition of the putatively primitive as more advanced and more mature? Was his grandfather suggesting that he was more mature as a citizen, even though as a former slave his citizenship had only recently been won? Can how to live as an excluded minority at the margins of the republic be separated from how to live in the republic as a whole? Does citizenship, for everyone, require masquerade? "Who knows," Ellison writes, "but that, on the lower frequencies, I speak for you."[20]

Predating Nietzsche and Dostoyevsky, Melville's protagonist also withdraws and consequently thinks against the trend of his time: first in captivity with the Typee and then in a British prison in *Omoo.* It would be imprecise, however, to say that Melville's Tommo withdraws in order to think. He is instead allowed a vantage for critical reflection by the situations of remove in which he finds himself. The device of withdrawal seems less devicelike in Melville's first novels: the physical remove is part of the central narrative and reads as less authorially figured. But despite this seeming naturalness, Melville's stories accomplish the epistemic work of the more overtly deployed structure of *Invisible Man.* Remove from the world allows a critical perspective. Shipping itself, throughout Melville's writing, provides this remove and a vantage point outside the everyday and hegemonic from which to think.[21] But in the earliest novels the remove of the texts is more profound: from mainland civilization, through the liminal world on board the ships moving between mainlands, and into the culture of another world. Inhabiting the world of the Marquesan Islanders compels disapproval of the values and practices of Melville's home world. In *Typee* and *Omoo,* for example, his criticisms of the missionaries are stringent and widely recognized.[22] The protagonist insists that his captors in *Typee,* living in isolation, are more Christian than the Christians who hope to find and convert them (*Typee,* 238). An example of this would be the care with which Tommo is fed. He was unable to master the technique of wrapping the gooey staple of the island diet around his finger. So Kory-Kory, who was his attendant, fed him. "He brought us various kinds of food; and, as if I were an infant, insisted upon feeding me with his own hands" (*Typee,* 109). And throughout *Omoo,* Melville presents the missionaries, the "mickonaree," as colonials more interested in their own comforts than in spreading the good news (*Omoo,* 494–506, 508). Following these observations, it seems only sensible in *Moby-Dick* when Ishmael joins Queequeg and prays to his companion's idol. "And what," he asks, "do I wish that Queequeg would do to me? Why, unite with me in my particular Presbyterian form of worship. Consequently, I must unite with him in his; ergo I must turn idolator" (*Moby-Dick,* 849). This pluralizing of the sacred troubles the assumption of progress, just as the pluralizing and confounding of maturity and infancy do. Dimensions of modern worship compel engagement of the pagan form, and this engagement boomerangs back on and contradicts the injunctions meant to shore up monotheism. Again resonating with *Invisible Man,* is it the principles of Christianity like the principles of the republic that matter here? And how do we see the principles of our own world when we find a way, momentarily at least, to desituate ourselves?

Let us consider, further, the temporal structures of Melville's and Ellison's travelogues as an unhinging of the metaphysical frame of reference and thus of the onto-theology of progress. Hannah Arendt understands the remove from everyday activity as calling forth and enabling a dimension of self—as, that is, enacting what she terms the thinking ego poised between past and future. Unexpected clashes between past and future, and by extension between savage and civilized, create a space of remove. Arendt is explicating Nietzsche's as well as Kafka's descriptions of thinking when there is no outside to thought: no promise of a better future, or of a noumenal realm of any sort. Instead, the past pushes forward against the future, and the future pushes back on the past, for this is the experience of the thinking ego and not of the biographical or biological self moving in a linear pattern from birth to death. The thinking ego looks back and selects from the past to make sense of the present moment and push forward.[23] In Kafka's version, the past and future are two antagonists colliding against each other in thought: "The first supports him in his fight with the second, for he wants to push him forward, and in the same way the second supports him in his fight with the first, since he drives him back."[24] For Nietzsche the collision where past and future meet is titled the *Augenblick*—the blink of an eye, which is also translated as the gateway "Now"[25] or the gateway "Moment" in *Zarathustra.*[26] Nietzsche saw the demise of progress and the two-world frame of reference as a crisis. He feared that the loss of our faith in progress, in relation to thinking, would stymie action: "Alas, the time is coming when man will no longer shoot the arrow of his longing beyond man."[27] But in Arendt's formulation of the condition and problem, "man lives in this in-between, and what he calls the present is a life-long fight against the dead weight of the past, driving him forward with hope, and the fear of the future (whose only certainty is death), driving him backward toward 'the quiet of the past.'"[28] And it is for Arendt a fight to be taken up: it is how we shoot beyond ourselves. As Ellison's protagonist tells us, thinking is a prelude to action: "a hibernation is a covert preparation for a more overt action."[29] When we withdraw and think, we prepare to muddle along in the face of confusion, "certain defeat," and the uncertainty of the future. We look back and revise and push onward and revise again.

In *Invisible Man* Ellison rewrites and performs variations on scenes from throughout Melville's work. The sermon "Blackness of Blackness" in the book's prologue takes us inside the all-black meetinghouse Ishmael peered into, and walked past, in *Moby-Dick*.[30] Taking us into the mind of his protagonist, Ellison takes us into what Melville calls the "hive of subtlety" that was Babo's head staked on a pole beckoning his former master, Benito Cereno, to follow him toward death.[31] Ellison riffs on an earlier moment in the tragedy of the revolt in his presentation of one of the many discomforting, and tragic, scenes in *Invisible Man*. As a college student, the protagonist takes Mr. Norton, a white trustee, into the black quarters and then to a juke joint filled with black inmates from an asylum. "They were supposed to be members of the professions toward which at various times I vaguely aspired myself," he explains, "and even though they never seemed to see me I could never believe that they were really patients."[32] In that they are "crazy," they are outside of and reflecting on the world the protagonist is trying to fit himself into: "Sometimes it appeared as though they played some vast and complicated game with me and the rest of the school folk, a game whose goal was laughter and whose rules and subtleties I could never grasp."[33] Overcome on many fronts, Mr. Norton repeatedly asks his chaperone for a "little stimulant," and they encounter the patients while in search of whiskey.[34] The protagonist will be expelled from college because of these events. We are reminded of Benito Cereno being handled with much more skill by Babo, "who, with one hand sustaining his master, with the other applied a cordial" (*Benito Cereno,* 700–701). The slaves had taken over the ship, and it was a ruse to make the American Captain Delano believe that the Spanish were still in control. Don Benito, too, needed repeated sips of a little stimulant to get through his performance. An exchange between the two captains after the revolt fails is one of two epigraphs at the beginning of *Invisible Man*. "'You are saved,' cried Captain Delano, more and more astonished and pained; 'you are saved: what has cast such a shadow upon you?'" And Don Benito, who in Melville's story lies melancholy and dying, responds, "The negro" (*Benito Cereno,* 754).

Ellison will later title an essay "The Shadow and the Act" and explore seeing and what an audience is ready to see. He asks what has happened to the public, the American public, if it is ready to see a black character in charge and never humiliated in a 1949 film of Faulkner's *Intruder in the Dust.* What has come out of the shadows? And how are such revelations performed? What remains hidden?[35] *Benito Cereno* is a point of reference throughout Ellison's work, but he recasts and redirects the shadows Melville presents in this story. He recasts, in other words, the revelations and concealments preoccupying Melville. *Invisible Man* is about how to act when the shadows of white supremacy obscure one's way. Ellison does not simply peep into the mind of Babo, or into the all-black meetinghouse; he writes from within the position of subjugated exclusion and reveals the unseen (or speaks the unspeakable unspoken from the position of the silenced). White supremacy is the question, too, in *Typee* and *Omoo* as well as *Benito Cereno.* Both of the earlier texts are about contact between the Marquesan Islanders and colonial powers from Europe and America. Once again, those on the margins of empire, in the shadows, have something to teach those at the hegemonic white center. The cultures are interwoven in *Omoo*—the English jail, for example, the "Calabooza Beretanee," is manned by Tahitian jailers who are delightfully lax. The prisoners "cheerfully acquiesce" to their authority (*Omoo,* 443–449). And in the confrontation held at bay in *Typee*—the islanders are not colonized in this story—we see the horizon of contact as well. In this text, however, their world is hegemonic and *they hold* the representatives of European and American power captive, the representatives of empire are *their guests.* White power is feared—they fear the French—but it is not in control in *Typee.* Melville's writing and thinking begin inside the Polynesian meetinghouse—inside the Ti and Taboo groves—of the other as dominant rather than dominated. Tommo was in the shadows there and struggled to speak where "the edge of the world" was its own center.

States of Artifice

When Melville writes Tommo and Toby into the world of the Marquesan Islanders, he is equipped with state-of-nature theory. He knows his readers will gaze through this lens as they peep with him at Polynesian life, and he plays with multiple reversals of the notion that civilization progresses from a more primitive state of nature.[36] Melville uses these references to challenge the historical trajectory of modernities that see themselves as progressing from a preconceived past; and his account will not be a simple reversal of savage and civilized. He does not present the encounter as a return to an Edenlike grace. The primitive will be allowed its own cultivation and will assume and act on its own dominance. Contrasting the islanders with the beginnings of discord and inequality through sexual competition in Rousseau's "Second Discourse,"[37] Melville writes that "you might have seen a throng of young females, not filled with envyings of each other's charms, nor displaying the ridiculous affectations of gentility, nor yet moving in whalebone corsets, like so many automatons, but free, inartificially happy, and unconstrained" (*Typee,* 152). He seems to naturalize their goodness in passages like this, but these allusions to canonical stories are not mere reversals or rebuttals that risk reconstructing narratives of progress or decline. Melville eschews these trajectories and naturalizing motifs. He, unlike Rousseau, situates his savages securely in their own artifice—they are language users, they are together in society. He presents not their innocence but their civilization as admirable. How are these seemingly perfect persons cunning and controlling? And how is Melville not reducing them to mere noble savages? They are lovely people—to look at and to be with—but they do hold Tommo and Toby captive. And they shrink a head or two here and there. They distinguish between friend and enemy; they cannot always decide who is which or how to treat a friend; and that is what makes them just like every "us" across the globe.

Melville notes that "the strict honesty which the inhabitants of nearly all of the Polynesian Islands manifest towards each other, is in striking contrast with the thieving propensities some of them evince in their intercourse with foreigners." They are not angels, but quite human, in contact with other civilizations. "It would almost seem that, according to their peculiar code of morals, the pilfering of a hatchet or a wrought nail from a European is looked upon as a praiseworthy action. Or rather, it may be presumed, that bearing in mind the wholesale forays made upon them by their nautical visitors, they consider the property of the latter as a fair object of reprisal" (*Typee,* 236). They are an alternative center. They stage and enact, and try to conserve and maintain, a picture of their world. Rather than view self- and world disclosure as a historical project predicated on assumptions of progress, the islanders practice these tasks as daily dimensions of politics. In contrast to Kennan Ferguson's argument in this volume, my contention is that Melville does not naturalize the Typee even though they have maintained their isolation in the first novel. Instead, states of artifice meet states of artifice. They frame us as much as we frame them. Let us consider how Tommo and his companion, Toby, encounter the islanders—or, rather, how they encounter Tommo and Toby.

The American companions are fugitives who have jumped ship together "clandestinely." Shipping itself is a removal from the world of everyday experience, as noted above; and now abandoning their duties to go adventuring on the island will instantiate an even further remove. Toby is an assumed name, and he would not tell his real name to anyone on the ship (*Typee,* 43). But Tommo and Toby were companionable. They each "had evidently moved in a different sphere of life" from their other shipmates. As Tommo explains, Toby's "conversation at times betrayed this, although he was anxious to conceal it" (ibid., 44). They both had a shared class understanding of being wronged by unacceptable treatment from their ship's captain: they were not being properly fed, the sick were not being cared for as they should be. Sensitive to the illegality and moral weight of leaving their posts, Tommo insists that the horrors of the ship were worth risking the dangers of terrain and cannibals to escape. He worries, though, about the possibility of "falling in with a foraging party of these same bloody-minded Typee, whose appetites, edged perhaps by the air of so elevated a region, might prompt them to devour one" (ibid., 43).

To escape their posts, Tommo and Toby plan to flee the bay where their ship was docked. They climb the mountains ringing the island and wait for the ship to leave. They would be able to spy its departure from this vantage point, and they were sure the mountains would be filled with abundant fresh fruit. They are wrong about finding fruit, however. They push up and down over high points and chasms in search of water and food. Starving, they realize they will have to climb down into the valleys where the islanders live, protected from the sea, and shipping, by the mountains. There is a problem, though, of reputation. Tommo and Toby know they could happen on the Typee or the Happar—they fear the Typee and very much dread an encounter with these most ferocious cannibals they have heard about so often. They forestall entering the valley because of this fear.

They follow paths that become dead ends. At one high vantage, where a path ends at the edge of a cliff, Toby asks if "every one that travels this path takes a jump here, eh?" (*Typee,* 59). At times Tommo prompts Toby onward; but at another time, when Tommo is despairing, Toby encourages him. Toby wakes up one morning energized and insists they are going to go back over the ascents and descents they have already traversed and return to and enter a settlement they had seen earlier. They will not return to the bay yet, but they will attempt this right-about retrograde. They are starving and tired, and Tommo is injured, so they advance toward the "crowning beauty of the prospect"—toward, that is, a view of the populated valley before them. These passages are proto-Nietzschean—stylistically and epistemically—and they signal confusions and consternations that complicate the distinction between tragedy and comedy. In passages that prefigure the narrative in *Thus Spoke Zarathustra,* Tommo and Toby are physically and emotionally exhausted by climbing and descending, by hoping and then despairing. They overcome adversity by carrying on through their despair. Tommo, at least, is transported out of his everyday experience and ready to see and hear and think differently. "Over all the landscape," he reports, "there reigned the most hushed repose, which I almost feared to break lest, like the enchanted gardens in a fairy tale, a single syllable might dissolve the spell" (ibid., 64–65). They prod themselves on, with hope, saying they will find the Happars in the valley and not the feared and bloody Typee.

Of course they descend to the Typee, but they do not find the fierce people forecasted by their reputation. And during this first meeting, they do not find the countenances they expect from simple savages. "One of them in particular," Tommo explains, "who appeared to be the highest in rank, placed himself directly facing me; looking at me with a rigidity of aspect under which I absolutely quailed. . . . Never before had I been subjected to so strange and steady a glance; it revealed nothing of the mind of the savage, but appeared to be reading my own." We could read these lines as an encounter with the inscrutable primitive. Or, by contrast, we could note that Tommo is surprised by being made an object of study. In this initial interview, the chief refuses a gift of tobacco. "He quietly rejected the proffered gift, and, without speaking, motioned me to return it to its place." Tommo was in no position, yet, to give and to have a gift honored by receipt. He is not allowed to frame the situation. "Was this act of the chief a token of his enmity? Typee or Happar? I asked within myself. I started, for at the same moment this question was asked by the strange being before me." Exchanging a glance of trepidation with Toby, "I paused for a second and know not by what impulse it was that I answered 'Typee.' The piece of dusty statuary nodded in approval, and then murmured 'Mortarkee?' 'Mortarkee,' said I, without further hesitation—'Typee mortarkee.'" And, having announced the Typee to be good: "What a transition! The dark figures around us leaped to their feet, clapped their hands in transport, and shouted again and again the talismanic syllables, the utterance of which appeared to have settled everything" (*Typee*, 89–90). Did he get lucky? Or had Tommo entered into the world of the Typee enough to know what the right answer would be? Had he sufficiently left behind the strictures of his own world's certainty?

The principal chief raged against the Happar and all joined in. The rovers were fed and cared for, they were treated with respect as guests, and they made fast friends. Now in a position to reciprocate his host's congeniality, now allowed to meet on a more equal footing, the protagonist too takes the name we know him by in this text. The chief "gave me to understand that his name was 'Mehevi,' and that, in return, he wished me to communicate my appellation. I hesitated for an instant, thinking that it might be difficult for him to pronounce my real name, and then with the most praiseworthy intentions intimated that I was known as 'Tom.'" But this name the chief could not say. "'Tommo,' 'Tomma,' 'Tommee,' everything but plain 'Tom.' As he persisted in garnishing the word with an additional syllable, I compromised the matter with him at the word 'Tommo': and by that name I went during the entire period of my stay in the valley" (*Typee*, 90–91).

After first meeting and helping care for Tommo and Toby when they entered the village, Chief Mehevi appears to them the next day in full warrior gear. Tommo is awestruck, and he does not recognize him. After Tommo and Toby had been attended to and visited by many people of the valley, "a superb-looking warrior stooped the towering plumes of his head-dress beneath the low portal, and entered the house. I saw at once that he was some distinguished personage, the natives regarding him with the utmost deference, and making room for him as he approached" (*Typee*, 96). But it wasn't merely the natives who were affected by his status. "His aspect," Tommo reports, "was imposing": "The splendid long drooping tail-feathers of the tropical bird, thickly interspersed with the gaudy plumage of the cock, were disposed in an immense upright semicircle upon his head, their lower extremities being fixed in a crescent of guinea-beads which spanned the forehead. Around his neck were several enormous necklaces of boars' tusks, polished like ivory, and disposed in such a manner as that the longest and largest were upon his capacious chest" (ibid., 96–97).

When they make eye contact, when Tommo meets "the strange gaze" he had met the preceding night and sees past the facade of power, he immediately knows that the warrior is Mehevi. "On addressing him, he advanced at once in the most cordial manner, and, greeting me warmly, seemed to enjoy not a little the effect his barbaric costume had produced upon me" (*Typee,* 98). Note not only Mehevi's conscious self-disclosure, but also his congenial awareness of the power of appearance as the Typee participate in the construction of their own reality.

Another warrior—taboo, but thus allowed to travel and carry news among the tribes of the valley and the outside world as well—also toyed with and relished his presentation of self when visiting the Typee. After walking in and pointedly ignoring Tommo, he later cordially discussed the rationale of his comportment with him, for he could speak English. "When I asked the now affable Marnoo why it was that he had not previously spoken to me, he eagerly enquired what I had been led to think of him from his conduct in this respect." Tommo tells him he had thought him a great chief, unaffected by seeing a white man. "At this declaration of the exalted opinion I had formed of him, he appeared vastly gratified, and gave me to understand that he had purposely behaved in that manner, in order to increase my astonishment, as soon as he should see proper to address me" (*Typee,* 167). Note how straightforwardly, and unabashedly, Mehevi and Marnoo effect artifice. Melville does not naturalize them. They use presentation of self—they manipulate emotion and perception with it—but they do not pretend that appearance is anything more than appearance. This is not, by any means, to say that appearances are not real. But these self-presentations for Mehevi and Marnoo are not ultimate truths, nor are they hiding ultimate truths. They are, like Tommo's assumption of his name, facilitating communication and part of being in a world. Mehevi and Marnoo are disclosing a world through self-disclosure. It is one in which they have elevated status, and they communicate this as they engage and acknowledge their white guest. By contrast, Tommo, because he is an outsider, often struggles and misfires as he attempts to fit himself into their world. Yet both sides work at communication and make a world together. It is striking, actually, how much understanding there is between the Typee and their subaltern visitors. They meet not as natural and civilized, but instead as form of life vis-à-vis form of life, as states of artifice in contact with each other without the assumption of a world-historical hierarchy.

"It's a Mutual, Joint-Stock World"

When Toby and Tommo are questioned by the Typee during their first night in the village, they are asked about the "movements of the French, against whom they seemed to cherish the most fierce hatred" (*Typee,* 94).[38] And the next day, when he is speaking with Mehevi, "that which engaged his attention was the late proceedings of the 'Franee,' as he called the French, in the neighboring bay of Nukuheva." They were able to communicate to the chief that there had been six warships in the bay when they left it. "When he received this intelligence, Mehevi, by the aid of his fingers, went through a long numerical calculation, as if estimating the number of Frenchmen the squadron might contain" (ibid., 98). It is very much "as if," though, for Tommo, and there is guessing on both sides until much later, when the English-speaking Marnoo arrives. With limited shared language, Toby and Tommo try to communicate that they need medicine from the Europeans for Tommo's leg. The Americans always worry that their indulgent hosts will suddenly be the cannibals they expected and eat them. But Mehevi and all remain steadfast in their role as hosts. Tommo is assigned a servant because he is lame. "I could not but be amused at the manner in which the chief addressed me upon this occasion," Tommo tells us, "talking to me for at least fifteen or twenty minutes as calmly as if I could understand every word that he said. I remarked this peculiarity very often afterward in many of the other islanders" (ibid., 100). Their assumption of their own hegemony was very strange to Tommo—surely, they must have thought, he will learn the language like every other child does. The Typee, however, were even more strange to Toby. They irked him in a way that they did not discomfit Tommo. He wanted to leave, to get help for Tommo's leg, and simply to escape, but he was rebuked. "As soon as we succeeded in making the natives understand our intention, they broke out into the most vehement opposition to the measure, and for a while I almost despaired of obtaining their consent. At the bare thought *of one of us leaving them,* they manifested the most lively concern" (*Typee,* 120; emphasis added).

Toby persists and tries to leave, but he is attacked by Happars and must come back. Leaving again, he promises to return with medicine, but he does not. What happens to him remains mysterious in the main body of the text, and Tommo fears that Toby has been killed. He decides to hide his own desire to leave after his request is angrily denied by Mehevi. He too will masquerade in his encounters with the Typee. But Tommo will share, rather than disparage and reject, their world. And he will not let them negate his past and his prospects.

Tommo will delight his hosts "by conforming to their style of dress" for a celebration (*Typee,* 192). He will court Fayaway and be allowed to violate the taboo on women in boats and take her sailing (ibid., 159). But he will disappoint his hosts and not be tattooed because he still plans to return to his own world. He will agree with them, and join them to an extent, but he will have his limits. After offering to have his arm rather than his face drawn on, he is angrily rebuffed by the Typee. He saw their desire to tattoo and make him a member of their group as a new danger. "I now felt convinced that in some luckless hour I should be disfigured in such a manner as never more to have the *face* to return to my countrymen, even should the opportunity offer" (*Typee,* 255; emphasis in original). To share worlds does not, and cannot, require wholesale capitulation of one world to the other unless we assume a better world that should be progressed toward and realized. I write without this epistemic certainty, and Melville does so as well. In contrast to Ferguson, I am arguing that tattooing Tommo's face would have rendered him, in Ellison's terms, invisible. Recall Ellison's protagonist telling us, "I've never been more loved or appreciated than when I tried to 'justify' and affirm someone's mistaken beliefs; or when I tried to give my friends the incorrect, absurd answers they wished to hear."[39] Tommo did not give his Typee friends what they wanted. By saying no, he refuses to deny the world and past from which he came, and he refuses to relinquish his hopes and prospects. He refuses to deny himself because others cannot see him. He emerges from both worlds, rather than from one or the other.

John Bryant notes that Melville "depicts, with clarity, the bafflement of the encounter between western and Pacific minds."[40] And he is right: the failures of understanding are many, and certainty is elusive. But to hope for too much certainty is to proceed with the assumptions of what is in *Typee* the marginalized modern. In *All Things Shining,* Hubert Dreyfus and Sean Dorrance Kelly explore what Karl Jaspers identified as the Axial Revolution across world religious systems, the idea "that there is a good beyond what we can find in the everyday conception of human flourishing; that there is a transcendent good that is the nature of the Divine." Dreyfus and Kelly make a case for inhabiting everyday flourishing without recourse to this form of the real and find resources for their project in the story of Ahab's pursuits. Instead of the truth of the whale, they argue with Melville in *Moby-Dick* the possibility "that there is no meaning to the universe hidden behind its surface events, that the surface events themselves—contradictory and mysterious and multiple as they may be—are nevertheless all the meaning there is." Mehevi and Marnoo, with their easily revealed ruses of self-presentation, comprehend the importance and sufficiency of the surface. Dreyfus and Kelly find this stance in Ishmael's ability "to live in these surface meanings and find a genuine range of joys and comforts there, without wishing they stood for something more."[41] The allure of exploring Melville's ability to dwell at the surface—rather than a transcendent level—as a religious question is strong, and it is the line of thought Hawthorne followed in his assessment of Melville's concern with "providence and futurity." He is never passive in his embrace of the contradictory and mysterious: "He can neither believe, nor be comfortable in his unbelief; and he is too honest and courageous not to try to do one or the other."[42] But *Typee* suggests that an origin of Melville's embrace of the indeterminate surfaces of everyday experience was political as well as theological, an outcome of living experience in the island polity. What Bryant sees as confusion is indicative of the ways in which Melville's *Typee* does not respond to, and satisfy, the two-world metaphysical framing. Melville lets confusion be. In the travelogue that is *Typee,* Melville reports on living a minority experience among self-satisfied actors who are trying to conserve their way of life. As William Spanos claims of *Moby-Dick* and the works that follow it, *Typee* too "de-structures" the Enlightenment comportment Heidegger terms the "age of the world picture" and reminds us that there are worlds, rather than the world, in which we flourish.[43] There are many ages, rather than the progressive age—many world pictures, rather than the world picture. Letting go of the assumption of progress and allowing, for the moment at least, the hegemony of the Typee world, what can we understand? What surfaces meet? How do they meet? And how do they fail to cohere? What can we see and not see?

In *Typee* the mystery of why Toby is allowed to escape and Tommo is not remains unresolved. We do know that Toby never gave himself over to the world of his captors, and hosts, in the way that Tommo did. Whereas both fear the sudden souring of hospitableness, Toby with vivid suppositions assumes they are being fed so assiduously to be fattened for consumption, and he worries they are being fed "baked baby" (*Typee*, 116–117). Toby is the figure of unreconstructed imperialism in the text. Alternatively, Tommo thinks "the horrible character imputed to these Typee appeared to me wholly undeserved" (ibid., 119). The absence of violence is the first sign that their reputation is strategic, that it is spread to save the Typee from the French. This interpretation is further substantiated by Mehevi's concern with "the Franee," and then later during Marnoo's visits after Toby has fled. Reporting to the Typee on the colonial forces surrounding them, Marnoo fell "back into an attitude of lofty command, exhorted the Typee to resist these encroachments; reminding them, with a fierce glance of exultation, that as yet the terror of their name had preserved them from attack, and with a scornful sneer he sketched in ironical terms the wondrous intrepidity of the French, who, with five war-canoes and hundreds of men, had not dared to assail the naked warriors of their valley" (ibid., 165). So it seems Tommo cannot leave and report how wonderful and peaceful the Typee actually are. Was letting Toby escape a mistake that will not be made again? Or is it something else? Mehevi threatens Marnoo's life and safety for simply asking if Tommo can go; Marnoo's status would be converted from friend to enemy. The aim of their elaborate ruse, the projection of ferocity, is an attempt to conserve their world.

Tommo ultimately escapes, and in large part did so because he made good friends with his host the old Marheyo. "When I thought of the loved friends who were thousands and thousands of miles from the savage island in which I was held captive, when I reflected that my dreadful fate would forever be concealed from them, and that with hope deferred they might continue to await my return long after my inanimate form had blended with the dust of the valley—I could not repress a shudder of anguish" (*Typee*, 281). But as he felt this anguish, he was being watched over with sympathy by Marheyo, who understood his longing for "home" and "mother." "Frequently suspending his employment, and noticing my melancholy eye fixed upon him, he would raise his hand with a gesture expressive of deep commiseration, and then moving towards me slowly would enter on tip-toes, fearful of disturbing the slumbering natives, and, taking the fan from my hand, would sit before me, swaying it gently to and fro and gazing earnestly into my face." Marheyo saw Tommo's face. Poised between savage and civilized—much like Arendt's thinking ego poised between past and future—Melville's protagonist has become of both worlds. He could not be of either one or the other.

> Just beyond the pi-pi, and disposed in a triangle before the entrance of the house, were three magnificent bread-fruit trees. . . . It is strange how inanimate objects will twine themselves into our affections, especially in the hour of affliction. Even now, amidst all the bustle and stir of the proud and busy city in which I am dwelling, the image of those three trees seems to come as vividly before my eyes as if they were actually present, and I still feel the soothing quiet pleasure which I then had in watching hour after hour their topmost boughs waving in the breeze. (Ibid., 282)

He is poised between friends and friends, Pacific island and American city, past and future. Whatever the reason for keeping him captive, his friend Marheyo, who saw through his masquerade of happiness, let him go when the time came. Their friendship was a point of contact, another surface, cutting across and through the strategic surface of the Typee's defenses. And Tommo tacked, and still tacks even as we read of him now, back and forth between revisions of revised past and future longings. There are always shadows. A mutual, joint-stock world is never monolithic and always the outcome of living, not merely lived, experience.

Conservation and Even Destruction

We have read Melville through Ellison with a focus on *Typee,* and now let us reorient and read Ellison through our reading of Melville's first novel. There we have learned that the pleasures and problems of collectivity are not easy surfaces to adventure along or to protect from adventurers. We have seen the savages resist the civilized with cultivated strategies. And we also know that the Typee were playing in the face of certain defeat. By recognizing the cultivation of the islanders before they are colonized, I do not mean to suggest that they will not be colonized. The islands will be secured by imperial forces. And this is how we American savages advance our hopes and prospects now as well. Heavily armed against others and among ourselves, we parse friends and enemies internationally and let ourselves be made into enemies of each other. It is a wonder that we can make friends and act on any sort of interconnectedness. But we do. Consider, for example, scenes in *Invisible Man*—during a riot—that replay the reversals of status Tommo experiences as guest and as captive of the Typee. I want to suggest that the protagonist's "hibernation"—his remove from the ordinary presumptions of his world—begins in these passages rather than with the move underground. These events knock him out of time and space. He will tack back and forth between leading and being led and be surprised by his own demotion to equality with those he has been trying to help. When the assumptions of progress supporting such hierarchies are relaxed, just as when Tommo's were, the meanings of actions are transfigured and the dominated find moments in which to rule. The presumed leader learns to follow by learning to see that which was formerly concealed. Citizens meet as citizens.

The riot is precipitated by the death of a black youth who was a leader in the Brotherhood but had left the party. Clifton was shot while resisting arrest. The protagonist delivers a speech at his funeral that helps incite Harlem, and the chaos reveals to him—as the youth must have realized—that the party had been using its black members for other "revolutionary" ends. Whatever the party's plans and prospects, Harlem explodes.

Stumbling into the melee, the protagonist is grazed by a bullet and befriended by a man in the crowd, Scofield, who tells him: "Man, you lucky you ain't dead. These sonsabitches is really shooting now." He "looked at the thin man, feeling a surge of friendship. He didn't know me, his help was disinterested."[44] Scofield gets him a drink and takes him along looting with a group of men who know each other. And there the protagonist meets Dupre. "He was a man who nothing in my life taught me to see, to understand, or respect, a man outside the scheme until now."[45] Dupre is a man who is very able—at leading and at doing—and he is seizing his chance. He does not fit the protagonist's progressive vision of the American dream. He is a poor man, with hope and a plan despite limited prospects—invisible to the protagonist of the novel until now. The protagonist has to give up his own advancement, his status, to see. The friends are grabbing shirts and "Dobbs hats." They are looting as if it were "a praiseworthy act," to recall the Marquesans pilfering from the Europeans (*Typee,* 236). And then the plan is proposed.

"Dupre looked down at me and kicked something—a pound of butter, sending it smearing across the hot street. 'We fixing to do something what needs to be done,' he said. 'First we get a flashlight for everybody. . . . *And let's have some organization, y'all.* Don't everybody be running over everybody else. Come on!'" They are going to burn down the tenement they live in. "I felt no need to lead or to leave them," the protagonist tells us; he "was glad to follow, was gripped by the need to see where and to what they would lead."[46] They were acting in concert. They all took buckets of "coal oil," kerosene, and went to the building outfitted with their flashlights. Despite being trained to lead by the Brotherhood, the protagonist tells us: "It didn't occur to me to interfere or to question. They had a plan." And they were going to see it through to the end. "Already I could see the women and children coming down the steps."[47] Dupre's pregnant wife tries to stop him and the others, but he refuses her. "'Now git on out the way, Lottie,' he said patiently. 'Why you have to start this now? We done been all over it and you know I ain't go'n change. . . . My kid died of the t-bees in that death trap, but I bet a man ain't no more go'n be *born* in there,' he said."[48] They had a small and ultimately doomed hope and prospect, but they acted nonetheless. The tragedy of the action is not to be denied here. They destroyed their home. But they did so triumphantly.

After helping them, the protagonist runs off thinking he needs to stop the Brotherhood. He still believes that they planned and are in some way exercising control of the riot. Despite the spontaneous organization that he sees unfolding before his eyes, he is still caught up in and trying to make sense of a narrative of history unfolding. He is in a new world, but still of his former world. He is happy and exhilarated by this unexpected encounter, but he cannot let himself capitulate to it. He thinks the Brotherhood would let Harlem burn for their ends, and that is probably the case. But Harlem was already ready to explode. When the protagonist was grasping to understand what was happening, what was going on, Dupre tried to school him out of his overschooled immaturity: "'Damn *who* started it,' Dupre said. 'All I want is for it to last for a while. . . . Don't nobody know how it started,' Dupre said. 'Somebody has to know,' I said."[49]

But Dupre is right. Again, the putative primitive has read the surfaces of possibility and acted on them. A world-historical perspective does not have to be ready to hand. The rioters do not need to have knowledge of the precise spur to action. There are many spurs waiting to aggravate, and the actors are ready to reveal who they are and disclose their world, even if to do so requires destruction. They spoke. Ellison's adventurer heard them. And as he joins with them in the event, in the moment, he learns to unlearn, as Tommo did among the Typee. The rioters each and all manifested their humanity and acted collectively. As citizens, they briefly saw each other's faces.

Uncertainty frustrates, and I have purposefully aggravated the reader of this essay by narrating rather than defining dissipation of the assumption of progress in Melville's and Ellison's texts. But I could not have done otherwise in this attempt to delineate the functions of progress in encounters between "the savage" and "the civilized." To embrace dissipation is to embrace dispersal—multiple and overlapping perspectives, movement across surfaces—and I did not want to lie by pretending an Archimedean remove at odds with my own argument. The assumption of progress is pervasive and relentless in our thinking and practices, and we cannot simply grab hold of it and escort it offstage. Instead, we have explored master narratives of progress and seen them unhinged. We have found smaller and innumerable assumptions of progress at issue as well: we hope and act, succeed and fail, and try again. Melville's protagonist did not find the primitives he expected, and Ellison's protagonist was not able to lead after all. Both are upended by the dominance of those whom they initially assume to be their inferiors. But without insisting on the richness of the impoverished lives of Dupre and Scofield, and without insisting on the cultivation of the savages Mehevi and Marheyo and Marnoo, we do not see and hear them. Can we go so far as to see "their" modernity in competition with "our" modernity? If the reader cannot envision Melville's savages as moderns, and see Ellison's destructive looters as citizens, let me then define this blindness as the assumption of progress this essay targets.

I am not thinking here of Ahab's modernity, which strives to find a godlike truth with final answers to replace the tattered Christian God, but a perspectival modernism granted us as gift by the recession from the world of God as guarantor. Machiavelli and Nietzsche are the canonical emissaries of this perspectivism, but Arendt, Dreyfus and Kelly, Spanos, Ellison, and Melville explore this modernity as a world of possibilities to be indulged rather than—or at least as well as—feared. Whereas Dreyfus and Kelly ascribe a pantheism to Melville, I have argued that he presents us with a rigorous temporal and ultimately spatial pluralism. To unhinge assumptions of progress is to change the ways we think and act. And Melville's experience in the Typee polity, related to us through the adventures of Tommo, disrupted his assumptions of hierarchy and hegemony. Taboo emerges on this perspectival reading as simply saying no as all cultures say no to something. Tommo's refusal to be tattooed, too, is simply saying no.[50] From the perspective of the South Seas as center of the world, Queequeg's selective engagement with Christianity is a parallel example. He left Father Mapple's chapel before the benediction and returned to his room to worship his own idol (*Moby-Dick*, 831, 846–849).

Melville does not describe an elementary relativism, nor does Ellison, in which we are either in one world or in another. The surfaces of past and future, old and new, meet and create new surfaces when we are in multiple worlds of revelation and concealment, of shadow and of act. By insisting on the modernity of the Typee, I do not want to suggest that we erase colonialism, as if a world-historical reverse-discrimination argument is in order. Oppression happened and is happening. But if we savages are to help ourselves, we need to take the equality of the other, and thus each other, as at least the thought of a possibility. We have to embrace the fact that we are dominated, and that we dominate, when we act in concert. Acting on that would be an act of democratic maturity: an end we can sketch the beginnings of among the not-yet-colonized Typee and in Ellison's well-ordered mob. Such acts could separate out, for a moment at least, the principles and practices of republics in contrast to the actualities of empires. Perhaps we could then consciously and deliberatively, even if provisionally, decide what we want to conserve and what we want to destroy. Compared to the passive sacrifice of ourselves and others to the "progressive" flow of so many haphazardly posited American futures, that might be mortarkee.

Notes

For their comments and provocations throughout the drafting of this chapter, I would like to thank Jason Frank, my anonymous reviewers, Stephen Engelmann, Mia Mihic Engelmann, Kennan Ferguson, Sarah Hoagland, Anne Leighton, Dylan Porter, and members of the Fall 2012 Honors Research Colloquium at Northeastern Illinois University. I am also indebted to the students in my spring 2012 Modern Political Theory class for their insights on the riot scenes in *Invisible Man*.

1. Herman Melville, *Omoo: A Narrrative of Adventures in the High Seas*

(1847), in *Typee, Omoo, Mardi* (New York: Library of America, 1982), 327–331; citations hereafter are given parenthetically in the text by title and page number.

2. Ralph Ellison, *Invisible Man* (1952; repr., New York: Vintage, 1995), 576.

3. Ibid., 577.

4. Herman Melville, *Typee: A Peep at Polynesian Life* (1846), in *Typee, Omoo, Mardi,* 286; citations hereafter are given parenthetically in the text by title and page number.

5. Ellison, *Invisible Man,* 579; emphasis in original.

6. Ibid., 573.

7. Cf. Ishmael's interpretation of the savage Queequeg after he saves a New England sailor who had been taunting him before falling overboard into cold waters. "He only asked for water—fresh water—something to wipe the brine off: that done, he put on dry clothes, lighted his pipe, and leaning against the bulwarks, and mildly eyeing those around him seemed to be saying to himself—'It's a mutual, joint-stock world, in all meridians. We cannibals must help these Christians.'" Herman Melville, *Moby-Dick; or, The Whale* (1851), in *Redburn, White-Jacket, Moby-Dick* (New York: Library of America, 1983), 859; citations hereafter are given parenthetically in the text by title and page number.

8. Hannah Arendt explicates Melville's *Billy Budd* and Dostoyevsky's *The Grand Inquisitor* in tandem in *On Revolution* (New York: Viking, 1963), 82–88. Her concern is with stammering and muteness—the inability to speak in the world from a position of absolute, transcendent goodness. Joining more recent critics of Melville, who will be addressed below, I explore what can be said and acted on without any form of transcendence, including the assumption of progress.

9. *Typee* and *Omoo* report on Melville's experiences, and they are novels that elaborate on and fictionalize these experiences. As John Bryant writes in his introduction to *Typee* (New York: Penguin, 1996), "We have no evidence of what Melville actually experienced, only what he wrote. And what he wrote is an anxious blend of fact and fiction" (xix). There is a tradition of trying to decipher and separate out the dimensions of this blend in *Typee* scholarship, and the appearance of the real-life Toby—a traveling companion in the story—after the initial publication of the text motivates this line of inquiry. The interpretation in this essay advances from the tale as Melville tells it.

10. In English publications of their work, Karl Jaspers and Hannah Arendt retain the German *Existenz* in part to distinguish their approach from contemporary existentialism. In "What Is Existenz Philosophy?"—which was first published in *Partisan Review* (Winter 1946): 35–54—Arendt distances her view from the overly subject-centered approach of the French existentialists and of Heidegger. Heidegger's phenomenological attempt at reconstruction of an ontological frame of reference is too subject-centered (and dangerous), in her view. And in mine,

this resistance to phenomenological reduction better captures lines of investigation joining Melville and the nineteenth-century existentialists. Arendt's *existenzisch* approach assumes a much more playful reality, one where surfaces meet and are formed.

11. Ellison, *Invisible Man,* 571; emphasis added.

12. Ibid., 3.

13. Ibid., 572–573.

14. Ibid., 16, 575.

15. Ibid., 571.

16. Ibid., 16.

17. Ibid.

18. Ibid., 17; emphasis in original.

19. Ibid., 574.

20. Ibid., 581.

21. What John Bryant terms "repose" in Melville's thinking dovetails with what I am explicating as the narrative device of withdrawal, a response to the demise of the two-world frame of reference. See his *Melville and Repose: The Rhetoric of Humor in the American Renaissance* (New York: Oxford University Press, 1993), 2–29, 46–160. Bryant elaborates humor as a dimension of this strategy for Melville, and repose can be found throughout Melville's oeuvre in many manifestations. As Hubert Dreyfus and Sean Dorrance Kelly note in *All Things Shining: Reading the Western Classics to Find Meaning in a Secular Age* (New York: Free Press, 2011), on board ship this reflection is enabled by the situation of remove per se. "'Brooding under the southern constellations,' one commentator reports Melville to have said, 'makes me receptive to new ideas'"(149).

22. Melville was contemporaneously celebrated by some, and vilified by others, for his criticisms of the missionaries and the colonial project generally. For example, see William Oland Bourne's defense of the missionaries in "Typee: The Traducers of Missions." This objection first appeared in 1846 in *Christian Parlour Magazine* and is reprinted in *Critical Essays on Herman Melville's* Typee, ed. Milton R. Stern (Boston: G. K. Hall, 1982), 38–52. By contrast, a review published the same year and attributed to Margaret Fuller suggests that *Typee*'s accounts of the missionaries should curtail contributions made to them. See Hershel Parker, ed., *The Recognition of Herman Melville: Selected Criticism since 1846* (Ann Arbor: University of Michigan Press, 1967), 3.

23. Hannah Arendt, "Preface: The Gap between Past and Future," in Arendt, *Between Past and Future: Eight Exercises in Political Thought* (New York: Viking, 1968), 9–14.

24. Ibid., 7; and Arendt, "Thinking," in Arendt, *The Life of the Mind*, ed. Mary McCarthy (New York: Harvest/HBJ, 1977), 202.

25. In her presentation of "The Vision and the Riddle," Arendt translates *der Augenblick* as *now* rather than *moment.* See Arendt, "Thinking," 204.

26. Walter Kaufmann presents the standard translation of *der Augenblick* as *moment.* See Friedrich Nietzsche, *Thus Spoke Zarathustra,* trans. Walter Kaufmann (New York: Viking, 1966), 58.

27. Ibid., 7.

28. Arendt, "Thinking," 205.

29. Ellison, *Invisible Man,* 13.

30. Ibid., 9–10; cf. Melville, *Moby-Dick,* 802–803.

31. Herman Melville, *Benito Cereno* (1855), in *Pierre, Israel Potter, The Piazza Tales, The Confidence-Man, Uncollected Prose, Billy Budd* (New York: Library of America, 1984), 755; citations hereafter are given parenthetically in the text by title and page number.

32. Ellison, *Invisible Man,* 74.

33. Ibid., 77.

34. Ibid., 69–71.

35. Ralph Ellison, "The Shadow and the Act," in Ellison, *Shadow and Act* (New York: Random House, 1964), 276–277.

36. Early critics elaborated Melville's presentation of the Typee as an investigation of the state of nature, and they presented and investigated this frame of reference repeatedly. But in complicating the simple reversal of savage and civilized, I am setting the argument of this essay apart from these readers. Theirs is often a simple reversal—Melville found an Eden, and their paradise is a critique of our modern savagery. See, for example, Richard Ruland, "Melville and the Fortunate Fall: Typee as Eden" in Stern, *Critical Essays on Melville's* Typee, 183–192. I am not so much arguing against this reversal as going beyond it. I am interested in how Melville posits the modernity of the Typee—in how they encounter each other on an equal footing—as we will see in this essay's conclusion.

37. Jean-Jacques Rousseau, "Discourse on the Origin of Inequality," in Rousseau, *The Basic Political Writings,* ed. Peter Gay (New York: Hackett, 1987), 63–65.

38. The heading for this section comes from Melville, *Moby-Dick,* 859.

39. Ellison, *Invisible Man,* 572–573.

40. Bryant, introduction to *Typee* (1996 ed.), xxix.

41. Dreyfus and Kelly, *All Things Shining,* 163–164.

42. From Nathaniel Hawthorne's notebooks, quoted in Laurie Robertson-Lorant, *Melville: A Biography* (1996; repr., Amherst: University of Massachusetts Press, 1998), 377.

43. William V. Spanos, *The Errant Art of Moby-Dick: The Canon, the Cold War, and the Struggle for American Studies* (Durham: Duke University Press, 1995), 63.

44. Ellison, *Invisible Man*, 538.

45. Ibid., 547.

46. Ibid., 542; emphasis in original.

47. Ibid., 546.

48. Ibid., 547; emphasis in original.

49. Ibid., 541; emphasis in original.

50. Two of the most thoughtful accounts of taboo, tattooing, and cannibalism in *Typee* and Melville's other novels of the South Seas—Michael Rogin's and Geoffrey Sanborn's—use psychoanalytic approaches that replicate an emphasis on the primitiveness of the islanders that I am trying to unhinge. An account of how the *existenzisch* approach of this essay pairs with their interpretations of *Typee* is outside the bounds of this essay because it would require an analysis of the onto-theology of the analytic frame. See Rogin, *Subversive Genealogy: The Politics and Art of Herman Melville* (New York: Knopf, 1983), 42–76, and Sanborn, *The Sign of the Cannibal: Melville and the Making of the Postcolonial Reader* (Durham: Duke University Press, 1998).

3

Chasing the Whale

Moby-Dick *as Political Theory*

George Shulman

> What we notice in stories is the nearness of the wound to the gift.
>
> —Jeanette Winterston

My aspiration in this essay is to read Melville's *Moby-Dick; or, The Whale* as a work of—not simply as a supplement to—political theory. By its dramatic form and content, *Moby-Dick* tells a story about politics and about theory; and through it, so will I.[1] Just as ancient tragedians were interlocutors to the polis, dramatizing inescapable heteronomy, haunting pasts, and irremediable conflict to a community avowing self-rule, so Melville retells dominant romances of liberal emancipation and national redemption as tragedy-in-the-making. Whereas Sophocles created an alter-city—what James Baldwin called a disagreeable mirror—Melville is among American literary artists who conjure fictional worlds elsewhere—on a whaling ship or a raft—to illuminate enigmas closer to home. His novel exalts what he calls "democratic dignity" while dramatizing what prevailing political rhetoric of democratic self-rule finds unspeakable: American freedom is premised on multiple forms of domination and forgetting. But he composes a *tragedy* because his depiction of derangement in the American practice of democracy includes the paradox that democratic aspirations are inherently entangled in the risk of domination. Though theorists often assume celebratory *or* critical positions toward the democratic, and so cannot engage what is complex and poignant in its meaning, Melville avowedly remakes tragedy to enact what is noble, horrific, and self-defeating in the project of political self-rule.

I do not think *Moby-Dick* is only a tragedy; it is truly a genre-busting work, but I emphasize how it is an "alter-world," like Thebes in Greek tragedy, a fictional space or place at once related to and removed from "reality," in which to stage a tragedy—at once modern and American—of democratic dignity. Like works of canonical political theory, therefore, it should be seen not as a direct representation of the social world, but as a form of mediation by which a political community can reflect on its core axioms, constitutive practices, and fateful decisions, and so also as an artful speech act. Such acts are fraught because they engage audiences whose background conditions—cultural grammars and historical traumas—are disavowed, unspoken. This is why rationalist approaches to persuasion fail, and why experiments with fiction and genre matter to political theory. For as readers professing democratic ideals are positioned as witnesses of tragedy in an alter-world, they can identify with and yet gain distance from its characters and the fate they coauthor, and in this way readers may reflect on their own history and narrative horizon, circumstances, and choices.[2]

By attending not only to *what* is said by characters and narrator, but also to *how* the text orients readers, we can see Melville reshape tragedy for a democratic (and American) audience. *Characters* can and do argue perspectives, but *the novel* personifies and enacts arguments in ways that viscerally render their pathos and meaning. Moreover, while characters speak in the unequivocal terms of prophecy, the text creates experiences of fraught ambiguity; readers must credit the inescapability of the questions that characters ask, the credibility of their answers—and how they create a tragedy. In sum, my central intuition is that the text does not so much philosophically advocate a "tragic perspective" on politics or life as dramatize a "tragedy" its audience blindly coauthors.[3]

This distinction between the tragic and tragedy warrants further introduction here, though I must earn it by the reading that follows. We should begin with the inherited meanings of the genre of "tragedy" that Melville revises: it dramatizes the nobility and defeat of human efforts to know or master their world, the elemental powers suffusing it, or themselves as subjects. For Nietzsche tragedy is thus the "Apollonian" form by which citizens, having contacted the senseless power of "Dionysian" energies, are enabled to affirm art, boundaries, and action in new ways. In Plato's *Republic* regimes thus are ruined by an excess of their animating eros—freedom in democracy—whereas for Aristotle tragic heroes are destroyed by a flaw inseparable from their virtue. In Hegel, tragedy dramatizes how conflicting values or rival gods divide cities and dismember protagonists, because choosing one means grievous loss of another. The genre also defeats a democratic and enlightenment "romance" of mastering temporality: tragedy denies the pastness of a past that instead haunts the present. In each regard we can imagine Aristotle's hope that tragedy yields catharsis of "pity and terror" about the *vita activa.*

It is no wonder, therefore, that Melville takes up tragedy to dramatize the vicissitudes of democratic dignity, but among academics a genre that creates certain experiences—of conflict, excess, haunting, and self-destruction—has become a philosophic perspective. As Eric Bentley noted fifty years ago, "In the twentieth century there has been a tendency to dehydrate tragedy and make of it an ideological scheme only, a 'tragic view of life.' As such it has *advocates,* and the scheme of thought reveals itself as a mere *polemic:* the idea of tragedy is being used as a stick to beat someone with. In America that someone is usually the Liberal . . . accused of undue rationalism and optimism." The tragic is thus a rhetorical device in literary and theoretical polemics that includes readings of *Moby-Dick* by cold war and more recent literary critics. I will dispute them because Bentley's deeper point inspires me: "the tragic" is a kind of "knowingness" that forecloses the experiences dramatically rendered in and as tragedy; "the tragic" is a conclusion about the meaning of a structure of experience called tragedy, though the genre does not dictate the lesson of the experiences it performs but releases audiences to the burden and freedom of judgment and action.[4]

It may seem impossible to "dehydrate" a whaling story, but we do if we make it "an ideological scheme only." For even readers who call it a tragedy typically juxtapose a pathological Ahab and an admirable Ishmael, who models the democratic values that Ahab only betrays. Some cold war critics thus made Ahab personify the ideological extremist or totalitarian and identified Ishmael with a pluralism tied to the democratic—and "American." For others, Ahab embodied "destructive Emersonianism" as an excess linked to American individualism. Later, Ahab personified the ugly truth of Promethean modernism, Enlightenment rationalism, masculine aggression, American nationalism, or ideas of (even democratic) sovereignty, which *must* mean domination. Since 9/11, some likewise argue, the national subject became a wounded Ahab, symbolized a monstrous evil threatening freedom, and organized politics as a crusade to kill it. In contrast, critics repeatedly take Ishmael to model a needed—even redemptive—turn toward an ethos of finitude valuing the ordinary, horizontal, proximate, local.

In my reading, Melville does not condemn Ahab to endorse Ishmael, partly because he does not resolve the meaning of the other key character, the whale. By making it a symbol both of nature's ambivalent meaning and (after Hobbes) of reified human power, he depicts Ahab's "monomania" both as mad and as a valid expression of "democratic dignity" opposing the powers—cosmic and political—that injure it. No wonder a crew of "renegades and castaways" identify with his injury and rage and embrace his plot to kill the whale.[5] Together they dramatize not only how American nationalism takes imperial form, or only the bond between Lockean liberalism and the crusades against despotic power that recurrently organize American politics, but also how admirable desires for freedom (and justice) are readily enmeshed in domination. Ahab models not only an imperial or Promethean pathology we can avoid or overcome, but a democratic paradox we must undergo. That is because he performs aspects of democratic politics and theorizing that are at once crucial and dangerous: he symbolizes objects that threaten democratic values and practices, he creates plots to imagine opposition, he affirms aggression, and he seeks to mobilize counter-sovereignty.

If I risk a certain perversity in defending Ahab, my rejoinder is that splitting Ahab and Ishmael means choosing Ahab's dichotomizing mode of practicing theory and politics. The only real alternative to the pathologies represented by Ahab—for they are real dangers—is to own and rework, not disavow, the suffering, longings, ambitions, and arts he personifies. To read the novel not as a melodrama, or as a philosophic treatise defending a single (even "tragic") point of view, but as a tragedy is to experience the mutually constituting tension between "Ahab" and "Ishmael" as modalities of democratic life, at once incommensurate and necessary. By making every position plausible and problematic, the text leaves readers not with a self-evident message, but with a challenge of political judgment for how we theorize our circumstances and make them conditions of action. Positioned as witnesses of a tragedy, we are called to judge if *we* are enacting what we witness, and if so, what choices remain in our hands. *Moby-Dick* enacts and so bequeaths the difficulties in conceiving and practicing democratic dignity.[6]

Forms of Address: Between Job and Ishmael

To see how *Moby-Dick* engenders an experiential apprehension of tragedy in American political life, let us begin with how the novel addresses readers: in the final epigraph we are addressed by the survivor, who informs Job that all he values is lost; but this messenger becomes the narrator, who begins, "Call me Ishmael." Framing the novel, these forms of address position readers in a tragedy. We must begin at the end to understand the beginning.

As the *Pequod* sinks, we are told of a grand gesture of human defiance: Tashtego, the Indian harpooner, perches on a topmast, "his red arm and a hammer hovered backwardly uplifted in the open air, in the act of nailing [Ahab's] flag faster and yet faster to the subsiding spar." A sky hawk "tauntingly" pecks at the flag, but its wing is caught by his hammer, so that "the bird of heaven, with archangelic shrieks, and his imperial beak thrust upwards, and his whole captive form folded in the flag of Ahab, went down with his ship, which, like Satan, would not sink to hell till she had dragged a living part of heaven along with her." But then we witness human insignificance: "now small fowls flew screaming over the yet yawning gulf; a sullen white surf beat against its steep sides; then all collapsed, and the great shroud of the sea rolled on as it rolled five thousand years ago" (636–637). We have been prepared to feel disturbed by human evanescence and futility, inspired by defiance until the end, and maybe satisfied by the symmetry that Ahab's predatory (modern, imperial, masculine, American) ship is sunk by its prey. Perhaps we take both pleasure and relief in the idea that the apocalyptic end, which Ahab sought, has arrived for us to witness. But of course this end is not the end; we read an epilogue whose epigraph quotes the book of Job—"And I only am escaped alone to tell thee"—as if to refuse oblivion the last word.[7]

This epigraph makes the end a beginning, for readers holding the book are addressed here by that messenger; *we* are positioned here *as Job*, given the message of catastrophic loss that initiates his grief, rage, and struggle with his god. The sinking is to initiate our own Jobian moment, as if our own world were lost with that ship, even while we survive. The novel explicitly invokes the biblical text closest to Greek tragedy, but this reference also connects readers to Ahab, who has been modeled as a Job figure. The catastrophic consequences of his response to his own grievous injury, it is suggested here, now initiate our own Jobian crisis, if we accept the novel as a message. But how to construe it? To grasp Ahab's theory about suffering, his defiant plotting, and the destruction he causes, to see how we are implicated, and to imagine how we might depart from his fate, we need to see how he echoes and yet departs from Job.[8]

Despite Christian efforts to moralize the text, Job vividly rejects the Hebrew theodicy that, by construing human suffering as punishment for sin, justifies God. Though a theodicy thus "humanizes" creation by attuning it to human aspirations for sense and justice, Job insists that God is indifferent to humans. But he also regrets and resents his life, wishing he had not been born. Granting his demand for an encounter, God speaks "out of the whirlwind":

> Do you dare to deny my judgment?
> Am I wrong because you are right?
> Is your arm like the arm of God? . . .
> Unleash your savage justice.
> Cut down the rich and mighty . . .
> Pluck the wicked from their perch.
> Push them into the grave.
> Throw them, screaming to hell.
> Then I will admit that your own strength can save you. . . .
> Will you catch the Serpent ["Leviathan" in the King James version]
> with a fishhook . . .
> Will he come to terms of surrender
> and promise to be your slave? . . .
> Will merchants bid for his carcass
> and parcel him out to shops?
> Will you riddle his skin with spears,
> split his head with harpoons?
> Go ahead: attack him:
> you will never try it again.
> Look: hope is a lie:
> you would faint at the very sight of him . . .
> Who under all the heavens could fight against him and live?
> . . . Power beats in his neck,
> and terror dances before him. . . .
> No one on earth is his equal—a creature without fear.
> He looks down on the highest.
> He is king over all the proud beasts.[9]

God's leviathan here symbolizes the divine and demonic power of a creator and creation whose aliveness are "beyond good and evil," inscrutable, and indifferent to human longings for justice. God's performance (and the poet's ravishing poetry) affirms this boundlessly creative power, but also the validity of Job's protest. Like Greek tragedy, the text enacts conflict between human (political) and divine (aesthetic, ontological) perspectives, incommensurate yet crucial to value.[10]

Melville represents Ahab as Job's heir in his anguish and outraged protest at an inhuman universe. In his famous review, "Hawthorne and His Mosses," Melville noted how "philosophers" devalued Shakespeare as "merely a dramatist," when his "dark" characters reveal "the very axis of reality" by "insinuating the things we feel to be so terrifically true that it were all but madness for any good man, in his own proper character, to utter or even hint of." As King Lear, "tormented into desperation . . . tears off the mask and speaks the sane madness of vital truth," so Ahab, maybe imitating Hamlet, addresses a whale head: "You have seen such horrors as would make Abraham an infidel"—as if to mock any ethical rationalism. Musing that "the ancestry and posterity of Grief go further than the ancestry and posterity of Joy," he imagines that if we "trail the genealogies of . . . high mortal miseries" to reach "the sourceless primogenitures of the gods," we will see "that the gods themselves are not for ever glad. The ineffaceable, sad birth-mark in the brow of man, is but the stamp of sorrow in the signers" (519). Ishmael affirms this melancholy wisdom: "The mortal man who hath more of joy than sorrow in him, that mortal man cannot be true—not true, or undeveloped" (477). Against an emerging utilitarian culture, Ahab invokes the persisting capacity for violent harm, and what we still call "depraved indifference," in nature and human affairs.[11]

But between Job and Ahab stands the modernity of Hobbes and Marx, who signal how Ahab departs from Job. For they took up God's challenge to Job: saving themselves by "their own right arm," by poesis and praxis, they become modern Prometheans who displace God. After Hobbes, leviathan signifies not natural-sacred alterity, but the state as a reified institution and imagined community, "the political body" as an invented compact, an artifact open to remaking or failure. It is an object of fantasy inside us, as we are inside it as a worldly power authored by us yet independent of our will. The "reality" of this whale is both intersubjectively constituted and recalcitrantly other, at once a material object and fantastic fiction, whose estranged power and charged meaning elicit and organize our love and hate. In turn, then, Marx protests how human beings "become the playthings of alien power" lodged in gods, states, and capital; they must reclaim the power they alienate to the worldly leviathans they author. Because redemption means killing the whales in which they mistakenly misplace their sovereignty, they must proudly affirm their equality and aggression to forge a counter-sovereignty.

Melville's Ishmael announces this faith early on, for as he surveys the crew and officers to suggest why no one stopped—and so many embraced—Ahab's hijacking of the ship, he openly positions us toward the aspirations and disaster he will render. The first mate, Starbuck, is a truly decent man, but his "sort of bravery . . . cannot withstand those more terrific, because more spiritual terrors, which sometimes menace you from the concentrating brow of an enraged and mighty man." If Ishmael here notes "the incompetence of mere unaided virtue or right-mindedness," he also grants how the crew is "morally enfeebled" by the other two officers (222). "Scarce might I have the heart" to depict such "sorrowful; nay shocking" failure, he says, but "man, in the ideal, is so noble, and so sparkling, such a grand and glowing creature, that over any ignominious blemish in him all his fellows should run to throw their costliest robes." Though men "seem detestable as joint-stock companies and nations . . . that immaculate manliness we feel within ourselves . . . remains intact though all outer character seems gone" (146).

This "we" comprises only men, whose sense of dignity is masculinized as he celebrates not "the dignity of kings and robes, but that abounding dignity which has no robed investiture. Thou shalt see it shining in the arm that wields a pick or drives a spike; that democratic dignity which, on all hands, radiates without end from God; Himself! The great God absolute! The center and circumference of all democracy! His omnipresence, our divine equality!"(146). Equality is here incarnated as an inherent dignity in those lacking other "investiture." Or, rather, this god of equality *dignifies* those without title to rule by birth, wealth, or learning, and so also dignifies any aspect of life deemed ordinary, not only labor.[12]

Ishmael prays that he can imbue a "shaggy" Ahab and "mongrel" crew with the stature of tragedy because he, too, worships equality:

> If, then, to meanest mariners, and renegades, and castaways, I shall hereafter ascribe high qualities, though dark; weave around them trag-

> ic graces if even the most mournful, perchance the most abased among them all shall at times lift himself to the exalted mounts; if I shall touch that workman's arm with some ethereal light; if I shall spread a rainbow over his disastrous set of sun; then against all mortal critics bear me out in it, thou just Spirit of Equality, which has spread one royal mantle of humanity over all my kind! Bear me out . . . thou great democratic God! who didst not refuse to the swart convict, Bunyan, the pale poetic pearl; Thou who didst clothe with doubly hammered leaves of finest gold the stumped and paupered arm of old Cervantes; Thou who didst pick up Andrew Jackson from the pebbles . . . [and] thunder him higher than a throne! Thou who, in all thy mighty earthly marchings, ever cullest thy selectest champion from the kingly commons, bear me out in it, O God! (146–147)[13]

Ishmael here invokes the iconography of Jesus, and the examples of Bunyan and Cervantes on the one hand, and of Andrew Jackson on the other hand, to exemplify "election" by the "great democratic God" of equality. Ahab and Ishmael as narrator are such "champions" culled from the "kingly commons." Despite grievous flaws, they champion the "abounding dignity" in people and practices devalued by aristocratic prejudice, bourgeois propriety, or hierarchical discourse. Ishmael thus writes to "bear out" a god who affirms what is "grand and glowing" in human beings, to entitle and encourage them to dispute distinctions of rank, presumptions of incapacity, and expectations of both possibility and impossibility. He must dramatize an excess he links to false prophecy, and the failure in "valor" of those who succumb to it, yet in a way that affirms their faith in equality.

Imagine, then, that Melville casts his Ahab as the heir of Job: he survives traumatic injury, denies it was random bad luck, and links God to evil, but this "grand, ungodly god-like man" also plots defiant, violent action to vindicate democratic dignity. He is thus an avatar of anti-theist (democratic, revolutionary) modern politics, and the Hebrew king whose insatiable desire for land and power symbolizes the self-destruction of a chosen people. In both regards, the epigraph implies that our own world went down with the *Pequod.* But if we digest how Ahab departed from Job, and how he is a "representative man" for us, we might imagine how to depart from him. That depends on analyzing the identity of the messenger and the form of his message.

By luck, Ishmael had witnessed from a distance how the ship, smashed by Moby Dick, was sucked down in a vortex, and he was saved when it ejected the coffin that his lover, Queequeg, had once made. Floating on it, the survivor says he was picked up by the "devious-cruising" *Rachel*, whose name evokes the wife of Jacob, the patriarch renamed Israel. Jeremiah calls Israel a "Rachel" weeping for her children when they are exiled to Babylon by a just God punishing their idolatrous infidelity. The epilogue concludes by noting how that ship "only found another orphan." This last word in *Moby-Dick* mirrors its first words, "Call me Ishmael."

But who is Ishmael? He was Abraham's first son, conceived with the bondswoman Hagar when Sarah was barren but cast out of the household without Abraham's blessing. As his name means "God will hear," he is saved from dying in the wilderness by God's angel, who says both that he will found a nation and that he will be a "wild" man whose "hand shall be against every man, and every man's hand shall be against him." The Bible links him to Canaanites and Egyptians, whereas Isaac, conceived by Sarah, gains the blessing as the next founding father of God's "chosen people." In America whites call themselves Isaacs; as the chosen people and good sons of Founding Fathers, they claim title to dispossess or enslave others they call Ishmael.

So when the narrator says, "Call me Ishmael," he implicitly addresses readers as Isaacs and offers a counteridentification. Partly, he signals that he stands with—or in ethnographic humility, not against—the pagans, "savages," and "cannibals" whose polytheistic worship Isaacs call idolatry. Partly, he signals rejection of the white supremacy that ranks white over red and black. Partly, he signals affirmation of aspects of human being that the enfranchised associate with those they cast out: wild, savage, and inscrutable are words he repeats like a mantra, as if to remind us of what and not only whom Issacs disavow, just as his wedding to Queequeg denies their sexual norms. Lastly, members of the two dominant American political parties (Whig and Democrat) called those who formed antislavery third parties Ishmaelites. Agonal by chosen name, our narrator stands with those cast out by ruling conventions, though he resists idealizing a counterworship. Affirming "doubt of all things earthly and intuitions of some things heavenly," he is "neither believer nor infidel but a man who regards both with equal eye" (423).

The messenger addressing Job at the end has renamed himself Ishmael and begins his story by positioning readers as Isaacs, to whom he offers not an emancipatory national romance, we come to realize, but the testimony of the sole survivor of a catastrophe. His text of witness makes us witness the destruction of an American whaling ship and its monomaniac captain, American officers, and multinational crew. If his testimony succeeds, we will have learned what is at stake: the meaning and fate of a self-declared democracy allied, maybe fatally, with slavery, imperial expansion, and an industrial civilization in violent war with nature.

His testimony is not accusing, however, but reparative and reconstructive; as we can grasp only at the end, he writes to make meaningful and to come to terms with a catastrophe he participated in making, was transformed by undergoing, and miraculously survived. Partly, then, his testimony tries to understand and make credible what he calls the "monomania" of Ahab and the support of a crew, including his earlier self. Partly, he represents the experiences that altered his assumptions about life and the Christian-capitalist civilization that enfranchised him. In sum, he narrates the transformation he signals by addressing us as Ishmael, as if to show how identification is not a sign of fated ethnoracial descent, but a political choice to resist or rework prevailing our inherited or presumed subjectivity. Readers who identify as elect may, in turn, claim Ahab's story as their own and perform their own shift from lucky survivor to critical witness.[14]

But the epigraph announcing destruction to Job can be construed in two different ways. By one interpretation, there is consolation, and other more obvious political resources, in the idea of a survivor and his testimony. For if catastrophe could not be averted *in the story*, in the world beyond the text a prophetic witness, who testifies to the danger of self-destruction by a republic bent on empire and invested in slavery, and who models a saving counteridentification, suggests the possibility of forestalling what otherwise will be a fate we coauthor. By a reading perhaps more faithful to the Job poem and the genre of tragedy, however, the catastrophe already has happened. We are summoned not to forestall it, but to accept its irreversible actuality as the condition of action now.[15]

After World War I, for example, D. H. Lawrence claimed that *Moby-Dick* announced the self-destruction of the European tradition of "idealistic half-ness" that, in religious and secular forms, separated spirit from matter, soul from body, and subject from object. Until we accept that the European project has died, and by our own hand in pursuing it, he argues, we will produce "post-mortem effects" rather than a new form of life. Similarly, Tocqueville had addressed French aristocrats, and James Baldwin would address whites, about refusing to face the end of regimes that enfranchised only them. Postmortem effects are counterrevolution and fascism in Europe, and culture war and defensive nationalism in the United States. For each critic, a possibility for new possibilities requires making "doom" a condition of action.[16]

But Melville, by contrast, simply depicts a textual sinking whose ambiguous worldly meaning—has it happened or can it be averted in the world beyond the text?—is not resolved. This ambiguity contrasts with his characters, who speak forms of prophecy. Ahab announces both Moby-Dick's certain meaning and that his plot of revenge will succeed. "The prophecy was that I should be dismembered; and —Aye! I lost this leg. I now prophesy that I will dismember my dismemberer." Calling himself "the prophet and the fulfiller," he boasts "that's more than ye, ye great gods, ever were" (201–202). His confidence mirrors Elijah, who prophesies Ahab's wounding and his death, and Father Mapple, who praises prophets for resisting evil no matter the cost. Granted, Ahab is a Promethean who claims a power (to fulfill prophecy) that Elijah and Mapple must leave to their God. But the issue of false prophecy goes to the core of politics: can audiences (the crew, or readers of the book) judge unequivocal yet opposing prophecies that define the whale, announce what time it is, and declare what is to be done? If forms of prophetic address foreclose gaps between word and world, intention and act, present and future, event and its meaning, Melville reopens them through testimony whose meaning, enigmatic as the whale, we must decipher and compose but cannot complete. Such testimony is given form as a tragedy; for as Charles Olson claims, Ishmael is less a narrator than "the chorus through whom Ahab's tragedy is seen."[17]

Framing the Tragedy: Fates, Scripts, and Protagonists

Looking back, Ishmael speaks as a witness, but he uses metaphors from drama to voice his questions about the meaning of his voyage. He imagines the world as a stage and presumes that motives are embedded in scripts and so in fates: he jokes, "Doubtless, my going on this whaling voyage formed part of the grand programme of Providence that was drawn up a long time ago" (29). He imagines the poster:

Grand Contested Election for Presidency of the United States.
WHALING VOYAGE BY ONE ISHMAEL.
BLOODY BATTLE IN AFFGHANISTAN.

We are struck by its uncanny timeliness—our era also seems framed by a disputed presidential election and war in Afghanistan, while a monomaniacal crusade mediates the global and national. Calling "the Fates" "stage managers," he wonders why they "put me down for this shabby part in a whaling voyage," but adds, "I think I can see a little into the springs and motives which being cunningly presented to me under various disguises, induced me to set about performing the part I did, besides cajoling me into the delusion that it was a choice resulting from my own unbiased freewill and discriminating judgment" (29).

One "motive" is escaping a "damp drizzly November in my soul," which was so bad that going to sea "is my substitute for pistol and ball," as if life on land is a soul death prompting suicide (25). A second is that all humans seem attracted to the sea, which he calls "the image of the ungraspable phantom of life; and this is the key to it all" (27). A third is "the overwhelming idea of the great whale himself. Such a portentous and mysterious monster" embodies a desire to "explore forbidden seas" and "barbarous coasts." Drawn by "wild conceits" of opening "the great flood-gates of the wonder-world" (29–30), he would escape the death-in-life of imprisonment on land by enacting a pursuit of knowledge. But motives are scripted, and here he voices (in highbrow tones) the imperial romance of the frontier myth, which promises rebirth by contacting the forbidden, savage, and sublime. "America" as an imagined community is formed by just this association of alterity with freedom: no wonder he imagines his adventure a destiny made manifest! As he realizes, this regenerative promise recruits men discontented in the father's house to battles that—as Melville claims about whaling—extend the civilization whose imprisoning grip they mean to slip. He thus retells as tragedy the myth of new frontiers and the "delusions" of "free will" it supports.[18]

So the *Pequod* is an American ship, with the same number of crewmen as states, and its nation-building project subverts the distinctions—between civilized and savage, free and slave—that authorize it. As the Pequot tribe, exterminated in King Philip's War, were infamous for brutality, so the crew mans a "cannibal" craft. Each officer commands a whaleboat and harpooner: Starbuck of New England directs Queequeg, a Pacific Islander; short, chubby Stubb, a Southerner, stands on the shoulders of Dagoo, an African; and Flask, a Westerner, commands Tashtego, an Indian. The 1846 Mexican War thus joined northern and southern wings of Jacksonian "democracy" to pursue what Alan Heimert calls "the imperial sublime," an "image of greatness" appealing to "the American passion for the grand, the vast, and the marvelous." As the Pacific replaces the prairie, whaling ships—"sweatshops of the Pacific," says Charles Olson—prefigure the industrialization and worldwide extension of American power. An ordinary voyage thus mediates geopolitics and national elections; because his personal choices bespeak (and then expose) the myth of freedom offered by his industrializing Christian culture, Ishmael's minor role takes him to the deranged center of American life.[19]

Melville makes a tragedy from the avowedly "shabby"—in the words of Tocqueville, "petty and paltry" as well as "anti-poetic"—stuff of democracy. When Ishmael muses, "Ahab, my captain, still moves before me in all his Nantucket grimness and shagginess," he promises, "I must not conceal that I have only to do with a poor old whale-hunter like him; and, therefore, all outward majestical trappings and housings are denied me. Oh, Ahab, what shall be grand in thee" must be "plucked at from the skies, and dived for in the deep, and featured in the unbodied air!" But what is "grand" in a champion culled from the common (179)?[20]

First are "over-bearing" qualities of mind and a "determinate, unsurrendurable wilfulness, in the fixed and fearless, forward dedication of that glance" (155). Second, he speaks for the core faith of "the democracy," as Jacksonians called it. That means, says Ahab, "I'd strike the sun if it insulted me. For could the sun do that, then could I do the other; since there is ever a sort of fair play herein, jealousy presiding over all creations. But not my master . . . is even that fair play. Who's over me? Truth hath no confines" (197). Though immersed in the "impersonal, a personality stands here. Though but a point at best . . . yet while I earthly live, the queenly personality lives in me, and feels her royal rights" (563). Therefore, "not white whale, nor man nor fiend can so much as graze old Ahab in his own proper and inaccessible being" (623). Because he affirms the striving to persevere in all things but refuses to revere *any* limit (even fairness) to a freedom he deems regal, his sense of entitlement entails a grand—readily inflated—sense of grievance at every symbol of limitation. In turn we are led to ask: does his monomania about the whale that injured him therefore reflect a hubris inherent in democratic dignity as such? An excess or pathology owing to a contingent, remediable understanding? The ambiguous connection between democratic dignity and monomania is thus the basis of the tragedy Melville tells.

In the novel's central chapters Melville uses stage directions and a script format (character names, colon, spoken lines) to set a dramatic form of scenes, dialogues, and monologues. The "Quarter-Deck" chapter begins "Enter Ahab; then all" to stage Ahab recruiting the crew to his project. They cry out assent, except Starbuck. "I am game for his crooked jaw, and for the jaws of Death, too, Captain Ahab, if it fairly comes in the way of the business we follow; but I came here to hunt whales, not my commander's vengeance. How many barrels will thy vengeance yield even if thou gettest it, Captain Ahab? It will not fetch thee much in our Nantucket market." Ahab says, "Come closer . . . thou requirest a little lower layer," and he declares, "If money's to be the measurer, man, and the accountants have computed their great counting-house the globe, by girdling it with guineas . . . then, let me tell thee, that my vengeance will fetch a great premium *here*," as he "smites his chest." Starbuck is horrified: "Vengeance on a dumb brute . . . that simply smote thee from blindest instinct! Madness! To be enraged with a dumb thing, Captain Ahab, seems blasphemous" (196–197; emphasis in original).

Starbuck sees blasphemy because Ahab invests malevolent agency in a dumb brute and because he takes vengeance out of God's hands; Ahab confirms it. Refusing to subject human aspiration to the calculation of accountants, he also rejects criteria of profitability compared to his own valuation of what matters. Ahab supplants capitalist logic, which hunts all whales, by the logic of revenge (and erotic love) that focuses on one. Those who hired him "were bent on profitable cruises," says Ishmael, whereas "he was intent on audacious, immitigable, and supernatural revenge." The "calculating" Quaker owners—one is named Bildad, Job's "false comforter"—noted his change after losing his leg, but "for those very reasons" deemed him "better qualified . . . for a pursuit so full of rage and wildness as the bloody hunt of whales" (158). The worldly asceticism of Christian Isaacs would join profit to the service of God, but acquisition must draw energy from "lower layers" they imagine they can master. Ahab, however, has other plans. His wounding has led him to reject the sovereignty of their God and market as well as their family values. He is the dark double of capitalist Christian society; baptizing his harpoon to the devil, not God, he mocks its deceptive pieties and exposes its monomaniac core.[21]

But "hark ye yet again—the little lower layer," Ahab repeats, to explain the ambition animating his hunt and inspiring his crew.

> All visible objects, man, are but as pasteboard masks. But in each event—in the living act, the undoubted deed—there, some unknown but still reasoning thing puts forth the mouldings of its features from behind the unreasoning mask. If man will strike, strike through the mask! How can the prisoner reach outside except by thrusting through the wall? To me, the white whale is that wall, shoved near to me. Sometimes I think there's naught beyond. But 'tis enough. He tasks me; he heaps me; I see in him outrageous strength, with inscrutable malice sinewing it. That inscrutable thing is chiefly what I hate; and be the white whale agent, or . . . principal, I will wreak that hate upon him. (197)

The material world of visible appearances is devalued as a "pasteboard mask," both false and unsatisfying, but hated as a "wall" whose "unreasoning" materiality imprisons him by resisting his will. Behind it he posits "an unknown but reasoning thing" animated by "inscrutable malice" he experiences as real and suffers. Hating inscrutability as much as malice, he would "strike through"—to experience and master if not know—the invisible power driving the visible world.[22]

Whereas God displayed his leviathan to Job, for whom appearances do not wall off or mask a hidden (divine or demonic) reality, but rather embody it, Ahab inherits a Cartesian universe splitting an animated subject from a material world reduced to deadened pasteboard by the absence of divine presence. Rather than accept this dismembering division, he posits a hidden and animating but demonic core, and in this way reanimates the world as a meaningful (albeit demonic) whole and reunites humans with it, albeit in enraged struggle. At this ontological level he protests the visible-invisible and subject-object splits constituting modernity, and he plots overcoming them by a violent apocalypse. He would humanize the world, so it is ruled by and for men, not by hidden demonism and inscrutable gods.

In retrospect, Ishmael describes how Ahab crosses from a "wisdom that is woe" to a "woe that is madness" (478):

> He came to identify with [the whale] not only all his bodily woes, but . . . that intangible malignity which has been from the beginning; to whose dominion even the modern Christians ascribe one-half of the worlds. . . . All that most maddens and torments . . . all the subtle demonisms of life and thought; all evil, to crazy Ahab, *were visibly personified, and made practically assailable in Moby Dick.* He piled upon the whale's white hump the sum of all the general rage and hate felt by his whole race from Adam on down; and then, as if his chest had been a mortar, he burst his hot heart's shell upon it. (219; emphasis added)

Against Starbuck's view of Ahab as a paranoid attributing malevolent purpose to a dumb brute, Ishmael pointedly notes that the conduct of the whale was widely seen as "unexampled, intelligent malignity" (218). Granting how Ahab's hatred was fueled by a "morbid" character, Ishmael still credits both the malevolent agency of the whale and how humans must symbolize what "maddens and torments" them. Jobian Ahab rages at the injustice of arbitrary suffering and the indifference of gods or life to it, but by "personifying" evil, he gives suffering a "cause," that is, an explanation, and a "practically assailable" target the crew can "strike." Grievance at "life" is irremediable and so paralyzing, but it is generative—of political plots and action, and so of tragedy—when mediated by the whale.

Melville shows how Ahab's allegory and defiance resonate politically: he elicits Starbuck's "enchanted, tacit acquiescence"; he "shocked" into the other mates the "same fiery emotion accumulated in the Leyden jar of his own magnetic life" (199); and the crew respond to his "heaven-insulting purpose" as an affirmation that dignity entails enmity toward whatever power denies it (143). Looking back, Ishmael sees "this grey-headed, ungodly old man, chasing with curses a Job's whale round the world, at the head of a crew . . . of mongrel renegades, and castaways, and cannibals" who seemed "specially picked and packed by some infernal fatality to help him to his monomaniac" as well as "supernatural revenge" (221–222).

Each is an *Isolato* "not acknowledging the common continent of men," for each inhabits "a separate continent of his own" (151). Atomized in Tocqueville's sense, they are "federated along one keel" because, "aboundingly responding to his ire," they are so "possessed" that "his hate seemed almost theirs" (151, 222). His "irresistible dictatorship" is plebiscitary (178). Because they join him "to lay the world's grievances before that bar from which not very many . . . ever come back" (151–152), he credibly can say to himself, "My cogged circle fits into all their various wheels" (201), and say to them, "I do not order ye; ye will it" (199). As Heimert infers, "Whoever willfully defies authority, Melville seems to say, when he stands in open rebellion, will find response in the democratic soul." As captain and crew become head and heart of a political body, democracy becomes a dramatic protagonist. But what is the tragedy?[23]

Democratic Dignity as Excess

One answer to this question is that excess or pathology in Ahab's conception of democratic dignity is revealed as he crosses over from the wisdom that is woe to the woe that is madness. As George Kateb defines it, "Dignity resides in being, to some important degree, a person of one's own creating, making, choosing, rather than in being merely a creature or a socially manufactured, conditioned, manipulated thing." Ahab thus reveals the structure of feeling and ideological grammar whereby equality invests people in ideas of self-determination and, by extension, Tocqueville (though not Kateb) argues, in ideas of popular sovereignty.[24]

For Tocqueville equality fosters a subject who seeks "the reason of things for oneself and in oneself alone," and who therefore would "strike through the form to the substance"; it is but a step to Ahab's quest to strike through visible appearances to grasp the underlying truth they seem to mask. Tocqueville also argues that equality creates subjects who feel "they owe nothing to any man, expect nothing from any man" and "imagine that their whole destiny is in their own hands"; it is a step to what Quentin Anderson later called an "imperial self" (and nation!). As Starbuck notes, "Ahab would be a democrat to all above" but "lords it over all below" because, when knowing is a form of mastery and agency is the exercise of sovereignty, others are mere obstacles or instruments, and life seems endlessly insulting in its reminders of our finitude.[25]

Here is the inversion whereby democratic dignity, practiced as what D. H. Lawrence calls "masterlessness," is wed to resentment and entangled in domination. In Nina Baym's apt phrase, a "melodrama of beset manhood" then scripts national politics: democratic dignity is a masculine fantasy of self-sufficiency that mobilizes men's aggression against symbols of emasculation, while excluding actual women from the circle of their "we." They enact melodrama, not tragedy, because Ahabian self-reliance pathologizes human incompletion and interdependence. Monomania thus appears when the dream to have no master encounters resistance, which men demonize as an intentionally enslaving, symbolically charged, yet "practically assailable" object that they kill to regain freedom.[26]

Political leaders thus tell melodramatic stories about democracy to address a national subject in gendered terms. In Michael Rogin's account, rights-bearing white men recurrently protest enslaving power and soul death by scripting a "political romance" in which idealized freedom is endangered by monstrous threats. Attributing difficulty not to the core market and familial institutions of liberal society, but to their subversion, reformers emplot "countersubversive" crusades to redeem liberalism and its emancipatory promise. Killing antiliberal objects—such as evil empire, big government, or terrorism in recent history—offers personal and political rebirth by calling forth the heroic agency, capacity for sacrifice, and national unity that self-declared sons lament they have lost.[27]

Rogin's Melville dramatizes such melodramatic romance as a problematic monomania that he links to every important position in antebellum political life. Ahab surely evokes Jacksonian expansionists, who hoped to bury sectional conflict over slavery by joining southern and northern whites in a war against the territorial limits and savagery that obstructed their Manifest Destiny. (Like Ahab with his hickory harpoon, they would unify a crew and fulfill what they prophesied.) But by 1850, as Melville wrote *Moby-Dick,* this romance intensified division, so that Ahab also bespeaks both John Calhoun, who attacked the national state as a monstrous threat to the freedom to own slaves, and the abolitionist Theodore Parker, who attacked the Union for protecting a "hydra-headed slave power conspiracy." Their romances of idealized liberty risked dismembering the Union. Rogin thus concludes, "Ahab derived from no single source alone," but is "a reproach to and culmination of" every voice in the antebellum political world.[28]

Ahab thus personifies an imperialist national subject mobilizing multinational subalterns in a global project that promises freedom but entails domination and generates self-destruction. In this regard, Melville sustains the critics who identify America with the Hebrew king. Within the national frame, the disturbing connection of freedom and domination also marks movements of reform that construe dignity as masterlessness. But we miss Melville's own "lower layer" if "Ahab" means only a pathological view of freedom. He enacts a tragedy because his claim to exemplarity bespeaks crucial (not only pathological) aspects of a democratic ethos, and of ourselves. Identifying with or as him then becomes a step toward gaining critical distance on dangers that inhere in what we value.

The Tragedy in Democratic Dignity

In what ways, then, does Melville suggest that Ahab is exemplary of democratic dignity? One answer to this question lies in how we are positioned toward him by the ontological and political dimensions of the text. One frame dramatizes how we make meaningful and engage the elemental sublime forces of life called Dionysian by Nietzsche. In this mythic or cosmic frame, he becomes a "grand, ungodly god-like man" who survives traumatic injury by wedding rigid allegorizing about life to enraged, violent action. Critics thus take him to personify the resentful pathologies of the will to truth, or of an inflated autonomy derived from liberal individualism, Enlightenment reason, Promethean modernism, or modern patriarchy. Insofar as his idea of masterlessness denies human finitude, he does enact resentment of what Nietzsche calls fundamental prerequisites of life. Insofar as his vision of malignity projects one determinate meaning onto nature, he seems trapped within the fiction of deep truth he posits. Typically, critics then praise the contrary orientation of an Ishmael who affirms human finitude, forswears projects to know or master being, and embraces visible, sensuous materiality.[29]

But this either-or makes two mistakes. First, Ishmael sees Ahab's vision of depravity as credible, the wisdom of woe. Nor does Melville simply pathologize Ahab's melancholy or rage. As Eric Bentley notes: "Margaret Fuller once said that she accepted the universe, and Thomas Carlyle commented, 'Gad, she'd better!' But . . . the tragic poets were on her side. Carlyle's remark is pure cynicism. He sees man as puny and the universe as a sort of Frederick the Great. . . . In reasoning thus, Carlyle misses the something that is everything. The king can only kill the soldier, he cannot dictate his attitude. Margaret Fuller did NOT have to accept the universe. Prometheus did not accept it either. . . . What is it to 'accept' the universe?"[30] Even if we must "accept" that feelings of vulnerability, terror, and rage are inescapable, there remains a choice about our attitude toward them. Melville's tragedy dignifies, even exalts, and not only faults, the attitude Ahab lives out.[31]

Second, therefore, simply to endorse Ishmael's contrary stance toward being is to avoid the very ambiguities about "attitude" that a tragedy must render viscerally. The text renders "as a real presence a mystery that lies beyond its own powers of explanation," Richard Brodhead argues, so we can feel life's inscrutability and Ahab's urgent insistence on making it meaningful, as well as life's cruelty and so the pathos of his protest. Only if we allow ourselves to suffer (as in undergo) his injury and longing can we grasp both the truth in his optic and posture and the difficulty of resisting his insistence on fixed meaning and dignity as mastery. But a "knowingness" about the right ("tragic") attitude toward life precludes this surrender to Ahab, which is in fact, though paradoxically, a condition of gaining real distance from him.[32]

At the same time, this novel-as-tragedy unfolds in a political dimension that also does not resolve the meaning of Ahab's example. Like Freud on paranoia, Melville depicts monomania as a defense that rescues Ahab from the traumatic helplessness and collapse of libido that followed his injury; in political terms, as Ahab moves from paralysis to dramatic action by linking wound to a cause and grievance to a project, he performs C. Wright Mills's axiom that politics links "private grievance" to "public cause." Unable to see meaning emerging immanently in ordinary life, he imposes a transcendent, allegorical meaning on it; because visible appearances seem "pasteboard," he posits an organizing truth behind them. Marxism, populism, or feminism—not only a "paranoid style" on the right—thus link visible world and invisible powers, and make appearances meaningful, by a deep truth naming "practically assailable" causes of suffering and enslavement. For this reason Eve Sedgwick aptly linked "strong" theory on the left to what Melanie Klein named "the paranoid-schizoid position."[33]

Ahab thus dramatizes how political rhetoric and theory invoke whales to signify the material and symbolic aspects of reified power, to protest its sovereignty and malignity. In turn, one can argue, such monomania justifies counter-sovereignties that weld people professing democratic aspirations into a despotic (and depoliticized) unity. But a survivor linked to Indians and slaves then may signal Melville's hope that democratic dignity can be saved from a dream of masterless freedom and joined instead to the "mortal inter-indebtedness" Ahab scorned (527). Melville then may echo Tocqueville: given modern heterogeneity, those who endorse the wholeness, inviolability, or sovereignty of a national or political subject will produce despotism. *Moby-Dick* in effect contrasts a Marxian or populist Ahab, whose melodramatic plot promises to unify an atomized or divided society, to a Tocquevillean Ishmael for whom dismemberment is the inescapable basis of political freedom. If we are led to "regret the world of reality" by fictions of redemptive purpose, as Tocqueville claims, then giving them up is the key condition for cultivating arts of association grounded in palpable ("horizontal") bonds and discrete projects with concrete others. But Melville's tragedy complicates such a postnational romance.[34]

For if we say a whale named Moby-Dick also survives, the defeat of Ahabian monomania leaves not an ethically chastened democratic dignity, but a Leviathan "megastate." If "the whale" signifies the symbolic and material power of a state tied to capital, why must Ahab accept dismembering damage to the personal and political body? If he models a tension between democratic dignity and the worldly powers that injure it, then democratic life may be underwritten (not only jeopardized) by his claim to judge what is real to and best for him, his claiming of authority to name what denies that dignity, and his determination to "bear out" his view by mobilizing action in concert.

Melville's ambiguity about the whale as a political object is therefore crucial to finding Ahab in our own political practices: as democratic dignity is a project of knowledge that analyzes the ruling powers that work through or behind appearances as common sense interprets them, so we depict "global capital," "neoliberalism," or "the state" as charged objects. As Ishmael wonders if the whale reveals blank indifference rather than intentional malignity, so we debate whether we vainly project intentionality to secure culpability. A tragedy implies that democratic projects cannot avoid conceiving collective objects as "practically assailable causes" to hold to account and remake or destroy. Given the independent power of such whales, moreover, practices of freedom can no more be severed from counter-sovereignty, and from the domination it risks if not entails, than from indignation and aggression. As democratic dignity is both enacted and endangered because it must "charge" whales with meaning and assail them, so we are impelled to ask how *we* conceive and challenge "practically assailable causes."

In ontological and political dimensions, then, Melville does not demean or endorse Ahab's vision, partly because he never resolves the meaning of the whale. The onto-frame does not teach acceptance (rather than resentment) of life, while the political frame endorses mutiny against (not obedience to) any sovereignty. Rather, the text conjures affect and choice in each frame, mediating the other in complex ways. Sustaining these tensions is one way he creates tragedy. A second way is implicating characters who seem antithetical. Consider then how he positions us with Ishmael, not as separate from Ahab, but as a chorus digesting a fraught but fruitful relationship.

Though "Ahab's quenchless feud seemed mine" (223), Ishmael now discerns another motive: "It was the whiteness of the whale that above all things appalled me." An absence of color, this blankness denotes the "inscrutability" and "indifference" in "the heartless voids and immensities of the universe," which "stab us from behind with the thought of annihilation." This "colorless all-color atheism" also reveals that colorful appearances are our projection. Indeed, "nature absolutely paints like the harlot whose allurements cover nothing but the charnel-house within." Accordingly, "though in many aspects this visible world seems formed in love . . . the invisible spheres were formed in fright" (230–231). Ahab paints nature with a color—Melville says elsewhere "blackness ten times black"—but a colorless void of constitutive nothingness is Ishmael's real horror. Still, "not ignoring what is good, I am quick to perceive a horror, and could still be social with it—would they let me—since it is but well to be on friendly terms with all the inmates of the place one lodges in" (30). How then does Ishmael (as a narrator) redeem his participation (as a character) in hunting rather than befriending horror?[35]

First, he embraces a pluralistic polytheism to engage a universe whose protean excess sustains multiple moods, optics, ways of life. Second, he rejects Ahab's investment in seeing darkness and seeking mastery: "Look not too long in the face of the fire . . . when its redness makes all things look ghastly . . . give not thyself up, then, to fire, lest it invert thee, deaden thee; as for the time it did me. There is a wisdom that is woe; but there is a woe that is madness" (477–478). Third, he embraces the sensuous, material world, and interdependence among the incomplete beings he embeds within it: when "my own individuality was now merged in a joint stock company," "my free will had received a mortal wound" because "another's mistake or misfortune might plunge innocent me into unmerited disaster and death."

But he also finds pleasure in a "Siamese connexion with a plurality of other mortals" (365).

Opposing what F. O. Matthiessen calls Ahab's "destructive Emersonianism" and its "relentless rejection of the claim of the ordinary," Ishmael lets go of the frontier myth that opposed "slavish shore" to freedom. "By many prolonged, repeated experiences, I have perceived that . . . man must eventually lower, or at least shift, his conceit of attainable felicity; not placing it . . . in the intellect or the fancy; but in the wife, the heart, the bed, the table, the saddle, the fire-side, the country" (469). Ironic, not pious, toward these, he also has become forbearing—even cynical—toward the life that injures him: "There are certain queer times and occasions in this strange mixed affair we call life when a man takes this whole universe for a vast practical joke, though the wit thereof he but dimly discerns, and more than suspects that the joke is at nobody's expense but his own." Even death consists of "jolly punches in the side bestowed by the unseen and unaccountable old joker. . . . There is nothing like the perils of whaling to breed this free and easy sort of genial, desperado philosophy, and with it I now regarded this whole voyage of the *Pequod,* and the great White Whale as its object" (265). Calling life a joke, not a tragedy, he endorses a philosophy that is genial, not embittered or fanatic, and desperado, refusing the claims to authority that justify obedience in the name of defiance.[36]

In 1983 Rogin argued that Ishmael flees not only political romance, but politics, as his sentimental education means retreating to "attainable felicity" and irony in a private realm whose "slavish" conventionality once drove him to sea—or into political projects. Now, we might say that Ishmael reimagines politics in relation to an everyday life he has learned to accept as the only real ground of political possibility. Seeking alternatives to rationalism, we may echo his turn from the Ahabian—Promethean, modernist, paranoid—aspirations of what Sheldon Wolin called "epic" theory, which would depict society as a whole and its systemic derangement. If Ahab can be said to dramatize the derangement in such accounts of derangement, we turn to the nonsovereign, aleatory, and local as we profess to reimagine (not escape) politics. The radically democratic then appears not in plots of revolutionary transcendence to transform a whole, but as felicitous breaks in practices of daily life. Maybe the appeal of architectonic theory receded with sixties radicalism: as worldly shifts from hope to disappointment made epic theory seem hubristic and imperial, vain in both senses, of course theorists now echo Ishmael.[37]

But Melville writes a tragedy: Ahab is the "dark character" who utters "the sane madness of vital truth" that a utilitarian or neoliberal culture leaves unspoken; Ishmael learns how this truth is destructive when its limitations are denied, but his reparative ethos turns us toward the horrors Ahab sees as well as those he creates: "It is well to be on friendly terms with all the inmates of the place one lodges in." What are "friendly" terms?

If "Ahab" connotes theorizing that posits a cause of suffering and a political project to address it, can we ever simply exorcize him, or, as Prospero says of Caliban and Shakespeare implies of Prospero, must we "own this dark thing" as a needful but dangerous aspect of our practice? After all, theorists (and citizens) contesting forms of domination must conceive and poeticize plots, though it is best to expose their seams in ways wounded Ahab truly could not. He collapsed the difference between art and life, the grave danger from which few of us are immune. Still, to think that Melville could disown Ahab is to imagine his novel without a plot. Indeed, in Ahab's passionate poetry to mobilize the crew, and in his driven but skillful plotting of the *Pequod*'s path to a climactic encounter with the whale, does he not represent crucial aspects of Melville's art, and of political mobilization more broadly? As Ahab says his plot is the "keel" of the ship, his story is the keel of Melville's novel; and as his poetry moves the crew, Melville moves his readers—albeit by a story that ends by killing off Ahab and sinking the ship. Even to endorse Ishmael's turn to the ordinary, Melville must narrate the epic arc of that shift in scale.[38]

But Ishmael's bond to Ahab is deeper than the formality of the performative contradiction that makes Ishmaelian ethos depend on epic narrative and paradigm shift. Just consider how the survivor becomes the genial desperado addressing us: he is turned from conventionality not only by his marriage to Queequeg, but also by Ahab's defense of the "queenly personality" against domination, by his insistence that his wound be meaningful, and by his willingness to risk his life for the truth he lived by. Ishmael is attracted to the aggression in Ahab's intention to avenge—say rectify—the injustice he resents, and so to his defiance of cosmic and worldly authority. Ahab's transgressive energy is thrilling and liberating, like a whale breaching. Carry this claim further: at first melancholic and suicidal, cut off from the energies of life, Ishmael requires, and is even saved by, Ahab and his plot. Rogin thus notes, "The failure of the observer to rejoin the living world, and to join it together," is what draws Ishmael to participate in the hunt."[39] Leaving his own dismembered condition as an observer of life, bodiless, bloodless, he rejoins the world as a participant, first with Queequeg and then "welded" with other *Isolatoes* in a political project with admittedly disastrous results.

To follow the sequence in Nietzsche's "Three Metamorphoses," he begins as "the camel" suffering the despair created by dutifulness, which makes life a desert without nourishment, because it must say "yes" to the demands imposed on it. But "in the loneliest desert" a "metamorphosis occurs: the spirit becomes a lion who would conquer his freedom and be master in his own desert. Here he seeks out his last master. . . . 'Thou Shalt' is the name of the great dragon. But the spirit of the lion says, 'I will.'" The Ahabian lion defies the authority-demanding, soul-destroying dutifulness and the internal piety seeking that burden. "The creation of freedom for oneself . . . is within the power of the lion" because "a sacred 'No' even to duty" prepares the way "to assume the right to new values," which is "the most terrifying assumption for a reverent spirit that would bear much." But the lion cannot "create new values"; it can only open space for such creation. The spirit "must become a child" because in "the game of creation a sacred 'yes' is needed." Ahab is wed to "no" by his pain and defiance, but Ishmael need not be trapped if he finds a "yes" to enfold the lion's valuable but dangerous negativity.[40]

Ishmael would have remained a camel bound to pious dutifulness if he had not identified with Ahab's lion, but he also works through that identification by experiencing its costs. In turn, to face the dangers in our practice of democratic axioms, Ishmael's testimony must move us to find ourselves in Ahab's view of life's cruelty, his anguish over injury and longing for integrity, his need for an assailable cause and his denial that he imagines the malignancy he attacks, his enraged sense of injustice and his ambition to enact it. If we invest in killing the whale, we can experience the meaning of aggression and its consequences. Melville creates an Ahab who would destroy his other, but Melville defeats that wish to reveal the reality surviving it, and, likewise, if we surrender to Ahab's project and suffer its defeat, we experience both enraged agency and the realities resisting it. If we feel the horror Ahab sees, his enraged longing to remedy it, and the horror he makes, we can register our loss in his. After Ahab, though, we cannot return to the false comfort offered by jeremiads about God's justice, or by idealizations of democratic sovereignty. How might we rework the democratic dignity he enacted and desecrated? One issue is meaning making or plotting, the other is aggression and sovereignty, and in neither regard is "Ishmael" a sufficient alternative.[41]

Reworking Democratic Dignity

Begin with Toni Morrison's illuminating effort to redeem Ahab. The whale is taken to connote nature and the state, she notes, but whiteness, as the sovereign category in a regime of domination, is the "singular whale" that "transcends all the others." An abstraction (from color, particularity, and embodiment) that is horrific, whiteness does mean dismemberment: because "the trauma of racism is, for the racist and the victim, severe fragmentation," Ahab's monomania is not reducible to "male" or "adolescent" vengeance "over a lost leg." Rather, he "diverts and converts" a multiracial crew from capitalist labor to a revolutionary project. "If, indeed, a white, nineteenth-century, American male took on not abolition, not the amelioration of racist institutions . . . but the very concept of whiteness as an inhuman idea, he would be very alone, very desperate, and very doomed. Madness would be the only appropriate description of such audacity." As "the only white male American heroic enough to slay the monster that was devouring the world as he knew it," Ahab is her Melvillean hero and avatar.[42]

There are many reasons to reject Morrison's reading. Ishmael, not Ahab, links horror to whiteness, and to identify Ahab only with abolition is to ignore how he also bespeaks Jacksonian expansionists and Calhoun. Most important, Melville does not endorse Ahab (as Parker, let alone Jackson or Calhoun) but relates all these figures at "a lower layer" to dramatize the resentful motivation and Manichean allegory Ishmael calls monomania. Melville is not Ahab or Ishmael, and he is both. Still, Morrison's focus on race is revelatory. First, she depicts a structure of reified power and takes seriously dismemberment as a trope depicting its psychic effect and political meaning. Second, therefore, her Ahab rebels against domination and abstraction, not life as such, and she rightly ties Melville to that negativity. For Melville declares, "All who say yes, lie," and affirms those who "speak NO! In Thunder." He expresses that "no" in Ahab, but also in his character Babo, the black Ahab who leads a slave insurrection in *Benito Cereno.* Here again he dramatizes the integrity in implacable defiance, though also its cost in self-destruction—and mere reversal of master and slave. Morrison affirms insurrectionary rage because she sees the whale as a despotic, injurious political object, but she elides how Ahab's assertion of democratic dignity is entangled in domination. Can the truth in democratic rage be valued and yet contained?[43]

This possibility appears in the way that James Baldwin affirms the truth in Ahabian anger, while rejecting Ahab's way of living it:

> It began to seem that one would have to hold in the mind forever two ideas which seemed to be in opposition. The first idea was acceptance, the acceptance totally without rancor, of life as it is and men as they are: in the light of this idea it goes without saying that injustice is a commonplace. But this did not mean that one could be complacent, for the second idea was of equal power: one must never . . . accept these injustices as commonplace but must fight them with all one's strength. This fight begins, however, in the heart and it now had been laid to my charge to keep my own heart free of hatred and despair.[44]

To accept life as it is "without rancor" means accepting that injustice is commonplace, yet he refuses to submit to it. He echoes Morrison's sympathy with Ahab's rage, but he widens the frame by which to judge it. Given the rule of whiteness, he argues, "the image of . . . the 'nigger,' black, benighted, brutal, consumed with hatred," is internalized by blacks (and whites). If blacks surrender to it, "life has no other possible reality" than "achieving their vengeance and their own destruction" by enacting the "nightmare" that whites project on them. Instead, he would illuminate "the altogether savage paradox" that "the Negro" is "compelled to accept the fact that this dark and dangerous and unloved stranger is part of himself forever," because "only this recognition sets him in any wise free." Democratic dignity requires this paradoxical, "precarious adjustment," whereby our darkness is "exploited" in "ironic" and "honorable" ways.[45]

To move from Morrison's idealization of Ahab by way of Baldwin is to suggest the idea of "owning" Ahab's anger, so we are not in denial of its truth, or ruled by it, but use it creatively and honorably. For democratic dignity requires Ahabian negativity to contest domination by internal thou shalts and leviathanic authorities, but it also must credit both the danger in defiance and "the claim of the ordinary." Conversely, a genial, desperado philosophy gains political traction only by acknowledging—not disavowing—the frame it draws from the powers and plots conjured by Ahabian art.

It is tempting to say, then, that the novel works agonistically; it situates us not so much between or above incommensurable positions as in a space that emerges (or we create) by undergoing or living their tension. "Instead of adhering to a uniform conception of reality and seeking to represent it in his fiction," Richard Brodhead says, Melville "tries out various modes of representation and explores different versions of the real." These are "radically incommensurate and arranged in such a way that from within one we simply cannot see the other," but because he gives neither the "status of an independent actuality," readers and citizens become "conscious of representation as a function of the imagination that creates it."[46] Juxtaposition helps us grasp how a democratic politics is at once underwritten and jeopardized by Ahabian energies—and by Ishmaelian virtues. Rather than split a "tragic" position from its others, a tragedy shows the value and danger in every position, virtue, ideal.

Moby-Dick thus leaves us with the problem of false prophecy, that is, of political judgment. It bequeaths to us the task of salvaging the good we value from the danger we witness in pity and terror, as we argue over "practically assailable" causes and fruitful action, for reasons and with results that no one discerns clearly, though many claim to. Melville notes only how the "measureless self-deception" of prophets and demagogues parallels "their measureless power of deceiving and bedevilling" others, but we would add that artists also use—and would redeem—this power (360). He exercises it partly by affirming the premise of democratic dignity and partly by dramatizing its self-destruction, which means by "weaving" "tragic graces"—both "mournful" and "exalted"—around "meanest mariners" and the "crazed" captain they take as a champion (146). His tragedy of democratic dignity thus stages the vicissitudes of this faith, rendering what is noble and dangerous in it as a legacy audiences must decide how to bear out.

But the novel reminds us to politically contextualize our own academic debates about modern Prometheanism. For Ishmael grasps the danger of fire midway in the text, but the ship sails on to destruction. Melville's tragedy impels us to ask: Do we remain on a deadly path, and is it in our power to inflect it? Hear Ishmael's perception as he turns:

> As they narrated to each other their unholy adventures, their tales of terror told in words of mirth; as their uncivilized laughter forked upwards out of them, like flames in the furnace; as to and fro, in their front, the harpooners wildly gesticulated with their huge pronged forks and dippers; as the wind howled on, and the sea leaped, and the ship groaned and dived, and yet steadfastly shot her red hell further and further into the blackness of the sea and the night . . . then the rushing *Pequod,* freighted with savages, and laden with fire, and burning a corpse, and plunging into that blackness of darkness, seemed the material counterpart of her monomaniac commander's soul. . . . Whatever swift, rushing thing I stood on was not so much bound to any haven ahead as rushing from all havens astern." (476)

Notes

1. By tracing relationships among tragedy, literature, and theory, my essay is deeply indebted to Peter Euben, *The Tragedy of Political Theory* (Princeton: Princeton University Press, 1990), and Michael Rogin, *Subversive Genealogy: The Politics and Art of Herman Melville* (New York: Knopf, 1983).

2. What Wendy Brown says of theory thus suggests a bond between literary art and political theory: "This meaning-making enterprise . . . depicts a world that does not quite exist, that is not quite the world we inhabit. But this is theory's incomparable value, not its failure," because "its revelatory and speculative work" requires "working to one side of direct referents." Wendy Brown, "At the Edge: The Future of Political Theory," in Brown, *Edgework* (Princeton: Princeton University Press, 2005), 80. In Melville's words, "It is with fiction as with religion: it should present another world, yet one to which we feel the tie." Theory and literature open space between a given world as we are conditioned to perceive it and possibilities of living otherwise.

3. To the degree that political theorists make *theory* mean *argument* to validate so-called empirical and so-called normative claims, my contrasting approach is to explore how Melville *dramatizes* rather than *argues,* by creating a fictional yet compelling alter-world. To the degree that the political theory canon is "detextualized" by severing *what* a text says from *how* it makes meaning, and to the degree that this canon thus excludes literature, as if theory and literary art were incommensurate, I emphasize how "fictionality" and fantasy do crucial truth-telling work in both.

4. Eric Bentley, *The Life of the Drama* (1964; repr., New York: Applause The-

atre Books, 1991), 278; emphasis in original. My reading must clarify the difference between "tragedy" and "the tragic," and also the difference that difference makes, and if I dehydrate the text, I have failed.

5. Herman Melville, *Moby-Dick; or, The Whale* (New York: Library of America, 2010), 146 (paperback classic ed.); references hereafter are included parenthetically in the text.

6. In addition to Michael Rogin's *Subversive Genealogy,* I am especially indebted to several readings of the novel: D. H. Lawrence, *Studies in Classic American Literature* (1923; repr., New York: Penguin, 1990); Newton Arvin, *Herman Melville* (1950; repr., Westport, Conn.: Greenwood Press, 1972); Richard Brodhead, *Hawthorne, Melville, and the Novel* (Chicago: University of Chicago Press, 1976); Eyal Peretz, *Literature, Disaster, and the Enigma of Power: A Reading of* Moby-Dick (Stanford: Stanford University Press, 2002); C. L. R. James, *Mariners, Renegades and Castaways: The Story of Herman Melville and the World We Live In* (1953; repr., Hanover, N.H.: Dartmouth College Press, 2001); Charles Olson, *Call Me Ishmael* (Baltimore: Johns Hopkins University Press, 1997).

7. In one sense the sinking is a fiction of apocalypse as a final "un-veiling," while in reality, beyond the text, life goes on. The fiction offers readers the satisfaction of an end, but the real calamity may be that "it is going to continue and continue," as the sign of a bedraggled homeless man in a *New Yorker* cartoon declared. The very fiction of a traumatic event may deny the ongoing-ness of the "crisis ordinary," as Lauren Berlant puts it in *Cruel Optimism* (Durham: Duke University Press, 2011). She depicts "not 'the waning of affect' but the waning of genre. Life can no longer be lived phantasmatically as melodrama, as Aristotelian tragedy spread to ordinary people, as a predictable arc that is shaped by acts, facts, or fates." As a result, she also rejects the idea of extraordinary evil. Berlant, "Thinking about Feeling Historical" in *Emotion, Space, and Society* 1, no. 1 (2008): 7.

8. On Job (as well as Jonah), see Ilana Pardes, *Melville's Bibles* (Berkeley: University of California Press, 2008).

9. From Stephen Mitchell's translation, *The Book of Job* (1987; repr., New York: HarperCollins, 1992).

10. In Eric Santner's words, "The world in which we find ourselves has ultimate, though also ultimately inscrutable, semantic power. . . . Something is always appearing from the ground of being that imposes itself on us with the sheer force of its validity, even if it finally has no safely construable significance." Ahab and Job seek a determinate meaning. Slavoj Žižek, Eric L. Santner, and Kenneth Reinhard, *The Neighbor: Three Inquiries in Political Thinking* (Chicago: University of Chicago Press, 2005), 94.

11. Melville links the "power of blackness" in Hawthorne to "that Calvinistic sense of innate depravity and Original Sin, from whose visitations, in some shape

or other, no deeply thinking mind is always and wholly free. For in certain moods, no man can weigh this world without throwing in something somehow like Original Sin, to strike the uneven balance." See Melville, "Hawthorne and His Mosses," in *Moby-Dick,* Norton Critical Ed., 2nd ed. (New York: Norton, 2002), 522. As Dostoevsky created Ivan Karamazov to protest a creation rife with innocent suffering, but also to dramatize what it means to "reject" life on those (or any) grounds, so Ahab shows the validity, and baleful consequences, of Melville's own grief and rage.

12. Note the resonance with Jacques Rancière's views of the demos and of democracy.

13. To depict Shakespeare's genius as unapproachable, Melville asserts, is to contradict the assumptions of one who would "carry republican progressiveness into literature as well as into life." Though many doubt the emergence of such genius among us, "great geniuses are parts of their time; they themselves are the times." They will appear in vernacular forms that go unrecognized, just as "it is of a piece with the Jews, for while their Shiloh was meekly walking in their streets, they were still praying for his magnificent coming, looking for him on a chariot who was already among them on an ass." Melville, "Hawthorne and His Mosses," 524.

14. It is important to credit that identification as an Ishmael has always been a crucial trope in the dominant culture, ever since members of the Boston Tea Party dressed as Indians. The enfranchised can shift identity, to occupy temporarily the position of outcasts, red or black, who remain marked subjects fixed in social place. Since antebellum days, artists and countercultural critics have used this cross-dressing to protest bourgeois society. Do they simply invert and so sustain the fantasies embedded in the racial sign? Do they merely use the meaning of the other for their own purposes, or do they politically address racial hierarchy? In the literature on *Moby-Dick,* however, only C. L. R. James questions Ishmael's professed identity, calling him an "intellectual Ahab" who equivocally oscillates between attachment to Ahab and to the crew. James does not identify Ishmael with the crew, but rather sees Ishmael as a political liberal, one who is unwilling to fully identify with workers and subalterns, whose multinational and multiracial character in fact represents the only alternative to the Ahab-Ishmael dyad, an alternative Melville dramatized but could not explicitly endorse. James, *Mariners, Renegades and Castaways,* 40–41.

15. According to Slavoj Žižek, "We should first perceive it [disaster] as our fate, as unavoidable, and then, projecting ourselves into it, adopting its standpoint, we should retroactively insert into its past . . . counterfactual possibilities ('If we had done this and that, the calamity we are now experiencing would not have occurred!') upon which we then act today. We have to accept that, at the level of possibilities, our future is doomed, that the catastrophe will take place, that it is our

destiny—and then, against the background of this acceptance, mobilize ourselves to perform the act which will change destiny itself and thereby insert a new possibility into the past. Paradoxically, the only way to prevent the disaster is to accept it as inevitable. . . . What this means is that one should fearlessly rehabilitate the idea of preventive action. . . . If we postpone our action until we have full knowledge of the catastrophe, we will have acquired that knowledge only when it is too late. That is to say, the certainty on which an act relies is not a matter of knowledge, but a matter of *belief*." Žižek, *First as Tragedy, Then as Farce* (New York: Verso, 2009), 151; emphasis in original.

16. Lawrence, *Studies in Classic American Literature*, 170. Lawrence's Melville apprehended "the terrible fatality. Doom. Doom! Of what? The doom of our white day. . . . His white soul, doomed. His great white epoch, doomed. Himself, doomed. The idealist, doomed. The spirit, doomed." How? Because "monomaniacs of the idea" will be destroyed by the effort to master "the deepest blood-nature" of life. Calling the *Pequod* "the ship of the white American soul," Lawrence puts Ahab among the "fanatics" of "white mental consciousness," who recruit "the dark races and pale to help us, red, yellow, and black, east and west, Quaker and fire-worshiper, we get them all to help us" in "this ghastly maniacal hunt of ourselves, which is our doom and suicide" (ibid., 169). In 1954, after Hitler, Stalin, and Hiroshima, C. L. R. James takes up Lawrence's themes while detained on Ellis Island by a Leviathan National Security State. "The voyage of the *Pequod* is the voyage of modern civilization seeking its destiny . . . heading for a crisis which will be a world crisis, a total crisis in every sense of that word. . . . That which was madness in a book one hundred years ago is the living madness of the age in which we live. . . . We shall conquer it or it will destroy us." See James, *Mariners, Renegades and Castaways*, 19, 34, 12.

17. Olson, *Call Me Ishmael*, 57.

18. We hear his Emersonian assumption that knowledge depends on experience: "There is no earthly way of finding out precisely what the whale really looks like" except "by going a whaling yourself; but by so doing, you run no small risk of being eternally stove and sunk by . . . this Leviathan." Like Nietzsche, he links living death to landlocked imprisonment, and philosophy to life-giving exploration of infinite seas: "The port would fain give succor; the port is safety, comfort, hearthstone, supper, warm blankets, friends, all that's kind to our moralities. But . . . know ye . . . that mortally intolerable truth: that all deep, earnest thinking is but the intrepid effort of the soul to keep the open independence of her sea; while the wildest winds of heaven and earth conspire to cast her on the treacherous, slavish shore[.] But as in landlessness alone resides the highest truth, shoreless, indefinite as God—so, better is it to perish in that howling infinite than be ingloriously dashed upon the lee, even if that were safety!" (136).

19. Alan Heimert, "*Moby-Dick* and American Political Symbolism," *American Quarterly* 15, no. 4 (Winter 1963): 506; Olson, *Call Me Ishmael*, 23. As Michael Rogin says, "Ahab and his crew do not escape into nature. The *Pequod* brings with it the interracial society, structure of authority, and industrial apparatus of nineteenth-century America" (*Subversive Genealogy*, 108). Start with whaling itself: whale oil was a central commodity in the emerging industrial order, crucial to lighting homes and cities. (Fossil fuel, discovered in 1859 in Pennsylvania, had displaced whale oil by 1890.) In 1846 over 900 whaling ships worked what was called the fishery; 735 originated in the United States, mostly in New Bedford or Nantucket (these figures from Olson, *Call Me Ishmael*, 20–25). The text shows the violent industrial production by which nature is made a commodity for market. Horrific violence on sentient creatures is a condition of civilized life: we "butcher" whales "to light the gay bridals . . . of men" and "illuminate the solemn churches that preach unconditional inoffensiveness by all to all." This murderous labor is also mortally risky: "For god's sake," Ishmael urges, "be economical with your lamps" because "not a gallon you burn, but at least one drop of a man's blood was spilled for it" (Melville, *Moby-Dick*, 282). In other words, the hinge of the cosmic and political dimensions of the novel is not only "the whale" as a confounding symbol, but also a plot depicting the commodification of nature by exploited industrial labor.

20. Alexis de Tocqueville, *Democracy in America*, 2 vols. (1835–1840; repr., New York: Vintage, 1990), 2:74, 318.

21. For C. L. R. James, Ahab is a critic of capitalist-industrial civilization, yet "Melville's whole point is to show the intimate, the close, the logical relation" of Ahab's madness "to what the world has hitherto accepted as sane and reasonable, to the values by which all good men have lived" (James, *Mariners, Renegades and Castaways*, 13).

22. Commentators are divided on Ahab's motivation: Is the problem his *desire* to know what no mortal can, and his rage that he cannot? Or is his problem his *claim to know* the nature of nature, the one determinate meaning of life?

23. Heimert, "*Moby-Dick* and American Political Symbolism," 526. We note how the young Marx calls philosophy "the head" and the proletariat "the heart" of one collective body seeking a revolution so that "man revolves about himself as his own true sun." Karl Marx, "Contribution to the Critique," in *The Marx-Engels Reader*, ed. Robert C. Tucker, 2nd ed. (New York: Norton, 1978), 65, 54.

24. George Kateb, *The Inner Ocean: Individualism and Democratic Culture* (Ithaca: Cornell University Press, 1992), 90.

25. Melville's Ahab parallels Tocqueville's account of democratic dignity. First, Ahab personifies the precepts of the Cartesian philosophy that democrats practice: "to evade the bondage of system and habit, of family maxims, class opinions, and, in some degree, of national prejudice; to accept tradition only as a means of infor-

mation, and existing facts only as a lesson to be used in doing otherwise and doing better; to seek the reason of things for oneself and in oneself alone. . . . As everyone shuts himself up tightly within himself and insists upon judging the world from there," he "readily conclude[s] that everything in the world may be explained, and nothing in it transcends the limits of the understanding" (*Democracy in America,* 2:3–4). Second, the ideal of equality seems to exalt not only acquisitive individualism, but a romantic view of integral subjectivity. Third, democratic social conditions link subjectivity to freedom as an absolute sovereignty that Tocqueville describes as rupturing the continuity of generations and the web of relationships making community. Nature, other persons, or communities appear as illegitimate limitations of personal or popular sovereignty. "The woof of time is every instant broken and the track of generations effaced" as the citizens in a democratic era feel "they owe nothing to any man, expect nothing from any man; they acquire the habit of always considering themselves as standing alone, and they are apt to imagine that their whole destiny is in their own hands." Such self-reliance has the worldly effect of "hiding his descendants and separating his contemporaries from him; it throws him back forever upon himself alone and threatens in the end to confine him entirely within the solitude of his own heart" (*Democracy in America,* 2:99). As Ahab curses "mortal inter-indebtedness," so citizens "must be reminded that they live with others" and indeed that they are impotent if alone and powerful only if acting in concert. Refusing this political truth, however, democratic dignity creates allegories of evil that attribute the absence of an idealized freedom to malevolent powers that hold men captive. As C. L. R. James later argued, therefore, "The society of free individualism gives birth to totalitarianism and is unable to defend itself against it" (*Mariners, Renegades and Castaways,* 54). Like Tocqueville and Marx, James's Melville depicts the paradoxical inversion whereby liberal modernity promises emancipation and progress but produces despotism and barbarism.

26. Lawrence, *Studies in Classic American Literature,* 9; Nina Baym, "Melodramas of Beset Manhood: How Theories of American Fiction Exclude Women Authors," *American Quarterly* 33, no. 2 (1981): 123–139. On melodrama, see Peter Brook, *The Melodramatic Imagination* (New Haven: Yale University Press, 1976); Bentley, *The Life of the Drama;* and Elizabeth Anker, *Orgies of Feeling* (Durham: Duke University Press, forthcoming). In Lacan's terms, dismemberment signifies castration as the separation that makes humans incomplete. *Lack* is the "traumatic kernel" of every subject, disavowed by fantasies of wholeness and the evil power that ruins it. If it could be removed, we would be whole again. But claims about disavowed traumatic kernels typically disavow actual traumas, a tension that Melville sustains.

27. For Tocqueville acquisitive and individualistic daily life is "anti-poetic" be-

cause it cannot support figurations of the ideal. But for people in a democratic era, a vibrant "source of poetry" is available in "the grand image of themselves" as a nation (*Democracy in America,* 2:74). He thus depicts atomized liberal men seeking and finding a redemptive meaning (and political unity) in a poetry that abstracts from the palpable bonds he calls "the real and true" to project an ideal nation and "monsters" that threaten it. Authors and audiences, he argues, are joined by a taste for abstraction and idealization that is both literary and political: "Each citizen is habitually engaged in the contemplation of a very puny object: namely himself. . . . When he has been drawn out of his own sphere, therefore, he always expects that some amazing object will be offered to his attention; and it is on these terms alone that he consents to tear himself for a moment from the petty complicated cares that form the charm and excitement of his life. . . . Authors, on their part, . . . inflate their imaginations, and expanding them beyond all bounds, they not infrequently abandon the great to reach the gigantic. By these means they hope to attract the observation of the multitude" (*Democracy in America,* 2:77).

28. Rogin, *Subversive Genealogy,* 130. Heimert cites Andrew Jackson, who called the national bank a "huge sea-serpent" whose "leviathan folds" envelop the republic, and who promised that "the bank is trying to kill me but I will kill it." Heimert also cites a critic of Theodore Parker: "He is possessed with inveterate monomania, which presents to his diseased mind all objects under one image. He is haunted by a specter . . . and this phantom he pursues with reckless speech of a wild huntsman, trampling on every obstacle to his headlong course" (Heimert, "*Moby-Dick* and American Political Symbolism," 517). Accordingly, Rogin argues, "The relationship between American politics and American literary art is very nearly the reverse of that normally proposed." For "if by realism is meant sensitivity to class and social constraint," American political rhetoric is not realist. In turn, the absence of realist politics shapes literary form: to render inflated language, demonized objects, allegorical symbolism, melodramatic narrative, Melville forgoes realistic mimetic strategies; Rogin, *Subversive Genealogy,* 19. The Parker quote is from Rogin, *Subversive Genealogy,* 136.

29. For two powerful statements of the argument radically juxtaposing Ahab to Ishmael, see F. O. Matthiessen, *American Renaissance: Art and Expression in the Age of Emerson and Whitman* (New York: Oxford University Press, 1941); and Hubert Dreyfus and Sean Dorrance Kelley, *All Things Shining* (New York: Free Press, 2011).

30. Bentley, *The Life of the Drama,* 283. As Brodhead says, Melville depicts "a world so fully inhuman that Ahab's rite of cosmic defiance seems like a noble and necessary response" (*Hawthorne, Melville, and the Novel,* 151). If accepting the universe in every regard and moment is the highest good, however, then rage is simply the symptom of a nonacceptance to reject and overcome. The alternative is

to accept rage as an understandable response to some aspects of life. The political question, therefore, is not so much if we are enraged, but how we explain it and channel it, and how we judge the explanations and actions of others. In a certain sense, acceptance may signal disconnection from the reality of a situation, not unjustifiable resentment.

31. There are credible reasons for the crew to assent to the hunt. They pile on the whale the grinding difficulty of life and the endlessly sacrificial—and violent—human labor needed to sustain it. Melville depicts pastoral harmony and human conviviality, but he sees inescapable enmity between humans and nature as well as the "sharkish" qualities joining them.

32. Brodhead, *Hawthorne, Melville, and the Novel,* 129.

33. C. Wright Mills, "Private Troubles, Public Issues," in Mills, *Power, Politics and People,* ed. Irving L. Horowitz (New York: Ballantine, 1963), 395. In "Paranoid Reading and Reparative Reading," in *Touching Feeling: Affect, Pedagogy, Performativity* (Durham: Duke University Press, 2003), Eve Kosofsky Sedgwick argues that "paranoia has by now candidly become less a diagnosis than a prescription. In a world where no one needs to be delusional to find systematic oppression, to theorize out of anything but a paranoid stance has come to seem naive, pious, or complacent" (125–126). In what Klein calls the paranoid-schizoid position, theorists anticipate—look for and find—injustice and systemic harm, partly because organized harm is ubiquitous and partly because aggression is split off from awareness and projected outward. Strong theory invests meaning, but in negatively charged and polarized ways. In contrast, Sedgwick uses Klein to argue that to inhabit "the depressive position" is to repair the worldly damage aggression causes, partly by reclaiming disowned parts of the self, and partly by refusing polarizing ways of thinking and acting. By assuming that complexity defeats any claim to grasp a whole whale, and by assuming inescapable ambivalence in oneself, impurity in each object of attachment, and imperfection in every norm and act, we turn from psychic splitting, intellectual dichotomy, melodramas of victimization, and heroized political antagonism. This depressive position is "no less acute, no less realistic, no less attached to a project of survival, and neither more nor less delusional or fantasmatic" than the paranoid position, Sedgwick insists, but involves "a different range of affects, ambitions, and risks" (*Touching Feeling,* 150). She encourages theorists on the left to turn from the paranoid to the depressive position, a move I associate with Ishmael. But as she notes that politics is likely to require both positions, or to occur at their intersection or in the interval between them, so I am arguing that Melville does not and cannot simply reject Ahab. Also see Sedgwick, "Melanie Klein and the Difference Affect Makes," *South Atlantic Quarterly* 106, no. 3 (Summer 2007): 625–642.

34. Tocqueville, *Democracy in America,* 2:78.

35. "What the white whale was to Ahab, has been hinted at; what, at times, he was to me as yet remains unsaid." The "at times" suggests that he does not have only this *one* view, but that it is crucial to dramatize: "But how can I hope to explain myself here; and yet . . . explain myself I must, else all these chapters might be naught" (Melville, *Moby-Dick,* 159).

36. Matthiessen, *American Renaissance,* 512. Ahab "cannot understand that the meaning he sees is a product of his imagination," Brodhead claims, whereas Ishmael "generates meanings from within the processes of actual experience, entertaining these not as final truth but for the sense they make of that experience" (*Hawthorne, Melville, and the Novel,* 156). Ahab claims purposeful causality and intentionality, and so follows fixed fates on "iron rails," but Ishmael sees the prevalence of chance, mocks intentionality, notes the wayward, and aspires to attainable felicity. Ahab openly claims authority, but Ishmael parodies all forms of authority; Ahab is grim and audacious, while Ishmael is sly and exuberant; Ahab is consumed by one idea, while Ishmael is digressive, open promiscuously to many; Ahab attacks, while Ishmael disarms, to "make friends with horror." Inclusionary, Ishmael sees the violence but also the beauty in nature and human capacities for idiocy and savagery as well as care, grief, and wonder.

37. Sheldon Wolin, "Political Theory as a Vocation," *American Political Science Review* 63, no. 4 (1969): 1062–1082.

38. In the political theory canon, Hobbes is not the only figure whose visionary capacity is tied to wounded rage. In *The Tempest,* the embittered Prospero wields (but finally snaps) a wand that represents the generative but problematic power of words and images to bewitch people and organize their lives. In More's *Utopia,* the character Morus depicts politics on a stage and counsels using "indirect philosophy" to work with and within a ruling script, whereas Hythlodaeus insists we must make a new play or remain captive to the "madness" normalized by the one now dominant. Ahab dramatizes what is problematic in what Wolin calls an architectonic mode of theorizing, but as Wolin notes, a political theory invested in the ordinary is "in a bind: it wants to be local and restricted, but structures of power—political, economic, and cultural—are national and global. To theorize the inside one must theorize the outside." Sheldon Wolin, "What Time Is It?" *Theory & Event* 1, no. 1 (1997), http://muse.jhu.edu/journals/theory_and_event/.

39. Rogin, *Subversive Genealogy,* 111.

40. Friedrich Nietzsche, *Thus Spoke Zarathustra* (1885), trans. Walter Kaufmann (1954; repr., New York: Penguin, 1996), 26–27.

41. Melville's text uses Ahab's aggression to enact what D. W. Winnicott calls "successful destruction," when an enraged child mentally or internally destroys its other, but survival of that other enables the child to experience both its subjectivity and the fact that reality is outside it. Infantile omnipotence (Lawrence says

masterlessness) is defeated as aggression is both affirmed and limited, and as the border between inside and outside is felt, so the outside is experienced as real, independent of the self and its projections. Because the other credits but contains the child's anger, the child discovers the world's resilience, and its own. Likewise, Melville's text is a "holding" environment as identification with Ahab engenders an experience of democratic subjectivity and of the world as an independent reality. On the use of Winnicott's idea, see Jessica Benjamin, *The Bonds of Love* (New York: Pantheon, 1988).

42. Toni Morrison, "Unspeakable Things Unspoken: The Afro-American Presence in American Literature," *Michigan Quarterly Review* 28, no. 1 (Winter 1989): 15–18. Her Ahab plays the prophet depicted by Father Mapple, whose sermon on Jonah Ishmael hears before he ships out. The prophet is "to preach truth to the face of falsehood," for "delight" is only "to him . . . who against the proud gods and commodores of this earth, ever stands forth his own inexorable self. . . . Delight is to him, who gives no quarter in the truth . . . and destroys all sin though he pluck it out from under the robes of Senators [e.g., Daniel Webster, advocate of the Fugitive Slave Act] and Judges [Lemuel Shaw, Melville's father-in-law, who ruled it constitutional]. Delight . . . is to him who acknowledges no law or lord, but the Lord his God, and is only a patriot to heaven" (Melville, *Moby-Dick*, 75).

43. Melville, "Hawthorne and His Mosses," 522. American artists respond very differently to Ahab's anger. The director John Huston sounds like Morrison: "Ahab speaks for Melville, and through him he is raging at the deity. This point . . . was never commented on by any critic who saw the picture, even by those who championed it. They failed to recognize that the work was a blasphemy. The message of *Moby-Dick* was hate. The whale is the mask of a malignant deity who torments mankind. Ahab pits himself against this evil power. Melville doesn't choose to call the power Satan, but God." Critics expected him to portray Ahab "as a raging madman," but he "rejected that." Joseph Persico, "Interview with John Huston," *American Heritage* 33 (May 1992): 13. In contrast, Laurie Anderson confessed that she could not deal with this anger when she made the story into an opera. See Samuel Otter's "Leviathanic Revelations," in *Ungraspable Phantom: Essays on* Moby-Dick, ed. John Bryant, Mary K. Bercaw Edwards, and Timothy Marr (Kent, Ohio: Kent State University Press, 2006).

44. James Baldwin, "Notes of a Native Son," in *Notes of a Native Son* (1955; repr., New York: Bantam, 1979), 95.

45. Baldwin, "Many Thousands Gone," in *Notes of a Native Son*, 29–34.

46. Brodhead, *Hawthorne, Melville, and the Novel*, 125.

4

Ahab, American

Susan McWilliams

When scholars talk about the dilemmas of American political life in *Moby-Dick,* they tend to focus on the dilemmas faced by the ship's crew: the narrator who wants us to call him Ishmael, Starbuck, Stubb, Flask, and so on.[1] Captain Ahab, in the literature, is largely approached as a monarchical or autonomous force—someone who comes in and exposes the weaknesses of the American polity by imposing on it, from above or outside. For C. L. R. James, for instance, Ahab is the "embodiment of the totalitarian type," a man "by nature a dictatorial personality" who is thus able to manipulate a relatively incompetent and incoherent crew.[2] Michael Rogin describes Ahab as the sole founder of a new, artificial Leviathan, who draws "on his destructive intimacy with nature, on the savage's instinctual power, and on a transforming, technological magic" to control the ship's sailors—thus symbolically changing the nation by reversing the course and mission of John Winthrop's *Arbella.*[3] John Alvis sees Ahab as a Caesarist demagogue who successfully subjugates a crew that lacks the religious or intellectual fortitude to resist him.[4] To others Ahab represents not any type or group of human beings per se but, rather, large and impersonal social forces: industrial capitalism, high Calvinism, modern warfare technology, and so on.[5] And a fair number of writers have approached Ahab as if he is either evil or the devil incarnate.[6] All these approaches, and others like them, draw attention to the ways in which Captain Ahab stands apart, or stands differently, from the ordinary American or the American population en masse. In most assessments of his character, in other words, Captain Ahab is portrayed in some critical way as *not one of us:* foreign in the literal sense, foreign in the psychological sense, or both. Ahab seems to most to represent behavior that is beyond the bounds of ordinary sympathy and outside the strictures of everyday society.

It is true that in some ways the book supports this kind of reading; early on in the book, Melville has Captain Peleg describe Ahab as a "grand, ungodly, god-like man," a description on which many commentators have seized.[7] And of course the great spectacle of Ahab's demise invites us to focus on the extraordinary size of his excesses and his flaws. But this familiar cast on the name Ahab leaves at least something to be desired, since in many ways Melville goes out of his way to stress that Ahab is not an impersonal or otherworldly force at all but an ordinary human being, someone who "responds humanly to other characters" and whose recognizably human qualities more than balance out his most extreme behaviors.[8] For instance, just seconds after Peleg describes Ahab in those semidivine terms, he backtracks, emphasizing the extent of Ahab's "humanities." Ahab, he says, is a "good captain" and a "good man" with a good family; "he has a wife—not three voyages wedded—a sweet, resigned girl," says Peleg, and "by that sweet girl that old man has a child."[9] If Ahab seems strange or alien at first glance, we quickly learn that he harks from a place much closer to home.

More specifically, Melville stresses the extent to which Ahab is not a foreign force but part of a well-established class of American citizens, with long roots in the nation's history. Those roots are part occupational; early in *Moby-Dick* Melville cites one of Daniel Webster's addresses to the Senate, an address in which Webster describes Nantucket whaling as one of the oldest and most estimable American industries, one that deserves "public encouragement."[10] More fundamentally, those roots are genealogical. Melville even intimates that Ahab shares a bloodline with Benjamin Franklin; "better than royal blood," Ishmael says, Nantucketers like Ahab have the blood of the American Founders in their veins.[11] Peleg underscores this genealogy in his discourse on Ahab; he tells Ishmael that, although Ahab has the name of a biblical king, "Ahab did not name himself"; in other words, if he seems aristocratic, it is by a kind of accident, and only a matter of appearance. Ahab, he emphasizes, is no noble; he is a Quaker, born and raised in that most egalitarian of early American religions. Shortly thereafter, when Ishmael foreshadows the story he is about to tell, a story of "meanest mariners" in which "men may seem detestable" and be marked by "ignominious blemish," he insists that even the tale's darkest characters are meant to be understood in the light of "democratic dignity," in "that abounding dignity which has no robed investiture." Even "the most mournful, perchance the most abased, of them all," Ishmael says, should be approached in the "Spirit of Equality," in service to a "great democratic God."[12]

It is worth considering Ahab along the lines that Ishmael suggests in the foregoing passage—not as an embodiment of impersonal force, tyranny, or pathology, but rather without any kind of "robed investiture." Such a reading, as Ishmael indicates, allows us not just to see Ahab in a new light but also to see Melville's more general teachings about the broader potential for democratic flourishing in the United States. I believe that the text more than justifies this kind of reading, not only for the reasons I have already suggested, but also because of a signal fact that has often gotten lost in treatments of Ahab's character. That is: two of Ahab's most definitive characteristics—his isolation and his desire for domination—do not differentiate him from the other characters in the book but rather underscore how much he is like them. Among the *Pequod*'s crew in particular, those traits are the rule rather than the exception, a fact that helps explain why the crew members are so quick to adopt Ahab's way of thinking: in large measure, it is already their own.[13] Moreover, in various places Melville suggests that those qualities, which many have rightly identified as the integral components of Ahab's character, are decidedly or distinctively American qualities—that is, qualities that are endemic to the American population. If Ahab is noteworthy in these regards, then, it is largely because Americans as a whole are noteworthy in these regards. (For a view that complements this argument even as it diverges from it, see George Shulman's excellent contribution to this volume.)

What's more, in the opening pages of *Moby-Dick* Melville twice calls our attention to the idea that, rather than treating Ahab's character as odd or singular, he will treat it as a reflection, albeit a distilled or exaggerated one, of the character of the society that surrounds him. Early on, Ishmael notes that on a whaling ship the captain "gets his atmosphere at second hand from the sailors on the forecastle." "He thinks he breathes it first; but not so. In much the same way do the commonality lead their leaders in many other things, at the same time the leaders little suspect it."[14] Before Captain Ahab is introduced, Melville already has suggested that he is not the sole or preeminent source of the atmosphere on the ship; his very breath is recycled from the lungs of the crew. It seems that even when we think he is in charge, or when Ahab himself thinks that his behavior is leading the direction of the ship, it may be in fact a lagging indicator of other, more widespread social phenomena.

But perhaps Melville's most clever hint along these lines appears among the book's prefatory "extracts." There he includes a line of Oliver Goldsmith's that has been modified to read: "If you should write a fable for little fishes, you would make them speak like great whales." As Melville presents it, the quotation suggests that in stories meant to instruct, the key characters are going to be exaggerated, made to appear bigger or more dramatic than their counterparts in real life. If you would create a story about a whale to instruct a school of fish about themselves, by the same principle you would create a story about "a mighty pageant creature" to instruct a school of ordinary citizens about themselves.[15] You would exaggerate your character to better draw attention to a more pedestrian subject.[16] But Melville's implication particularly stands out if you compare his modification of the line to what Goldsmith actually said, since in the original that meaning is absent: "Why, Mr. Johnson, [writing fables] is not so easy as you seem to think; for if *you* were to make little fishes talk, they would talk like WHALES. "[17] Melville transforms the quotation so that it takes on a more general and imperative tone, one that indicates his own approach; it suggests that when we see whales or other imposing figures (like Ahab) in the book, we are to understand that they are speaking to, and about, much more ordinary selves.

In this essay I focus on the ways in which Ahab is an ordinary self, or an ordinary American citizen, by the standards of *Moby-Dick.* Although we might not be inclined to think of them as average or "normal" qualities, Ahab's isolation and desire for domination are presented in the book as qualities that are widespread in the population, and qualities that have a great deal to do with one another. We can, to this extent, understand Ahab as an exaggerated caricature of the American character, a caricature that—in Ahab's grand decline and defeat—sets into relief what Melville considered to be a great danger for and within American political life, and perhaps modern, mass democratic life more broadly.

By looking at Ahab in that light, I argue that in *Moby-Dick* we can see Melville worry that the United States is weakened by what he calls its "*Isolato*" culture: a culture in which norms and circumstances conspire to isolate individuals from one another. In such a culture, Melville thinks, the idea of independence becomes so overemphasized that the fact of human interdependence becomes dangerously underemphasized. In such a culture individuals become increasingly incapable of forging the most basic interpersonal connections, and they become more broadly incapable of engaging in public discussions about the direction of their common life; they become, in the simplest case, bad citizens. To that extent Melville echoes Alexis de Tocqueville's fear that American democracy inclines toward a kind of individualism that breeds a stance of political indifference and enervates public life. But Melville suggests further that in an *Isolato* culture individuals who feel cut off from each other—and from deliberative political possibilities—tend to understand their options for action solely in terms of violence and domination. The grand threat of an *Isolato* culture is that when the individuals within it act, they tend to act with a kind of brutality that is self-denying and ultimately self-destroying. If we read Ahab's story as a story of American character, what we read is a story about a particular kind of modern democratic self-delusion: a kind of self-delusion that emanates from certain individualist conceits of democratic life, but which culminates in a desperate struggle for dominance that stands to destroy a democratic citizenry in the end.

The Life of Solitude

Almost every description of Ahab in *Moby-Dick*, from the beginning of the book to the end, turns on Ahab's solitude. It is clear that even before his first encounter with Moby Dick, Ahab was a solitary man, not inclined to spend much time with others. As a sea captain, he has long been known for his profound detachment; though he has always been a great egalitarian, a person in whom "there seemed not to lurk the smallest social arrogance," Ahab has never been able to talk to other people. For instance, unlike other captains, Ahab does not forbid discussion at his dining table, but at mealtimes he himself falls dumb, unable to participate in any conversation with others. As Ishmael puts it: "Socially, Ahab was inaccessible. Though nominally included in the census of Christendom, he was still an alien to it. He lived in the world, as the last of the Grisly Bears lived in settled Missouri. And as when Spring and Summer had departed, that wild Logan of the woods, burying himself in the hollow of a tree, lived out the winter there, sucking his own paws."[18] Ahab's insularity is one of his definitive and most shaping qualities.[19]

But even though the extent of Ahab's isolation is striking, among the characters in *Moby-Dick* it is hardly unusual. One of the first things that

Ishmael emphasizes, and then reemphasizes again and again, is that nearly everyone in his story is what he calls an "*Isolato.*" Almost all on the *Pequod,* he says, are *Isolatoes,* "not acknowledging the common continent of men, but each *Isolato* living on a separate continent of his own." And in this regard the crew of the *Pequod* is itself only a reflection of a broader culture; on the American shore, Ishmael notices how even men who have extensive and meaningful common histories will sit around at a "social breakfast table" in an awkward silence, "looking round as sheepishly at each other as though they had never been out of sight of some sheepfold among the Green Mountains." The same isolationism persists in church, where Ishmael describes the parishioners "purposely sitting apart from the other" in silence, "insular and incommunicable," preached to by a minister who stands before them in his own "physical isolation." Even the loquacious Captain Peleg strikes Ishmael as fundamentally "insular" and "distrustful" of others.[20] On land and at sea, almost everyone Ishmael encounters is an *Isolato,* just like Ahab.

Tellingly, almost all the characters in *Moby-Dick* who do not seem to be *Isolatoes* are not American citizens.[21] Ishmael is struck by how easily Queequeg, the "uncivilized" cannibal from the South Pacific, is able to make a heartfelt proclamation of deep and abiding friendship. "In a countryman," Ishmael reflects, "this sudden flame of friendship would have seemed far too premature, a thing to be much distrusted." But for Queequeg, "those old rules would not apply." Melville's suggestion here is clear: among Americans, deep human connections are so unusual that they are suspect; keeping interpersonal distance is the norm. Some kind of social isolationism is the peculiar national standard. Melville underscores this point even more forcefully by comparing the atmosphere on American whaling ships to that on foreign whaling ships. In contrast to the *Isolato* culture of the American whaling ship, Ishmael wonders at the "abounding good cheer" and sociability of an English whaling ship, a ship filled with "eating, and drinking, and laughing." And those "famous, hospitable ships" of the English, he says, are meager in their sociability compared to Dutch whaling ships, where "high livers" are "flooded with whole pipes, barrels, quarts, and gills of good gin and good cheer." The character of whaling ships, he concludes, are "incidental and particular" to the countries that launch them.[22] By the same logic, it seems that Ahab's character, at least as far as his habits of solitude go, is incidental and particular to the country that launched him.

Although many scholars have tried to tie Ahab's isolated ways to other, more particular conditions—that he is an orphan, that he is a Quaker, that he is a whaler, that he is a captain, that he has been disabled—Melville makes clear that none of those may be regarded as a definitive "cause" of his solitude.[23] Characters in the book who were not orphaned are called *Isolatoes;* characters in the book who are not Quakers are called *Isolatoes;* women and children and others who never set foot on whaling ships fit the description of *Isolatoes;* all the crew members on Ahab's ship who do not share his rank are *Isolatoes;* and people who are not disabled are called *Isolatoes.* Even if we may regard all those particular qualities as aggravating the habits of solitude that shape Ahab's life, none can be considered to represent a singular, causal link. Perhaps to underscore the point, the book also introduces at least a couple of foreign whaleship captains who share Ahab's rank and profession—and who even have lost limbs to Moby Dick!—but who do not seem to share Ahab's tendency toward social isolation and insularity.[24] In highlighting Ahab's habits of solitude when emphasizing his Americanness, Melville suggests that the two are deeply connected.

In fact, Melville repeatedly implies a link between American life and social isolation. The *Pequod,* peopled by *Isolatoes,* is just like "the American army and military and merchant navies, and the engineering forces employed in the construction of the American Canals and Railroads," says Ishmael. In each case, he explains, the population is made up of people whose ancestry is international, but who have landed in a single place and find themselves engaged in common work. Yet even as they daily toil and strive together, they live without "acknowledging the common continent of men." They act as if they still live on independent islands, although they all now sleep on the same piece of land. They have been "federated along one keel"—the language of "federation" is telling, of course, another indication that Melville is focused on the United States—but they remain separate, each in a place of isolation and solitude. For Americans, who are all somehow detached from their ancestry and tied to different histories, detachment has become the normal way of life. This way of life finds itself expressed throughout the American nation, and in its whaling ships. Melville again signals this in a prefatory "extract" that he modified from an original text, this time James Rhodes's *Cruise in a Whale Boat:* "It is generally well known that out of the crews of Whaling vessels (American) few ever return in the ships on board of which they departed."[25] In the original text, the word "American" is absent.[26] Again, Melville misquotes to make his own meaning clear: that detachment and separation—not to mention some amount of disloyalty—are the marks of the American whaleship in particular, and the marks of American life more generally.

In a funny way, then, Melville echoes Ralph Waldo Emerson's assertion a decade earlier that a signal "sign of our times" in the United States is a set of norms and circumstances that isolate individuals from one another. In this environment, Emerson says, "everything that tends to insulate the individual" is valued and protected, and the idea that "help must come from the bosom alone" is accepted across the board.[27] The picture that Melville draws of American citizens in *Moby-Dick* is a kind of Emersonian paradise in those terms, a society in which individual insulation is the standard mode of being. But in Melville's telling, quite opposed to Emerson's well-known vision, a society in which solitude is the standard becomes a society of people whose way of thinking about themselves is deeply problematic.

Disdaining Dependence

Specifically, Melville suggests that in a society where solitude is a way of life, and the idea of solitude is valued, the fact and idea of human interdependence are concomitantly devalued. No one exemplifies this more than Captain Ahab, who is humiliated by and furious about his injury in large part because it has made him tangibly dependent on others. He needs doctors to help tend to his wounds; he needs a carpenter to craft and repair his false leg; he needs other crew members to assist him in climbing ladders during the ritual of "gamming" that takes place when two whaleships meet each other at sea. Without others, Ahab is quite literally without a leg to stand on. This state of things infuriates him. At one point, while waiting for the carpenter to fix his false leg, Ahab makes the nature of his most pressing complaint clear. He yells, "Here I am, proud as a Greek god, and yet standing debtor to this blockhead for a bone to stand on! Cursed be that mortal inter-indebtedness which will not do away with ledgers. I would be as free as air; and I'm down in the whole world's books."[28] What Ahab says he hates about his injury, more than anything else, is the way in which it seems to have turned him into a dependent creature. For Ahab, a man who has long been habituated to a norm or standard of solitude, being so obviously dependent on other people seems a humiliation. Ahab's life of solitude has prepared him to mistrust all interdependence, even or especially his own, and his mistrust along those lines is one of his signature qualities.[29] Having spent a life in which his insularity has helped define his identity and status, Ahab experiences his visible dependence almost as if it is a loss of his humanity. For him, being human means being able to live a life apart.

But, notably, Ahab is not the only *Isolato* on the ship who is troubled by the idea and fact of his dependence on others. Ishmael, for instance, becomes quite anxious when he finds himself tied to Queequeg by a monkey rope as they work to insert the ship's blubber hook into a recently caught whale. Hitched to Queequeg, Ishmael begins to panic. "I seemed to distinctly perceive that my own individuality was now merged in a joint stock company of two," he recalls later. "My free will had received a mortal wound." With no way to "get rid of the dangerous liabilities which the hempen bond entailed," Ishmael reports feeling their mutual dependence to be "so gross an injustice" that it could not possibly be sanctioned by Providence. Although he eventually comes to terms with the situation, he never forgets that first reaction: his association of interdependence with danger, degradation, and injustice. He remarks elsewhere that once you have cultivated an idea of "man, in the ideal," as a "grand and glowing creature" set apart from others, then the idea of men as "joint stock-companies"—that is, interdependent beings who share risk and liability—"may seem detestable."[30] In other words, Ishmael says, when you are used to the idea of humans as heroically independent creatures, the idea of humans as interdependent creatures seems decidedly second-rate. For those ensconced in *Isolato* ways of being and thinking, interdependence becomes disdainful, and dependence becomes equivalent to dishonor.

The moments during which Ishmael and Queequeg are linked by a monkey rope are even more telling, though, because Queequeg—the non-American who alone seems to resist the *Isolato* culture of the ship—does not seem to be bothered by the experience in the least. While Ishmael is busy convincing himself that the situation represents a mortal blow to his free will, Queequeg goes about his business. Undisturbed by the idea of being tied to another, Queequeg is able to act with what others on the ship consider unparalleled calmness and bravery. Throughout the book, in fact, Melville stresses both the fact that Queequeg thinks differently about interdependence than the other men on the ship, and the fact that his different thinking gives him a kind of strength and ability to act that the *Isolatoes* lack. For instance, before they board the *Pequod,* Ishmael and Queequeg wind up in a minor altercation that ends when a man gets blown off a dock and begins to drown. While all the Americans at the scene stand and watch in horrified silence, Queequeg dives into the water and saves the flailing man. After the rescue, the American bystanders want to fawn over his bravery, but Queequeg just asks for a glass of water and stands at the edge of the crowd. Ishmael watches Queequeg in this pose and says that he "seemed to be saying to himself—'It's a mutual, joint-stock world, in all meridians. We cannibals must help these Christians.'"[31] Again, then, Melville associates Queequeg's distinctiveness with his acceptance of the idea that it is a "mutual, joint-stock world"—that is, a world in which all humans are interdependent and liable for each other. And Melville underscores that this distinctive outlook has something to do with the fact that Queequeg remains a "cannibal"; he has not been Americanized.[32]

Queequeg, in contrast to Ahab and the other men on the *Pequod,* does not experience his own dependence as either disturbing or paralyzing. Even when an illness brings him to death's door, and he becomes almost totally dependent on other members of the crew to keep him alive, Queequeg remains calm and good-spirited. He even asks the ship's carpenter to fashion him a coffin that will resemble those used on his native island. Quite unlike Ahab, who rages and roils when the carpenter works on a project that signifies his frailty and dependence, Queequeg seems nothing but grateful to the man who has so worked on his behalf. And later, when he recovers from his illness, Queequeg is not bothered—as other men on the ship are—by the frailty and dependence that the coffin signifies; rather, "with a wild whimsiness," he turns it into a sea chest. Queequeg both acknowledges his own interdependent status in the world and does not fear or lament it. And critically, it is at this moment in the story that we learn that Ahab is both mystified by and envious of Queequeg. Ishmael describes Ahab watching Queequeg on the dock, as if the latter's body spoke "a mystical treatise on the art of attaining truth." Staring at Queequeg, Ahab exclaims, "Oh, devilish tantalization of the gods!"[33]

For Ahab, Queequeg is alluring because he represents an appealing way of being; he embodies the possibility of ailing and depending on others without suffering humiliation.[34] Put another way, Ahab knows that Queequeg possesses a critical quality that he, Ahab, does not. And he also seems to know that this quality enables Queequeg to have, even in moments of total dependence, a kind of spiritual clarity or contentment and a kind of inner strength. But Ahab has trouble learning what, according to Ishmael, Queequeg has to teach: the idea that every individual has a "Siamese connexion with a plurality of other mortals," and to acknowledge that is the first step toward an "unappalled" life of courage and contentment. According to Ishmael, Queequeg demonstrates that though acknowledging interdependence is frightening because it involves the acceptance of human frailty—since it forces you to realize that "if your banker breaks, you snap; if your apothecary by mistake sends you poison in your pills, you die"—it also is liberating in that it brings you closer to the truth of the human condition. Queequeg's "good cheer," so unusual on the ship, comes from his appreciation of human interdependence.[35] It is a lesson that Ahab seems unable to learn. Committed to habits of isolation and a kind of thinking that idealizes solitude, he tends to resist even the idea of his own interdependent human condition.

Melville underscores the idea that for Ahab—and, indeed, for his fellow American *Isolatoes*—the way of thinking that accompanies the habit of solitude is a way of thinking that both neglects and devalues the idea of human interdependence. Further, in *Moby-Dick* this proves to be a way of thinking that is less than desirable: a way of thinking that brings neither knowledge nor strength nor spiritual contentment. Melville associates the *Isolato* way of thinking with anxiety, paralysis, and rage. This stands in contrast to the bravery, wisdom, and contentment that Melville associates with the acceptance of human interdependence. By this token, if Emerson is right in thinking that Americans are wedded to the idea of human independence, Melville worries that Americans are dangerously divorced from the fact of human interdependence. And the result of that divorce may well be a nation that drowns in rage and anxiety. For Melville the *Isolato* model that seems to define American thinking leads down an unfavorable path; his descriptions of Ahab's rage and desolation, and his bewildered envy of that foreign harpooner, begin to make that clear.

The Desolation of Solitude

To be fair, at some moments Ahab seems to come close to recognizing the limitation of the way he thinks and the cost that his *Isolato* ways have imposed on him. In one of *Moby-Dick*'s most memorable scenes, in a chapter titled "The Symphony," Ahab laments his life to Starbuck, and what he laments in particular is the "the desolation of solitude it has been." His life, he says, seems to have forced a burdensome isolation on him, one that has compelled him to exist "against all natural lovings and longings." As he sheds a tear, he describes living without any kind of close or extended human companionship. It is a kind of "Guinea-coast slavery," he tells Starbuck, to be so solitary in the world. He imagines, he says, that his "one small brain" and "one single heart" are "turned round and round in this world, like yonder windlass," with nothing to grasp, and nothing to which they may be fixed.

At one point in this set of pained reflections, Ahab even implores Starbuck to look into his eyes—"let me look into a human eye," he says; "it is better than to gaze into sea or sky; better than to gaze upon God"—so that he might finally find some human connection. The eye is the "magic glass," he tells Starbuck, and he hopes that looking into his first mate's eyes may finally bring him some true communion, some sense of connection to others, and some sense of being at home in the world. "Close!" he yells to Starbuck. "Stand close to me." Starbuck obliges and, as his eyes meet Ahab's, begins to speak of his own "loving" and "longing" in the world. But at that, Ahab looks away—"like a blighted fruit tree," Ishmael says, casting "his last, cindered apple to the soil." Ahab turns away from Starbuck, and Starbuck promptly runs off. Finding his first mate gone, Ahab crosses the deck "to gaze over on the other side," where he stares at the "two reflected, fixed eyes in the water there."[36] He begins the final chase for Moby Dick the next morning.

There are a couple of critical things to notice about this passage, which I agree with many others is pivotal within *Moby-Dick*.[37] The first is that this attempt at human connection, despite Ahab's heartfelt plea for it, is not in the end successful. It culminates not in an embrace, not in any profession of mutual interdependence or purpose—not in any kind of human togetherness. It ends with Starbuck stealing away and Ahab staring into the ocean, both men seeming more isolated than ever. Despite what both Ahab and Starbuck acknowledge in that moment as a basic human need for connection with others, they cannot achieve it. It is a grim and foreboding failure, one underscored by the description of Starbuck as "blanched to a corpse's hue with despair" as he hurries off the deck.[38]

To that end, this chapter of the book encapsulates Melville's idea that people who have become habituated to a life of isolation might not be able to overcome that isolation in any meaningful way, even when desperation or necessity demands it. If this is as close as two *Isolatoes* may get to sounding in true harmony—a suggestion Melville makes by titling this chapter "The Symphony"—it is clear how poorly they do.[39] Their voices do not come together in a pleasing or brilliant consonance; they remain separate and halting, reaching a discordant end. These *Isolatoes* are unable to find a common sound, even when they search for it. The conclusion is grim, but it is a common refrain in Melville's writing. None of Melville's *Isolatoes*—in *Moby-Dick* or elsewhere—succeed socially or find human connection, despite their desire or need to do so.[40] The individual who has become so isolated suffers a kind of distortion over time, a distortion that renders him or her incapable of full access to the human community.[41]

In the exchange between Ahab and Starbuck, Melville offers a hint about how he understands the nature of that distortion and what it entails. When looking into Starbuck's eyes, Ahab calls them a "magic glass." But in those words, what sounds like a poetic tribute to human communion is actually a disturbing revelation: earlier in the voyage, Ahab describes a "magician's glass" as something that "to each and every man in turn but mirrors back his own mysterious self." What Ahab actually sees in Starbuck's eyes—what any human might literally see, looking in another's eyes—is his own reflection. Ahab experiences the eyes not as the window to another's soul but as a mirror to his own. It is by that account no wonder that when he turns away from Starbuck, he turns to stare into the sea. His view there is the same; indeed, early in *Moby-Dick* Ishmael says that Narcissus was tormented by "the same image" that "we ourselves see in all rivers and oceans": our own.[42] The particular distortion of Ahab's vision is that he has become so isolated that he cannot see, in an almost literal way, outside himself. And Starbuck's vision is not much better. His first response, when Ahab looks into his eyes, is to start talking about himself: his own yearning, his own loneliness, his own desire to return to Nantucket. Starbuck, too, is an *Isolato,* and, in his own way, he has trouble reaching outside his inner being. It is not merely that these men devalue interdependence, intellectually speaking; it is also that they have trouble expressing their interdependence and acting with that interdependence in mind, practically speaking.

What Ahab *can* speak, as he does in this exchange, is the language of "Guinea-coast slavery." The great irony of the master of the ship—whose rule depends on enforcing his authoritarian, almost totalizing control over others—claiming a position of enslavement is not to be missed.[43] Especially in nineteenth-century America, this is not an innocent linguistic inversion.[44] It suggests at the very least a kind of political blindness, an inability to see outside the self. (This is not a blindness of Ahab's alone; at the beginning of the book Ishmael speaks in similarly problematic terms when he asks, "Who ain't a slave?")[45] That he would call his own isolation an enslavement demonstrates his neglect of the very proximate existence of *actual* slaves. Ahab's isolation corresponds, in Melville's telling, with a failure to understand the most evident political dynamics of his time and place—largely because he does not seem to be able to acknowledge the reality of anyone's position other than his own. And, of course, that kind of neglect of the experience of others itself provides support for the legal and political institution of slavery.

Through this exchange, Melville develops the notion that Ahab's isolation—and the isolation of others on the *Pequod*—is not just a kind of material fact but involves the development of a particular way of seeing. It is a way of seeing that lacks the quality of mutual recognition, the very quality that Ralph Ellison, among others, has singled out as essential to the maintenance of any democratic covenant in general, and to "the ethical authority of American law" in particular, since mutual recognition involves an acknowledgment of the common humanity that justifies democratic citizenship.[46] Both Ahab and Starbuck, having lives in which social isolation is a norm, have adjusted their vision accordingly and adjusted it in a way that makes it difficult if not impossible for them to see each other in full. Each has been thrown back on himself enough to be confined, to borrow Alexis de Tocqueville's phrase, "within the solitude of his own heart."[47] In another, each man sees only himself, just a reflection of his solitary pains. This makes effective communication and joint action difficult at best, since both depend on some recognition of others and of the common continent of humanity.

This way of seeing is endemic on the *Pequod*. As Melville presents it, it is the way of seeing that develops among people who assume their own isolation from others, and who by some degree of circumstance and choice have long been divorced from a sense of commonality. It finds no clearer example than when Ahab nails a gold doubloon to the mainmast, announcing that he will award it to the first sailor who spots Moby Dick. The doubloon comes from Ecuador, and it is an unremarkable coin in that it has a border announcing its provenance and an artistic design of national significance in the middle.[48] But every single man on the ship, when looking at the doubloon, reads himself and his own story into the coin's design. As each person on the ship comes by to look at the gold coin, it becomes clear that the doubloon merely reflects the aspirations and attachments of the person who gazes on it.[49] No one on the *Pequod* speaks with anyone else about the coin, not to compare interpretations of the design and certainly not to reflect together about what the doubloon's presence itself might signify for the voyage as a whole. Melville portrays the crew members as locked into their solitary worlds, confined mostly to conversation within their own heads. Here, as elsewhere in the novel, the characters do not engage in discussions with one another so much as they give speeches to themselves.[50]

Of course, in their failure to come together to see what the doubloon might mean for them as a community, the *Isolatoes* on the *Pequod* demonstrate one of the reasons that their voyage ends in such spectacular failure. By looking and speaking only within themselves, they neglect the chance to develop a more holistic, communal sense of the state of the ship—a sense that might come from more interpersonal connection and communication. This kind of failure is first made clear in *Moby-Dick* when Ahab announces his intention to pursue the white whale; there are varying degrees of discomfort among the crew, but no man on the crew discusses his hesitations with another.[51] Melville even separates the reactions of different crew members into different chapters and headings, drawing attention to the extent of their mutual isolation. In a community of *Isolatoes*, it seems, there is a predictable reluctance to engage in the kind of shared discussion and public deliberation that may exert an informing or even moderating force on policy. Presuming that they, too, have developed habits of seeing and thinking that lack the quality of mutual recognition, they may even be unable to imagine such a public or common discussion in the first place. Many are able to run from Ahab, quite literally—they run apart "in a terror of dismay" when he reasserts his plans later in the book—but none is able to communicate with another or translate his dread into some kind of organized response.[52] This impotence gets worse over time; monologues become more frequent as the story progresses, gradually replacing dialogue and multivoiced conversation almost entirely.[53] Again, on this count, Melville's *Isolatoes* sound a great deal like Tocqueville's description of the kind of American individualism he feared; in "the habit of always considering themselves as standing alone," Americans constitute a populace who live divorced from the public sphere, disconnected from the political.[54] They fail to act well as interdependent beings because they fail to see each other as interdependent beings.

Notably, despite the emphasis in thinkers like Tocqueville and Winthrop on the potential for religion to furnish the kind of spirit of interdependence that the men on the *Pequod* lack, their common Christian background does little to furnish them with the sense of community they need.[55] Not only is their worship on land defined by its "insular and incommunicable" rituals marked by "physical isolation," as I discuss above, but also Melville suggests that their religiosity at sea is more reminiscent of some "Christian hermit of old times" whose worship takes place only in the context of a much more powerful—definitive—separation from society at large.[56] Stubb make this point powerfully clear when he shouts, "That's Christianity!" in response to a speech by the ship's cook, the thrust of which is that, just as it is hopeless to keep sharks from being sharks, it is hopeless to keep men from their own sharklike inclinations.[57] It is a speech that suggests that self-restraint and democratic self-governance are nearly impossible. Melville presents the "Christianity" of the crew, then, as something of a farce; whatever truly Christian sentiments they once harbored have been overpowered by the isolating (and ultimately self-absorbing) forces of their lives. Again and again, despite an ancestral religion that insists on treating the other as self, the men on the *Pequod* are stymied by their repeated failures even to engage each other.

Among the crew, perhaps the greatest failure along these lines is Starbuck's, which Melville describes in meticulous detail. Even when Starbuck thinks of trying to stop Captain Ahab, he never considers sounding out anyone else on the ship or looking for others who might agree with him, much less trying to enlist anyone else's help (and Melville makes clear that there are at least some other people on the ship who would aid his cause).[58] Starbuck feels so isolated—"I stand alone here upon an open sea," he cries—that he thinks his only option is to commit a ghastly crime: to sneak into Ahab's cabin and shoot him. But he rejects that course of action, understandably reluctant to become a murderer.[59] Yet, having made the decision that private violence is beyond him, he goes no further. He neglects to think about the possibility of any common or public option for resisting Ahab. Rather, he effectively throws up his hands, giving himself up to whatever might happen. Having decided that he cannot stop Ahab by himself, with violence, Starbuck comes to believe that he can do nothing.

In some ways, Starbuck's feelings of terrible disconnection bring this analysis back to an earlier point, since they echo the feelings of terrible disconnection that Ahab expresses when he bewails the isolations of his own life. Each man is accustomed to imagining that he stands alone in the world. But standing alone has, by definition, a lonely element to it. Thus, Ahab says that at times he imagines himself as a tiny being, tossed around in a cold universe by the winds of chance. And Starbuck despairs of the cruel hand that fate has dealt him, as he imagines himself entirely alone, in the middle of the yawning and watery Pacific. Although the two men seem often set in a kind of opposition, they share in the *Isolato*'s lament. It is the lament of the man who is cut off from any sense of common human action or purpose, hampered by a disdain for the idea of human interdependence, a failure to fully recognize others, and an inability to forge meaningful human connection.

Moreover, it is telling that, during the moment in which he feels this kind of disconnection most acutely, Starbuck contemplates murderous violence. Believing that he is alone in the world, he understands his ability to act to be limited to the most naked kind of brutality. He believes, in short, that the only way he might connect with the world enough to change it is by imposing on it by force. Though Starbuck does not go down that path, his sense of the set of actions available to him is telling. It seems difficult and almost unnatural for him to contemplate collective or deliberative action, but it seems effortless for him to consider the path of inaction on the one hand, and the path of violent, dominating action on the other.

The Drive to Domination

Of course, those are precisely the two paths of action that Ahab believes are available to him when it comes to the white whale. As he says over and again, in his mind the only two options are between doing nothing and risking the lives of the entire crew to kill the white whale. He cannot—and will not—consider any other possibilities for more moderate or deliberative action, as he makes most clear when he tells Starbuck that the decision to pursue Moby Dick is his alone. He can choose either inaction or domination, he says, and points a musket at Starbuck's head to indicate that he has chosen the latter path.[60] Ahab's sense of his own options mirrors Starbuck's sense of his options, and it draws further attention to the fact that Ahab's way of thinking is not unusual on the ship he commands. Melville indicates that if collective or deliberative joint action seems difficult or even unnatural to *Isolatoes*, they have little trouble imagining action that is violent or domineering. *Isolatoes* tend either toward the path of inaction—exhibiting the kind of indifference to the public sphere that Tocqueville feared—or toward the path of action through undeliberative force.

Needless to say, Ahab chooses the path of domination and force. But tellingly, he justifies his choice time and again by arguing to the crew that it is only by force that men can overcome their isolation and solitude. Men live behind "pasteboard masks," he says, and the only way to escape the solitary confines of living behind the mask is to "strike through the mask" with some kind of violent action. "How can the prisoner reach outside except by thrusting through the wall?" he asks.[61] For Ahab, who assumes human isolation, choosing violence is superior to choosing inaction because at least violence—even destructive violence—may have the potential to transform or even overcome the pains and limitations of human isolation. Dominating someone forges a kind of connection with him, albeit a nonideal one. And sharing in an act of domination does the same. But perhaps more important, violence seems to hold out the possibility for one individual to assert a singular place in the world, to transcend the boundaries of the isolated self. Ahab's thinking along these lines is what one critic has called "bad transcendental thinking," but it is the kind of transcendental thinking that Melville posits as natural, or at least probable, for the *Isolato*.[62]

Melville stresses this when he has Ahab say, as some of the crew members begin to rally to his cause, that they all must join in because "stand up amid the general hurricane, thy one tost sapling cannot."[63] The image Ahab uses is revealing, largely because it is almost exactly the language he uses to describe the desolation of his own solitude. But this time, Ahab locates himself on the side of the hurricane gales. For Ahab, the world seems a place of impersonal forces that exert power by domination. And in such a world, the individual can have power only to the extent that he can become—or, to a lesser extent, become part of—a dominating force. The alternative is to be subject to the whims of an impersonal world, to be dependent and therefore, in Ahab's mind, humiliated. Unable to come to terms with the fact of human interdependence, Ahab can conceive of the world only as a struggle for domination, in which the central dynamic is to humiliate or be humiliated.[64] In such stories one is either dominant or humiliated, rendered either powerful by the use of force or impotent by inaction.

To be certain, Ahab's well-documented quest for domination is an attempt to reassert his own individual power, to "prove" that his evidently disabled and dependent condition is only a kind of illusion. If, by killing the white whale, Ahab were able to triumph in a battle over nature itself, he would be able to reclaim the old fantasy of himself as an independent presence in the world.[65] His attempt to achieve a kind of cosmic transcendence by force is an attempt to make a definitive statement of independence. This is clear in the language he uses when, partway through the journey, he starts worshipping fire.[66] Ahab announces that he is modeling himself after fire; he, too, will seek to reassert control over his own destiny through destructive force and domination. In addition, he says, he worships fire because fire is a "hermit immemorial"—a solitary figure exerting independent force in the world, even in the face of "unanticipated grief." For Ahab, fire seems to embody the possibility of existing in the world on essentially independent terms, overcoming setbacks and losses without needing any help; fire seems to him to demonstrate that such independence can come only through the pursuit of a kind of destructive domination. Ahab even announces that the flames are his "fiery father," the representation of his "genealogy."[67] He has chosen to follow the path of fire, as he understands that path to exist.

Quite obviously, in making this proclamation Ahab demonstrates the extent to which his self-knowledge has become distorted; he quite literally disowns his human forebears. His claim represents an attempt to distance himself from his species and shows the extent to which his way of thinking has led him to disdain humanity altogether—even his own.[68] Here Melville indicates the extent to which Ahab's aspirations to independence (and his accompanying disdain for the idea of interdependence) have distorted his thinking. Ahab's desire to be an independent power in the world, a desire that he believes can be realized through the destructive domination of others, amounts in the end to a desire to be something other than human. As Catherine Zuckert has indicated, such a desire in fact represents an abrogation of responsibility; he would rather take his whole ship down than admit his own mortal limits and the limits of his understanding.[69] Ishmael underscores this when he opines that any person who takes his bearings from a fire is suffering from an "unnatural hallucination" of lies. "Look not too long in the face of the fire, O man!" he cries. If Ahab has become an exemplar of "madness," Ishmael suggests, it is because his way of seeing the world culminates in hallucinatory thinking. But, notably, Ishmael says this after relating his own experience of staring too long into the flames of the tryworks on the ship; he thus makes clear that the temptations of fire watching—the temptations of hallucination and destructive action—are not temptations to Ahab alone. It is easy, on the *Pequod,* to want to stare into the fire and to embrace all it represents.[70]

Again, it is important to realize that Ahab's way of thinking—albeit exaggerated—is not exceptional on the *Pequod.* As a number of critics have noticed, the *Pequod*'s crew seems inclined to violence from the beginning, always seeking domination through a kind of unrestrained and even totalizing warfare.[71] Virtually the only time Melville describes a long conversation within the crew itself, it culminates in a brutal knife fight. Even the Quakers among them are "fighting Quakers," Ishmael says; they are "Quakers with a vengeance" who seek not consensus but domination.[72] They alternate between periods of inaction and periods of naked aggression, with, as I have mentioned, little conversation in between—and when they do have conversations, it is often only after they have recently killed a whale.[73] To the extent they have a common life, that life is organized not around mutual recognition but around mutual violence. Their behavior suggests a general belief in the idea that domination by force is the primary if not only course of action available in the world—at least, the only action besides inaction.

Moreover, as Zuckert has argued, Ahab represents the aim of modern science, with its emphasis on the conquest and mastery of nature.[74] He would assert his mastery over nature not just in spite of but because of his awareness that nature is in fact the master of men, an inclination that Melville stresses is common among whalers.[75] "But a moment's consideration will teach, that however baby man may brag of his science and skill," he writes, "yet for ever and for ever, . . . the sea will insult and murder him." Ahab is just one of many who would, by virtue of setting sail, engage this "foe" who is likely to consume him in the end.[76] All the men on the *Pequod* are men who have a strong desire to exert themselves against a hostile nature.

Ahab's vision thus has deep resonance within a crew that, on many levels, sees the world in the same terms he does. They, too, seem accustomed to thinking in terms of a dichotomy between impotence by inaction and domination by force. At that level of fundamentals, Ahab's way of thinking is the crew's way of thinking. Many of them are already inclined to pursue a risky and violent course in the world. And even those men on the ship who have some sense that the violence in Ahab's plan is ill-advised—men like Starbuck, who might be inclined to choose inaction—have trouble resisting because they have trouble imagining or actualizing some kind of joint response. And, as I have mentioned, they even have trouble recognizing each other's discomfort in the first place; they are too locked into their private isolations. Therefore, even though Ahab's plan reveals itself to be a plan based on "measureless self-deception," as Ishmael suggests, Ahab seems to have an equally "measureless power of deceiving and bedeviling so many others" because their way of thinking, like his, already inclines to that exact kind of self-deception.[77] To that degree, it is easy to explain why, as so many scholars have noted, it actually takes Ahab very little effort to convince the crew to go along with his plan.[78] He does not have to convince them as much as he has to speak in a language that is already theirs.[79]

And theirs is a language and way of thinking that, according to Melville, is decidedly American. Throughout the book, American ships are depicted as most notable for the erratic violence of their pursuits. For instance, Ishmael says that *only* American ships have made a habit of pursuing sperm whales to violent ends; "among those whaling nations not sailing under the American flag," most have "never hostilely encountered the Sperm Whale." Ishmael even considers whether the "positive havoc" wreaked on sperm whales by American ships alone—American ships, he says, kill thirteen thousand sperm whales a year just in the Pacific Northwest—may be enough to make the species go extinct. The figure is shocking in part because Ishmael has just described at length how difficult and risky it is to capture a single sperm whale; any reasonable deliberation or calculation of risk would dispose a ship's crew to pursue more mainstream and accessible prey. American whaling ships are posited throughout the book as inclined toward particularly reckless courses of violent action—nurtured, Ishmael speculates, by the "agrarian freebooting impressions" that exist across the American nation, even "in the land-locked heart of our America."[80] The aggressive spirit of the law of the American whaleship, Ishmael indicates elsewhere, is only exaggeration—or maybe even a prophecy—of the nation's future.[81] Melville suggests that in their inclination toward violent action, and their willingness to take a violent path rather than to do nothing or to consider a more moderate course, the crew members of the *Pequod* only reflect the general inclinations that exist in the American nation more broadly. By that standard, Ahab does not seem like such an outlier.

Nor does Ahab's "dominate or be dominated" psychology seem so unusual when seen against the background of racialized slavery in America, which Melville mentions many times throughout the book. The idea that one must dominate or be dominated, humiliate or be humiliated, is central to the master-slave relationship. Ahab's own desire to capture "the whiteness of the whale"—to capture and claim the whitest being in the world—has evident resonance in a society where whiteness is generally accepted as a legitimate reason to dominate others.[82] (Here, too, Queequeg, with his effortless interracial friendships, stands in the book as a visible alternative to the American way of seeing things.)[83] In a society that legalizes the enslavement of some humans by others on nothing but the basis of skin color, the tenor of Ahab's quest is hardly beyond the pale.

Ahab and the other *Isolatoes* on the *Pequod* constitute what Melville elsewhere called a "ruthless democracy"—a society in which common action seems possible only through destruction, domination, and violence.[84] They seem incapable of considering the more moderate courses of action that lie between doing nothing and doing something dangerously violent. Melville's clear suggestion is that this failure emanates from the standards of an *Isolato* culture in which the idea of human interdependence seems disgraceful, and deliberative or common action thus becomes difficult. In denying or obscuring the interdependent elements of their humanity, Ahab and the crew of the *Pequod* have trouble acting humanely. Caught up in a way of life and a way of thinking that put all their emphasis on the human individual, they are not good at thinking about themselves as a human community. That their journey ends with the destruction of their community at large is, without doubt, a suggestion of exactly how significant Melville thinks their intellectual and cultural failure is.

One of *Moby-Dick*'s most haunting moments comes near the end of its story, when Ahab realizes that he is doomed. "Oh, lonely death on lonely life!" he cries, bemoaning his isolation to the last.[85] But the folly of his final remarks should not be missed. Even in his moment of reckoning Ahab fails to see his connection to others of his kind.[86] Ahab is dying with dozens of other men; they are all going down together. As he has long failed to see the extent to which their lives were bound in common, he fails to see that their deaths are in common as well. His final moments crystallize his great flaw: his deep inability to recognize the extent to which his life is, in fact, inextricably bound to the lives of his crew members.[87] Even as he dies, Ahab is unable to see or articulate his connection to humanity, in either proximate or universal terms.

Ahab's last minutes crystallize the failure of thought and vision that mark his actions throughout the story of *Moby-Dick*. But they also in large measure crystallize the failure of thought and vision that mark the action (and sometimes the inaction) of the *Pequod*'s crew. Throughout the ship's voyage, the men on board repeatedly neglect to recognize their interdependence and fail to see the full range of possibilities available to them for common deliberation and action. They accede to Ahab's vision so readily because it is premised on their own way of thinking: a way of thinking that dichotomizes inaction and violent action and sees no possibility for public or common life in between. They, too, are *Isolatoes* living lonely lives: lives that have schooled them to disdain the idea of interdependence and have ill-equipped them for constructive political action.

Indeed, for Melville, the ultimate failure of the *Isolato*'s way of seeing and being in the world is a deeply political failure. Inclined to think in terms of the self and disinclined to think in terms of interdependence or commonality, the *Isolato* tends to see opportunity for joint action only in the basest and most violent terms. These are not only terms that erode the fellow feelings that undergird democratic life, but also terms that reduce human interaction to a struggle for dominance in which the idea of equality fades into the background. It is perhaps no wonder that a society of *Isolatoes* is also a slaveholding society; *Isolatoes* are basically impotent when it comes to cultivating the mutual recognition that is necessary to sustain democratic governance. They tend only to the polarities of private indifference or public dominance; as such, they readily submit to the despotism of others or become despots themselves.

The real difficulty is, as Melville intimates throughout the book, that the *Isolato* way of thinking emanates from the conditions and conceits of modern democratic life itself—most specifically in its American form. In *Moby-Dick* Melville describes a country filled with men and women of varied (and often mysterious) ancestry who have inherited a belief in striking out on one's own—and who still, for understandable reasons, have trouble seeing each other as a unified nation. It is a nation that, as Melville depicts it, has come to value independence because the circumstances of American life encourage independence. And in such circumstances, even the experience of making their own laws—Melville emphasizes that American whalemen are unusual in having been "their own legislators and lawyers"—has resulted not in an appreciation of common life, but, rather, in the conviction that each man ought to set his own rules by whatever means are available to him.[88] In *Moby-Dick* the danger to American democratic life very much comes from within American democratic life, and the danger to American citizenship very much comes from within the citizenry.

In his most definitive qualities, Ahab is not an outlier on his ship or in his nation.[89] Rather, he is quite evidently a paradigmatic, if exaggerated, caricature of certain tendencies within the American citizenry. If we read his story in that light, we see set in relief Melville's anxieties about what he saw as an ascendant *Isolato* culture in American life—a culture that threatens to undermine the foundations of responsible democratic citizenship. In his description of Ahab and the other men on the *Pequod,* Melville echoes Tocqueville's worry about the extent to which modern democracy—in its circumstances and its norms—could isolate the individual, the extent to which it "throws him back forever upon himself alone."[90] Like Tocqueville, Melville worries about the extent to which such isolation could result in a population marked by public inaction and indifference. But in addition, Melville worries that when *Isolatoes* do act, they act out in a violent struggle for domination that is destructive and self-defeating. For Melville, at bottom the *Isolato* way of thinking is hallucinatory, representing a denial of the fundamental interdependence of the human community—a denial that leads in the end not only to the destruction of democratic ideals but also to the destruction of the community altogether.

It is telling, toward that end, that the one moment in which Ahab says his "purpose keels up in him" and he considers giving up his quest is the moment in which he holds the black cabin boy Pip's hand.[91] Pip, having been brought to the edge of death in an accident—and then reminded by that sharklike Stubb that he could be sold in Alabama—has become what most of the people on the boat regard as insane. And yet he often seems saner than the rest. On a number of occasions, Pip's words suggest that he alone among the crew sees the pervasive self-absorption in their chase, such as when he suggests that everyone's obsession with the doubloon is only so much navel-gazing; both racially and in his words, he is a constant reminder of the failure of both Ahab and his crew to find any degree of social cohesion.[92] Ahab's brief recognition of Pip's humanity indicates that the captain—and thus the dangerous political psychology he represents—is not incapable of being saved. There is always the potential for the recognition of the true inter-indebtedness of the human species, and in that potential lies the true hope of democratic life.

And yet in the end, Ahab dies without some final revelation or change of heart, suggesting that Melville is not sanguine about the prospects for true democratic flourishing in America. Admittedly, Ishmael survives—and he survives with a clearer understanding of human interconnectedness both at the universal and at the community level. He says he has come to understand how all humans are inextricably bound to a plurality of other humans, and that fate is not individual but shared. He declares a new appreciation for the interdependence of the "kingly commons." But Ishmael's enlightenment comes only after the wholesale destruction of the community of which he has been part; although he survives by riding on his friend Queequeg's coffin, his is in fact a rather lonely fate. At the end of the novel, he is picked up by another American ship, which finds "another orphan"—another lonely and disconnected soul—to add to the national collection.[93]

Notes

This chapter previously appeared, in a slightly different form, in the *Review of Politics* 74, no. 2 (March 2012): 233–260. (Copyright by the University of Notre Dame). It is reprinted here with the permission of Cambridge University Press.

1. See, for instance, Elizabeth D. Samet, *Willing Obedience: Citizens, Soldiers, and the Progress of Consent in America, 1776–1898* (Stanford: Stanford University Press, 2004), 64.

2. C. L. R. James, *Mariners, Renegades and Castaways: The Story of Herman Melville and the World We Live In* (1953; repr., Hanover, N.H.: Dartmouth College Press, 2001), 15.

3. Michael Paul Rogin, *Subversive Genealogy: The Politics and Art of Herman Melville* (New York: Knopf, 1983), 139–140.

4. John Alvis, "*Moby-Dick* and Melville's Quarrel with America," *Interpretation: A Journal of Political Philosophy* 23, no. 2 (1993): 223–247.

5. Inger Hunnerup Dalsgaard, "'The Leyden Jar' and 'The Iron Way' Conjoined: *Moby-Dick*, the Classical and Modern Schism of Science and Technology," in *Melville "Among the Nations": Proceedings of an International Conference,*

Athens, Greece, July 2–6, 1997, ed. Sanford E. Marovitz and A. C. Christodoulou (Kent, Ohio: Kent State University Press, 2001), 252; Giles Gunn, "Enamored against Thee by Strange Minds: Recovering the Relations between Religion and the Enlightenment in Nineteenth- and Twentieth-Century American Literature," in *Knowledge and Belief in America: Enlightenment Traditions and Modern Religious Thought,* ed. William M. Shea and Peter A. Huff (Cambridge: Cambridge University Press, 1995), 76; R. Bruce Bickley Jr., "'Civilized Barbarity': Melville and the Dark Paradoxes of Waging Modern War," in *War and Words: Horror and Heroism in the Literature of Warfare,* ed. Sara Munson Deats et al. (Lanham, Md.: Lexington Books, 2004), 131.

6. See, for instance, Linda Costanzo Cahir, *Solitude and Society in the Works of Herman Melville and Edith Wharton* (Westport, Conn.: Greenwood Press, 1999), 25; Rollo May, *The Cry for Myth* (New York: Norton, 1991), 279; Henry A. Murray, "In Nomine Diaboli" (1951), in *Herman Melville,* Moby-Dick, ed. Nick Selby (New York: Columbia University Press, 1998), 80.

7. Herman Melville, *Moby-Dick* (New York: Library of America, 1991), 108.

8. Melville, as James McIntosh puts it, works at "humanizing" Ahab throughout the book. See McIntosh, "The Mariner's Multiple Quest," in *New Essays on* Moby-Dick, ed. Richard H. Brodhead (Cambridge: Cambridge University Press, 1986), 40.

9. Melville, *Moby-Dick,* 109. In both the title of and introduction to her book *Captain Ahab Had a Wife* (Chapel Hill: University of North Carolina Press, 2000), Lisa Norling picks up on the fact that little attention is given to this kind of pedestrian or domestic detail in Ahab's life, despite multiple mentions in the novel.

10. Melville, *Moby-Dick,* 21. The entire speech appears in Daniel Webster, *Speeches and Forensic Arguments* (Boston: Perkins and Marvin, 1830), 433–435. William Ellery Sedgwick notes that when Melville wrote *Moby-Dick,* "the American whale fishery expressed the best in the American character. It also exemplified the peculiarities of our national life." See Sedgwick, *Herman Melville: The Tragedy of Mind* (Cambridge: Harvard University Press, 1945), 90.

11. Melville, *Moby-Dick,* 141. Melville is correct that Benjamin Franklin's grandmother, Mary Morrill (or Morrel) was one of the founding female residents of Ahab's native Nantucket. See Henry Whittemore, *Genealogical Guide to the Early Settlers of America: With a Brief History of Those of the First Generation* (Baltimore: Genealogical Publishing Co., 1967), 196.

12. Melville, *Moby-Dick,* 108, 146.

13. Kim Leilani Evans has argued that if Ahab has power over the crew, "it is because they share, at some level, his motivations." See Evans, *Whale!* (Minneapolis: University of Minnesota Press, 2003), 107.

14. Melville, *Moby-Dick,* 29.

15. Ibid., 17, 102.

16. This is an argument that Oliver Goldsmith does make in his essay "On the Use of Hyperbole." See *The Works of Oliver Goldsmith,* ed. Peter Cunningham (New York: Harper and Brothers, 1900), 6:83–86.

17. The original remark appears in John Forster, *The Life and Times of Oliver Goldsmith,* 2 vols. (London: Chapman and Hall, 1871), 2:191; emphases in original.

18. Melville, *Moby-Dick,* 181, 185.

19. F. O. Matthiessen describes this as Ahab's "self-enclosed" character in his *American Renaissance: Art and Expression in the Age of Emerson and Whitman* (New York: Oxford University Press, 1941), 459.

20. Melville, *Moby-Dick,* 151, 56, 60, 65, 99.

21. The only exception to this rule is the black cabin boy, Pip, a Connecticut native who seems, as a result of an accident that left him in the throes of what all on the ship deem "insanity," to grasp the interconnectedness of all things. Jason Frank explores Pip in "Pathologies of Freedom in Melville's America," in *Radical Future Pasts: Untimely Essays in Political Theory,* ed. Romand Coles, Mark Reinhardt, and George Shulman (Lexington: University Press of Kentucky, forthcoming).

22. Melville, *Moby-Dick,* 78, 498–499.

23. For example, Wilson Carey McWilliams suggests that "the circumstances of his birth would have made it difficult for him to form emotional bonds with the world," and that Ahab's Quaker religion taught him "to be a man of 'stillness and seclusion,'" and thus contributed to his solitary ways. See McWilliams, *The Idea of Fraternity in America* (Berkeley: University of California Press, 1973), 342. James contends that Ahab's isolation stems from his rank, itself "inseparable from the function of authority in the modern world." See James, *Mariners, Renegades and Castaways,* 79. And August J. Nigro argues that Ahab's "dismemberment also leads to Ahab's external separation from community" in his *The Diagonal Line: Separation and Reparation in American Literature* (Cranbury, N.J.: Associated University Presses, 1984), 78.

24. The great example along these lines is Captain Boomer, the captain of an English whaling ship called the *Samuel Enderby* who lost his arm to Moby Dick. As Robert Zoellner has observed, Boomer's reaction to his injury is "opposite" to Ahab's. Boomer responds to his injury by drawing closer to his men, enhancing the already convivial and affectionate character of relationships on his ship. See Zoellner, *The Salt-Sea Mastodon: A Reading of* Moby-Dick (Berkeley: University of California Press, 1973), 116.

25. Melville, *Moby-Dick,* 151, 22.

26. The original volume is James Allen Rhodes, *A Cruise in a Whale Boat, by a Party of Fugitives; or, Reminiscences and Adventures during a Year in the Pacific*

Ocean, and the Interior of South America (New York: New York Publishing Co., 1848).

27. Ralph Waldo Emerson, "The American Scholar," in *Selected Writings of Ralph Waldo Emerson,* ed. William Gilman (New York: Signet, 2003), 244.

28. Melville, *Moby-Dick,* 527.

29. See Richard Manley Blau, *The Body Impolitic: A Reading of Four Novels by Herman Melville* (Amsterdam: Rodopoi N.V., 1979), 79; John Michael, *Identity and the Failure of America: From Thomas Jefferson to the War on Terror* (Minneapolis: University of Minnesota Press, 2008), 100; and Rogin, *Subversive Genealogies,* 138. Joseph Adamson writes that Ahab "responds with shame and rage to any situation in which he finds himself incapacitated" or "dependent on others." See Adamson, *Melville, Shame, and the Evil Eye: A Psychoanalytic Reading* (Albany: State University of New York Press, 1997), 93.

30. Melville, *Moby-Dick,* 365, 146. Elsewhere he repeats this message by saying that if you think about man from the point of view of the "moons of Saturn"—a very non-earthbound position—the idea of "man alone" is a vision of "a wonder, a grandeur, and a woe." But from the same viewpoint, men as a collective "seem a mob of unnecessary duplicates" (521).

31. Ibid., 89. Queequeg repeats this feat later in the book when he rescues Tashtego after the latter falls overboard into the massive head of a sperm whale (390–391).

32. Aside from Queequeg's un-Americanized behavior and mannerisms, Melville also draws attention to the fact that Queequeg continues to worship an idol named Yojo according to his ancestral customs. Queequeg takes the bearings for his thought from a set of traditions that seem completely unfamiliar to all the Americans in the novel. See Zoellner, *The Salt-Sea Mastodon,* 70.

33. Melville, *Moby-Dick,* 537.

34. See Samuel Otter, *Melville's Anatomies: Bodies, Discourse, and Ideology in Antebellum America* (Berkeley: University of California Press, 1999), 164.

35. Melville, *Moby-Dick,* 365.

36. Ibid., 602–606.

37. See, most notably, Leo Marx, *The Machine in the Garden: Technology and the Pastoral Ideal in America* (New York: Oxford University Press, 1964), 315. See also Joan Burbick, *Healing the Republic: The Language of Health and the Culture of Nationalism* (Cambridge: Cambridge University Press, 1994), 173; James, *Mariners, Renegades and Castaways,* 79; and Ian Maguire, "'Who Ain't a Slave?': *Moby-Dick* and the Ideology of Free Labor," *Journal of American Studies* 37, no. 2 (August 2003): 300.

38. Melville, *Moby-Dick,* 605.

39. There is no doubt that Melville considers Starbuck an *Isolato,* and not only

because Ishmael says that everyone on the ship could fit that appellation. Elsewhere Ishmael singles Starbuck out as an *Isolato,* remarking on "the wild watery loneliness of his life." And Starbuck himself at one point says that he regards himself "alone here upon an open sea," a comment that I discuss in more detail below. Ibid., 144, 572.

40. R. E. Watters writes that "in Melville's opinion, prolonged isolation either chills the heart or corrupts the mind—or both." See Watters, "Melville's 'Isolatoes,'" *PMLA* 60, no. 4 (December 1945): 1140.

41. See R. E. Watters, "Melville's 'Sociality,'" *American Literature* 17, no. 1 (March 1945): 34.

42. Melville, *Moby-Dick,* 604, 484, 27.

43. See Michelle Ann Stephens, *Black Empire: The Masculine Global Imaginary of Caribbean Intellectuals in the United States, 1914–1962* (Durham: Duke University Press, 2005), 252.

44. See Maguire, "'Who Ain't a Slave?,'" 289.

45. Melville, *Moby-Dick,* 28.

46. Greg Crane, "Ralph Ellison's Constitutional Faith," in *The Cambridge Companion to Ralph Ellison,* ed. Ross Posnock (Cambridge: Cambridge University Press, 2005), 114. "Responsibility rests upon recognition," says the Invisible Man, "and recognition is a form of agreement." See Ralph Ellison, *Invisible Man* (1952; repr., New York: Vintage, 1995), 14. Ellison drew many of his themes from Melville's work; notably, the epigraph to that book comes from Melville's *Benito Cereno.*

47. Alexis de Tocqueville, *Democracy in America,* trans. Phillips Bradley, 2 vols. (1835–1840; repr., New York: Vintage Books, 1990), 2:99.

48. The coin described is an eight-escudo gold piece, which was minted by Ecuador between 1838 and 1841 (and in a smaller version between 1841 and 1843), during the very contentious early years of that state's existence as a republic. See Paul Royster, "Melville's Economy of Language," in *Ideology and Classic American Literature,* ed. Sacvan Bercovitch and Myra Jehlen (Cambridge: Cambridge University Press, 1986), 317. See also Chester L. Krause and Clifford Mishler, *Standard Catalog of World Coins: Spain, Portugal, and the New World* (Iola, Wisc.: Krause, 2002), in which the coin is listed as KM 23.1.

49. See Christopher Sten, *Sounding the Whale:* Moby-Dick *as Epic Novel* (Kent, Ohio: Kent State University Press, 1996), 64.

50. Robert Milder sees in the book "a series of parallel soliloquies" in *Exiled Royalties: Melville and the Life We Imagine* (New York: Oxford University Press, 2006), 73.

51. The only interaction there is amounts to a kind of violent frenzy, about which I say more later.

52. Melville, *Moby-Dick*, 565.

53. P. Adams Sitney, "Ahab's Name: A Reading of 'The Symphony,'" in *Herman Melville's* Moby-Dick, ed. Harold Bloom (New York: Chelsea House, 1986), 144.

54. Tocqueville, *Democracy in America*, 2:98.

55. It is telling that Queequeg, whom I describe throughout this paper as providing an alternative vision to that of Ahab and the other Americans, tells Ishmael that he sees Christianity as a corrupting force (Melville, *Moby-Dick*, 83).

56. Ibid., 186–187.

57. Ibid., 338. See also Zoellner, *The Salt-Sea Mastodon*, 223.

58. For instance, Stubb suspects that the devil has something to do with Ahab's quest for the white whale. See Melville, *Moby-Dick*, 371. Notably, Stubb happens to walk by Starbuck during the scene I am about to describe: he seems to reinforce the idea that Starbuck is unable even to consider working in concert with others on the ship. For his part, Stubb is oblivious to Starbuck's agonies.

59. Ibid., 572.

60. This exchange echoes a moment much earlier in the text, during which Ahab lambastes Stubb; as my argument elsewhere would lead one to expect, Stubb decides to tell no one about Ahab's aggression and does nothing.

61. Ibid., 197.

62. John Bryant, "*Moby-Dick* as Revolution," in *The Cambridge Companion to Herman Melville*, ed. Robert S. Levine (Cambridge: Cambridge University Press, 1998), 74.

63. Melville, *Moby-Dick*, 197.

64. See David Leverenz, "Selection from *Manhood and the American Renaissance*," in Selby, *Herman Melville*, Moby-Dick, 131. Interestingly, psychologists today consider the "humiliate or be humiliated" dynamic so well embodied by Ahab to be a central feature of sadomasochistic personality type. See, for instance, Peggy J. Kleinplatz and Charles Moser, eds., *Sadomasochism: Powerful Pleasures* (Binghamton, N.Y.: Harrington Park Press, 2006), 287.

65. David T. Mitchell and Sharon L. Snyder, *Narrative Prosthesis: Disability and the Dependencies of Discourse* (Ann Arbor: University of Michigan Press, 2000), 138.

66. Gabriele Schwab says that Ahab's "god of fire is a god of destruction who steers his destiny" and thus is in that respect Ahab's great ideal. See Schwab, *Subjects without Selves: Transitional Texts in Modern Fiction* (Cambridge: Harvard University Press, 1994), 56.

67. Melville, *Moby-Dick*, 564.

68. William Hamilton explores Ahab's "defiance of humanity" in *Melville and the Gods* (Atlanta: Scholars Press, 1985), 58.

69. Catherine H. Zuckert, *Natural Right and the American Imagination: Po-*

litical Philosophy in Novel Form (Lanham, Md.: Rowman and Littlefield, 1990), 111–112.

70. Melville, *Moby-Dick*, 477. Notably, in this passage Ishmael remarks that it is only on an American whaler with a tryworks located so prominently that it is easy for men to stare into its fire (474).

71. See Julian Markels, *Melville and the Politics of Identity: From* King Lear *to* Moby-Dick (Champaign: University of Illinois Press, 1993), 68. See also James Gilligan, *Violence: Reflections on a National Epidemic* (New York: Vintage Books, 1997), 23; and Harold Kaplan, *Democratic Humanism and American Literature* (New Brunswick, N. J.: Transaction, 2005), 170.

72. Melville, *Moby-Dick*, 102.

73. For instance, only right after they kill a whale do Stubb and Flask have a conversation about the direction in which the ship is heading; ibid., 369–374.

74. Zuckert, *Natural Right and the American Imagination*, 108.

75. Richard H. Brodhead, *The School of Hawthorne* (New York: Oxford University Press, 1986), 37.

76. Melville, *Moby-Dick*, 316–317.

77. Ibid., 360.

78. Richard H. Brodhead, "Trying All Things: An Introduction to *Moby-Dick*," in *New Essays on* Moby-Dick, or the Whale, ed. Richard H. Brodhead (Cambridge: Cambridge University Press, 1986), 47.

79. See Michael West, *Transcendental Wordplay: America's Romantic Punsters and the Search for the Language of Nature* (Athens: Ohio University Press, 2000), 329. Similarly, James Fentress Gardner writes that "the whole ship's company could be swept along by Ahab, regarding his mad quest as their own" because "all are partly moved by the spiritual principle . . . that Ahab centrally *represents*." See Gardner, "Melville's Vision of America: A New Interpretation of *Moby Dick*," *Proceedings* (Myrin Institute) 32 (1977): 39; emphasis in original. Zuckert, too, argues that Ahab is able to attain the crew's sympathies because "they, too, wish savagely and naturally to strike back"—although in her telling, this is less a particularly American trait than a natural human one. See Zuckert, *Natural Right and the American Imagination*, 102.

80. Melville, *Moby-Dick*, 215, 516, 284.

81. See the discussion of the rule of "fast-fish and loose-fish," ibid., 446–449.

82. Ibid., 223. D. H. Lawrence calls Moby Dick "the deepest blood-being of the white race" in *Studies in Classic American Literature* (1923; repr., New York: Viking, 1951), 173. Toni Morrison makes a similar argument in "Unspeakable Things Unspoken: The Afro-American Presence in American Literature," *Michigan Quarterly Review* 28, no. 1 (Winter 1989): 15–16.

83. See Carolyn L. Karcher, "A Jonah's Warning to America in *Moby-Dick*," in Bloom, *Herman Melville's* Moby-Dick, 67–92.

84. See Timothy B. Powell, *Ruthless Democracy: A Multicultural Interpretation of the American Renaissance* (Princeton: Princeton University Press, 2000), 153–176.

85. Melville, *Moby-Dick*, 636.

86. Wilson Carey McWilliams observes that "whatever else his death is, it is not lonely" in *The Idea of Fraternity in America*, 341.

87. William Ellery Sedgwick says that in this way, Ahab's "whole inward truth is reflected in the manner of his death." See Sedgwick, *Herman Melville: The Tragedy of Mind*, 117.

88. Melville, *Moby-Dick*, 446.

89. Thomas Woodson writes that to dismiss Ahab as "a madman, a Satan or a Byronic egotist is too simple." See Woodson, "Ahab's Greatness: Prometheus as Narcissus," in *Critical Essays on Herman Melville's* Moby-Dick, ed. Brian Higgins and Hershel Parker (New York: G. K. Hall, 1992), 440.

90. Tocqueville, *Democracy in America*, 2:99.

91. Melville, *Moby-Dick*, 593.

92. John Bryant, *Melville and Repose: The Rhetoric of Humor in the American Renaissance* (New York: Oxford University Press, 1993), 225.

93. Melville, *Moby-Dick*, 147, 638.

5

"Mighty Lordships in the Heart of the Republic"

The Anti-Rent Subtext to Pierre

Roger W. Hecht

In the "Enceladus" section of book XXV of Herman Melville's novel *Pierre,* the titular hero of the book, Pierre Glendinning, has a dream. Physically and morally exhausted from his unsuccessful attempt to write a "great, deep book," Pierre slips into a trance in which "a remarkable dream or vision came to him":[1] "The actual artificial objects around him slid from him, and were replaced by a baseless yet most imposing spectacle of natural scenery. But though a baseless vision in itself, this airy spectacle assumed very familiar features to Pierre. It was the phantasmagoria of the Mount of Titans, a singular height standing quite detached in a wide solitude not far from the grand range of dark blue hills encircling his ancestral manor" (396–397). That a comforting vision of home might arise in Pierre's tortured mind should be of no surprise. After all, he had recently given up his inheritance and his family's wealth and prestige for a life of poverty and artistic frustration in the cause of preserving the family's honor. It is indeed an ironic situation in which Pierre finds himself. Raised in an environment where the honor of the Glendinning patriarchs was held sacred, Pierre learns that his own father may have sired an illegitimate daughter, Isabel, who lives in poverty in the shadows of Saddle Meadow, the family estate. Pierre is determined to protect both the dignity of his half sister, by publicly acknowledging her as a Glendinning, and his father's reputation and that of the Glendinning family name, by shielding him from the charge of illegitimacy. To do so, he takes the extreme step of pretending to marry Isabel in order legitimately to bring her into the Glendinning family circle, engaging in a deeper level of illegitimacy through implied incest, all at the cost of his mother's outrage and his own impending marriage to Lucy Tartan. Disowned and disinherited, Pierre takes Isabel to the city, where he trades the comfort of rural wealth for the misery of urban poverty. His effort to support his new family through writing fails. It should be no surprise, then, that in his darkest moment, Pierre's tormented mind should find comfort in a vision of the "soft haze-canopied summer's noon" (397) of the home he left behind.

Pierre's pastoral vision, however, is soon disturbed by new details. The pastures and hills, "thickly sown with small white amaranthine flowers" that make the hillsides appear "glittering white, and in June still show like banks of snow" undermine the ability of the family's tenant farmers to raise their cattle and pay their rents. The flowers are inedible and the land has lost its agricultural value, yet the tenant farmers are still beholden to their "annual tribute of upland grasses, in the Juny-load; rolls of butter in the October crock; and steers and heifers on the October hoof; with turkeys in the Christmas sleigh." In Pierre's now darkened vision, the desperate tenant farmers, perhaps facing evictions from failure to pay their rent, beg their landlady, Pierre's mother, "Free us of the amaranth, good lady, or be pleased to abate our rent!" (398).

At first glace, the struggles of tenant farmers may appear to have little to do with Pierre's scandalous family dramas that preoccupied Melville for much of the novel and so preoccupied his hostile critics, who roundly attacked him for his "sacrilegious speculations" on the "holy relations of the family," his "morbid thoughts" and "provoking perversion," even going so far as to pronounce him "crazy" and "deranged."[2] What could a farmer's complaint have to do with Pierre's own struggles to find sustenance in the city and define himself as a writer of great literature, or his conflicts with his powerful mother, or his attempts to protect his family name from its association with illegitimacy? As it turns out, the question of family legitimacy and the struggles of tenant farmers are in fact very closely linked. The tenant farmers' plea to "abate our rent" alludes to New York's Anti-Rent Wars, which were just winding down at the time Melville was composing *Pierre*. This decade-long struggle between tenant farmers and New York landholding families offers an important but usually overlooked context for understanding the politics of Melville's ambitious and challenging novel.

Tenant farmers on the estates of New York's largest landowning families—the Rensselaers and the Livingstons—bore a host of complaints about leases that they considered "feudal" and "opposed to the spirit of the institution" of democracy. Beginning in 1839, farmers in the Helderberg hills west of Albany began a rent strike to pressure Stephen Van Rensselaer IV to renegotiate their leases, with the option to purchase their farms outright. Over the next six years, the conflict spread across eleven counties stretching along the Hudson River valley and throughout the Catskills. The Anti-Renters adopted a number of different strategies to press their demands, including further rent strikes, direct confrontation with authorities, legislative action, and challenging the legitimacy of the landlords' titles in court. It is this last concern, the legitimacy of family titles, that links Pierre's family struggles with the plight of the Glendinnings' suffering farmers. Though now it is barely recognized as a historical footnote, the Anti-Rent conflict resonated both in New York and in national politics in the decades leading to the Civil War, speaking to issues involving the expropriation and division of property, political and economic privilege, the rights of workers and the landless, and the question of who owns the fruits of one's labors. In *Pierre* references to the Anti-Rent conflict invoke a host of tensions threatening American democracy, including the expropriation of land by force from the Cherokee and from Mexico, slavery in the South and the exploitation of labor in the North, the expansion of political rights for white men and the inequality of conditions for women, blacks, and Native Americans, and the power of market capitalism to undermine basic institutions, such as the family. The Anti-Rent conflict provides the local platform for much of the larger social and political criticism scholars have found in *Pierre.* In this essay I will show how the Anti-Renters' concerns are reflected in Melville's own interrogation of the legitimacy of property as a whole. Melville makes the illegitimacy of the Glendinning family titles analogous to the illegitimacy of the Glendinnings' property titles. Just as Melville demystifies property relations, exposing the corruption and violence with which property is secured and maintained, he demystifies the authority of the Glendinning family by exposing Pierre's father's past and his mother's desperate efforts to police it in the novel's present. In doing so, Melville exposes the process and consequences of maintaining "mighty lordships in the heart of a republic"—powerful families whose wealth and power undermine the promise of democracy. Melville does not instruct his readers how to challenge these "mighty lordships," but he does help readers understand the stakes of maintaining such an ambiguous and paradoxical presence in the heart of a putative democracy.

The Anti-Rent Wars

The Anti-Rent Wars began in 1839, but discontent among the tenant farmers extends almost to the origins of the leasehold system, which is rooted in colonial Dutch and English land grants. Many patentees, such as the Rensselaers, built huge family estates modeled after the English manor system. The colonial governments granted tens of millions of acres to patentees, some of whom were speculators profiting from the sale of land, some of whom chose to lease the land to farmers. By 1776 over two million acres were leased to roughly seven thousand tenant families.[3] The terms of their leases contained numerous restrictions. Farmers were compelled to purchase their supplies from manor commissaries, process their grain at manor mills, and commit to the landlord a set number of days' labor in addition to paying an annual rent in wheat and livestock, the "annual tribute" Melville refers to in Pierre's dream.[4] The Revolution threatened to destroy the manor system, especially with the abolition of primogeniture and feudal tenures. The New York landlords who sided with the Revolution survived the transition by creating ingenious new leases. Some landlords, such as the Livingstons, employed life leases, in which the tenant remained on the property for the lifetimes of up to three signatories. If a farmer included the name of his youngest grandchild, a farm could stay in the family for three generations and could, in theory, be renewed for as many lives indefinitely. These leases, however, contained many restrictions on the tenants' economic activities.[5] The Rensselaers preferred what was called a "durable lease" or an "incomplete sale." Under this kind of lease, farmers owned the title to their farms, paid taxes, and had control over their soil, but they paid an annual rent of fourteen bushels of winter wheat and four fat fowls, in addition to providing a day's service to the landlord.[6] All leases also contained a "quarter sale" provision: a 25 percent penalty payable to the landlord should the farmer sell his leasehold to someone else. Ostensibly the quarter sale was a provision to maintain social stability by preventing farmers from speculating on leased lands. In effect, it prevented farmers from capitalizing on their improvements to the land (for example, cleared land, wells, fences, buildings). One of the few ways farmers could profit from the labor they invested in the land beyond the sale of produce was to sell their leases to new farmers with the value of their improvements added. The landlords wanted to maintain and control a stable population in the communities they owned, and they wanted to keep the value of improved lands for themselves. The quarter sale was designed to keep farmers on the land by denying them the profits of selling their leases. Melville likens these leases to treaty promises made to the Cherokee, binding the farmers to their leaseholds "so long as the grass grows and water runs" (16). Rather than an assurance of security, these leases were a kind of imprisonment. At the same time, farmers suspected the landlords of evicting farmers, then re-leasing the cleared land at a higher rent, robbing the farmers of the value of their improvements. The quarter sale provision was one of the strongest points of contention among the rebelling farmers, who believed that an individual has the right to own the products of his labor.[7]

For as long as the leasehold system had existed, however, farmers found ways to resist. Individually, farmers delayed paying the landlords; they "wheedled, pleaded, dragged their feet, and ignored rules that proprietors sought to enforce" and grumbled about "living in a state of vassalage."[8] An unsteady peace between landlords and tenants was maintained through what the historian Reeve Huston calls "a theatre of benevolence and deference," in which landlords would offer generosity and leniency to their tenants, and the tenants in turn would provide deference to the landlords' social and political status.[9] Such public performance only asserted the sense of inequality between the two parties and merely muted but did not quash the tenants' resentments. Localized insurgencies and squatter's movements did arise in the decades before and following the Revolution, giving voice to the tenants' doubts about the landlords' titles and their beliefs that "independent proprietorship was the natural status of free men, and that as long as unimproved land existed, everyone willing to improve it had a claim to a portion of it."[10] Through a combination of eviction and use of the state militia, these insurgencies were put down.

The turning point came in 1839, with the death of Stephen Van Rensselaer III. In his will he divided between his two sons, Stephen IV and William, his estate and approximately $400,000 in debt, which roughly equaled the amount of unpaid rent owed by his tenants. While William continued his father's policy of leniency, collecting partial rents and offering abatement in the case of extreme hardship, Stephen IV pressed to immediately collect rents. When he refused to meet with a committee of tenants to discuss the farmers' hardships and then rejected their proposed terms for renegotiating their leases, the first Anti-Rent War was born. The starting point was in the Helderberg hills west of Albany. Tenants initially resisted sheriff's officers issuing warrants to delinquent farmers with such long-standing repertoires of popular resistance as harassment, vandalism, and threats of personal violence. Over the course of several months, the sheriff's officers attempted to press their warrants with greater force, and the farmers pushed back with greater force still. At one point a posse of five hundred deputies was met by a force of three thousand farmers armed with clubs. This repeated resistance was eventually met with force from the state militia; though a shot was never fired, the sheriff was allowed to distribute his warrants unobstructed.[11] Over the next five years the movement continued to grow, as Anti-Rent associations formed throughout the leasehold district. The more militant farmers persisted in the use of aggressive tactics, forming companies of "Indians" dressed in calico robes and leather masks to harass authorities and interfere with distress auctions. At the same time, the associations pressed their demands in the legislature and the courts.

In the legislature the Anti-Renters argued that the landlords were "an aristocracy encouraged and protected by law which enjoyed privilege denied to other men" and that lease clauses that allowed the landlords to seize tenants' property subjected them to "feudal slavery," which was "inconsistent with a code of equal laws."[12] The Anti-Renters sought legislation that would nullify the most odious elements of their leases, especially the quarter sale provision. In the courts the Anti-Renters argued that the landlords' titles were themselves fraudulent, that they should be nullified, and that the estates should be broken up and distributed to the tenants, who had earned their rights to the land through their labor.[13] They argued for the invalidation of the Rensselaers' titles on several grounds: that the borders of their land were never defined; that the English patent to the grant was not properly executed; that the proprietors of the Rensselaer estate at the time had usurped the manor from its rightful heirs; that the size of the manor had been fraudulently tripled.[14] They claimed other irregularities in the titles of other landlords as well. Reeve Huston notes that titles to the leasehold estates were "notoriously weak" and sometimes plagued by "outright fraud."[15] For instance, Huston describes how Robert Livingston received patents for two tracts of land totaling 2,600 acres. Although the two plots were miles apart, they were listed as adjacent on their confirmatory patent. Livingston claimed the two plots as well as all the land in between, thus creating the 160,000-acre Livingston Manor.[16] Unfortunately for the tenants, common law barred them from challenging their landlords' titles in court.[17] Though the title challenge could not be pursued in court, it was an important moral challenge to the validity of the leasehold system. If property titles are illegitimate, then the social and political systems built on them are equally illegitimate.

Legitimacy and the Land

Melville embraces and expands this challenge to titles posed by the Anti-Renters to consider the effect of property on democracy as a whole. Book I of the novel, "Pierre Just Emerging from His Teens," establishes Pierre's relationship to his estate and to his family circle. There is, however, something unsettling about both. The description of the land is shrouded in the discourse of the picturesque, popularized at the time through gift books containing images and articles by such figures as the painter Thomas Cole, landscape architect A. J. Downing, and writer E. L. Magoon. This picturesque discourse establishes a moral bond between topography and individual character. The viewer of the picturesque, whose taste and education enable an elevated relationship with nature, has a greater claim to owning the land.[18] This is a position advanced by James Fenimore Cooper in the Littlepage trilogy of novels, written in defense of the New York landlords. "The earth is beautiful," claims Mordaunt Littlepage, hero of the novel *The Chainbearer,* "but it is most beautiful in the eye of those who have the largest stake in it."[19] As Tracy B. Strong notes in his contribution to this volume, Melville understands Americans' tendency to think of their nation as innocent, and how this "delusion" helps mask the structures of domination and the consequences of power. The aesthetic and spiritual discourses surrounding Nature are part of the way Americans have affirmed the claim to both innocence and power. In parodying the picturesque discourse that naturalizes the landlord's place in the landscape, Melville works to delegitimize the relationship between the land and the landlords. At the same time, the Glendinning family, who claims title to own and rule over Saddle Meadows, is riven by illegitimacy that undermines any title it claims to moral authority. In exposing both, Melville critiques the powers of the "mighty lordship" class of New York landlords and exposes the dangers they pose to republican democracy. Consider first the strange, hyperbolic language describing Saddle Meadows:

> In the country then Nature planted our Pierre; because Nature intended a rare and original development in Pierre. . . . She blew her wind-clarion from the blue hills, and Pierre neighed out lyrical thoughts, as at the trumpet-blast, a war-horse paws himself into a lyric of foam. She whispered through her deep groves at eve, and gentle whispers of humanness, and sweet whispers of love, ran through Pierre's thought-veins, musical as water over pebbles. She lifted her spangled crest of a thickly-starred night, and forth at that glimpse of their divine Captain and Lord, ten thousand mailed thoughts of heroicness started up in Pierre's soul, and glared round for some insulted good cause to defend. (19–20)

Samuel Otter notes the "displacements, overstatements, anticlimaxes, and the mingling of categories" that permeate Melville's panegyric.[20] On one level, such a passage is clearly a parody of picturesque discourse.[21] It strains to the breaking point the already overstressed language of Emerson's *Nature,* in which the landscape "satisfies the soul," and the viewer "is placed in the centre of beings, and a ray of relation passes from every other being to him," where heroic acts "cause the place and the bystanders to shine."[22] Nature can have these effects because Emerson changes Nature from property to *a property,* "a poetical sense of mind": "There is a property in the horizon which no man has but he whose eye can integrate all the parts, that is, the poet. This is the best part of these men's farms, yet to this their land-deeds give them no title."[23] Emerson uses the language of land deeds and titles to suggest that Nature's spiritual powers of poetic self-actualization work in spite of property relations, that the love of Nature transcends property. Melville's parody of the discourse of Nature, however, shows us that the landscape aesthetic is a function *of* property. Pierre is no "transparent eyeball" intersecting with the forces of the universe; he is the future heir of an enormous estate. Whereas Emerson, by aestheticizing Nature, attempts to elide the problems of property (commodity is the lowest end of *Nature* and receives the least amount of attention), the beauty of the country appeals to Pierre precisely *because* of its "very long uninterrupted possession by his race" (13). Much of book I is a demystification of property—specifically, the property of the large New York estates. Melville establishes Pierre's intense personal and proprietary identification with the landscape, but as he does so, he also exposes how an aristocratic culture was established in America, the social inequalities it perpetrates, and the violence needed to maintain it.

For Pierre, Saddle Meadows is "a talisman" that makes "the whole earthly landscape" and the Glendinning family inextricable: "For remembering that on those hills his own fine fathers had gazed; through those woods, over these lawns, by that stream, along these tangled paths, many a grand-dame of his had merrily strolled when a girl; vividly recalling these things, Pierre deemed that part of the earth a love-token; so that his very horizon was to him a memorial ring" (13). The connection between the land and Pierre's family is, in his mind, a fact of Nature, such that "it was a choice of fate that Pierre had been born and bred in the country" (19).[24] But, as Melville notes, it is not fate but history that placed Pierre in Saddle Meadows. The Glendinnings had held control of Saddle Meadows for generations, since "the earlier days of the colony" (10), since the time of Pierre's great-grandfather, through a title deeded from "three kings—Indian kings" (17) and passed through the family line. The family and property history is rife with violence and bloodshed. Beginning with the Indian battle that left Pierre's great-grandfather mortally wounded—who sat "unhorsed on his saddle in the grass, with his dying voice, still cheering his men in the fray," which begat the name Saddle Meadows, "a name likewise extended to the mansion and the village" (10)—and continuing through the Revolution, when Pierre's grandfather "annihilated two Indian savages by making reciprocal bludgeons of their heads" (38), the land is marked by violence. Melville questions the legitimacy of the Glendinnings' "long uninterrupted possession" of the land by highlighting the expropriation and displacement of the Native inhabitants, conducted not only by removing their persons but by renaming the place, erasing entirely their presence. The Glendinnings' possession is maintained by subsequent violence, which is not merely one of Pierre's relics of the past. Melville draws a direct line between the Glendinning family estate and the recent Anti-Rent War, in which patroons sent "regular armies, with staffs of officers, crossing rivers with artillery, and marching through primeval woods, and threading vast rocky defiles . . . to destrain upon three thousand farmer-tenants of one landlord, at a blow" (16). This allusion to the first major conflict of the Anti-Rent Wars exposes the reach of the aristocracy's power, in which the state serves to protect the interest of the landed class and not the interest of the tenants.[25]

The power of such an aristocracy in a nation that prides itself on its democratic institutions is indeed very troubling. Melville points out that landed families in America, such as the "oriental-like English planter families of Virginia and the South" and "the most ancient and magnificent Dutch Manors at the North" (15–16), were not eliminated during the Revolution but are still intact. They are, in fact, older, more established, and more naturalized than the "manufactured" peerages in England (15).[26] Melville gives them a sinister air. The Virginia families are "oriental-like," whereas the Dutch are "steeped in a Hindooish haze" (16). As John Carlos Rowe notes, in the nineteenth century Westerners popularly associated the Orient with "chaotic and irrational despotism," violence, arbitrary rule, and moral corruption.[27] Such behavior we will later see displayed by Mary Glendinning, Pierre's mother. Through a paradoxical analogy, Melville links this "oriental," morally corrupt aristocracy to the corrosion of democracy. It is a political zombie, springing to life out of death. Comparing a democracy to an acid that "produc[es] new things by corroding the old" and noting how verdigris is produced through the reaction of acids to copper, Melville exposes a paradox of nineteenth-century American politics:

> Now in general nothing can be more significant of decay than the idea of corrosion; yet on the other hand, nothing can more vividly suggest luxuriance of life, than the idea of green as a color; for green is the peculiar signet of all-fertile Nature herself. Herein by apt analogy we behold the marked anomalousness of America . . . when we consider how strangely she contradicts all prior notions of human things; and how wonderfully to her, Death itself becomes transmuted into Life. So that political institutions, which in other lands seem above all things intensely artificial, with America seem to possess the divine virtue of natural law; for the most mighty of nature's laws is this, that out of Death she brings Life. (13–14)

In America, it seems, democracy is not corroding old forms to create new forms of government; it is corroding itself, and a landed aristocracy is the form this corrosion is taking. John Locke famously claimed that in the beginning "all the world was *America*,"[28] in that the civilized world was once in the "state of Nature" in which all men were "equal and independent" because they equally shared in the produce of the earth that God had given them.[29] For Locke, the basis of this equality is property, which men create by applying labor to the earth, creating value in the form of crops and other products of improvement. Such improvement, according to Locke, is a divine command: "God and his reason commanded [man] to subdue the earth, *i.e.* improve it for the benefit of life, and therein lay out something upon it that was his own, his labour. He that in obedience to this command of God, subdued, tilled and sowed any part of it, thereby annexed to it something that was his property, which another had no title to, nor could without injury take from him."[30] What assured equality under this system is that the size of a man's possession was to be limited by "what he could make use of." If a man produced more than he and his family could use, the surplus would spoil, which would offend God. So long as one man's possession did not inhibit his neighbor from enjoying his own property, equality was assured. Such land and political equality are key to the Jeffersonian "fee-simple empire" of independent yeoman farmers, a central icon of the American ideal. Because of money, however, Locke allows for the limitless accumulation of property. "It is plain," Locke states, "that men have agreed to a disproportionate and unequal possession of the earth."[31] So rather than establishing equality, property creates its opposite. The verdigris, whose green color is a "signet," a sign of Nature, not Nature itself, suggests not only the "luxuriance of life," but luxury, the manifestation of excessive wealth, which is a morally corrosive force. It is worth noting that verdigris is a poison. So here Melville exposes a paradox underlying American politics: whereas Europeans engage in revolutions to tear down their "artificial" aristocracies to pursue their dreams of equal rights, America, despite its claims to democracy, has been developing an aristocracy and making it seem like a natural product of the republic itself: "In America, the vast mass of families be as the blades of grass, yet some few there are that stand as the oak; which instead of decaying, annually puts forth new branches; whereby Time, instead of subtracting, is made to capitulate into a multiple virtue" (14).

How is it, then, that an aristocracy can not only survive, but also thrive in a democracy? To answer this question, Melville points to the law: acts of Congress that expropriate Indian lands, displacing the native inhabitants, clearing the territory for white settlement; and leases, with their restrictions and hated quarter sales, those "haughty rent-deeds" that are held by a "thousand farmer tenants, so long as the grass grows and water runs; which hints of a surprising eternity for a deed, and seems to make lawyer's ink unobliterable as the sea" (16). Melville's use of the phrase "so long as the grass grows and water runs" points directly to the duplicitous language used by President Andrew Jackson to assure the Creek Nation of their safety in the Indian Territory west of the Mississippi, linking the displacement of Native Americans with the exploitation of the tenant farmers. Just as the government (and the Glendinning patriarchs) used the law and violence to clear territory of Indians, so too do the patroons use the law and violence to keep their tenants in line. But unlike the government, which reneged on its promise to the Creek that they and their children would live in their new territory "as long as the grass grows and water runs," the landlords make sure their tenants are "held" to their leases through "lawyer's ink"—the force of law. Though the leases, with their restrictions and quarter sale provisions designed to keep tenants on their farms for "a surprising eternity," suggest that the lease obligations are unreasonable, the ink with which they are written is as "unobliterable as the sea."[32] The principal argument by which the landlords and their supporters defended themselves was the unassailability of the contract. Even if a contract is unfair, it must be enforced.[33] Here Melville suggests how the law works in collusion with the aristocracy at the expense of democracy: "Whatever one may think of the existence of such mighty lordships in the heart of a republic, and however we may wonder at their thus surviving . . . yet survive and exist they do" (16–17).

One effect of the survival of "such mighty lordships" is the unchecked arbitrary power of the landlord and the immiseration of the tenants. Mary Glendinning evicts Delly Ulver, not for failing to meet her rent obligations, but for having a child out of wedlock. Mrs. Glendinning assumes this power as a right of her possession as an aristocrat, earned through the family's "long uninterrupted possession" of Saddle Meadows.[34] James Fenimore Cooper, whose Littlepage trilogy of novels gives voice to the landlords' point of view, grants this same authority to oversee and supervise the lives of their tenants to the proprietors of large estates by virtue of their taste and education. Advised by his parents to build a "substantial" house on his property and live alongside his tenants, Mordaunt Littlepage is told, "Nothing contributes so much to the civilization of a country as to dot it with a gentry. . . . It is impossible for those who have never been witnesses of the result to appreciate the effect produced by one gentleman's family in a neighborhood, in the way of manners, tastes, general intelligence, and civilization at large."[35] For Delly Ulver, the effect is arbitrary eviction and poverty. Mary Glendinning takes on the role of judge, juror, and moral arbiter of her tenants. Of Ned, the father of Delly's child, she declares, "No such profligate shall pollute this place" (117). In response to Pierre's concern about the misery of Delly and her baby, Mary Glendinning replies, "The mother deserves it," and that her baby appropriately suffers because "the sins of the father shall be visited upon the children to the third generation" (121). In the same way that landlords reserve the right to enforce contracts regardless of their consequences on the tenants' lives, Mary insists on the power to enforce God's law regardless of its effect on individuals. Cautioned by the Reverend Falsgrave to temper her wrath, suggesting that though the consequence of sin is hereditary, "it does not follow that our personal and active loathing of sin, should descend from the sinful sinner to the sinless child," Mary retorts, "If . . . we receive the child as we would any other, feel for it in all respects the same, and attach no ignominy to it—how then is the Bible to be fulfilled?" (121–122). Mary feels entitled to define the moral law; she also overrules the authority who might place limits on her power. The future impoverishment of Delly and her child is of no concern, so long as the estate is no longer polluted.

Mary Glendinning's outrage over Ned and Delly's pollution of the sanctity of Saddle Meadows helps expose the problem of profligacy and illegitimacy within the Glendinning family, the suppressed consciousness of past ill deeds that, once brought to the surface, threatens the family's reputation and authority. The power of the title Glendinning lies in the family genealogy of heroism, patriotism, culture, and purity. Pierre's great-grandfather and grandfather were war heroes, and his cultivated, gentlemanly father maintained a "gentlemanhood" combined with "the primeval gentleness and golden humanities of religion." Training in these "noble qualities" was meant to prepare Pierre to take his place as "heir to their forests and farms" (11). Yet the family title is as insubstantial as the family's property titles. As John Carlos Rowe observes, every character in *Pierre*—his ancestors, his parents, his half sister, his entire family structure—is revealed to be "inherently illegitimate."[36] Rowe points out that the "history of aristocratic pretension" described by Melville "is designed to mask [the family's] artificial origins, which on close examination generally betray . . . theft, piracy, and military conquest."[37] There is little patriotic about the Glendinning family history. The family's military achievement serves to enlarge the Glendinning family power, not "the ideals of social democracy,"[38] but the story helps maintain the veneer of respectability and in turn helps authorize the estate. By exposing the Glendinnings' respectability as a veneer only, Melville exposes to interrogation the legitimacy of all the "mighty lordships," both in the North and in the South.

Moral Authority and Aristocracy

In exposing the illegitimacy of family narrative, Melville delegitimizes the aristocracy's public authority. In exposing illegitimacy within the family itself—the impropriety of the relationship between Pierre and his mother, his father's infidelity, and the implied incest between Pierre and his illegitimate half sister—Melville shreds the aristocracy's source of moral authority, revealing a family structure that is unnatural and corrupt to the core. Reviewers of *Pierre* were particularly outraged by the novel's "monstrously unnatural" incest plot.[39] The reviewer for the *New York Herald* chastised Melville by proclaiming that "Nature . . . is the proper model of every true artist. Fancy must be kept at proper bounds."[40] These reviewers understood that the Glendinning family dynamic violated all propriety and precepts of the domestic code that dominated nineteenth-century American society. The conventions of domesticity made the home the locus of "finer sympathies, tastes, and moral and religious feelings"; it was the natural refuge from the unnatural, "calculating world" of trade and commerce.[41] The official rhetoric of domesticity, expressed in domestic novels and domestic instruction books, made the home the center of traditional values and practices. Maintaining the home was a woman's "natural vocation," and she was expected to cheerfully inhabit "the shady green lanes" of domestic life.[42] The family estate was likened by domestic promoters to "the aptest earthly manifestation of the heavenly kingdom,"[43] and the conduct within this kingdom—everything from household duties to appropriate sexual relations between spouses—was highly regulated through the domestic discourse. It is no surprise, then, that the *New York Herald* found Melville's violations of the "holy relations of the family" so shocking.[44]

Though the most obvious violation of the domestic code is Pierre's faux marriage to his half sister, Isabel, this expression of incest seems foreshadowed by the unusual intimacy between Pierre and his mother that pushes all limits on the natural domestic mother-son relationship. His banter while helping his mother "finish [her] toilette" casts him simultaneously as a maid-in-waiting, a helpful brother, and a lover. Putting a bow around her neck and crossing the ends at the front, he says, "I am going to try to tack it with a kiss, sister,—there!—oh, what a pity that sort of fastening won't always hold!—where's the cameo with the fawns, I gave you last night?—Ah! on the slab—you were going to wear it then?—Thank you, my considerate and most politic sister—there!—but stop—here's a ringlet gone romping—so now, dear sister, give that Assyrian toss to your head" (20–21). Pierre's "lover-like adoration" of his mother is matched on her part by "the proudest delights and witcheries" that are possible "for the most conquering virgin to feel." Pierre's "inexpressible tenderness and attentiveness" culminate for Mary in her own "grand climacteric" (22). The sexual pathology in this scene suggests a high degree of corruption within the Glendinning family. Pierre's efforts to rescue Isabel by presenting her as his wife, thus giving her the legitimacy of the Glendinning name, only mirror and replicate the incestuous behavior performed with his mother. Even Pierre's impending marriage to his betrothed, Lucy Tartan, carries hints of incest. Reminding Pierre of his future bride, Mary says, "You, Pierre, are going to be married before long, I trust, not to a Capulet, but to one of our own Montagues; and so Romeo's evil fortune will hardly be yours" (25). Though Lucy Tartan is not a blood relative of Pierre's, but the daughter of a close friend of his father's, the implication is that Pierre's marriage must be within the family line—"one of our own Montagues"—not to a Capulet. While it is likely that Mary Glendinning probably has class in mind, that Pierre will marry one of his own kind, her admonishment strongly suggests that a proper marriage line (one that will protect the property lines) is with another Glendinning. Her words certainly foreshadow Pierre's faux marriage to Isabel, one of Pierre's own Montagues, indeed.

Mary Glendinning's vigilant efforts to police Pierre's sense of the family's reputation, as well as any evidence of illegitimacy in Saddle Meadows, indicate that she is fully aware of the threat to the family's legitimacy. She reminds Pierre of his father's standing, a standard she expects Pierre to uphold: "Never rave, Pierre; and never rant. Your father never did either; nor is it written of Socrates; and both were very wise men. Your father was profoundly in love—that I know to my certain knowledge—but I never heard him rant about it. He was always exceedingly gentlemanly: and gentlemen never rant" (25–26). She further polices her husband's image by keeping the chair portrait, a painting executed by the elder Pierre's cousin that, according to "a very wonderful work on Physiognomy," revealed that "he was secretly in love" with a "French young lady" (96), out of sight. She displays instead a portrait that she thinks "correctly" conveys his "finest, and noblest combined expression" (88), but not necessarily his true self. Evicting Ned and Delly, however, does little to suppress suggestions of her own family's illegitimacy; rather, it brings it closer to the surface. When Pierre attempts to broach the issue indirectly, asking the Reverend Falsgrave seemingly rhetorical questions, Mary Glendinning attempts to redirect the subject. When Pierre asks, "Should I honor my father, if I knew him to be a seducer?" Mary responds, "Pierre, Pierre! There is no need of these argumentative assumptions. You very immensely forget yourself this morning" (124). Pierre's interrogations lead to Mary's evasions. Once Pierre leaves the room, Mary quickly returns to her original purpose of evicting Ned and Delly, as if evicting them will make all questions of illegitimacy go away and secure the future of all the Glendinnings' moral and property titles.

Evicting Ned and Delly does not, of course, erase the issue of illegitimacy. Nor do Pierre's efforts to preserve his father's good name and Isabel's legitimacy by keeping the truth of her origins from Mary Glendinning (to preserve her feelings) while pretending to marry Isabel to include her in the ranks of the Glendinning clan. Rather, the enormity of the illegitimacy within the Glendinning family is so great that the family collapses from the weight of its contradictions. In honoring both his father's and Isabel's reputations, Pierre loses his place as the legitimate heir of Saddle Meadows. In her outrage over Pierre's actions, Mary Glendinning disowns him; the shock of it eventually kills her. Pierre's later murder of Glen Stanly, the newly established heir of Saddle Meadows, in the streets of New York City and his subsequent suicide in the Tombs put an end to the Glendinning line. The marriage between Pierre and Isabel is "fictitious" (207), a ruse designed to lend legitimacy to a relationship that is, at its base, illegitimate. Fictitious too are any of the family's other claims to legitimacy, be they moral or political.

In Pierre's dream in book XXV the vision does not linger on the complaining farmer very long; it drifts over the hillsides, where the view changes from the "delectable" picturesque bower to a "Titanic" sublime mountainscape, in which "frequent rents among the mass of leaves revealed horrible glimpses of dark-dripping rock, and the mysterious mouths of wolfish caves" (398). Eventually, the vision settles on a pile of rocks that Pierre had christened Enceladus, "the most potent of all the giants, writhing from out of the imprisoning earth" (400). In Greek mythology, Enceladus was a giant, son of Gaia and Uranus, who warred against the Olympian gods along with the other Titans. Wounded by a spear thrown by Athena, Enceladus was buried under Mount Etna in Sicily. Pierre recalls an expedition of collegians who took it upon themselves to excavate this rock formation to see if it was "a daemonic freak of nature, or some stern thing of antediluvian art" (400). By the time the collegians gave up on their task, they had revealed a formation resembling the Titan's "mighty chest, . . . his mutilated shoulders, and the stumps of his once audacious arms." More important, they uncover "his shame" (401). Though that shame could be seen as Enceladus's defeat and the helplessness of being trapped under the earth, the shame could be the shame of incest: "Old Titan's self was the son of incestuous Coelus and Terra, the son of incestuous Heaven and Earth. And Titan married his mother Terra, another and accumulatively incestuous match. And thereof Enceladus was one issue. So Enceladus was both the son and grandson of incest" (402). Pierre identifies with Enceladus because of his "reckless sky-assaulting mood," by which he attempted "to regain his paternal birthright" and failed. The tales of incest also bind Pierre and the half-buried, raging Titan. Perhaps the Enceladus figure points to what we are to make of "mighty lordships in the heart of the republic." Enceladus was a potent giant, but where we find him in America is pinned to the ground, his arm a mere stump, his torso mutilated. Nature "performed an amputation" on the Titan, leaving him "impotent." By the time Melville composed *Pierre*, the New York landlords were in steep decline. In 1846 Anti-Rent activists were instrumental in electing John Young governor. In turn, Governor Young pardoned three men convicted of the murder of Osman Steele, the deputy, and proposed legislation to test the landlords' titles.[45] The constitutional convention that same year also abolished quarter sales and perpetual leases.[46] By 1852 the Rensselaer family, driven to bankruptcy from the pressures of the Anti-Renters' rent boycott, had sold their estate to land speculators.[47] Other major landlords, feeling similar pressures, began selling off their estates to their tenants.[48] In New York the landed aristocracy had become nearly as impotent as Enceladus. Melville never tells his readers what to make of these "mighty lordships," but Enceladus could be a hint. America's incestuous Titans, the feudal landholding families, may collapse, like the Glendinnings, into mere stumps, entombed under the weight of their own contradictions. What Melville doesn't give us, however, are Olympians to toss mountains on top of them. That would be the role republicans must fill.

Notes

1. Herman Melville, *Pierre; or, The Ambiguities,* in *Pierre, Israel Potter, The Piazza Tales, The Confidence-Man, Uncollected Prose, Billy Budd* (New York: Library of America, 1984). All quoted passages from *Pierre* are taken from this edition; page numbers are given parenthetically in the text.

2. See reviews from *Literary World, New York Herald,* and *New York Day Book* in Brian Higgins and Hershel Parker, comps., *Critical Essays on Herman Melville's* Pierre; or, The Ambiguities (Boston: G. K. Hall, 1983), 42, 55, 50.

3. Reeve Huston, *Land and Freedom: Rural Society, Popular Protest, and Party Politics in Antebellum New York* (New York: Oxford University Press, 2000), 13.

4. Henry Christman, *Tin Horns and Calico: An Episode in the Emergence of American Democracy* (New York: Collier Books, 1945), 22–23.

5. David Maldwyn Ellis, *Landlords and Farmers in the Hudson-Mohawk Region, 1790–1850* (Ithaca: Cornell University Press, 1946), 226–228.

6. Christman, *Tin Horns and Calico,* 26.

7. Huston, *Land and Freedom,* 27–28.

8. Ibid., 24, 33.

9. Ibid., 28.

10. Ibid., 33.

11. Ibid., 92–94.

12. Ibid., 111.

13. Ibid., 115.

14. Ibid., 112. The Anti-Renters' challenges to the landlords' titles are spelled out in great detail in C. Pepper Jr., *Manor of Rensselaerwyck* (Albany: J. Munsell, 1846).

15. Huston, *Land and Freedom,* 19.

16. Ibid., 19.

17. Ibid., 101.

18. The relationship between landscape aesthetic and politics is explored in Roger Hecht, "Rents in the Landscape: The Anti-Rent War in Melville's *Pierre,*" *American Transcendental Quarterly* 19, no. 1 (March 2005): 37–50.

19. James Fenimore Cooper, *The Chainbearer,* in *Works of James Fenimore Cooper,* 10 vols. (New York: Collier, 1891), 6:285.

20. Samuel Otter, "The Eden of Saddle Meadows: Landscape and Ideology in *Pierre,*" *American Literature* 66, no. 1 (March 1994): 56.

21. Samuel Otter argues that Melville's parody of picturesque landscape representation is a critique of the larger "antebellum 'picturesque project,' the effort to construct and empower the American difference through representations of the land" (ibid., 57). Otter explores how sentimentalizing landscape through picturesque representation presents America as a new Eden rather than a site of historical struggle in which entire populations are displaced or enslaved; ibid., 65–81.

22. Ralph Waldo Emerson, *Nature,* in *The Complete Essays and Other Writings of Ralph Waldo Emerson,* ed. Brooks Atkinson (New York: Modern Library, 1940), 9–14.

23. Ibid., 5–6.

24. For an analysis of the relationship between property and Pierre's subjectivity, see Jeffory A. Clymer, "Property and Selfhood in Herman Melville's *Pierre,*" *Nineteenth-Century Literature* 61, no. 2 (September 2006): 171–199.

25. The allusion also echoes other conflicts between authorities and the "Calico Indians," Anti-Rent militants who fought directly against agents of the landlords seeking to evict farmers from their leaseholds, this conflict culminating in the death of a deputy sheriff, Osman Steele, in Delaware Country in 1845. In response, Governor Silas Wright proclaimed three counties to be in a state of insurrection and declared martial law. In the crackdown that followed, over 250 men were arrested and indicted for the murder, though only two were convicted for their involvement. Their death sentences were later set aside by Governor John Young. Huston, *Land and Freedom,* 149–150, 179.

26. Nicola Nixon argues that *Pierre*'s "uncompromising" form—its lack of narrative continuity—is a reflection of the ideological fissures in the Union in the 1850s. By linking the northern and southern feudal aristocracies, Melville intends to remind northern readers of their own complicity with southern slavery. See Nixon, "Compromising Politics and Herman Melville's *Pierre,*" *American Literature* 69, no. 4 (1997): 726.

27. John Carlos Rowe, *At Emerson's Tomb: The Politics of Classic American Literature* (New York: Columbia University Press, 1997), 78–79.

28. John Locke, *Second Treatise of Government* (1690), ed. C. B. Macpherson (Indianapolis: Hackett, 1980), 29.

29. Ibid., 8.

30. Ibid., 21.

31. Ibid., 29.

32. Clymer points out how Melville exposes the problem of theft and legitimacy

through the use and naturalization of legalistic phrases. Conquered Indians are described as the "conveyancers" of their land, whereas tenant contracts are described in terms of broken Native treaties. He notes, "The will to empire proceeds most efficiently under the terms and language of law." Clymer, "Property and Selfhood in Herman Melville's *Pierre*," 175–178.

33. James Fenimore Cooper wrote his defense of the landlords in his Littlepage trilogy of novels. In his preface to *The Redskins* he strongly decries efforts by the state legislature to address the Anti-Renters' concerns, arguing that they "cannot impair the obligation of contracts!" Cooper, *The Redskins,* in *Works of James Fenimore Cooper,* 6:464.

34. The geographer Denis Cosgrove describes this linkage between property and moral leadership as "the lordship of the eye." Referring to the ideologies encoded in English topographical poetry and landscape painting, Cosgrove states, "A well-managed country house and its lands form a self-sufficient world. . . . The whole system is hierarchically organised. . . . Its harmony rests ultimately on its subordination to the care and authority of one all-powerful lord" who has moral authority over his estate. See Cosgrove, *Social Formation and Symbolic Landscape* (1984; repr., Madison: University of Wisconsin Press, 1998), 196.

35. Cooper, *The Redskins,* in *Works of James Fenimore Cooper,* 6:452.

36. Rowe, *At Emerson's Tomb,* 76.

37. Ibid., 77. Michael Paul Rogin notes how, in the first decades of the nineteenth century, political leaders traded on the names and reputations of revolutionary figures to establish their own reputations or the reputations of their causes. These leaders "aimed, on the model of the revolutionary fathers, to return to emotional sources of power and generate heroic authority." See Rogin, *Subversive Genealogy: The Politics and Art of Herman Melville* (New York: Knopf, 1983), 19.

38. Rowe, *At Emerson's Tomb,* 81.

39. *New York Evening Mirror,* August 27, 1852, quoted in Higgins and Parker, *Critical Essays,* 45.

40. *New York Herald,* September 18, 1852, quoted in Higgins and Parker, *Critical Essays,* 53.

41. Nancy F. Cott, *The Bonds of Womanhood: "Women's Sphere" in New England, 1780–1835* (New Haven: Yale University Press, 1977), 64.

42. Ibid., 74, 67.

43. Catherine E. Beecher and Harriet Beecher Stowe, *American Woman's Home* (1869; repr., Hartford, Conn.: Harriet Beecher Stowe Center, 1975), 19.

44. *Literary World,* August 21, 1852, quoted in Higgins and Parker, *Critical Essays,* 42.

45. Huston, *Land and Freedom,* 179–180.

46. Ibid., 160.

47. Ibid., 195–197.

48. These changes weren't entirely victories for the Anti-Rent farmers. Huston notes that large estates were often purchased by politically well-connected land speculators, who were as adept as the old landlords at making use of the machinery of law to ensure their power. The collapse of the feudal system of patroonery ushered in a purer form of capitalism, which was not necessarily more democratic. Ibid., 196–200.

6

Melville and the Cadaverous Triumphs of Transcendentalism

Shannon L. Mariotti

Generations of scholars have tried to solve the puzzle of Melville's relationship with transcendentalism. There are many hints that Melville's writings engage transcendental ideas in general and the works of Emerson and Thoreau in particular. This is not surprising, given that Emerson, Thoreau, and Melville (along with Hawthorne and Whitman) were often grouped together as rising figures making a name for American literature, had common friends and acquaintances, and published in some of the same venues. Emerson, Thoreau, and Melville were connected through figures in the literary world such as Horace Greeley, of the *New York Tribune,* and especially Evert Duyckinck, editor of the *Literary World.*[1] There were more personal connections as well, most significantly Nathaniel Hawthorne: he was a close friend to Melville and, as a onetime Concord resident, was also well acquainted with Emerson and Thoreau.[2]

But though it's difficult to escape the sense that some of Melville's writings respond to Emerson or to Thoreau, there is less scholarly consensus on what he seems to be saying about them. In addition, because of the paucity of biographical details about Melville's life, extensive letters, or journals, characterizing his reception of transcendentalism runs longer on possibilities than it does on proof. Some scholars have seen the influence of Emerson writ large on Melville's entire corpus, tracing his use of transcendental ideas and images and weighing and measuring his overall attitude toward "the sage of Concord" in different ways. Much of this literature follows in the footsteps of F. O. Matthiessen, who thought that Melville was both "attracted and repelled" by Emerson: attracted primarily by his views on art and creativity and his nonconformism, but repelled by his abstraction, asceticism, and relentless optimism, as well as his views on fate and necessity.[3] Other scholars have identified particular ways that Melville connects with Emerson or Thoreau in specific texts. For example, Melville's novel *The Confidence-Man* (1857) seems to engage transcendental themes, and scholars have also shown how the characters of Mark Winsome and his disciple Egbert may be modeled on Emerson and Thoreau.[4] In addition, previous scholars have connected Melville's short story "Cock-A-Doodle-Doo!" with Thoreau's writings.[5]

But the greatest amount of scholarship on Melville's reception of transcendentalism focuses on "Bartleby the Scrivener." Some scholars have connected this text with Emerson's essay "The Transcendentalist," a lecture first delivered in 1842 and published as part of *Nature, Addresses, and Lectures* in 1849.[6] Others link it to "Self-Reliance," published in *Essays: First Series* in 1841.[7] Exploring connections with the other famous Concordian, many scholars place "Bartleby" in dialogue with Thoreau's essay on civil disobedience.[8] Some of the most valuable recent analyses of "Bartleby" have continued to explore this line of argument, showing how Bartleby, like Thoreau, represents the problems of alienating modern mass society,[9] explicating how the story radically subverts Thoreau's thoughts on authority,[10] or exploring how Thoreau is one of the figures captured in Bartleby's overdetermined plurality.[11] As Kevin Attell's contribution to this volume also highlights, "Bartleby" has proven especially rich terrain for contrasting interpretations.

Based on an analysis of all the available evidence of connections among Melville, Emerson, and Thoreau, this essay intervenes in the existing scholarship to make a new argument in a different way. I analyze two stories, published in consecutive months—"Bartleby the Scrivener" and "Cock-A-Doodle-Doo!"—that can be seen as companion pieces in which Melville advances a skeptical critique of transcendental practices of awakening. Both stories were written in the years immediately following Melville's introduction to transcendentalism in 1849: "Bartleby" was published in *Putnam's* magazine in November 1853, and "Cock-A-Doodle-Doo!" was published in December of the same year in *Harper's New Monthly Magazine*. In ways that are more lamenting and stir pathos in "Bartleby" and more comedic and stir amusement in "Cock," Melville constructs a narrative in which characters experiment with transcendental practices of awakening, but in ways that lead only to death. As I will show, "Bartleby" engages primarily with Emerson's thought, whereas "Cock-A-Doodle-Doo!" responds to Thoreau. But in different ways, both stories—with lament and longing, as well as hilarity and absurdity—register Melville's skepticism that transcendental practices could ever fully address the problems that people face in their immediate, material world. Through these narratives, Melville problematizes the theory and practice of self-reliance, the abstracting tendencies that might be associated with transcendentalism, and the idea that we can awaken to a new morning above and beyond the immediate and particular material realm of worldly embodiment, mortality, and suffering.

In "Bartleby" this exploration of the impossibilities and costs of transcendentalism plays out in terms of Emerson's idealist gaze and his self-described visual practice of "focal distancing."[12] Melville began to be exposed to Emerson's ideas in 1849 and 1850, just a few years before he wrote "Bartleby." We know from one of Melville's letters that he "had only glanced at a book of his once in Putnam's store—that was all I knew of him, till I heard him lecture" in 1849.[13] But by 1850 he was sufficiently interested in Emerson to spend part of a visit with Hawthorne reading his essays (though he did not actually purchase any of Emerson's books until more than a decade later).[14] By the time he wrote "Bartleby," however, Melville was well versed enough in Emerson's thought to engage his ideas critically, though he twisted the transcendentalist's practices in ways that indicate his own skepticism and doubt. For example, Bartleby seems to mimic Emerson's ways of seeing, but for the scrivener this practice is associated only with strained eyes and "dead-wall reveries." Drawing on another Emersonian practice and modeling his advice to "stay at home with the self," as opposed to "travelling," Bartleby becomes increasingly stationary in the story, moving less and less until his immobility makes it hard to tell whether he is alive or dead. And, most important, throughout the story, in ways that are often connected with these other practices, Melville expresses skepticism regarding Emerson's dismissive attitude toward particularity, embodiment, and the material aspects of our immediate lives. Whereas most scholars have focused their attention on Bartleby's most famous statement, "I would prefer not to," my essay draws out the implications of another phrase the scrivener repeats: "I am not particular."

In the companion story to "Bartleby," Melville uses the themes of death and mourning to critique the dangers and delusions of transcendental awakening and morning in an even more extreme, absolute, and certain way. I read "Cock-A-Doodle-Doo!" as a parody of the kind of "lusty bragging" that Thoreau trumpets in "Walking" as well as *Walden.* "Walking" was published posthumously, in June 1862, in the *Atlantic Monthly,* nine years after Melville published "Cock." But we also know that Thoreau was delivering lyceum lectures based on "Walking" as early as 1851 and 1852: Melville may have heard about these lectures through mutual friends. There are also parallels between "Cock" and *Walden,* and even though *Walden* was not published until 1854, Thoreau was known to be reworking and revising it for many years before that, and it is not impossible that Melville had heard about this work. As we will see, Melville echoes Thoreau's language in several ways. But most significantly, in "Cock" Melville critiques what he sees as the folly of Thoreau's ideas by subversively employing the sounds and symbol of the chanticleer: whereas in Thoreau's writings the cock symbolizes morning and the experience of awakening, in Melville's story it highlights the dangers of the delusion that people can transcend the material world of pain, suffering, and death. And there are dire political consequences to this kind of forgetting: the cock's crow works like a different kind of "opiate of the masses," pacifying the characters' sense of impending crisis and enabling them instead to passively accept their material deprivation rather than actively working to change it.

Despite similar themes, however, there are striking differences of tone between "Cock" and "Bartleby" that seem to reflect the nature of Melville's engagement with Emerson, on the one hand, and with Thoreau, on the other hand, and speak to the different ways Melville weighs and measures these two thinkers: Emerson is to be taken seriously even if his thinking is sometimes deeply flawed, although Thoreau may merit only a more comic treatment. "Bartleby" is funny at points, but its dominant tone is still one of tragedy, whereas "Cock" has a tone of insane hilarity throughout. It's hard *not* to take "Bartleby" seriously, while it's hard to take "Cock" too seriously. In the broadest terms, then, these two stories represent the two poles of Melville's attitude toward transcendentalism. As Hawthorne famously said, Melville could "neither believe, nor be comfortable in his unbelief," and yet "he is too honest and courageous not to try to do one or the other."[15] In "Bartleby" we see more of the discomfort; in "Cock" we simply see the unbelief.

Melville's critique of transcendentalism is different in "Bartleby" in large part because of how the bourgeois lawyer is framed as an unreliable narrator. The lawyer is presented to us as a conventional man who obeys the same forms of authority that Bartleby prefers not to recognize. So we feel sympathy for how the scrivener might be misunderstood, and we become suspicious of the lawyer's critical reading of Bartleby. In this way, the story contains an element of uncertainty about its own critique of transcendentalism and is itself uncomfortable with the skepticism that is displayed toward Bartleby's practices throughout the story. In "Bartleby" we sense Melville trying to believe, but failing: ultimately, he constructs a narrative that performs his own uncomfortable, stubborn unbelief in transcendentalism. But in "Cock" it is more uncomplicated: Melville honestly doesn't believe in Thoreau's brand of transcendentalism. Whatever compelled him about Emerson doesn't extend in the same way to Thoreau. Taken together, however, these two stories give us the fullest picture of Melville's reception of the two figures most closely associated with transcendentalism.

"Bartleby" and Emerson's Transparent Eye-Ball

To understand Melville's critical engagement with Emerson we must first analyze the key aspects of his transcendental theory and practice of self-reliance that are at work in "Bartleby." Emerson understands self-reliance through two related practices, both of which are part and parcel of his enactment of transcendentalism: borrowing Emerson's own phrases, we might call the first practice "staying at home" and the second, a visual practice, "focal distancing." Both concepts designate ways of moving past immediate particularity and connecting with the universal: this motion of moving up and over, of *transcending* the immediate material particularity that surrounds us and projecting ourselves toward a realm of more distant universal ideals characterized by "truth," "reason," and a balancing "compensation," defines Emerson's practice of transcendentalism. Emerson tends to present particularity as a disagreeable thing to be overcome through processes of abstraction by which we move past the things that immediately surround us in the foreground of our lives and tap into the universal that is the pathway to the transcendental. Emerson sees the world in terms of two realms: there is the world that surrounds us, the "buzz and din" of the material realm characterized by "disagreeable particulars," a realm of confusion, superficiality, alienation, and conformity.[16] Throughout his writings, Emerson adds to this list of "disagreeable appearances" that we should strive to see beyond: men and women and their social life, poverty, labor, sleep, fear, fortune, tragedy, moaning women, hard-eyed husbands, swine, spiders, snakes, pests, madhouses, prisons, enemies, government, social art, luxury, "every establishment, every mass."[17] He contrasts "the inharmonious and trivial particulars" with the "musical perfection" of "the Ideal journeying always within us, the heaven without rent or seam," and in his writings this transcendental realm variously goes under the name of Universal Spirit, Universal Mind, Consciousness, Genius, Aboriginal Self, Over-Soul, Spiritual Laws, Reason, or God.[18]

Paradoxically, because of the way that Emerson thinks the universal exists deep within us as well as in a more distant realm beyond the things that immediately surround us, we can access it by moving beyond particularity in two different ways. First, we can access the universal by remaining stationary and "staying at home" with the self to move beyond the particular contexts of our own lives, falling back into our aboriginal self, abandoning ourselves to childlike intuition, and tapping into this shared Universal Spirit flowing within all humans. Self-reliance is not about searching outside ourselves, but about developing confidence in the universal that lies within each of us, to connect with a more timeless and eternal strain of genius. As Emerson notes, "Thus all concentrates; let us not rove; let us sit at home with the cause," and "So let us always sit. . . . All men have my blood, and I have all men's."[19] Emerson advocates staying with the self as a pathway to greater self-confidence and self-trust, because he thinks there are worlds within each of us and we can travel within ourselves. As he says, "The soul is no traveler; the wise man stays at home."[20] Here we are, says Emerson, "and if we tarry a little, we may come to learn that here is best . . . and the Supreme Being, shall not be absent from the chamber where thou sittest."[21] In this way, his injunctions to keep our seats evoke Buddhist practices of seated meditation, in which one tries to avoid flying off into distraction and instead hone one's powers of concentration: Emerson's advice to sit at home with the self seems sympathetic to this kind of meditation, in which one strives for a kind of awakening by settling and grounding the self.

But if one pathway to transcendence involves falling back into the aboriginal universal self, another involves focusing our gaze above and beyond the things that immediately surround us in order to visualize the universal. Visual practices enable us to focus our gaze on the more harmonious ideal realm of compensation that Emerson thinks exists above and beyond the "buzz and din" of the confused, superficial, material world. For Emerson, if you can see past such things and "conform your life to the pure idea in your mind," a "correspondent revolution in things" will occur, and the "temporary," "disagreeable appearances" will "vanish" and "be no more seen."[22] In one famous passage from *Nature,* Emerson describes a moment of transcendent vision when he leaves the material realm so fully that he becomes vision itself, at one with the Universal Spirit: he rises above the streets and the village and is uplifted into "blithe air" and "infinite space," the "tranquil landscape," the "distant line of the horizon": "I become a transparent eyeball. I am nothing. I see all. The currents of the Universal Being circulate through me; I am part or particle of God. . . . In the tranquil landscape, and especially in the distant line of the horizon, man beholds somewhat as beautiful as his own nature."[23] In such moments, "the eye of Reason opens." Emerson consistently uses images of distant horizons, landscapes, stars, the cosmos, and the sky to describe this universal realm on which we should focus our gaze. Emerson says we are too "near-sighted"—meaning that we see well only what lies close by us in an immediate way—and advocates this practice of focal distancing so we can learn to see that more distant realm clearly. Otherwise, Emerson asks, "of what use is genius, if the organ is too convex or too concave, and cannot find a focal distance within the actual horizon of human life?"[24]

What was Melville's attitude toward these ideas? Melville's critique of Emerson, as it plays out in "Bartleby," takes place against a backdrop of sympathy for the transcendentalist's noble fight against the force of convention. This is part of what accounts for the story's pathos. As the narrative progresses, Bartleby increasingly takes on the qualities Emerson encourages: self-reliance, self-trust, and an unconventional reliance on his own preferences and intuitions. Melville admired these aspects of Emerson's work. Indeed, his marginal comments in his copy of Emerson's *Essays, First* and *Second Series* are most laudatory when Emerson speaks of honesty, self-trust, unconventionality, and the poetic imagination. For example, when Emerson writes, "Self trust is the essence of heroism," Melville writes next to it, "This is noble." Next to a passage where Emerson is critical of our conventionality, Melville agrees: "Nothing can be truer or better said."[25] In "Illusions" Emerson writes, "I look upon the simple and childish virtues of veracity and honesty as the root of all that is sublime in character. Speak as you think, be what you are, pay your debts of all kinds." Next to this, Melville applauds him: "True & admirable! Bravo!"[26] At another point he simply exclaims, "Bully for Emerson!—Good."[27] As additional testaments to his admiration, after hearing Emerson lecture for the first time in February 1849, Melville wrote a letter to Evert Duyckinck, saying, "I have heard Emerson since I have been here. Say what they will, he's a great man."[28] A month later, in a March 3 letter to Duyckinck, Melville famously compliments Emerson as a fellow "thought-diver" of intellectual daring and originality: "I love all men who *dive.* Any fish can swim near the surface, but it takes a great whale to go down stairs five miles or more."[29]

But ultimately, as Melville insisted to Duyckinck, he himself did not "oscillate in Emerson's rainbow," and he was also skeptical of the man who seemed to be "full of transcendentalism, myths & oracular gibberish."[30] Melville's marginal comments are far more critical of Emerson's relentless optimism. For example, next to a passage where Emerson describes evil as only temporary rather than absolute, Melville writes, "He still bethinks himself of his optimism—he must make that good somehow against the eternal hell itself."[31] In "Prudence" Emerson writes, "Trust men, and they will be true to you; treat them greatly and they will show themselves great, though they may make an exception in your favor to all their rules of trade." Melville responds: "God help the poor fellow who squares his life according to this." In the same work Emerson writes: "The drover, the sailor, buffets it [the storm] all day, and his health renews itself at as vigorous a pulse under the sleet, as under the sun of June." Melville responds, "To one who has weathered Cape Horn as a common sailor what stuff all this is."[32]

How do Melville's skepticism, his doubt, and his reservations play out in "Bartleby"? Melville critiques Emerson's theory and practice of transcendental awakening by having the scrivener parody these themes of self-reliance, of focal distancing past particularity toward universals, and of sitting at home with the self.[33] Bartleby comes to take on more and more of the qualities that Emerson evokes as pathways to a kind of transcendental awakening. But Melville seems critical of what Sharon Cameron has called Emerson's "impersonal," portraying Bartleby as excessively self-reliant, impossibly abstracted and detached from the human world.[34] The outcome that greets the man who would prefer not to is quite different from the one Emerson anticipates and Bartleby seems to meet only with tragedy, not transcendence, and death, not awakening. Melville's story ultimately indicates that a wholly unconventional life is not a human life at all: it leads only to the "cadaverous triumph" of death.

We should remember that the story itself seems to signal the moment when Bartleby's process of transcendence and awakening begins. Bartleby starts out as an extremely industrious copyist. Indeed, he works at a furious pace initially and also seems to partake in all the usual processes of cross-checking that are expected of all the scriveners: "At first, Bartleby did an extraordinary quantity of writing. As if long famished for something to copy, he seemed to gorge himself on documents. There was no pause for digestion. He ran a day and night line too, copying by sun-light and by candle-light" ("Bartleby," 642). But then Bartleby begins to change. Like Jesus, resurrected and arising from death, "It was on the third day, I think," that Bartleby begins to undergo a process of transcendental awakening: the lawyer calls to Bartleby and is met with his reply, in a "mild, firm voice": "I would prefer not to" (ibid., 643).

Does Bartleby decide to stop copying others' words as a way of following Emerson's advice that "imitation is suicide"? In a radically self-reliant way, Bartleby places himself outside the pull of all forms of conventional authority and, as Emerson encourages, acts fully on the basis of his own intuition. Bartleby doesn't refuse, protest, or say no, all of which would still place him within the parameters of the lawyer's doctrine of assumptions: even though he would be *rejecting* those assumptions, he would still be acting on the basis of their logics. In a way that is not tinged by *ressentiment* or a sense of victimization, Bartleby simply asserts his own preferences with a "cadaverously gentlemanly *nonchalance*," and with the seeming expectation that his assertions will have at least as much authority as the lawyer's assumptions ("Bartleby," 650; emphasis in original). As the lawyer realizes, "He was more a man of preferences than assumptions" ("Bartleby," 659). On the third day Bartleby places himself wholly outside the realm of copying the conventions of others, rejecting what the lawyer calls "common sense" and acting in a radically and—as Melville will show—impossibly self-reliant way.

We get a deeper sense of how Melville uses the figure of Bartleby to critique Emersonian transcendentalism by analyzing a short phrase that he repeats three times: "I am not particular." The lawyer asks Bartleby if he would like a clerkship and he replies, "No, I would not like a clerkship; but I am not particular" ("Bartleby," 666). Then the lawyer asks if Bartleby would like to be a bartender. He replies, "I would not like it at all; though, as I said before, I am not particular" (ibid., 667). Finally, the lawyer asks

Bartleby if he would like to travel to Europe as a companion to entertain "some young gentleman with your conversation," to which Bartleby replies, "Not at all. . . . I like to be stationary. But I am not particular" (ibid.).

Bartleby seems to have awakened to Emerson's universal realm, which lies over and above the immediate material world of particularity, becoming like Emerson's "transparent eye-ball." In that famous passage from *Nature,* Emerson says: "I become a transparent eye-ball. I am nothing. I see all. The currents of the Universal Being circulate through me."[35] But in Melville's story this transcendence is portrayed skeptically. Though the narrator himself may be unable to understand Bartleby's process of awakening, it is undeniable that the story constructs the scrivener as less and less recognizably human and less attached to the world of humans. The narrator describes him as a "pale and motionless young man" and a "poor, pale, passive mortal" who only grows more and more insubstantial throughout the story as he increasingly loses his grounding in the ordinary material world. Bartleby doesn't seem to have any needs, desires, or human appetites. There was not "any thing ordinarily human about him" ("Bartleby," 643). Bartleby is like an impersonal spirit, an outline of a person, blank, not filled in, "like a very ghost," as the lawyer says (ibid., 648). If Bartleby becomes like a "transparent eye-ball" who has moved into the Universal Spirit, in Melville's story this primarily means that he becomes wholly detached from the only things that *matter,* from humans and the world itself, a figure who simply "seemed alone, absolutely alone in the universe" (ibid., 657).

Bartleby doesn't even fulfill that most basic appetite of hunger in normal ways, but subsists wholly on gingersnaps. As the lawyer discovers, the office boy, nicknamed "Ginger-Nut" because of his love for these small, spicy cookies, keeps Bartleby supplied with this unusual form of sustenance. Bartleby never drinks beer, tea, or coffee "like other men" and "never eats a dinner, properly speaking; he must be a vegetarian, then; but no, he never eats even vegetables, he eats nothing but ginger-nuts" ("Bartleby," 646). Toward the end of the story, when Bartleby has been imprisoned for vagrancy, his detachment from convention extends even to refusing to eat a meal: though the lawyer has provided money for his dinner, Bartleby refuses it, saying, "It would disagree with me; I am unused to dinners" (ibid., 670).

Bartleby's strange diet becomes even more interesting when we realize that Melville once linked Emerson with gingerbread. In one of his letters, Melville mockingly defends Emerson against Duyckinck's criticisms of his asceticism: "You complain that Emerson tho' a denizen of the land of gingerbread, is above munching a plain cake in company of jolly fellows & swiging off his ale like you & me."[36] But Melville says, "My dear Sir, that's his misfortune not his fault. His belly, Sir, is in his chest, and his brains descend down into his neck, and offer an obstacle to a draughtful of ale or a mouthful of cake."[37] Melville's critique of Emerson comes through in the depiction of this pale figure who is also more brain than belly. Bartleby, like Emerson, seems to be a denizen of the land of gingerbread, but this ends badly for him: when he is in the Tombs and his one food source is cut off, he may simply have starved to death.

Ultimately, for all his admiration of Emerson, Melville found an element of absurdity in the abstracted, ascetic quality of his thought and in his detachment from the rough-and-tumble conditions of the material world. Melville captures this critique in a kind of summarizing marginal comment: "This is admirable, as many other thoughts of Mr. Emerson's are. His gross and astonishing errors & illusions spring from a self-conceit so intensely intellectual and calm that at first one hesitates to call it by its right name. Another species of Mr. Emerson's errors, or rather, blindness, proceeds from a defect in the region of the heart."[38] Not only is Emerson, in Melville's view, more mind than body, but he is also more about the intellect than the heart. In Melville's view, for all of Emerson's insight, there is also a profound "blindness" to his perspective. Indeed, Melville's skepticism about Emerson's transcendental mode of vision plays out in "Bartleby."

Eyes and vision figure prominently in "Bartleby," but in a way that reflects Melville's concerns about Emerson's tendency to look up and over "disagreeable particularity" and to "dispose" of "the most disagreeable facts." Indeed, we know from Melville's marginalia that he was especially critical of this aspect of Emerson's thought. For example, in "The Poet," Emerson writes: "Also, we use defects and deformities to a sacred purpose, so expressing our sense that the evils of the world are such only to the evil eye." In response, Melville expresses frustration: "What does the man mean? If Mr. Emerson travelling in Egypt should find the plague-spot come out on him—would he consider that an evil sight or not? And if evil, would his eye be evil because it seemed evil to his eye, or rather to his sense using the eye as an instrument?" In another part of "The Poet" where Emerson writes that the poet, because he can "reattach things to nature and the Whole," thus also "disposes very easily of the most disagreeable facts,"

Melville underlines this and comments: "So it would seem."[39] But Melville registers his skepticism about Emerson's visual practice most fully through Bartleby's "dead-wall reveries."

There is not much worth looking at in the lawyer's office, and yet after he begins his process of supposed awakening, Bartleby spends much of his time staring at the walls, an appropriate thing to do given that his workplace is on Wall Street. The lawyer's chambers are bounded by a white wall on one side—"This view might have been considered rather tame than otherwise, deficient in what landscape artists call 'life'"—and in the other direction, his "windows commanded an unobstructed view of a lofty brick wall, black by age and everlasting shade; which wall required no spy-glass to bring out its lurking beauties, but for the benefit of all near-sighted spectators, was pushed up to within ten feet of my window panes" ("Bartleby," 636). As the lawyer notes, "For long periods he would stand looking out, at his pale window behind the screen, upon the dead brick wall" (ibid., 652). The lawyer will hear only silence and motionlessness and know that "behind his screen he must be standing in one of those dead-wall reveries of his" (ibid., 653). Bartleby seems to represent Emerson's "transparent eyeball," which is "nothing" but "sees all," but in Melville's story, even when we appreciate how this portrayal is mediated through the lawyer, it still just takes the form of staring at a brick wall. The scrivener may be trying to take Emerson's advice to avoid being "near-sighted," to look past his immediate realm and focus his gaze on the more harmonious distant horizon that lies beyond it. But in Melville's story something that Emerson sees as a pathway to awakening seems like a dead end.

Eyes and vision figure into the story in another way as well. In his misguided way, the lawyer at one point thinks he has "solved" the problem of Bartleby's preference not to: maybe it's because his eyes are strained by copying! The lawyer worries that Bartleby's furious copying in the first few days of his employment ruined his eyesight. This echoes Emerson's fear for his own eyesight, a constant worry of his after he contracted what seems to have been uveitis, a rheumatic inflammation of the eye, in 1825. Emerson refers to his persistent fear of losing his eyesight in the famous passage about the transparent eyeball in *Nature,* where he writes that he feels "that nothing can befall me in life,—no disgrace, no calamity, (leaving me my eyes,) which nature cannot repair."[40] The lawyer's concern with Bartleby's eyesight may allude to Emerson's concerns with losing vision, both literally and in terms of the practice of focal distancing. As the lawyer says, "I looked steadfastly at him, and perceived that his eyes looked dull and glazed. Instantly it occurred to me, that his unexampled diligence in copying by his dim window for the first few weeks of his stay with me might have temporarily impaired his vision" ("Bartleby," 656). But after several days of rest, Bartleby still will not copy: "Whether Bartleby's eyes improved or not, I could not say. To all appearance, I thought they did. But when I asked him if they did, he vouchsafed no answer. At all events, he would do no copying" (ibid.). Indeed, the lawyer persists in thinking that the problem is all about Bartleby's eyes, even after he has abandoned Bartleby and moved to a new office. Returning to try to coax Bartleby to leave the old office, the lawyer asks: "How would a bar-tender's business suit you? There is no trying of the eyesight in that" (ibid., 667). The lawyer's own conventional subject position might prevent him from understanding Bartleby. But given the inscrutability of the scrivener's dead-wall reveries, in this instance the lawyer can be forgiven for thinking the problem with Bartleby might be physical. This is another way that the story performs a kind of uncertainty about the critiques of transcendentalism that the narrative itself advances.

There is also a more macroscopic way that the story abstracts away from, and shifts the reader's line of sight away from, the material context of the story. Just as Emerson lists "disagreeable" particular things that are then glanced over, so does Melville give hints of the immediate conditions that make up Bartleby's context. After all, the story is subtitled "A Tale of Wall-Street." But the material and ideological conditions of Wall Street are never the *focus* of the story: they are always only a subtitle, a subtext. Following Emerson's line of sight, the story seems to direct our attention away from these conditions and to portray Bartleby as a transcendental character abstracted from all particularity. But scholars have worked to redirect our attention to Bartleby's immediate historical context, unearthing the hidden ideology of capitalist production in the story, reminding us of the scrivener's alienating conditions of employment, that his job is on Wall Street working for a lawyer associated with John Jacob Astor, that his firm is located near a place where there were recently labor strikes, that he may be living in the lawyer's offices because he is actually homeless, and the list could go on.[41] But despite all the minor chords these elements strike in the story, the major key works to portray Bartleby as somehow disconnected from this larger material context, perhaps because of the way it is narrated through the eyes of the unreliable narrator, the bourgeois lawyer who is himself clueless about the conditions of his laborers. This deflection of immediate material conditions represents another way that Melville critiques transcendentalism's abstraction.

Bartleby's detachment, his preference not to participate in worldly activities, is also captured by his motionlessness and by his static residence in his "hermitage." From the very first word used to describe Bartleby, the overriding characteristic that defines him is his lack of movement. He is characterized by a "great stillness," and the lawyer first describes him as "a motionless young man" who "never went anywhere" ("Bartleby," 642, 646). He is a "fixture": "Like the last column of some ruined temple, he remained standing mute and solitary in the middle of the otherwise deserted room" (ibid., 658). Even when Bartleby is imprisoned in the Tombs, he takes up the same stationary habits he displayed in the office: "He slowly moved to the other side of the inclosure and took up a position fronting the dead-wall" (ibid., 670). While he is in the lawyer's chambers, Bartleby stays mostly in his "hermitage," which is how the area behind the green screen is described throughout the story. Bartleby "sat in his hermitage, oblivious to every thing but his own peculiar business there" (ibid., 646).

The scrivener's retreat from activity and movement, as well as the world of relationships, obligations, and conventions, registers Melville's skepticism about Emerson's counsel to explore the universe within the self, to find the Supreme Being in the chamber where you sit. We know from his marginal comments that Melville was critical of Emerson's praise of self-reliance when it also extended to disparaging the benefits to be gained from studying other cultures and simply "staying at home with the self." Writing of Americans going to Europe in search of culture, Emerson queried, "You do not think you will find anything which you have not seen at home?" and Melville responded, "Yet, possibly, Rome or Athens has something to show or suggest that Chicago has not."[42] Even though the lawyer might not fully understand Bartleby's motives, the scrivener's life appears deeply impoverished by most conceivable measures.

Melville's uncomfortable unbelief in Emerson's transcendental practices, his state of simultaneous attraction and repulsion, is captured most concisely in Bartleby's "cadaverous triumph." If Bartleby demonstrates the momentarily disruptive power that an assertion of preferences can have—throwing a wrench in the machinery of custom—his wholesale protest against all conventions, his radical form of self-reliance, also places him beyond human society and outside the world. For Melville, there is ultimately a deep poverty and futility attached to transcendental practices of awakening: there is no life at all wholly detached from the obligations and conventions that condition our human and worldly existence. As other scholars have noted, the ultimate end that Bartleby meets—dying in the prison known as the Tombs and surrounded by high walls—is foreshadowed by the pale existence he leads in the lawyer's office.[43] The man who used to work in the "Dead Letter office"—"Dead letters! Does it not sound like dead men?" ("Bartleby," 672)—lived a life that increasingly resembled a death. Indeed, the lawyer initially thinks Bartleby is just sleeping when he finally does die.

"Cock-A-Doodle-Doo!" and Thoreau's Chanticleer

Melville's connections with Thoreau are far less direct. We don't have any proof that Melville ever met Thoreau, though it seems that he was at least familiar with some of Thoreau's works. We know that Melville borrowed *A Week on the Concord and Merrimack Rivers* from Evert Duyckinck. We also know that parts of Thoreau's *A Yankee in Canada* appeared in *Putnam's* the same year as "Bartleby," published anonymously, though "Thoreau's authorship could have been an open secret, as Melville's anonymous authorship frequently was."[44] But this is the nature of the evidence linking Melville with Thoreau: there is only speculation, hearsay, and gossip, and much of it reflects the same mocking, lighthearted, and comical tone of "Cock" itself.[45]

There is an anecdote about Melville and Hawthorne that indicates the jesting quality that the two might have used in speaking about Thoreau. In March 1851, Hawthorne visited Melville at his farm in Pittsfield, Massachusetts. Years later Thomas F. Wolfe recounted an anecdote he had heard from Melville about this visit: "March weather prevented walks abroad, so the pair spent most of the week in smoking and talking metaphysics in the barn,—Hawthorne usually lounging upon a carpenter's bench. When he was leaving, he jocosely declared that he would write a report of their psychological discussions for publication in a book to be called 'A Week on a Work-Bench in a Barn,' the title being a travesty upon that of Thoreau's then recent book, 'A Week on Concord River.'"[46]

But if this story is mocking and lighthearted, it is also familiar and even affectionate, not malicious. Indeed, Hawthorne probably portrayed

Thoreau in more positive ways to Melville. Hawthorne was a fan of *Walden* and "found it one of the few works he could recommend while in England as having original 'American characteristics.'"[47] As Hershel Parker writes, "A good deal of Melville's early impressions of Thoreau came from Hawthorne, as did his impression of Emerson the man. The previous year at the red cottage they had talked about Emerson, but now they talked about the Concord man who had climbed Greylock—'the most unmalleable fellow alive' although a good walking companion, Hawthorne had decided long before."[48] This unmalleability actually seems to have been a point of sympathy between Thoreau and Hawthorne, given that Hawthorne later described himself to his soon-to-be wife using the exact same terms: as Hawthorne wrote to Sophia, "I am a most unmalleable man."[49] Ultimately, Hawthorne "felt himself in fuller sympathy with [Thoreau] than with Emerson."[50] Duyckinck also "had strong opinions about Thoreau, and over the period of four years, probably found occasion to express some of them to Melville."[51] But Duyckinck did not hold a very high opinion of Thoreau at all and published a negative review of *A Week on the Concord and Merrimack Rivers* in the *Literary World* that mocked Thoreau: "He deprecates churches and preachers. Will he allow us to uphold them? Or does he belong to the family of Malvolios, whose conceit was so engrossing that it threatened to deprive the world of cakes and ale?"[52] Reflecting the dominant mood of the day, Duyckinck thought of Thoreau "as a cranky imitator of Emerson."[53]

Melville's treatment of Thoreau in "Cock" bears the marks of both these influences.[54] The disposition of "unmalleability" that Hawthorne liked is not so far from the unwavering and self-righteous commitment to rising above the world of cakes and ale that Duyckinck abhorred in Thoreau. Thoreau's absolutism forms the basis for the critique that Melville makes of Thoreau in "Cock": as we will see, the characters of this story do not waver from their single-minded pursuit of transcendence and awakening even as their lives fall apart, even as death and destruction pile up as a result of their neglect of their human finitude and worldly embeddedness. In "Cock" Melville emphasizes the costs of an unmalleable disposition.

We get our first clue that "Cock-A-Doodle-Doo!" critically engages Thoreau through the story's pairing of the crowing of the chanticleer with the theme of "morning," being "awake," and arising from the "doleful dumps," all of which are recurrent themes in Thoreau's writings. For example, in the "Where I Lived and What I Lived For" chapter of *Walden*, Thoreau makes one of many connections among the chanticleer, morning, and awakening: "As I have said, I do not propose to write an ode to dejection, but to brag as lustily as chanticleer in the morning, standing on his roost, if only to wake my neighbors up."[55] We see more images of the rooster in the "Sounds" chapter: Thoreau speaks of walking in the winter woods, which resound with the crowing of the cock: his "health is ever good, his lungs are sound, his spirits never flag."[56] Thoreau is invigorated by the sound: "Who would not be early to rise, and rise earlier and earlier every successive day of his life, till he became unspeakably healthy, wealthy, and wise?"[57]

In "Walking" we see more references to the cock's crow and the way it can lift our spirits and stimulate our own awakening. As Thoreau writes, "Unless our philosophy hears the cock crow in every barn-yard within our horizon, it is belated. That sound commonly reminds us that we are growing rusty and antique in our employments and habits of thought."[58] Unlike us, it seems, the cock, according to Thoreau, "has not fallen astern; he has got up early, and kept up early, and to be where he is, is to be in season, in the foremost rank of time. It is an expression of the health and soundness of Nature, a brag for all the world—healthiness as of a spring burst forth—a new fountain of the Muses, to celebrate this last instant of time."[59] Thoreau also speaks of being uplifted from the "doleful dumps," which is also a recurrent phrase in "Cock-A-Doodle-Doo!" As Thoreau writes, "The merit of this bird's strain is in its freedom from all plaintiveness. The singer can easily move us to tears or to laughter, but where is he who can excite in us a pure morning joy? When, in doleful dumps, breaking the awful stillness of our wooden side-walk on a Sunday—or perchance a watcher in the house of mourning—I hear a cockerel crow far or near, I think to myself there is one of us well at any rate, and with a sudden gush return to my senses."[60]

Another sound, beyond the crowing of the chanticleer, figures prominently into both Thoreau's writings and Melville's short story: the whistle of the railroad. We might draw parallels between Thoreau's references to the railroad in the "Sounds" chapter of *Walden* and Melville's repeated references to the train in "Cock," not just in terms of how each portrays the whistle itself but in the language each uses to depict the transfer of goods brought by the train. The call-and-response language that Thoreau uses to relate the exchange of commodities is also echoed in "Cock." Thoreau describes how the sounds of the locomotive echo through the woods: "Here come your groceries, country; your rations, countrymen! Nor is there any man so independent on his farm that he can say them nay. And here's your pay for them! screams the countryman's whistle."[61] In another passage Thoreau writes, "And hark! here comes the cattle-train bearing the cattle of a thousand hills, sheepcots, stables, and cow-yards in the air, drovers with their sticks, and shepherd boys in the midst of their flocks, all but the mountain pastures, whirled along like leaves blown from the mountains by the September gales."[62] These sounds of the cock and of the railroad, the two primary sounds that echo throughout Thoreau's writings, both figure prominently in "Cock," as the narrator brags lustily about his own awakening.

But Melville imports the symbols, sounds, and sights that appear throughout Thoreau's writings to mockingly and bitingly critique them. Melville's story begins with the narrator in a very depressed state. Unable to sleep, he goes outside early one morning and looks around him at a landscape that seems in ruin and decay: "All round me were tokens of a divided empire" where old and new, dying and growing, mingled together ("Cock," 1203). Whereas the transcendentalist would view nature as a unified and harmonious whole, Melville here emphasizes breakage, division, decay, and death. The narrator describes two locomotive crashes in which his friends died, but he mockingly questions the transcendentalist idea of the universe as a balanced whole where even bad things are part of the workings of fate and part of a larger, compensatory unity: "Yet what's the use of complaining," he asks. "Don't the very heavens themselves ordain these things—else they could not happen?" (ibid., 1204). Even the cows come in for some criticizing: in contrast to Thoreau's usual raptures about Nature, the narrator looks at the beasts coming out of the barn into the pasture and says, "What a miserable-looking set, to be sure!" (ibid., 1206). The narrator goes on to rail against the railroad: "Great improvements of the age! What! to call the facilitators of death and murder an improvement! Who wants to travel so fast? My grandfather did not, and he was no fool" (ibid., 1205). Another passage follows the pattern of the "Sounds" chapter of *Walden,* which Melville renders in an even more exclamatory style: "Hark! Here comes that old dragon again . . . snort! puff! scream!—here he comes straight-bent through these vernal woods, like the Asiatic cholera cantering on a camel. Stand aside! here he comes, the chartered murderer! the death monopolizer! judge, jury, and hangman all together, whose victims die always without benefit of clergy. For two hundred and fifty miles that iron fiend goes yelling through the land, crying 'More! more! more!'" (ibid.).

But then the mood changes completely and the more philosophical critique of Thoreau's practice of awakening begins on the level of substance, not just style. Throughout the story, the cock has the power to shake the narrator out of his melancholy. He hears the most magnificent crow from a rooster that he has ever heard, which lifts him completely from his negative and depressed state. He experiences what Thoreau might call morning, no matter what the clocks say: "Hark! By Jove, what's that? . . . Hark again! How clear! how musical! how prolonged! What a triumphant thanksgiving of a cock-crow! . . . Why, why, I begin to feel a little in sorts again. It ain't so very misty after all. The sun yonder is beginning to show himself: I feel warmer. Hark! There again! Did ever such a blessed cock so ring out over the earth before!" ("Cock," 1206). The narrator thinks that the bird "plainly says—'*Never say die!*'" and feels his "blood bound": "I feel wild. What? Jumping on this rotten old log here, to flap my elbows and crow too? And just now in the doleful dumps. And all this from the simple crowing of a cock. Marvelous cock!" (ibid., 1206–1207; emphasis in original).

But it is through this repeated pattern of events that Melville critiques Thoreau. Something terrible happens, the narrator falls into the doleful dumps, but then he hears the cock crow and his spirits are lifted up and over the material realm of decay, decline, and debt: "If at times I would relapse into my doleful dumps, straightway at the sound of the exultant and defiant crow, my soul, too, would turn chanticleer, and clap her wings, and throw back her throat, and breathe forth a cheerful challenge to all the world of woes" ("Cock," 1215). And yet for Melville, these experiences of exhilaration and transcendence are just delusions that cannot defeat death. Indeed, these momentary spiritual lifts may even *hasten* the onset of negative conditions because, while held in thrall to the crowing of the cock, the characters in the story fail to attend to their immediate world concerns, such as finding ways to sustain and care for sick bodies and pay the bills. It becomes clear that the narrator is in debt, but his fascination with these momentary experiences of transcendence and awakening pacify any sense of concern and quell any motivation to work toward changing his worldly conditions. His spirits aren't even dampened by the creditor to whom he owes money, who comes to dun him. The narrator glibly asks the bill collector to roll up the bill so he can light his pipe with it (ibid., 1208). "'My friend,' said I, 'what a charming morning! How sweet the country looks! Pray, did you hear that extraordinary cock-crow this morning? Take a glass of my stout!'" (ibid., 1209).

The dun keeps coming to the narrator's door with bills, but no matter. The narrator has a hefty mortgage on his house and is forced to take out another mortgage to pay more debts, but no matter. The dun commences a civil process against him and serves him with the document rolled up in his cigar, but no matter ("Cock," 1215). Nothing *matters* anymore: the cock's crow causes him to transcend this dismal material world: "Arrived home, I read the process, and felt a twinge of melancholy. Hard world! Hard world! . . . Hark! like a clarion! yea, like a jolly bolt of thunder with bells to it—came the all-glorious and defiant crow! Ye gods, how it set me up again! . . . Plain as cock could speak, it said: 'Let the world and all aboard of it go to pot. Do you be jolly, and never say die. What's the world compared to you? What is it, anyhow, but a lump of loam? Do you be jolly!'" (ibid., 1216). The bird's crow causes the narrator to abstract away from what Emerson would call the "disagreeable particulars" that surround him in the world. The cock gives him "reinvigorated spirits" and a "dauntless sort of feeling." He thinks over all his problems but still feels "as though I could meet Death, and invite him to dinner, and toast the Catacombs with him, in pure overflow of self-reliance and a sense of universal security" (ibid., 1210). These last few words regarding self-reliance and universal security, it nearly goes without saying, are strongly marked with the imprint of transcendentalism.

The same dynamic whereby people become deluded about their desperate material conditions because of the euphoria they experience when the cock crows becomes even more pronounced when the narrator actually meets the rooster. One day, while sitting and "reading Burton's Anatomy of Melancholy," the narrator learns that Merrymusk, the poor man who comes to split his wood, is the owner of the bird. Soon the narrator visits Merrymusk's hovel to see this magnificent cock and tries to buy him from the woodcutter, who calls the bird Trumpet. But the desperately poor man won't sell him at any price. Indeed, the cock's crow seems to be all that is keeping the whole family alive. Everyone in the family is sick and near death, but they are all hysterically happy all the time and completely ignorant of their terrible material circumstances, because they get to listen to the chanticleer all day. The sick wife and the four sick children lie in bed together beyond a curtain that divides the room. Trumpet lives in the house and keeps coming into the sickroom to hop on the bed and crow. The narrator asks Merrymusk if it's a good idea to have the cock crowing all the time in a sickroom, but Merrymusk insists it revitalizes them all: "Don't *you* like it? Don't it do *you* good? Ain't it inspiring? Don't it impart pluck? Give stuff against despair?" ("Cock," 1222). The children's "little sickly" voices plead for Trumpet to sound again, and the roof shakes as he crows. The cock jumps on the sickbed: "All their wasted eyes gazed at him with a wild and spiritual delight. They seemed to sun themselves in the radiant plumage of the cock. 'Better than a 'pothecary, eh?' said Merrymusk. 'This is Dr. Cock himself'" (ibid., 1223). The narrator asks Merrymusk if there is any hope for his wife's recovery: "Not the least." What about the children then? "Very little." The narrator muses, "It must be a doleful life, then, for all concerned. This lonely solitude—this shanty—hard work—hard times" (ibid.). But no, Merrymusk insists, it's not so bad at all because he has Trumpet, who crows through the darkest moments. With this in mind, the narrator goes home, rejoicing, inspired by the cock crowing, and finds that nothing bothers him anymore, either. He has to take out another mortgage on his plantation, and some of his relatives die. But all he does is buy more beer, some stout and porter. He doesn't wear mourning for his dead family members but, out of respect for the dead, "for three days drank stout in preference to porter, stout being of the darker color" (ibid., 1224).

In the final scene of the story, awakening and death are wrapped up in each other in the most dramatic fashion. Everyone is mortally ill: "the whole house was a hospital." Merrymusk lies on a heap of old clothes on the floor. And yet Merrymusk, his wife, and the children insist they are fine and keep asking the cock to crow: "Crow, Trumpet." "All well" turn out to be Merrymusk's last words: "His head fell back. . . . Merrymusk was dead" ("Cock," 1224). The cock now continues hopping about the house, crowing, as the family continues dying off one by one. The wife listens to the cock crow, then dies, and the cock crows once again. Trumpet then perches on the bed where the dead wife and her children lie and the "pallor of the children was changed to radiance." The cock jumps up onto the children's bed and crows over and over again, "bent upon crowing the souls of the children out of their wasted bodies." Finally, "They were dead. The cock shook his plumage over them. The cock crew. It was now like a Bravo! like a Hurrah! like a Three-times-three! hip! hip! He strode out of the shanty" (ibid. 1225). The narrator follows the cock out of the hovel, and then the bird "flew upon the apex of the dwelling, spread wide his wings, sounded one supernatural note, and dropped at my feet. The cock was dead" (ibid.). The narrator buries them all together and plants a stone on their gravesite. And the story ends with wild crowing: the narrator notes, "Never since then have I felt the doleful dumps, but under all circumstances crow late and early and with a continual crow. COCK-A-DOODLE-DOO!—OO!—OO!—OO!—OO!—" (ibid. 1226). In this way "Cock" ends with an even more cadaverous triumph than "Bartleby." The landscape is littered with corpses, but it still resounds with the lusty bragging of the chanticleer, taken up by the narrator himself after the cock itself expires.

The experience of *morning* doesn't prevent *mourning*, though the Trumpet of awakening might sound throughout that process, and the path of transcendentalism still leads to the grave. And indeed, despite the comic tones of the story, Melville makes a sharp critique of the dangers of these delusions of transcendence. As long as the characters hear the call of morning, they ignore the world around them and their material and human lives worsen. As long as they are uplifted into this illusory euphoria of awakening, they don't work toward any productive change of the material and ideological conditions of their lives. Poverty figures prominently in the story, both in the narrator's debt and the family's desperate sickness. But none of them displays any critical awareness of the causes of this desperation or seems motivated to work toward changing these conditions, because of the opiate of the chanticleer and the delusion of awakening to a morning beyond this world. This is the ultimate critique Melville makes of both Emerson and Thoreau: in his view, transcendentalism fosters a kind of quietistic, complacent, passive, and comfortable disposition that makes us think we can rise above our own bodies, human needs, material conditions, and worldly conventions. But for Melville there is no escaping these aspects of life except through death. In fact, in his parodies of both Emerson and Thoreau, trying to practice these forms of transcendental awakening leads only more directly to death, given the ways that they entice his characters, from Bartleby to Merrymusk, to move above and beyond immediate material particularity in ways that lead to the neglect of the body, of relationships, of obligations, of humanity, and of the world itself.

But as "Cock" also demonstrates, Melville tends to lump Emerson and Thoreau into the same category in a way that blurs important distinctions between them, ascribing to Thoreau the same practices and transcending aims that he seems to critique in Emerson.[63] Instead, if Emerson's practices aim to transcend the immediate particularities of the material world, Thoreau's practices aim to descend into it. If Emerson's moments of awakening come through transcending the immediacy of the here and now, moving up and over material particularities, then Thoreau's moments of awakening come from digging more deeply into those immediate particularities. If Emerson is properly understood in terms of these transcending motions and visual practices, Thoreau is really more of a "descendentalist," moving down and more deeply to be awakened by the world immediately around him. In these ways Melville actually has more sympathies with Thoreau than he himself seems to have appreciated, and both Melville and Thoreau are similarly critical of Emerson's abstract idealism in similar ways. But Melville is not attentive to these distinctions, unsurprisingly perhaps, given how the conventional wisdom of the day said that Thoreau was a weak imitator of Emerson and given how Melville might have known about Thoreau primarily through hearsay and the gossip of mutual acquaintances, whereas we know he actually did read Emerson's work and hear him lecture.

Cadaverous Triumphs and Mourning Morning

Melville seems sensitive to many of the same problems that Emerson and Thoreau are concerned with, but deeply skeptical of the lusty bragging about transcendence and awakening that he hears from them. Melville seems attracted by these thinkers' emphasis on creative originality and unorthodox self-trust and compelled by the call both Emerson and Thoreau issue to engage in practices intended to awaken to a morning beyond the conventional authorities of their day. He seems to find Emerson especially attractive in this regard, while not taking Thoreau quite as seriously. Melville wants to affirm the critiques of convention and authority that Emerson and Thoreau advance, to sympathize with the feelings of alienation and estrangement that both convey. But he can't share their optimism: Melville criticizes transcendental theory and practice as a dangerous and deluded denial of our necessarily embodied and embedded condition in a world of pain and suffering. In "Bartleby" and "Cock," any transcendence of this world is a transcendence unto death, and any illusion of triumphant awakening is ultimately cadaverous.

A passage from "Cock-A-Doodle-Doo!" captures Melville's reluctant doubt nicely. The narrator describes how world affairs of late have been characterized by some "rascally despotisms" being "knocked on the head" by "high-spirited revolts" while some "high-spirited travelers" have also been "knocked on the head." Likewise, the narrator's "private affairs were also full of despotisms, casualties, and knockings on the head," and the world forced him into a "toiling posture" that "brought my head pretty well earthward, as if I were in the act of butting it against the world." But rather than asserting that these hard material realities can be overcome, Melville's narrator says he "marked the fact, but only grinned at it with a ghastly grin" ("Cock," 1203). All in all, Melville seems to think that we do have the capacity to revolt and knock the rascals and despots of the world on the head, but nothing we do can awaken us from or transcend the pain and suffering of our immediate material world: nothing we do can protect us from just being knocked back on the head in response.

Notes

I am grateful to Jason Frank, Walt Herbert, Elizabeth Stockton, Isis Leslie, and David Rando for their careful reading and helpful suggestions, all of which greatly strengthened the essay. Thanks to Susan McWilliams and the other participants of the APSA panel titled "American Tragedy: The Political Thought of Herman Melville." Finally, Wouter Van Erve valuably contributed to this project as my research assistant during the summer of 2010.

1. Duyckinck corresponded with both Thoreau and Melville and was once a good friend to Melville, though they later had a falling-out, seemingly because Duyckinck was deeply critical and skeptical of Emerson and began to see too much transcendentalism in Melville's writing. Duyckinck was also probably familiar with Thoreau's anonymous contributions to various magazines and journals, and his own paper printed a review of *A Week on the Concord and Merrimack Rivers.* Duyckinck also had one of the best private libraries in the country at the time, and Melville borrowed books from him, including Thoreau's *Week*, "because Duyckinck told him there was a section on Mount Greylock in it." Hershel Parker, *Herman Melville: A Biography*, vol. 1, *1819–1851* (Baltimore: Johns Hopkins University Press, 1996), 740. See also Parker, *Herman Melville: A Biography*, vol. 2, *1851–1891* (Baltimore: Johns Hopkins University Press, 2002). Horace Greeley was another common acquaintance: Greeley "had known Melville's brother Gansevoort rather well" and "began using his New York *Tribune* to 'get Thoreau's name before the public and create an audience for him' as early as 1848." Hershel Parker,

"Melville's Satire of Emerson and Thoreau: An Evaluation of the Evidence," *American Transcendental Quarterly* 7, no. 2 (1970): 65.

2. Nathaniel Hawthorne was one of Melville's closest friends and also one of the writers he most admired. But Hawthorne also represented a strong connection to Concord and to Emerson and Thoreau, renting Emerson's family home in Concord and writing *Mosses from an Old Manse* there, which Melville read along with its allusion to Thoreau in the dedication. In addition, Hawthorne and Thoreau were walking and boating partners, and Hawthorne even purchased the small boat Thoreau built, *The Lilypad*. Elizabeth Peabody, Sophia Hawthorne's sister, was another point of connection: for example, she edited the volume titled *Aesthetic Papers*, in which Thoreau's "Resistance to Civil Government" was first published.

3. Matthiessen sees Melville's writing as a "reaction" to Emersonian transcendentalism. F. O. Matthiessen, *American Renaissance: Art and Expression in the Age of Emerson and Whitman* (New York: Oxford University Press, 1941), 184. Others amplify the attraction angle and downplay the repulsion, such as Perry Miller, who argues that both *Moby-Dick* and *Pierre* are to the end "'defiantly' and 'unrepentantly' Transcendental." Perry Miller, "Melville and Transcendentalism," *Virginia Quarterly Review* 29 (Autumn 1953): 556–575. In more recent variations on this theme, John Williams discusses *Mardi*, *Redburn*, *White-Jacket*, and *Moby-Dick* to argue that these works derive their force from the "white fire" of transcendentalism and to show how Melville responded to, absorbed, and transformed ideas and images from Emerson. John B. Williams, *White Fire: The Influence of Emerson on Melville* (Long Beach: California State University, Long Beach, 1991). Similarly, Michael McLoughlin argues that Melville saw self-reliance and nonconformity in a positive light in his early "Transcendental novels of the sea," but he then developed an increasingly antitranscendentalist philosophical position in his later works. Michael McLoughlin, *Dead Letters to the New World: Melville, Emerson, and American Transcendentalism* (New York: Routledge, 2003).

4. In a 1946 piece tracing Melville's reception of transcendentalism in this novel, Egbert Oliver argues that the character Mark Winsome, the mystic, parodies Emerson "with pointed directness" to criticize Emerson's view on the beneficence of Nature, his cold intellectualism and asceticism, his indifference toward poverty, and his lack of compassion, and he asserts that his disciple, Egbert, is "explicitly based" on Henry David Thoreau. Egbert S. Oliver, "Melville's Picture of Emerson and Thoreau in *The Confidence-Man*," *College English* 8, no. 2 (November 1946): 61–72. For different reasons, Hershel Parker is also persuaded that Mark Winsome represents a satire on Emerson's sense of man's innate goodness and thinks evidence can be marshaled to argue that Egbert the disciple is a caricature of Thoreau. Parker, "Melville's Satire," 3. Elizabeth Foster also argues that Winsome is a portrait of Emerson, though she disagrees that Egbert caricatures Thoreau: Foster

thinks that *both* Winsome and Egbert represent Emerson's philosophy; Winsome represents the metaphysics and the abstract philosophy, and Egbert represents the ethics and the practical effects. Melville, *The Confidence-Man,* ed. Elizabeth S. Foster (New York: Hendricks House, 1954), lxix.

5. In a 1948 piece Egbert Oliver argues that Thoreau's *A Week on the Concord and Merrimack Rivers* was the "source" for "Cock-A-Doodle-Doo!"—motivating Melville's satire and furnishing the language, symbols, and details of the story. Egbert S. Oliver, "'Cock-A-Doodle-Doo!' and Transcendental Hocus-Pocus," *New England Quarterly* 21, no. 2 (June 1948): 204–216. William Bysshe Stein agrees that "Cock" is a satire on Thoreau, but he argues instead that it was "directly" inspired by "Walking" and that Melville "was thinking of" this essay when he composed his short story. William Bysshe Stein, "Melville Roasts Thoreau's Cock," *Modern Language Notes* 74 (March 1959): 218–219. Sidney Moss, however, disagrees with the thesis that "Cock" is a satire on Thoreau, seeing it instead as a comedic celebration of life and arguing that, at the time, Thoreau wasn't even well known enough to be parodied. Sidney Moss, "'Cock-A-Doodle-Doo!' and Some Legends in Melville Scholarship," *American Literature* 40, no. 2 (May 1968): 192–210. Hershel Parker disagrees with Moss on these points and thinks Melville was indeed on occasion satirizing transcendentalism, but he also valuably reminds us that "with such contextual arguments we are always partly at the mercy of what record, if any, chances to survive." Parker, "Melville's Satire," 66.

6. Christopher W. Sten, "Bartleby the Transcendentalist: Melville's Dead Letter to Emerson," *Modern Language Quarterly* 35 (1974): 30–44. For example, Sten argues that "a comparative examination" suggests that Melville had read "The Transcendentalist" and speculates that he "read it with care." First, Sten contends that Melville used Emerson's depiction of the idealist in this essay as a model for the spiritual Bartleby, who shuns the material world. Second, Melville used Emerson's "materialist" as a model for the lawyer, an agent of the economic institutions of Wall Street. And finally, Melville used Emerson's "self-dependence" as a model for Bartleby's ethics: Emerson's "I do not wish" statements are seen as a model for Bartleby's refusals. Ultimately, Sten sees the figure of Bartleby as Melville's critique of Emerson's transcendentalism: the scrivener's extreme rejection of the material world and "his attempt to be absolutely free, pure, and self-reliant—leads to his premature death," which shows how a "seemingly innocent ethical theory, even the apparently healthy 'American' one of self-reliance, can in practice be quite deadly" (ibid., 39). But, though this would seem to be the centerpiece of his argument, Sten also notes that it is "difficult to detail the similarities between Melville's portrayal of Bartleby and Emerson's portrayal of the idealist because Bartleby, virtually speechless and impassive, gives us little from which to intuit his philosophical position" (ibid., 36). Still, he goes on to say, "Bartleby's ethics,

like his metaphysics, are evidently those of the Transcendentalist, for he is similarly 'self-dependent'" (ibid., 38). My own argument is somewhat in sympathy with Sten's, but whereas Sten bases his argument on parallels between Emerson's refusals and Bartleby's refusals, I show how Melville's engagement with Emerson plays out through a critique of transcendental practices of awakening, such as "sitting at home," the visual practice of "focal distancing," and abstraction generally.

7. Francine Puk also argues that Emerson's transcendental doctrines were "uppermost in Melville's mind when he wrote 'Bartleby,'" but she thinks the "source" essay was actually "Self-Reliance": for her, Melville's story "rebuts" and "refutes" Emerson by critically exploring the destructive consequences of a radical application of his dictum that "what I must do is all that concerns me, not what people think." Francine S. Puk, "Bartleby the Scrivener: A Study in Self-Reliance," *Delta* 7 (1978): 7–20.

8. Egbert Oliver sees Thoreau as the "source" for "Bartleby" and thinks that the scrivener's aloofness, withdrawal, and noncooperation are modeled on Thoreau's passive resistance and refusals. Egbert S. Oliver, "A Second Look at 'Bartleby,'" *College English* 6 (1945): 431–439. Similarly, Robert Morseberger argues that it "seems almost inevitable" that Melville had Thoreau's work "distinctly in mind" in writing his story because Bartleby's denial "has an affirmative quality, as it did when Thoreau refused to pay taxes to a government that supported slavery and war." Robert Morseberger, "'I Prefer Not To': Melville and the Theme of Withdrawal," *University College Quarterly* 10 (January 1965): 25. Frederick Busch sees "Bartleby" as a tale of modern political alienation, in which Bartleby carries out the threat of passive resistance and disobedience that Thoreau articulates in "Civil Disobedience." Frederick Busch, "Thoreau and Melville as Cellmates," *Modern Fiction Studies* 23 (Summer 1973): 239–242.

9. Michael Rogin's *Subversive Genealogy: The Politics and Art of Herman Melville* (New York: Knopf, 1983) is significant for my purposes, given some key similarities but sharp differences between our interpretations of "Bartleby." Rogin undertakes a reading of "Bartleby" that is situated in the economic, political, and historical context of modernization. For Rogin, following György Lukács's analysis of the "modern hero," Bartleby's absence of personal history and particular qualities and his inability to enter into relationships or have contact with the world situate him in modernity and mark him as an inhabitant of the American mass society that Tocqueville feared. Rogin asserts, "The power of Melville's short story comes from its abstractness. By resituating *Bartleby* historically, we can see it as a comment on the historical triumph of abstraction" (ibid., 194). Rogin shows how the "failure of political reforms, alluded to in *Bartleby,* confines the scrivener and his employer in the office they share. Economic relations replace political dreams," and Bartleby's employer is "master over a refractory slave" who first copies him and

then "withdraws his labor," appropriating the "lawyer's identity by refusing to copy him" and thus gaining a "cadaverous triumph" over the lawyer (ibid.). But Rogin also sees the scrivener as Melville's critical psychological analysis—and subversion—of Thoreau's civil disobedience and passive resistance. Rogin sees Bartleby's "I prefer not to" as an echo of Thoreau's "I simply wish to refuse allegiance." Ultimately, Rogin sees Bartleby as an inverted copy of Thoreau that Melville uses to expose "the passive aggression which lies behind nonviolent resistance" and to highlight the pure negativity of Bartleby's position and its resistance to colonization, but also its ultimately destructive consequences (ibid., 195). I agree with Rogin that "Bartleby" highlights a deep tension between the abstracting tendencies of modernity and immediate material particularity, but I see this dynamic playing out in a different way in the story. If Rogin views Melville as critically engaging the abstracting tendencies of modernity through the figure of Bartleby and his lack of particular qualities—"I am not particular," the scrivener insists several times—I also see this concern with abstract universals and material particularity as part and parcel of Melville's critical engagement with Emerson's own transcending idealist gaze, which itself bears some features of the violent tendencies that Rogin associates with modern industrialism. Thus, our concern with the way themes of abstraction are criticized in the story is sympathetic, but Rogin and I make different arguments about how Melville undertakes these challenges and how they relate to his reception of transcendentalism. If Rogin sees the figure of Bartleby as a subversion of Thoreau and his practice of civil disobedience, I see Melville as engaging these concerns with abstraction through a parallel between Bartleby and Emerson.

10. Gregory Jay also sees Melville's "Bartleby" as a subversion of Thoreau's "Civil Disobedience" that takes shape around the very different ways each text responds to the problem of authority. For Jay, Thoreau also refuses the authority of the state, the conventional economy, and mainstream society, but in a way that is fraught by a gender anxiety that fears emasculation and asserts manhood through disobedience, thus still working within the conventions of authority he aims to subvert. In contrast, Bartleby's negation is more radical and wholesale, and his "withdrawal from writing and his refusal to copy may well be read as a willed disobedience to every prescription in his culture's 'general text.'" Gregory S. Jay, *America the Scrivener: Deconstruction and the Subject of Literary History* (Ithaca: Cornell University Press, 1990), 21.

11. Branka Arsi makes seven and a half wholly different interpretations of what might be going on in this short story, linking Bartleby to passivity, the impersonal, melancholy and madness, drugs, addiction, sexuality, ethics, and friendship. Importantly, Arsi doesn't try to pin Bartleby down, to categorize him, but sees the story as open to all these sometimes competing and even contradictory possibili-

ties; she does, however, briefly discuss the links between Bartleby and Thoreau, though they are not a focus of her argument. Branka Arsi, *Passive Constitutions: 7½ Times Bartleby* (Stanford: Stanford University Press, 2007).

12. I explore Emerson's practice of "focal distancing" in greater depth and analyze different implications of this idealist gaze elsewhere. See Shannon Mariotti, "The Death of the First-Born Son: Emerson's 'Focal Distancing,' Du Bois' 'Second Sight,' and Disruptive Particularity," *Political Theory* 37, no. 3 (June 2009): 351–374; Mariotti, "Emerson's Transcendental Gaze and the 'Disagreeable Particulars' of Slavery: Vision and the Costs of Idealism," in *A Political Companion to Ralph Waldo Emerson,* ed. Alan M. Levine and Daniel S. Malachuk (Lexington: University Press of Kentucky, 2011); and Mariotti, *Thoreau's Democratic Withdrawal: Alienation, Participation, and Modernity* (Madison: University of Wisconsin Press, 2010).

13. Parker, *Herman Melville: A Biography,* 1:618.

14. Sophia Hawthorne wrote in a letter to her sister Elizabeth that one morning Melville "shut himself into the boudoir & read Mr. Emerson's Essays in presence of our beautiful picture." This picture was an engraving of Raphael's *The Transformation,* a gift from Emerson. Looking at this picture, Hershel Parker notes, also "occasioned some stories from Hawthorne, and especially from Sophia, about their stay in the Old Manse in Concord and their acquaintance with Emerson and his followers, such as Thoreau and the young William Ellery Channing." Ibid., 776.

15. Also cited in Andrew Delbanco, *Melville: His World and Work* (New York: Knopf, 2005), 252–253.

16. I discuss the following texts in my discussion of Emerson: Ralph Waldo Emerson, "The Transcendentalist," in *Nature, Addresses, and Lectures,* vol. 1 of *The Collected Works of Ralph Waldo Emerson,* ed. Alfred R. Ferguson (Cambridge: Belknap Press of Harvard University Press, 1971); Emerson, "Experience," in *Essays: Second Series,* ed. Joseph Slater (Cambridge: Belknap Press of Harvard University Press, 1983); Emerson, "Self-Reliance" and "Heroism," in *Essays: First Series,* ed. Joseph Slater (Cambridge: Belknap Press of Harvard University Press, 1979); Emerson, *Nature,* in Ferguson, *Nature, Addresses, and Lectures.*

17. Emerson, "Transcendentalist," 203.

18. Emerson, "Experience," 41.

19. Emerson, "Self-Reliance," 41.

20. Ibid., 46.

21. Emerson, "Heroism," 152.

22. Emerson, *Nature,* 45.

23. Ibid., 10.

24. Emerson, "Experience," 30.

25. William Braswell, "Melville as a Critic of Emerson," *American Literature* 9 (November 1937): 326.

26. Ibid., 325.

27. For a full list of Emerson's marginalia, see Jay Leyda, *The Melville Log: A Documentary Life of Herman Melville, 1819–1891,* 2 vols. (1951; repr., New York: Gordian Press, 1969), and Braswell, "Melville as a Critic of Emerson." Melville made many marginal comments in dialogue with Emerson's ideas, but sixteen of the thirty essays remain unmarked, including "Compensation," "Self-Reliance," and "The Over-Soul." This may mean that Melville did not read these essays, that he read them but did not mark them, or (more likely) that he had already read them and so did not reread them when he purchased his own volumes.

28. Leyda, *The Melville Log,* 1:287. Melville heard Emerson on February 5, 1849, in James F. Clarke's Freeman Place chapel in Boston, in a lecture titled "Mind & Manners in the 19th Century."

29. Quoted in Parker, *Herman Melville: A Biography,* 1:618; emphasis in original.

30. Ibid. Melville's resistance to the optimistic, universalizing tendencies of romanticism and idealism also comes through in a letter he wrote to Nathaniel Hawthorne in the summer of 1851 regarding Goethe's injunction to "live in the all." Melville writes: "This 'all' feeling, there is some truth in it. You must have often felt it, lying on the grass on a warm summer's day. Your legs seem to send shoots into the earth. Your hair feels like leaves upon your head. This is the *all* feeling. But what plays the mischief with the truth is that men will insist upon the universal application of a temporary feeling or opinion." *The Letters of Herman Melville,* ed. Merrell R. Davis and William H. Gilman (New Haven: Yale University Press, 1960), 131. Thanks to Walt Herbert for bringing this letter to my attention.

31. Braswell, "Melville as a Critic of Emerson," 330.

32. Leyda, *The Melville Log,* 2:648.

33. Herman Melville, "Bartleby the Scrivener," in *Pierre, Israel Potter, The Piazza Tales, The Confidence-Man, Uncollected Prose, Billy Budd* (New York: Library of America, 1984); hereafter cited parenthetically in the text by title and page number.

34. Sharon Cameron, "The Way of Life by Abandonment: Emerson's Impersonal," in Cameron, *Impersonality: Seven Essays* (Chicago: University of Chicago Press, 2007).

35. Emerson, *Nature,* 10.

36. Leyda, *The Melville Log,* 1:291.

37. Braswell, "Melville as a Critic of Emerson," 323.

38. Ibid., 330.

39. Ibid., 324.

40. Emerson, *Nature,* 10.

41. For valuable historically situated and deeply contextual analyses of "Bartleby," see, in addition to Michael Rogin's *Subversive Genealogy,* Barbara Foley's "From Wall Street to Astor Place: Historicizing Melville's 'Bartleby,'" *American Literature* 72, no. 2 (March 2000): 87–116; David Kuebrich's "Melville's Doctrine of Assumptions: The Hidden Ideology of Capitalist Production in 'Bartleby,'" *New England Quarterly* 69, no. 3 (September 1996): 381–405; Michael Gilmore's "'Bartleby the Scrivener' and the Transformation of the Economy" in Gilmore, *American Romanticism and the Marketplace* (Chicago: University of Chicago Press, 1985); Louise Barnett's "Bartleby as Alienated Worker," *Studies in Short Fiction* 11 (Fall 1974): 379–395; Leo Marx's "Melville's Parable of the Walls," in *Bartleby the Inscrutable: A Collection of Commentary on Herman Melville's Tale "Bartleby the Scrivener,"* ed. M. T. Inge (Hamden, Conn.: Archon Books, 1970).

42. Braswell, "Melville as a Critic of Emerson," 326.

43. See, for example, Ronald Wesley Hoag, "The Corpse in the Office: Mortality, Mutability, and Salvation in 'Bartleby the Scrivener,'" *ESQ* 38, no. 2 (1992): 119–142.

44. Parker, "Melville's Satire," 66.

45. Herman Melville, "Cock-A-Doodle-Doo!," in *Pierre, Israel Potter, The Piazza Tales, The Confidence-Man, Uncollected Prose, Billy Budd;* hereafter cited parenthetically in the text by title and page number.

46. Parker, *Herman Melville: A Biography,* 1:827.

47. Matthiessen, *American Renaissance,* 196.

48. Parker, *Herman Melville: A Biography,* 1:827.

49. Matthiessen, *American Renaissance,* 230.

50. Ibid., 196.

51. Parker, "Melville's Satire," 65.

52. Parker, *Herman Melville: A Biography,* 1:744.

53. Ibid.

54. If the figure of Bartleby reflects a kind of abstract, cerebral, and impersonal motionlessness that might be associated with Emerson, Thoreau seems more embodied, full of movement, virility, and a kind of surging life force that might also be associated with masculinity and the phallus. Yet "Cock-A-Doodle-Doo!" mocks the kind of lusty male bragging that Thoreau himself, as we saw above, celebrated. The term *cock* would have had these connotations in Melville's day. As the *Oxford English Dictionary* indicates, the word *cock* has long applied to the male of a species of fowl; the earliest written reference goes back to circa 897. But it has also been used figuratively to apply to human males at least since Chaucer's time and to designate someone with pluck and spirit. But the word has also been a slang

term for a penis since at least 1618. These especially male qualities of vitality are evoked in Melville's story, in an entirely unsubtle way, through the figure of the cock. Indeed, it is impossible to forget that the central figure of Melville's story is a *cock.* There are pages and pages of admiring descriptions of the bird, and it is never described in any other term: never a rooster, not a bird, not even a chanticleer, but always simply a cock.

55. Thoreau, *Walden* (1854), ed. J. Lyndon Shanley (Princeton: Princeton University Press, 1971), 204, 84.

56. Ibid., 127.

57. Ibid.

58. Thoreau, "Walking," in *Collected Essays and Poems*, ed. Elizabeth Hall Witherell (New York: Library of America, 2001), 254.

59. Ibid., 254.

60. Ibid.

61. Thoreau, *Walden,* 115.

62. Ibid., 121.

63. For further discussion of key differences between Emerson and Thoreau, see Mariotti, *Thoreau's Democratic Withdrawal.*

7

Language and Labor, Silence and Stasis

Bartleby among the Philosophers

Kevin Attell

> The Stoic [placed felicity] in philosophic pride,
> By him called virtue; and his virtuous man,
> Wise, perfect in himself, and all possessing,
> Equal to God, oft shames not to prefer,
> As fearing God nor man, contemning all
> Wealth, pleasure, pain or torment, death and life,
> Which when he lists, he leaves, or boasts he can,
> For all his tedious talk is but vain boast,
> Or subtle shifts conviction to evade.
>
> —John Milton, *Paradise Regained*

Is there a single short story of the American nineteenth century that has generated as much critical commentary over the last half century, and from such a wide range of disciplinary perspectives, as "Bartleby the Scrivener"? To mention just a few examples: Bartleby the impassive employee has been seen as an alienated proletarian laborer and his inertia in the law office as a figure for a revolutionary disruption of commerce and the capitalist system; Bartleby and his employer have been traced to various real people, including Melville's friends Eli James Fly and George J. Adler and several of the many lawyers in Melville's family; Bartleby has been read as an ironic portrait of Thoreau in his civil disobedience, of Emerson and his aloof transcendental sages, and of Melville himself, the maniacally prolific writer (his entire career as a novelist lasting only twelve years) who eventually fell into silence and a dull desk job (see, for example, Shannon L. Mariotti's essay in this volume); Bartleby has been cast as an existentialist antihero; he has played Oedipus to the lawyer's Laius in psychoanalytical readings; he has served as a case study in anorexia, catatonia, and schizophrenia; deconstructive critics have seen the scrivener as an allegorical figure for *différance,* the unstoppable movement and displacement within signifying systems that undermine all appeals to stable meaning; and in its narrative of mysterious suffering and final self-sacrifice, Bartleby's story has been read as a Passion or *imitatio Christi.*[1] Bartleby, that is to say, has been many things to many people, a sort of Galatea, as J. Hillis Miller suggests in his book *Versions of Pygmalion,* with all the ambivalences that that object of desire entails.[2]

Perhaps more curious than this explosion of critical interest is the great fortune—possibly greater than that of any other single text in American literature—"Bartleby" has enjoyed among European philosophers over the last thirty years. That "Bartleby the Scrivener" is in some way a philosophical story has of course been an axiom of the critical commentary for quite some time. And indeed, as the epigraph to this essay suggests, Bartleby's signature phrase—"I would prefer not to"—might plausibly be read as an oblique reference, via Milton, to the same Stoic philosophy alluded to even more elliptically by the bust of Cicero that momentarily occupies Bartleby's gaze in the lawyer's office.[3] Limiting oneself, however, to major contemporary Continental theorists who have commented on the tale, one must list Maurice Blanchot, Gilles Deleuze, Jacques Derrida, Giorgio Agamben, Michael Hardt and Antonio Negri, and Slavoj Žižek. And here Galatea becomes a Rorschach test, as commentary on "Bartleby" affords the occasion for these thinkers to present key ideas from their own conceptual repertoires as well as elliptically polemicize with one another.

Out of this constellation of philosophical readings of "Bartleby" two main lines of interpretation emerge. On the one hand, there is the question of language and the withdrawal of language (or language of withdrawal) represented by both Bartleby's signature phrase and his eventual silence; on the other, there is the question of human action or labor and its disruption or reformulation in Bartleby's mechanical repetition as a copyist and final unwillingness to do even this. Two rubrics, then, and two negations: language and silence, labor and stasis.

Language and Silence

Gilles Deleuze

Deleuze's essay "Bartleby; or, The Formula" first appeared in 1989 as an afterword to a French translation of "Bartleby," "The Encantadas," and "The Bell-Tower," and it was later revised and republished in *Critique et clinique* in 1993. As the title of the piece suggests, Deleuze's central point of concern is what he calls Bartleby's "formula," that is, his signature phrase. He begins the piece, however, by setting out some general reading protocols, namely, that "Bartleby" is neither a metaphorical nor a symbolic tale but rather a "violently comical text," and that as a comical text it is absolutely *literal*.[4] The tale, he writes, "means only what it says, literally. And what it says and repeats is *I would prefer not to.*"[5] Though this opening gesture is made quickly, it is worth emphasizing how important this concept of literality is for Deleuze's reading and for the argument he ultimately makes for the politically disruptive power of Melville's text. For it is here that we are notified that what follows will be a reading of Bartleby's formula as a linguistic-syntactic operation. The "violence" of Bartleby's comedy is the linguistic—*literal*—violence that this formula wreaks on all hegemonic and majoritarian linguistic and political formations, whether they be those of—in expanding concentric circles—the law office, Wall Street, New York's Halls of Justice, America, or the West. As Deleuze points out, Bartleby's preference not to do anything but copy, and eventually not even to copy at all, disrupts the smooth functioning of the law office; it confounds the attorney, provokes the other employees to near violence, and even causes the attorney to move his offices to another location when Bartleby obstinately will not leave after being fired. And the operator or focal point of this disruptiveness is, of course, the formula "I would prefer not to." "Without a doubt," he writes, "the formula is ravaging, devastating, and leaves nothing standing in its wake."[6]

Why does the phrase wreak such havoc? Deleuze argues that the famous phrase functions as an "agrammatical formula," that is, as a construction that lies at or just beyond the limit of a set of syntactically-grammatically correct expressions. Though Bartleby's "I would prefer not to" is not in fact ungrammatical or incorrect, Deleuze nevertheless notes that there is a "certain mannerism, a certain solemnity" in the phrase, and that the attorney and his other employees find it "queer" and do not—or claim not to—ever use it.[7] The phrase seems indeed to ring oddly in the hearers' ears, and in this sense, Deleuze argues, it "has the same force, the same role, as an *agrammatical* formula," standing by analogy as the "limit of a series such as 'I would prefer this. I would prefer not to do that. That is not what I would prefer . . .'"[8]

There are two distinct frames within which Deleuze situates the disruptive power of Bartleby's quasi-agrammatical formula, though they can each be seen as a modulation or recalibration of the other. They might be called the *linguistic frame* and the *literary frame.* On the one hand, Deleuze analyzes the ambiguous logical or propositional status of the formula itself, emphasizing the difficulties involved in assigning it any clear linguistic status as an utterance. On the other hand, the unease that the formula produces at the level of the sentence stands as an example or metonymy of the unease Melville's entire literary practice produces in the field of English-language literature. This latter is a question of what Deleuze calls "minor literature," and it will, for Deleuze, place Melville squarely within a tradition that also includes, among others, Beckett, Celine, Artaud, and, above all, Kafka.

First, let us take the linguistic frame. At the level of the statement, Deleuze argues, the disruptive power of the formula lies in its being an utterance that cannot be easily placed in any system of either (1) propositional and representational truth or (2) performative speech. In the first case, as a statement concerning two possibilities (that is, what would be preferred and what would not be preferred), Deleuze notes that it is neither an affirmation nor a negation. Unlike, say, "I do not want to" or "I refuse to," or even "I would rather," Bartleby's formula never settles on any affirmation—including, and especially, the affirmation of his preference solely to keep copying: "You *will* not?" asks the lawyer; "I *prefer* not," replies Bartleby ("Bartleby," 648; emphases in original). Indeed, Bartleby never states a preference *for* copying, and soon enough that activity, too, gets swept up into the space of inactivity that is Bartleby's defining gesture. In a sense Bartleby's eventual ceasing even to copy is already written into the formula, which "not only abolishes the term it refers to, and that it rejects, but also abolishes the other term it seemed to preserve, and that becomes impossible. In fact, it renders them indistinct."[9] As a statement the formula "excludes all alternatives, and devours what it claims to preserve no less than it distances itself from everything else. . . . [It] hollows out a zone of indetermination that renders words indistinguishable, that creates a vacuum within language [*langage*]."[10] What is expressed in the formula, then, is not a will for the negative or a nihilism, but something even stranger, something that entails no will at all. In the formula we see "not a will to nothingness, but the growth of a nothingness of the will. . . . Pure patient passivity, as Blanchot would say. Being as being, and nothing more."[11] "I would prefer not to" is the index of a patience and a passivity beyond even the dialectic between passivity and activity, between choosing to and choosing not to.

Blanchot invokes Bartleby as a figure for such a radical passivity in *The Writing of the Disaster* (1980), in which he anticipates in a very condensed form Deleuze's analysis of the formula's neither-active-nor-passive grammatical construction. And like Deleuze, Blanchot proposes that Bartleby's phrase expresses a patience and a passivity that are more radically neutral than merely the negation of any given positive activity. Indeed, being bound by our philosophical tradition to thinking of passivity as simply the "contrary of activity" is, for Blanchot, a defining characteristic of the "ever-restricted field of our reflections," beginning, presumably, as early as the principle of noncontradiction.[12] By contrast, Blanchot's reflections, here and in many other texts, are tasked with the thinking of a nondialectical and nonoppositional negativity, of a patience that "opens me entirely, all the way to a passivity which is the *pas* ['not'] in the utterly passive, and which has therefore abandoned the level of life where *passive* would simply be the opposite of *active*."[13]

In this sense, Blanchot introduces the insight that Deleuze will later develop, in that he identifies in the grammar of Bartleby's formula, which has "none of the simplicity of a refusal," precisely this step beyond refusal or will-to-the-negative and into the radically neutral.[14] He writes: "This is the core of refusal which Bartleby the scrivener's inexorable 'I would prefer not to' expresses: an abstention which has never had to be decided upon, which precedes all decisions and which is not so much a denial as, more than that, an abdication. . . . 'I will not do it' would still have signified an energetic determination, calling forth an equally energetic contradiction. 'I would prefer not to . . .' belongs to the infiniteness of patience; no dialectical intervention can take hold of such passivity."[15] This "pure patient passivity," then, is the strange ontological ground, neither positive nor negative, out of which the peculiar grammar of Bartleby's formula arises. To what is Bartleby referring when he says, "I would prefer not to"? It is true that at first it is to correcting his copy, but as the formula eventually overtakes every specific option presented to Bartleby, it becomes evident that the radical though "not particular" ("Bartleby," 667) negation of Bartleby's quasi-agrammatical phrase encompasses all specific references and propositions, that is to say, the entire logic of symbolic representation itself. This, on Deleuze's reading, is the first way in which the formula hollows out a zone of indetermination or vacuum within language.

In addition to upsetting the notion of a propositional model of linguistic truth, however, the phrase is equally disruptive of the logic of the speech act, as analyzed most famously by J. L. Austin in *How to Do Things with Words*. In this text Austin makes a fundamental distinction between what he calls the "constative" function of language—broadly speaking, the use of language to make statements—and the "performative" function. Performative utterances are not statements of fact or descriptions of states of affairs; rather, they are acts of language—speech acts—that by virtue of their own taking place bring about facts or states of affairs. Performative speech acts, then, cannot be evaluated as either true or false on the model of a propositional or constative statement, and for this reason Austin instead proposes the notions of "felicity" and "infelicity." The infelicitous speech act is not a false utterance but one that does not work; it "misfires" and is therefore voided or vitiated.

The specific nature of Austin's criteria for the felicitous speech act is directly relevant for Deleuze's reading of Bartleby's formula, and this is because a speech act can be felicitous only if it is uttered under certain necessary conventional conditions.[16] The point to emphasize here is not the completeness or imperviousness of Austin's "felicity conditions" but the way the logic of the performative blurs the distinction between words and things. Instead of the word either accurately or inaccurately representing the thing, in the performative act we have a functional interdependence of the spoken word and the seemingly extralinguistic world in which it is embedded. Performative utterances are not true or false; they either work or do not work depending on whether they are uttered properly in certain necessary conventional socio-politico-linguistic conditions.

This, Deleuze argues, is the second linguistic logic that Bartleby's formula unsettles, and it is perhaps in its disruption of the performative function of language that the formula most directly enters into that "passive resistance" that the lawyer claims "so aggravates an earnest person"

("Bartleby," 646). In stubbornly reiterating his formula, Bartleby views with complete indifference all the conditions necessary for the speech act to function and thus severely undermines not only the logic of the speech act itself, but all the conventions of the social contract. As Bartleby's repeated response to every command, order, request, pronouncement, and promise of the lawyer, the formula seems to neglect and thus short-circuit all the social and conventional presuppositions that are required for the felicitous speech act to take place. Bartleby is the attorney's employee; his context is the law office; he has a professional, economic, social, contractual relation to the lawyer, his boss; and yet his obstinately repeated formula demolishes everything the lawyer might reasonably expect of his employee as a result of his speech acts.[17]

The lawyer in fact rightly interprets why his speech acts misfire. He has wrongly believed that Bartleby is a full participant in the act, that he and Bartleby have assumed the same conventions, and that a new state of affairs (say, Bartleby's dismissal and departure) would be smoothly ushered in by the felicitous performative. As the lawyer complacently muses to himself after calmly firing Bartleby, "Without loudly bidding Bartleby depart—as an inferior genius might have done—I *assumed* the ground that depart he must; and upon that assumption built all I had to say" ("Bartleby," 658; emphasis in original). Yet when that procedure turns out to have failed, the lawyer is quick to pinpoint the reason: "My procedure seemed as sagacious as ever,—but only in theory. How it would prove in practice—there was the rub. It was truly a beautiful thought to have assumed Bartleby's departure; but after all, that assumption was simply my own, and none of Bartleby's. The great point was, not whether I had assumed that he would quit me, but whether he would prefer so to do. He was more a man of preferences than assumptions" (ibid., 658–659). All the way up to and including the ultimate performative utterance that an employer holds in reserve—namely, "You are fired!"—"the formula," Deleuze writes, "stymies all speech acts, and at the same time, it makes Bartleby a pure outsider [*exclu*] to whom no social position can be attributed. This is what the attorney glimpses with dread: all his hopes of bringing Bartleby back to reason are dashed because they rest on a *logic of presuppositions* according to which an employer 'expects' to be obeyed, or a kind friend listened to, whereas Bartleby has invented a new logic, a *logic of preference*, which is enough to undermine the presuppositions of language as a whole."[18]

Bartleby's response to the lawyer's speech brings the performance, so to speak, to a crashing halt. The "doctrine of preference" implicit in his formula cannot be assimilated to what Melville calls "the doctrine of assumptions" ("Bartleby," 660), the presuppositional and conventional logic of the performative function of language, just as that very same utterance eludes any constative statement of preference for one thing over another. Thus, when viewed through the lens of either propositional logic or the pragmatics of the speech act, Bartleby's formula stands outside both constative and performative "grammar" and chips away at the very foundation of every linguistic category. As both constative and performative "agrammaticality," the formula impassively, disruptively sits there, like Bartleby himself on the banister, as a radically indeterminate linguistic event, bringing language as a whole face to face with its prereferential, preperformative, perhaps prelinguistic presuppositions.

This *linguistic frame* for Deleuze's reading of the story is preliminary to his analysis of the tale's *literary frame.* The uncomfortable linguistic status of the formula is centrally important to Deleuze's reading because it leads to his argument concerning the "foreign" languages that "minor literatures" open up within major languages and literatures: "The formula at first," he writes, "seems like a bad translation of a foreign language," but, in fact, the truth is something like the inverse of this hypothesis: "Perhaps it is the formula that carves out a kind of foreign language within language."[19] This suggestion alludes directly to an argument put forth by Deleuze and Félix Guattari in their 1975 monograph *Kafka: Toward a Minor Literature.*

For Deleuze and Guattari minor literature is a writing that creates something like an estrangement of language within the major language, a peculiar literary practice that they argue must be the starting point for any consideration of nonhegemonic writing. Deleuze and Guattari schematize three of its key characteristics, all of which will later be evoked in Deleuze's reading of Melville. In minor literatures, they argue, (1) "language is affected with a high coefficient of deterritorialization," that is to say, writers of a major language who are either displaced from the rich native soil of that language or are not members of the dominant ethnic or national identity of its speakers operate a deterritorialization on the language; (2) "everything in them is political" because, in contrast to major literatures, wherein the social milieu serves as a seemingly neutral and unproblematic backdrop against which individual or private concerns can be dramatized and narrated, the situation of minor literature is "completely different; its cramped space forces each individual intrigue to connect immediately to politics"; and (3) "everything takes on a collective value" because the impoverished conditions under which the minor author works mean that his or her authorial activity and expression are expropriated and subsumed into the collective.[20] Minor literature, in short, is a recognizable type of avant-garde or experimental literature, one whose experiments are determined by these specific conditions of lexical-syntactic impoverishment, lack of psychological interiority, and authorial collectivity or impersonality. And without having to follow Deleuze and Guattari too far into their own system or their reading of Kafka's texts, one can see clearly enough how this concept of minor literature works directly against what are traditionally some of the most valorized notions about great literature: its verbal richness, its psychological depth, and the personal genius of the individuals who write it.

This is the "literary" background for Deleuze's suggestion that Bartleby's agrammatical formula is the utterance of some sort of foreign language—an American English—within English. "Is this not," he asks rhetorically, "the schizophrenic vocation of American literature: to make the English language, by means of driftings, deviations, de-taxes or surtaxes (as opposed to the standard syntax), slip in this manner? To introduce a bit of psychosis into English neurosis?"[21] With its urban law office setting, its symmetrically organized clerks, Turkey and Nippers, its figure of patriarchal authority in the lawyer, the tale "starts off as in an English novel, in Dickens's London."[22] But Bartleby arrives, "contaminates everything" with his utterance, breaks this scene to pieces, and institutes the fractal geometry of a minor literature: "Everything began à l'anglaise but continues à l'américaine. . . . The American patchwork becomes the law of Melville's oeuvre, devoid of a center, of an upside down or right side up."[23]

In this overturning of the English novel by the American, Deleuze sees an analogy—in fact, something more than an analogy—to the American revolutionary project at its most radical, thus drawing a parallel between American literary and political form, both of which take on the shades of the "minor." He writes that "what Kafka would say about 'small nations' is what Melville had already said about the great American nation: it must become a patchwork of all small nations."[24] It is a universal political project whose exemplary figure may indeed be the patchwork itself, "the American invention *par excellence*, for the Americans invented patchwork, just as the

Swiss are said to have invented the cuckoo clock."[25] This last comment may be a joke at the expense of the Swiss, but the point being made is about all of Europe (or at least the major powers), with its political imaginary so rooted in blood and soil. Though its promise may not ultimately have been met, America nevertheless "sought to create a revolution whose strength would lie in a universal immigration, émigrés of the world."[26] And in terms that may be debatable but are nevertheless defensible (and perhaps even orthodox), this is the way Deleuze understands the early American political imagination: "Even before their independence, Americans were thinking about the combination of States, the State-form most compatible with their vocation. But their vocation was not to reconstitute an 'old State secret,' a nation, a family, a heritage, or a father. It was above all to constitute a universe, a society of brothers, a federation of men and goods, a community of anarchist individuals, inspired by Jefferson, by Thoreau, by Melville."[27]

Though as big as a continent, this is the foreign country where Melville's "minor literature" is written, written as if in a foreign language within the English canon. And while Bartleby's mutism—his broken and unresponsive speech—has often been read as a sort of pathology, his formula here stands instead as a radical cure for the America of 1853 (or 1989): "Even in his catatonic or anorexic state, Bartleby is not the patient, but the doctor of a sick America, the *Medicine-Man,* the new Christ or the brother to us all."[28]

As intimations of a new community, a new type of sociality, a new ethics, Bartleby and his formula assume in Deleuze's reading something like the contours of a philosophical self-portrait, a gesture that is shared to some degree by all the thinkers discussed in this chapter. Let us now turn to Derrida, who also reads in Bartleby's reluctance to respond a figure for an ethical-political problem, namely—and paradoxically—*responsibility.*

Jacques Derrida

Like Deleuze, Derrida in his discussion of Bartleby in *The Gift of Death* (1990) is most interested in the grammar of Bartleby's utterance, and he suggests in very similar terms that the phrase is like what Deleuze has termed agrammaticality.[29] Bartleby's equivocal phrase, he argues, may not state anything determinate, but it nevertheless "doesn't say absolutely nothing. *I would prefer not to* looks like an incomplete sentence. Its indeterminacy creates a tension: it opens onto a sort of reserve of incompleteness; it announces a temporary or provisional reserve, one involving a proviso. Can we not find there the secret of a hypothetical reference to some indecipherable providence or prudence?"[30] There are two claims being made here for the formula: (1) that the indeterminacy of the statement's modality *itself* constitutes the statement's reference, and (2) that the referent of this indeterminate grammatical openness is some sort of providence or prudence. Both these cryptic claims become clearer when they are placed in the context of Derrida's extended discussion of one of the most fundamental, and shocking, episodes in the Scriptures. Deleuze is not the first to draw an analogy between Bartleby and Christ, but Derrida is probably the first to draw one between Bartleby and Abraham, particularly Abraham in the terrible episode of the near sacrifice of Isaac on Mount Moriah. Indeed, Derrida's Bartleby appears only briefly at the end of his long reading of this episode and stands there more or less as a modern proxy for Abraham.

Abraham's sacrifice of Isaac is especially disconcerting because it is presented as an archetypal example of a moral or ethical dilemma, indeed as perhaps *the* moral or ethical dilemma, insofar as it places in irreducible conflict Abraham's responsibility to God, on the one hand, and his responsibility to his beloved son (and everyone else in his family, for that matter, or even every other person on earth) on the other. Abraham obeys God, honors his duty to obey God's command, and consents to commit a terrible act, and yet, unlike, say, Agamemnon, he is "never considered a hero. He doesn't make us shed tears and doesn't inspire admiration: rather stupefied horror, a terror that is also secret."[31] Terror, secret, responsibility, alterity: these are the coordinates of Derrida's discussion of Abraham's sacrifice, which the following few pages will review before returning to Bartleby's indeterminate phrase, which for Derrida is fundamentally a repetition or modulation of Abraham's almost total silence while undertaking the terrible task of offering God the gift of his son's death.

Upon receiving his command, Abraham keeps his intention to sacrifice Isaac a secret, but he keeps this secret in a very specific way. As Derrida notes (following Kierkegaard's reading of the episode), Abraham offers a "strange reply" to Isaac when he asks his father where they will find the lamb for the sacrifice.[32] "It can't be said," he writes, "that Abraham doesn't respond to him. He says God will provide. God will provide a lamb for the holocaust (['burnt offering'] Genesis 22:8). Abraham thus keeps his secret at the same time as he replies to Isaac. He doesn't keep silent and he doesn't lie. He doesn't speak nontruth."[33] And yet in his, to say the least, evasive reply, Abraham does not quite speak the truth, either. His utterance lies on the border between truth and untruth, between speaking and not speaking, and by not entering fully into the sphere of speech, by not communicating to others the terrible fact of his decision to kill Isaac, Abraham commits a transgression that is both linguistic and ethical. In fact, in the terms of Derrida's discussion, the two are one and the same: "Because, in this way, he doesn't speak, Abraham transgresses the ethical order. . . . By keeping the secret, Abraham, betrays ethics."[34] But what exactly does Derrida mean by the ethical order here? And why is the refusal to speak a betrayal of ethics?

At issue is a distinction (again from Kierkegaard) between the "singular" and the "general," the latter being the proper sphere of ethics insofar as it roughly corresponds to what we might call the "social," or at least the sphere in which individual singularities share a common space. And the medium of that sharing—in a sense, the substance of that common space itself—is language. By speaking (and this necessarily means speaking to others), the individual enters into and acknowledges the domain of the general at the same time he or she renounces the absoluteness of his or her singularity. Language puts the self in relation to others, and in this sense it is the ethical medium par excellence. The general is the space of commonality made both possible and necessary by language, and it is precisely what is disrupted by Abraham's refusal to speak and reveal his secret. Derrida writes: "To the extent that, in not saying the essential thing, namely the secret bond between God and him, Abraham doesn't speak, he assumes the responsibility that consists in always being alone, retrenched in one's singularity at the moment of decision. . . . But as soon as one speaks, as soon as one enters the medium of language, one loses that very singularity. . . . Speaking relieves us, Kierkegaard notes, for it 'translates' into the general."[35] By revealing his secret, Abraham would, in this sense, be shirking his responsibility to God by seeking a very tempting "relief" in the sphere of the ethical, where reasons might be given, where justifications might be offered, where forgiveness might be sought, where, in short, Abraham might confront this terrible divine imperative by bringing it out into the open. But Abraham refuses to speak, refuses to respond to Isaac. Derrida's question for Abraham here is the same one the baffled lawyer asks Bartleby: "*Why* do you refuse?" ("Bartleby," 644; emphasis in original). Why does Abraham withdraw from what would seem to be, at the very least, his ethical responsibility?

Derrida's argument plays on two apparently distinct and indeed incompatible senses of the term *responsibility*. On the one hand, there is the intimate responsibility that one is bound to as a solitary individual, a responsibility that is one's and one's alone and that cannot be mitigated or collectivized by any appeal to others (say, in the form of asking for advice or approval or assurance that one is making the right decision). On the other hand, there is the etymological sense of responsibility, the responsibility before others with whom one has a more or less mutual and symmetrical (and ultimately linguistic) relation—a relation that is at base a responsibility to respond to the other. It is this latter responsibility that Abraham evasively betrays when he answers-without-answering Isaac's question. Abraham is caught between two responsibilities, each of which appears to be a betrayal of the other.

In this characteristic gesture, Derrida identifies and puts pressure on an irresolvable aporia in this keyword for so many of the Western philosophical tradition's accounts of ethics. And it is precisely this aporetic impasse that is dramatized in the story of Abraham and Isaac, which, on Derrida's account, "can be read as a narrative development of the paradox that inhabits the concept of duty or of absolute responsibility. This concept puts us into relation (but without relating to it, in a double secret) with the absolute other, with the absolute singularity of the other, whose name here is God."[36] It is worth emphasizing Derrida's identification of one of this story's protagonists—namely, God—with absolute otherness or the absolute other, for God or the absolute other serves a very specific logical function in this text's analysis—or better, deconstruction—of the ethical category of responsibility.[37] What then is the role and significance of Abraham's secret bond to this absolute and singular other, which seems to be in fatal conflict with his ethical bond to others "in general"? What does it mean, precisely, to say that God is the *absolute* other? Obeying God's command is, the Scripture suggests, an absolute responsibility, but is it not impossible to respond to God?

Indeed, as Derrida notes, Abraham does not respond to God beyond the almost tautological and certainly self-reflexive statement "Here I am," a response that, in the asymmetry it establishes with its addressee, suggests that insofar as God is the absolute other, he is not of the order of language. On one reading—say, a more or less negative theological one—this asymmetry would be a result of God's absolutely unique and transcendent position outside even the sphere of positive existence, and certainly outside the common space of the general (that is, the world). But in Abraham's inability to respond to God as the absolute other, can we not, Derrida suggests, see a situation that is similar or indeed identical to what is the most common experience of the ethical "in general," and one that would recast the absolute other or God not as a transcendent essence, but as the very otherness that distances each of the infinitely numerous finite beings within the space of the general?[38] Or, in the case of Bartleby, can we not see how, in the space behind his green screen, "privacy and society [are] conjoined" ("Bartleby," 642)? The general—as the sphere of responsibility and responsiveness—proves, in truth, to be no less essentially characterized by the impossibility to respond to the other, since for every singular other (loved ones, friends, peers, pets) to whom I am able to respond and be responsible, there are countless others to whom I cannot and never will be able to respond or act ethically.

And what can one say about this? Abraham does not speak about his sacrifice, does not offer justifications or reasons; this is his secret, his Bartleby-like withdrawal from responsibility "in general" and from the relief, as Kierkegaard puts it, of displacing his responsibility onto the general or "ethical." The general, however, harbors within it something of the absolute and secret, and this is because any single relation or responsibility that is acknowledged or met necessarily entails the neglect of infinite others. Because I am a finite being, it is impossible for me to respond to the infinite number of finite others; the impossibility of the absolute is a constitutive element of the general. To choose to save one other is to sacrifice the other others—indeed, infinite others. "And I can never justify this sacrifice," writes Derrida. "I must [like Abraham—and by extension Bartleby] always hold my peace about it. Whether I want to or not, I will never be able to justify the fact that I prefer or sacrifice any one (any other) to the other. I will always be in secret, held to secrecy in respect of this, for nothing can be said about it."[39] Even the most ethical choice boils down, ultimately, to a *preference,* and this "remains finally unjustifiable (this is Abraham's hyperethical sacrifice), as unjustifiable as the infinite sacrifices I make at each moment."[40]

What is to be read in the episode of Abraham's archetypal encounter with the transcendent God's impossible and unanswerable command is for Derrida nothing other than the structure of everyday ethical experience, which, though in terms perhaps less hyperbolic, nevertheless reproduces the aporetic and unsettling ethical dilemma of Mount Moriah all the time. This is an assertion that Derrida fleshes out in the final moments of the chapter, where the distinction between the absolute otherness of God and the otherness of others in general finally collapses (or is deconstructed) and the transcendence of the divine sphere is presented as nothing other than the structure of the profane world (or vice versa, if you wish). On the one hand, "God, as wholly other, is to be found everywhere there is something of the wholly other,"[41] and on the other, "there is no longer any ethical generality that does not fall prey to the paradox of Abraham."[42] That is the secret Abraham keeps when he elusively responds without responding and speaks without speaking.

Bartleby's formula, whether as Deleuze's quasi-agrammaticality or Derrida's pseudo-incomplete sentence, is, of course, another unresponsive response, a statement that borders on senselessness or silence—or at least appears to harbor a secret. For Derrida this is a perfect repetition of Abraham's speaking-without-speaking, whose ultimate referent, so to speak, is the aporetic impasse of ethics and responsibility. "Just as Abraham doesn't speak a human language," he writes,

> just as he speaks in tongues or in a language that is foreign to every other human language, and in order to do that responds without responding, speaks without saying anything either true or false, says nothing determinate that would be equivalent to a statement, a promise, or a lie, in the same way Bartleby's "I would prefer not to" takes responsibility for a response without response. It evokes the future without either predicting or promising; it utters nothing fixed, determinable, positive or negative. The modality of this repeated utterance that says nothing, promises nothing, neither refuses nor accepts anything, the tense of this singularly insignificant statement, reminds one of a nonlanguage or a secret language. Is it not as if Bartleby were also speaking "in tongues"?[43]

For Derrida Bartleby's secret language brings the canonical language of ethics—and especially of ethical responsibility—to an aporetic impasse, forcing it to confront, as if in a "dead-wall revery" ("Bartleby," 656), its internal ambivalences and limits. Indeed, for the thinkers I have discussed thus far, as Bartleby's "ravishing, devastating" formula collapses into agrammaticality or glossolalia or silence, it brings its hearers and readers—the lawyer, us—face to face with the uncertain and fugitive foundations of the political-ethical order.

Labor and Stasis

As we move from the question of "language and silence" to the question of "labor and stasis," the dominant voices become Italian. This is perhaps not surprising, since in no other western European country was the question of labor so central to philosophical debates of the last few decades of the twentieth century, a period in which the national philosophical milieu was dominated by Marxism and post-Marxism, the most relevant strand of which, for the present discussion, was known as *Autonomia*.[44] *Autonomia* is something of a blanket term—and a contested one at that—used collectively to name several related leftist movements in Italy in the 1960s and 1970s that were distinct from, and to varying degrees hostile to, the Italian Communist Party (PCI), at the time the largest communist party in Europe and a major force in the Italian parliament. Arising out of and comprising workers' movements, feminist movements, and student movements, *Autonomia* is a larger phenomenon than can be adequately accounted for here.[45] One particular issue, however—namely, the call for a "refusal of work" within the workers' movement—must briefly be reviewed as a context for the Bartlebys of this section.

Though the broad notion of the refusal of work has had many proponents and has gone through a number of modulations within the Marxist and anarchist traditions—from Lafargue's "droit à la paresse" to the Situationist slogan "Ne travaillez jamais"—it is the formulation of the "strategy of refusal" by the Italian Marxist theorist Mario Tronti that most directly concerns us here. Though his relation to the party fluctuated, Tronti never left the PCI; his thought, however, and in particular the texts collected in his 1966 book *Workers and Capital,* had an enormous influence on the autonomist development of the workers' movement. In a famous phrase Tronti asserts, "To struggle against capital, the working class must struggle against itself insofar as it is capital."[46] In contrast to the notion that the working class must reclaim its laboring activity and the fruits of its labor from the capitalist class, and in contrast even to the idea of an eventual workers' self-management of the entire cycle of production, Tronti's *operaismo* (workerism) seeks to refuse the notion of "work" at its very core, and this is because such a notion has the class relation already written into it. He writes: "Productive labour [as distinct from labor power] . . . exists not only in relation to capital, but also in relation to the capitalists as a class. It is in this latter relationship that it exists as the working class."[47] The working class is constituted as such by the conversion of its labor power into "work" in the capitalist social formation. "What are workers doing," Tronti asks, "when they struggle against their employers? Aren't they, above all else, saying 'No' to the transformation of their labor power into labor?"[48] This "no," this refusal of work, entails a reconsideration of the very nature of human productivity and the human capacity for action. Ultimately, the refusal of work, which is to say, the refusal of the conversion of human activity into labor, is not an appeal to idleness or passivity, but rather an effort to develop human capacities for productivity and self-constitution (at both the individual and collective level) in ways entirely free from—autonomous from—the capitalist social formation as well as the state form. As Nicholas Thoburn puts it, Tronti "proposes that to be alienated from work, its form, function and subject, becomes the founding condition of revolutionary politics. Politics is hence not the reclamation of work against an 'external' control, but a *refusal* of work and the very subject of worker."[49]

Michael Hardt and Antonio Negri

Tronti's *operaismo* sets the stage for Hardt and Negri's portrayal of Bartleby as an icon of the refusal of work in *Empire* (2000), for their Bartleby is an equivocal figure in which lie certain implicit critiques of *Autonomia* and workerism, which in turn have a long and dense history in Negri's writings from the 1960s to the 1990s. As they write in a subchapter titled "Refusal": "[Bartleby's] refusal certainly is the beginning of a liberatory politics, but it is only a beginning."[50] To understand this engagement with autonomist theory better, we must review the ontology of human labor and production that lies beneath Hardt and Negri's evocation of Bartleby's passivity and the limits of his "refusal."

Though it also owes a great deal to the Marxian materialist conception of history, Hardt and Negri's ontology of human productivity is grounded above all in Negri's reading of Spinoza, especially in his 1981 book *The Sav-*

age Anomaly. In this book Negri lays the groundwork for his Spinozist identification of being with the ceaseless power of production, a concept that in this text derives from the Spinozan figures of *potentia* and *conatus* but will later be codified in what is perhaps Negri's signal concept: constituent power. He writes, "Production as a constitutive ontology. Spinoza founds this possibility of philosophy, or rather of the destruction of philosophy, with absolute coherence. Constitutive ontology recognizes production within the structure of being. It is not possible to say being, except in terms of production."[51] But what is the nature of this production and this productivity?

On the one hand, what is being produced is nothing less than human existence itself. As we read in Hardt and Negri's most recent book, *Commonwealth,* where it is viewed under the lenses of "immaterial labor" and "biopolitical production," this ontology sees in human labor (that is to say, human activity as such) "not the production of objects for subjects, as commodity production is often understood, but the production of subjectivity itself."[52] For Hardt and Negri biopolitical production, in its revolutionary and liberated form, is the free, spontaneous, and vital production of human existence in a collective praxis (the subject—and indeed object—of this collective praxis is what they term, following Spinoza, the "multitude").[53] Thus, the product of this production is none other than the producer, in an autogenetic and autarchic dynamic in which the collectivity of humanity—the multitude—is a self-constituting artifact.

On the other hand—and this is the more important point for the present discussion—this human productivity is ceaseless, unstoppable, excessive, and exuberant. For Hardt and Negri this ceaselessness is central to the nature of the human capacity for productive activity, which is "a power of self-valorization that exceeds itself, flows over onto the other, and through this investment, constitutes an expansive commonality. The common actions of labor, intelligence, passion, and affect configure a *constituent power*."[54] Just as it is impossible to speak of being without speaking of production, so too is it impossible to speak of collective existence without speaking of living labor and constituent power. As we read in Negri's 1992 book *Insurgencies* (whose translated Italian title is, precisely, *Constituent Power*), "Living labor constitutes the world, by creatively modeling, *ex novo,* the material it touches," and "constituent power is a creative strength of being. That is, of concrete figures of reality, values, institutions, and logics of the order of reality. Constituent power constitutes society and identifies the social and the political in an ontological nexus."[55] The internal articulations among these near-synonyms within Hardt and Negri's argumentation over numerous texts need not be mapped in detail here; what is crucial is that in whatever guise it assumes, this basic human capacity for productivity is (1) ceaseless and (2) ontological. And on both those scores, Bartleby make a gesture in the right direction, but he ultimately comes up short; his refusal is "the beginning of a liberatory politics, but it is only a beginning."[56]

What then is the step not taken by the scrivener? What is it that Bartleby does not do? In short, he does not *produce.* To be sure, ceasing to work for the lawyer is the first step away from his alienation in the capitalist mode of production, but he does not then redirect his capacity for production into the collective and free praxis that works toward the construction of a "new mode of life and above all a new community,"[57] which is in turn a "new regime of *production.*"[58] For Hardt and Negri Bartleby's refusal of work is "absolute";[59] he remains inert, passive, and alone—in short, a "suicide."[60] "Bartleby in his pure passivity and his refusal of any particulars presents us with a figure of generic being, being as such, being and nothing more. And in the course of the story he strips down so much—approximating ever more closely naked humanity, naked life, naked being—that eventually he withers away, evaporates in the infamous Manhattan prison, the Tombs."[61]

This passage shows how the ontological gesture in "Bartleby" is ultimately incompatible with the Spinozan "metaphysics of production"[62] valorized by Hardt and Negri, and indeed they write of Bartleby's self-immolation precisely as a failure to be fully Spinozan: "As Spinoza says, if we simply cut the tyrannical head off the social body, we will be left with the deformed corpse of society. What we need is to create a new social body, which is a project that goes well beyond refusal."[63] In contrast to taking on this positive project, Bartleby simply refuses absolutely, and in stripping away everything to arrive at "being and nothing more," Bartleby vanishes to a point where the productive capacities of man—the power to act—have been jettisoned to arrive at an anterior or underlying pure and passive "being as such." The ontology implicit in "Bartleby," in short, is based on what Hardt and Negri would find to be a mistaken metaphysics, one in which pure and passive being precedes production and activity—a being that is simply and inertly *there.* That this is in large part a critique of a Heideggerian conception of being—and of the Heideggerian philosophical project of a fundamental ontology[64]—is perhaps clear enough, but this characterization of Bartleby's negative and passive inertia is even more pointedly and more specifically a polemical rejoinder to Agamben's reading of Bartleby, to which we will now turn.

Giorgio Agamben

"I'm a Spinozan, whereas the ontology and the metaphysics of Agamben are Heideggerian," Negri states in a 2005 interview.[65] Agamben's relation to Heidegger, with whom he studied briefly in the late 1960s, is a complex one, but Negri's claim here is accurate enough. For Negri, Agamben's Heideggerianism entails a reduction of being to a neutral, impassive, and impotent bare fact: "being and nothing more." Whether this is a legitimate characterization of Heidegger's thought itself is a question that must be left open here; but it *is* a mischaracterization of Agamben's "ontology and metaphysics" and of what is perhaps the key concept in Agamben's philosophical lexicon, *impotentiality*. As we will see, it is absolutely true that for Agamben Bartleby is a figure for impotentiality, but this is not, as Negri suggests, mere passivity.

Agamben begins his 1993 essay "Bartleby, or On Contingency" by noting that Bartleby belongs to a literary constellation that includes such dark stars as Akaky Akakievich, Bouvard and Pécuchet, Simon Tanner, Prince Myshkin, and Kafka's courtroom clerks.[66] But this figure is, he suggests, perhaps only a dim outline of the truer image we might get when Bartleby is placed in his proper philosophical constellation. The first section of Agamben's essay, titled "The Scribe, or On Creation," seeks to map out this strange house of the zodiac, and in a typically eclectic and erudite survey of Byzantine and medieval Christian, Cabbalistic, and Islamic texts, Agamben traces the ways in which thinkers from these traditions have commented on the Aristotelian question of the passage from potentiality to act (from *dunamis* to *energeia*), the process by which things emerge out of nonbeing into being—that is to say, the question of creation. "This," Agamben writes, "is the philosophical constellation to which Bartleby the scrivener belongs. As a scribe who has stopped writing, Bartleby is the extreme figure of the Nothing from which all creation derives; and at the same time, he constitutes the most implacable vindication of this Nothing as pure, absolute potentiality."[67] But what is the nature of this Nothing and this pure, absolute potentiality? And why is Bartleby's ceasing to write the critical gesture for understanding the act of *creation*?

The first and critical assertion Agamben makes about potentiality is its constitutive co-belonging—and ultimate identity—with what he calls "impotentiality." The essential intimacy of potentiality and impotentiality is the key point in Aristotle's polemic with the Megarians in book Theta of the *Metaphysics.* Against the Megarian position that all potentialities are always actualized and that the only potentialities that exist are those that pass into act, Aristotle asserts that for there to be potentiality at all, and therefore for any sort of change to happen, the potentiality to be or do something must also equally entail the potentiality not to be or do that thing. "Every potentiality (*dunamis*)," he writes, "is impotentiality (*adunamia*) of the same and with respect to the same" (*Metaphysics* 1046a 32). If this were not the case, then all potentialities would immediately realize themselves as particular actualities and all potentialities-not-to would always have been absolute impossibilities, or more simply, there would *be* only a static and unchanging actuality. This potentiality-not-to is what Aristotle calls *adunamia* or "impotentiality." In Agamben's usage, then, "impotentiality" (*impotenza*) does not mean inability, impossibility, or mere passivity, but rather the potentiality not to (be or do), which is the constitutive counterpart to every potentiality to be or do. For Agamben the necessity of an impotentiality in every potentiality is the "cardinal point on which [Aristotle's] entire theory of *dunamis* turns," and it is on this basis that he develops his own doctrine of potentiality.[68]

The inherently two-sided structure of potentiality-impotentiality means that actuality is not just the realization and fulfillment of the potentiality-to-be, but also the paradoxically negative "fulfillment" of the potentiality-to-not-be. If it is the case that in the passage to act potentiality modifies itself not by simply effacing its impotential side, but rather by turning that side back on itself in such a way that it too remains in some way as a constitutive element of the act—that is to say, of being—then the nature of being or act needs to be rethought as something more complex than simply the realization of positive potentialities. In a way that resonates with the issues informing the preceding discussion, Agamben goes about this reevaluation of (im)potentiality and act by considering the nature of *work,* conceived in its most fundamental sense as the activity that realizes potentialities.

In the essay "The Work of Man," Agamben notes that the term *energeia*—which is derived from the word *ergon* ("work"; Italian "*opera*") and literally means "being at work"—"was, in all probability, created by Aristotle, who uses it in functional opposition to *dunamis*."[69] In the *Nicomachean Ethics* Aristotle considers the way certain "works" or activities provide the criteria for defining certain types of beings. For example, the flute player is defined by playing the flute, the sculptor by making statues (and the scrivener by copying). But problems arise when we ask about the human being as such. The sculptor clearly produces *agalmata,* but what is the "work of man" as man? Is there no distinct *ergon* into which the potentiality of the human as such realizes itself? This quandary in the Aristotelian argument provides Agamben with the basis for his account of the human not as a being endowed with this or that particular potentiality or capability (or any corresponding "work") but as a being of "pure potentiality." Because of the impossibility of "identifying the *energeia,* the being-at-work of man as man, independently of and beyond the concrete social figures that he can assume,"[70] Agamben suggests that in Aristotle we can discern "the idea of an *argia,* of an essential inactivity [*inoperosità*] of man."[71] *Inoperosità* (another keyword in Agamben's vocabulary, and translated variously as inactivity, inoperativeness, and inoperativity) is the distinctive potentiality of man insofar as what characterizes the human as such is not the capacity to do or be this or that, but precisely the capacity *not* to (be or do), a potentiality that exists autonomously and indifferently to any particular actuality or "work." Just as actuality must be thought of not merely as the realization of potentiality but also as the "act of impotentiality," so the *ergon* and *energeia* of man must be thought of as the work of inoperativity.[72] Contrary to the sort of misreading we find in Hardt and Negri's critique of what they see as Agamben's quietism, then, this does not mean mere passivity, but rather indicates a kind of "working that in every act realizes its own *shabbat* and in every work is capable of exposing its own inactivity and its own potentiality."[73]

Bartleby's oddly passive activity, or active passivity, or undecidable position between passivity and activity is for Agamben the supreme figure for this "work of man," and for this reason he stands as the brightest—or, as it were, darkest—star in the constellation of literary-philosophical figures with which Agamben opens his essay. Though it is certainly the case that for Agamben Bartleby's "I would prefer not to" establishes the linguistic framework for suspension of the logic of will and necessity, truth and untruth, being and nonbeing, the decisive moment in the tale comes when Bartleby finally ceases to copy.[74] For this is the point at which Bartleby passes from being a scrivener who copies, and indeed *only* copies—that is to say, whose being is defined by his copying—to being a scrivener who does not copy but nevertheless retains the potentiality for copying. Bartleby's paradoxical "work" after he has ceased to work is to move from the ceaseless and determinate actualization of his potentiality-to-copy to an experience of his potential-to-and-not-to-copy. As Agamben puts it: "In [his] obstinate copying . . . there is no potential not to be. . . . This is why the scrivener must stop copying, why he must give up his work."[75]

Bartleby does not just *not work;* he has *ceased* to work. But he has certainly not ceased to be capable of that work; indeed, his capability—his virtuosity even—as a scrivener is never in doubt. As his formula so insistently puts it, it is not that he cannot work but rather that he prefers not to. And this is why his inoperativity (again, not to be confused with inability) is a figure for pure potentiality. Bartleby's nonwork withholds itself from the passage into act of which it is fully capable and remains in the mode of a pure having, in which what is seized and held is not any *ergon* or *energeia,* but the potentiality to be or not be, the capacity to pass or not pass into the act, which, contra Negri, is the true "a priori of every act of production."[76] For Agamben, in the moment of not exercising his capacity, Bartleby "writes nothing but [his] potentiality to not-write," and in his inoperativity Bartleby has settled into the most fundamental level of creation, the obscure zone in which creation, so to speak, happens.[77]

This in turn is why Bartleby's work in the Dead Letter office proves so decisive for him. In keeping with his optimistic reading of the tale even in its sepulchral finale, Agamben writes that the "undelivered letters are the ciphers of joyous events that could have been but never took place." For Agamben these letters reveal themselves to be not only "works" but also "acts of impotentiality." They are indeed *erga* inscribed on the blank sheet of paper and thus mark the "passage from potentiality to actuality," but they therefore equally mark the "non-occurrence of something" as well;[78] that is to say, in the vision of the undelivered letter, the letter that never arrives, Bartleby sees not only the *ergon* of a realized *dunamis,* but also the possibility that was never realized in any work. And the experience of that point of contingency—the suspended moment of potentiality as such—is what the scrivener who does not write retrieves in his obscure gesture.

The stakes of such a reconfiguration of our conception of work, of thinking of work as the act of impotentiality as well as of potentiality, are high. In remaining balanced at the pivot point between potentiality and impotentiality, Bartleby thus moves toward "the construction of an experience of the possible as such"[79] and thus "risks not so much the truth of his own statements as the very mode of his existence; he undergoes an anthropological change that is just as decisive in his subjective history as the liberation of the hand by the erect position was for the primate or as was, for the reptile, the transformation of the front limbs that changed it into a bird."[80] First behind his green screen in the law office, then balanced on the banister in the stairwell, and finally in the Tombs, Bartleby situates himself ever more securely on this point of contingency, an intervallic space that reveals itself, under Agamben's lens, to be anything but melancholy: "In the end, the walled courtyard is not a sad place. There is sky and there is grass. And the creature knows perfectly well 'where it is.'"[81] In the figure of the scribe who does not exercise his capacity to write (or who exercises his capacity not to write) Agamben presents us with a Bartleby who achieves the "*restitutio in integrum* of possibility,"[82] which is in turn the starting point for an "anthropological change" that will unite human action with the human's definitive, constitutive, and creative impotentiality.

Slavoj Žižek

The final theorist we will discuss is Slavoj Žižek, who—in terms more explicit and imperative than those of any of the theorists discussed above—calls for a "Bartleby politics," which in turn is a synonym for what he perhaps equally opaquely calls a "politics of subtraction." Paradoxically, however, in contrast certainly to Deleuze and Agamben, Žižek does not really engage or closely read the text of "Bartleby" in the course of his presentation of the politics of subtraction.[83] Indeed, he seems to take for granted that a sort of constellation of political-philosophical Bartlebys has already come into view and that its basic contours are familiar enough to his readers that he can allude to it—polemically as we will see—without elaborating on the tale itself. This, however, does not mean that he does not stake a particular claim within the Bartleby-political debate; in fact, he does. What then does Žižek's own Bartleby politics look like? Perhaps the best way begin to answer this in the present context is to examine how Žižek positions his own Bartleby politics against that of the two theorists with which this section opened: Hardt and Negri.

As noted above, Hardt and Negri see Bartleby's refusal as a figure for both a thwarted *Autonomia* and an Agambenian-Heideggerian passivity (as they see it), and thus appeal to an immanent Spinozan productivity as the step Bartleby must, but does not, take. Though the Agambenian response to this is that they misconstrue the nature of potentiality and thus fall into a sort of Megarianism, Žižek in *The Parallax View* suggests that Hardt and Negri forcibly, if surreptitiously, attempt to efface any and all negativity within the immanent productivity of the multitude. It is a point that has great resonances with the Agambenian valorization of the impotentiality that inheres within all potentialities, but unlike Agamben, Žižek appeals to the force of the negative as it is conceived within the Hegelian-Marxist tradition. In short, one might say that for both Agamben and Žižek, Hardt and Negri's insistently productivist and "active" Spinozism neglects or indeed forcibly represses the work of negativity. Contra Hardt and Negri's view that Bartleby's refusal constitutes "the first move of, as it were, clearing the table, of acquiring a distance toward the existing social universe," Žižek suggests that Bartleby's gesture is instead the index of "a kind of *arche*, the underlying principle that sustains the entire movement: far from 'overcoming' it, the subsequent work of construction, rather, gives body to it."[84] Žižek's question concerns the *direction* of the inquiry, that is, whether attention is directed toward the future resolution and self-overcoming of the dialectic or toward the first principle grounding or sustaining it and the ways this principle can become intelligible.

This sustaining principle is what Žižek elaborates over the course of this text as the "parallax gap," an irreducible incompleteness of perspective or instability of ground, a "minimal difference" dividing everything from itself at its most fundamental level, which Žižek acknowledges is very close to the Derridean notion of *différance* but which is also akin to the more clearly Hegelian idea of negativity, the driver, as it were, of the dialectic (and I have already suggested a proximity to Agambenian impotentiality).[85] In contrast to a thinking oriented toward the working through of the dialectic toward its telos (in either its Hegelian or Marxist modulations)—that is, toward the dialectic's reconciliation with itself in the absolute—"the wager of [Žižek's] book is that, far from posing an irreducible obstacle to dialectics, the notion of the parallax gap provides the key which enables us to discern its subversive core."[86] For Žižek, Bartleby's attitude is not merely an initial abstract step toward a second, decisive one of "forming a new alternative order; it is the very source and background of this order, its permanent foundation."[87]

The reason this point is so important for the debate between Hardt and Negri and Žižek is that in their conceptualization of an affirmative biopolitics of the multitude, Hardt and Negri seek both to derive the coming immanent order of the multitude from within the workings of the dialectical unfolding of the capitalist order and to imagine the body of the multitude as an immanent absolute positivity. In their vision of the final triumph of the multitude's total biopolitical self-production, Hardt and Negri embrace, in Jodi Dean's words, "an ethics of affirmation that eliminates negativity from the political. Politics becomes immanent, part of the nature of things."[88] Bartleby's refusal, in this model, is a half measure because it remains stuck in negativity and does not reverse itself into positive productivity. But for Žižek this final reversal to the immanent and positive productivity of a free and unhindered multitude—what Hardt and Negri refer to as "absolute democracy"—effectively attempts to kick away the ladder of the dialectic that led to it, allowing them to imagine an absolute democracy without (or at least implicitly without) negativity.

In *In Defense of Lost Causes,* Žižek further develops this argument (and indeed it is in this book that he actually uses the term "Bartleby politics"). Here he evokes once again the way that for Hardt and Negri Bartleby's refusal remains stuck at a "suicidal marginal position with no consequences,"[89] but he elaborates this dynamic in terms of a critical tension between the Hegelian categories of abstract and determinate negation, categories that he finds implicitly operative in Hardt and Negri's overtly anti-Hegelian thought. Arguing that Hardt and Negri covertly "tak[e] over the underlying Marxist schema of historical progress,"[90] Žižek proposes that for them "Bartleby's 'I would prefer not to' is a Hegelian 'abstract negation' which should then be overcome by the patient positive work of the 'determinate negation' of the existing social universe."[91] In presenting Bartleby in these terms, Hardt and Negri unintentionally not only make "the most standard (pseudo-) Hegelian critical point," but also reveal a fault line in their thinking on the way the positive biopolitics of the multitude arises out of the conditions of capital (that is, becomes in-itself) and then finally overcomes those conditions (that is, becomes for-itself).[92]

Biopolitical production promises, for Hardt and Negri, a stage of human praxis and production that is finally unsubsumable by capital, insofar as it is, in Žižek's gloss, "'directly' socialized, socialized in its very content, which is why it no longer needs the social form of capital imposed onto it."[93] This biopolitical praxis of the multitude, in turn, "opens up the possibility of 'absolute democracy,' it cannot be enslaved, because *it is immediately, in itself, the form (and practice) of social freedom.*"[94] Žižek, however, points again to Hardt and Negri's implicit assumption of a historical teleology and its "wager that one can repeat at the postmodern level the classical Marxist gesture and enact the 'determinate negation' of capitalism," an ultimate determinate negation in which the revolutionary dialectic finally comes to rest in the immanent self-production of the multitude or general intellect in an "absolute democracy."[95]

There is much to say about the details of this expansive and often arcane debate, but the central issue here—since Bartleby is a figure for it—is the role of negativity in these models of resistance and refusal. Bartleby, for Hardt and Negri, does not make it to the last stage because he is stuck in negativity—he *is* negativity—for which there is no clear place in the immanent collective praxis of the multitude, which has more or less overcome the dialectic and entered into a new absolute space that, in an important sense of the term, would be postpolitical. But for Žižek, not only is this beatific vision symptomatic of a current line of leftist thinking that, he argues, is animated by a tacit acceptance of the victory of capital and renunciation of oppositional (that is, class) politics, but it implicitly operates on an immanentist ontology of an absolute that has purified itself of the negative.[96]

By contrast, Žižek argues for an ontology of irreducible negativity, the fundamental level of which, in Žižek's Lacanian terminology, is called the "Real," which he glosses as "not the inaccessible Thing, but the *gap* which prevents our access to it, the 'rock' of the antagonism which distorts our view of the perceived object through a partial perspective . . . the very gap, passage, which separates one perspective from another, the gap (in this case: social antagonism) which makes the two perspectives radically *incommensurable.*"[97] Whether and to what degree this gap is to be identified with *différance,* Lacanian lack, or Hegelian negativity—or any combination of these— is a question that lies too far afield from the present discussion, but insofar as it is the first principle on which Žižek's political ontology is based, and the principle by virtue of which Žižek distinguishes his Bartleby politics from that imagined by Hardt and Negri, it marks the stark divergence in their conceptions of the nature of the absolute (or, in the precise terminology of the *Phenomenology of Spirit*'s final chapter, "absolute knowing," the self-arrival of spirit at the end of its journey through history). As Adrian

Johnston puts it, for Žižek "absolute knowing, as the self-relating of pure negativity, entails the insight that there is no such position of conclusive stability; the reconciliation achieved by absolute knowing amounts to the acceptance of an insurmountable incompleteness, an irresolvable driving tension that cannot finally be put to rest through the one last *Aufhebung*."[98]

What, then, of Bartleby and of Bartleby politics? Bartleby, in his withdrawal, short-circuits the traditional progression of sublation by insisting on the persistence and, so to speak, presence of the negative in every social or indeed ontological formation. Along these lines, Žižek, too, draws attention to the fact that Bartleby's phrase is not really a refusal or straight negation. "Bartleby does not negate the predicate; rather he affirms a non-predicate," and in doing so steps into a "new space outside the hegemonic position *and* its negation."[99] In distinction from a politics of resistance or protest, which is caught up in a dialectical unfolding that is ceaselessly engaged in a chase for its own tail, insofar as it seeks the final negation and reconciling *Aufhebung*, Bartleby's is a "gesture of subtraction at its purest, the reduction of all qualitative differences to a purely formal minimal difference," which instead illuminates or makes visible (and, most important, affirms) the irreducible parallax sustaining the entire dialectical edifice.[100] As Žižek summarily puts it, in terms that resonate strongly with the logic of impotentiality proposed by Agamben: "The difference between Bartleby's gesture of withdrawal and the formation of a new order is . . . that of parallax: the very frantic and engaged activity of constructing a new order is sustained by an underlying 'I would prefer not to' which forever reverberates in it—or, as Hegel might have put it, the new postrevolutionary order does not negate its founding gesture, the explosion of the destructive fury that wipes away the Old; it merely *gives body* to this negativity. The difficulty of imagining the New is the difficulty of imagining Bartleby in power."[101]

For Žižek and Agamben, in his obscure and minimal existence Bartleby is the embodiment, or the placeholder, of a negativity or potentiality that *exists and persists as such*, and does not simply efface itself or disappear in the onto-political drama of becoming. The tension Bartleby creates on this stage is not that between two opposing or successive positivities, but that between all positivities—all "somethings"—and the negativity or "nothing" that persists within them, not "the gap between two 'somethings' [but] the gap that separates a something from a nothing, from the void of its own place."[102]

This is the field that Žižek's politics of subtraction is intended to open up and—to borrow a Heideggerian term—dwell in. And in doing so, in subtracting or withdrawing itself radically from the dynamic of direct resistance to (but also definition by) the ruling hegemonic power, the subject of a Žižekian Bartleby politics seeks to remove the keystone from the political edifice, causing it to collapse. "Subtraction *is* the 'negation of negation' (or 'determinate negation'), in other words, instead of directly negating-destroying the ruling power, remaining within its field, it undermines this very field, opening up a new positive space."[103] Bartleby's withdrawal for Žižek is not a passivity and acceptance of the hegemony of the ruling order, but rather a passive aggressiveness whose radicalness renders it more threatening to that order than any direct resistance. As Žižek writes, in a passage that visualizes the triumph—if not the precise concrete performance—of a politics of subtraction: "Imagine the proverbial house of cards or a pile of wooden pieces which rely on one another in such a complex way that, if one single card or piece of wood is pulled out—*subtracted*—the whole edifice collapses: *this* is the true art of subtraction."[104] And Bartleby, on Žižek's reading, is the great virtuoso, and indeed namesake, of this subtractive political "art."

Admittedly, this account of Žižek's Bartleby politics, like that of every philosophical Bartleby discussed in this chapter, has focused on what might be called the first principles of the philosophical-political argument, certainly to the neglect of many practical and concrete questions. Whether these accounts are more about philosophy than politics is a question that will be left open here; nevertheless, in surveying the ways in which Melville's foundling scrivener has been adopted by the theorists discussed in the preceding pages, one finds that it is indeed at the point of political-philosophical first principles that Bartleby tends to intervene, appearing, as it were, motionless on the "office threshold, the door being open" ("Bartleby," 641–642), as if he had always been there, "a perpetual sentry in the corner" (ibid., 646). Why is Bartleby so emblematic for these thinkers? The answer lies, unsurprisingly, in his impassivity, his neutrality, his negativity, his preference-not-to—everything that is conveyed in his "mildly cadaverous reply" (ibid., 655) to the lawyer. And as the foregoing discussion has sought to show, these thinkers' interpretations and appropriations of Melville's tale, as brilliant and perceptive as they all are, can be read as a series of Rorschach tests, in which projected onto the inkblot of the scrivener (who, unlike Turkey, was never "incautious in dipping his pen into his inkstand" [ibid., 637]) we can see illuminated the often obscure conceptual cores of their political ontologies.

Or perhaps he is more like a constellation of stars, a clear sparkling *B*. This essay began by noting how Bartleby in the 150 years or so since his death has been many things to many people. And so perhaps he would not be surprised to find himself cast in this role as a new sign of the zodiac in the *coelum stellatum* of contemporary philosophy.

Notes

1. For a comprehensive overview and bibliography of the criticism, to which this very brief distillation is greatly indebted, see the chapter on "Bartleby" in Lea Bertani Vozar Newman, *A Reader's Guide to the Short Stories of Herman Melville* (Boston: G. K. Hall, 1986), 19–78.

2. J. Hillis Miller, *Versions of Pygmalion* (Cambridge: Harvard University Press, 1990). Additionally, in a sort of inversion of Bartleby being many things to many people, in Enrique Vila-Matas's marvelous *Bartleby & Co.*, many people become versions of Bartleby. In this book's idiosyncratic pantheon of "writers of the No," Vila-Matas constructs an international canon of Bartlebys, including Robert Walser, Franz Kafka, Felipe Alfau, Samuel Beckett, Joseph Joubert, Bobi Bazlen, B. Traven, and many more. Vila-Matas, *Bartleby & Co.*, trans. Jonathan Dunne (New York: New Directions, 2000).

3. In his copy of *The Poetical Works of John Milton*, Melville did not mark these lines (which are IV:300–308). He did, however, mark lines 289–290 and 316–318. See Robin Grey, ed., *Melville and Milton* (Pittsburgh: Duquesne University Press, 2004), 176.

4. Gilles Deleuze, *Essays Critical and Clinical*, trans. Daniel W. Smith and Michael A. Greco (Minneapolis: University of Minnesota Press, 1997), 68.

5. Ibid; emphasis in original.

6. Ibid., 70.

7. Deleuze suggests that in this case the "usual formula would instead be *I had rather not*" (*Essays*, 68; emphasis in original), though the grammar of this phrase, in fact, is much harder to map and, to some American ears at least, would sound no less odd than Bartleby's formula. Moreover, even though it appears not to have anything like the disruptive force of the famous formula, Bartleby's grammatically strangest phrase is probably "I know you . . . and I want nothing to say to you." Herman Melville, "Bartleby the Scrivener," in *Pierre, Israel Potter, The Piazza Tales, The Confidence-Man, Uncollected Prose, Billy Budd* (New York:

Library of America, 1984), 669; hereafter cited parenthetically in the text by title and page number.

8. Deleuze, *Essays,* 68–69; emphasis in original.

9. Ibid., 71.

10. Ibid., 73.

11. Ibid., 71.

12. Maurice Blanchot, *The Writing of the Disaster,* trans. Ann Smock (Lincoln: University of Nebraska Press, 1986), 15.

13. Ibid., 13; emphases in original.

14. Ibid., 141.

15. Ibid., 17.

16. For Austin's schema of these conditions, see *How to Do Things with Words* (Cambridge: Harvard University Press, 1962), 14–15.

17. Indeed, as the tension between Bartleby and the lawyer escalates, Bartleby is described as being precisely *alone,* that is, outside all social relations and conventions. Upon his announcement that he has given up copying permanently, Bartleby seems, in the lawyer's words, to be "alone, absolutely alone in the universe. A bit of wreck in the mid Atlantic" ("Bartleby," 657). And after being fired and instructed to leave the offices, Bartleby "answered not a word; like the last column of some ruined temple, he remained standing mute and solitary in the middle of the otherwise deserted room" (ibid., 658).

18. Deleuze, *Essays,* 73; emphases in original.

19. Ibid., 71.

20. Gilles Deleuze and Félix Guattari, *Kafka: Toward a Minor Literature,* trans. Dana Polan (Minneapolis: University of Minnesota Press, 1986), 16–17.

21. Deleuze, *Essays,* 72.

22. Ibid., 77.

23. Ibid.

24. Ibid., 89.

25. Ibid., 86–87.

26. Ibid., 86.

27. Ibid., 85.

28. Ibid., 90; emphasis in original.

29. Bartleby also makes a cameo appearance in another text by Derrida, the 1991 lecture "Resistances," where the neither-active-nor-passive response of his formula is read as a figure for the repetition compulsion in psychoanalysis. The psychoanalytic context of that reading, however, puts the Bartleby of "Resistances" too far afield of the more political-ethical argument at issue here. See Jacques Derrida, *Resistances of Psychoanalysis,* trans. Peggy Kamuf, Pascale-Anne Brault, and Michael Naas (Stanford: Stanford University Press, 1998), 24.

30. Jacques Derrida, *The Gift of Death and Literature in Secret,* 2nd ed., trans. David Wills (Chicago: University of Chicago Press, 2008), 75.

31. Ibid., 79–80.

32. In truth, this chapter is in large part a reading of Kierkegaard's reading of Abraham's sacrifice in *Fear and Trembling* (1843), and indeed at times Derrida writes in a sort of free, indirect style that makes it difficult to separate his and Kierkegaard's claims. Nevertheless, whether it is the text of Genesis or of *Fear and Trembling* that Derrida is reading, the argument is transposed into and subsumed by Derrida's own distinctive conceptual vocabulary.

33. Derrida, *The Gift of Death,* 59–60.

34. Ibid., 60.

35. Ibid., 60–61.

36. Ibid., 67.

37. And this identification in Derrida is not a mere passing comment: "The other as absolute other, namely God" (ibid., 67); "God is the name of the absolute other as other and as unique" (ibid., 68); "the absolute other: God if you wish" (ibid., 69).

38. This is a distinction that Martin Hägglund has helpfully glossed as that between what Hegel defined as a "positive infinity" and a "negative infinity." See his discussion in Hägglund, *Radical Atheism: Derrida and the Time of Life* (Stanford: Stanford University Press, 2008), 92–96.

39. Derrida, *The Gift of Death,* 71.

40. Ibid.

41. Ibid., 78.

42. Ibid., 78–79.

43. Ibid., 75.

44. This national division should, however, not be taken as a particularly rigid one, since many of the autonomist movements mentioned below were greatly influenced by the work of, among others, Foucault and Deleuze and Guattari (and vice versa).

45. For accounts of *Autonomia,* see Steve Wright, *Storming Heaven: Class Composition and Struggle in Italian Autonomist Marxism* (London: Pluto Press, 2002), and chap. 2 of George Katsiaficas's *The Subversion of Politics: European Autonomous Movements and the Decolonization of Everyday Life* (Atlantic Highlands, N.J.: Humanities Press, 1997), as well as the collection of primary and secondary sources in Sylvère Lotringer and Christian Marazzi, eds., *Autonomia: Post-Political Politics* (Los Angeles: Semiotext(e), 2007).

46. Mario Tronti, *Operai e Capitale* (Turin: Einaudi, 1966), 260; my translation.

47. Lotringer and Marazzi, *Autonomia,* 29.

48. Tronti, *Operai e Capitale,* 30; my translation

49. Nicholas Thoburn, *Deleuze, Marx and Politics* (London: Routledge, 2003), 111; emphasis in original.

50. Michael Hardt and Antonio Negri, *Empire* (Cambridge: Harvard University Press, 2000), 204.

51. Antonio Negri, *The Savage Anomaly*, trans. Michael Hardt (Minneapolis: University of Minnesota Press, 1991), 224.

52. Michael Hardt and Antonio Negri, *Commonwealth* (Cambridge: Harvard University Press, 2009), x.

53. With this last term, the titles of each of the books constituting Hardt and Negri's trilogy have been named. The middle volume is *Multitude: War and Democracy in the Age of Empire* (New York: Penguin, 2004), in which this further gloss on biopolitical-immaterial production is offered: "Material production—the production, for example, of cars, televisions, clothing, and food—creates the *means of social life*. . . . Immaterial production, by contrast, including the production of ideas, images, knowledges, communication, cooperation, and affective relations, tends to create not the means of social life but *social life itself*. Immaterial production is biopolitical" (146; emphases in original).

54. Hardt and Negri, *Empire*, 358; emphasis in original.

55. Antonio Negri, *Insurgencies: Constituent Power and the Modern State*, trans. Maurizia Boscagli (Minneapolis: University of Minnesota Press, 1999), 326–327.

56. Hardt and Negri, *Empire*, 204.

57. Ibid.

58. Ibid., 205; emphasis in original.

59. Ibid., 203.

60. Ibid., 204.

61. Ibid., 203.

62. Negri, *Savage Anomaly*, 228.

63. Hardt and Negri, *Empire*, 204.

64. "[Heidegger] brings phenomenology back to classical ontology not in order to develop a means to reconstruct being through human productive capacities but rather as a meditation on our telluric condition, our powerlessness, and death. All that can be constructed, all that resistances and struggles produce, is here instead disempowered and found 'thrown' onto the surface of being." Hardt and Negri, *Commonwealth*, 29.

65. Max Henniger and Antonio Negri, "From Sociological to Ontological Inquiry: An Interview with Antonio Negri," *Italian Culture* 23 (2005): 162. For a more detailed discussion of the division between Negri and Agamben, see my "Potentiality, Actuality, Constituent Power," *diacritics* 39, no. 3 (2009): 35–53.

66. Agamben's essay first appeared alongside an Italian translation of Deleuze's

Bartleby essay in a volume called *Bartleby, la formula della creazione* (Macerata: Quodlibet, 1993). Agamben's Bartleby essay, however, is an expansion of a brief but important chapter (titled "Bartleby") in Agamben, *The Coming Community*, trans. Michael Hardt (Minneapolis: University of Minnesota Press, 1993), which was published in 1990—and there is an even earlier piece by Agamben called "Bartleby Writes No More" published in the communist newspaper *Il Manifesto* in 1988.

67. Giorgio Agamben, *Potentialities: Collected Essays in Philosophy*, ed. and trans. Daniel Heller-Roazen (Stanford: Stanford University Press, 1999), 253–254.

68. Giorgio Agamben, *Homo Sacer: Sovereign Power and Bare Life*, trans. Daniel Heller-Roazen (Stanford: Stanford University Press, 1998), 45.

69. Giorgio Agamben, "The Work of Man," trans. Kevin Attell, in *Sovereignty & Life*, ed. Matthew Calarco and Steven DeCaroli (Stanford: Stanford University Press, 2007), 1.

70. Ibid., 2.

71. Ibid.

72. Agamben, *Potentialities*, 183.

73. Agamben, "Work of Man," 10.

74. Among the arguments Agamben puts forth concerning the linguistic features of the formula, perhaps the most crucial is his alignment of Bartleby's "I would prefer not to" with the Greek expression "*ou mallon*, 'no more than,' the technical term with which the Skeptics denoted their most characteristic experience: *epokhē*, 'suspension'" (Agamben, *Potentialities*, 256). Used, for example, in an assertion such as "Scylla exists no more than a chimera," *ou mallon* grammatically makes neither positive nor negative claims concerning the truth or falsity, being or nonbeing, of a given proposition. It suspends all propositions and "predicates nothing of nothing" (ibid., 257).

75. Ibid., 268.

76. Hardt and Negri, *Empire*, 366.

77. Agamben, *The Coming Community*, 37.

78. Agamben, *Potentialities*, 269.

79. Ibid., 249.

80. Ibid., 260; translation modified.

81. Ibid., 271.

82. Ibid., 267.

83. A point noted by Jodi Dean in *Žižek's Politics* (New York: Routledge, 2006), 197.

84. Slavoj Žižek, *The Parallax View* (Cambridge: MIT Press, 2006), 382.

85. Ibid., 11.

86. Ibid., 4.

87. Ibid., 382.
88. Dean, *Žižek's Politics*, 120.
89. Slavoj Žižek, *In Defense of Lost Causes* (New York: Verso, 2008), 353.
90. Ibid., 352.
91. Ibid., 353.
92. Ibid.
93. Ibid., 357.
94. Ibid., 356; emphasis in original.
95. Ibid., 338.
96. Ibid., 337–339.
97. Žižek, *Parallax View*, 281; emphases in original.
98. Adrian Johnston, *Žižek's Ontology: A Transcendental Materialist Theory of Subjectivity* (Evanston: Northwestern University Press, 2008), 235.
99. Žižek, *Parallax View*, 381–382; emphasis in original.
100. Ibid., 382.
101. Ibid.; emphasis in original.
102. Ibid.
103. Žižek, *In Defense of Lost Causes*, 409; emphasis in original.
104. Ibid., 409–410; emphases in original.

8

Melville's "Permanent Riotocracy"

Michael Jonik

> All now was turned to jollity and game,
> To luxurie and riot, feast and dance.
>
> —John Milton, *Paradise Lost*

> We find ourselves in a *time of riots* wherein a rebirth of History, as opposed to the pure and simple repetition of the worst, is signalled and takes shape. Our masters know this better than us: they are secretly trembling and building up their weaponry, in the form both of their judicial arsenal and the armed taskforces charged with planetary order. There is an urgent need to reconstruct or create our own.
>
> —Alain Badiou, *The Rebirth of History: Times of Riots and Uprisings*

Outlandish Politics

Like "Bartleby" or *Benito Cereno,* Herman Melville's "The Encantadas; or, Enchanted Isles" is part of his 1856 collection *The Piazza Tales.* Yet rather than cohering into a narrative like these other tales, "The Encantadas" is a series of "sketches": they trace variously the topography, geology, and natural and political history of the Galápagos and, in so doing, aggregate fragments from a variety of source materials. One part *Tempest* and one part *Voyage of the* Beagle, one part sardonic travel narrative and one part decolonial allegory, they resist representational closure or wholeness and gesture toward the ongoing, aleatoric processes for which the archipelago became better known. Melville invites us to take them in parts and in relation to each other, as a world within itself and a world in scattershot, a world just burst forth from a volcano, still shrouded in smoke, and an old, weathered world, hesitant to begin again. Gilles Deleuze, in cinematic terms, thus remarks that in "The Encantadas" we find "a new perspective, an archipelago-perspectivism that conjugates the panoramic shot and the tracking shot."[1] Such an "archipelago-perspectivism" includes the geographical and natural historical "shots" that "The Encantadas" comprises, in which the form of the archipelago evinces both fragmentariness and ongoing process. The archipelago—as a topology, topography, and active trope—allows for an alternative or subversive taxonomy[2] in which literary and scientific forms of representation are rendered multiple and incomplete. They remain, as Melville writes in *Moby-Dick*, "unpainted to the last."[3]

An archipelago-perspectivism likewise informs the later sketches that deal with the islands' "human" or political history. They constellate yet another set of Melvillean "*Isolatoes*": the explorers (Cowley, Colnett, and Porter), "passing voyagers and compilers,"[4] and whalers and tortoise hunters who charted and colonized the islands; the West Indian buccaneers and pirate-utopians who used them as a safe haven, or "sea Alsatia" ("Encantadas," 792); the irascible Dog-King and diabolical Hermit Oberlus, who used their "darksome glens" (ibid., 806) for their dark designs; the Chola widow, Hunilla, for whom the islands serve as a stage for her silent tragedy; and, not least, all those "runaways, castaways, solitaries" (ibid., 815) who have left behind abandoned abodes, scattered relics, and solemn gravestones—the "signs of vanishing humanity" (ibid., 817). Melville's society in "The Encantadas," "learned in all the lore of the outlandish life" (ibid., 788), thus comprises so many "outlandish individuals," such as Queequeg, so many "outlandish strangers" (*Moby-Dick*, 827, 1027).[5] They join the "outlandish beings" of the Galápagos—the tortoises, lizards, snakes, salamanders, gray albatrosses, "ant-eaters," and "man-haters"—to form an outlandish collective, an "incomputable host of fiends" ("Encantadas," 781).

Put differently, in Melville's Galápagos, the archipelago serves as the topology of a non-identitarian community. It evokes a politics of relation—an "outlandish politics"—that draws together solitaries in their differences, yet is open-ended and not governed by a unifying (territorial) identity or wholeness.[6] Melville's outlandish politics signifies an unsettling otherness that does not perpetuate identity but seeks to estrange it or make it extravagant. If, as he writes in *Mardi*, "all mankind are egotists. The world revolves upon an I; and we upon ourselves; for we are our own worlds," he creates compelling scenarios in which isolated selves become confederated to all those "strangers, from outlandish distant climes, going clad in furs."[7] Even Bartleby, who seems to merge with his office walls, estranges the spaces he occupies. He's not your typical New Yorker but a "bit of wreck in the mid Atlantic."[8] An outlandish politics knocks the ego world off its identity axis. It is a politics that does not consist in an instituted, consolidated paternal authority or state-controlled system, but multiplies into an "archipelago of brothers, a community of explorers,"[9] mutually implicated in the struggle for universal emancipation, the struggle to dissolve the paternal function. From the slave insurrection of *Benito Cereno* and the mutinies that hang over *Billy Budd*, to the series of texts that deal manifestly or implicitly with the American Revolution, the Haitian Revolution, the South American independence movements, the Revolutions of 1848 and the Italian *Risorgimento*, and the American Civil War and Reconstruction, Melville's writing bears witness to this struggle and the possibilities and perils of the new community it seeks to bring forth.[10] In texts that do not directly recall moments of political rupture, Melville interrogates how forms of domination imbricate political, social, or scientific systems, how these systems come to disintegrate, and what novel alternatives might be created in their wake. In *White-Jacket*, for example, both the centralizing force of a paternal figure and the micropolitics by which paternal power saturates an institution (in terms of naval discipline, hierarchy, codes of honor, corporal punishment, colonialism, impressment) come under intense scrutiny in the name of liberty and "The Rights of Man." Melville enacts a multifarious exploration of the politics of the fraternal relation, in search of what he calls the "proper fraternal feeling,"[11] if not the "infinite fraternity of feeling" he describes in a letter to Hawthorne.[12] Scenes of brotherly love suffuse his work to the extent that *philos* and *eros* often become indistinguishable.[13] He lauds the "Grand Parliament of the best Bachelors in universal London" in his mock symposium, "The Paradise of Bachelors," yet sets it against the blank stares of the factory women in "The Tartarus of Maids" to perform a striking juxtaposition of gender inequality.[14] In the prismatic histories of works such as *Benito Cereno, Israel Potter,* and *Clarel,* there are refracted the symbolic shards of the disintegrating fraternal orders of the Old World. In *Battle-Pieces,* Melville memorializes the fratricidal convulsions of the Civil War: "the strife of brothers" and the "mistrust" of "Fathers" he details in his poem "The Armies of the Wilderness"; the "generous boys" who "lie down midway on a bloody bed" in "On the Slain Collegians"; as well as the survivors who, "like castaway sailors," "at last crawl, spent, to shore" in "The College Colonel."[15]

Melville's "The Encantadas" participates in these broader questions of revolution and community that animate Melville's politics. To explore how, I will focus primarily here on his two later sketches: "Sketch Sixth: Barrington Isle and the Buccaneers," in which he describes a seventeenth-century "pirates' utopia" in the Galápagos in external but predatory relation to the Spanish Empire, and "Sketch Seventh: Charles' Isle and the Dog-King," in which he provides a striking dramatization in postrevolutionary South America of the dynamics of insurrection and the political ambiguities that follow. On the one hand, my contention is that these sketches could be put among the broader group of Melville's works that continue to resonate with—if not challenge and reformulate—programs of collective resistance and give tread to emergent conceptions of nonidentity-based community, such as the transnational, the cosmopolitan, or the common. Yet, at the same time as Melville's characters in "The Encantadas" instantiate possibilities of egalitarian collectivity built around insurgency, mutiny, and revolution, or become departicularized to void themselves of binding identity coordinates, they also adumbrate how the formation of a resilient non-identitarian community is not without its attendant risks. Like many of his works, "The Encantadas" stages the ambiguities of political power in a manner that disallows clear-cut valorizations between order and anarchy, the state system and its heterotopic spaces, violence and justice, monarchical authority and democratic individuality, libertarian exploitation and communist collectivity, if not utopia and dystopia. Even if they provide an alternative to settled colonial identities, characters like the Dog-King and Hermit Oberlus are far from egoless utopian saviors, and the pirate-poets who make the Galápagos their "bowers of ease" ("Encantadas," 786) are at once murderers and marauders.

The key political question "The Encantadas" raises thus is: What will separate the universal fraternity from its diabolical counterpart, the masquerade of false brothers?[16] Or, more formally: What will inoculate this community from the return of paternal power or its concomitant addictions to personal identity? As the father is deposed, what will keep a new father from emerging and seizing control? As Melville writes in *Clarel* concerning the revolutions in 1848:

What if the kings in Forty-eight
Fled like the gods? even as the gods
Shall do, return they made; and sate,
And fortified their strong abodes.[17]

The return of paternal power remains the problematic that emergent collectives face to bring about and sustain themselves against violent expressions of counterrevolutionary force. This is the daily struggle in Tahrir Square and Wall Street, in Damascus and Athens, on the archipelago of Bahrain and anywhere else where new collectives strive for political representation. Yet, at the same time, is there not also a "pathology of masterlessness"—a *mastery of masterlessness* that marks the incessant quest for liberty but cannot ensure that the flight from tyranny will end in a happy home? It is the irony of D. H. Lawrence's double formula in *Studies in Classic American Literature:* "'Henceforth be masterless.' Henceforth be mastered."[18] Or, as Lacan sardonically quipped to the May 1968 revolutionaries: "What you aspire to as revolutionaries is a new master. You will get one."[19] Although these questions assuredly point to debates outside the scope of this essay, what is pressing is to ask what we can learn from Melville for our own "time of riots" about the possibilities of new planetary organization, even if found scattered on the plutonian shores of the Galápagos.

The Surgings of Revolt

In "Charles' Isle and the Dog-King," Melville relates an outlandish history, a history that his narrator, Salvator R. Tarnmoor, "gathered long ago from a shipmate learned in all the lore of outlandish life" ("Encantadas," 788). In it a "certain Creole adventurer," for his valor in effecting the "successful revolt of the Spanish provinces from Old Spain," is rewarded by Peru with his "pick of the Enchanted Isles" (ibid.). He chooses Charles' Island, on the condition that its "deed must stipulate that thenceforth Charles' Isle is not only the sole property of the Creole, but is forever free of Peru, even as Peru of Spain" (ibid., 789). He proclaims himself "Supreme Lord of the Island, one of the princes of the powers of the earth." Upon finding it unsatisfactory to rule over a kingdom without any subjects, he invites "subjects to his as yet unpopulated kingdom." Yet these subjects quickly realize the virulent paranoia of their new monarch, who fully earns his title, the "Dog-King," by disbanding his human guard and raising an "army now solely consisting of [a] dog-regiment." "Armed to the teeth," Melville writes, "the Creole now goes in state, surrounded by his canine janizaries, whose terrific bayings prove quite as serviceable as bayonets in keeping down the surgings of revolt." The two bodies of the king become merged into the symbolic hybrid of a dog-body—not exactly the "merry monarch" one might expect for an island named after Charles II. The Dog-King's "grim dogs" not only become a "disciplined cavalry" but are classed above the settlers in the natural-social hierarchy, "much as, from the ramparts, the soldiers of a garrison, thrown into a conquered town, eye the inglorious citizen-mob over which they are set to watch" (ibid., 789–790).

Yet, after building a capital city from out of the Galápagos's lava floors and cinders, the pilgrims themselves begin to exhibit their own "untoward character." The Dog-King declares martial law, shooting the "plotters and malignant traitors" until realizing, in a hyperbolized moment of Malthusian clarity, that through such a "dispensation of justice" he will completely depopulate his empire. By necessity, he proceeds to lure and capture deserters, castaways, and other desperados to repeople it. These new immigrants come to enjoy a "petted" status (not unlike the "foreign-born Praetorians, unwisely introduced into the Roman state, and still more unwisely made favorites of the emperors"); nonetheless, they break out into a "terrible mutiny" that leads to a bloody slaughter of dogs, the Dog-King's ignominious overthrow, and the proclamation of a new republic ("Encantadas," 790–791). The deposed Creole is then sent out, an ironic Napoleon, to a mainland exile in Peru. There "he watched every arrival from the Encantadas, to hear news of the failure of the Republic, the consequent penitence of the rebels, and his own recall to royalty. Doubtless he deemed the Republic but a miserable experiment which would soon explode" (ibid., 791). Such a recall to power never happens, however, because, as Melville relates, "the insurgents had confederated themselves into a democracy neither Grecian, Roman, nor American. Nay, it was no democracy at all, but a permanent *Riotocracy,* which gloried in having no law but lawlessness. . . . Charles' Island was proclaimed the asylum of the oppressed of all navies. Each runaway tar was hailed as a martyr in the cause of freedom, and became immediately installed a ragged citizen of this universal nation. . . . It became Anathema—a sea Alsatia—the unassailed lurking-place of all sorts of desperadoes, who in the name of liberty did just what they pleased" (ibid., 791–792).

Melville critics have read the story of the Dog-King as a cautionary parable for the fate of postrevolutionary societies. To be sure, the Dog-King—a successful revolutionary—once given the possibility to rule, cynically repeats the very autocratic system he had helped overthrow. History, far from a progress of universal emancipation realized in a revolution, seems to "stammer" as a brutal repetition of constriction and fragmentation. The history of postcolonial South America would seem to bear this out, leading Chris Sten to remark: "What is reflected in this brief history is not so much the nation building that followed the revolutions of 1808–1826 in South America, but the fragmentation that came after, a fragmentation seen not just in warlordism but in the breakup of Bolívar's Gran Colombia and the United Provinces of the Rio de la Plata into their earlier constituents, the first into Venezuela, Colombia, and Ecuador, and the second into Argentina, Uruguay, Paraguay, and Bolivia."[20] In the wake of decolonization, the newly formed South American republics became marked by political disintegration, economic depression, and widespread instability.[21] Even Darwin, whose reflections on South American society punctuate his observations of its geology and manifold species, remarked upon visiting postrevolutionary Argentina that the stability the government did enjoy was "owing" to the "tyrannical habits" of its governors, "for tyranny seems as yet better adapted to these countries than republicanism. The governor's favorite occupation is hunting Indians: a short time since he slaughtered forty-eight, and sold the children at the rate of three or four pounds apiece."[22] In this atmosphere of post-independence "political buccaneering," there arose local charismatic warlords, or *caudillos,* who set up networks of power and, like seafaring pirates, would provide vigilante "stability" for profit.[23]

The Dog-King consolidates the despotic tendencies of many such figures, including those of the "liberator" Bolívar, who, "though unwavering in his republican convictions, became aware early on of the problem of authority in the new nations he liberated, and he was to move towards ever more authoritarian constitutions."[24] Bolívar deeply distrusted popular sovereignty and worked to prevent democratic elections, which he thought to be "the greatest scourge of republics and [to] produce only anarchy" and insisted on a strong, centralized government with "all the stability of monarchical regimes."[25] His plan for a unified South America ultimately failed, however, which led him to famously surmise: "America is ungovernable. Those who have served the revolution have ploughed the sea."[26] Yet Melville's Dog-

King probably even more closely resembles General José de Vilamil,[27] a Creole from New Orleans and hero in the Ecuadorian revolutionary cause.[28] Vilamil served as the first governor of the Galápagos for Ecuador, founding a penal colony on Charles' Island in 1832, which Darwin then visited in September 1835. As Darwin records in his *Voyage:* "This archipelago has long been frequented, first by the Bucaniers, and latterly by whalers, but it is only within the last six years that a small colony has been established here. The inhabitants are between two and three hundred in number; they are nearly all people of colour, who have been banished for political crimes from the Republic of the Equator."[29] In a more imaginative register—one appropriate to the enchanted landscapes of Melville's Galápagos—the Dog-King also evokes Shakespeare's *The Tempest* and *Timon of Athens.* Yet, on Charles' Island, Melville's Prospero has turned misanthrope, and his sprites have become an army of dogs; he is at once a Timonist "man-hater" and a churlish Diogenes.[30]

The point, however, is not to pinpoint a particular historical or literary source (or set of sources) for the Dog-King, but to show how all these varied sources, which become animate in his strange hybrid personae, embody the paradoxes of the struggle for emancipation. To this end, it is instructive to briefly contrast the episode next to Melville's other characters who participated in South American liberation. In *White-Jacket,* for one, Melville describes Jack Chase's motivation for his initial desertion of the *Neversink* in terms of his revolutionary involvement in Peru: "But with what purpose had he deserted? to riot in some abandoned sea-port? for love of some worthless signorita? Not at all. He abandoned the frigate from far higher and nobler, nay, glorious motives. Though bowing to naval discipline afloat; yet ashore, he was a stickler for the Rights of Man, and the liberties of the world. He went to draw a partisan blade in the civil commotions of Peru; and befriend, heart and soul, what he deemed the cause of the Right" (*White-Jacket,* 365). In the chapter "The Advocate" in *Moby-Dick,* Ishmael credits Nantucket whalemen with opening the Pacific to commerce and exacerbating the end of Spanish colonization in South America: "Until the whale fisher rounded Cape Horn, no commerce but colonial, scarcely any intercourse but colonial, was carried on between Europe and the long line of opulent Spanish provinces on the Pacific coast. It was the whalemen who first broke through the jealous policy of the crown, touching those colonies; and, if space permitted, it might be distinctly shown how from those whalemen at last eventuated the liberation of Peru, Chili, and Bolivia from the yoke of Old Spain, and the establishment of eternal democracy in those parts" (*Moby-Dick*, 910). In "The Encantadas" Melville rewrites the "glorious intentions" of Jack Chase and the "eternal democracy"[31] of the newly liberated republics in Ishmael's ironical description as the malevolent motives of the crafty Dog-King, and the permanent riotocracy that followed in his wake. By replacing the stereotypical freedom-fighting revolutionary with his self-interested Dog-King, Melville would seem to make a farce of postrevolutionary repetition: the revolution is seemingly permanent only insofar as it signifies a permanent substitution of new masters.

The Dog-King could join the distinguished group of postrevolutionary figures in Melville's works who defy easy classification or "ideological reductionism."[32] There is Benjamin Franklin, caricatured in *Israel Potter* as an archpatriarch, sly through excessive benevolence.[33] There is Garibaldi, the Italian patriot, a major figure in Melville's poems about the Italian *Risorgimento* contained in his late, unfinished *Burgundy Club*.[34] Garibaldi, seemingly unrelenting in his emancipatory fervor (to the extent that he wanted to destroy the papacy and declined Lincoln's offer to lead the Union forces in 1862 because the president would not abolish slavery), famously ceded his revolutionary winnings to the king of Italy for the ultimate cause of unification.[35] Like these other historical revolutionaries–cum–Melville characters, the Dog-King mocks the enlightened "progress" from monarchy to republic to which his century of revolutions, and the century before him, claimed to bear witness. He does not found a universal republic but a "miserable republic." Despite claims that his kingdom will be free from Peru as Peru was from Spain, he does not put an end to systems of colonial oppression or prevent the restoration of paternal authority but re-creates them in miniature. He becomes a gross hybrid of the emancipatory promise of revolution and its terrible failure (for which the repeated counterrevolutionary retrenchments of the French Revolution served for many, including Melville, as a haunting model). This duplicity persistently hangs over Melville's politics and accents his manifold scenes of insurgency, revolution, and mutiny. Insurgents merge with counterinsurgents, liberators become kings, and masters cannot be distinguished from slaves, nor misanthropes from philanthropists. In the 1850s of "The Encantadas," the increasingly disunited United States itself verged on a "miserable republic about to explode."

Michael Rogin, whose *Subversive Genealogy* is in many ways still the most potent and sustained work to consider the question of Melville's revolutionary inheritance, catalogues the duplicitous mutinies through which Melville's political vision becomes dramatized: "The *San Dominick* slaves carry out the only successful mutiny in all of Melville's fiction. There is near-mutiny on the *Neversink,* comic mutiny on the *Julia,* failed mutiny on the *Town-Ho,* alleged mutiny on the *Bellipotent,* and desertion from the *Dolly.* The metaphoric slaves on all those ships fail to overthrow their masters. . . . *Benito Cereno* recontains a slave revolt inside a masquerade."[36] Even had Rogin included within his survey the successful insurgents who create the "permanent *Riotocracy*" instantiated on Charles' Island, the list would still read like a catalogue of revolutionary failures. Even in the successful mutiny of *Benito Cereno,* as he asserts, "the slaves overthrew their masters only to reenact their own enslavement. Melville fictionalized a mutiny that the slaves had fictionalized before him."[37] At the same time, critics should be careful not to map this too hastily to a univocal tragic political orientation throughout Melville's writing. Rather, what emerges does not cohere into a single, consistent political position. For what is at stake in all these scenes of mutiny is Melville's subtle diagnosis of the structure of the workings of revolt—what Robert S. Levine has described apropos of the American Revolution in *Israel Potter* as his ability to "restage" the revolutionary moment "in all of its sublime multiplicity and confusion, helping us to realize how little we know about the trajectories of history even as we discern that those trajectories might have gone in different directions."[38] Melville, in effect, offers simultaneously multiple and dynamic political perspectives—an archipelago of political perspectives. He does not seek to resolve them but to prompt us again and again to rethink how political situations are formed of heterogeneous elements and colliding imperatives, and how new political formations are always in the making. To this end, Melville's work directly engaged the contradictory historical forces of the nineteenth century; he sought to populate his works with embodiments of these forces, as well as with the outcasts, orphans, and insurgents that inhabit the outside of nineteenth-century narratives of historical progress, capitalist hegemony, and Christian society. This perhaps is Melville's radical political gesture: to stage for his century—if not proleptically for our own—the masquerades of power that put on faces of benevolence, charity, or even mere personhood to cover grotesque visages of exploitation. If throughout Melville's work there is enacted an "immanent critique" of the deep relational structure of political power, it is not one that demands a shift in totality, but a faithfulness to ever-shifting pluralities. As such, Melville's permanent riotocracy joins a series of scenes of resistance across his writing that have collectively animated a boisterous mob of writers and philosophers intent on resisting still-rampant forms of imperialism and societal control. It is to them that I will now turn, shifting focus from the vexed history of the Dog-King to the riotous community that replaces him.

Desperado Philosophy

Invoking C. L. R James, Amy Kaplan, in her recent article "Transnational Melville," asks: "Are all [Melville's] motley crews of mariners, renegades, and castaways federated along the keel of destruction? Or do they represent other democratic potentialities?" She goes on to conjecture that "the lawlessness [of the insurgents] bespeaks other kinds of confederating, where 'any fugitive would be welcome' and 'each runaway tar' would be 'installed as ragged citizen of this universal nation.'"[39] She links Melville's "permanent *Riotocracy*" to an analogous passage in *White-Jacket,* a passage that serves as her formula of transnationality. There Melville writes, "We sailors sail not in vain. We expatriate ourselves to nationalize with the universe."[40] For Kaplan this expatriation is not just to leave the father or fatherland, or to be reborn into a metaphysical All-ness; it also harbors concrete political potential. In a time when catastrophes such as 9/11, Katrina, and the global financial crisis have "revealed our shared vulnerability" and "the illusion of national sovereignty," "a transnational approach to literature and culture must propose alternatives, [it must] imagine such future modes of confederating."[41]

In a passage from *Redburn,* "America" replaces the universe of *White-Jacket* as the alembic of the departicularized community to come: "You cannot spill a drop of American blood without spilling the blood of the whole world. . . . We are not a nation, so much as a world; for unless we may claim all the world for our sire, like Melchisedec, we are without father or mother. . . . We are the heirs of all time, and with all nations we divide our inheritance" (*Redburn,* 185).[42] On the basis of passages like this one, Deleuze celebrates Melville's characters as instantiations of a political program freed of the "Oedipal phantasm."[43] In his *Essays Critical and Clinical* and across his oeuvre, Deleuze adopts figures from the vast orphanage of

Melville's writing as figures of the clash of universal fraternity with paternal authority. He charts how the paternal function, "the heart of the representative system," becomes dissolved into the immanent strife of "the disorder of haecceities."[44] Ishmael is borne up on Queequeg's coffin amid the wreckage of the law of the Father, amid the wreckage of reason. Ahab, by pursuing paternal authority and willful preference to their extremes, brings about the destruction of this authority. He prefers "to will *nothingness* rather than *not* will."[45] *Moby-Dick*'s secret motto, then, as Melville confides to Hawthorne, is Ahab's formula: "*Ego non baptizo te in nomine patris, sed in nomine diaboli!*" (*Moby-Dick*, 1315). Scenes of paternal overcoming suffuse Melville's work: Bartleby's formula, as Deleuze argues, "strip[s] the father of his exemplary speech, just as it strips the son of his ability to reproduce or copy. . . . Redburn renounces the image of the father in favor of the ambiguous traits of the mysterious brother. Pierre does not imitate his father but reaches the zone of proximity where he can no longer be distinguished from his half sister."[46] Likewise, the self-abnegating fealty of Billy Budd leaves Captain Vere, on his deathbed, only to "mutter" to his attendant the name of the executed youth. Deleuze's Melville is a tenacious critic of how forms of paternity—even those wearing the masks of "love" (Christian charity, philanthropy, family identity)—surreptitiously foreclose the fraternal relation. "Now what Vere and the attorney demonstrate is that there are no good fathers. There are only monstrous, devouring fathers, and petrified, fatherless sons. If humanity can be saved . . . it will only be through the dissolution or decomposition of the paternal function."[47] For Deleuze Melville's confrontations of figures of "Primary Nature" such as Bartleby or Budd with paternal authority seek to open a space for a fraternal humanity to come: "To liberate man from the father function, to give birth to the new man or the man without particularities, to reunite the original and humanity by constituting a society of brothers as a new universality. In the society of brothers, alliance replaces filiation and the blood pact replaces consanguinity. Man is indeed the blood brother of his fellow man, and woman his blood sister: according to Melville, this is the *community of celibates,* drawing its members into an unlimited becoming."[48] The "community of celibates" becomes released from the settled rituals of inherited identity by offering an alternative to grounded, predetermined relations centered on the paternal bloodline. It fosters new, open-ended alliances—new blood pacts between brothers and sisters—as if to reinstate the dream of Enlightenment universal fraternity foreclosed by the plutocratic realities of Western democracy, the dream of Thomas Paine, Anacharsis Clootz, and Olympe de Gouges. At the same time, Deleuze's community of celibates gestures toward a nonreproductive futurity that rejects heteronormative institutions like the family and the nation-state as the sine qua non of community, as well as their inherent dependencies on concepts of identity such as personhood, private property, and territory.

Melville often presents his people to come in the dress of a universal citizenry, as an "Anacharsis Clootz deputation from all the isles of the sea, and all the ends of the earth" (*Moby-Dick*, 921), "an assortment of tribes and complexions" (*Billy Budd,* 1353), a masquerade of representative humanity, a "piebald parliament . . . of all kinds of that multiform species, man" (*The Confidence-Man*, 848). C. L. R. James, for his part, finds Melville's Anacharsis Clootz formulations to be "decisive."[49] Clootz's anonymous mob becomes synonymous with James's "meanest mariners, castaways and renegades" who constitute the *Pequod*'s laboring crew. They operate in stark contrast to Ahab's "queenly personality"—a contrast that "Melville traces at every level from the basic human function to the philosophic conceptions of society."[50] Federated along the keel of the heterotope of the ship, or set loose into the ports of the faceless multitude, Melville's characters participate in the undoing of fixed narratives of nation, class, race, or self-identity. Donald Pease puts this forcefully, again launching James's trident configuration:

> As participants in a transnational social movement, the "mariners, renegades, and castaways" did not belong to a national community. The irreducible differences and inequivalent cultural features characterizing the "mariners, castaways, and renegades" refused to conform to a state's monocultural taxonomy and could not be integrated within a nationalizing telos. . . . Forever in between arrival and departure, the elements comprising the composite figure "mariners, renegades, and castaways" perform a process of endless surrogation. Each term names the movement of a "we" that is responsible for its constitution and that traces the presence within it of an alterity irreducible to an "I."[51]

So if, as Marx writes in *The Holy Family,* Napoleon "perfected the Terror by substituting permanent war for permanent revolution,"[52] Melville's renegades in "The Encantadas" perfect the process of decolonization by substituting democratic reterritorialization with permanent riotocracy. The process of unbelonging, of "endless surrogation," hyperextends the already disjoint revolutionary temporality. It seemingly disallows the reinstitution of yet another autocratic regime, at the same time that it prevents anything like the "democratic" redistribution and protection of private property enacted by the Federalists in the wake of the American Revolution. "Nay, it was no democracy at all, neither Grecian, Roman, nor American." As such, it resists the world-historical conjurations of the ghosts of dead Romans, Roman costumes, or Roman phrases.[53] It is an insurrection without institution, a process of making permanent a series of interruptions to any foundational national narrative. The question becomes how revolutionary time might become extended (or made permanent) to prevent the return of patriarchal forms of power, to hold open new spaces for resistance and communal arrangement.

It is interesting that the Trotskyite C. L. R. James, in his reading of "The Encantadas" in *Mariners, Renegades and Castaways,* does not remark on the phrase "permanent *Riotocracy*" or on the Dog-King sketch, relating, rather, the hopeless struggle of humanity to the "crowning curse" of the Galápagos tortoises, their "straightforwardness in a belittered world."[54] For James "The Encantadas" does not harbor the revolutionary potential or latent modes of confederating that Kaplan recognizes; rather, it encapsulates Melville's vanquished faith in human progress. As James summarizes: "[Melville] takes politics and religion, love, friendship and faith; one by one he places them in *Las Encantadas* and shows how they are destroyed. He does not complain. He is even good-tempered, but the destruction is not less thorough."[55] Yet the argument here is that, as the "asylum of the oppressed of all navies," the "martyr[s] in the cause of freedom," or the "ragged citizen[s] of this universal nation," the insurgents who overthrow the Dog-King indeed form another anonymous mob that models the creation of the "world-federation" James envisages on the decks of the *Pequod.*[56] They form a new politics of relation that resists allegiance to any nation, fixed site of identity, or predetermined spatio-geographical distribution. The law of lawlessness instead demands a constant reconfederating as new members join and others leave. The apparent paradox of this temporary community's permanence is a testament to the resilience of its viable yet flexible system of managing its perpetual becoming-other. It is a shifting multiplicity, an open archipelago. Its "ragged citizens" are left unfinished, like the "ragged edges" of truth in *Billy Budd* (1431).

To signify this dis-order, Melville creates the neologism *riotocracy.* Riotocracy perhaps modulates the word *rotocracy* (connoting the power of those in charge of "rotten boroughs"[57] and essentially a synonym for *mobocracy*) or could be merely Melville's fanciful construction to express the power of his rioters. In any case, it empowers the double sense of *riot* as both a general unruliness and a carefree abandonment to merriment. In Melville's riotocracy, both Milton's sense of jollity and Badiou's sense of protest preside. If, as "no democracy," it also admits to the brute fact that for all the liberating revolutions the eighteenth and nineteenth centuries had witnessed, in many cases it has been only permanent *aristocracy* that has prevailed and that has formed the seemingly implacable bases of global capitalist modernity. In its externality to the state, Melville's permanent riotocracy invokes a figure of commonality opposed to the formation of this modernity. Its insurgents, "in the name of liberty," rather, "did just what they pleased." It fits Peter Lamborn Wilson/Hakim Bey's descriptions of a "pirates' utopia" or "temporary autonomous zone": "a mini-society living consciously outside the law and determined to keep it up, even if only for a short but merry life."[58]

In the sketch immediately preceding the story of the Dog-King, "Barrington Isle and the Buccaneers," Melville describes a similar scene of anarchic cooperation in the Galápagos archipelago:

> As a secure retreat, an undiscoverable hiding place, no spot in those days could have been better fitted. In the centre of a vast and silent sea, but very little traversed; surrounded by islands, whose inhospitable aspect might well drive away the chance navigator; and yet within a few days' sail of the opulent countries which they made their prey, the unmolested buccaneers found here that tranquillity which they fiercely denied to every civilized harbor in that part of the world. Here . . . those old marauders came, and lay snugly out of all harm's reach. But not only was the place a harbor of safety, and a bower of ease, but for utility in other things it was most admirable. ("Encantadas," 786)

The Encantadas, as a pirates' utopia, exist as a place off the grid of state control, hidden in "enfolded immensities [that] escape the measuring rod."[59] The enchanting, displacing effect of the Galápagos Islands—as shrouded in fog, surrounded by trick currents, given to ocular deceptions—itself enables the inhabitants to avoid all "entanglements with 'permanent solutions'"; it makes possible such confederations, living under temporary articles or no articles at all, off the map, "out of all harm's reach." Their temporary status is further demonstrated, as Melville continues, quoting (or rewriting) from "a sentimental voyager long ago,"[60] in that "it is highly improbable that the buccaneers ever erected dwelling-houses upon the isle" (ibid.). The only permanent trace of their "bowers of ease" is the "romantic seats" that evince for Melville's narrator "[no] other motive than one of pure peacefulness and kindly fellowship with nature" (ibid., 787). They join the broader community of singularities dispersed across Melville's writing—the loose confederations of landless runaways, castaways, and nomads who sail outside the measured grid of state control. Like the outlandish *Isolatoes* who eschew "the common continent of men" in *Moby-Dick* (921), they seek out new commonalities on the romantic seats of their bowers of ease. Out of such shared situations, Melville further explores how individualities form their "Siamese connexion[s]" with the "plurality of other mortals" (*Moby-Dick,* 1135); out of such shared situations, he further enacts his politics of the "kingly commons" (ibid., 917).

Like Bartleby or the crew of the *Pequod,* then, Melville's riotocrats and pirate-utopians in "The Encantadas" could serve as conceptual personae for current critical formulations of the "common."[61] The common, to hazard a provisional definition, is the inventive, nonhomogenizing activity of producing not a community of individuals who group themselves along the lines of a unified identity, but a composition of singularities in a common relationship.[62] The common becomes distanced from any nostalgic gemeinschaft whose constitution is based on a continual reinscription of timeless mythoi into its own self-identity. It is based not on individuals who share identities (of which the nation-state is the prime example—Pease's "monocultural taxonomy"), but on singularities who enact an indeterminate, processual sharing of differences. The constitution of the common presupposes active, open-ended cooperation as its logical condition of possibility and at once its outcome, and it thus is oriented toward opening new social relations.

For Cesare Casarino, such scenes of commonality in Melville's work point to a thought of the outside of capitalist modernity and its pernicious binaries of identity. In *Modernity at Sea,* Casarino explores how by turning

Melville and Marx into a "cosy loving pair"—or, more specifically, "by reading Melville's *Moby-Dick* and Marx's *Grundrisse* along and through each other." As Casarino writes: "*Moby-Dick* and the *Grundrisse* [are] works that attempt to come to terms with the outside of the history of modernity. . . . If the history of modernity is above all the history of capitalism, any thought of resistance to such a history is above all a thought of resistance to capital. To resist capital is to dare to think its outside, and for both Marx and Melville, such an outside makes itself felt in history through the explosive corporeal potentiality of labor, through a crisis-ridden and joyous collective body of *potentia*."[63] Rather than implicating the *Pequod*'s crew in a dialectics of class struggle or between master and slave (as C. L. R. James does), Casarino posits a dialectical excess constituted by the shared capabilities "incarnated in the living flesh of labor."[64] Put differently, both Melville and Marx show that the potential productive force of labor in bodies ceases to be the dialectical counterpart to capitalism's demand that the body's labor be commodified. The *Pequod*'s crew becomes "taken off the clock"[65] as a pure *potentia* of collective bodies of labor who model an alternative to capitalism by opening new loci of exchange, or new material, corporeal experiments. Such corporeal *potentia* modulates into "*amor potentiae*"[66] insofar as it takes as its experiment the formation of new modes of love and of being-with. Thus the homosocial relationship between Ishmael and Queequeg not only provides a counterforce to reified forms of heterosexual love, but serves to break up the complicity of capital with an oppressive heteronormativity. Their love becomes a shared experiment "without any teleological horizon"—it is "to live 'in the place of the other' . . . to live as *potentia* and *multitudo*."[67] This leads Casarino past James's dialectical-materialist and homoerotic paean to the body of labor in *Moby-Dick*—which, according to Casarino, "leaves Ahab's version of the events intact and does not translate into an investigation of the crew's own projects in the novel."[68] Rather, Casarino seeks to find in the *Pequod*'s crew a "collective body of subjectivity" that is "both *potentia* and *multitudo*—and as such it implies and needs no interiority. *This is a subjectivity without subjects*."[69]

Casarino's "subjectivity without subjects"—like Deleuze's community of celibates—is an opened-ended, experimental mode of being in common. Both Casarino and Deleuze go beyond the picture of fraternity Wilson Carey McWilliams develops in his seminal chapter on Melville in *The Idea of Fraternity in America*.[70] Whereas McWilliams likewise limns a society of the "Fatherless" in Melville's writing, he persistently reproduces the identity structures that predetermine "particularities."[71] In these alternative pictures of commonality, "fraternity" becomes not so much "essential for the realization of man's nature"[72] (as it is in McWilliams's terms) as an anonym for an open-ended—and indeed genderless—process of becoming freed from cardinal identity constraints like consanguinity, essentialism, or monolithic understandings of human nature: all the baptisms in water, blood, or fire that confer onto docile singularities the name of the Father. If McWilliams's duty-bound figure of fraternity becomes reducible to a nostalgia for the *imitatio Christi*,[73] Deleuze ironically instates a departicularized Bartleby as "the new Christ or brother of us all."[74] For Casarino fraternity becomes an activation of mutual corporeal potential, at once "crisis-ridden" and "joyous."

A similar critique might be leveled against Rogin, who, despite his expansive analysis of Melville's symbolic, societal, and historical implications, ironically performs the problematic of paternal inheritance as he endeavors to subvert it. Whereas his aim is to understand revolution through Melville's own "double revolutionary descent,"[75] his persistent conflation of Melville's writing and his biography serves to neutralize the force of his political explosiveness by redirecting it back onto speculative episodes in an Oedipal family drama. The temptation to biographize, which remains a critical reflex in Melville studies, runs the risk of reproducing a heteronormative politics and hermeneutical piety organized around the authorial (paternal) personality. This is the case with many of the usual loci of Melvillean political critique, especially those concerning questions of sexuality, such as the sperm-squeezing scene of emancipatory *jouissance* in "A Squeeze of the Hand," not to mention the Gorgon's head of the overdetermined relationship between Melville and Hawthorne. These have often led to fetishizations of Melville's own sexuality at the expense of sharing in or transferring the emancipatory potential for new modes of being-with. Theorists of the common pursue a picture of Melvillean fraternity in the other direction: one that does not ahistoricize Melville by taking him out of enmeshed historical networks, but emphasizes how Melville offers new "collective bodies of subjectivity" and new heterotopic possibilities of relation and distributions of collective power that might unbind forms of capitalist domination that use identity (family, state, ethnicity, "society," religion, personhood, sexuality, *ressentiment*) as their ideological covers.

A Paradise of Flowers and a Tartarus of Clinkers

Like Casarino's laboring crew aboard the *Pequod*, the pirates who take asylum in the Encantadas form an outside to global capitalist modernity, or perhaps its inexorable underside. If their collective labor is to "[ravage] the Pacific side of the Spanish colonies" and prey on the "opulent countries" along the Spanish Main, their collective reward is to "measure their silks of Asia with long Toledos for their yard-sticks" and to enjoy the "tranquillity" of their Galápagos retreat ("Encantadas," 786). The islands become a privileged destination, precisely because they are not considered a destination for state power at all—like the many pirate utopias of the sixteenth and seventeenth centuries, they exist outside the controlled cartographical space of empire and global exchange. As a result, they preempt the foundational discourses of the state itself—no Columbus would come to claim this fallen earth, to settle it, to cultivate it, or to "civilize" it. When Melville's narrator at the close of Sketch Seventh naively suggests saving the "shipwrecked men" of Charles' Island, his knowing captain advises them to steer clear, to "brace up" and "keep the light astern" (ibid., 792).

If in other sketches, such as "Norfolk Isle and the Chola Widow," Melville draws on Defoe's *Robinson Crusoe* and its reuptake of the Selkirk typology, here he gestures toward a lesser-known work of Defoe, his *General History of the Pyrates* (1724).[76] Among Defoe's biographies of famous buccaneers is a provocatively detailed pirates' utopia off the coast of Madagascar called Libertalia, a proto-socialist commune, operating much like Melville's Galápagos retreat.

There Defoe describes a multinational "Nest of Pyrates" with "all the Necessaries of Life" where captured slaves are set free and the death penalty condemned, where money "was of no Use because every Thing was in common, and no Hedge bounded any particular Man's Property."[77] Even if Defoe's Libertalia would ultimately fail, his pirate-utopians endure not as ruthless criminals, but as nonconformists who put under suspicion the prevailing narratives of historical progression and global capitalist expansion at the very bases of their eighteenth-century society. Melville's buccaneers in Sketch Sixth, like those in Defoe's *General History*, also resist the hasty generalization or stereotyping that would determinately incarcerate them as outcasts of history. As Melville continues, shortly after the passage cited above:

> That the buccaneers perpetrated the greatest outrages is very true; that some of them were mere cut-throats is not to be denied; but we know that here and there among their host was a Dampier, a Wafer, and a Cowley, and likewise other men, whose worst reproach was their desperate fortunes; whom persecution, or adversity, or secret and unavengeable wrongs, had driven from Christian society to seek the melancholy solitude or the guilty adventures of the sea. . . . All of the buccaneers were not unmitigated monsters. . . . Could it be possible, that they robbed and murdered one day, revelled the next, and rested themselves by turning meditative philosophers, rural poets, and seat-builders the third? Not very improbable, after all. For consider the vacillations of a man. Still strange as it may seem, I must also abide by the more charitable thought; namely, that among these adventurers were some gentlemanly, companionable souls, capable of genuine tranquility and virtue. ("Encantadas," 787–788)

Again we witness Melville's refusal to consolidate into a unified political or ideological position. Melville's marauders become the next day meditative philosophers, pastoral poets, if not landscape designers. Like Ishmael's "genial, desperado philosophy" through which imperiled sailors learn to laugh in the face of death and realize the multiformity of "this strange mixed affair we call life" (*Moby-Dick,* 1035), or like his algorithm for human mental multiformity in *The Confidence-Man* that "many men have many minds" (*Confidence-Man,* 846), in "The Encantadas" Melville's premise is that it is "not very improbable" that these pirates too will subvert our expectations with their own multiformity, for why not, "given the vacillations of man" ("Encantadas," 788)?

What is more, Melville's archipelago-perspectivism includes the vacillations of these pirates' utopias themselves. Like Libertalia, Melville's sea Alsatias, despite their claims to permanent impermanency, could not last. As is the case with any utopia, Melville's pirates' utopias might anamorphose into their dystopian counterparts, as the "map" of utopia engraved by Ambrosius Holbein and used as the frontispiece to the 1518 edition of More's *Utopia* anamorphoses into a barren skull. This is curiously registered in the history of the Galápagos. In 1820 a boat steerer from the Nantucket whaler the *Essex,* a ship always in the back of Melville's mind, had set a wildfire that blackened the whole of Charles' Island. The Dog-King sketch strangely foretells the autocratic regime of a sugar plantation owner, assassinated in 1904 by his insurgent workers. The Galápagos has been subject to other misanthropes since, from Europeans and Americans seeking refuge in the Ecuadorian tax haven (today's misanthropic pirates' utopia) to ecotourists and their ongoing colonialism. As Melville says, there are "two sides to a tortoise" ("Encantadas," 769). Every paradise of flowers has its tartarus of clinkers, as every paradise of bachelors has its tartarus of maids. The utopia of escape, of following the line, can become a dystopia of nomadism, the liquid modernity of Zygmunt Bauman in which rootlessness has become a formula for universal alienation. The pathology of masterlessness becomes another form of mastery. The fate of the "Runaways, Castaways, Solitaries" Melville describes in the final sketch of "The Encantadas" attests to this: "The Enchanted Isles [have] become the voluntary tarrying places of all sorts of refugees; some of whom too sadly experience the fact that flight from tyranny does not itself insure a safe asylum, far less a happy home" (ibid., 816).

For Deleuze the only "real danger" to the "society without fathers" is the "return of the father."[78] From this vantage point, he renders inseparable the failures of the "two revolutions, the American and the Soviet, the pragmatic and the dialectal":[79] "Just as many Bolsheviks could hear the diabolical powers knocking at the door in 1917, the pragmatists, like Melville before them, could see the masquerade that the society of brothers would lead to. Long before Lawrence, Melville and Thoreau were diagnosing the American evil, the new cement that would rebuild the wall: paternal authority and filthy charity."[80] This paternal authority and charity merge in the protean figure of the Melvillean confidence man. "What malignant power," Deleuze asks, "has turned the trust into a company as cruel as the abominable 'universal nation' founded by the [Dog-King] in *The Encantadas?*"[81] Even if it is not, to be precise, the "Dog-Man" who founds the universal nation, we can see Deleuze's point: that in the wake of the dissolution of transcendental paternal sovereignty, immanent fraternity always risks becoming a masquerade of false brothers. Melville's novel *The Confidence-Man,* already begun while he was finishing "The Encantadas," becomes an extended exploration of this risk, the duplicity of fraternity. The novel's key term is *trust,* which is both an expression of human bonding and a cover for the dissimulations that inhabit capitalism at every point where money is to be made. Confidence might always reveal itself as a con game. The society without fathers can "resort to manipulation" and thus become nourished by an "ir-remediable mistrust among particular individuals."[82] We must take it on faith that our contracts will not be broken, that our credit will be good. As Deleuze asks: "Are these false brothers sent by a diabolical father to restore his power over *overly credulous* Americans? . . . The novel is so complex that one could just as easily say the opposite: this long procession of con men would become a comic version of authentic brothers, such as *overly suspicious* Americans see them, or rather have already become incapable of seeing them."[83] At the same time, charity might also slip into a form of paternalism, a Christian charity, that demands "the fusion of souls in the name of [a] great love."[84] For Melville it becomes equally misanthropic to love a philanthropist as it is philanthropic to hate a misanthrope.

It is on these fronts that Deleuze locates the struggle for emancipation in Melville's work and the enduring promise of his proto-pragmatism. Melville not only recognizes the duplicity of fraternity as both a community to come and a masquerade. He also works to resist, by means of a pragmatist ethics, the "particularities that pit man against man" and, through a radical empiricism, any reintegration into wholeness or unity that would serve to negate singularity or stymie one's ability to create oneself and one's world anew. Bartleby, for Deleuze, becomes the most radical of empiricists: the hero of both the disintegration of representation and the repartitioning of the sensible order in its wake. Melville, Deleuze attests, "is already sketching out the traits of the pragmatism that will be its continuation. It is first of all the affirmation of a world in process, an archipelago."[85] For this to come about, the "knowing subject"—the constituted subject of phenomenology or the solitary political subject capable of individual agency—will have had to become dissolved into "a community of explorers, the brothers of the archipelago, who replace knowledge with belief, or rather with 'confidence.'"[86] Deleuze seemingly endows Melville's federated world with what were to him the more attractive features of William James's "pluralistic universe": "things are 'with' one another in many ways, but nothing includes everything, or dominates over everything. The word 'and' trails along after every sentence. Something always escapes."[87] Relations are externalized, as "a wall of loose, uncemented stones";[88] truth remains rough and unfinished. The "cement" of consolidating paternal authority never hardens to seal off the wall. We might rewrite Melville's formula from *White-Jacket* along the lines of James's radical empiricism as "We expatriate to trans-nationalize in the pluriverse."

For Jacques Rancière, however, in his trenchant assessment of Deleuze's reading of Melville in *The Flesh of Words*, this image of the "wall of loose, uncemented stones" serves rather as precisely the aporia of an emancipatory politics to be elicited from Melville's writing. Rancière writes:

> Under the mask of Bartleby, Deleuze opens to us the open road of comrades, the great drunkenness of joyous multitudes freed from the law of the Father, the path of a certain Deleuzism that is perhaps only the "festival of donkeys" of Deleuze's thinking. But this road leads us to a contradiction: the wall of loose stones, the wall of non-passage. . . . And this wall of loose stones is like those . . . aerial bridges that Zarathustra had to cast toward the future, at the risk of seeing them resemble the counterfeits that enchanters and fools made of them. But, of course, the strength of every strong thought is also its ability to arrange its aporia itself, the point where it can no longer pass. And this is exactly what Deleuze does here when, in one single gesture, he clears the way of Deleuzism and sends it into the wall.[89]

Given the duplicity of the society of brothers, it is easy to see how Rancière might hear in the drunken joyous multitude the incessantly repeating Ye-a! Ye-a's! of a Nietzschean festival of donkeys. For Rancière nomadic thought might risk becoming caricatured as a "universal mobilism to which it is so easily likened. For universal mobilism is also a quietism, an indifferentism."[90] The question for Rancière in this context remains a pressing one: "How can one make a difference in the political community with this indifference?"[91] And, given that the "oxymoronic figure" of a wall of loose stones is also a roadblock for the people to come, does this interminably postpone the promised fraternity?

These will remain, at least for now, open questions. What is at stake is whether we will shrink back before this wall as if it were altogether impassable, or whether we will find new ways to dismantle it, if not to kick it down. The challenge remains to find new ways of being-with that do not become totalizing, that can remain incomplete, contingent, and under construction, and new ways of perpetually reorganizing the loose, uncemented stones. Melville's outlandish politics, as multivocal, polyvalent, and pluralist (in James's sense), does this as it draws together contradictory forces and rarely resolves them into a finished whole or places the crowning "architectural finial" (*Billy Budd,* 1431). Melville's politics keeps its "ragged edges" (ibid.). This disallows any univocal political position as well as any correspondence between his own personal political views and those of the players in his work—to the contrary, for example, of Rogin's claim that Vere's actions symbolize Melville's own late accession to authority.[92] If the failed promise of the French Revolution haunts his work, or if he flirts with a Burkean position in *Billy Budd,* this is not tantamount to a de facto antirevolutionary political position. If the scroll of *Mardi* contains a series of formulaic Burkean pronouncements, at the same time the cast of *Mardi* vehemently disclaims authorship of them and tears them to "shreds" (*Mardi,* 1187). Dennis Berthold's fine comment on Melville's late works *The Burgundy Club* and *Billy Budd* may thus hold for his work more generally: "As multivocal, dialogical dramas, they are less important as statements of Melville's actual political beliefs than as hermeneutical texts that unmask art's ideological function, exposing the process that transforms emotion into art, event into history, and people into icons."[93] That art can draw together contraries so that we might better understand complex ideological dynamisms, that we can, through this understanding, find new ways to counterforce exploitation and the return of paternal power, that we can find new modes of confederating without consolidating all the solitaries of our fragmentary world: these are perhaps the challenges, but also the hope, that Melville's writing gives us. It is to inaugurate, again and again, as Edoaurd Glissant would say, a new "poetics of relation," and a new politics of relation. In his work resounds the promise of pragmatism, the "double principle of archipelago and hope."[94] It calls forth to new riots and to new festivals, to a new planetary order and to a new humanity.

Notes

1. Gilles Deleuze, "Bartleby; or, The Formula," in Deleuze, *Essays Critical and Clinical,* trans. Daniel W. Smith and Michael A. Greco (Minneapolis: University of Minnesota, 1997), 87.

2. See Denise Tanyol, "The Alternative Taxonomies of Melville's 'The Encantadas,'" *New England Quarterly,* 80, no. 2 (July 2007): 242–279.

3. Herman Melville, *Redburn, White-Jacket, Moby-Dick* (New York: Library of America, 1983), 1077. Subsequent citations to this edition will made parenthetically in the text by title and page number.

4. Herman Melville, "The Encantadas; or, Enchanted Isles," in *Pierre, Israel*

Potter, The Piazza Tales, The Confidence-Man, Uncollected Prose, and Billy Budd (New York: Library of America, 1984), 785; hereinafter cited as *Pierre . . . Billy Budd.* Subsequent citations to this edition of the story will be made parenthetically in the text by title and page number.

5. See also Melville's description of "all manner of interesting and outlandish characters" one might encounter in reading Francis Parkman's *The California and Oregon Trail* in his review, "Mr. Parkman's Tour," in *The Piazza Tales and Other Prose Pieces, 1839–1860,* ed. Harrison Hayford, Alma A. MacDougall, and G. Thomas Tanselle (Evanston and Chicago: Northwestern University Press and the Newberry Library, 1987), 233.

6. See also Deleuze's comments on the word *outlandish* in Melville's writing, in his interview with Claire Parnet in his *Abecedaire,* under the heading "'A' for Animal." Deleuze, speaking of "deterritorialization" as a philosophical concept that does not yet exist, finds in Melville the correlate (exact translation) for *outlandish:* "For example, I later realized that in Melville, the word 'outlandish' is always coming up. . . . 'Outlandish' is exactly the deterritorialized. Word for word." Gilles Deleuze, Claire Parnet, and Pierre-André Boutang, *Gilles Deleuze from A to* Z (DVD), trans. Charles J. Stivale (Cambridge: Semiotexte/MIT Press, 2011), 13:51–14:12.

7. Herman Melville, *Typee, Omoo, Mardi* (New York: Library of America, 1982), 1216. Subsequent citations to this edition will be made parenthetically in the text by title and page number.

8. Herman Melville, "Bartleby the Scrivener," in *Pierre . . . Billy Budd,* 657.

9. Deleuze, *Essays,* 86.

10. See Tracy B. Strong's extensive analysis of *Benito Cereno* (including its symbolic evocations of the Haitian Revolution) and Jason Frank's provocative diagnosis of the "fear of mutiny, insurrection, and revolution" that "haunts" *Billy Budd* elsewhere in this volume.

11. Herman Melville, "I and My Chimney," in *Pierre . . . Billy Budd,* 1299.

12. Melville to Hawthorne, November 17, 1851, in Herman Melville, *Correspondence,* ed. Lynn Horth (Evanston and Chicago: Northwestern University Press and the Newberry Library, 1993), 212.

13. Similar scenes of brotherly love appear in "Hawthorne and His Mosses," *Moby-Dick, Pierre, Clarel,* and *Billy Budd.*

14. Herman Melville, "The Paradise of Bachelors and the Tartarus of Maids," in *Pierre . . . Billy Budd,* 1261.

15. Herman Melville, *Tales, Poems, and Other Writings,* ed. John Bryant (New York: Modern Library, 2001), 347, 359, 356.

16. See also Deleuze, *Essays,* 89.

17. Herman Melville, *Clarel: A Poem and Pilgrimage in the Holy Land,* ed.

Harrison Hayford, Hershel Parker, and G. Thomas Tanselle (Evanston and Chicago: Northwestern University Press and the Newberry Library, 1991), 148.

18. D. H. Lawrence, *Studies in Classic American Literature* (1923; repr., New York: Viking, 1972), 8. Or, as he puts it in his matter-of-fact pronouncement: "Liberty is all very well, but men cannot live without masters. There is always a master" (4).

19. Jacques Lacan, quoted in Slavoj Žižek, "Occupy Wall Street: What Is to Be Done Next?" *Guardian,* April 24, 2012, www.guardian.co.uk/commentisfree/cifamerica/2012/apr/24/occupy-wall-street-what-is-to-be-done-next.

20. Christopher Sten, "'Facts Picked Up in the Pacific': Fragmentation, Deformation, and the (Cultural) Uses of Enchantment in 'The Encantadas,'" in "*Whole Oceans Away": Melville and the Pacific,* ed. Jill Barnum, Wyn Kelley, and Christopher Sten (Kent, Ohio: Kent State University Press, 2008), 220.

21. Edwin Williamson, *The Penguin History of Latin America* (London: Penguin, 2009), 237.

22. Charles Darwin, *The Voyage of the* Beagle (1839; repr., New York: Penguin, 1989), 125; see also 135–137 for Darwin's assessment of the "violent revolution" in Argentina. Darwin is among the unacknowledged sources of the "Encantadas" sketches, classed among the "barren bootless allusions from some few passing voyagers or compilers," as Melville admits in Sketch Fifth ("Encantadas," 785). See also Hester Blum, *A View from the Masthead* (Chapel Hill: University of North Carolina Press, 2008), 133–157.

23. Williamson, *Penguin History,* 237.

24. Ibid., 231.

25. Ibid.

26. Quoted ibid., 232.

27. See the editorial notes on "The Encantadas" in Melville's *The Piazza Tales* (Northwestern ed.), 612.

28. Ibid., 613. Vilamil was not Cuban, as the Dog-King was, which leads Chris Sten to surmise that "significantly, Cuba, the home of the Creole in this seventh sketch, showed no promise of gaining independence in the decades before Melville's time. Despite sporadic slave revolts, which were brutally suppressed by the Spanish, Cuba remained a Spanish colony until the end of the nineteenth century and the Spanish-American War. Clearly the Dog-King saw no promise to staying in Cuba and sought to improve his lot elsewhere" (Sten, "Facts Picked Up in the Pacific," 220).

29. Darwin, *Voyage of the* Beagle, 271.

30. See Hennig Cohen, "Melville and Diogenes the Cynic," in *Melville "Among the Nations": Proceedings of an International Conference; Volos, Greece, July 2–6, 1997,* ed. Sanford E. Marovitz and A. C. Chistodoulou (Kent, Ohio: Kent State University Press, 2001), 135.

31. As the note to this passage in the Norton Critical Edition relates, the description of these new republics in terms of "eternal democracy" was a "contemporary catchphrase." See Melville, *Moby-Dick*, 2nd ed., ed. Hershel Parker and Harrison Hayford (New York: W. W. Norton, 2001), 99.

32. See Dennis Berthold, "Melville, Garibaldi, and the Medusa of Revolution," *American Literary History* 9, no. 3 (Autumn 1997): 449.

33. In addition to Franklin there are other "relics of primogeniture" from the American Revolution present in Melville's work: for example, the badge of the Cincinnatus that Major Jack Gentian wears in Melville's unfinished late work, *The Burgundy Club*, which evokes Melville's own revolutionary genealogy. See Michael Paul Rogin, *Subversive Genealogy: The Politics and Art of Herman Melville* (New York: Knopf, 1983), 290.

34. Garibaldi's relationship to Melville has admirably been developed by Berthold, in "Melville, Garibaldi, and the Medusa of Revolution."

35. Less well known is Garibaldi's involvement in the South American independence movements, specifically in resisting Las Rosas in Argentina in the 1840s. An interesting biographical twist, though most likely apocryphal, would uncannily link these figures: Garibaldi met with the famous lover of Bolívar, Manuela Sáenz, while she was living as an outcast in Paita, Peru. As the story goes, so had Herman Melville a few years earlier, when the *Acushnet* was docked in nearby Tumbes, right before heading to the Galápagos. Tantalizing as this may be, Hershel Parker disclaims the meeting, finding no documentary evidence to support it. Gabriel García Márquez, however, mentions the visits from both Garibaldi and Melville in *The General in His Labyrinth: A Novel*, trans. Edith Grossman (New York: Knopf, 1990), 261. See Parker, *Herman Melville: A Biography*, vol. 1, *1819–1851* (Baltimore: Johns Hopkins University Press, 1996), 203. There is also a recent French film, *Manuela Sáenz: Simon Bolivar's Love Story*, which reimagines their meeting (placing it, for what it's worth, in 1856). In the film Melville's visit prompts Sáenz to revisit her lover Bolívar's letters, which elicits a flood of passionate memories of their revolutionary times together.

36. Rogin, *Subversive Genealogy*, 210.

37. Ibid., 213. See also Helen Lock, "The Paradox Slave Mutiny in Herman Melville, Charles Johnson, and Frederick Douglass," *College Literature* 30, no. 4 (Fall 2003): 54–70.

38. Robert S. Levine, "The Revolutionary Aesthetics of *Israel Potter*," in *Melville and Aesthetics*, ed. Samuel Otter and Geoffrey Sanborn (New York: Palgrave Macmillan, 2011), 170. Levine holds *Israel Potter* to be "a comically antic work that mixes fictional with historical characters, skews historical chronologies, and depicts such celebrated figures as Franklin, Jones, and Allen as tricksters, plotters, and killers" (170).

39. Amy Kaplan, "Transnational Melville," *Leviathan: A Journal of Melville Studies* 12, no. 1 (2010): 51.

40. Ibid., 42, 51; Melville, *White-Jacket*, 427.

41. Kaplan, "Transnational Melville," 51–52. Kaplan also adduces the multiple perspectives that a "transnational Melville" offers: "From Melville, we learn that transnational approaches to literature and history must account for both: expatriation, border-crossing, and cosmopolitanism, as well as colonial violence, empire-building, and the bloodshed of revolutions and counter-revolutions" (51).

42. Cf. Melville, *Redburn*, 297.

43. Deleuze, *Essays*, 85.

44. Jacques Rancière, *The Flesh of Words: The Politics of Writing*, trans. Charlotte Mandell (Stanford: Stanford University Press, 2004), 159, 157.

45. Friedrich Nietzsche, *On the Genealogy of Morality*, ed. Keith Ansell-Pearson, trans. Carol Diethe (Cambridge: Cambridge University Press, 2007), 68.

46. Deleuze, *Essays*, 77–78.

47. Ibid., 81, 84.

48. Ibid., 84; emphasis in original.

49. C. L. R. James, *Mariners, Renegades and Castaways: The Story of Herman Melville and the World We Live In* (1985; repr., Hanover, N.H.: Dartmouth College Press, 2001), 19.

50. Ibid., 28.

51. Donald Pease, "Doing Justice to C. L. R. James's *Mariners, Renegades and Castaways*," *boundary 2* 27, no. 2 (Summer 2000): 18–19.

52. Karl Marx and Friedrich Engels, *Marx/Engels Collected Works*, vol. 4, *1844–45* (New York: International Publishers, 1975), 123.

53. Karl Marx, "The Eighteenth Brumaire of Louis Bonaparte," in *The Marx and Engels Reader*, ed. Robert C. Tucker (New York: W. W. Norton, 1978), 595.

54. James, *Mariners, Renegades and Castaways*, 109.

55. Ibid., 110.

56. Ibid., 20.

57. See "rotocracy, n.," in OED Online, www.oed.com/view/Entry/167767?redirectedFrom=rotocracy.

58. Peter Lamborn Wilson, *Pirate Utopias: Moorish Corsairs and European Renegadoes*, rev. ed. (Brooklyn, N.Y.: Autonomedia, 2003); Hakim Bey, *T.A.Z.: The Temporary Autonomous Zone, Ontological Anarchy, Poetic Terrorism* (Brooklyn, N.Y.: Autonomedia, 2003), 67.

59. Bey, *T.A.Z.*,71.

60. According to the editors of the Northwestern-Newberry edition of *Piazza Tales*, Melville's "sentimental voyager" is in fact the British explorer James Colnett, from whom Melville liberally adapts his Sketch Sixth, emphasizing the egalitarian

tendencies of the buccaneers. See Melville, *The Piazza Tales* (Northwestern ed.), 603, 610–611.

61. Following Deleuze's influential treatment of "Bartleby," Giorgio Agamben, Michael Hardt and Antonio Negri, and Cesare Casarino (among others) have invoked Melville's characters as modeling the "common" as an impersonal community of singularities. Exemplary are Giorgio Agamben's *The Coming Community*, trans. Michael Hardt (Minneapolis: University of Minnesota Press, 1993); Michael Hardt and Antonio Negri's *Empire* (Cambridge: Harvard University Press, 2001); Antonio Negri and Cesare Casarino's *In Praise of the Common* (Minneapolis: University of Minnesota Press, 1993); and Cesare Casarino's *Modernity at Sea: Melville, Marx, Conrad in Crisis* (Minneapolis: University of Minnesota Press, 2002). See Kevin Attell's contribution to this volume.

62. Michael Hardt and Antonio Negri, *Commonwealth* (Cambridge: Harvard University Press, 2009), 183.

63. Casarino, *Modernity at Sea*, xxi.

64. Ibid., xxii.

65. Ibid., 58.

66. Ibid., xxv.

67. Ibid., 163.

68. Ibid., 118.

69. Ibid., 114; emphasis in original.

70. Wilson Carey McWilliams, "Herman Melville: The Pilgrim," in McWilliams, *The Idea of Fraternity in America* (Berkeley: University of California Press, 1973).

71. It is noteworthy in this context that McWilliams understands Melville's *Isolatoes* as "like most lonely men" rather than as departicularized figures. Ibid., 338.

72. Ibid., 354.

73. Ibid., 364.

74. Deleuze, *Essays*, 90.

75. Rogin, *Subversive Genealogy*, 162.

76. Daniel Defoe, *A General History of the Pyrates* (1724), ed. Manuel Schonhorn (Mineola, N.Y.: Dover, 1999).

77. Ibid., 430, 435, 427.

78. Deleuze, *Essays*, 88.

79. Ibid.

80. Ibid.

81. Ibid., 89.

82. Rogin, *Subversive Genealogy*, 203.

83. Deleuze, *Essays*, 89; emphases in original.

84. Ibid., 87.

85. Ibid., 86.

86. Ibid., 86–87.

87. William James, *A Pluralistic Universe* (1909), in James, *Writings, 1902–1910* (New York: Library of America, 1988), 776.

88. Deleuze, *Essays*, 86.

89. Rancière, *The Flesh of Words*, 164.

90. Ibid., 162.

91. Ibid., 163.

92. On this topic I would mark my point of departure from critics like Larry Reynolds who have taken Melville's diagnosis of revolutionary violence and paternal authority to be an endorsement of political conservatism or state authority, buttressing their arguments with scenes from Melville's biography or (in Reynolds's case) with circumstantial contact with events in New York City in the second half of the nineteenth century. See Reynolds, *Righteous Violence: Revolution, Slavery, and the American Renaissance* (Athens: University of Georgia Press, 2011), 182–200.

93. Berthold, "Melville, Garibaldi, and the Medusa of Revolution," 449.

94. Deleuze, *Essays*, 87.

9

What Babo Saw

Benito Cereno *and "the World We Live In"*

Lawrie Balfour

> The miracle of Herman Melville is this: that a hundred years ago in two novels . . . and two or three stories, he painted a picture of the world in which we live, which is to this day unsurpassed.
>
> —C. L. R. James, *Mariners, Renegades and Castaways: The Story of Herman Melville and the World We Live In*

> Over the bleached bones and jumbled residue of numerous civilizations are written the pathetic words: "Too late."
>
> —Martin Luther King Jr., "A Time to Break Silence"

In 1952, while awaiting possible deportation in a prison on Ellis Island, the Trinidadian intellectual and radical activist C. L. R. James wrote a book-length study of Herman Melville and the totalitarian reach of the cold war state. James's book focuses on *Moby-Dick,* from which it borrows its title, and on Melville's unfulfilled allegiance to the fate of the *Pequod*'s polyglot, multiracial crew. Though Melville shrinks from embracing democratic revolt, James nevertheless looks to him as the poet of the "renegades and castaways and savages" who counter the sickness of modern existence with their humor and their deep sense of history and who prefigure the multinational crew of detainees on Ellis Island.[1] In *Benito Cereno,* a novella first published serially in 1855 and then as part of *The Piazza Tales* a year later, James discerns both the power of Melville's democratic art and the point of its deterioration into mere "propaganda." Melville's narration of an American sea captain's incapacity to comprehend the meaning of an insurrection aboard a slave ship represents "every single belief cherished by an advanced civilization . . . about a backward people," James argues, even if it is ultimately a mystery story with a point to prove rather than the inauguration of something genuinely new.[2]

James is not alone in finding resources for democratic thinking in Melville's fiction and in *Benito Cereno* specifically. Indeed, Melville has been called "one of the principal interpreters of the American obsession with race and commitment to racism," a touchstone for twentieth- and twenty-first-century artists attempting to conceive the possibilities for and obstacles inhibiting multiracial democracy.[3] Perhaps most famously, Ralph Ellison begins *Invisible Man* with an epigraph from the concluding section of *Benito Cereno:* "'You are saved,' cried Captain Delano, more and more astonished and pained; 'You are saved; what has cast such a shadow upon you?'" Ellison omits Captain Cereno's reply, but it would be familiar to Melville's readers: "the negro." The ambiguity of that shadow—is it thrown by a single black individual, or does it represent a more abstract conception of blackness, or both?—conjures a long history in which racialized violence, democracy, and denial intertwine. It also suggests the lasting power of Melville's imaginative destabilization of prevailing fictions of race.[4] Accordingly, this essay seeks to highlight those dimensions of *Benito Cereno* that, by reflecting on the political challenges of Melville's time, most acutely limn the challenges of democratic life today. I consider how his attention to the rituals that cloaked the viciously inegalitarian racial order of the mid-nineteenth century in the mantle of civility calls our attention to a regressive politics of friendship at work in our "postracial" era.

Melville's novella recounts a slave revolt on a Spanish ship off the coast of Chile in 1799. The ship's history is revealed largely through the eyes of a quintessentially American captain, Amasa Delano, who happens on the drifting *San Dominick* and attempts to rescue the ragged vessel and its human cargo and crew. The scene Delano encounters is one of apparent disarray, as the blacks and whites on board "in one language, and as with one voice, all poured out a common tale of suffering."[5] In his innocence—and his confident sense of American superiority not only to the slaves on board but also to the Old World Catholics who are the captain and crew—Delano fails to recognize that the disorder he attributes to the Spanish captain Benito Cereno's leadership disguises an elaborate pantomime orchestrated by Babo, a Senegalese slave and mastermind of the revolt. It is the slaves who rule, until the moment when Cereno attempts to escape with the departing Delano, Babo pursues him with a knife, and the extent of the insurrection is unveiled.

Whereas other commentators have examined Melville's story as a powerful apprehension that the price of racial domination would soon come due, I explore Melville's prescience about the character of the postrevolutionary racial order that would emerge from American slavery. Melville's ironic treatment of the American seaman enables him to disclose, simultaneously, what Delano saw and what the slaves would have foreseen. Crucially, the latter would have known that the generosity and openness so characteristic of the American character were inseparable from an insatiable demand for gratitude, that easy friendship could and would at any moment give way to cruelty, that white witness to the horrors of slavery could not be disentangled from the pleasures of voyeurism. This does not mean that *Benito Cereno* explores what Elizabeth Alexander calls "the black interior."[6] The reader, in fact, learns nothing of the thoughts or feelings or losses sustained by the Africans on board the *San Dominick,* and Babo dies, emphatically, in silence. Nonetheless, *Benito Cereno* gestures toward practices of racial domination that are not only insusceptible to remedy by dint of white goodwill but are, in fact, sustained by it.

More specifically, the novella raises pointed questions about the viability of friendship as a mechanism for democratic revival in the aftermath of slavery and Jim Crow. One of the most disquieting elements of Melville's story is its insight into the ways in which a brutal, racially hierarchical order was maintained through performances of friendship. What are the legacies of such performances? To what extent do political theoretical commitments to the value of social trust obscure this history or reinspirit its legacies? In a period defined by segregated neighborhoods and schools and widening racial inequalities, on the one hand, and the hegemony of color-blind discourse and policies, on the other, can the habits and rituals of friendship enable American citizens to negotiate the difficult choices and inevitable losses of collective life? If the regressive racial policies of the post–civil rights era are undergirded by a "friendship orthodoxy" that insists on citizens' essential sameness under the skin and feeds a culture of blame, can the idea of political friendship be reworked in progressive ways?[7] I approach these questions by reading *Benito Cereno* alongside Danielle Allen's *Talking to Strangers,* which makes a vigorous case for the democratic importance, in the post–civil rights era, of treating one's fellow citizens like friends. Although Melville published his story with an "eye on the gathering storm," I conclude that the novella's great, troubling success may consist most dramatically in its capacity to foreshadow dangers that would linger long *after* the storm.[8]

Imagining Slave Insurrection

For today's readers, it may be hard to understand how Melville's story could be evaluated in isolation from its historical context or why his critical sense of events around him evaded so many astute critics for so long. Composed in the middle of a decade that began with the Fugitive Slave Law and ended with John Brown on the gallows, *Benito Cereno* first appeared in serial form in *Putnam's Monthly,* an antislavery journal.[9] Yet, as Carolyn Karcher remarks, "Until the mid-1960s, there was almost no interest in Melville's racial views, and very little recognition of the prominent place that social criticism occupies in his writings."[10] Early commentary on the novella, which reads Babo as the embodiment of evil, has been supplanted more recently by an appreciation of Melville's multiple social-critical targets. The text's critique of prevailing racial ideologies, its references to Haiti, its implicit condemnation of American slavery and expansionism, and its exploration of the kinship of American and Spanish imperial aspirations have generated a vast scholarship.[11] Recognizing that it would be a mistake to pin Melville to any one of these as his dominant preoccupation, I concur with Sandra Zagarell's conclusion that "the novella's comparisons range throughout modern Western history, often pivoting, as if in warning, on the rebelliousness of subordinated populations."[12]

Although much of the action is seen, or not, from the perspective of the myopic American captain, Melville weaves references to historical events throughout the story. Taking inspiration from the historical captain Amasa Delano's *Narrative of Voyages and Travels, in the Northern and Southern Hemispheres,* which was published in 1817, Melville redacts the original in ways that call into question the world that Delano—both historical and fictional—represents. Perhaps most obviously, by changing the name of Cereno's ship from the *Tryal* to the *San Dominick* and shifting the time of the revolt from 1805 to 1799, Melville sets his tale in the context of the age of revolution, generally, and the liberation of Haiti, most especially.[13] As recent commentators have noted, furthermore, Melville would have been familiar with the slave revolts on the *Amistad* (1839) and *Creole* (1841) as well as the slave uprisings that terrified the southern states and the debates about the expansion of slavery and the status of fugitives that roiled the nation.[14] More, the story's reference to the *San Dominick* as a "slumbering volcano" (698) may direct the reader to Frederick Douglass's 1849 "Slumbering Volcano" speech and foretell the inevitability of slave insurrection.[15] Melville does not tell us for certain, however. As Joyce Sparer Adler remarks, "Far from developing his thought in glaring black and white, Melville beclouded it, challenging American readers to 'pierce' in this work, as they needed to in life, the surface and also the upper substratum of slavery in order to arrive at its skeletal reality."[16]

In its portraits of key figures, *Benito Cereno* also examines and undermines prevailing views about slavery and race. Delano stands for the liberal racialism of many northern abolitionists, opposed to slavery but not to the idea of racial hierarchy.[17] Cereno, though emblematic of Old World attitudes, is also, in the view of many scholars, a stand-in for slavery's southern defenders. As Michael Rogin remarks, "Melville's slave mutiny as masquerade inserted itself between two opposed perspectives on the master-slave relationship in antebellum America, and unsettled both."[18] Further, Melville differentiates the slave characters, giving them individual histories that defy white characters' repeated references to them as "the blacks" or "his blacks" or "the negro." Though James's characterization of Babo as "the most heroic character in Melville's fiction" is not persuasive, Melville parodies Delano's incapacity to recognize Babo's genius ("that hive of subtlety"), exposes the costs of Cereno's inability to transform his own experience of bondage into insight into the slaves' desires, and raises uneasy questions about *which* characters engage in "ferocious piratical revolt" (734).[19] Indeed, Sterling Stuckey and Joshua Leslie make a compelling case that Melville's reading of Mungo Park and others inculcated in him a sense of West African cultural traditions that enabled him to produce complex accounts of even the unnamed characters—the African women, the oakum pickers, and the hatchet polishers.[20]

To say that *Benito Cereno* is a work of social commentary is not to unravel, once and for all, the puzzle of precisely *what* Melville's message might be. Indeed, the story signals its inscrutability from the first. Calling readers' attention to what cannot be known, Melville sketches an opening scene that is inaccessible to at least three of the senses: it is gray, mute, and calm (673).

He also muddies the narrator's point of view by writing in a flat, apparently detached tone across the novella's three sections. In the first and longest section, the action is narrated in the third person, but the perspective seems to be the occluded vantage of Delano himself.[21] The second section consists of excerpts from Benito Cereno's deposition after the American and Spanish sailors have retaken the ship and captured or killed the insurrectionary slaves. Drawing from the historical documents in Delano's *Narrative*, this section testifies to extraordinary events in a manner that both mimics and undermines the objectivity of legal documents. The third section returns to the third person but no longer seems to issue from the viewpoint of the American captain. Throughout the novella, moreover, Melville deploys devices that hide the meaning of events from the reader's view. One of the most effective of these is his extravagant use of double negatives, which, Eric Sundquist argues, signal the tautology that "asserts the virtual equivalence of potentially different authorities or meanings."[22]As Philip Fisher observes, furthermore, Melville intensifies both the critique and its ambiguity through the use of inclusive either/or sentences in which the second term preserves rather than negates the first: "For Melville this *either/or* that is protected from denial is the syntax of the superimposed space of American slavery. It is the political space of what we call occupation rather than conquest. Each gesture and every single fact has a double location that can only be experienced by means of what appears to the eye and to the mind as an *either/or*."[23] Through a series of overlapping truths—Babo is slave and master, Cereno master and slave—Melville signals that it is impossible, finally, to cut the "intricate knot," to get to the bottom of things, and, most important, either to realize the promise of liberation or to restore, unchanged, the upended order. "What Melville represents," in Fisher's view, "is the simple fact that there might be no fundamental sense to the belief that slavery could be, in the strong sense, 'abolished.'"[24] And in this regard *Benito Cereno* may be most valuable not for its prediction of the cataclysm of the Civil War so much as for its illumination of the "low-grade civil wars" that both preceded and followed the epic struggle of 1861–1865, right up to the present day.[25]

Troubling Friendship

Among the many themes that have captured the attention of commentators on *Benito Cereno*, friendship may be one of the most salient and least remarked. Even as the story advertises its gloominess with repeated reference to shadows, grayness, and specters, it is also permeated with allusions to friendship, civility, and sociality. These allusions do not serve to lighten the atmosphere, however. Instead, Melville's reflections on the costs—both current and impending—of chattel slavery set the terms through which friendships, both interracial and intraracial, develop. And gestures of friendship are the currency through which the action advances. It may even be in these performances of friendship that the story is most ominous. For in this regard, *Benito Cereno* offers more than a cautionary tale about democratic politics in the age of human bondage and imperial expansion: it also provides a vantage from which to regard the politics of friendship and the potential role of friendship in democratic politics after slavery.

Three central "friendships" structure the narrative of *Benito Cereno:* Benito Cereno and Alexandro Aranda, Cereno and Babo, and Cereno and Delano. Presented in overlapping or layered fashion, rather than entirely discrete from one another, they might be said to represent the story's past, present, and future, respectively.[26] Despite obvious differences among them, furthermore, they are all entangled in the traffic in human beings and mediated by racial hierarchy. That this is true even of the oldest friendship, the abiding love that Cereno expresses for Aranda, raises unsettling questions about the possibilities of *intra*racial friendship in a time of white supremacy. Murdered during the mutiny, Aranda haunts the action as his skeleton hangs behind a shroud from the prow of the *San Dominick.* His friendship with Cereno goes back to the latter's youth, according to the deposition (743), but his introduction in the story is *preceded* by his slaves'. When Cereno declares to Delano that he is the owner of everything on board the ship, he makes an exception for "the main company of blacks, who belonged to my late friend, Alexandro Aranda" (689). As the conversation proceeds awkwardly, Delano attempts to extract more information from Cereno, incorporating the slaves into an elaborate euphemism about the death of the Spanish captain's friend: "'And may I ask, Don Benito, whether—since awhile ago you spoke of some cabin passengers—the friend, whose loss so afflicts you, at the outset of the voyage accompanied his blacks?'" (689). In a final twist, when Aranda exits the story in the company of Benito Cereno, their reunion is effected by the absent body of Babo, which has been "burned to ashes" in punishment for the revolt (755). Only his head remains. Stuck on a pole in the Lima Plaza, where it could meet "unabashed, the gaze of the whites," Babo's head rejoins Aranda's bones, which are buried at St. Bartholomew's Church, and Cereno's body, interred in a monastery beyond the church, by holding both resting places in its regard (755).

Whereas Melville offers the reader—and Delano—only glimpses of the friendship between Aranda and Cereno, he lavishes attention on the elaborate pantomime of devotion presented by Babo and his master. As Delano regards the pair, his distaste for slavery, or at least the Spanish variety, melts. Babo, he notes, fulfills his duties "with that affectionate zeal which transmutes into something filial or fraternal acts in themselves but menial; and which has gained for the negro the repute of making the most pleasing body servant in the world; one, too, whom a master need be on no stiffly superior terms with, but may treat with familiar trust; less a servant than a devoted companion" (680). If Delano disapproves of slavery's "ugly passions," he admires the sociable passions it instills and says of Babo: "Faithful fellow! . . . Don Benito, I envy you such a friend; slave I cannot call him" (685). Whether "presenting himself as a crutch" (732) for his master or explaining away an injury vindictively inflicted by Cereno, Babo demonstrates a virtuosic command of the conviviality through which slavery was sustained. Although the story is replete with happy images of interracial friendship, in other words, it does not countenance anything approximating the equality of Queequeg and Ishmael, sharing first the marriage bed and then the monkey rope.[27] Instead, the reader encounters master and man tethered together by something more like a leash. Babo, after all, is introduced with a face "like a shepherd's dog" (678), and the narrator continues by observing that "Captain Delano took to negroes, not philanthropically, but genially, just as other men to Newfoundland dogs" (716). The question, of course, is: who is leading whom? Although Delano is deceived about who commands the *San Dominick,* the faked friendship he witnesses between Babo and Cereno copies precisely the everyday performances of familial and friendly relations that were part and parcel of the order of slavery. Babo's self-fashioning as a loving and loyal friend to Cereno exposes an order based in "violence and ventriloquism," feigned enjoyment and affection.[28] Intimations of interracial friendship or friendliness, furthermore, also provide the mechanism through which the rebels advance the plot, as when the oakum pickers relieve the tension engendered by Delano's momentary suspicions "with gestures friendly and familiar, almost jocose, bidding him, in substance, not be a fool" (711). The performance reaches a climax when Babo, "a dagger in his hand, was seen on the rail overhead, poised, in the act of leaping, as if with desperate fidelity to befriend his master to the last" (733).

Of all of the relationships that drive *Benito Cereno,* the halting friendship between Delano and Cereno is the only one that unfolds across all three sections of the story. The first and longest section relates how Delano's repeated gestures of sympathy and friendship are rebuffed by the mysteriously unhappy Cereno. During his day on board the *San Dominick,* Delano continually makes overtures to Cereno. When they are, repeatedly, not rewarded, Melville wryly observes, "He was not a little concerned at what he could not help taking for the time to be Don Benito's unfriendly indifference towards himself" (680). This is not to say that the captains are wholly equal in Delano's eyes. While the American captain sees his colleague as "my poor friend," he also regards him as "the Spaniard," an envoy from a world that is dark in its own right and atavistic in its religious customs and its treatment of slaves. Indeed, one of the story's most ingenious elements is its exposure of the degree to which rituals of friendship, for Delano, rely on a presumption of hierarchies that not only divide ship captains from bondsmen and crew but also sustain a vertical order between the captains themselves. Crucially, that order depends on rituals of friendship, and these rituals make possible Babo's ingenious inversions. For example, one of the most harrowing scenes of the novella—when Babo drapes Cereno in the Spanish flag and proceeds to shave him—begins with an invitation to Delano to join the two men in the cuddy, which the American approves as a "sociable plan" (714). Delano's insistent reversion to the language of friendship appears to defy common sense, but my reading in this regard departs slightly from Zagarell's comment that Delano's attachment to a "code of gentility" prevalent in Victorian America is "conspicuously irrelevant to the situation he actually faces."[29] Though Delano's interpretation of the action within a framework of friendship, reciprocated and rebuffed, blinds him to the meaning of the action, Melville reveals that it is entirely appropriate to the world of American mastery he inhabits. When Cereno clings to the departing Delano's hand "across the black's body" and bids him good-bye as "my best friend," Melville lays bare the ugly terms on which relationships among white men played out within the political and social economy of slavery (732).

Melville also figures friendship as a primary currency of white intercourse *after* revolution and restoration. During Cereno's brief spell of relative tranquility and health on the return journey, "ere the decided relapse which came, the two captains had many cordial conversations—their fraternal unreserve in singular contrast with former withdrawments" (753). Strikingly, Cereno repeatedly calls Delano "my best friend," despite his admission that the American was able to foil the slaves only because of his hopeless obtuseness. Against the backdrop of the two captains' repeated failures of communication on board the *San Dominick,* moreover, Melville's portrayal of the them speaking with intimacy and affection calls into question the terms on which friendships are undertaken.

Further, Melville hints that the promiscuity of Delano's friendship, his democratic openness to all, goes hand in hand with a failure to feel the injustice of slavery. Just as he distributes freshwater to the thirsty men and women on board the *San Dominick* "with republican impartiality" (712), disregarding differences of rank and race, Delano seems equally determined to share his geniality with everyone and everything he encounters. The American captain's expressions of friendship, significantly, are not insincere. Indeed, Melville reveals them to be sincere *and* fatuous. Their dubious value is expressed by Delano's readiness to extend the title "friend" beyond the human world, thereby exposing the ease with which he forgets the suffering of others, the fragility of his bonds of friendship. Attempting to cheer the morbid Cereno in the final pages of the story, Delano looks to the sky and sea and remarks: "'These mild trades that now fan your cheek, . . . do they not come with a human-like healing to you? Warm friends, steadfast friends are the trades'" (754). The political implications of this paean to benign nature are troubling. As Wilson Carey McWilliams notes, Delano—and the North he exemplifies—"could express emotion and seek solidarity only with nonhuman things, with a personalized 'Nature' or with 'natural men' deprived of human personality."[30] Further, Glenn Altshuler reminds us, the friendly winds Delano invokes are the trades that carried slaves from Africa to the Americas.[31]

Present-day readers may be able to see through Melville's superficially positive figurations of interracial and intraracial friendship and apprehend "the skeletal reality" he sketches with such devastating power. But what seems obvious in the alien costume of a nineteenth-century slave ship may remain elusive when we turn to the conditions of democratic life today. In

Benjamin DeMott's view, modern Americans are as blind as Delano to the regressive function of friendship in the post–civil rights era. *The Trouble with Friendship: Why Americans Can't Think Straight about Race* eviscerates the reactionary politics of today's "friendship orthodoxy," which underwrites a form of politics that personalizes entrenched structures of racial inequality and relieves white citizens of any sense of responsibility. Three assumptions, DeMott argues, feed the idea that friendship is the cure for what ails interracial relations: (1) a conception of shared humanity that gives rise to a belief in shared values and feelings; (2) an understanding of racial disparities as the consequence of "personal animosity" rather than structural injustice; (3) a view of public assistance efforts as unnecessary relics of the past.[32] Together these assumptions paper over a history of caste distinction whose effects have not been fully acknowledged, much less effaced. In effect, they bring Delano's blindnesses into the twenty-first century: "How is possible to sustain faith in sameness and sympathy between the races when one knows at first hand the texture of today's American cityscape—the ocular evidence that gives the lie to versions of black America as solidly middle class? What are the sequences of thought and feeling that enable men and women neither callous nor credulous to confront, day after day, in their lived experience, manifest inequity while clinging to the myth of sameness and escaping altogether the sense of personal misconduct?"[33]

Can friendship be saved? Should it be? In spite of the ills DeMott associates with appeals to interracial friendship, one of the most exciting recent books in democratic theory, and one of the few to take racial inequality as a fundamental concern, is premised on a vigorous defense of the importance of friendship as a vehicle for revitalizing democratic citizenship. Danielle Allen's *Talking to Strangers* develops from the observation that "congealed distrust" among citizens signals a fundamental breakdown in the polity.[34] In the absence of habits of interaction among strangers, Americans are incapable of negotiating the losses inherent in majority rule and becoming a genuinely democratic people. What American citizens need, Allen avers, are "more muscular habits of trust production."[35] In her elaboration on what this entails, furthermore, she develops a conception of friendship that counters the terms on which the "friendship orthodoxy" is grounded.

First, Allen dispenses with arguments about shared humanity that depend on what DeMott calls "sameness-under-the-skin." Her democratic society is defined by its heterogeneity, the manyness of the citizenry who engage together in the difficult enterprise of becoming a people. "Wholeness," not "oneness," is the metaphor that captures this aspiration. And it cannot be realized through the disavowal of difference or the pretense that citizens are not situated in such a way that their interests may and often do conflict. Accordingly, Allen advances a conception of political friendship premised on self-interest rather than its denial. In view of the inevitability of sacrifice, of giving something up for others in democratic life, political friendship sustains a form of autonomy that "consists . . . of getting one's way in concert with others, and as modified by them."[36] Reinvigorating democracy, then, involves the cultivation of a capacity to transform the pursuit of one's interests into practices, habits, rituals that enable citizens to interact *as if* they were friends.

Second, Allen does not reduce racial inequality among citizens to personal animosity or argue that they need to develop stronger *emotional* attachments to one another. Drawing on Aristotle and Ellison, she emphasizes the rituals and practices that enable citizens to treat each other with respect. Recognizing the inevitable gap between the freedom and autonomy democracy promises and the actual experiences of democratic citizens, Allen maintains that these rituals serve a critical, political purpose. "Since the purpose of rituals is to create, justify, and maintain particular social arrangements, they are the foundation also of political structures, and an individual comes to know intimately central aspects of the overall form of his community by living through them."[37] Becoming a more democratic people entails replacing the habits of domination and acquiescence with "new citizenly techniques . . . [that] integrate into one citizenship the healthy political habits of both the dominators and the dominated."[38] In this light, we see one danger of precisely the kind of friendship exhibited by "the generous Captain Amasa Delano." Friendship requires not only a willingness to sacrifice for others but also an openness to being the beneficiary of such sacrifice: "we must . . . confront the counterintuitive idea that citizens who give often and generously to other citizens may be distrusted, despite their equitability."[39] An unwillingness to be indebted to others (or to acknowledge one's indebtedness) may simply be a ploy to reinforce one's power, and it reflects a resistance to the vulnerability and lack of sovereignty that are the condition of all democratic citizens. Fugitive glimpses of human beings' "mortal inter-indebtedness," a term Jason Frank aptly draws from *Moby-Dick* in the introduction to this volume, point toward an alternative conception of democratic sociality.[40] It is a conception, crucially, that cannot be realized under conditions of racial domination.

Third, Allen counters Delano's and her own contemporaries' desire to put the past behind them with an insistence on the democratic value of historical consciousness. Her argument begins with a retelling of the integration of Little Rock's Central High School in 1957 and the "new constitution" that was "inaugurated" through the actions of the young women and men who braved murderous crowds to refound the polity more democratically.[41] Countering scripts in which it is African Americans who play the role of the supplicant and whites the part of the benefactor, Allen presses us to consider whether the Little Rock Nine and their allies were in fact "philanthropists."[42] She reverses prevailing understandings of who has been dependent on whom across the arc of U.S. history. Concerned that this history remains "undigested," she traces the political consequences of such indigestion: the invisible costs some citizens are expected to pay to mitigate the unowned vulnerabilities of others.[43]

Despite the many strengths of Allen's case, Melville's story sounds an uneasy echo. Where Allen's argument shifts between the habits of domination and the challenges of manyness, *Benito Cereno* (in contrast to *Moby-Dick*) adheres to the former and leaves little room for a heterogeneous world not permeated by the residual traces of hierarchy. Although Melville ingeniously disturbs assumptions about the racial order of his day, he cannot conceive that his characters will experience their *interchangeability*—black for white, master for slave—as *equality*.[44] The centrality of friendship to the action of *Benito Cereno* raises questions about the vexed character of the rituals to which Allen turns to alleviate the effects of racial domination. The novella both "dramatizes the epistemological fancy footwork Delano must perform in order *not* to understand what is amiss on the *San Dominick*" and shows how much of that footwork is bound up with sending and interpreting signals of friendship.[45] In other words, Melville sketches a world in which gestures of friendship and rituals of sociality not only modify the distrust of strangers but also inhibit reflection or vision. They blind Delano to the truth of what is happening on board the slave ship even as they enable him to perpetuate his blindness about the character of slavery itself. Indeed, Delano comes closest to apprehending what is happening on the *San Dominick* at those moments when his gestures of friendship fall flat. He stifles any possible insight when "a thousand trustful associations," like the sight of his old boat, reassure him that his own goodwill is legible to those around him (708).

Further, Melville's story queries the likelihood that citizens might cultivate "habits of 'antagonistic cooperation'" in such a way that sacrifices are acknowledged and reciprocated, when perceptions of self-interest and sacrifice are themselves shaped by expectations about one's position in a racialized economic and political order.[46] Though Allen rightly challenges the idea that self-interest is reducible to wealth maximization, Delano perceives his own pursuit of profit, including profit derived from the trade in human beings that he professes to abhor, to be something akin to what she calls "equitable self-interest." (He only wants his fair share!) Indeed, the dark side of Delano's conviviality makes vivid Samuel Delany's observation that social capital is "a truly outrageous metaphor."[47] *Benito Cereno* suggests why the insecurity that Allen identifies as the shared condition of democratic citizens remains politically undecided; it may move us to new forms of citizenly friendship, but it may also, perhaps more readily, reinforce our commitment to the undemocratic relationships of old. Melville's story eerily inquires of us: Would we know the difference? In the shadow of *Benito Cereno,* Allen's gloss on Ellison's claim that "our fellow citizens *are* the boat, and we in turn the planks for them" both demands something more strenuous than easy assurances that "we are all in the same boat" or Delano's promiscuous friendship *and* elides a question raised so pointedly by the insurrection on the *San Dominick:* What kind of boat?[48]

What Babo Saw

Benito Cereno concludes with the display of Babo's head, regarding white passersby as well as the remains of his former master and his master's friend. What are readers to make of "his voiceless end" (755)? As several commentators note, at the very moment when the reader sees the action from Babo's point of view, he has been permanently silenced. The action, as Dana Nelson suggests, is "arrested" in a way that may prevent emancipation from the dynamic of black-white relations Melville so effectively undermines through the inversions of the plot.[49] Further, it vivifies the fact that the black characters never speak in their own voices at any point in the story. Not only are all Babo's words thoroughly scripted, even if he is the author of that script, but Melville prefigures Babo's fate through the character of Atufal, who in an especially elaborate masquerade is required to ask Cereno's pardon and instead regards him with "unquailing muteness" (690).[50] As Jean Fagin Yellin concludes, "Melville did not pretend to speak for the black man, but he dramatized the perception that his voice had not been heard."[51] Neither singly nor collectively. Melville does report the gestures of the oakum pickers, the clang of the hatchet polishers, and the "blithe songs of the inspirited negroes" (726), but the effect is to amplify the absence of their individual voices. Perhaps most obviously, Melville omits any discussion of friendships *among* the slaves, despite the fact that their elaborate cooperation drives the plot.[52]

What might Babo and his allies have said, if they could? What did they see? Unhindered by the blinders of mastery, Babo would not only have understood the inherent barbarity of his condition, but would probably have foreseen the obstacles to a postrevolutionary order shared by former slaves and masters alike. Although he utters no words after the unveiling of the plot, it is unlikely that he would have expressed surprise at the viciousness of the retaking of the *San Dominick* from the former slaves, during which shackled captives were killed by sailors (752); or at the spectacle of his own execution, beheading, and burning; or at the breeziness of Delano's insistence that the events on the *San Dominick* should be left in the past. Least of all would Babo have been surprised that the same man who had admired his services, to the point of offering to buy him, would not hesitate to grind the fugitive slave into the hull of a boat with his boot (733).

Babo might also have expected that Delano's liberality in extending the title of "friend" to all would carry a substantial price tag. If the captain's gifts are freely given, the gestures are meant to be received with appropriate gratitude and the giver's generosity recognized. In the historical Delano's *Narrative,* the captain reports that he "was mortified and very much hurt" by Cereno's unwillingness to compensate him for his efforts.[53] The recollections of "the generous Captain Delano" are tinged with self-pity for "such misery and ingratitude as I have suffered at different periods, and in general, from the very persons to whom I have rendered the greatest services."[54] Even when Melville relates that "the noble Captain Delano" struggled to put an end to the needless massacre of captured slaves, the story leaves open the question of whether his mercy reflects humanitarian motives or his interest in the fate of the ship's "cargo" as a source of his own repayment. Melville forces us to consider how certainly we can discern the gap between a gesture of common humanity and a cold calculation of profit.

Where Melville dramatizes Delano's easy slide from generosity to resentment vis-à-vis the insufficiently grateful Cereno, he also drops clues to the kinds of expectations that would become the cost of black freedom in the United States. In its most pointed form, Patrick Buchanan's "Brief for Whitey" summarizes the puzzled reaction of future Delanos to the articulation of African American grievances: "Where is the gratitude?"[55] To be sure, Buchanan represents an extreme view, but it is also a view that crystallizes a tradition of friendship tethered to expressions of generosity and expectations of thanks, to the maintenance of hierarchy between benefactor and supplicant. Such a tradition manifests itself not only in the stance of open racists but also in the responses of generations of "friends of the Negro," who expect acknowledgment for their forward thinking on matters of race. Maybe this attitude even ensnares Melville himself, whose final poem in *Battle Pieces* asks, "Can Africa pay back this blood / Spilt on Potomac's shore?"[56] As Karcher notes, the poem "reverses the role of debtor and creditor, victim and perpetrator, blaming Africans for having caused the war to end their enslavement in America and placing a higher value on the blood of white soldiers than on that of black slaves."[57] It presages what Saidiya Hartman calls "the debt of emancipation" and the rise of new habits of domination and submission.[58]

Babo might also have justly mocked Ishmael's famous expression of shared subjection—"Who ain't a slave? Tell me that"[59]—as politically sterile. Certainly, Cereno's experience of subjection fills him with horror, but it does nothing to enlighten him about the plight of the women and men in his charge. Despite their physical intimacy throughout most of the first section of the story, Babo never represents brotherhood for Cereno. Rather, Babo is a vision so fiendish that he continues to inspire fainting spells in the captain long after the insurrection has been suppressed. Delano, for his part, proves no more equipped than Cereno to broaden his sense of human concern, whether as a consequence of his democratic character or as a result of his experience in Babo's thrall.[60]

Nor is he equipped either to remember or to forget the plight of the slaves who were killed, imprisoned, or reenslaved for their aspiration to freedom. "The past is passed; why moralize upon it?" (754). Delano's attempt to cheer his melancholy friend summarizes his own actions, across the arc of the story, as he continually responds to slights and stifles his suspicions of Cereno's intentions toward him. Repeatedly, Delano is portrayed "drowning criticism in compassion, after a fresh repetition of his sympathies" (686), or reassuring himself with the reminder that "yes, this is a strange craft; a strange history, too, and strange folks on board. But—nothing more" (710). Delano's ritual suppression of unease not only heightens that of the reader but also reveals what his advice to Cereno disavows. Keeping the past at bay is not a once-and-for-all accomplishment but a task that requires continual vigilance on the part of the former masters and their allies. For the formerly enslaved, it might entail the imperative to "get over it," "stop whining," or simply "cease to be the special favorite of the laws." For Delano's heirs, it would involve an insistent repetition of the mantra that "the past is passed," which has been deployed so effectively to forestall discussion of affirmative action, reparations, or even modest race-conscious proposals.[61] The call to leave the past in the past might also manifest itself in the continuing force of the immunity-by-friendship defense through which relationships with African Americans reinscribe white innocence, even in the face of stark evidence of racial injustice. Neither Melville nor Babo predicts such developments, but I expect that neither would be surprised by them.

"Whatever else [Melville's] works were 'about,'" writes Ellison, "they also managed to be about democracy."[62] *Benito Cereno* was about the conditions of American democracy in the 1850s, to be sure, and it looked ahead to see that the American appetite for slavery and expansion was propelling the nation toward disaster. That *Benito Cereno* traffics in partial truths and resists easy conclusions also suggests another way to read it as a democratic story. It calls on readers both to reflect on the circumstances as Melville laid them out and to heed Allen's admonition, following Aristotle: "You've heard me, you understand. Now judge."[63] In this way we might say that the living value of Melville's tale resides equally in what it tells us about his time and in what it withholds. This call to judgment, moreover, is not limited to the relatively safe enterprise of reflecting on the past. Much of *Benito Cereno*'s power emerges from the uncanny sharpness with which it prefigures the legacy that the age of enslavement would leave to future generations and demands a rethinking of our own circumstances. Part of that legacy, Melville intimates, is a history of friendships—interracial and intraracial—that transpire across and through the subject bodies of black women and men. This is not to say that political friendship has no role to play in remaking

American democratic life after the civil wars of the nineteenth and twentieth centuries. But it presses us to be particularly alert to the ways in which friendship might yet sustain the relations those wars were meant to undo.

Notes

The epigraph from Martin Luther King Jr. is in "A Time to Break Silence," in *A Testament of Hope: The Essential Writings and Speeches of Martin Luther King, Jr.*, ed. James Melvin Washington (San Francisco: Harper, 1990), 243. I was reminded of this passage by George Lipsitz, "Afterword: Racially Writing the Republic and Racially Righting the Republic," in *Racially Writing the Republic: Racists, Race Rebels, and Transformations of American Identity*, ed. Bruce Baum and Duchess Harris (Durham: Duke University Press, 2009), 297.

I would like to acknowledge the thoughtful suggestions of participants in the 2011 American Political Science Association Annual Meeting session "American Tragedy: The Political Thought of Herman Melville," Molly Farneth, Roger Herbert, Adam Hughes, Susan McWilliams, Mark Reinhardt, Tracy Strong, and, especially, Jason Frank, who offered keen ideas about how to make the argument sharper.

1. C. L. R. James, *Mariners, Renegades and Castaways: The Story of Herman Melville and the World We Live In* (1953; repr., Hanover, N.H.: Dartmouth College Press, 2001), 114.

2. Ibid., 111.

3. Arnold Rampersad, "Melville and Race," in *Herman Melville: A Collection of Critical Essays*, ed. Myra Jehlen (Englewood Cliffs, N.J.: Prentice-Hall, 1994), 173.

4. See, for example, Toni Morrison's reference to *Benito Cereno* in her meditation on the nomination of Clarence Thomas to the Supreme Court. Toni Morrison, "Introduction: Friday on the Potomac," in *Race-ing Justice, En-gendering Power: Essays on Anita Hill, Clarence Thomas, and the Construction of Social Reality*, ed. Toni Morrison (New York: Pantheon, 1992), xv.

5. Herman Melville, *Benito Cereno*, in *Pierre, Israel Potter, The Piazza Tales, The Confidence-Man, Uncollected Prose, Billy Budd* (New York: Library of America, 1984), 676. Subsequent references to this work will be given parenthetically in the text.

6. Elizabeth Alexander, *The Black Interior: Essays* (St. Paul: Graywolf Press, 2004).

7. Benjamin DeMott, *The Trouble with Friendship: Why Americans Can't Think Straight about Race* (New Haven: Yale University Press, 1995).

8. Andrew Delbanco uses this phrase to describe Melville's acuity as a so-

cial analyst during the period in which he wrote *Benito Cereno.* Delbanco further maintains that "in our own time of terror and torture, *Benito Cereno* has emerged as the most salient of Melville's works: a tale of desperate men in the grip of a vengeful fury that those whom they hate cannot begin to understand." Andrew Delbanco, *Melville: His World and Work* (New York: Knopf, 2005), 231.

9. Jean Fagan Yellin, *The Intricate Knot: Black Figures in American Literature, 1776–1863* (New York: New York University Press, 1972), 216.

10. Carolyn L. Karcher, *Shadow over the Promised Land: Slavery, Race, and Violence in Melville's America* (Baton Rouge: Louisiana State University Press, 1980), ix.

11. There is an extensive literature debating Melville's racial views and his commitment to abolition as revealed both in *Benito Cereno* and in the larger body of his work. For an incisive summary of these debates, see Dana D. Nelson, *The Word in Black and White: Reading "Race" in American Literature, 1638–1867* (New York: Oxford University Press, 1993), 164–165n1.

12. Sandra A. Zagarell, "Reenvisioning America: Melville's *Benito Cereno*," in *Critical Essays on Herman Melville's* Benito Cereno, ed. Robert E. Burkholder (New York: G. K. Hall, 1992), 139.

13. He also changes the name of Delano's ship from the *Perseverance* to the *Bachelor's Delight,* which, Zagarell notes, was the name of the ship sailed by the buccaneer William Ambrose Cowley. Ibid., 141.

14. As many scholars have noted, Melville's personal life was intimately tied to the politics of the Fugitive Slave Law. His father-in-law, Massachusetts Supreme Court chief justice Lemuel Shaw, famously opposed slavery but felt compelled to abide by the law and, in 1851, ordered Thomas Sims returned to his master.

15. William Gleason, "Volcanoes and Meteors: Douglass, Melville, and the Poetics of Insurrection," in *Frederick Douglass and Herman Melville: Essays in Relation,* ed. Robert S. Levine and Samuel Otter (Chapel Hill: University of North Carolina Press, 2008), 120. Gleason cites Robert K. Wallace, *Douglass and Melville: Anchored Together in Neighborly Style* (New Bedford, Mass.: Spinner, 2005), as the source of this connection.

16. Joyce Sparer Adler, "*Benito Cereno:* Slavery and Violence in the Americas," in Burkholder, *Critical Essays on Herman Melville's* Benito Cereno, 76.

17. See Eric J. Sundquist, *To Wake the Nations: Race in the Making of American Literature* (Cambridge: Harvard University Press, 1993), 152.

18. Michael Paul Rogin, *Subversive Genealogy: The Politics and Art of Herman Melville* (New York: Knopf, 1983), 211.

19. James, *Mariners, Renegades and Castaways,* 112.

20. Sterling Stuckey and Joshua Leslie, "The Death of Benito Cereno: A Reading of Herman Melville on Slavery," in Stuckey, *Going through the Storm: The*

Influence of African American Art in History (New York: Oxford University Press, 1994), 153–170.

21. In chapter 10 of this volume, Tracy Strong aptly observes that this part of the novella is written "from, although mostly not in, the third-person point of view of Captain Amasa Delano." Tracy B. Strong, "'Follow Your Leader': Melville's *Benito Cereno* and the Case of Two Ships."

22. Sundquist, *To Wake the Nations,* 155–163.

23. Philip Fisher, "Democratic Social Space: Whitman, Melville, and the Promise of American Transparency," *Representations* 24 (Autumn 1988): 93; emphases in original.

24. Ibid., 88.

25. Danielle S. Allen, *Talking to Strangers: Anxieties of Citizenship since* Brown v. Board of Education (Chicago: University of Chicago Press, 2004), xvii.

26. In the sequence of action that begins with Cereno's leap into Delano's departing boat, continues with Babo's armed pursuit of the captain and his capture by Delano, and ends with the unveiling of Aranda's skeleton, Melville writes: "All this, with what preceded, and what followed, occurred with such involutions of rapidity, that past, present, and future seemed one" (733).

27. For an exploration of the sublimity of Ishmael and Queequeg's friendship and its antirevolutionary implications, in contrast with the friendship imagined in Frederick Douglass's *Heroic Slave,* see John Stauffer, "Interracial Friendship and the Aesthetics of Freedom," in Levine and Otter, *Frederick Douglass and Herman Melville,* 134–158. For an account of the unadmitted erotic economy of interracial friendships in American cinema, see Robert Gooding-Williams, "Black Cupids, White Desires," in Gooding-Williams, *Look, a Negro! Philosophical Essays on Race, Culture, and Politics* (New York: Routledge, 2005), 17–33.

28. Saidiya V. Hartman, *Scenes of Subjection: Terror, Slavery, and Self-Making in Nineteenth-Century America* (New York: Oxford University Press, 1997).

29. Zagarell, "Reenvisioning America," 129–130.

30. Wilson Carey McWilliams, *The Idea of Fraternity in America* (Berkeley: University of California Press, 1973), 370. McWilliams's observation can be extended beyond Melville's implied critique of Emersonianism to encompass Delano's fondness for his boat, the *Rover,* which, "as a Newfoundland dog," had often been laid up on the beach at his New England home and which "evoked a thousand trustful associations" (708). I was alerted to this passage by James H. Kavanagh, "That Hive of Subtlety: *Benito Cereno* and the Liberal Hero," in *Ideology and Classic American Literature,* ed. Sacvan Bercovitch and Myra Jehlen (Cambridge: Cambridge University Press, 1986), 368–369.

31. Glenn C. Altshuler, "Whose Foot on Whose Throat? A Re-examination of Melville's *Benito Cereno,*" *CLA Journal* 18 (March 1975): 391.

32. DeMott, *The Trouble with Friendship,* 8.

33. Ibid., 145.

34. Allen, *Talking to Strangers,* xiii.

35. Ibid., 84.

36. Ibid., 133.

37. Ibid., 28.

38. Ibid., 116.

39. Ibid., 134.

40. Jason Frank, "Introduction: American Tragedy: The Political Thought of Herman Melville," this volume.

41. Allen, *Talking to Strangers,* 6.

42. Allen explores this idea through the Invisible Man's ruminations on whether African Americans living under Jim Crow are philanthropists or scapegoats. Ibid., 101–118.

43. Ibid., 7.

44. On interchangeability and its limits, see Nelson, *The Word in Black and White.*

45. Zagarell, "Reenvisioning America," 128; emphasis in original.

46. Allen, *Talking to Strangers,* 118. The term is Ellison's.

47. Samuel R. Delany, ". . . Three, Two, One, Contact: Times Square Red," in Delany, *Times Square Red, Times Square Blue* (New York: New York University Press, 1999), 199. Thanks to Mark Reinhardt for pointing me to Delany's counter-narrative of cross-class contact.

48. Allen, *Talking to Strangers,* 45; emphasis in original. DeMott offers his own critique of the claim that "we're all in the same boat." DeMott, *The Trouble with Friendship,* 29–32.

49. Nelson, *The Word in Black and White,* 110.

50. Such silences multiply, as Strong points out elsewhere in this volume, over the course of Melville's career. They register his growing doubtfulness "as to the possibilities of *expressing* what was wrong with America." Strong, "Follow Your Leader"; emphasis in original.

51. Yellin, *The Intricate Knot,* 224. Alternatively, we might say that Melville's story "speak[s] about the unspeakable without presuming to speak it directly." Mark Reinhardt, "Who Speaks for Margaret Garner? Slavery, Silence, and the Politics of Ventriloquism," *Critical Inquiry* 29 (Autumn 2002): 85.

52. Matthew Rebhorn makes a convincing case for the centrality of nonverbal communication in *Benito Cereno,* but the novella allows only glimpses of how "the languages of embodiment" circulate among the black characters on the *San Dominick.* Matthew Rebhorn, "Minding the Body: *Benito Cereno* and Melville's Embodied Reading Practice," *Studies in the Novel* 41 (Summer 2009): 157–177.

53. Amasa Delano, "From a Narrative of Voyages and Travels, in the Northern and Southern Hemispheres: Comprising Three Voyages Round the World, Together with a Voyage of Survey and Discovery in the Pacific Ocean and Oriental Islands," in *Benito Cereno*, ed. Wyn Kelley (Boston: Bedford/St. Martin's, 2008), 120.

54. Ibid., 122.

55. Patrick J. Buchanan, "A Brief for Whitey," March 21, 2008, http://buchanan.org/blog/pjb-a-brief-for-whitey-969. Thanks to P. J. Brendese for bringing Buchanan's essay to my attention. P. J. Brendese, "The Race of a More Perfect Union: James Baldwin, Segregated Memory, and the Presidential Race," *Theory & Event* 15, no. 1 (2012), http://muse.jhu.edu/journals/theory_and_event/toc/tae.15.1.html.

56. Herman Melville, "A Meditation," in *Battle Pieces and Aspects of the War*, ed. Sidney Kaplan (1960; repr., Amherst: University of Massachusetts Press, 1972), 242.

57. Carolyn L. Karcher, "White Fratricide, Black Liberation: Melville, Douglass, and Civil War Memory," in Levine and Otter, *Frederick Douglass and Herman Melville*, 354.

58. Hartman, *Scenes of Subjection*, 130–134. Although I am generally persuaded by Hartman's argument, I depart from her characterization of emancipation as a "nonevent" (116).

59. Herman Melville, *Moby-Dick* (New York: Oxford University Press, 2008), 4.

60. Nelson, *The Word in Black and White*, 127.

61. Eduardo Bonilla-Silva writes that this is one of the basic story lines of white American discourse in the post–civil rights era. Eduardo Bonilla-Silva, *Racism without Racists: Color-Blind Racism and the Persistence of Racial Inequality in the United States* (Lanham, Md.: Rowman and Littlefield, 2003).

62. Ralph Ellison, "Twentieth-Century Fiction and the Black Mask of Humanity," in Ellison, *Shadow and Act* (New York: Random House, 1964), 40–41.

63. Allen, *Talking to Strangers*, 186.

10

"Follow Your Leader"

Melville's Benito Cereno *and the Case of Two Ships*

Tracy B. Strong

> Conceive the sailors to be wrangling with one another for control of the helm. . . . And they put the others to death or cast them out from the ship, and then, after binding and stupefying the worthy shipmaster with mandragora or intoxication or otherwise, they take command of the ship, consume its stores and, drinking and feasting, make such a voyage of it as is to be expected from such, and as if that were not enough, they praise and celebrate as a navigator, a pilot, a master of shipcraft, the man who is most cunning to lend a hand in persuading or constraining the shipmaster to let them rule.
>
> —Plato, *Republic*, Book VI

> I sometimes wonder that we can be so frivolous, I may almost say, as to attend to the gross and somewhat foreign form of servitude called Negro Slavery, there are so many keen and subtle masters that enslave both north and south.
>
> —Henry David Thoreau, *Walden*, "Economy"

The metaphor of a ship for the polity is, as the epigraph from Plato shows, as old as Western political thought. It was especially prominent in American political discourse in the middle of the nineteenth century: as Alan Heimert has pointed out, there was a widespread fear about the direction in which the country was going, most often expressed as the fear that the American ship of state was running aground or being sucked into a giant maelstrom.[1] President Polk's provocation of the war with Mexico, the relentless expansionism, and the increasing tension over slavery all called into question the nature of the American experiment. The ship of state could be foundering, and, as an author of his times and a widely traveled seafarer, Melville often chose, therefore, to place his tales on ships. Indeed, except for *Pierre,* all his novels take place aboard or in relation to ships: they were his frame for America. Appealing to his "shipmates and world-mates," he writes in *White-Jacket* (1850): "We mortals are all on board a fast-sailing . . . world-frigate."[2]

In the case of *Benito Cereno,* we have *two* ships, linked by a longboat, throughout the book in some kind of contact with each other. The one is captained by a New Englander; the other, while appearing to be Spanish, is in fact run by slaves. Joined together as if they might be thought to form the two main sections of America, the two are, as we shall see, less different than they might at first appear. Central to the question of a ship, as Plato tells us, is the question of the captain and thus the question of sovereignty. The captain—as Melville will have the American captain observe in *Benito Cereno*—has absolute authority while at sea. It follows that the character of the captain and his relation to his crew may be reflected in the character of the ship, that is, of the polity. Such embodiment produced doubts in Melville: at the end of *White-Jacket,* a novel that is in part about the just way to run the ship of state, he indicates that trusting everything to the captain is a mistake.[3]

If the ship is the polity, what were Melville's expectations for his own country? In his youth Melville had held to a version of the doctrine of Manifest Destiny. In *White-Jacket* he writes that Americans are "the chosen people, the Israel of our time." Even here, however, his doubts are already present, as he goes on to say that the "political messiah . . . has come in us, *if we would but give utterance to his promptings.*"[4] As he matured, he came to worry greatly about the course his country was taking; America was a country that knew little of who or what it was, for, as he wrote in *Redburn,* it had neither mother nor father.[5] His distress that America either does not know or has a dangerous idea of itself remained an important American trope. As Robert Frost put it a century later:

MIST
I don't believe the sleepers in this house
Know where they are.

SMOKE
They've been here long enough
To push the woods back from around the house
And part them in the middle with a path.

MIST
And still I doubt if they know where they are.
And I begin to fear they never will.[6]

America did, however, have those who claimed to lead it, and the direction these leaders—its captains—sought to take was of major political concern in the middle of the nineteenth century (as it remains to this day).

In 1850 white Americans worked out a compromise concerning the status of the land arrogated from Mexico.[7] To keep the country united, the slave trade was abolished in the District of Columbia, though the practice of slavery was retained; California was admitted as a free state; the new Southwest territories were to decide on the question of slavery by vote; the Fugitive Slave Act, however, required all citizens to assist in the recapture of escaped slaves. The result was a short-term papering over of the divisions in the country. It is in this context that the novella *Benito Cereno* first appeared in 1855, serialized in three issues of *Putnam's Monthly Magazine,* an antislavery publication with a distinguished stable of authors. (Thoreau's *Cape Cod* first appeared there.) Stunningly, the last issue of the serialization included an anonymous, heavily ironic article titled "About Niggers," which depicted blacks both as happy and with "terrible capacities for revenge," referring specifically to the revolt in San Domingo.[8] The anonymous article thus ironically exemplified (and, in my reading, undermined) the very ideology of white supremacy that Melville had taken up (and undermined) in his novella.

Melville republished his work in 1856 in a slightly revised version in *The Piazza Tales.* The story is adapted from the real-life account of the American Captain Amasa Delano in the eighteenth chapter of his *Narrative of the Voyages and Travels, in the Northern and Southern Hemispheres.*[9] In Melville's account, the *Bachelor's Delight,* captained by Delano, encounters a Spanish ship, the *San Dominick,* off the coast of southern Chile. The Spanish vessel is in seriously bad repair. Delano goes over to it to offer help and finds a ship whose personnel consists mainly of blacks, albeit with a white captain, Don Benito Cereno, and very few other white sailors. Cereno tells a tale of disaster and death from storms, fever, and scurvy to account for the condition of the boat. He is assisted in all things by the African Babo, a small and physically unprepossessing man, who appears to be his body servant and never leaves his side, even when Delano asks for a private conversation with Cereno. Although the condition of the ship and a number of incidents raise doubts in Delano's mind—he fears at times that Cereno is a pirate who means to take over his ship—he is never moved to action. As Delano leaves the *San Dominick,* Cereno jumps into the longboat; Babo jumps in after him, dagger in hand. Delano thinks first that Cereno means to kill him, then realizes that Babo means to kill Cereno. Babo is captured and the truth appears: the slaves had taken over the ship, killing the owner, Don Aranda, and most of the whites, keeping only Captain Cereno, those with the necessary skill as navigators, and a few others for show in case they were to encounter another ship. The entire experience aboard the *San Dominick* has been a piece of theater, carefully worked out by Babo, intended to dupe those commanding any ship they might encounter.[10] The Spanish ship is recaptured. Taken to Lima, the capital city of the Viceroyalty of Peru, the slaves are tried and eventually executed; three months after the trial, the historical Cereno dies.[11]

Let me proceed by increments. The story is at least about the fact that the kind-souled, well-mannered, and unfailingly affirmative Delano[12] has (like most of the first-time readers of the opening part of the novella)[13] only the dimmest comprehension of the hatred that might have led the slaves to take over the ship. Nor does Delano ever come to an acknowledgment of the lot of the slaves that led to rebellion: at most he is interested in securing his salvage rights. If Delano is indifferent, however, the story makes it progressively more difficult for the reader to be so. It was thus certainly not a random choice that led Ralph Ellison to choose as an epigraph for *Invisible Man* this quotation from *Benito Cereno:* "'You are saved,' cried Captain Delano, more and more astonished and pained; 'you are saved: what has cast such a shadow upon you?'" Cereno's reply, tellingly not given in Ellison's epigraph, is "the negro."[14] Because of the question of race, we are *not* saved, we remain in the shadow.

What is meant by this question and this response? There is little doubt that race is an important question in Melville's novella. Cereno is certainly referring at least to Babo, the self-liberated slave with whom he appears joined throughout the first part of the story. Race is what orients Delano toward everything that he sees, does, and feels; it also orients him toward everything that he does not see, do, and feel. As one peruses the secondary literature, it is problematically clear that the judgments about what Melville was saying about race vary enormously. They go from readings of the novella as being about human depravity and evil (as embodied in Babo), to a justification or acceptance of slavery, to an avoidance of the question of slavery, to an indictment of slavery wherein Babo becomes a kind of revolutionary hero and martyr.[15] I shall consider another kind of appropriation: the source of the range of interpretations derives, I think, not from lack of clarity or oversight on Melville's part but from the fact that his novella is written precisely to get his readers to question first their own attitudes and behaviors in racial matters and then, more important, the source of those attitudes and behaviors.

Consider the lack of any authoritative authorial voice. Of the three separate sections, the first, three-quarters of the book, is written from, although mostly not in, the third-person point of view of Captain Amasa Delano (and is several times longer than Delano's account in his book). I say *from* (not *in*), because for the most part the effect is as if a camera were following him around recording from his point of view both what he does and what he sees. This point of view is complicated by the fact that occasionally the narrative voice (of the camera, as it were) offers ironic reflections on Delano's character. We find straight off that Delano might have been uneasy were he not "a person of a singularly undistrustful good nature." The narrator goes on to ask "whether, in view of what humanity is capable, such a trait implies, along with a benevolent heart, more than ordinary quickness and accuracy of intellectual perception" and indicates that this "may be left to the wise to determine" (673). The irony alerts us to Delano's lack of wisdom, although the syntax and double negatives allow a casual reader to pass over the passage, much as Delano passes through the world around him without really seeing it.[16]

On occasion, his anxieties lead him to question his position. After an incident that produces a "qualmish sort of emotion" (708), Delano interrogates himself—notably he thinks of himself in the third person, seeing himself as he thinks a camera might—only to conclude that it is "too nonsensical to think [that someone would] murder Amasa Delano. . . . His conscience is clean" (709). Delano suspects Cereno of malfeasance because he simply cannot conceive of the possibility that African slaves might have been able to take over a ship—this despite the fact that by setting the story in 1799 (rather than 1805, when the original account took place) and by renaming the Spanish ship *San Dominick,* Melville reminds us of the proximity of the slave rebellion in Haiti (1791–1798) and anticipates the subsequent freeing of the slaves in Santo Domingo in 1800.[17] One would think that these events would be more present to Delano. As Lawrie Balfour shows in her contribution to this volume, what matters most to Delano are courtesies and good manners—what one owes to a stranger—and these courtesies are precisely what allow him to sustain relations of racist domination. That his conscience is "clean" merely means that he is unable and unwilling to perceive the reality of the situation—so also was the conscience of many a New Englander "clean" about the matter of slavery (just as Thoreau had pointed out in his 1849 "Civil Disobedience").[18]

Delano encounters a world that is in effect a stage set for a ghastly play, although he does not know it to be theater. As in the case of a classical three-level Elizabethan stage, on the highest deck are four symmetrically arranged "elderly grizzled negroes," apparently occupied at picking oakum (hemp fibers to be used for caulking) from junk (old or inferior rope).[19] Below and in front of them, "separated by regular spaces," are "the cross-legged figures of six other blacks; each with a rusty hatchet in his hand." Below and in the center of this tableau, leaning against the mast, are Delano and Babo. This is the setting for what will turn out to be a staged play (677–678).[20]

This first section forms the bulk of the book. The second section consists of Cereno's deposition before the court. Melville's version of the deposition is often word for word from the original but adds great emphasis on the weakness of Cereno (he is borne in on a litter, accompanied by a monk—whose name, Infelez, calls to mind *infeliz,* "unhappy"), a weakness and company not found in the original. That account (both in Delano's book and in Melville's story) is notably certified by "His Majesty's Notary": by explicitly omitting Delano's account (present in Delano's book), however, Melville focuses attention on what is referred to as Cereno's account of a "fictitious story" dictated to Cereno by Babo after the takeover (747). In Delano's book Cereno refers immediately to a signed contract ("by the deponent and the sailors who could write," Babo and Atufal doing so "in their own language"). In Melville the agreement among the slaves now in possession of the ship—that Cereno will take them to Senegal and that they will kill no more whites—is at first purely verbal; Melville presumably postpones the drafting of the contract in the novella to call attention to the fact that whites cannot conceive of valid contracts with slaves: it is only after further threats by the blacks to kill some of the crew (the cook in particular) that Cereno, "endeavoring not to omit any means to preserve the lives of the remaining whites, . . . agreed to draw up a paper" in which he also formally made the ship over to them (744–745).

In this section the story is told purely from the point of view of the members of a slave-accepting system. It is clear that the written agreement between the blacks and the whites is of no serious importance to the court, which presumes it was extorted, despite the fact that the whites had first refused to agree to any contract. No credence is given to the blacks' description of this refusal. On the other hand, the court remarks that the blacks indeed had a plan to poison Cereno, on the grounds that "the negroes have said it" (749; again on 750). As the passage about the testimony of the blacks is not in Cereno's actual deposition, Melville presumably added it as an ironic counterpoint to the unwillingness of whites to acknowledge the validity of any contract with blacks.

The narrative technique of the book is frequently reiterated across Melville's work. There are official stories and unofficial stories. The separate accounts of the same event (here three, four if you count Delano's original book, which was well known) serve to call into question, that is, to politicize, the very idea of an event. In *Israel Potter*, for instance, Melville's intertextuality manages both to call upon *and* to critique authoritative books and figures, including the Bible, the Odyssey, Benjamin Franklin's *Poor Richard's Almanack*, Irving's "Rip Van Winkle," Cervantes's *Don Quixote*—and this is only a start. As he says in *Billy Budd:* "The symmetry of form attainable in pure fiction cannot so readily be achieved in a narration essentially having less to do with fable than with fact. Truth uncompromisingly told will always have its ragged edges; hence the conclusion of such a narration is apt to be less finished than an architectural finial."[21]

Benito Cereno has many "ragged edges." The first two parts consist of a staged play and an ostentatiously "official" account of the meaning of the play. The third and last part is entirely Melville's invention. Overall, the tripartite division is intended to cast doubt on at least the first two versions of the events. As if to raise the question, Melville is careful to note "it is hoped" that the deposition will "shed light on the preceding narrative" (738). The stamp of authoritative state approval in and to the second part clues us to the fact that this is the dominant power's version of events. Part III opens with an "If" of interrogation—here it is a question *if* the deposition did in fact "serve as the key to fit into the lock of the complications which precede it": the presumption is that the answer must be "not entirely" (752–753). We have thus in the second part a questioning of the first part and in the last part a questioning of the two previous parts. Importantly, we find that even the identification necessary for the conviction of Babo as ringleader depended on the accounts of the surviving sailors, as Cereno had refused or been unable to speak of Babo or even look at him. Cereno's refusal suggests that as he was constantly joined to Babo, he may have in some sense *also* been ringleader. Thus: "On the testimony of the sailors alone rested the legal identity of Babo" (755).[22]

So is the novella about slavery? At one level it obviously is. Though against abolitionism (which he saw as another kind of racism), Melville detested slavery.[23] He was, however, well aware that preaching the message of the moral corruption induced by slavery would be of no avail to the broader public. That approach had been tried for decades. So he elected in this book to verbally so complicate the character of Delano that many or most of his white readers would be swept along by the events, as was Delano, without even grasping what was going on. The eventual revelation to Delano ("the negro") thus functions as a revelation to the reader also.

Yet the slavery that this book is about is not just the slavery that existed in America in 1855 and over which a war was soon to be fought. All is mixed, without precise definition. The novella starts with an assertion of the color *gray:* Melville gives us both a lack of distinction between black and white and a lack of distinctness—there are vapors, like the fog and mist Robert Frost saw obscuring America's view of itself. The *San Dominick* appears as a "white-washed monastery" (675) apparently occupied by (Dominican) Black Friar monks (that is, whites who are dressed in black).[24] No appearance is secure: we are told that Atufal, who appears as a chained slave, was "a king in his own country" and that Babo, who, as we find out, is the leader, was a slave in his country. (Slavery is not exclusive to America.) The two figures on the carving on the stern of the *San Dominick* are engaged in a combat that will be mirrored in the struggle in the longboat after Cereno jumps into it. Both are masked, and the "dark satyr" holds a "writhing figure" down, his foot on the other's neck (676). If a parallel is intended with the scene in the longboat, it is Delano who becomes the "dark satyr" as he there holds Babo down with his foot.

It is thus significant that at no time during the story is the institution of American chattel slavery the explicit central focus of the book or directly called into question. On a rare occasion, Delano muses that "this slavery breeds ugly passions in man"—but, despite the fact that he is from Massachusetts, the most abolitionist of the states, the focus of his distress is what he takes to be Cereno's insolent behavior (721). As we shall see, I do not take this lack, as did F. O. Matthiessen, to be an oversight—I take it to be importantly purposeful, for Melville seeks to go, as it were, *below* the institution of American slavery.[25] The simple condemnation of American slavery, especially by a New Englander, is easy—so easy that Melville, as had Thoreau, thought it self-serving. He not only explores the effects of slavery in *Benito Cereno* but seeks to bring to light what in human relations gives rise to slavery and what slavery gives rise to in human relations.[26]

There are many ways to read this story. One can read the novella, as does Michael Rogin, against the events of 1848 in Europe, as revealing the difficulties political theory has in dealing with slavery, and more narrowly as a reproach by Melville to his friend Hawthorne for the latter's support of Franklin Pierce (and Pierce's support of the 1854 Kansas-Nebraska Act, which repealed the Missouri Compromise).[27] Along these lines, it is clear, as Jason Frank shows in his introduction to this volume, that Melville offers a far more complex analysis of slavery than the well-known section of Hegel's *Phenomenology of Spirit,* in which, despite everything, the ultimate victory of the slaves is dialectically assured. In the end, with Hegel we do not have to worry too much about the institution of slavery, for it is, ultimately, historically progressive; for Melville, there is no such assurance.[28]

It does seem to me the case, then, that we cannot do justice to *Benito Cereno* if we limit it to being about American slavery. It is also, we can say, about the tendency Americans have to think of their nation as innocent and blessed. It is not so much that Delano has standard "white" opinions of blacks but that he is self-deluded, a delusion that Americans tend to share, thinks Melville, about themselves generally. And this delusion is not without its dangers; there are hints and more than hints of this: by renaming Delano's ship the *Bachelor's Delight,* Melville has given it the name of the ship of a well-known seventeenth-century pirate, James Kelley.[29] Though the slaves may or may not technically be pirates (as they have taken over a ship and are using it for their own purposes), Melville gives an ironic credence to the possibility that the true pirate here may be the American ship.[30] As he remarks in *Israel Potter,* "Intrepid, unprincipled, reckless, predatory, with boundless ambition, civilized in externals but a savage at heart, America is, or may yet be, the Paul Jones of nations."[31]

It is also certainly the case that Delano manifests all the prejudices of certain American whites regarding the basic docility and gentleness of blacks. For example, in 1852, three years before the publication of *Benito Cereno,* Harriet Beecher Stowe could write in her best-selling *Uncle Tom's Cabin* that when the "negro race [will] no longer [be] despised and trodden down, [it] will, perhaps, show forth some of the latest and most magnificent revelations of human life. Certainly they will, in their gentleness, their lowly docility of heart, their aptitude to response on a superior mind and rest on a higher power, their childish simplicity of affection, and facility of forgiveness."[32] Melville entertains no such illusions about *any* human being, black or white.

While *Benito Cereno* is indeed about slavery, it is not only about chattel slavery as practiced in America and elsewhere.[33] If one reads this book as being about only the *institution* of slavery, one must read it as simply a dialectic between oppressor and oppressed, as having a bipartite structure. Yet there is another way of reading. Babo, now a leader, had been a slave who was then enslaved by Don Aranda. Cereno, once in command, is now a slave. If the book is about slavery, it is about slavery as a *consequence* of the fact of domination, and it is thus about the meaning of how one follows one who is in power. (That Thoreau had the same distress can be seen from my second epigraph.) Let us say, then, that at least one of the principal subjects of *Benito Cereno* is the question of the actual practice of authority—here of "following your leader." This question lies under and informs any consideration of the master-slave dialectic, for Melville, it seems to me, understood that one cannot rest human affairs on a happy outcome of the dialectic. If one reads the book as being about leading and following, one must read it as having a second three-part structure, now centered on the three protagonists and loosely corresponding to the three-part narrative structure.

The final section, as noted above, starts with a conversation between Delano and Cereno, to which I now turn. After the trial and the account of the slave takeover, Delano wishes to know from Cereno how the latter was taken in by the evil brewing under his nose. Cereno notes that had he been more acute, it might in fact have cost him his life. Indeed, "malign machinations and deceptions impose" themselves on all human beings—he could not have done otherwise. The captain of a ship might be thought to be the model of what we mean by a "leader." Yet here we have a story about a man who was obliged to accept a pose as being in control, while going along with evil because his safety required it (754).

As the longboat of the *Bachelor's Delight* approaches the *San Dominick,* the sailors and Amasa Delano notice that "rudely painted or chalked, as in a sailor freak,[34] along the forward side of a sort of pedestal below the canvas [that covered the figurehead], was the sentence, '*Seguid vuestro jefe,*' (follow your leader)" (676). We learn later that the original figurehead was that of Christopher Columbus, the "discoverer" of the New World who landed first on the island now called San Domingo and who introduced slavery to the Americas, *and* that that figurehead was replaced by the slaves with the defleshed, whitened bones of the murdered owner, Don Aranda.[35] Toward the end of the first section of Melville's story, after Babo and the other slaves have been exposed and the battle to retake the ship has commenced, the shroud falls from the figurehead of Cereno's erstwhile ship to reveal the skeleton of the slave owner in conjunction with its chalked message, "Follow your leader" (734). And here is how the book ends:

> Some months after, dragged to the gibbet at the tail of a mule, the black met his voiceless end. The body was burned to ashes; but for many days, the head, that hive of subtlety, fixed on a pole in the Plaza, met, unabashed, the gaze of the whites; and across the Plaza looked toward St. Bartholomew's church, in whose vaults slept, then, as now, the recovered bones of Aranda; and across the Rimac bridge looked toward the monastery, on Mount Agonia without; where, three months after being dismissed by the court, Benito Cereno, borne on the bier, did, indeed, follow his leader. (755)

The last sentence (103 words!), with its slow and relentless cadence of a funeral dirge, has the effect of tying all the elements of the story together into a whole. The whole centers on the following of one's leader. (We were given a clue to this when Melville has the first mate, leading the boarding of the *San Dominick*, apparently gratuitously cry out: "Follow your leader" [737].) *Benito Cereno* is about, among other things, what being a leader or captain is, how one is to recognize one, and the mistakes that can be made in following him.

We are told at the end that Cereno does indeed "follow his leader." But precisely whom is he following? In Melville's account of his deposition before the court, he indicates that Babo had shown him a skeleton "which had been substituted for the ship's proper figure-head, the image of Christopher Colon . . . ; that the negro Babo had asked him whose skeleton that was, and whether, from its whiteness, he should not think it a white's; that, upon his covering his face, the negro Babo, coming close, said words to this effect: 'Keep faith with the blacks from here to Senegal, or you shall in spirit, as now in body, follow your leader,' pointing to the prow." Babo then repeats this requirement to each to the surviving Spaniards (744).[36] The leader could be Columbus. It could be Don Aranda (now skeletonized by Babo and the others—with a hint of cannibalism). It could be Babo. It could be the church to which Cereno retires. It could be the Spanish sovereign, Charles V, who had retired to a monastery: all are instances of leading and thus of sovereignty itself.[37]

In the actual deposition there is no mention of the change of figureheads; the various references to following a leader do not appear: these are all Melville's additions. And as they bracket the story, appearing first with the passage about the figurehead and the warning from Babo, then the dropping of the shroud and the boarding of the first mate, down to the last words of the story, it would seem that Melville has clued us here to a central concern of his work. If the novella is about following a leader, what is Melville's understanding of a leader? As Catherine Zuckert and John Schaar have separately pointed out, there are three images of leadership in the novella: Delano, Cereno, and Babo.[38] Let us take them in sequence.

Delano self-identifies in Melville's account and is identified in Cereno's actual deposition as a person of "good nature, compassion, and charity" (754). As noted, he is unfailingly courteous and concerned with good manners, shutting out the occasional doubts that the odd happenings on the *San Dominick* arouse in him. This is despite the fact that the white sailors try repeatedly to signal to him that something is wrong. His inability to grasp the situation is summed up in his encounter with an "aged sailor" whose hands are "full of ropes, which he was working into a large knot . . .

[which] seemed a combination of a double-bowline-knot, treble-crown-knot, back-handed-well-knot, knot-in-and-out-knot, and jamming-knot." Captain Delano addresses the knotter in Spanish: "'What are you knotting there, my man?' 'The knot,' was the brief reply, without looking up. 'So it seems; but what is it for?' 'For someone else to undo,' muttered back the old man." The knotter urges Delano in the first English-language words heard in the novella to "undo it, cut it, quick." Despite the fact that he apparently has recognized each of the component knots, Delano is no Alexander. He picks up the great knot, but does not know what to do with it ("knot in hand, and knot in head") and surrenders it to "an elderly negro" who tosses it overboard (707–708). Delano finds "all this . . . very queer" but soon gets over his qualms. The knot stands for what Delano does not understand, or rather that of which he has only the dimmest sense as something being wrong.[39] Thus, he "ignore[s] the symptoms" (708). Such ignorance is his trait. Despite the fact that he noticed that the *San Dominick* flew no colors, it never occurs to him that if Babo can use the Spanish flag as a shaving smock, it is unlikely that he, Delano, is now aboard a ship under Spanish command.

Additionally, he is self-satisfied in his ability to overcome his doubts. In his final conversation with Cereno, he claims that these traits are in the end a good thing, as without them he would have openly questioned the status of the Spanish ship and, in turn, would have certainly been murdered by the slaves. "Had it been otherwise, doubtless . . . some of my interferences might have ended unhappily enough. . . . Those feelings . . . enabled me to get the better of momentary distrust, at times when acuteness might have cost me my life" (754). Delano is a New Englander of a distinguished family. (Franklin Delano Roosevelt will be one of his descendants.) At the beginning, he arrives on a scene that is chaotic to the point practically of anarchy. It is decidedly not the way a ship should be run—one imagines him coming on the ship Plato describes in the epigraph to this essay. If it had been his world, it would have been his role to restore order and set things right. We know from the account that he gives in his book that he had previously managed to set things in order on his ship with some "refractory" crew by "giving them good wholesome floggings; and at other times treating them with the best I had."[40] He clearly knows what supposedly proper order is: in his book he explicitly details all of the qualities that he thinks leadership and rule should have—and in the case of the *San Dominick* is unable to exercise any of them.[41]

Why so? He is kept from doing anything because he is unable to learn from the past how to deal with a new situation. Like Americans in general in Melville's understanding, he knows of nothing and cares for nothing but the present. The past is simply not available for him in his present circumstances—which is one reason Melville took care in the story to change names and dates so that the immediate past *should have been* present, as it should also be to the reader. Delano thus must fall back on the courtesy he fancies one owes a stranger, even one whose behavior is as strange as Cereno's. In his conversation with Cereno after the trial, just before Delano wonders why "the negro" continues to cast such a shadow on Cereno, Cereno has consoled Delano for having mistaken him for the dangerous person: "You were in time undeceived. Would that . . . it was so ever, and with all men." Delano responds: "You generalize, Don Benito; and mournfully enough. But the past is passed; why moralize on it? Forget it. See, yon bright sun has forgotten it all, and the blue sea, and the blue sky; these have turned over new leaves." The "bright sun" contrasts with the fog and gray of the opening: colors (that is, black and white) are now clearly visible, and the world has come back to the order that Delano thinks it should have. Much as in Thomas Cole's 1836 painting *The Oxbow,* the sun of civilization has pushed back the clouds of savagery and order is reestablished.[42] That order is one in which whites rule and blacks obey. A true citizen of "Nature's nation,"[43] Delano has, in other words, learned *nothing* from the experience with Cereno and Babo, except perhaps to be more anxious about the dangers of blacks revolting if they were treated too trustingly (as had Don Aranda).[44] (In Delano's book, in fact, the incident of the *San Dominick* is not mentioned again and Delano passes immediately on to other matters, opening the next chapter with a business-as-usual "I shall now finish my account of the coast of Chili by giving some description" of various islands.)[45] Nothing is retained, except the desire for salvage rights. It is against men such as Delano that Melville puts this passage at the very close of the "Supplement" to his *Battle-Pieces:* "Let us pray that the terrible historic tragedy of our time may not have been enacted without instructing our whole beloved country through terror and pity."[46]

What are we to make of Cereno? The matter is not easy. Take this case. Carl Schmitt had risen to be one of the most prominent German legal scholars during the Weimar period and in 1933 had joined the Nazi Party. In 1938 he had been severely criticized in SS publications and had been relieved of his official non-university positions. Protected by Goering, he continued to teach and publish at the University of Berlin.[47] He did not resign from the party and never apologized after the war. In a letter apparently written on his fiftieth birthday, in 1938, Schmitt signed himself as "Benito Cereno," seeming to identify his lot during Nazism with that of Cereno.[48] He continued to use the name for himself in various letters and exchanges with Ernst Jünger throughout the war.[49] Schmitt refered to Benito Cereno as "the hero of Herman Melville's story" and noted that "in Germany he [Benito Cereno] has become a symbol of the situation of intelligence in a system of mass politics [*einem Massen-System*]."[50] What is striking here is the reference to Cereno as the *Held*—the hero. Schmitt noted in a letter of March 11–12, 1941, to Ernst Jünger that "B C tells himself: better to die from them than for them." The only place that this might make sense with reference to Melville's story is the moment when Cereno leaps into the boat. He may indeed die, as Babo has clearly indicated that he will kill Cereno (or try to) if Cereno gives the play away. (And Babo does leap in after him.) In this sense, Hitler and the SS would be Babo, and Schmitt's self-identification with Cereno a sign that he thought resistance to the state to be justified but would be at the risk of one's life (and thus he was excused in the postwar period).[51] In this reading Cereno (and Schmitt) are the aristocratic elite, now dominated by the corrupted masses led by evil itself.[52] And, indeed, Schmitt closed his *Ex Captivitate Salus* by portraying himself as the "last conscious representative of the *jus publicum Europaeum,* its last teacher and researcher in an existential sense, [experiencing] its end as does Benito Cereno the voyage of the pirate ship."[53] Cereno is the old Europe taken over first by the dangerous masses, unable to find an intelligent leader, enslaved to the crowd, and helpless face-to-face with an uncomprehending, powerful, but fundamentally stupid America unappreciative of excellence. The novel then is more about class and its fate in mass society than it is about race.

There is a truth to this: Cereno is enslaved; Delano is unthinking. Melville's story does not exempt the New World from the sins of the Old: I noted above the allusions to Charles V and more extensively to the bringing of institutions like slavery to the New World. (Lima was built on the backs of slave labor in the gold mines.) It is harder, however, to find in Cereno the aristocratic elite that seems at the basis of Schmitt's interest. He appears initially to Delano as "half-lunatic": indeed, "no landsman could have dreamed that in him there was lodged a dictatorship beyond which, while at sea, there was no earthly appeal" (680, 681). It is noteworthy that while Delano is deluded in almost all of his perceptions of the situation about the Spanish ship, he is not deluded in his sense of what a ship's captain should be: he recognizes clearly that Cereno does not correspond to it. Cereno is no hero, despite Schmitt's need to call him one. The problem for Melville may rather lie in what Delano thinks a leader should be. (And here I recall that in *White-Jacket* Melville goes out of his way to attack the practice of flogging as well as the expectation that one should trust the captain in everything.) The parallels drawn by Melville serve rather to indicate that he does not find the American polity, as exemplified in Delano, to be exceptionally exempt from the sins of the Old World. But what are those sins?

Don Benito Cereno replies to Delano's greeting of the healing sun and the turning over of "new leaves" with the following. The leaves can start anew "because they have no memory . . . because they are not human." (The implication is that Delano lacks something as a human being.) To Delano's insistence that the "mild trades [winds] that now fan your check, do they not come with a human-like healing to you?" Cereno replies that "their steadfastness but waft[s] me to my tomb." It is at this point that the central teaching of the novella appears. It is the passage used by Ellison as an epigraph that I mentioned at the outset.

> "You are saved," cried Captain Delano, more and more astonished and pained; "you aresaved; what has cast such a shadow upon you?"
>
> "The negro." (754)

The next line is "There was silence." Cereno's answer—explicitly—puts an end to all conversation. There is not another word of direct speech in the novella, as if with this nothing more could be said, as if words had failed. At the outset of the story, at the end of the third paragraph, we were warned that there were "shadows present, foreshadowing deeper shadows to come" (673). We now encounter them.

The shadow for Cereno is "the negro." In Spanish, *negro* means not only a black person, but also blackness, jet blackness. Blackness is associated by Melville with "those deep far-away things in [a person]; those occasional flashings-forth of the intuitive Truth . . . ; those short quick probings at the very axis of reality."[54] What do Cereno's last words mean? Some readers have taken them to mean that Cereno has acknowledged what Delano could not, that the enslavement of others is wrong, a reading that could be that of present-day Delanos.[55] A more obvious reading is that the caster of the shadow is simply Babo and that he, Cereno, is incapable of doing anything, even of saying anything, about this fact. It is no accident that Ellison used this passage for *Invisible Man* without Cereno's answer: the novel that follows becomes the answer to Delano's question. Cereno will keep Babo invisible and unspoken of except by his own death. Saying "the negro" *is* a "flashing-forth of [an] intuitive Truth": however, it is a truth Cereno cannot acknowledge. It leaves him speechless, and thus he refuses or rather is unable to acknowledge the actuality of his insight (an insight that never occurs in any form to Delano). The actuality of "the negro" calls into question for different reasons the ability of both Cereno and Delano to say anything appropriate to the circumstances.

Most centrally, what is the relation of this shadow to the repeated injunction to "follow your leader"? To explore this, I turn to the third of the leader figures: Babo. Throughout the story he is presented as joined to Benito Cereno. They are leaning on each other in their first appearance to Delano, who finds in the tableau an example of the proper and admirable relation of whites to blacks. At the end it is not even clear that Babo and Cereno may not have died at the same time, for Babo is executed "some months" after the trial and Cereno dies "three months after being dismissed by the court" (755). Yet this union has multiple dimensions. Joyce Adler has given an excellent analysis of its complexity. On the one hand, she notes, the two are "inseparable." From the scene in which Babo kneels to fix Cereno's shoe buckle, to the shaving scene and more, "in all these scenes, which are like photographic stills, master and slave are bound together, their social connection constituting their chain." Beyond this inseparability, however, they are also "irreconcilable": Babo seeks to kill Cereno after the latter leaps into the boat; Cereno will not confront or even face Babo at the trial. Finally, the two are "interchangeable": the two cross the plaza at the end in the same direction. Master and slave are not a question of race but of domination. From all this, violence in inevitable.[56]

We know from the beginning of Rousseau's *Social Contract* that "he who believes himself to be the master of another is just as much the slave as they." Melville's point here is similar. As long as one has domination over the other, Cereno and Babo are not individually free, or free of each other.

Note that when Cereno jumps into the longboat, even though he, in effect, breaks the contract he has made with Babo to take the blacks to Senegal, the two nonetheless remain tied to each other. This is why the story starts in gray, the colors indistinct from each other. There are no masters without slaves, no slaves without masters. Once Babo takes over the ship and makes Cereno the equivalent of his slave, he is just as much caught in this web as was Cereno before the revolt. This is the reason that Melville *appears* ambivalent about the slavery question: he understood that turning things upside down only reproduced the previous dynamics. Not for him was the too easy condemnation so loved by Northerners in *Uncle Tom's Cabin.* (This is one of the reasons Ralph Ellison thought that Twain and Melville were the best writers on slavery in nineteenth-century America and paid no attention to Stowe, except to dismiss a performance of *Uncle Tom's Cabin.*)[57]

Nonetheless, one cannot stop here, for to do so would reduce the abilities and courage of Babo and the other blacks to insignificance. We must also ask about Babo as the third example of leadership. Adler catches part of this in her essay: "His blackness marks him as the man taken by force from Africa to be a slave in the Americas. He has a rich intelligence: he has the qualities of mind of a master psychologist, strategist, general, playwright, impresario and poet. Melville endows him with his own poetic insight into the symbolic implications that can be found in significant figures and objects: the skeleton, the black giant who may throw off his chains and will not ask pardon, the padlock and the key, the Spanish flag used as a rag."[58]

One could add that he writes and speaks Spanish. It is the case that of the three, Babo appears by far the most perceptive and able. We know him, however, only through his deeds—alone of the three, he is not given a point of view, except at the very end, where his "head . . . fixed on a pole, met . . . the gaze of the whites" (755). Delano is the eye for the reader in the first section; Cereno's deposition offers his account in the second (an account, as I noted, stamped with official approval from the powers that be). But at the end we learn of Babo only that "seeing all was over, he uttered no sound, and could not be forced to. His aspect seemed to say, since I cannot do deeds, I will not speak words" (755). The words he spoke earlier in the story were the words of a script that he made up for himself in accordance with the expectations of the audience; they are not authentically his own. As there is no one able to hear whatever Babo has to say as himself, there are (as yet) no words for this situation. The contract with Cereno has not been honored (and should not have been): after which there is nothing that can be said. As I observed earlier, in note 22, there is controversy over the resonances of "Babo." While it is clear that Melville took the term from Delano's account, it is also clear that he kept the name and did not change it, as he did a number of other names. Indeed, he fuses Babo with his son Mure (who does not appear at all) and does not have Babo die during the retaking of the ship. One possible reason Melville may have wanted to keep the character Babo is that his name resonates with the Greek term for those they could not understand, the *barbaroi,* the antonym to those of the *pólis,* those whose speech is of the *logos*—so Babo has nothing of his own to say. Our word *babble* possibly comes from this root. Demosthenes (*Orations* 3.10) is clear that the *barbaroi* do not speak Greek and relates *barbaroi* to language. For Melville, the name becomes a badge of the recognition of the distance to an acknowledgment of the other who is the enslaved.

In *Moby-Dick* the sailors come to follow Ahab enthusiastically: the result, for all but Ishmael, is death, and he is saved only by a coffin. There are three cases in *Benito Cereno* where the injunction to follow one's leader appears: they also are all associated with death. The first are the words chalked by Babo on the ship's prow. These are associated with him and the murders by the slaves. Babo warns the white survivors to keep their promise to help; if they don't, they will "follow their leader." The second is the cry of the first mate during the retaking of the *San Dominick.* These are associated with the slaughter of the blacks and the reestablishment of a legal order that allows slavery, and thus with the actions of Amasa Delano. The third is associated with Benito Cereno in death, as he in life does indeed follow his leader. Who the leader is has no single answer. The issue, rather, is the *following* of one's leader.

I noted at the start that Melville writes the first part of the story more or less from the point of view of Delano. This perspective is one of a rather obtuse person, overly satisfied with his version of the state of the world. At times perceptions of the situation are given narrative voice. By and large, Delano and the narrator share similar perceptions: the doubling simply keeps one from too easily moving away from seeing the world as Delano does, for his vision seems confirmed (if occasionally undercut) by a more abstractly authorial voice. This is a device that Melville uses quite often, notably in "The Paradise of Bachelors and the Tartarus of Maids" and "Bartleby the Scrivener." It consists in giving the reader a point of view that must then be discarded, even though it appears at times to be confirmed.

At the beginning of the story, the reader's point of view follows that of Captain Delano. As the story goes along, the reader finds himself or herself more and more distant from Delano. At the end of the story the reader is left with the head of Babo—his body having been burned—a "hive of subtlety" that continues its gaze and which, having no words for what has happened, speaks volumes. As Melville moved through his career's work, he became increasingly doubtful about the possibilities of expressing what was wrong with America. Bartleby, famously, has nothing to say to the other presences in the story. In "The Tartarus of Maids" the women are not allowed to talk. In "The Bell-Tower" workers are replaced by a speechless automaton "without a soul"; a giant bell is cast, during which the architect murders a man, and a fragment of the murder shows up as a flaw in the bell (much as the ship's bell in *Benito Cereno* has a flaw: the resonances are obviously to the Liberty Bell).[59] The automaton kills the architect and is destroyed by the townspeople. The great, flawed bell is rung for the first time and destroys the tower. The last lines of the story: "So the blind slave obeyed its blinder lord, but, in obedience, slew him. So the creator was killed by the creature. So the bell was too heavy for the tower. So the bell's main weakness was where man's blood had flawed it. And so pride went before the fall."[60] So also liberty as Americans practice it may destroy their polity.

In all this Melville's strategy is to prod the reader to move from an initial comfortable position to a more complex understanding. Babo and the slaves are clearly presented as having murdered, often viciously: sailors were tied up and thrown alive overboard; Don Aranda was murdered and possibly cannibalized. Melville in no ways hides their violence. The same is true for the whites: during the retaking of the ship the sailors behave savagely toward the surviving blacks, to the point that Delano must stop them the next day. Likewise, the violence meted out to Babo and the other slaves is cruel; it is, however, "official" violence. Slavery is in itself cruel. The movement of the novella is thus a form of political education: it impresses on the reader the ease with which one accepts one's prejudices as natural, and the difficulty in abandoning them. *The important point is that this difficulty is made all the greater by virtue of the fact that one is not clear for what one abandons them* (thus, Babo has no words of his own). If, in the case of the Civil War, a shadow may be expiated and lifted from the land, *it will still not be clear in which direction the land is headed.* As Lincoln remarked at the opening of his June 16, 1858, "House Divided" speech: "If we could know *where* we are, and *whither* we are tending, we could then better judge *what* to do and *how* to do it."[61] The end of *Battle-Pieces* is a poem titled "America." It closes like this, partially echoing the last conversation of Delano and Cereno:

While the shadow, chased by light,
Fled along the far-drawn height,
And left her on the crag.[62]

At the time of the writing of *Benito Cereno,* what was clear was that leaders—the leaders of that time—were not to be followed. (He also has leaders in general in mind and, as noted, at that moment Franklin Pierce in particular, whose signing of the Kansas-Nebraska Act had opened the whole country to slavery.) The question Melville poses is whether we can see legal savagery in the same light as we see supposedly "extralegal" savagery. To do so would be to see ourselves as others—the slaves—see us, and this is what is lacking in all the white characters in this story.

There is great violence in this story, violence by blacks and whites. This shadow is on this story, as was the shadow, Melville knew, on the land. The shadow, then, is not slavery or blackness or Babo: what underlies all these is the following of a leader, simply because he is the leader. "Follow the leader" is child's play: this is what Melville finds the most distressing. And his position is sorrowfully complex. In "The Portent," the first poem in *Battle-Pieces,* Melville writes:

Hanging from the beam,
Slowly swaying (such the law),
Gaunt the shadow on your green
Shenandoah!
The cut is on the crown
(Lo, John Brown),
And the stabs shall heal no more.[63]

Harpers Ferry, the site of Brown's raid, is on the Shenandoah River. Brown was wounded by a sword during his capture. The next poem in *Battle-Pieces* is the 1860 "Misgivings," which opens:

> When ocean-clouds over inland hills
> Sweep storming in late autumn brown,
> And horror the sodden valley fills,
> And the spire falls crashing in the town,
> I muse upon my country's ills—
> The tempest bursting from the waste of Time
> On the world's fairest hope linked with man's foulest crime.

The silences that envelop this story point to an increasing distress Melville has with his country. He writes the first three-quarters of the novella in such a manner that readers will be caught up in their own refusal to acknowledge the evil of slavery—much as Delano denies it. It is not that they do not know that slavery is evil, but that they do not, cannot, acknowledge it.[64] Melville thus understands that simply telling his countrymen that they are in denial would be of little effect or import. As with the nation, the reader comes too late to see his or her "complicity in moral blindness."[65] One should, in reading the novella, have a certain embarrassment at what one has assumed. At the end, though, there is silence.

Shortly before his execution, John Brown gave a handwritten note to his jailor: "I, John Brown, am now quite *certain* that the crimes of this *guilty, land: will* never be purged *away;* but with Blood. I had *as I now think: vainly* flattered myself that without *very much* bloodshed; it might be done."[66] Melville knew it also: so it is when leaders are followed simply because they are the leaders. Despite or because of his hatred of slavery, Melville found in Brown's raid the bursting of a tempest on the land. (We have already seen the crashing spire in "Misgivings" and falling bell in "The Bell-Tower.") Babo has no words of his own. Neither Cereno, nor Delano, nor Brown is able to find words for "man's foulest crime." Perhaps there could not have been any. For, if we can adequately express nothing, if we cannot find words for our actuality, then only violence will suffice: war was but five years away.

Notes

I should like to thank Babette Babich for a helpful reading of this text and in particular for her suggestions about Plato and the name Babo. Forrest Robinson provided comments that expanded several issues more than I had done. Jason Frank's careful reading opened up many doors, and the essay is much better for his intelligence and generosity. Lawrie Balfour pointed to paths for rethinking two key issues.

1. Alan Heimert, "*Moby-Dick* and American Political Symbolism," *American Quarterly* 15, no. 4 (Winter 1963): 499–500. Heimert extensively explores the ship metaphor in American literature and political writing.

2. Herman Melville, *White-Jacket,* in Melville, *Redburn, White-Jacket, Moby-Dick* (New York: Library of America, 1983), 768–769; further citations to these three works are to this edition.

3. Ibid., 768.

4. Ibid., 506; emphasis added. The term *Manifest Destiny* was coined in the 1830s by the writer John J. O'Sullivan. He is the subject of one of the chapters of the Ph.D. thesis of one of my students, Adam Gomez, "An Almost Chosen People" (University of California at San Diego, 2010).

5. Melville, *Redburn,* 185. As an example of these doubts, Melville contributed seven satirical articles to the journal *Yankee Doodle* on General Zachary Taylor's role in the Mexican-American War. In the third, for instance, Taylor spends a day in the saddle despite the fact that a tack has been placed point upward on it. On dismounting, his trousers tear and his buttocks are laid bare. "Though Valiant as the Cid, the old hero is as modest as any miss. Instantly muffling up with his coat tails the exposed part, he hurried into his tent." See Luther Stearns Mansfield, "Melville's Comic Articles on Zachary Taylor," *American Literature* 9, no. 4 (January 1938): 415. Mansfield tends to read them as supportive of Taylor; I find them mocking. *Yankee Doodle* ran weekly from October 10, 1846, to October 3, 1847. Based in New York, it satirized American politics, especially with regard to James Polk.

6. Robert Frost, "A Cabin in the Clearing," in Frost, *Collected Poems, Prose, and Plays* (New York: Library of America, 1995), 427.

7. Mexico was obliged to cede Texas and gave over the rest of the Southwest for $18 million—less than half the prewar offer.

8. I owe this reference to Matthew Rebhorn, "Minding the Body: *Benito Cereno* and Melville's Embodied Reading Practice," *Studies in the Novel* 41, no. 2 (Summer 2009): 169–170. Looking up the *Putnam's* article "About Niggers" online, we find that when the whites on an island shout "Liberty! Liberty! To Arms! . . . it penetrated the thick tympanums of these degraded niggers . . . and they

discovered . . . that liberty does not mean slavery!" *Putnam's Monthly Magazine,* December 1855, 609, http://digital.library.cornell.edu/cgi/t/text/text-idx?c=putn;cc=putn;view=toc;subview=short;idno=putn0006-6.

9. Amasa Delano, *A Narrative of Voyages and Travels, in the Northern and Southern Hemispheres* (1817; repr., Stockbridge, Mass.: Berkshire House, 1994). Citations are to the original edition, which is available on Google Books. I shall be concerned on occasion with the differences between the two accounts. They are well detailed in Michael Rogin, *Subversive Genealogy: The Politics and Art of Herman Melville* (New York: Knopf, 1983), 208–220; in Sandra A. Zagarell, "Re-envisioning America: Melville's *Benito Cereno,*" *ESQ: A Journal of the American Renaissance* 30 (1984): 245–249; and especially in Margaret M. Vanderhaar, "A Re-examination of *Benito Cereno,*" *American Literature* 40, no. 2 (May 1968): 179–191.

10. The theatricality of the story is one of the basic points made by Michael Rogin.

11. Lima was the administrative capital of Spanish colonies on the western coast of South America south of Bolivia. In the actual events, Babo is killed during the retaking of the ship and Delano gives a deposition that goes unreported in Melville's story. Additionally, Cereno does not die but tries to make Delano out to be a pirate in an attempt to deny him salvage rights. See Delano, *A Narrative,* 334, 342–344.

12. Michael McLoughlin, following E. F. Carlisle, argues that Delano is meant as a critique of Emerson and transcendentalism in McLoughlin, *Dead Letters to the New World: Melville, Emerson and American Transcendentalism* (New York: Routledge, 2003), 122. This is a bit one-sided, as Melville, if not without some questioning, was in no doubt about Emerson's extraordinary qualities. See Herman Melville to Evert Duyckinck, March 3, 1849, in *Correspondence,* ed. Lynn Horth (Evanston and Chicago: Northwestern University Press and the Newberry Library, 1993), 121–122.

13. The point is very well made by James Kavanagh in "'That Hive of Subtlety': *Benito Cereno* as Ideological Critique," *Bucknell Review* 28, no. 1 (1984): 127–157. Kavanagh points out that "the analysis of 'Benito Cereno' must begin by breaking absolutely the seductive grip of 'identification' between the reader and Amasa Delano, a grip not even loosened by the seemingly negative judgments of the American Captain carried in phrases like 'moral simplicity' and 'weak-wittedness.'" He adduces a number of critics who have failed to accomplish this break, on whom the effect of Melville's irony seems to have gone unnoticed.

14. Herman Melville, *Benito Cereno,* in *Pierre, Israel Potter, The Piazza Tales, The Confidence-Man, Uncollected Prose, and Billy Budd.* (New York: Library of America, 1984), 754. All citations to *Benito Cereno* are given parenthetically in the

text and refer to this edition. Works other than *Benito Cereno* in this volume will be cited by title and the volume cited as *Pierre . . . Billy Budd.* See also *The Collected Essays of Ralph Ellison,* ed. John F. Callahan (New York: Modern Library, 1995), 88.

15. Some account of this can be found in Allan Moore Emery, "The Topicality of Depravity in *Benito Cereno,*" *American Literature* 55, no. 3 (October 1983): 316–331. See also Kavanagh's comments in "That Hive of Subtlety" on those critics who think that Melville is simply saying that there is a beast in us all.

16. The four previous sentences draw directly from remarks offered to me by Professor Forrest Robinson. I am grateful for his comments.

17. The original name of the Spanish boat was *Tryal,* and that of the American was *Perseverance.*

18. Henry David Thoreau, "Civil Disobedience," in *Walden and Civil Disobedience,* ed. Owen Thomas (New York: Norton, 1966), 228.

19. This was typically work imposed on jailed convicts.

20. On the gothic qualities of the whole scene, see McLoughlin, *Dead Letters,* 120–121.

21. Melville, *Billy Budd,* in *Pierre . . . Billy Budd,* 1431. Architectural finials were once believed to deter witches from landing on one's roof. I owe some of the thoughts in the next paragraph to Forrest Robinson.

22. See the important discussion in Joyce Sparer Adler, *War in Melville's Imagination* (New York: New York University Press, 1981), 88–110. There is, incidentally, some controversy in the literature about the origins of the name Babo. Whatever reason Melville might have had for retaining this name, the name is in Delano's deposition as that of the ringleader. See Delano, *A Narrative,* 335. See also Robert Cochran, "Babo's Name in *Benito Cereno:* An Unnecessary Controversy?" *American Literature* 48, no. 2 (May 1976): 217–219. I discuss the name below.

23. See the discussion in Wilson Carey McWilliams, *The Idea of Fraternity in America* (Berkeley: University of California Press, 1973), 369; Eric J. Sundquist, "*Benito Cereno* and New World Slavery," in *Reconstructing American Literary History,* ed. Sacvan Bercovitch (Cambridge: Harvard University Press, 1986), 93–122.

24. Melville backgrounds a very complex relation between the New World and the Old by a set of images that refer the reader to the Spain of Charles V (who, like Cereno, left his position of power to end his life in a monastery). See the seminal article by H. Bruce Franklin, "Apparent Symbol of Despotic Command: Melville's Benito Cereno," *New England Quarterly* 34, no. 4 (November 1961): 462–477. See also, on the lack of color, Darryl Hattenhauer, "'Follow Your Leader': Knowing One's Place in *Benito Cereno,*" *Rocky Mountain Review of Language and Literature* 45, nos. 1/2 (1991): 7–17, esp. 8–9, and Rogin, *Subversive Genealogy,* 208,

who relates it to Hegel's "gray on gray" in from the introduction to his *Philosophy of History*.

25. F. O. Matthiessen, *American Renaissance: Art and Expression in the Age of Emerson and Whitman* (New York: Oxford University Press, 1941), 508: "Melville's failure to recognize [the fact of slavery] makes his tragedy comparatively superficial." Also cited in John Schaar, "The Uses of Literature for the Study of Politics: The Case of Melville's *Benito Cereno*," in Schaar, *Legitimacy in the Modern State* (New Brunswick, N.J.: Transaction, 1981), 84. Matthiessen found *Benito Cereno* to be a failure and pretty much dismissed the work, a rare mistake by a great critic.

26. Schaar, "The Uses of Literature," 67–68, gets at this point in his consideration of the importance of the "world of domination."

27. Rogin, *Subversive Genealogy*, 208–220. The act gave the territories an opening to decide on the question of slavery by popular vote: this produced a bloody war in Kansas as settlers of both persuasions rushed to the territory. Lincoln's speech against the act in Peoria on October 18, 1854, marks the real beginning of his national career. Hawthorne wrote a campaign biography of Pierce.

28. See the interesting discussion in Elizabeth Wright, "The New Psychoanalysis and Literary Criticism: A Reading of Hawthorne and Melville," *Poetics Today* 3, no. 2 (Spring 1982): 98–100.

29. In the late seventeenth century Kelley became a pirate after being freed from a slave ship; his piracy was conducted mainly in the same waters as the events in this novella. He was eventually captured in Boston (with Captain William Kidd) and hanged in London in 1701.

30. See Carolyn L. Karcher, "The Riddle of the Sphinx: Melville's *Benito Cereno* and the *Amistad* Case," in *Critical Essays on Herman Melville's* Benito Cereno, ed. Robert Burkholder (New York: G. K. Hall, 1992), 196–228, which analyzes very carefully the parallels and disjunctures between this case and that of the *Amistad*, wherein blacks had taken over the ship that was taking them to slavery. They were acquitted of piracy at their trial in Boston (John Adams was their lawyer), as their abduction had been against their will and the takeover had happened outside American jurisdiction. On the name change, see ibid., 213–214.

31. Melville, *Israel Potter*, in *Pierre . . . Billy Budd*, 561. The distinction between privateer (which Jones called himself) and pirate was a matter of perspective.

32. Harriet Beecher Stowe, *Uncle Tom's Cabin; or, Life among the Lowly* (1852; repr., New York: Penguin, 1986), 275. See James Baldwin, "Everybody's Protest Novel," in his *Notes of a Native Son* (1955; repr., Boston: Beacon, 1984), 13–19. Those who compare *Adventures of Huckleberry Finn* unfavorably to Stowe's book on the question of the portrayal of blacks should think again. On this see my "Glad

to Find Out Who I Was: Mark Twain on What Can Be Learned on a Raft," *Journal of Law, Philosophy and Culture* 5, no. 1 (2010): 151–177.

33. See similar thoughts in Schaar, "The Uses of Literature."

34. *Freak* can mean a prank or a sportive fancy.

35. According to Cereno's deposition Aranda was murdered and simply thrown overboard.

36. This passage is not in Delano's book.

37. See the similar thoughts in H. Bruce Franklin, "Past, Present and Future Seemed One" in Burkholder, *Critical Essays*, 231. Franklin makes an extensive case for the figure of Charles V of Spain. See also Franklin, "Apparent Symbol of Despotic Command."

38. Catherine H. Zuckert, "Leadership—Natural and Conventional—in Melville's *Benito Cereno*," *Interpretation* 26, no. 2 (Winter 1999): 239–255. This is a helpful article even if I do disagree with its conclusion that Babo is the example of a democratic leader (assuming at face value that this is all she means). See also Schaar, "The Uses of Literature."

39. See Wright, "The New Psychoanalysis," 102–104. For a perhaps overly complex reading of the suppressed erotic in this scene, see Myron Tuman, *Melville's Gay Father and the Knot of Filicidal Desire: On Men and Their Demons* (n.p.: Cybereditions, 2006).

40. Delano, *A Narrative*, 320.

41. In chapters 16 and 17 of his book he spends a good deal of time laying out the proper qualifications of a sea captain.

42. An image of *The Oxbow* can be seen at http://xroads.virginia.edu/~cap/nature/oxbow.gif.

43. The phrase is Perry Miller's: "Thus, superficial appearances to the contrary, America is not crass, materialistic: it is Nature's nation, possessing a heart that watches and receives." See Miller, *Errand into Wilderness* (Cambridge: Harvard University Press, 1956), 210, as well as his *Nature's Nation* (Cambridge: Harvard University Press, 1967).

44. Increased vigilance and severity of treatment were consequences of the rebellion of Nat Turner (1831). Delano expresses surprise several times at the laxity of the treatment of the Africans.

45. Delano, *A Narrative*, 354.

46. Melville, "Supplement" to *Battle-Pieces and Aspects of the War* (1866; repr., New York: Da Capo, 1995), 260; also cited by Schaar, "The Uses of Literature."

47. See my introduction to Carl Schmitt, *The Concept of the Political* (German ed. 1932; 1st English ed. 1976), trans. George Schwab, rev. ed. (Chicago: University of Chicago Press, 2007); and the excellent Thomas O. Beebee, "Carl Schmitt's Myth of Benito Cereno," *Seminar: A Journal of Germanic Studies* 42,

no. 2 (2006): 114–134, as well as my "Sacred Spirit of Politics: Thomas Hobbes, Carl Schmitt and St. Paul" in *Jahrbuch Politisches Denken* (2010), 245–294, and chapter 6 of my *Politics without Vision: Thinking without a Banister in the Twentieth Century* (Chicago: University of Chicago Press, 2012), 218–262.

48. Copies of the letter were sent to several people after the war, among them Armin Mohler, who printed it in the publication of his correspondence with Schmitt. Schmitt had apparently wanted this letter to become the epigraph to a reissue of his book on Hobbes, *Der Leviathan in der Staatslehre des Thomas Hobbes. Sinn und Fehlschlag eines politischen Symbols* (Hamburg: Hanseatische Verlaganstalt, 1938).

49. See Schmitt to Jünger, February 25, 1941, and March 11–12, 1941 (signed "Grüss Ihres Cereno"), in Carl Schmitt, *Ernst Jünger–Carl Schmitt. Briefe 1930–1983* (Stuttgart: Klett-Cota, 1999). I was reminded of the Jünger references by Beebee's article "Carl Schmitt's Myth of Benito Cereno."

50. Carl Schmitt, *Ex Captivitate Salus. Erfahrungen der Zeit, 1945–1947* (1950; repr., Berlin: Duncker and Humblot, 2002), 21–22.

51. Schmitt wanted his March 11–12, 1941, letter to Jünger used as an epigraph to his book *Leviathan* and conceived of that book, despite its anti-Semitism, as an act of resistance to Nazism. See my *Politics without Vision*, chap. 6, and my introduction to Schmitt, *The Leviathan in the State Theory of Thomas Hobbes: Meaning and Failure of a Political Symbol*, trans. George Schwab and Erna Hilfstein (original German ed. 1938; 1996; repr., Chicago: University of Chicago Press, 2008).

52. It is certainly no accident that José Ortega y Gasset's *The Revolt of the Masses*, first published in 1930, had been a best seller in Germany.

53. Schmitt, *Ex Captivitate Salus*, 75.

54. Melville, "Hawthorne and His Mosses," in *Pierre . . . Billy Budd*, 1159.

55. See, for instance, William D. Richardson, *Melville's* Benito Cereno: *An Interpretation with Annotated Text and Concordance* (Durham: Carolina Academic Press, 1987), 86. Also cited in Beebee, "Carl Schmitt's Myth of Benito Cereno." See also Richard Faber, "*Benito Cereno* oder die Entmythologisierun Euro-Americas. Zur Kritik Carl Schmitts und seiner Schule," in *Kultursoziologie. Symptom des Zeitgeistes?* ed. Richard Faber (Würzburg: Königshausen & Neumann, 1989), 82, who also refers to Babo as the hero of the story. Beebee also cites this article.

56. Joyce Sparer Adler, "*Benito Cereno:* Slavery and Violence in the Americas," in Burkholder, *Critical Essays*, 82–83.

57. Ralph Ellison, introduction to the 1982 reissue of *Invisible Man*, reprinted in *The Collected Essays of Ralph Ellison*, 487, 483.

58. Adler, *War in Melville's Imagination*, 88.

59. I was led to look to these works by Franklin, "Past, Present and Future."

60. Melville, "The Bell-Tower," in *Pierre . . . Billy Budd,* 833.

61. The text of this speech can be found, for example, at www.pbs.org/wgbh/aia/part4/4h2934t.html; emphasis added. Similarly, Emerson had opened his great essay "Experience" (1844) with the question "Where do we find ourselves?"

62. Melville, *Battle-Pieces,* 162. Adler cites the same poem in *War in Melville's Imagination,* 158.

63. Melville, "The Portent," in *Battle-Pieces,* xix. Richard Cox and Paul Dowling have published an interesting study of *Battle-Pieces* in "Herman Melville's Civil War: Lincolnian Prudence in Poetry," *Political Science Reviewer* 29 (2000): 192–295.

64. I can *know* you are late, you can *know* you are late, you can *know* that I *know* you are late; but unless you *acknowledge* it by *doing something* (saying, "I'm sorry"), the situation is not adequately dealt with.

65. Herman Melville, "Misgivings," in *Battle-Pieces.* I owe the phrase "complicity in moral blindness" to a personal communication from Forrest Robinson.

66. David S. Reynolds, *John Brown, Abolitionist* (New York: Knopf, 2005), 395; emphases in original.

11

The Metaphysics of Indian-Hating Revisited

Thomas Dumm

In his recent study of Abraham Lincoln and the abolition of American slavery, Eric Foner argues that by the concluding months of the American Civil War, Lincoln had undergone a sea change in his attitude toward African Americans. Once firmly committed to the idea of colonization, believing that the inferiority of blacks made their presence in a postslavery society problematic, Lincoln abandoned the idea, not only because of its impracticality, but because he no longer held such a firmly racist attitude toward blacks. Lincoln wasn't the only one. The movement toward the abolition of slavery that culminated in the Thirteenth Amendment to the Constitution reflected a remarkable transformation of attitudes on the part of white Americans regarding the natural rights of blacks, so that even the question of suffrage was able to be raised, opening the possibility of their participation in American life.

But Foner notices something less than transformative in Lincoln's view of natural rights. "The continuing evolution of Lincoln's attitudes regarding blacks stands in stark contrast to the lack of change when it came to Native Americans," he writes.[1] Lincoln shared a common assumption that Indians could not be civilized. Moreover, he believed that Indians constituted a primary obstacle to the Republican vision of a free-labor, free-market, unified nation-state; they had their own senses of sovereign nationhood, promised to them by succeeding U.S. governments, promises broken many times over. Foner mentions only in passing one other interesting piece of information. Lincoln's paternal grandfather, for whom he was named, was killed by an Indian while working on his Kentucky farm, "an event witnessed by the seven-year-old Thomas Lincoln [Abraham's father]."[2]

Foner disavows the idea that Lincoln was an Indian-hater, noting that he once commuted the death sentences of several hundred condemned Indians who had been convicted of the massacre of settlers (though he allowed thirty-eight of the sentences to stand, which resulted in one of the largest mass executions in American history). Yet to think that young Abraham Lincoln, who became in adulthood almost a stranger to his father, would not have heard extensively of this family tragedy, that his father would not have imparted to him his personal knowledge of the killing of his grandfather, and that the grandson would then not have been strongly affected by it, is not plausible. Foner may be correct that Lincoln didn't have a personal hatred for Indians. But that is not to say that he was not invested in what Herman Melville describes in *The Confidence-Man* as "the metaphysics of Indian-hating."

In what follows I want to revisit Melville's presentation of the metaphysics of Indian-hating to think through the *form* of hate he describes. The formal characteristic of Indian-hating, I will argue, consists of two features: metaphysicians of Indian-hating characterize acts of violence committed against themselves as attacks on innocents, and their innocence is deeply related to their sense of moral superiority to those acting against them. This characteristic makes the metaphysics easily transferable to others who resist the metaphysician. Melville characterizes the metaphysical only implicitly, but he reaches deeper than the popular meaning of the day, the idea of metaphysics simply being obtuse philosophy. Melville was instead seeking to understand the origins of a permanent human emotion, that of hatred, and its changing object that becomes fixed, an obsession. In this sense his understanding is as close to Freud's as it may have been to Plato's.

In a sense, Melville is continuing an exploration of the relationship of woundedness and hatred that he began in *Moby-Dick.* When Ahab famously attributes to the white whale some sort of superhuman agency, he is projecting onto Moby-Dick, to the whale, the very violent impulses that he himself exhibits in the floating charnel house known as the *Pequod.* Ahab's obsessive hatred leads to his destruction and that of his crew, but what is of interest in relationship to Melville's later exploration of hatred is his acknowledgment of the madness of his obsession and his refusal to give it up. In a key scene shortly before the chase begins, he refuses the mad Pip's assistance, saying, "There is that in thee, poor lad, which I feel too curing of my malady. Like cures like, and for this hunt, my malady becomes my most desired health."[3] Ahab's sickness is his health.

And there is another passage in *Moby-Dick* that more directly presents the metaphysical quandary faced by Ahab. In explaining, over the protests of Starbuck, why he must seek the whale, Ahab writes: "All visible objects, man, are but as pasteboard masks. But in each event—in the living act, the undoubted deed—there, some unknown but still reasoning thing puts forth the mouldings of its features from behind the unreasoning mask. If man will strike, strike through the mask! How can the prisoner reach outside except by thrusting through the wall?"[4] This is the metaphysical quest Ahab has undertaken, to get to the root of the reason that Moby Dick took his leg, to find in the whale the source of all evil. One could well call this earlier effort the metaphysics of whale fishing.

In what follows I will provide two examples of the ongoing presence of this metaphysics in American life, first one culled from Laura Ingalls Wilder's classic children's book, *Little House on the Prairie,* and then one from the rationale put forward by Vice President Dick Cheney for the way the war on terror should be prosecuted.

Melville's Indian

Melville's *The Confidence-Man* has been read as a satire of transcendentalism, as a deep-seated primitive Christian critique of Christian hypocrisy, and as a gloriously complicated condemnation of American capitalism.[5] Melville may have sensed, given the increasingly poor sales of his previous works, *Moby-Dick, Pierre, Israel Potter,* and *The Piazza Tales,* that this was likely to be his last published novel.[6] Hence, he seems to have written it as much for himself and his small group of loyal readers as for a general public. The language is picturesque, the plot is chaotic and episodic, and the novel doesn't end so much as stop.

The Confidence-Man consists of a series of encounters on a steamboat, the *Fidèle,* as it is voyaging down the Mississippi River to New Orleans "on a first of April."[7] The confidence man referred to in the title appears throughout the novel in a variety of disguises: as an elderly crippled black man, a man in mourning, a man in a gray coat, an herb doctor, a man in a yellow vest, and others (852–853).[8] All these characters share in "confidence." Melville contrasts these confidence men with hardheaded empiricists, men of faith who have a deep pessimism concerning the possibilities of earthly goodness, and others, as he tells his tale. The style of the novel harks back to

British satire of the century before, and the attempt seems to be to assume a Swiftian pose—the confidence man preys on the naive. Moreover, in the shape-shifting of the man on the boat we are to assume an allegorical reference to the greatest shape-shifter of all, Satan.

Many of the characters inhabiting this novel are based on famous con men, religious frauds, and other real people. But the Indian-hater of Melville's account is not a confidence man at all. He is a supposedly heroic figure, Colonel John Moredock, an actual historical person who had previously been portrayed by James Hall, who wrote several books about the American frontier in the 1830s and 1840s. Chapter 26—the full title of which is "Containing the Metaphysics of Indian-Hating, According to the Views of One Evidently Not So Prepossessed as Rousseau in Favor of Savages"—discusses the character of the American Indian and explains why backwoodsmen hate him with such virulence. Chapter 27, "Some Account of a Man of Questionable Morality, but Who, Nevertheless, Would Seem Entitled to the Esteem of That Eminent English Moralist Who Said He Liked a Good Hater," is specifically a retelling of Hall's discussion of Moredock in an 1835 book of sketches Hall wrote about the American West.

Hall's essay is not only a portrait of Moredock. It is an attempt to explain Moredock's hatred within the context of the pioneer culture of the time. Hall writes of the relative enlightenment of the nineteenth-century pioneer in comparison to that at the age of initial settlement. "America," he writes, "was settled in an age when certain rights, called those of discovery and conquest, were universally acknowledged; and when the possession of a country was readily conceded to the strongest."[9] But even as the civilization advanced and more moral understandings of right and wrong prevailed, pioneers, living as they did away from the sources of civilization, were only slightly affected by this advance. Living close to Indians, they "form[ed] a barrier between savage and civilized men." The pioneer does not believe "that an Indian, or any other man has a right to monopolize the hunting grounds, which he considers free to all. When the Indian disputes the propriety of this invasion upon his ancient heritage, the white man feels himself injured, and stands, as the southern folks say, upon his reserved rights." Moreover, every pioneer child is raised with tales of the conflict between Indians and his or her parents. Everyone grows up with stories of scalpings and massacres. "The impressions which we have described are handed down from generation to generation, and remain in full force long after all danger from the savages has ceased, and all intercourse with them has been discontinued." Hall is here describing precisely the experience of Lincoln, whose father would probably have handed down the tale of the death of Lincoln's grandfather.

Hall then tells about the life and times of Moredock. Moredock's entire family was slaughtered by Indians when he was a child. He vowed then that he would hunt down all who killed them, and eventually, after killing all those Indians responsible, he simply continued his career as an Indian killer. "He resolved never to spare an Indian, and though he made no boast of this determination, and seldom avowed it, it became the ruling passion of his life." Hall warns us not to infer "that Colonel Moredock was unsocial, ferocious, or by nature cruel. On the contrary, he was a man of warm feelings, and excellent disposition."

In placing Moredock firmly within the narrative of his novel, Melville uses the words of Hall himself. That is, the Indian-hating chapter is composed of a speech that is a secondhand account of someone who heard Hall himself discussing Moredock. This double distancing by Melville is indeed part of the larger masquerade Melville presents throughout the novel. Moredock's hatred is thus taken by Melville to be witnessed by multiple others, providing ambiguous voices telling an almost mythical tale of the frontier. That he allegorizes the Indians as disciples of the devil is fairly well accepted by most Melville scholars. Yet Melville's attitude about "savages" was in real life much more sympathetic. Of course, the relationship of Melville to the question of good versus evil is much more complex than to allow any simple conclusion concerning his attitudes. To make Indians into demons is not to relieve the other masqueraders of their bad behavior. Indeed, if anything, Melville blurs the distinctions between the various deceivers, gullible victims of con men, and the more directly evil demons—perhaps we could even say the more honestly evil characters who also are floating down the river on the *Fidèle*.

One of the frustrating qualities of *The Confidence-Man* is its impossibly complicated plot line, made more so by the multiple voices that serially inhabit the tale. Moreover, there are flashbacks and asides, characters appearing in disguise, accusations of fraud (sometimes by frauds), and so forth. In this instance, the lines can be particularly confusing. Moredock's story is told to a cosmopolitan by a stranger. In an earlier chapter (chapter 25) the cosmopolitan had an argument with a misanthrope. The stranger begins the conversation by explaining to the cosmopolitan that he has observed the cosmopolitan's argument with the misanthrope, and he suggests that the misanthrope reminds him of Colonel John Moredock. The stranger seeks to distinguish Moredock from the misanthrope, noting that Moredock's hatred wasn't directed to the human race generally, but instead to Indians specifically, "silky bearded and curly headed, and to all but Indians juicy as a peach. But Indians—how the late John Moredock, Indian-hater of Illinois, hated Indians, to be sure!" (990). After introducing the subject, the stranger goes on to suggest that he tell the story of Moredock as a friend of his father's, James Hall, the judge, told it.

So we have the telling of a telling of a telling of a story. Hall's nonfictional rendering of Moredock becomes fictionalized by way of proxy. Who knows who the stranger is? Perhaps he is the biggest liar of all who, to fool us even more, decides to tell the truth. Rather than dream following dream, deceit follows deceit. Here epistemic uncertainty is driven by a willful psychology of lies, ontologizing the triumph of an evil that is not so much banal as it is picturesque.[10]

According to the stranger, the way Hall explains the logic of Indian-hating is straightforward, practically a syllogism. Even though not all Indians are bad, because you can never know for sure, you must assume that any Indian you deal with may be bad. Part of the proof Melville adduces, in Hall's words, is as follows.

> At any rate, it has been observed that when an Indian becomes a genuine proselyte of Christianity (such cases, however, not being very many; though, indeed, entire tribes are sometimes nominally brought to the true light,) he will not in that case conceal his enlightened conviction, that his race's portion by nature is total depravity; and, in that way, as much as admits that the backwoodsman's worst idea of it is not very far from true; while, on the other hand, those red men who are the greatest sticklers for the theory of Indian virtue, and Indian loving-kindness, are sometimes the arrantest horse-thieves and tomahawkers among them. So, at least, avers the backwoodsman. And though, knowing the Indian nature, as he thinks he does, he fancies he is not ignorant that an Indian may in some points deceive himself almost as effectually as in bush-tactics he can another, yet his theory and his practice as above contrasted seem to involve an inconsistency so extreme, that

> the backwoodsman only accounts for it on the supposition that when a tomahawking red-man advances the notion of the benignity of the red race, it is but part and parcel with that subtle strategy which he finds so useful in war, in hunting, and the general conduct of life. (997)

For the Indian, then, there is no winning for losing. If he converts to Christianity, a sign of his conversion is his enlightened understanding of his depraved past. If he fails to convert, then no matter how good he may claim to be, he is mistaken. He is either lying to the white man or, in an especially depraved sense, lying to both the white man and himself. The Indian has no choice when this is his choice. That is to say, unlike the white man, who has a world of choices in front of him, he cannot be particular.[11] In this sense only someone who behaves as brutally as the devil, in effect acting in response to the devil, is capable of resisting and overcoming the Indian's cunning.

The paradigmatic Indian whom Judge Hall tells of is a chief named Mocmohoc, who for many years harassed a colony of settlers composed of the extended families of seven cousins, the Wrights and the Weavers. Eventually reduced to five cousins because of the ongoing attacks by Mocmohoc and his tribe, the settlers finally succeeded in making a treaty with him. Mocmohoc not only treated with them, but seemed genuinely pleased to become their friends. But still suspicious, the five agreed never to enter Mocmohoc's wigwam together, so that if he was insincere, the remaining cousins could wreak their vengeance. Nonetheless, over time, Mocmohoc won them over, and he invited them all to a feast of bear's meat. He then killed them all. Many years later, when reproached for this act of treachery by a hunter he is holding captive, Mocmohoc responds, "Treachery? Pale face! 'Twas they who broke their covenant first, in coming all together; they that broke it first, in trusting Mocmohoc" (999).

The effect that such depravity has on those who observe the Indian is considerable. Not all backwoodsmen are victims, but they all know someone or of someone who has been victimized. "What avails, then, that some one Indian, or some two or three, treat a backwoodsman friendly-like? He fears me, he thinks. Take my rifle from me, give him motive, and what will come? Or if not so, how know I what involuntary preparations may be going on in him for things as unbeknown in present time to him as me—a sort of chemical preparation in the soul for malice, as chemical preparation in the body for malady" (999–1000).

These lines say much. A chemical preparation in the soul, involuntary preparations, in the face of free will there is a compulsion on the part of the Indian that, even though he resist with all his will, may overcome him. And what may even be worse, should the Indian achieve a measure of success in resisting his inner self, there is no way that he will be trusted anyway. Despite this thorough examination of the soul of the Indian, the settler cannot know him, and, even more astonishing, the Indian cannot know himself. The settler may be ignorant, but his quandary is no different from that of anyone else who has realized that no one can know the pain of others. But Judge Hall seems to suggest something more, that the Indian cannot even know his own pain, and his self-ignorance will lead to self-destruction, even if that self-destruction is at the hands of the settler.

What is replayed here is the most common problem of skepticism, the inability to know others. But in this example the Indian is animalized, rendered practically insentient. He is a force of nature; for the Indian-hater the very idea that an Indian can be thought of as a human being is oxymoronic. In fighting against his savage nature, the Indian cannot help becoming a coward. To resist your own nature requires not bravery, but submission to the superior culture of the white man, his Christianity. This leads the judge to his final observation concerning the Indian. "A coward friend, he makes a valiant foe" (1000).

At this point Judge Hall discusses the Indian-hater par excellence. Of the type, he argues, the purest is he who leaves his kin, goes deep into the forest primeval, and acts out "a calm and cloistered scheme of strategical, implacable, and lonesome vengeance" (1000). The emphasis might be on the word "cloistered," for the Indian-hater par excellence is one whose biography can never be told, who lives in intense solitude. Such a man is almost a parody of Emerson's self-reliant individual. (It may even be the case that this was at least a part of Melville's intent.) It is here that Melville has the judge turn more specifically to the story of John Moredock. The judge emphasizes how the perfection of self-reliant distance from others is not the case for Moredock. Though he was an Indian-hater, he had a heart, something that is curiously true of almost all real Indian-haters, who live through a contradiction, "namely, that nearly all Indian-haters, have at bottom, loving hearts; at any rate, more generous than the average" (1005). He had a wife and children, and even was considered to be a potential candidate for governor of Illinois, but he declined, knowing that the pomp of high office would interfere with his ability to kill more Indians, distracting him from his solitary task.

What are we to make of this tale? It would seem that the metaphysics of Indian-hating involves some deep contradictions, to borrow from dialectics. Loving yet hateful, suspicious yet openhearted, the Indian-hater can hate Indians only on condition that he be a lover of Christian mankind. He also, though, must be the sort of Christian who places suspicion above faith. But there is also the issue of grievance. Indian-haters must assume what William James was later to call "vicious naivety," that is, an innocence that is not so innocent, that cloaks aggressive hatred in a sense of moral superiority and just vengeance.

In using the Indians this way, in making them into an entire race of confidence men, Melville is adding another chapter to his critique of the practicability of Christianity. That the Indian-hater is someone whom Melville uses to illustrate the unrealistic view of the world that a weak-minded Christian confidence might hold, presenting the Indian-hater as realistic in comparison, is but one dimension of his critique of American confidence. Another dimension of Melville's critique of confidence has to do with its total complicity with genocidal evil, an evil that wraps itself in the cloak of Christian love.

At least as long as Christianity persists, Melville seems to be saying, so will this metaphysics. And so it is. The continued presence of such metaphysics in the United States, even after the almost total decimation of the Indian tribes, suggests that, like other forms of hatred, it is able to outlast its original object. But this persistence is also transmogrified over time, as substitute objects of hatred and the hidden expression of other desires come into play. In that, Indian-hating either parallels Christianity, which responds to the world with its own powers, on its own terms, so to speak, and constantly finds new objects, or is one of the forms that Christianity assumes in a frontier society.

Beyond the troubled notion of a Christianity that persists formally while losing sight of its original object of hatred, the devil, Melville presents us with an image of knowledge that finds itself in keeping with, or perhaps even prophesying, a larger theme of Western experience, that of the descent into nihilism. But nihilism itself has a long trajectory, and perhaps there are steps along the way.

The Ingalls in Indian Territory

Along with hatred and repulsion, the metaphysics of Indian-hating is driven by fear and desire. Indeed, fear and desire are the twins of hatred and repulsion. It is a bit like the story of the bear hunter who kills a bear, is mauled by another bear, heals, seeks revenge—and so the next year he kills the bear that mauled him. But then he is mauled by another bear. He eventually kills that bear and is mauled again by yet another bear. This goes on for a number of bears over the course of a number of years. Eventually, after he kills yet another bear, he is tapped on the shoulder, and the biggest bear of all says to him, "You don't really come here for the hunting, do you?" This is the sort of dark comedy that Melville is able to extract from his relating the tale of Moredock. It is a desire that turns absurd. That which is forbidden exerts this sort of psychic power, in that we always seem to want most that which is denied to us, no matter how much harm it causes us, or perhaps because of the harm it causes us. Melville's Indian-hater enjoys hating Indians, but the terrible price he pays is that there is no escaping this pleasure, and hence it becomes a pleasure that is no longer a pleasure.

What Charles Ingalls wanted was land. As settlers closed in on his family living in the woods of Wisconsin, Ingalls concluded that it would be good to move to the western country. "In the West the land was level, and there were no trees. The grass grew thick and high. There the wild animals wandered and fed as though they were in a pasture that stretched much farther than a man could see. And there were no settlers."[12] The narrator immediately explains, "Only Indians lived there."[13]

As is made clear in the conclusion of the story, Ingalls had decided, apparently in a mistaken faith in politicians who had said that the Indian Territory of Oklahoma was about to be opened to settlement, to jump the gun and get there first. His working assumption, like that of the others who squatted on the Indian Territory, was that the Indians had no serious right to inhabit the land despite the treaties that had been made, and that if settlers like Ingalls would stake claims to the land, eventually the government of the United States would be compelled to protect them from the Indians. But Ingalls's timing was off. At the end of *Little House on the Prairie* the Ingalls family have left their house and are moving on, northward toward Minnesota.

But the arc of this narrative is effectively framed not so much by Pa

Ingalls's restlessness as by Laura Ingalls's desire. This desire is first (predictably) planted in her by her father. "Pa promised that when they came to the West, Laura should see a papoose. 'What is a papoose?' she asked him, and he said, 'A papoose is a little, brown, Indian baby.'"[14] Laura's curiosity about papooses grows throughout the book and is coupled to more general, vague discussions of Indians. The expression of unconscious desire embedded in these discussions is remarkable. Consider this discussion between Laura and her mother as they are eating supper while spending their first night on the land they were settling on the prairie.

> "Where is a papoose, Ma?" Laura asked.
>
> "Don't speak with your mouth full, Laura," said Ma.
>
> So Laura chewed and swallowed, and she said, "I want to see a papoose."
>
> "Mercy on us!" Ma said. "Whatever makes you want to see Indians? We will see enough of them. More than we want to, I wouldn't wonder."
>
> "They wouldn't hurt us, would they?" Mary asked. Mary was always good; she never spoke with her mouth full.
>
> "No!" Ma said. "Don't get such an idea into your head."
>
> "Why don't you like Indians, Ma?" Laura asked, and she caught a drip of molasses with her tongue.
>
> "I just don't like them; and don't lick your fingers, Laura," said Ma.
>
> "This is Indian country, isn't it?" Laura said. "What did we come to their country for, if you don't like them?"
>
> Ma said she didn't know whether this was Indian country or not. She didn't know where the Kansas line was. But whether or not, the Indians would not be here long. Pa had word from a man in Washington that the Indian Territory would be open to settlement soon. It might already be open to settlement. They could not know, because Washington was so far away.[15]

In *The History of Manners,* Norbert Elias notes a dynamic in the emergence of manners as a civilizing process. Manners initially were developed among the late medieval nobility so they could distinguish themselves from the very highest classes of royalty. Having less wealth, they invented other forms of distinction. Then those of the highest rank took note, and manners penetrated to the upper classes. And so manners were further refined by the nobility in an attempt to retain their distinction. Though the back-and-forth of codes of etiquette was for some time chaotic, Elias suggests that over time certain lines of development emerged. "These include," he writes, "for example, what may be described as an advance of the threshold of embarrassment and shame, as 'refinement,' or as 'civilization.'"[16] This internalization of distinctions crossing ranks bound medieval society together.

The carrying of manners to the frontier, it would seem, involves precisely a raising of the threshold of shame. Even within the limited frame of the Ingalls family, Laura is less civilized than Mary; Mary is older, of course, and also more refined. So the questioning about Indians comes from Laura, who is less ashamed, less embarrassed to ask. Her mother is the teacher of her children, and of her husband (for she was born and bred in the East). She is the teacher of shame, and of its eventual internalization into guilt. Having absorbed the lesson of manners far more completely, Ma is unwilling to explain her reasons for hating Indians to the girls. But hate them she does.

But there is also a coupling of the desire to *see* with the act of *eating*. Laura shifts from asking what a papoose is to wanting to see one, immediately after swallowing her food, without yet being given an explanation about what a papoose is by her Ma. Her father had already told her that a papoose is a "little, brown, Indian baby," but here she wants to learn from her mother. And her mother resists, as if implicitly realizing the danger of Laura's desire. The repetition of the question, the persistence of her inquiry, which eventually elicits a longer response from Ma, communicates a deep nervousness regarding the boundaries they are crossing. The entire conversation is framed by questions concerning territorial lines. Laura wants to know whether they are in Indian country, and her mother tells her that she doesn't know, perhaps that it doesn't matter anyway.

The next major discussion of Indians occurs when two Indians invade the house while Pa is hunting. Ma feeds them cornbread after they sign for her to do so, and they take Pa's tobacco with them. When Pa comes home, he explains that they did the right thing to feed them. But Laura, whom Pa had warned not to let the dog, Jack, off the leash, inadvertently lets Pa know she had thought to do just that. Pa is angry.

> "Do you know what would have happened if you had turned Jack loose?" Pa asked.

> "No, Pa," they whispered.
>
> "He would have bitten those Indians," said Pa. "Then there would have been trouble. Bad trouble. Do you understand?"
>
> "Yes, Pa," they said. But they did not understand.
>
> "Would they have killed Jack?" Laura asked.
>
> "Yes. And that's not all. You girls remember this: You do as you're told, no matter what happens." . . .
>
> "Do as you're told," said Pa, "and no harm will come to you."[17]

Absolute obedience of the young girls in a situation of potential danger is his lesson to them. But there is more going on here than even the possibility of a confrontation over the dog (though such a confrontation is to occur later in the narrative).

One of the distinctive features of the Indians who come to the house is their strong odor. When Laura goes into the house she smells them first. "Laura ran toward Ma, but just as she reached the hearth, she smelled a horribly bad smell, and she looked up at the Indians."[18] Laura soon realizes why they smell so bad. "Around their waists each of the Indians wore a leather thong, and the furry skin of a small animal hung down in front. The fur was striped black and white, and now Laura knew what made that smell. The skins were fresh skunk skins."[19] Aside from the obvious use of skunk skins as codpieces, there is another symbolic role played by the presence of the skunk skins. Many Native American tribes tell tales of how the skunk was a monster that was brought down to size by one hero or another, sometimes being a symbol of evil.[20] That the skunk skins are worn as codpieces indicates a threat of evil that has undertones of sexual violence. Pa seems aware of this fact. At one point during the evening after the Indians came to the house he says, "The main thing is to be on good terms with the Indians. We don't want to wake up one night with a band of the screeching dev—."[21] At this point Ma shushes him, presumably so that he won't frighten the girls. But the association of the Indians with demons is completely consistent with Melville's depiction of the rationale for Indian-hating. For the Indian-hater it is impossible to be on good terms with the Indians. The tension that comes from trying to do so while knowing that they might turn into devils at any moment is unbearable.

One wonders what Pa is thinking. Despite the obvious signs of danger, he continues to make excursions away from the house. He goes to Independence, Missouri, some forty miles away, to trade furs for supplies and farming tools. Those trips also keep him informed of the latest developments concerning the status of the Indian Territory. The tensions with the Indians continue to build. Indeed, in the winter months preceding the planting season, two more Indians appear while Pa is away, and they almost make off with the furs Pa had been gathering to trade for farming supplies. (The Indian seizing the furs was stopped by his companion. The implication was that to take the furs was to cross some line that should not be crossed. Apparently, the Indians had good reason for tracing a delicate path as well.)[22]

When Pa comes home and is informed of this incident, he "looked sober." That evening he plays a song on his fiddle about an Indian maid named Alfarata, which contains the lines "Fleeting years have borne away / The voice of Alfarata." Laura asks where the voice went. "Oh I suppose she went West," Ma answered. "That's what Indians do." This leads Laura to further questions about the Indians, which eventually result in Pa's providing a fuller explanation, though not quite a complete one.

> "When white settlers come into a country, the Indians have to move on. The government is going to move these Indians farther west, any time now. That's why we're here, Laura. White people are going to settle all this country, and we get the best land because we get here first and take our pick. Now do you understand?"
>
> "Yes, Pa," Laura said. "But, Pa, I thought this was Indian Territory. Won't it make the Indians mad to have to—"
>
> "No more questions, Laura," Pa said, firmly. "Go to sleep."[23]

This question, however, lingers through the rest of the story.

Eventually, the Indians do get mad and threaten to go on the warpath. Only the intervention of a leader of the Osage tribe, named Soldat du Chêne, prevents a war from breaking out, which would have increased the possibility of the Ingalls family being massacred.[24] Two days after the war party breaks up, a procession of Osage Indians passes the Ingalls homestead. The procession stretches as far as the eye can see, and it takes all day for the Indians to depart. Eventually, Laura gets her wish and sees a papoose, riding in a basket on the side of a pony with its mother. She looks deep into the baby's black eyes.

> "Pa," she said, "get me that little Indian baby!"
>
> "Hush, Laura!" Pa told her sternly.
>
> The little baby was going by. Its head turned and its eyes kept looking into Laura's eyes.
>
> "Oh, I want it! I want it!" Laura begged. The baby was going farther and farther away, but it did not stop looking back at Laura. "It wants to stay with me," Laura begged. "Please, Pa, please!"[25]

Fear has quickly been transformed into desire. Laura persists, even in her shame, and begins to cry.

> Ma said she had never heard of such a thing. "For shame, Laura," she said, but Laura could not stop crying. "Why on earth do you want an Indian baby, of all things!" Ma asked her.
>
> "Its eyes are so black," Laura sobbed. She could not say what she meant.
>
> "Why, Laura," Ma said, "you don't want another baby. We have a baby, our own baby."
>
> "I want the other one, too!" Laura sobbed, loudly.[26]

Laura cannot say what she means, which is to say she cannot say why she wants what she wants. But want that baby she does. This desire to *have* that which she has been wanting to *see,* to *see* that which she originally wanted to *know,* a desire to know that is incited by her father's comments, conflates knowledge, scopophilia, and possession into a single urge. She would add that baby to her collection—baby Carrie, and the papoose, the "other one, too." It is a hunger she feels, a deep desire to possess, a desire that will be satisfied only temporarily and will require further fulfillment as time passes.

Laura is not an Indian-hater in Melville's sense. But she is a member of a family of Indian-haters. It is apparent that she seems to be attempting to break with the family through the vehicle of desiring to possess the baby. Perhaps the desire to possess is not so far from the desire to destroy. But the generational shift is clear. Take the baby. Eat that baby, and move on.

Laura is indifferent to the baby's mother. This indifference is remarkable only if we think that she is seeing these Indians as fellow humans. She is not. They have become things to her. But then again, so is her own little sister, further down the internal civilizational order of her family.

That evening, as the long procession finally comes to an end, the family seem to realize that they have been witnesses (at least) to something wrong. "Then the very last pony went by. But Pa and Ma and Laura and Mary still stayed in the doorway, looking, until that long line of Indians slowly pulled itself over the western edge of the world. And nothing was left but silence and emptiness. All the world seemed quiet and lonely. . . . [Laura] sat a long time on the doorstep, looking into the empty west where the Indians had gone."[27] The quiet that the Ingallses now sense is not a relief to them. None of them is hungry; they all feel, as Ma says, "let down."[28] This is what loneliness is about, the loneliness of being absent in presence.[29] Everyone alone. Yet they are alone together.

Why are they let down? Let down by whom? Ma and Pa are unable or unwilling to acknowledge their own complicity in this sad chapter. It is simply something that the Indians must bear. But they still feel their guilt, in the form of a loss of appetite.[30]

None of this guilt is resolved. Instead, the next chapter begins, "After the Indians had gone, a great peace settled on the prairie."[31] The page is turned, spring arrives, the burnt-over prairie turns green as if overnight, and a period of bucolic planting and caring for plants begins. "Pretty soon they would all begin to live like kings."[32] Only they won't. Within a few months they will be on their way again, ordered out of Indian Territory by the U.S. government. Pa, hearing the news, will immediately make the decision to have the family leave the little house and homestead where they had spent the year. They take off the next day. But before they leave, he expresses his outrage. "I'll not stay here to be taken away by the soldiers like an outlaw! If some blasted politicians in Washington hadn't sent word it would be all right to settle here, I'd never have been three miles over the line into Indian Territory. But I'm not waiting for the soldiers to take us out. We're going now!"[33] In expressing his sense of betrayal, Pa conveniently ignores the fact that he knew, when he entered Indian Territory, that he was squatting there. He never questioned his own sense of the inevitability of the fate of the Indians, his confidence in the government's bad faith, and his reliance on the politicians' willingness to break promises to the Indians. So when those politicians, in a rare gesture, keep their promise (for a while) to the tribes in the Indian Territory, *he* feels betrayed. This sense of betrayal can easily be transferred to the Indians themselves. Here in miniature we see the seeding of the metaphysics of Indian-hating in Charles Ingalls.

So they leave. But there is one last peculiarity embedded in the final chapter of *Little House on the Prairie.* As the family settles in for their first night back on the plain, again on the move, Pa breaks out his fiddle. He begins by playing "Oh, Susanna," Stephen Foster's song of the Gold Rush. Of course, the Gold Rush was that great leap that inspired so many to go West. But it is the next two songs that Pa chooses to play that are most telling. First he plays "Dixie," a song that originated in black minstrelsy of the 1850s and then became the unofficial anthem of the Confederacy. Then he plays "Battle Cry of Freedom," an 1862 patriotic song of the Union. It is as though he is enacting the tableau of race and reunion so powerfully explained by David Blight in his historical masterpiece of the same name.[34] Blight shows how the reconciliation of southern and northern Americans in the post–Civil War era entailed a dramatic and drastic revision of the reasons for and outcome of the Civil War, one that subordinated the emancipation narrative of the war for one of "brother against brother" quarrels concerning autonomy versus unity. What happened by way of this forgetting of the reason for the war was the repression of liberated African Americans. If the war was fought over differences that were exclusively between white Americans, then the reconciliation of North and South, it follows, would involve only them. Of course, that involvement would entail the oppression of those who were the very reason for their war.

What might this strategic forgetting have to do with the metaphysics of Indian-hating? It turns out: everything. In the essay that concludes volume 1 of *Democracy in America,* Alexis de Tocqueville writes about "the three races that inhabit the United States."[35] For Tocqueville "the Negro" and "white man," however unhappily, are destined to be with each other even when and if slavery is abolished. And even if the Negro remains servile, he will nonetheless survive. But the Indian is destined to be destroyed. Tocqueville writes at length of the process by which the penetration of the wilderness by European settlers disturbed the game on which the Indians depend; the settlements are made on territories ill-secured by the tribes, since they possess those lands collectively, if at all. "The Indians, who had lived until then in a sort of abundance, find it difficult to subsist, and have still more difficulty in procuring the objects of exchange that they need. By making their game flee, it is almost as if one had made the fields of our farmers sterile. Soon the means of existence is almost entirely lacking in them."[36] Tocqueville remarks on these matters sorrowfully, as though a natural calamity were occurring. (The tone of his comments is similar to the language used by investment bankers when the markets crashed as a consequence of their fraudulent practices; they referred to the crash as a financial tsunami, something no one could have predicted, a sort of act of God.)

William Connolly has noted that Tocqueville's posture enabled the destruction of Indians to proceed under the guise of the civilizing process. He notes, "Tocqueville registers, then, in carefully crafted language, the construction of 'America,' a civi-territorial complex in which the crucial dimensions of territory and civilization reinforce each other until they accumulate enough force together to propel the 'triumphal progress of civilization across the wilderness.' What of those wandering nomads who are, well, not dispossessed from territory they never possessed but displaced from a wilderness upon which they wandered? Tocqueville disposes of them sadly and regretfully, for they are dead to civilization even before the advance of civilization progressively kills them off."[37] Connolly's description of Tocqueville's sorrow could be transferred completely and clearly to the Ingalls family, who feel empty and lonely when the Indians leave, knowing, without acknowledging, that their role in the civilizing process entailed driving the Indians away. Yet by the end of the next and final chapter, they are cheered by the songs of the Civil War, not the war that was fought, but the fictional war between quarreling brothers, in which the ever-present bodies of black Americans are ignored in the name of national harmony.

In the End All the World Will Be America

"Thus in the beginning all the world was America, and moreso than that is now," John Locke writes in his *Second Treatise of Government*.[38] Locke's state of nature was imaginary, but his imagination, as well as that of most of those who employed the concept, was sparked by the fact of the European encounter with the inhabitants of the Americas. Locke referred to Indians repeatedly and seems to have been fascinated with them, as though there were a way they might hold a key to all of political understanding. His state of nature was much more gentle than that imagined by Thomas Hobbes, at least in part because of better knowledge of the ways of the tribes of North America. Hobbes projected the idea of a war of all against all, not the loose associations that Locke could see as being the beginnings of civil society. Immediately following his description of life in the state of nature being nasty, brutish, and short, Hobbes writes, "It may per adventure be thought, there was never such a time, nor condition of warre as this; and I believe it was never generally so, over all the world: but there are many places, where they live so now. For the savage people in many places of *America*, except the government of small Families, the concord whereof depend on naturall lust, have no government at all; and live this day in the brutish manner, as I said before."[39] In fact, a pregovernmental civil society is not so far from the manner in which many of the tribes seemed to govern themselves. Thomas Paine would later model his early governmental form directly on the way Indians governed themselves.

Let us think again about the theoretical justification for killing Indians, going back to Melville's text. "What avails, then, that some one Indian, or some two or three, treat a backwoodsman friendly-like? He fears me, he thinks. Take my rifle from me, give him motive, and what will come? Or if not so, how know I what involuntary preparations may be going on in him for things as unbeknown in present time to him as me—a sort of chemical preparation in the soul for malice, as chemical preparation in the body for malady" (999–1000). What chance is one to take when someone who looks innocuous enough, and who professes to be a good human being, even if not a Christian, is nonetheless, perhaps even without knowing so, evil? What does it mean that the preparation for death include a chemical preparation? Is it only a poison, or is it even something more?

In the context of Indian-hating, what would it mean for all the world to be America *now,* that is, for us to imagine, like Locke (perhaps even more so, like Hobbes) that there is a brutish world of universal war, filled with untrustworthy savages? Could it be something like this? "If there is a one percent chance that Pakistani scientists are helping al Qaeda build or develop a nuclear weapon, we have to treat it as a certainty in terms of our response."[40] This "one percent doctrine," as it is known, was first articulated by Richard Cheney, the vice president of the United States, following the attacks of September 11, 2001. It is a particular response to globalization, which in this context means the return of the entire world to a state of nature. Before the 9/11 attacks Secretary of Defense Donald Rumsfeld, in a memorandum titled "National Security Issues—Post Cold War Threats," speculated about the equalizing power of contemporary technology. "The post Cold-War liberalization of trade in advanced technology goods and services has made it possible for the poorest nations on earth to rapidly acquire the most destructive military technology ever devised, including nuclear, chemical, and biological weapons and their means of delivery. We cannot prevent them from doing so."[41] Following the attacks of 9/11 the problem became even more difficult to address. Now it wasn't simply poor states, but nonstate actors who would be able to collude with poor states to attack the United States. In this reversal, the world is filled with Indians, nonstate actors if ever there were, untrustworthy heathens, tribes of non-Christian terrorists, filled with passion, undisciplined, but also uncompromising, willing to die for their beliefs, or at least for their reactive hate against those who in their innocence have unleashed death. Modern America is now besieged by the denizens of a world that is imagined in terms that are all too like the America imagined by the contract theorists.

And here the deepest irony of the historical unfolding as the metaphysics of Indian-hating comes into view. It can be found in this final projection of American paranoid power. Where once the world was like America, in Locke's and Hobbes's states of nature, now it is the case that all the world is again like America, except for . . . America. We look out on a world that has returned to the state of nature imagined by Hobbes and Locke.

It is a fantastic vision, in the most straightforwardly etymological sense of the term. That is, it is a vision of the world that is a fantasy. It always has been a fantasy. That the United States has for so long deferred its historical accounting for the debt it has incurred by the destruction of the Indians does not mean it will not in the end be called to account. Melville knew this. He anticipated the prophecy that Lincoln thundered in his otherwise conciliatory Second Inaugural Address, in which Lincoln said of the war, "Yet, if God wills that it continue until all the wealth piled by the bondsman's two hundred and fifty years of unrequited toil shall be sunk, and until every drop of blood drawn with the lash shall be paid by another drawn with the sword, as was said three thousand years ago, so still it must be said 'the judgments of the Lord are true and righteous altogether.'" It is a terrible legacy. Lincoln was able to weigh the tragedy of slavery, but not that of the vast harm of those other others. Possession against death or possession as the step after death, these are the choices for this culture. Laura still desires that baby.

Lincoln's failure of sympathetic imagination helped point the United States toward its tragic future, one in which the rest of the world passes us by, as though we are the haunted house of the neighborhood of nations.

(This must be whispered, for as we know, Lincoln is a great man.) But Melville, who lived through Lincoln's administration, and others, knew better. He brought *The Confidence-Man* to an end without a real conclusion because he knew Americans would never disembark from the *Fidèle*. We remain in the thrall of the confidence man. And the boat drifts ever farther south.

That this metaphysical heritage of hatred found its clear articulation in what I suspect is Melville's least often read novel is completely consistent with his understanding of the tragedy of American ignorance. A prophet then, he remains a prophet now. Once again, it seems, in the United States' collective outrage, indignation, sense of injury, and self-deception, the country finds itself surrounded. We are not surrounded by heathens, but by our own past. Melville anticipated Lincoln on this matter as well. He presents us with a terrible heritage, but an honest one. For that, we need to thank him, reluctantly.

Notes

1. Eric Foner, *The Fiery Trial: Abraham Lincoln and American Slavery* (New York: Norton, 2010), 261.

2. Ibid.

3. Melville, *Moby-Dick*, in *Redburn, White-Jacket, Moby-Dick* (New York: Library of America, 1983), 1363.

4. Ibid., 967.

5. See, respectively, Charles Olson, *Call Me Ishmael!* (1947; repr., Baltimore: Johns Hopkins University Press, 1997); Hershel Parker, *Herman Melville: A Biography*, vol. 2, *1851–1891* (Baltimore: Johns Hopkins University Press, 2002); and Michael Rogin, *Subversive Genealogy: The Politics and Art of Herman Melville* (New York: Knopf, 1983).

6. In the chronology in the Library of America edition of *The Confidence-Man*, in 1887 it is noted that there was no printing of Melville's books by Harper's after 1876, and that his lifetime total sales of the eight books Harper's published—*Typee, Mardi, Redburn, Pierre, Battle-Pieces, Omoo, White-Jacket*, and *Moby-Dick*—was thirty-five thousand copies in the United States and sixteen thousand in Britain. *The Confidence-Man* was not published by Harper's, which didn't want it, but by Dix & Edwards in New York and Longman in Britain.

7. Melville, *The Confidence-Man: His Masquerade*, in *Pierre, Israel Potter, The Piazza Tales, The Confidence-Man, Uncollected Prose, Billy Budd* (New York:

Library of America, 1984), 841. All further references to this novel are to this edition and will be given parenthetically in the text.

8. I have relied extensively on the second edition of the Norton Critical Edition of *The Confidence-Man* for help in interpreting what I believe is Melville's most twisted, metaphorical, and difficultly plotted novel. While it would be too cumbersome to refer constantly to the notes in that edition, I nonetheless owe the editors of that edition a deep debt, and I will refer to some of the interpretations explicitly throughout the essay. See Melville, *The Confidence-Man: His Masquerade*, ed. Hershel Parker and Mark Niemeyer, 2nd ed. (New York: Norton, 2006), 21.

9. James Hall, *Sketches of History, Life, and Manners, in the West* (Philadelphia: Harrison Hall, 1835), 456–461, quoted in Melville, *The Confidence-Man* (Norton ed.). All subsequent quotations can be found in those pages.

10. For a parallel view of the power of domination as a source of evil, but with a specific reference to slavery, see Tracy B. Strong's contribution to this volume, "'Follow Your Leader': Melville's *Benito Cereno* and the Case of Two Ships."

11. Shannon Mariotti searches out the implications of a similar paradox in her analysis not of Bartleby's famous declaration, "I would prefer not to," but of a less well analyzed statement he makes, "I am not particular," in "Melville and the Cadaverous Triumphs of Transcendentalism," in this volume.

12. Laura Ingalls Wilder, *Little House on the Prairie* (1935), ill. Garth Williams (1953; repr., New York: Harper Trophy, 1971), 2.

13. Ibid.

14. Ibid., 6.

15. Ibid., 46–47.

16. Norbert Elias, *The History of Manners*, vol. 1 of *The Civilizing Process*, trans. Edmund Jephcott (1978; repr., New York: Pantheon Books, 1982), 101.

17. Wilder, *Little House*, 146.

18. Ibid., 137.

19. Ibid., 138.

20. See, for instance, Robert (Bobby) Lake-Thom, Medicine Grizzly Bear, *Spirits of the Earth: A Guide to Native American Nature Symbols, Stories, and Ceremonies* (New York: Plume Books, 1997), 95.

21. Wilder, *Little House*, 144.

22. Ibid., 233–234.

23. Ibid., 236–237.

24. Soldat du Chêne is the appellation that Laura Ingalls Wilder gives to the Indian, who supposedly speaks French. It is quite likely, however, that the name is a more general term for Indian chief. If there were Osage who spoke French, they probably learned it from Louisiana Creoles. On the identity of the Indian in ques-

tion, see Stephanie Vavra, *Who Really Saved Laura Ingalls? Soldat du Chêne or a soldat du chien?* (Morrison, Ill.: Quill Works, 2001).

25. Wilder, *Little House,* 308.

26. Ibid., 309–310.

27. Ibid., 311.

28. Ibid.

29. For an extended discussion, see Thomas Dumm, *Loneliness as a Way of Life* (Cambridge: Harvard University Press, 2008).

30. For the Ingallses to lose their appetites is indeed a signal of crisis. Those who are familiar with the series are aware of the enormous role that food—the hunting and slaughter of animals, the baking, the roasting, the boiling, the planting of crops, the gathering of nuts and fruits, in short, the emphasis on the American cornucopia of wild game and fertile lands—has in the lives of all involved. In fact, the entire narrative has to do with trying to find a suitable and sustainable life that is possible only by securing food.

31. Wilder, *Little House,* 312.

32. Ibid., 315.

33. Ibid., 316.

34. David Blight, *Race and Reunion: The Civil War in American Memory* (Cambridge: Harvard University Press, 2002).

35. Alexis de Tocqueville, *Democracy in America,* trans. Harvey Mansfield and Delba Winthrop, 2 vols. (1835–1840; repr., Chicago: University of Chicago Press, 2000), 1:302–396.

36. Ibid., 1:309–310.

37. William E. Connolly, *The Ethos of Pluralization* (Minneapolis: University of Minnesota Press, 1995), 168–169.

38. John Locke, *Two Treatises of Government,* ed. Peter Laslett (New York: New American Library, 1960), 343.

39. Thomas Hobbes, *Leviathan; or, The Matter, Forme, & Power of a Common-Wealth Ecclesiasticall and Civill,* ed. Ian Shapiro (1651; repr., New Haven: Yale University Press, 2010), 78; emphasis in original.

40. Ron Suskind, *The One Percent Doctrine: Deep Inside America's Pursuit of Its Enemies since 9/11* (New York: Simon and Shuster, 2006), 62.

41. Ibid., 64.

12

Melville's War Poetry and the Human Form

Roger Berkowitz

Forms, measured forms.

—Herman Melville, *Billy Budd*

Nothing can lift the heart of man
Like manhood in a fellow-man.
The thought of heaven's great King afar
But humbles us—too weak to scan;
But manly greatness men can span,
And feel the bonds that draw.

—Herman Melville, "On the Photograph of a Corps Commander"

At the climax of Melville's *Billy Budd, Sailor (An Inside Narrative),* Captain Vere is overseeing the trial and conviction of Billy Budd. Billy, Vere recognizes, is wholly innocent, a messenger of divine judgment. And still, for the captain forced to become judge, the necessary outcome of the impending trial is clear: "Struck dead by an angel of God! Yet the angel must hang!"[1]

Budd's conviction is frequently read as illustrating the conflict between formal state laws and natural law.[2] The conflict between natural and state law, however, is not the intellectual or moral fault line of *Billy Budd*. Vere's reasoned plea that the judges recognize the obligation of their magisterial buttons ultimately is unsuccessful. After his speech, the judges "moved in their seats, less convinced than agitated by the course of an argument troubling but the more the spontaneous conflict within" (*Billy Budd*, 1415). As Vere himself admits, in a contest between these two legal orders, natural law—according to which Billy is "a fellow-creature innocent before God, and whom we feel to be so"—must prevail. The appeal to positive law alone will not trump God's law.

It is here that Melville has Vere "abruptly chang[e] his tone" (*Billy Budd,* 1415). The captain's new tactic is to argue that it is war that necessitates Billy's hanging. "We proceed," Vere announces, "under the law of the Mutiny Act. In feature no child can resemble his father more than that Act resembles in spirit the thing from which it derives—War" (ibid., 1415–1416). The invocation of war is essential, because war—and with it the law—"looks but to the frontage, the appearance," and the form of actions. In war and law, form displaces content as the truth of the matter itself. The outward form trumps inward intent, which is why "Budd's intent or non-intent is nothing to the purpose" (ibid., 1416).

That form is a central conceit of *Billy Budd* is no secret, announced as it is in both the final chapter of the main narrative and in the first chapter of the supplemental sequel that Melville appends to the text. First, in the final chapter of the main text, form is given voice by Vere at the moment of Budd's hanging—after which Vere commands a "beating to quarters at an hour prior to the customary one." The reason for the ritual is given clearly: "'With mankind,' [Vere] would say, 'forms, measured forms, are everything; and that is the import couched in the story of Orpheus with his lyre spellbinding the wild denizens of the wood'" (*Billy Budd,* 1430). The spellbinding form of ritual, as is true of music, serves the purpose of discipline and war. Musical form, as Plato knew, is where one must erect the guardhouse of culture and order. It is the demand of formality that drives Vere and thus the narrative structure of *Billy Budd.*

Melville's novella puts form in question throughout in the contest between war and peace and the stylized fictionality of the narrative. But Melville explodes the formal closure only at the end by appending a short, three-chapter sequel to his tale, a sequel that begins by announcing the fictionality of form: "The symmetry of form attainable in pure fiction can not so readily be achieved in narration essentially having less to do with fable than with fact. Truth uncompromisingly told will always have ragged edges; hence the conclusion of such a narrative is apt to be less finished than an architectural finial" (*Billy Budd,* 1431). If war and the force of war on the *Bellipotent* require a formal closure that casts a spell that binds men to a common purpose, the humanity of fiction liberates man to the human passions, the philanthropic love of man that celebrates Billy Budd's uncanny goodness. Melville's vision of war is tragic, not simply in the human cost war exacts, but also in the opposing forces war unleashes. Destructive in its violence, war is also unifying in its formal beauty. War unmakes political life, but it also can bring new states to be. War, in Melville, epitomizes the excessive humanity of what dissolves forms and breaks customary procedures; yet war also demands a lawful formality that will straitjacket human passion into an equally human need for order.

The Forms of War

The importance of war in Melville's later writing has only occasionally been acknowledged. In her insightful essay "*Billy Budd* and Melville's Philosophy of War," Joyce Sparer Adler suggests an opposition between Vere and Melville's philosophies of war: "While to Vere war is a sacred, fated form and the *Bellipotent* (literally, the power of war) a place of worship whose military architecture is complete, to Melville that architecture is neither holy nor final. Vere would bind man's consciousness; Melville would awaken it."[3] There is, Adler argues, a gulf separating Vere's warrior ethic and Melville's humanism. Vere is the "symbolic figure . . . of civilized man. . . . His ultimate faith is in Force."[4] He is, she asserts, "appalling to Melville," an example of the tragedy of civilization in which the creative potentialities of man are wasted.[5] Vere becomes a one-sided acolyte—"the god whom Vere has been trained to worship is Mars."[6] War, in Adler's rendering of Melville, is "madness," a hell where one encounters the full "absence of morality."[7]

At times Adler acknowledges the contradictoriness of Melville's philosophy of war, containing both abhorrence and luminosity.[8] And Vere, too, she writes, has a certain humanity, so that "the contradiction within Vere is his very essence; the split in him is as central to his meaning as is the split in Ahab."[9] But Adler largely ignores these subtleties in her effort to recruit Vere and Melville to the side of a humanistic liberalism. In doing so, she misses the way that Melville's vision of war emerges as a deeply human endeavor, and humanity itself is seen to emerge only through man's bellicosity.

Another limitation of Adler's powerful reading of Melville's war philosophy is her complete oversight of *Battle-Pieces and Aspects of the War*, Melville's book-length collection of poetry inspired by the United States Civil War.[10] She is, of course, not alone in ignoring *Battle-Pieces*, poems that are often relegated to that barren decade after Melville abandoned writing prose in the aftermath of the critical and commercial failures of *Moby-Dick* (1851), *Pierre* (1852), and *The Confidence-Man* (1857), and before the posthumous publication of *Billy Budd* (1924). Melville wrote and published nothing for nearly a decade before *Battle-Pieces* (1866) appeared, and this barren period is typically seen as the end of Melville's writerly life, save for the "Indian summer" that brought forth the unfinished *Billy Budd.*

For Robert Penn Warren, who edited a collection of Melville's poetry, that poetry needs to be understood "against the backdrop of his defeat as a writer."[11] *Battle-Pieces* must also be seen against the backdrop of war. "War," as Warren remarks, "despite suffering and horror, fulfills certain deep-seated needs in men. . . . Men yearn for significance in life, for the thrill of meaning in action, for communion in a common cause, for the test of their fiber, paradoxically for both the affirmation of, and the death of, the self."[12] It would be one-sided to see war in Melville as simply a vessel promising a vital affirmation of life. And yet, Warren rightly notes that Melville's return to life as a writer occurred amid the wages of war. And so for readings of *Billy Budd,* set as it is amid war and on the *Bellipotent,* these wartime poems are a necessary key to Melville's later work.

Andrew Delbanco, Melville's most recent biographer, acknowledges that Melville's "turn to poetry amounted to an attempt to start his life anew amid a sense of failure."[13] For Delbanco that effort at rebirth was a failure: Melville "never satisfactorily" figured out how to present the Civil War in verse.[14] Delbanco finds the poems overly "constructed, with none of the adventurous freedom of Melville's stories and novels," and constrained by a "certain hampered carefulness."[15] In the seven pages Delbanco gives to *Battle-Pieces* in his nearly four-hundred-page biography, he concludes that William Dean Howells had it right in an 1867 review: Melville's poems are secondhand accounts of the war that ignore the war itself, poems filled with hot air, "not words and blood, but words alone."[16]

Modern readings of Melville's war poetry similarly tend toward pacifism. Michael Warner's "What Like a Bullet Can Undeceive?" argues that *Battle-Pieces* rejects war. For Warner, Melville's poetry reveals that "the whole idea of war fought for a cause, any cause, is made to seem absurd."[17] "War," he writes, "dramatizes the guilt of humanity," and Melville's "pastoral theodicy makes violence categorically illegitimate."[18] The very brilliance of a bullet can "undeceive" men and show the illegitimate violence of war. "The bullet strips away conviction and habit," leaving man bereft of any beliefs and values, metaphysically naked, possessed of "not a creed but a way of prescinding from creed."[19] Warner's account of Melville on war leaves us skeptical and disbelieving.

One way of politicizing Melville is to enlist him in a cause, be that cause pacifism or equality. Many of the essays in this volume, and also Jason Frank in his excellent introduction to it, imagine a political Melville who "articulates a political critique at the level of philosophical principle and deep cultural presupposition."[20] Melville's critical eye is enlisted in the enlightenment project of exposing hierarchies of oppression and mechanisms of white supremacy. I do not deny these political readings of Melville; and yet Melville's politics should not be reduced to a liberationist project of emancipation. For Melville politics is not simply about critique and unmasking. Politics in Melville is importantly about the telling of stories and rendering of forms that will bind us to our highest and most glorious human and national ideals.

As Robert Penn Warren reminds us, Melville's poetry in *Battle-Pieces* soars as an original metaphysical inquiry into the tragic polarities of the human condition as illumined by the act of war. The Civil War was precisely the "kind of big, athletic, overmastering subject which [Melville] always needed for his best work, and it was bloodily certified by actuality."[21] Melville's Civil War poetry collides grand ideologies with human passions, all tempered with a reverence for manly heroism that coexists with woeful destruction. In the clash and resolution of striving oppositions that fill his verse account of the Civil War, Melville achieved a "metaphysical style of his own."[22] It was a style born not only of struggle, nationalism, and rebirth, but of the equally bloody and heroic reality of the Civil War.

For Stanton Garner, Melville sought a "grand synthesis" that would present America and its rebirth from the purification of war. At bottom, the war confronts Melville as an anarchic challenge, the breakup of the Union and the extraordinary civilization-destroying violence. In response to the chaos of the war, *Battle-Pieces* is composed of a "complex of metaphors and images" that begin, repeat, and transform themselves "so that the reader is not fully aware of what the book is saying or how it is saying it until after he has read all of the poems."[23] There is, as David Devries and Hugh Egan argue, "a heteroglossic lyric style" that "confront[s] the bewildering horror of the Civil War."[24] And yet these multiple styles and voices are forged into a unit.

Amid such plurality, *Battle-Pieces* is a "coherent literary entity," a precisely thematized struggle between the formal claim of a resurrected unity contrasted with the metaphysical brutality of war. The poems reflect the dissolution of faith and the loss of political meaning as well as an affirmation of formal images—literally the "aspects of war"—that strike us with their heroic beauty. It is these aspects that Melville imbues with the compelling power to rebind a broken people that is the driving political vision of *Battle-Pieces.* War has a vital capacity to focus attention on formal acts of greatness. And it is this formal power to raise aspect above reason that animates *Battle-Pieces.*

America and Its Shadows

Of the many images that run through *Battle-Pieces,* none is more present than the shadow. The book begins with "The Portent," a poem telling of the shadow that John Brown cast on the American experiment. Another early poem, "The Conflict of Convictions," introduces the new Iron Dome, which replaced the original wooden dome that had earlier adorned the Capitol. Here the Iron Dome "fling[s]" its shadow across the land, marking the maturing and also hardening of the American nation:

> Power unanointed may come—
> Dominion (unsought by the free)
> And the Iron Dome,
> Stronger for stress and strain,
> Fling her huge shadow athwart the main;
> But the Founder's dream shall flee. (*Battle-Pieces,* 17)

The Iron Dome symbolizes both the loss of American innocence and the rise of brutal and imperial government, one whose bureaucratic inflexibility threatens the foundation of freedom. Together, the technological intransigence of the Iron Dome and the racial shadow of John Brown are the dual specters that threaten to undermine American freedom.

Finally, *Battle-Pieces* ends with "America"—at least tentatively (for *Battle-Pieces,* like *Billy Budd,* has a supplement that bursts its formal bounds—in which the double shadows of slavery and dominion are "chased by light").

A clear calm look. It spake of pain,
But such as purifies from stain—
Sharp pangs that never come again—
And triumph repressed by knowledge meet,
Power dedicate, and hope grown wise,
And youth matured for age's seat—
Law on her brow and empire in her eyes.
So she, with graver air and lifted flag;
While the shadow, chased by light,
Fled along the far-drawn height,
And left her on the crag. (*Battle-Pieces,* 162)

If the shadow of John Brown is the "Portent" that shatters the innocence of the American founding,[25] and the dominating shadow of the Iron Dome threatens to extinguish American freedom, the fleeing shadow in the face of "America" reborn leaves the country wiser, more mature, lawful, and safe on the heights. Purified by pain, triumphal in knowledge gained, and transposed from death to life, America shines, free from the shadows that haunted her.

As a whole, *Battle-Pieces* aspires to set the United States into verse as a country reborn from the ravages of war.[26] Or, at least, that is the book's formally coherent aspiration. The coherent narrative, however, clashes with and is even undermined by Melville's counterthemes of chaos, anarchy, and excess. Against the figures of formal order, there is also a celebration of dissonance, a polyphony that bursts the bounds of formal symmetry and thus continues to threaten the newly reborn nation.

America Re-formed

Melville presents *Battle-Pieces* as a unification of the plurality in his introductory note—a note set off from the whole by brackets and on an unnumbered page in the front matter. The note advises that the poems, composed singularly after the culmination of the war, "naturally fall into the order assumed." They consider "aspects which the strife as a memory assumes are as manifold as are the moods of involuntary meditation—moods variable, and at times widely at variance." It is this multiplicity that the poems represent to the reader, as Melville writes: "I seem, in most of these verses, to have but placed a harp in a window, and noted the contrasted airs which wayward winds have played upon the strings." And amid this limned multivocality, the collected poems "make up a whole, in varied amplitude." There is, at least at first glance, an ambition to paint the United States as a new nation, one birthed anew from out of the chaos of the Civil War.

If any poem in *Battle-Pieces* expresses Melville's hope that formal unity might overwhelm and give sense to a reemergent America, it is "Dupont's Round Fight." Here Melville immortalizes the exploits of Commodore Samuel Francis Dupont, who won one of the Union's first battles of the war—at a time in November 1861 when dangerous losses at the Battle of Bull Run threatened the evacuation of Washington, D.C., and even the destruction of the Union. In the naval battle Melville commemorates, Dupont sailed his fleet down one side of Point Royal, in South Carolina, firing at and defeating Fort Walker, than sailed up the other side and took Fort Beauregard. The symmetrical, circular course of Dupont's path led to one of Melville's strongest affirmations of the power of form in war. War honors not simply victory, but victory accompanied by "geometric beauty."

In time and measure perfect moves
All Art whose aim is sure;
Evolving rhyme and stars divine
Have rule, and they endure.
Nor less the Fleet that warred for Right,
And, warring so, prevailed,
In geometric beauty curved,
And in an orbit sailed.
The rebel at Port Royal felt
The Unity overawe,
And rued the spell. A type was here,
And victory of LAW. (*Battle-Pieces,* 30)

Dupont's victory at sea depends, like the victories of art and law, on the perfection of form, the evolving rhymes, the geometric beauty of the sailing ships, and the measured coherence of aesthetic, scientific, and moral unity. If Right is to prevail, and it must, and if the Union is to be preserved, and it shall, then there is a kind of measured destiny in the universe, a LAW, at which art must aim and magnify.

Milton Stern believes "Dupont's Round Fight" is a key to the "conservative nature of Melville's poetry."[27] Stern sees in Melville's portrait of Dupont the "type" of warrior later given form in Captain Vere, the last bastion of formal order in a world plagued by rebellion, chaos, and anarchy. Form, in Stern's reading of Melville, cannot simply be the measure of general laws. The threatening spirit animating the dissolution of institutions and authority, the chaos of the Civil War, like the revolutionary spirit of the times in *Billy Budd,* cannot be opposed by formal reason or written laws. Society is at war, and in war, form is paramount. But the form Melville invokes is LAW, in capital letters. Neither natural law nor positive law, the LAW of "Dupont's Round Fight" is the geometric law of symmetry that imposes form and gives sense and significance to the world.

Another of Melville's poems, "The House-Top. A Night Piece," works together with "Dupont's Round Fight" as a celebration of the draconian "victory of LAW" and the quelling of "the Atheist roar of riot." In "The House-Top," Melville clearly contrasts the perceived threat of anarchy to the redemption found in formal legality. In the draft riots of 1863 Melville finds chaos and anarchy, and the "Atheist roar of riot." He tallies the loss of common truths, the "civil charms / And priestly spells which late held hearts in awe," which "like a dream dissolve." And against this "sway of self" that returns man to his precivilized state ("And man rebounds whole aeons back in nature"), Melville welcomes the formal authority of draconian law:

> Wise Draco comes, deep in the midnight roll
> Of black artillery; he comes, though late;
> In code corroborating Calvin's creed
> And cynic tyrannies of honest kings;
> He comes, nor parlies, and the Town, redeemed,
> Gives thanks devout. (*Battle-Pieces,* 87)

"The House-Top" narrates the riots in New York City during the summer of 1863, themselves a response to the Enrollment Act. The act, passed by Lincoln and a Republican Congress, forced enlistment, and yet was deeply partisan and unpopular. For one thing, the act allowed men of means to hire substitutes to serve in their place or to pay a three-hundred-dollar commutation fee to avoid enlistment. This was at a time when the war was increasingly unpopular among whites who resented Lincoln's Emancipation

Proclamation—which from Melville's own Unionist perspective turned the object of the war away from the preservation of the Union toward the liberation of slaves. Recall that New York at the time (and even more than today) was, as Stanton Garner has reminded us, deeply divided by wealth and politics. Of the city's eight hundred thousand inhabitants, sixteen hundred had three-fifths of the income. The poor—including most of the city's two hundred thousand Irish, lived in rags and were subject to cholera, smallpox, typhoid, and malnutrition. It had been one thing to fight to preserve the Union, but when Lincoln reoriented the war as a war for the liberation of slaves, the democratic masses of New York rebelled.[28] There were daily riots that lasted until Lincoln sent in General John Adams Dix and the army to restore order.

In a note attached to the poem, Melville writes of the riots: "I dare not write the horrible and inconceivable atrocities." Though disagreements continue about the true extent of the riots, over one hundred civilians were killed and a number of free blacks were lynched. Rioters also ransacked the homes of wealthy Republicans. In Melville's concluding words, the town, New York City, was thankful for the draconian response of the army; only the army restored order and thus reaffirmed the foundational American belief in man's natural goodness:

> The grimy slur on the Republic's faith implied,
> Which holds that Man is naturally good,
> And—more—is Nature's Roman, never to be scourged. (*Battle-Pieces*, 87)

What Dix, interpreted as Draco, offers in the violent reaffirmation of the rule of law is the redemption of man's natural goodness, his being "Nature's Roman." Garner claims that Melville writes ironically in "The House-Top" (and also in "Dupont's Round Fight") and that the narrative voice is not his own, but he offers no support for this claim.[29] Whatever Melville may personally have made of the riots, "The House-Top" and "Dupont's Round Fight" display a major theme of his poetry, the political and legislative power of beautiful and strong formal action to bind people together in the face of the emergent threat of anarchy.

It is hard to read "The House-Top. A Night Piece" and not think forward to Melville's setting of *Billy Budd* amid the specter of the terror of the French Revolution and the "Red Flag," symbols of anarchy that inform every aspect of *Billy Budd,* which is set in 1797, the same year as the mutiny at the Nore, where British sailors struck for higher pay and won. Thereafter, British sailors increased their demands for revolutionary changes in the very structure of authority and privilege. It is the revolutionary demand for equality and for restitution of past iniquities, the spirit of the age, that animates the French revolutionaries, American abolitionists, and British seamen. The revolutionary assault on natural distinction and order is the omnipresent background against which Vere must act and judge to restore order on the *Bellipotent,* just as the threatened dissolution of the Union and the specter of anarchy are the political and metaphysical settings behind Melville's response to the Civil War.

What form connotes, especially as Melville expresses it in *Billy Budd,* is the legislating power of the visage, of the great deed. Melville introduces this theme of the legislating heroic act early in *Billy Budd,* in his textual digression on the topic of Admiral Horatio Nelson, "the greatest sailor since our world began." Nelson's greatness lay not in his wisdom, but in his recognition that "an excessive love of glory, impassioning a less burning impulse, the honest sense of duty, is the first" and highest virtue in a military man. That Nelson, like Achilles, "under the presentiment of the most magnificent of victories crowned by his own glorious death," adorned himself in his medals as if "for the altar" is proof of his greatness (*Billy Budd,* 1367). Nelson's greatness lies in his deed, the outward appearance of his act, the form as opposed to the content. Melville brushes off the question of Nelson's intentions. What matters is not the reasons that inspired Nelson—for example, if he acted to gain honor—but the outward appearance of the deed that, in being immortalized in song and myth, recalls to those who hear of it the truth of military greatness. Heroic action that is remembered and glorified, Melville suggests, lays out a truth through its formal power of being seen.

When Melville has Vere announce the entwinement of war, law, and form at the climax of Billy Budd's trial, he recalls for the reader the virtues that distinguished Nelson, specifically his love of glory that impassioned a dimmer impulse toward duty. The importance of appearance and form serves to instruct Vere as to the necessary course of action. Most directly, Vere recognizes that the actual appearance of Billy being hanged is essential to guard against a possible mutinous impulse among the crew. Explaining mitigating or exculpatory circumstances to the crew is insufficient.

They care only about Billy's deed, which, however explained, will remain to the crew a simple murder committed in a flagrant act of mutiny. Against the possibility of mutiny, a deed is necessary to reassert order. What Vere recognizes is that the formal act of punishment itself is needed to bring law into existence.

The Beautiful Visage

The importance of the formal visage is at the core of *Battle-Pieces and Aspects of the War.* Indeed, the word *aspect,* which in its original sense is an "act of looking," offers one key to reading Melville's Civil War poems. Melville's poetry not only offers multiple ways to look at the war—although it surely does that—but also expresses the various "Aspects of the War," or the ways in which war *looks.* War looks useful and also useless. It is ghastly and gallant. Sometimes war looks ugly; at other times war wears the regalia of the beautiful. In all these aspects, war appears not simply as an object to be considered, but as an active subject. The aspects of war are the ways that war shows itself and makes its presence felt.

Nowhere does the beautiful aspect of war appear more vividly than in "Rebel Color-Bearers at Shiloh. A plea against the vindictive cry raised by civilians shortly after the surrender at Appomattox." In this poem Melville writes of the resplendent bravery of the flag bearers "glorying in their show."

> The color-bearers facing death
> White in the whirling sulphurous wreath,
> Stand boldly out before the line;
> Right and left their glances go,
> Proud of each other, glorying in their show;
> Their battle-flags about them blow,
> And fold them as in flame divine:
> Such living robes are only seen
> Round martyrs burning on the green—
> And martyrs for the Wrong have been. (*Battle-Pieces,* 144)

The poem is inspired by an account Melville read of in the newspaper. A Union general was trapped and his regiment under attack. A Rebel party began to form across the bank of a river, and their color guard "stepped defiantly to the front as the engagement opened furiously." The Union sharpshooters requested permission to shoot, to which a Colonel Stuart replied, "No, no, they're too brave fellows to be killed" (*Battle-Pieces,* 252).

The "aspects" of Melville's Civil War come through in a number of poems that address the shining brightness of heroic deeds. "The Eagle of the Blue" celebrates not a man but a bird, an eagle that was "borne aloft on a perch beside the standard" of a Union regiment. The heroic eagle "went through successive battles and campaigns; was more than once under the surgeon's hands; and at the close of the contest found honorable repose in the capitol of Wisconsin" (*Battle-Pieces,* 250). Melville celebrates this bird who "exulteth in war" and is concerned, above all, with the power of his beauty:

> No painted plume—a sober hue,
> His beauty is his power;
> That eager calm of gaze intent
> Foresees the Sibyl's hour. (*Battle-Pieces,* 122)

The aspect of the eagle—sober, intent, and powerful—enraptures as does the frenzied Sibyl, the divinely inspired prophetess of ancient lore who speaks in the name of God. It is this eagle that, when "the very rebel looks and thrills" (*Battle-Pieces,* 123), sends shivers into the rebel forces, and gives them a preview of the fated Union victory. The eagle's powerful beauty may rupture the order of military rationality; at the same time, however, the grand bird offers an aspect, a visage, a form that elevates the spirit and binds the regiment to its common purpose.

If an eagle can raise the spirits of some and sow terror in others, only a man can truly shine in such a way that binds his fellow men to him and to each other. The formal power of manly beauty is on full display in "On the Photograph of a Corps Commander," Melville's paean either to General Ulysses S. Grant (as Megan Williams assumes) or, more likely, to General Winfield Scott Hancock (as Garner argues).[30] The corps commander's visage itself is ennobling and enabling, Melville writes:

> Nothing can lift the heart of man
> Like manhood in a fellow-man.
> The thought of heaven's great King afar

But humbles us—too weak to scan;
But manly greatness men can span,
And feel the bonds that draw. (*Battle-Pieces,* 106)

Whether the poem depicts Grant or Hancock, the corps commander is one of the few figures whose greatness shines through in *Battle-Pieces,* a bold reminder of Admiral Nelson's heroically productive deed. Another is the southern general Stonewall Jackson, who merits two poems that are the "greatest tribute in *Battle-Pieces* to any single Civil-War figure."[31] What Melville marvels about in Stonewall Jackson is his resolve: "Stonewall followed his star" (*Battle-Pieces,* 82). Taken by the simple fact of the man, Melville writes of the corps commander:

Ay, man is manly. Here you see
The warrior-carriage of the head,
And brave dilation of the frame;
And lighting all, the soul that led
In Spottsylvania's charge to victory,
Which justifies his fame. (*Battle-Pieces,* 105)

In "The Armies of the Wilderness," Melville lauds Grant not for his strategic brilliance or courage in battle, but simply as "a quiet Man, and plain in garb—"; he is "like a loaded mortar." Melville attends to his outward look and names him, admiringly, "the silent General" (*Battle-Pieces,* 99). Walt Whitman described Grant as "the typical Western man—the plainest, the most efficient."[32] Similarly, Garner describes Hancock as "the natural leader that a democracy is capable of producing, not a man born to rank and position but one who is worthy of it." Hancock is, Garner writes, thus a model for Billy Budd, the handsome soldier who commands respect through nothing other than his vibrant manhood. For Melville, Grant and Hancock were exemplars of the new democratic American. And all this is visible, Melville suggests, simply from a photograph—although, importantly, Melville himself visited with and experienced these paradigmatic democrats in the flesh.

What Melville emphasizes is not the experience of these men, but the force of their images. It is the corps commander's visage, his form, that braces those who see it for the pursuit of greatness—the picture is "a cheering picture." As the poet writes:

A cheering picture. It is good
To look upon a Chief like this,
In whom the spirit moulds the form.
Here favoring Nature, oft remiss,
With eagle mien expressive has endued
A man to kindle strains that warm. (*Battle-Pieces,* 105)

Robert Penn Warren rightly sees in "On the Photograph of the Corps Commander" Melville's humanity, his sensitivity to human values and human suffering over and above the claims of ideology and religion.[33] Melville can celebrate Stonewall Jackson and Robert E. Lee, even as he can the Union commander, not for what they fight for, but for who they are. What war brings home is the idea that alongside ideology and belief, right and wrong, and good and bad, these absolutes dissolve and what takes their place is the singularity of human character.

Forms and Violence

The attraction to the power of form is palpable in both *Battle-Pieces* and *Billy Budd.* And yet in both these works formal closure and coherence are upended. The famous "digression" that supplements and undoes the formal coherence of *Billy Budd* is well known and was discussed above. Less often remarked is the literal supplement that follows both the main text and even the notes in the original edition of *Battle-Pieces.* Melville begins his supplement in words that clearly prefigure chapter 28 of *Billy Budd,* written years later: "Were I fastidiously anxious for the symmetry of this book, it would close with the notes. But the times are such that patriotism—not free from solicitude—urges a claim overriding all literary scruples" (*Battle-Pieces,* 259). Why the overriding of literary scruples? And why, also, the overriding of the wartime focus on the external visage? For as long as war is the main event, Melville seems to hew to a martial reverence for formal coherence. Only with the end of the war, when it is time to "hymn the politicians," does he abandon formality and symmetry. It seems that literary and military scruples are united in the demand for form, whereas politics urges the overriding of such scruples.

Politics demands nuance—one thinks of Max Weber's praise of an ethic of responsibility against an ethic of conviction in his essay "Politics as a

Vocation." There is greatness in the judgment that affirms self-restraint just as there can be in bellicosity. Since the South will not repent for fighting for its convictions, the North must avoid the demand for voluntary humiliation. All that is needed, Melville writes, is that the "South have been taught by the terrors of civil war to feel that Secession, like Slavery, is against Destiny; that both now lie buried in one grave; that her fate is linked with ours; and that together we comprise the Nation" (*Battle-Pieces,* 260). The North must avoid triumphalism. It must admit that its victory was less from skill and bravery than from "superior resources and crushing numbers" (ibid., 266). And, too, the North must recall that many southern fighters were misled by their leaders and ancestors. And though we must sympathize with the "infant pupilage to freedom" that sets the freed slaves in need of assistance, Melville cautions that such humane kindness toward blacks "should not be allowed to exclude kindliness to communities who stand nearer to us in nature. For the future of the freed slaves we may well be concerned; but the future of the whole country, involving the future of the blacks, urges a paramount claim upon our anxiety" (ibid., 267).

Some have berated Melville here for preferring to mend fences with white Southerners to doing justice to freed slaves. They are right. The reconciliation Melville affirms can and does support the rejuvenated nationalism that reaffirms America as a white nation through the period of segregation. And yet the point of the supplement is precisely that in politics, unlike in war and literature, compromises have to be made, corners cut, and common sense practiced. What common sense told Melville is that to save the Union, an olive branch had to be extended to the South, and that the rebirth of the nation meant that "no consideration should tempt us to pervert the national victory into oppression for the vanquished" (*Battle-Pieces,* 269).

Also in *Billy Budd,* Melville's final digression is a response to practicalities in the world, to the fact that the actual world has ragged rather than symmetrical edges. The necessity of form, of beautiful narration, of heroism—when imposed on the real world—necessarily leads to injustices and to violence. Not all heroes will be the embodiment of absolute good, as is Billy, who willingly sacrifices his life to the king. Both Vere and Melville recognize that the imposition of form on the content of the real world is a violent one, but both also believe that such imposition is necessary and, more important, worthy of honor—at least in times of war.

Neither Vere nor Melville is lighthearted about the need for a formal reassertion of the law at the expense of justice. Vere expresses his own anguish throughout the trial. After he emerges from his secret conversation with Billy, his face is "one expressive of the agony of the strong" (*Billy Budd,* 1419). And Melville too expresses his own self-criticism by appending three short sections to the end of *Billy Budd* that self-consciously rupture the formal coherence of the story. Pure justice doesn't accord with legal institutions in a human world from which law has withdrawn. And even fiction, if it is to accurately reflect the truth of the world, cannot be pure.

In both its recognition of the absence of formal symmetry and its attempt to recollect formal laws through heroic deeds, Melville's *Battle-Pieces* remains, as does *Billy Budd,* an inescapably political book. As Hannah Arendt argues, Melville's reversal of the primordial crime in which Cain slew Abel is based on the recognition that goodness, like evil, is "strong, stronger perhaps even than wickedness." The strength of goodness and the "violence inherent in all strength and detrimental to all forms of political organization" means that if good goes unpunished, the consequences are as disastrous as when evil is left unpunished.[34] Violence done by absolute good—as much as violence done by absolute evil—can set in motion a chain of violence and wrongdoing. In the face of potential violence motivated by the revolutionary and reformist spirit of the age, Vere recognizes that order must be restored less by positive law than through a radical recollection of form. And yet Melville also questions whether such an assertion of form can be valid in the real world.

War, Brutality, and the Dream of Justice

The struggle between the ordering power of form in war and the violent destructiveness of war's formlessness is vivid in the best of Melville's Civil War poems, above all in "The Armies of the Wilderness." The two-part poem vividly struggles with the destructive and brutal truth of the Civil War through a description of the Battle of the Wilderness near Spottsylvania, Virginia, in 1863. Part 1 of the poem describes the scene of the opposing Union and Rebel camps as they prepare for battle; part 2 introduces General Grant, unnamed, as he plans the attack and then narrates the bloody and brutal battle itself. It is one of the longest poems in *Battle-Pieces* and has rightly been called the "most important crossroads in [Melville's] intellectual and moral response" to the Civil War. It is, as Garner writes, the poem in which "the truth of the war—the Satanic state in which the rule of law and civility is mocked by violent armies bent on feral destructiveness—is seen."[35]

"The Armies of the Wilderness" is also one of only a very few poems in *Battle-Pieces* that Melville could write by drawing from his personal experience. In April 1864 he and his brother, Allan Melville, traveled to the front, much as Walt Whitman had done in February. Unlike Whitman, Melville—still the adventurer from his days as a sailor—did not just watch the action, but participated as well, accepting an invitation from Colonel Charles Russell Lowe Jr. to ride along with a five-hundred-man expedition to track down and fight John Singleton Mosby, a commander of what then were called Partisan Rangers and today would be called guerrilla fighters. During the three-day and two-night mission, Melville lived among the soldiers as they tracked and attacked Mosby—and then fled, suffering casualties along the way. A highly fictionalized version of the Mosby expedition is included in *Battle-Pieces* as "The Scout toward Aldie," a long and thrilling poem that imagines Mosby as a human Moby Dick; as a mythic instantiation of inscrutable evil, Mosby lives in the wilderness, where he is pursued by brave yet foolish soldiers who risk everything and achieve little.[36]

After returning to Lowell's cavalry camp in Vienna, Virginia, Melville made his way to the main camps of the Army of the Potomac, then under the command of General Grant. Grant apparently received Melville, and the two discussed past battles. Melville toured the camps, where he also met General Winfield Scott Hancock, memorialized in "On the Photograph of a Corps Commander." There is, in Melville's depictions of Stonewall Jackson, Grant, and Hancock, a fortifying simplicity. These men are heroes. Eschewing grand theories and complicated theoretical justification, Melville affirms, simply, the truth of heroism. His heroes do not raise the firmament or "make the earth wholesome," as Emerson would have it.[37] Against Emerson's vision of the uses of heroes who elevate man, Melville's heroes bind men together. His heroes are immortalized for doing great deeds, and yet not once does *Battle-Pieces* descend to the melodrama of hagiography.

Against the simple force of beauty and calm that Melville invokes in his portraits of heroes, it is chaos and complexity that are the themes of "The Armies of the Wilderness" and also of *Battle-Pieces* more generally. The focus on the wilderness evokes the untamable vastness of nature. And the battle itself is pure chaos, in which simple vision and hard facts dissolve:

"Pursuer and pursued like ghosts disappear / In gloomed shade—their end who shall tell?" (*Battle-Pieces,* 102). It is the natural depths and byzantine mysteries of war that rise to the fore, and Melville struggles to find a language with which to speak about these horrors of war:

None can narrate that strife in the pines,
A seal is on it—Sabaean lore!
Obscure as the wood, the entangled rhyme
But hints at the maze of war— (*Battle-Pieces,* 103)

The maze of war is both carnal and moral, as in the pitch of battle it is easy to lose sight of right and wrong, good and bad. Indeed, Melville purposefully opens his poem by painting a landscape of the uncertain moral verities at war in the conflict. It is a "strife of brothers," and both sides cling fervently to belief in their cause:

On fronting slopes gleamed other camps
Where faith as firmly clung;
Ah, froward kin! so brave amiss—
 The zealots of the Wrong. (*Battle-Pieces,* 93)

Throughout *Battle-Pieces* Melville declares the Union forces to be fighting for right and the South to be for wrong. Again later in this poem we learn that "but Heaven lent strength, the Right strove well, / And emerged from the Wilderness." Yet the claims for right are always countered by an understanding that both sides have a claim for right: "YEA AND NAY— / EACH HATH ITS SAY" (*Battle-Pieces,* 18). Or as it is written in "The Armies of the Wilderness,"

Did the Fathers feel mistrust?
Can no final good be wrought?
Over and over, again and again
Must the fight for the Right be fought? (*Battle-Pieces,* 94)

Melville goes out of his way to humanize the Rebel soldiers, as in this early stanza describing how Union soldiers looked on their countrymen from the South across enemy lines.

Through the pointed glass our soldiers saw
The base-ball bounding sent;
They could have joined them in their sport
But for the vale's deep rent.
And others turned the reddish soil,
Like diggers of graves they bent:
The reddish soil and trenching toil
Begat presentiment. (*Battle-Pieces,* 93–94)

The presentiment in the digging of trenches is, of course, that the soil will soon shroud thousands of corpses. Approximately twenty-five thousand American soldiers were killed or wounded in three days of fighting in the wilderness around Virginia in a battle that has drawn sharp criticism from military historians and ethicists. Grant fought what some have called a "war of attrition," sending wave upon wave of Union troops to simply overwhelm the southern defenses. William McFeely writes that Grant "led his troops into the Wilderness and there produced a nightmare of inhumanity and inept military strategy that ranks with the worst such episodes in the history of warfare."[38] James McPherson has a different view, concluding that it was Robert E. Lee who turned the battle into a war of attrition by "skillfully matching Grant's moves and confronting him with an entrenched defense at every turn."[39] In either case, the cost of battle was colossal:

In glades they meet skull after skull
Where pine-cones lay—the rusted gun,
Green shoes full of bones, the mouldering coat
And cuddled-up skeleton. (*Battle-Pieces,* 101)

The challenge Melville confronts is to narrate what has come to be a new kind of war, one in which the simple truths and powerful acts have given way to mass movements and calculations of resources. In a war in which thousands upon thousands of men are sacrificed in a single battle in the midst of a nameless forest, the honor and dignity of the warrior yield to the brute force of numbers and steel. The color- and standard-bearers whom Melville celebrates in "Rebel Color-Bearers of Shiloh," the bold eagle of the "The Eagle of the Blue," and even the manliness of Grant and Stonewall Jackson pale in the face of the "The Armies of the Wilderness." The new kind of war heralds the eventual dimming of martial heroism.

The focus on armies is intentional, moving us beyond the dignity of soldiers to the swarming masses where twenty and thirty thousand roughly clad and ill-slept soldiers clash in the darkness. In such a battle, "plume and sash are vanities." They are useless, or at least useful only to "deck the pall of the dead." The cannon are dragged over the ground and have "trenched their scar" on the earth. And "black chimneys, gigantic in moor-like wastes," darken the sky, threatening to depeople the world: "The hearth is a houseless stone again— / Ah! where shall the people be sought?" All markings of human civilization are endangered in this wilderness war. The soldiers

> Kindle their fires with indentures and bonds,
> And old Lord Fairfax's parchment deeds;
> And Virginian gentlemen's libraries old—
> Books which only the scholar heeds—
> Are flung to his kennel. It is ravage and range,
> And gardens are left to weeds. (*Battle-Pieces,* 98)

"The Armies of the Wilderness" explores the decline of human civilization. Headstones are used for hearthstones to prepare celebratory feasts for the fighting men. And the tents of the camp are dim remnants of civilization that, like the Pleiades, which dim in the winter, itself is fading into a cold winter of barbarism. Indeed, there is in the progress of the war a dangerous regression.

> *Turned adrift into war*
> *Man runs wild on the plain,*
> *Like the jennets let loose*
> *On the Pampas—zebras again.* (*Battle-Pieces,* 98)

Just as the jennets, a breed of riding horse, reverted to being wild zebras after they were imported to the Americas and then let loose to run on the Pampas in South America, so too has man lost himself in the wilderness of modern warfare.

The great hero of "The Armies of the Wilderness" is the new kind of army itself, the large, mass, and impersonal force that is challenging the traditional pride of bravery and personality. Admiral Nelson's heroism is replaced by the force of numbers. Read in this way, the poem is a companion to "A Utilitarian View of the Monitor's Fight," a poem in which Melville sings of the highly modern and mechanical cadence of the new war, one that trades pageantry for "plain mechanic power." The iron-clad *Monitor* is the most potent symbol of the transformation in war brought about by the Civil War, and it also infects the poetry of war in *Battle-Pieces.* Melville makes this poetic resonance palpable in the first stanza:

> Plain be the phrase, yet apt the verse,
> More ponderous than nimble;
> For since grimed War here laid aside
> His Orient pomp, 'twould ill befit
> Overmuch to ply
> The rhyme's barbaric cymbal. (*Battle-Pieces,* 61)

The plainness and even clunkiness of Melville's prose is a big part of the poem's point.[40] There are poems in which Melville remains faithful to a romantic vision of war and symmetrical rhythmic meter, but much of *Battle-Pieces* boasts rhymes that are ponderous and grimy. The poems bespeak an effort to invent a poetry fitting to a new kind of war, a war whose power proceeds less from form than from mass—it is not moral superiority or excessive courage, but simply the advantage in human and natural resources, in Melville's accounting, that decides the war for North over South.

War is part of the human experience, and Melville's engagement with war in *Battle-Pieces* shows him struggling with and exhilarated by the savagery and the contest of the military ethic. And yet Melville also marks the change in war, its sacrifice of grandeur. Nowhere is that more apparent than in the final verse of "A Utilitarian View of the Monitor's Fight":

> War shall yet be, and to the end;
> But war-paint shows the streaks of weather;
> War yet shall be, but warriors
> Are now but operatives; War's made
> Less grand than Peace,
> And a singe runs through lace and feather. (*Battle-Pieces,* 62)

War is the "singe" that runs through the lace and feather of life, and yet that singe has itself lost at least part of its power. It still can burn and carry desolation, more than ever before, but war's fiery capacity to enliven and ennoble is clearly diminished. Once a matter of color-bearers and eagles, war is transforming and becoming a matter of brute efficiency. Once a contest of skill and strategy, war is becoming a matter of resources and production. The war music of old is being replaced by the barbaric cymbal, iron clashing against iron.

One need not be a romantic to recognize that war is, if not, as Heraclitus thought, the father of all things, at least central to the experience of being human. For Simone Weil, the good and the just are offspring of war, since justice makes sense only as an idea for which one will endure the most extreme sacrifice. Absent the glory and tragedy of war, there would be no spiritual cauldron in which to forge the mettle of justice. As Weil writes: "Only he who has measured the dominion of force, and knows how to respect it, is capable of love and justice."[41] What war teaches, Weil argues, is the experience of utter misery, the reduction of man to a mere thing, a plaything of fate. Only amid the fury of war, the savagery of strife, and the lashes of lightning do human beings confront the utter senselessness of our world, the very precondition that calls forth the dream of justice.

The experience of human misery is what first allows human beings to raise themselves to a higher plane, to "resort to the aid of illusion, fanaticism, to conceal the harshness of destiny from their eyes." As did Plato and Nietzsche before her, Weil understood that the "man who does not wear the armour of the lie cannot experience force without being touched by it to the very soul."[42] Only the lie of justice, the dream of a higher plane of human purpose, allows us humans to survive the existential threat of war. Justice, in other words, is that noble lie that we humans invent to make our warlike and strife-filled lives meaningful.

The hope that war can offer meaning to life is palpable in Melville's late writing, as he struggles to salvage both his own writing career and his pained nation. *Battle-Pieces* is, in large measure, an exploration of the continuing power of war to rejuvenate life. Melville celebrates that formal pomp and grandeur of war. He finds still in the Civil War the passions of loyalty and convictions of faith that can give and even restore meaning to life. He discovers in the war the possibilities not only for his own personal rebirth as a writer, but for the reconstitution of the United States as well.

In short, Melville finds the war stimulating in the way that wars have, since time immemorial, been essential prods to human greatness.

The power of greatness to bind men into peoples is celebrated in the same book that traces the rise of a utilitarian warfare that augurs the fading of heroic warfare. In such a world without heroes, brutality replaces ideals and totalitarian movements subvert the bonds that draw men together. Melville is alive to these threats. But *Battle-Pieces* is, in the end, an affirmation of the notion that amid the brutality of modern war, human greatness will shine forth. War is brutality. War is utility. War is technology. And war is inhumanity. But war is also a testament to humanity. In celebrating the manly deeds of great heroes, we can, Melville argues, bind ourselves to a grand vision of who we are.

Notes

1. Herman Melville, *Billy Budd, Sailor (An Inside Narrative)*, in *Pierre, Israel Potter, The Piazza Tales, The Confidence-Man, Uncollected Prose, Billy Budd* (New York: Library of America, 1984), 1406; hereafter cited parenthetically in the text by title and page number.

2. Robert Cover, *Justice Accused* (New Haven: Yale University Press, 1975); Robert Ferguson, *Law and Letters in American Culture* (Cambridge: Harvard University Press, 1984), 289.

3. Joyce Sparer Adler, "*Billy Budd* and Melville's Philosophy of War," *PMLA* 91, no. 2 (1976): 274.

4. Ibid.

5. Ibid., 275.

6. Ibid., 268.

7. Ibid., 268–269.

8. Ibid., 266.

9. Ibid., 274.

10. Herman Melville, *Battle-Pieces and Aspects of the War* (1866; repr., New York: Da Capo Press, 1995); hereafter cited parenthetically in the text by title.

11. *Selected Poems of Herman Melville: A Reader's Edition,* ed. Robert Penn Warren (Boston: David R. Godine, 2004), 4.

12. Ibid., 9.

13. Andrew Delbanco, *Melville: His World and Work* (New York: Knopf, 2005), 267.

14. Ibid., 268.

15. Ibid., 269.

16. Ibid., 273.

17. Michael Warner, "What Like a Bullet Can Undeceive?" *Public Culture* 15, no. 1 (Winter 2003): 44.

18. Ibid., 48.

19. Ibid., 53.

20. See Jason Frank, "Introduction: American Tragedy: The Political Thought of Herman Melville," in this volume.

21. Melville, *Selected Poems,* 11.

22. Ibid., 12.

23. Stanton Garner, *The Civil War World of Herman Melville* (Lawrence: University Press of Kansas, 1993), 33

24. David Devries and Hugh Egan, "'Entangled Rhyme': A Dialogic Reading of Melville's Battle-Pieces," *Leviathan: A Journal of Melville Studies* 9, no. 3 (October 2007): 17–33.

25. Garner, *The Civil War World,* 47.

26. See Thomas Dumm's essay in this volume, which argues that the reconciliation of North and South was predicated on suppressing the true racial cause of the war.

27. Milton R. Stern, introduction to Melville, *Billy Budd, Sailor (An Inside Narrative),* ed. Milton R. Stern (Indianapolis: Bobbs-Merrill, 1978), xvii.

28. Garner, *The Civil War World,* 250ff.

29. Ibid., 255.

30. Megan Williams, "'Sounding the Wilderness': Representation of the Heroic in Herman Melville's *Battle-Pieces and Aspects of the War,*" *Texas Studies in Literature and Language* 45, no. 2 (Summer 2003): 161; Garner, *The Civil War World,* 325.

31. Garner, *The Civil War World,* 243.

32. Ibid., 327.

33. Melville, *Selected Poems,* 19.

34. Hannah Arendt, *On Revolution* (1963; repr., New York: Penguin, 1987), 87.

35. Garner, *The Civil War World,* 328.

36. Ibid., 304–323.

37. Ralph Waldo Emerson, *Representative Men* (1850; repr., Boston: Houghton Mifflin, 1897), 9.

38. William McFeely's *Grant: A Biography* is quoted in Williams, "Sounding the Wilderness," 158.

39. James M. McPherson's *Battle Cry of Freedom* is quoted in Williams, "Sounding the Wilderness," 157.

40. Melville, *Selected Poems,* 17.

41. Simone Weil, *The* Iliad, *or the Poem of Force,* ed. Sian Miles, trans. Mary McCarthy (London: Weidenfeld & Nicolson, 1986), 192.

42. Ibid., 194.

13

The Lyre of Orpheus

Aesthetics and Authority in Billy Budd

Jason Frank

> Be a man's intellectual superiority what it will, it can never assume the practical, available supremacy over other men, without the aid of some sort of external arts and entrenchments.
>
> —Herman Melville, *Moby-Dick*

> "With mankind," he [Vere] would say, "forms, measured forms, are everything; and this is the import couched in the story of Orpheus, with his lyre spellbinding the wild denizens of the wood." And this he once applied to the disruption of forms going on across the Channel and the consequences thereof.
>
> —Herman Melville, *Billy Budd, Sailor (An Inside Narrative)*

Herman Melville worked on *Billy Budd, Sailor (An Inside Narrative)* for the last five years of his life—between 1886 and 1891—and since its posthumous discovery and publication in 1924 *Billy Budd* has often been read as Melville's last will and testament, the most mature articulation of his social and political thought. There is, of course, little agreement over the meaning of this subtle and enchanting testament, although past interpretations typically cluster into two competing approaches. The "testament of acceptance" school associates Melville's own position with Vere's and emphasizes the novella's concluding affirmation of necessity in this "moral dilemma involving aught of the tragic."[1] The opposing "testament of resistance" school exposes the irony of Melville's unreliable narrator and identifies a skeptical rejection of Vere's claims of authority, even to the point of doubting Vere's sanity.[2]

Billy Budd, one critic has recently noted, "taps commitments of ethical, political, and philosophical value that make its criticism peculiarly confessional and urgent."[3] At the center of these controversies is the contested meaning of Vere's famous judgment near the novella's conclusion: "*Struck* dead by an *angel of God!* Yet the *angel must hang!*" (1406; emphases in original). These interpretations often turn on the vicissitudes of legal judgment, in other words, and situate Melville's "inside narrative" within a broadly juridical, if not narrowly procedural, frame.

Judging Vere's judgment has also been the guiding hermeneutic of most of the political theory scholarship dedicated to the novella. Hannah Arendt, for example, embraces the wisdom of Vere's decision to "punish the violence of absolute innocence," represented by Budd, as an exemplification of her theoretical insight that "the absolute spells doom to everyone when it is introduced into the political realm." Arendt contrasts Budd's otherworldly "innocence" and "goodness" to Vere's personification of worldly "virtue," a political principle "which alone is capable of embodiment in lasting institutions."[4] Michael Rogin, by contrast, rejects Vere's decision as a grotesque sanctification of the state, which returns man to the unthinking nature of "beasts" rather than the "rights-granting nature of the Declaration of Independence." "Like Melville's fiction of the 1850s," Rogin writes, "*Billy Budd* confines us in a denuded, mundane world, from which all possibility of transformation has fled. But unlike the earlier stories, *Billy Budd* gives that world its blessing."[5] Arendt and Rogin judge Vere's judgment differently, but they agree that the political theory of the story is located primarily in its dramatization of judgment. Even for these political theorists *Billy Budd* remains very much a "judge's story."[6] It is as if most of what is of political theoretical significance in the novella were confined to three of its thirty chapters.

This essay takes a different approach. While the familiar focus on Vere's judgment provides an illuminating example of the dilemmas of legal and moral judgment in times of political crisis—in light of contemporary theoretical preoccupations, Melville's story may be said to dramatize the fraught exposure of procedural norms to the sovereign "state of exception"—this focus also quietly displaces another, perhaps deeper dilemma posed by the novella.[7] Melville situates the story's dilemma of judgment and legal procedure within a broader and more worldly theoretical rubric: the constitution and performative maintenance of political authority. Melville makes a political spectacle of legal judgment in *Billy Budd,* and even though Vere's drumhead court is "summarily convened," and even though Budd is secretly tried belowdecks in the commander's chambers, it retains aspects of a show trial. The many irregularities of Budd's improvised court-martial are as much a part of the political spectacle orchestrated by Vere as Budd's subsequent hanging at sea before the assembled crew (or, as Vere revealingly refers to them, "the people") (1416). Like many of Melville's shipboard novels, *Billy Budd* provides a detailed investigation of the everyday mechanisms and manifestations of male authority as they interweave across different registers of social and political life. Borrowing from the aesthetic political theory of Edmund Burke, on whom Vere is modeled, Melville's story dramatizes authority's inextricable reliance on "forms, measured forms," while also insisting that law itself be understood in its embedded relation to these myriad forms rather than isolated from them in unencumbered normative abstraction.[8] To adapt the familiar terms of H. L. A. Hart's legal positivism, we could say that *Billy Budd* is concerned less with the formal proceduralism of the "primary rules" of the law than the complexity of the secondary "rules of recognition" on which these laws depend.[9]

The problematic of authority in Melville's novella is, therefore, *before the law* in both senses of the term: it is at once *prior to* law and a question of law's appearance *in front of* its beholden subjects. Melville's novella offers a sustained reflection on the usually hidden interdependence of these two senses of being before the law and, in doing so, draws readers' attention to an often disavowed dilemma for democratic theorists past and present: the inescapably aesthetic dimensions of political authority.[10] I will read Melville's novella as a provocation for contemporary democratic theorists to be more carefully attentive to questions they typically reject as both normatively and historically antithetical to democratic politics.

"Before the Law" is, of course, also the title of a well-known parable by Franz Kafka included at the end of his novel *The Trial* (but also published separately in Kafka's lifetime).[11] Rogin suggests that *Billy Budd* "anticipates the Kafkaesque strand of literary modernism," having particularly important analogies to themes developed in Kafka's story "In the Penal Colony."[12] I want to suggest that Kafka's remarkable two-page parable "Before the Law" raises in condensed form theoretical issues about authority and aesthetics elaborated by Melville in his last work of fiction. A brief recounting of Kafka's parable can, therefore, provide preliminary orientation to the central themes of this essay.

In Kafka's parable "a man from the country" seeks to gain admittance to the law but is told by the doorkeeper that, though it is possible he might gain admittance later, he cannot be admitted "at the moment." This comes as unexpected news to the man from the country, who thinks, in transparent democratic fashion, that "the law should be accessible to every man and at all times." The door to the law remains open, and the man from the country peers inside. Seeing this, the doorkeeper laughs and suggests that the man from the country try to enter without his permission, but he warns that while he is powerful, he is but the first and lowest doorkeeper. "From hall to hall keepers stand at every door, one more powerful than the other. Even the third of these has an aspect that even I cannot bear to look at." Hearing this, the man from the country "looks more closely at the doorkeeper in his furred robe, with his huge pointed nose and long, thin, Tartar beard," and "decides he had better wait until he gets permission to enter." The man from the country is here interpellated as an obedient subject through his senses, as his first act of obedience is founded on the sensuous particulars of the doorkeeper's coat, nose, and beard, and what he *imagines* to be the "aspect" of the other doorkeepers beyond these immediate perceptions. And so the man from the country waits obediently for days and years, and "during these long years the man watches the doorkeeper almost incessantly." Indeed, he "forgets about the other doorkeepers, and this one seems to him the only barrier between himself and the law." The man from the country becomes so enthralled with the doorkeeper before him in his "prolonged watch" that he comes to know the fleas in the doorkeeper's fur collar and even begs these fleas to help him and to "persuade the doorkeeper to change his mind." But to no avail. Finally, as his sight begins to dim and the world darkens around him, the man from the country perceives a "radiance that streams immortally from the door of the law." The onset of his physical blindness is coupled with a revelatory insight. With his vision darkening, his hearing failing, and his body infirm—with the growing incapacitation of his senses—the man from the country asks a final question: "Everyone strives to attain the law . . . how does it come about, then, that in all these years no one has come seeking admittance but me?" To which the doorman loudly replies: "No one but you could gain admittance through this door, since this door was intended only for you. I am now going to shut it." The man from the country's awareness of his ambiguously voluntary complicity in his own subjection comes only with his death. "What like a bullet," as Melville puts a similar point in "Shiloh," "can undeceive?"[13]

Kafka's parable, like *Billy Budd,* dramatizes the creaturely life of the law, how law's authority is constituted and maintained by way of the senses and imagination, through the mechanisms of *aisthesis,* which Jacques Rancière theorizes in terms of the "partition of the perceptible" and the "community of sense."[14] The authority of law in both stories does not reproduce itself through knowledge of its origins or foundations—which forever escape apprehension, in any case—but only through its delegated and multiform appearances. In both tales the law never emerges to speak in its own name. The forever receding horizon of what comes before the law as its universal origin (or natural foundation) is resolved only through the myriad manifestations of what comes before the law as its singular sensuous appearance. The inaccessible foundation, as Derrida writes of the Kafka parable, continually "incites from its place of hiding," and this incitation comes through the appearance of those delegated to act on behalf of the law.[15] Elaborating a similar point, Richard Flathman writes that "from the moment that legislators, judges, police officers, CEOs and union officials, colonels and sergeants, provosts, deans, and teachers attempt to promote the authority and bindingness of rules, historicity, narrativity, and hence imagination and fiction are introduced into the very core of legal thought."[16] It is not what is hidden that Kafka's parable and Melville's novella illuminate, but the allure of what is enigmatically manifest. The soft collar of sensory enthrallment depicted in both stories is not the same as violence or even the threat of violence. Kafka's guardian does not *threaten* the man from the country, after all, but actually tempts him to disobey. The man from the country is kept waiting—and the authority of law sustained—through his own desire to gain eventual—impossible—admittance to the sublime law. The door of the law always remains open—he is not physically debarred—but he "decides to wait" when confronted with the doorman's appearance. Revealingly, the German is closer to "he decides to prefer to wait"—"*Entschliesst er sich, doch lieber zu warten, bis er die Erlaubnis zum Eintritt bekommt*"—a phrase that highlights the ambiguously nuanced account of volition, will, and consent in the parable. Melville, as we will see, gives a similarly nuanced account in the mesmeric agency depicted in *Billy Budd,* where authority operates through enthralling sensuous manifestations "spellbinding the wild denizens of the wood." Both Melville and Kafka redirect theoretical attention away from the question of law's originary authorization—they do not offer the critical justificatory theory of authority required by democratic theory—and toward its sensuous manifestations. These literary examinations of law's surface mechanisms—its "forms, measured forms"—might alert us to the sensory operation of law's everyday authority, and thereby enrich or give needed texture to the sometimes anemic discourse of contemporary democratic theory.

Characterology and Authority

Melville's preoccupations with the performative dimensions of authority are already evident in his first novels, with their sustained reflections on the intricate web of human relations aboard whaling ships (*Typee* and *Omoo*), merchant vessels (*Redburn*), and naval frigates (*White-Jacket*). His persistent reliance on the ubiquitous ship-of-state metaphor, which Alan Heimert has shown to be an essential component of the nineteenth-century American political imaginary, allowed Melville to explore the concrete and daily mechanisms of authoritative relations and draw broad conclusions about how these relations are created, sustained, and undone, without relying on the conceptual abstractions of most theoretical reflection on these themes.[17] Ships were useful for focused explorations of authority, because, as Melville writes in *Benito Cereno*, "ship captains enjoy a dictatorship beyond which, while at sea, there was no earthly appeal."[18] Thus, in many of his novels Melville examined "the qualities needed to command and direct with skill, fairness, and justice."[19] Melville recognized early on that serious investigation into the workings of authority required richer symbolic and literary resources than those provided by the prevailing liberal political discourses of nineteenth-century America, most notably those theoretical paradigms emphasizing the central role of individual consent or social utility. Though none of Melville's early novels matches the depth and subtlety of observation into the "little lower layer" of human motivation exemplified by "The Quarter-Deck" chapter of *Moby-Dick*, with its examination of the *Pequod* crew's terrible conversion to be "all with Ahab, in this matter of the whale," they do nonetheless indicate that from the beginning of his writing career, Melville recognized that the liberal language of rights, contract, and consent and the utilitarian calculus of aggregate pleasures and pains obscure as much as they reveal when it came to matters of authority.[20] Melville's sailors,

Elizabeth Samet has recently argued, are living and breathing "metonyms for the situation of all citizens in a republic."[21] His literary examinations of the practical terrain between reasoned consent and coercion, or between riotous mutiny and disciplinary violence, map the rough middle ground of authoritative relations often missing from theoretical discussions of these issues. The "pervasive theme in [*Billy Budd*] is the mode of communication of men in authority," as many readers have recognized, but this "mode of communication" is not narrowly discursive but broadly aesthetic.[22] Like the lyre of Orpheus invoked near the novella's end, authority "spellbinds" in part through mechanisms of sensuous captivation (1430).

Readers first glimpse these spellbinding mechanisms in Melville's treatment of character in the novella. Melville outlined a typology or, perhaps more precisely, a characterology, of authoritative relations in *Billy Budd*, which revolve around the three central figures of Budd, Claggart, and Vere.[23] In the case of Budd the interrelationship between the forever receding foundation of authority and its sensuous manifestation connects Nature to visible and sonorous beauty. It is well known that Melville associates Budd broadly with Nature—he is a foundling, an American Adam born "before Cain's city and citified man"—and also with Thomas Paine and the revolutionary ideals of universal natural rights (1362). Budd provides Melville with the opportunity to critically examine the Enlightenment and the American Romantic dream of grounding political authority in the harmonious order of nature. "You are going to take away my peacemaker," says Captain Graveling to Lieutenant Ratcliffe when Budd is impressed at the beginning of the novella from the merchant ship *The Rights of Man* and onto the naval frigate H.M.S. *Bellipotent* (1357). "Before I shipped that young fellow, my forecastle was a rat-pit of quarrels. It was black times, I tell you, aboard the *Rights* here. . . . But Billy came; and it was like a Catholic priest striking peace in an Irish shindy. Not that he preached to them or said or did anything in particular; but a virtue went out of him, sugaring the sour ones. They took to him like hornets to treacle" (1356). The authority that Budd exercises over the crew of *The Rights of Man* is natural and instinctive, based in free expression of love rather than persuasion or calculations of self-interest. Melville associates Budd's authority with Paine's idealization of a spontaneous social order based in the needs of Nature organized in civil society rather than built on the artificial government of men. Perhaps more interesting than Melville's ultimately skeptical treatment of political authority based in the dictates of natural law (which Arendt also emphasizes in her reading of the novel) is how he understands the sensuous mechanisms of this peacemaking power. In this, Melville leaves Paine behind and seems to pursue the aesthetic insights of Paine's central opponent in the "Revolution Controversy" of the 1790s, Edmund Burke.

In Melville's story Budd's authority is engendered through the sheer beauty of his physical presence, not through rhetorically persuasive speech, or the speech of reasoned deliberation or rational conviction. Indeed, Budd's authority transcends the unreliable worldly mediations of speech altogether, as dramatized by his speech impediment, a stutter. The men aboard *The Rights of Man* do not consent to Budd's authority. They are not convinced or persuaded into accepting it, but neither are they coerced. Like the "Handsome Sailor" invoked at the opening of the tale, of which Budd is taken to be a singular example, Budd in his harmony of outer form and inner nature elicits the "spontaneous tribute" of those gathered around him: "the crew," "the people," "the public" (1353). In a phrase that unites the theories of Paine and Burke, Melville writes of a "natural regality" that summons an "honest homage" (1353). This quality, Melville emphasizes, is not that "manufacturable thing known as respectability," but an immediate physical manifestation of inner goodness and innocence. "The moral nature was seldom out of keeping with the physical make" (1354). Melville describes with great care the details of Billy's body, the melodious song of his voice, and the unselfconscious virtuosity of his movements (1361). This immediate beauty and effortless grace cannot be faked, because it is an external and perfectly correspondent manifestation or expression of an inner truth, an expressive virtue of the heart. Throughout the story Melville establishes an elaborate connection between the innocence of Budd's being and the captivating beauty of his appearance, which could be effectively described in terms of seduction were it not a manifestation of pure innocence. Budd was not a seducer but what Melville describes as a "cynosure"; his authority is likened to the captivating but forever reliable guidance of the North Star (1354).

As Arendt also emphasizes, Melville associated this unmediated presence of the good with the incapacity of speech and violence. Just as "spontaneous," "immediate," and "unconscious" as Budd's manifestations of natural goodness is the violence with which he reacts in the face of injustice. "Quick as lightning Billy let fly his arm" aboard *The Rights of Man* when harassed without provocation by Red Whiskers (1357). Paralyzed by a "convulsed tongue-tie" in the face of Claggart's false accusations, Budd "quick as a flame from a discharged cannon at night" knocks Claggart, his senior officer, to the ground (1404). Budd is abandoned by the mediating power of speech, and his ensuing violence manifests the tyrannical spirit beyond the mediating letter of the law, the violence of the Word made flesh.[24] Bereft of a capacity for worldly mediation, he can only "speak with a blow." It is not, however, simply the violence of the absolute that Melville dramatizes in the story, the focus of Arendt's reading, but the captivating appearance of the absolute that works to veil the violence of its claim to transcend the conditions of worldly mediated authority.

If Budd's terrible innocence is incapable of "double meanings and insinuations," and "seemed to have little or none" of "self-consciousness" (1359), Claggart is malevolent duplicity personified. As a portrait of "radical evil," not only does Claggart suspect the motivations of everyone around him—he even suspects Budd of being a "mantrap under the ruddy-tipped daisies"—but his own motivations are a black hole of unintelligibility. Like Budd, a foundling with no known origin, Claggart has a mysterious past, but one shrouded by a dark veil of suspected criminality. Because of Melville's insistence on Claggart's inscrutability, and even taking into consideration the prurient "affair of the spilled soup," I am not persuaded by readings of the novel that explain Claggart's actions by reference to his repressed homosexual desire.[25] It is explanation or the legibility of motivation itself that Melville denies in his presentation of Claggart: "to pass from a normal nature to his, one must cross the deadly space between" (1383). If Budd's authority is engendered through an unmediated harmonization of its inner source and outer appearance, Claggart's power emerges from the unbridgeable gap between these registers of being. In his actions Claggart appears the most "rational," "efficient," and "deliberate" of men—the personification of utilitarian instrumental reason—but these outward instrumentalities serve obscure but suspected malevolent ends. Indeed, Melville suggests their power resides in part *in* this very unintelligibility (a theme also explored on a different register by that "inscrutable scrivener" Bartleby). Insight into Claggart's motives requires the "lexicon of the Holy Writ" and spiritual perception of the "Hebrew prophets," the narrator states, rather than the empirical legal code of "Coke and Blackstone" (1382). "Though [Claggart's] even temper and discreet bearing would seem to intimate a mind peculiarly subject to the law of reason, not the less in heart he would seem to riot in complete exemption from that law, having apparently little to do with reason further than to employ it as an ambidexter implement for effecting the irrational. . . . Toward the accomplishment of an aim which in wantonness of atrocity would seem to partake of the insane, he will direct a cool judgment sagacious and sound" (1383). Through Claggart Melville offers a penetrating critique of instrumental reason. The dark malevolence of Claggart's motivation is hidden behind his "constitutional sobriety," "ferreting genius," "ingratiating deference to superiors," and "austere patriotism." Claggart, Eichmann-like, possesses a scrupulous instrumental rationality that veils the insanity or evil of the ends it serves. Claggart's composed facade is, however, like Budd's harmonization of innocence and beauty, presented by the narrator as a product of nature. Against both Paine's Enlightenment rationalism and the expressive nature of his transcendentalist contemporaries, Melville was insistent on the natural existence of radical evil. Claggart's "evil nature" was "not engendered by vicious training or corrupting books or licentious living, but born with him and innate" (1383). Claggart was the kind of man of whom John Rawls would famously write, his nature is his misfortune.[26]

As the *Bellipotent*'s "master-at-arms," Claggart was "a sort of chief of police charged among other matters with the duty of preserving order on the populous lower gun decks." Melville sets up a clear contrast between the spontaneous social order of Budd's "peacemaking" aboard *The Rights of Man* and the covert and manipulative disciplinary mechanisms employed by Claggart and his "understrappers." Whatever authority Claggart exercises over the crew of the *Bellipotent*—and *power* is the more appropriate term—is a product of fear and manipulative but subtle coercion. "Of this maritime chief of police the ship's corporals so called, were the immediate subordinates, and competent ones; and this, as is to be noted in some business departments ashore, *almost to a degree inconsistent with entire moral volition*. His place put various converging wires of underground influence under the chief's control, capable when astutely worked through his understrappers of operating to the mysterious discomfort, if nothing worse, of any of the sea commonality" (1376; emphasis added). Melville signals the illegitimacy of Claggart's power as "inconsistent with entire moral volition," and in doing so also remarks on the illegitimacy of the authority that structures the American workplace, a prominent theme in some of Melville's other stories, but he also emphasizes that this power works without relying on the means of direct confrontation and enforcement. Indeed, the story as a whole, as I will return to below, can be read as an inquiry into the varying degrees that constitute the juridical category of "moral volition." The "converging wires of underground influence," which Claggart works so astutely, and which are personified later in the story by the man who darkly hints at mutinous conspiracy to Budd, do maintain order aboard the ship, but they do so by means of inarticulate threat and insinuation internalized as pervasive and "mysterious discomfort" among the "sea commonality." Under Claggart's power a counterfeit environment of obedience based in manipulation and fear is established so that even spontaneous expressions of passion and feeling are shaped by a guarded self-consciousness. The crew laugh at the jokes and ironic remarks of the master-at-arms, for example, but they do so with a "counterfeit glee." In his presence all are disfigured into flatterers and courtesans. The malevolent duplicity on which Claggart's power is based is contagiously disseminated as pervasive mistrust among the crew. Even Vere is struck with "strong suspicion clogged by strange dubieties" in Claggart's presence. In Claggart Melville dramatizes a form of power reminiscent of classical republican theories of despotism like Montesquieu's, based not simply on fear of the despot but more centrally on the distancing mistrust between subjects, and a corrupting sense of being constantly subject to another's arbitrary will.[27] While Claggart's malevolence is portrayed as naturally evil, his power works by first separating the outward actions and inner beliefs of those subjected to him, and then separating these subjects from each other. If Budd's authority achieves a spontaneous union of fraternity and goodwill, Claggart's power works by corrosive and ubiquitous mistrust.

Unlike the natural power and authority of Claggart and Budd, Vere's authority is expressly unnatural, artificial, constituted by men. Vere is not a natural leader, but the holder of a legally constituted office. In Vere Melville offers an account of political authority without appeal to Nature or God. This is stated clearly in one of Vere's many addresses to the corporals assembled to serve as judges in Budd's trial, addresses that many readers have taken to be the express articulation of the political theory of the story: "Do these buttons that we wear attest that our allegiance is to Nature? No, to the King. Though the ocean, which is inviolate Nature primeval, though this be the element where we move and have our being as sailors, yet as the

King's officers lies our duty in a sphere correspondingly natural? So little is that true, that in receiving our commissions we in the most important regards ceased to be natural free agents" (1414). Portraying the sailors as so many "fast fish" (to use his term from *Moby-Dick*), Melville places agency and volition at the center of these questions of authority. Melville's complex presentation of Vere's character, judgment, and action has made Vere the centerpiece of most interpretations of the novella. Is Vere "an unambiguous figure of legitimate authority," as F. O. Matthiessen would have it, or does Vere's claim that the crew have "ceased to be natural free agents" simply restate the lack of "moral volition" associated with Claggart's illegitimate power, as Richard Weisberg argues?[28] These competing interpretations focus on the sources of Vere's authority (the king) or the extent to which he abides by or violates authorized legal procedures in establishing the drumhead court to try Budd for Claggart's death. As Vere's invocation of signifying "buttons" already suggests, however, here too Melville is focused on examining not only the sources but the aesthetic manifestation of his authority, not just why but how authority is constituted, sustained, and contested. Melville explores this theme most elaborately in the case of Vere, not only because Vere is the superior officer and highest authority aboard the *Bellipotent*, but because Vere at once enacts and theoretically reflects on the inexorably aesthetic dimensions of political authority. It is Vere, after all, who applies the lessons of Orpheus's spellbinding lyre to the revolutionary threat emanating from France and the need for "forms, measured forms."

The contrast Melville draws between bookish, "starry Vere" and Admiral Lord Nelson is revealing in this regard. Nelson represents for the narrator another expression of natural authority, here taking the form not of the "Handsome Sailor" but of the military hero. "Nelson," the narrator states, was one "not indeed to terrorize the crew into base subjection, but to win them, by force of his mere presence and heroic personality, back to an allegiance if not as enthusiastic as his own yet as true" (1366). In the heroic figure of Nelson, Melville provides a contrast to the deflationary "Benthamites of war" whose reductive materialism and squinting focus on social utility obscure the importance of inspirational exemplarity and the aesthetics of glory to establishing military authority. The "martial utilitarians" can only criticize as "foolhardiness and vanity," for example, the fact that Nelson, dressed in full military regalia, stood high on the quarterdeck of the *Victory* during the Battle of Trafalgar (1366). It was "a sort of priestly motive," the narrator states, that "led him to dress his person in the jeweled vouchers of his own shining deeds." Nelson's "ornate publication of his person" stands as a "poetic reproach" to the "new order" of a purportedly disenchanted modernity organized around authorities who no longer rely on those "exaltations of sentiment" that are "vitalized into acts" (1367). The narrator accuses this "new order" of a self-deluded and self-destructive "iconoclasm" that echoes Burke's famous comments about the dangerous consequences of tearing off the finely wrought veils and moral drapery of public life.

Vere also does not "terrorize the crew into base subjection," but neither is his authority grounded in the charismatic "presence [of his] heroic personality." Throughout the novella Melville emphasizes the legal constitution and artifice of Vere's authority, but he suggests that here too authority is sustained through what Burke called "pleasing illusions."[29] Like Burke, Vere rejects the self-evidence of natural law and the social-contract theories he associates with the French Revolution. Authority cannot be consistently or rigorously based in abstract justifications like free and equal consent, or popular sovereignty without fraudulence. Vere, the narrator reports, opposed the radicals and freethinkers of the Revolution, not out of the narrow class interest of "protectors of privilege," or because he believed these ideas were only "insusceptible of embodiment in lasting institutions," but because the appeal to the unmediated authority of Nature was at "war with the peace of the world and the true welfare of mankind" (1371). While Vere is portrayed as a philosophical conservative, one who recognizes the centrality of "forms, measured forms," he is also presented as a knowing and reflective conservative. He personifies Burke and expressly admires Montaigne. Vere, the narrator reports, has "acquired settled convictions which were like a dike against those invading waters of novel opinion, social, political, and otherwise." But these convictions are merely "settled," not grounded on rational reflection or epistemic certainty. Moreover, Vere is known to act and judge with prudence "under unforeseen difficulties requiring prompt initiative" (1396). He does not automatically rely on the authority of "precedent," "custom," "propriety," or "usage." Far from it. Vere's criteria of judgment, as I will elaborate in the next section, are eminently worldly and political, drawing on multiple contexts of consideration and attuned to questions of worldly appearances and popular reception, even when it comes to the theatrical appearance and sensuous form of legal procedure and judgment itself.

Melville's three-part characterology of authority in *Billy Budd* provides an important background for understanding the theoretical stakes of his account of Budd's trial, which has become a premier canonical example in modern law and literature scholarship.[30] Budd, Claggart, and Vere exemplify three modalities of personal authority, but the insights Melville accumulates from these accounts, particularly in regard to the relationship between authority and appearance, carry over into his treatment of the impersonal authority of the law overseen by Vere. The interweaving portraits of the novel's central characters prime readers to recognize continuities of preoccupation once the story descends belowdecks to Vere's improvised legal proceedings in the wake of Claggart's death. This is not a question of the source of authority before the law—king or Nature—so much as the presentation of law itself as a means of staging or reconstituting worldly authority in a state of emergency.

Forms, Measured Forms

Melville modeled Budd's quickly improvised trial, sentence, and execution on the *Somers* mutiny of 1842. "True, the circumstances on board the *Somers* were different from those on board the *Bellipotent*," Melville writes, "but the urgency felt, well-warranted or otherwise, was much the same" (1417). In November 1842 three men were tried by a summary court aboard the U.S.S. *Somers,* a naval frigate fighting in the Mexican-American War, for plotting a mutiny against the ship's officers. Among these officers was Melville's cousin Lieutenant Guert Gansevoort, who also played a leading role in the subsequent court-martial. Like Budd, the accused men were tried, condemned, and hanged at sea, which provoked controversy at the time for its breach of procedural protocol. When the *Somers* arrived back in New York shortly after the hangings, the ship's commander and other officers were pilloried in the press for assuming dictatorial powers in their handling of the case.[31] The press also emphasized that there was very little evidence that a mutiny had, in fact, been planned. With this case providing the relevant historical context, some have read *Billy Budd* as Melville's attempted literary rehabilitation of his cousin's reputation, but this seems a rather low-sited end for such an ambitious novelist, and other historical analogies present themselves.

On May 4, 1886—the same year Melville began writing *Billy Budd*—a bomb exploded in Chicago's Haymarket Square during a labor rally. Dozens of policemen were injured in the blast, and seven eventually died. The event immediately became a resonant symbol of the class struggle dividing America during the Gilded Age. The police arrested eight labor activists for the bombing, and what was proclaimed "the trial of the century" began the following month in Chicago's Cook County Courthouse.[32] Some scholars have argued that *Billy Budd* should be understood as Melville's "imaginative response to the Haymarket affair,"[33] and there are many intriguing parallels. Like Vere, Judge Gary appealed to emergency provisions in his conduct of the trial, and in both trials what was fundamentally at issue transcended local circumstances to assume an almost world historical significance. Julius Grinnell, the state's attorney, made these broader stakes clear in the prosecution's opening statement: "Gentlemen, for the first time in the history of our country people are on trial for endeavoring to make Anarchy the rule."[34] According to the state's argument, and trumpeted daily by the unprecedented coverage in the press, what was at stake in the legal trial of eight suspected anarchists was nothing short of the rule of law itself. "If I appreciate this case correctly," another state attorney, George Ingham, told the jury, "the . . . question . . . is whether organized government shall perish from the earth, whether the day of civilization shall go down into the night of barbarism."[35] The trial, conviction, and sentencing of the "Haymarket martyrs" was not only an expression of the state's authority, but also a powerful means of securing that authority. What the backdrop of this overtly political and infamous show trial in Chicago helps reveal about Melville's novella is how legal procedures—"forms, measured forms"—can be orchestrated to address broader worldly contexts of political authority. Just as the Haymarket trial addressed multiple and interweaving contexts of authority—from local struggles between labor activists and the Chicago police, for example, to the internationalist context of threatened proletarian revolution against industrial capitalism itself—so is Budd's trial embedded in a dense network of overlapping authoritative relations—from personalized relations aboard the ship, to relations within the fleet at a time of war, to mutinous challenges to naval authority, to the place of all authority in the Age of Democratic Revolutions. The fear of mutiny, insurrection, and revolution haunts the novella from its beginning to its end, as does the related difficulty of sustaining authority in the midst of such pervasive threat. "The similarities of historical moment," Alan Trachtenberg has rightly noted, "resound too insistently to be ignored."[36] The danger of insurrection and what Melville elsewhere called "riotocracy" (see Michael Jonik's contribution to this volume) not only is invoked as background historical context, but also intimately shapes the dialogue and interactions of almost every scene; it shapes the emotional environment and mood in which the story unfolds.

Billy Budd is, among other things, an investigation of how abstractions of power—state sovereignty, police power, the rule of law—are created, sustained, and contested in and through everyday performance and manifestation. It is a study of the intricate interdependence of these overlapping networks of authority, which become more brilliantly illuminated in times of emergency and crisis. Vere's understanding of this basic interdependence—at once sophisticated and intuitive—shapes his judgments and reactions to the unfolding events of the story and makes *Billy Budd* less a "judge's story" than a phenomenological analytics of authority. Vere's sensitivity to the mood of the crew and the "lurking" threat of sedition is indicated at every juncture of his decision making in the wake of Claggart's death. In each instance, the narrator directs the reader's attention to the relevant "antecedents" of Vere's judgments: "The unhappy event [of Claggart's death] . . . could not have happened at a worse juncture. . . . For it was close on the heel of the suppressed insurrections, an aftertime very critical to naval authority, demanding from every English sea commander two qualities not readily interfusable, prudence and rigor" (1407). The emergency considerations of the Nore Mutiny of 1797—itself occurring in the "aftertime" of the war with France (1793), and that in the "aftertime" of the French Revolution itself (1789)—shape Vere's quick decision to summarily and secretly convene a drumhead court to try Budd, even though this course of action clearly breaks from "usage," which would require that Budd be imprisoned until the "ship rejoined the squadron" and then tried under the authority of the admiralty.

The narrator admits that in the "irregularities" of the legal proceedings improvised by Vere (most important, its avoidance of "publicity") "there lurked some resemblance to the policy adopted in those tragedies of the palace" characteristic of the state mysteries of monarchical authority so thoroughly discredited in an era of enlightened republicanism (1408). But while Vere was "a conscientious disciplinarian," the narrator reports, he was also "no lover of authority for mere authority's sake" (1371). Instead, the narrator presents Vere's judgments as carefully calibrated to their "reasonable" political consequences in the critical "aftertime" of revolutionary unrest. A political realist of a distinctive sort, Vere seems to take the first political question to be "the securing of order, protection, safety, trust, and the conditions of cooperation."[37] "Feeling that unless quick action was taken on it, the deed of the foretopman, so soon as it should be known on the gun decks, would tend to awaken any slumbering embers of the Nore among the crew, a sense of the urgency of the case overruled in Captain Vere every other consideration" (1409). Not only does Vere convene the trial immediately and secretly, but he deviates again from "general custom" in the irregular makeup of the court itself and in his frequent interventions in the court proceedings. All these "deviations" are components of Vere's orchestration of the formal legal proceedings to subdue the "slumbering embers" of the "murmuring" crew. Aboard the H.M.S. *Bellipotent,* the secrecy of the proceedings is ultimately an essential part of the show.

Questioning the formal legality of Vere's decision making at this point in the narrative, and within the procedures of trial itself—as Richard Weisberg, for example, has exhaustively done—seems somewhat beside the point. Scholars have persuasively "demonstrated that Vere was not empowered to try and execute Billy under the laws governing the case,"[38] but the emphasis of the story seems continually to draw the reader's attention away from strict construction. Time and again, Melville refers to the broader worldly contexts within which the legal proceedings are situated. In one of his many "formal and informal" interventions into the trial, for example, Vere argues that even in the "arbitrary" proceedings of a martial court, it is not the strict terms of the Mutiny Act that should be taken into consideration, so much as the broader political *end* that the act was designed to serve. He urges the judges to be attentive to the spirit over the letter of the law, and that spirit has a terrible visage, indeed: "In feature no child can resemble his father more than that Act resembles in spirit the thing from which it derives—War. . . . War looks but to the frontage, the appearance. And the Mutiny Act, War's child, takes after the father" (1416). Further indicating the political, and perhaps even indirectly democratic, considerations of his improvised legal proceedings, and their importance as a manifestation and means of perpetuating political authority, Vere identifies the intended audience for the trial as "'the people' (meaning the ship's company)" (1416). In a speech to the judges, Vere argues that they must take into primary consideration, more than legal precedent or due process, the reaction of "the people" to their ultimate judgment and sentence. "The people have native sense . . . how would they take it?" Vere asks. Again, Vere refers to the "recent outbreak at the Nore" as the relevant context: "Your clement sentence they [the people] would account pusillanimous. They would think that we flinch, that we are afraid of them—afraid of practicing a lawful rigor singularly demanded at this juncture, lest it should provoke new troubles. What shame to us such a conjecture on their part, and how deadly to discipline" (1416). Melville embeds the court's legal judgment, in other words, within the larger political context of anticipated popular response.

Vere's negotiation of legal proceedings in the story navigates between a rule-bound formalism and extralegal dictate, summed up by Melville's felicitous phrase "lawful rigor." But the improvisational approach that Vere takes to these legal proceedings would seem to be at odds with his pronouncement of the importance of "forms, measured forms." Indeed, several critics who have explored the centrality of Vere's invocation of "forms" to the political meaning of the story have done so to emphasize his (and Melville's) "acceptance of convention, law, expediency and authority."[39] In Vere's invocation of forms a number of critics have identified Melville's late and tragic concession to the "regularities of custom and law."[40] What these approaches do not sufficiently account for, however, is the specific mythic reference that exemplifies the broader theoretical point; they do not adequately engage the fact that it is the spellbinding power of "the lyre of Orpheus" that subdues the "wild denizens of the wood" and thereby demonstrates the import of mankind's need for "forms, measured forms."[41] A focus on the musical enchantment of these forms over their conventional or customary qualities brings to the fore the sensuous dimension of authority emphasized here. Moreover, this dimension is further highlighted by the events that precede and frame the narrator's invocation of Orpheus's lyre. Several stunning episodes of biblical murmuring and incipient insurrection punctuate the novel's final pages, following the announcement of Budd's condemnation and his hanging and burial at sea.[42] Each of these moments brings to the fore an assemblage of mesmeric agency and sensory soft compulsion that constitutes and sustains the novel's relations of authority.

The aftermath of Budd's trial suggests that Vere's overriding concerns with the specter of latent insubordination among "the people" were warranted and his judgment thereby (at least partially) vindicated, and this indeterminate latency of revolt is expanded on in the final pages of the novel as an object of sustained literary reflection. The first episode occurs after Vere announces the trial, judgment, and sentence of Budd to the assembled crew. "A confused murmur went up. It began to wax. All but instantly, then, at a sign, it was pierced and suppressed by shrill whistles of the boatswain and his mates" (1421). The officials' suppression of this first episode of inchoate "murmuring" and incipient or virtual insurrection by means of a "shrill whistle" suggests a sensuous recollection of form, a well-timed reorganization of the regimented community of sense that sustains authority aboard the H.M.S. *Bellipotent.* By means of these "shrill whistles" of the boatswain and his mates, the murmuring multitude is effectively reinterpellated into habitually subordinated subjectivity. The narrator suggests that this return to form is physically primed by the disciplined military habituation of the crew, because sailors, "of all men," are "the greatest sticklers for usage" (1421).

The mesmeric automatic nature of this collective response is echoed in three additional episodes that follow in quick succession. As Budd stands on the mainyard with the "ignominious hemp about his neck," he utters, or sings, his famous last words: "God bless Captain Vere!" This line, "delivered in the clear melody of a singing bird on the point of launching from a twig," had, the narrator continues, "a phenomenal effect, not unenhanced by the rare personal beauty of the young sailor" (1426). The melodious clarity of Budd's voice alongside his "now spiritualized" beauty also effects the spellbinding charm of Orpheus's lyre: "Without volition, as it were, as if indeed the ship's populace were but vehicles of some current electric, with one voice from alow and aloft came a resonant sympathetic echo: 'God bless Captain Vere!'" (1426). Melville's emphasis on this "current electric" and the "spontaneous echo" of the crew suggests a mode of resonant affective or infrasensible communication that recurs at several points in the novella (and also in "The Quarter-Deck" chapter of *Moby-Dick*) and signals his attempt to elucidate a practical state of mesmeric volition obscured by theoretical discussions of authority emphasizing voluntary consent or rational calculations of utility.[43] Vere's famously indeterminate response to Budd's final words suggests a similar condition: "either through stoic self-control or a sort of momentary paralysis induced by emotional shock, [Vere] stood erectly rigid as a musket in the ship-armorer's rack" (1427). The practical ambiguities of agency and volition are at the center of the novel and its treatment of authority and its expressly aesthetic mechanisms.

In the wave-washing silence that follows Budd's hanging, Melville offers the novel's most sustained examination of these prearticulate affective orientations and dispositions. The passage is worth quoting at length, as it elaborates on both the ambiguity of the significance of insubordinate murmuring and the sonorous dimensions of its emergence and dissipation:

> This emphasized silence was gradually disturbed by a sound not easily to be verbally rendered. Whoever has heard the freshet-wave of a torrent suddenly swelled by pouring showers not shared by the plain; whoever has heard the first muffled murmur of its sloping advance through the precipitous woods may form some conception of the sound now heard. The seeming remoteness of its source was because of its murmurous indistinctness, since it came from close by, even from the men passed on the ship's open deck. Being inarticulate, it was dubious in significance further than it seemed to indicate some capricious revulsion of thought or feeling such as mobs ashore are liable to, in the present instance possibly implying a sullen revocation on the men's part of their involuntarily echoing Billy's benediction. (1429)

The "spontaneous echo" is here replaced by another resonant but inarticulate murmuring and, as is true of the earlier example, this inchoate unsettlement of the ship's orderly community of sense is quickly reorganized by means of a disciplinary sonorous intervention. "But ere the murmur had time to wax into clamor it was met by strategic command, the more telling that it came with abrupt unexpectedness." "Shrill as a shriek of the sea hawk, the silver whistles of the boatswain and his mates pierced that ominous low sound, dissipating it; and yielding to the mechanism of discipline the throng was thinned by one-half" (1429).

As if to underscore the significance of this interference of sound and affective reorganization, Melville offers another example. As Budd's body is cast to sea in his hammock, Melville recounts a final incident of incipient insurrection dispelled by intervening sensory reorganization and the retrenchment of the reigning community of sense. Just as the body slides to sea, "a second strange human murmur was heard. . . . An uncertain movement began among them, in which some encroachment was made. It was tolerated but for a moment. For suddenly the drum beat to quarters, which familiar sound happening at least twice every day, had upon the present occasion a signal peremptoriness in it. True martial discipline long continued superinduces in average man a sort of impulse whose operation at the official word of command much resembles in its promptitude the effect of an instinct. The drumbeat dissolved the multitude" (1430). Dissolved them into what? A disaggregated collective of disciplined individuals? A regimen? A regime? The quick succession of these aural interventions depicted at the novel's end seems to attempt to mimic the very rhythmic reorganization they describe. In this final episode, which immediately precedes Vere's invocation of "forms, measured forms," Melville describes a form of subordinated subjectivity "toned by music and religious rites" that provides the corporeal or sensory *preconditions* of command (1430). The drumbeat that conclusively "dissolves the multitude" at the end of *Billy Budd* echoes the drumhead court convened to suppress "the slumbering embers of the Nore." Melville suggests a continuity or interdependence between these forms usually thought of in isolation—the rule of law, sensory enchantment, and disciplinary organization—that emphasizes not only the "acceptance of convention, law, expediency and authority," but the aesthetic means of constituting and sustaining that authority. As Elizabeth Samet writes in her study of the cultural negotiations of autonomy and obedience in nineteenth-century American literature, "In the traditional dynamics of command and obedience there is always something covert, mysterious, magnetic, and fundamentally unreasoning, something unaccounted for by rational theories of the rights of man."[44]

In each of these concluding episodes of murmuring, Melville dwells on an inchoate collective incipience—affective, shifting, episodic—that has not yet been organized as a legible articulation of resistance or subordination (a preoccupation prefigured in earlier stories such as "Bartleby" and *Benito Cereno*), a collective defined by affective orientation not yet cohered into the cogency of an articulation or a claim. His text lingers on these charged but indefinite moments, registering the subtle empirical contours of a typically unrecognized and ephemeral potentiality before it crosses over into legible experience or registers as an event. In these episodes Melville illuminates the fleeting potentiality and virtuality of resistance, and its sensory subordination and capture. He seems fascinated by the indeterminacy of such collective states, as they drift along in a kind of mesmeric attraction between voluntarism and habituated behavior. In each instance the emergence of some new, more threatening form is deftly assuaged and redirected through a sensory directive of whistle and drum. In each instance an order is restored through the sensory redirection of aesthetic experience.

This returns us, by way of conclusion, to Melville's reliance on Burke's theory of political authority in *Billy Budd.* It is widely accepted that the principles Vere espouses in the novella, particularly those statements Vere makes concerning the significance and political modernity of the French Revolution, echo Burke's *Reflections on the Revolution in France,* a book Melville first encountered in his adolescence and referred to explicitly in *Mardi.*[45] A Burkean conservatism has also been attributed to the narrator when, for example, he describes the Nore mutineers as replacing "the flag of founded law and freedom" with the "enemy's red meteor of unbridled and unbounded revolt . . . ignited into irrational combustion as by live cinders blown across the Channel from France in flames" (1363). Thomas Scorza has argued that Melville's critique of enlightened liberalism in *Billy Budd* actually occurred within "a more general critique of the whole of modernity" influenced by Burke's writing.[46] But what did Melville take from Burke? Was it Vere's prudent consequentialism, or his embrace of settled conventions and usage? The above discussion provides evidence that neither interpretation adequately characterizes Vere's actions in the novella, or Melville's pointed emphases on the choreography of sensation. I want to suggest that what Melville drew most clearly from Burke in *Billy Budd* is the latter's attention to the worldly context of law, its embedding in cultural and institutional networks of authority, and also the crucially aesthetic dimensions of that authority's constitution and maintenance over time. It is not simple violence or the threat of violence that lies behind the authority of the law—as Burke eloquently puts the point, the gallows do not stand behind "every vista"; rather, its authority is engendered through the means of what Melville described as "external arts and entrenchments."[47] These are not mere "ornaments" and "fictions" but the very vehicles enacting authority. Burke had a profound understanding of how political authority was actually maintained and supported through a dense network of adorned authoritative relations throughout society. "The public affections," as Burke put the point, "combined with manners, are required as supplements, sometimes as correctives, always as aids to the law."[48] All the "props of authority" that Paine summarily condemned under the name of a "Quixotic age of chivalrous nonsense" are argued by Melville to be not so easily gotten rid of.[49] To attempt to do without these "props" is to succumb to dangerous fantasies of autonomy, mastery, and sovereignty that Melville created Ahab to at once exemplify and critically expose, but that is another story.[50]

Melville's investigation of the interrelationship between authority and aesthetic form in *Billy Budd* carries through to the "ragged edges" of the novella's famous afterword and conclusion. "The symmetry of form attainable in pure fiction," Melville writes, "cannot so readily be achieved in a narration essentially having less to do with fable than with fact. Truth uncompromisingly told will always have its ragged edges; hence the conclusion of such a narration is apt to be less finished than an architectural finial" (1431). The "ragged edges" of Melville's "inside narrative" are contrasted at the novel's end with two subsequent tales of the tragic events aboard the H.M.S. *Bellipotent* during the year of the "Great Mutiny." "What Melville's tale tells," Barbara Johnson writes, is in the end "the snowballing of tale telling."[51] The narrator reports that the first of these concluding tales appeared in "an authorized weekly publication" of the British navy under the head "'News from the Mediterranean.'" In the alchemy of this official transcript Budd is converted into an alien and vindictive murderer, while Claggart appears as a "respectable," "responsible" "victim" with "strong patriotic impulse" (1433). Though this official narrative serves an authorizing function in "His Majesty's navy," it also disappears completely from public memory; "long ago superannuated and forgotten," this journalistic record is simply replaced by the next round of reported news and quickly buried in the archival ash heap of official history.

The second "record" also falsifies "the secret facts of the tragedy," but it effects a transmutation of a different sort. "Billy in the Darbies," the "rude" ballad with which the novel ends, springs from the naval world of the bluejackets themselves. Captivated by "the fresh young image of the Handsome sailor" and haunted by the "fact he was gone, and in a measure mysteriously gone," this "hidden transcript" of the events orally circulates a "knowledge" directly opposed to officialdom.[52] The "instinctive" sense of Budd's innocence and the injustice of his sacrifice are given poetic form by another foretopman gifted with an "artless poetic temperament." Written from the perspective of Budd on the night before his hanging, the sailor shanty imagines the final moments of Budd's life and his death. "But aren't it all sham?" Budd asks, "A blur's in my eyes; it is dreaming that I am." Unlike the official record, "Billy in the Darbies" converts "the striking incident" aboard the

Bellipotent into a lasting "monument" (1434). Here aesthetic form still captivates and spellbinds but serves the ends of popular subversion rather than authority. It resonates with the murmuring insubordination of the crew rather than their habituated obedience to "usage."

Thanks to Harrison Hayford and Merton M. Sealts's genetic analysis of Melville's manuscript, we know that the ballad with which the novel ends was actually the text that inspired the "inside narrative" itself. Melville began writing "Billy of the Darbies" in early 1896, and it is from these few lines that *Billy Budd, Sailor (An Inside Narrative)* would develop in Melville's notes over the next five years. In this sense, *Billy Budd* is itself the "monument" of its eponymous hero's death. Unlike monuments that provide sensuous markers of an authorizing discourse, however—think of Melville's ironic dedication of *Israel Potter* to "His Majesty the Bunker Hill Monument"—Budd's inside narrative neither sanctifies nor condemns.[53] The story at once invites and resists the allegorical readings that have so often been applied to it. Its self-proclaimed "ragged edges" and lack of formal "symmetry" bespeak the unresolved conflicts that are enacted in the text itself.

One last historical anecdote will bring this essay to its own ragged ending. On the box where he kept the manuscript of *Billy Budd*, Melville glued a piece of paper commanding him to "keep true to the dreams of thy YOUTH!" How to sustain a commitment to radical egalitarianism and affirm what Melville called "unconditional democracy in all things," while also recognizing—and to some extent equally affirming—the spellbinding allure of authority in everyday life? The common view of Melville as a democratic egalitarian in his youth and a conservative in his middle and old age effectively effaces the persistence of this conflict in *Billy Budd*. It is true that Melville was "one of early America's frankest commentators on the hopes and the failures of democracy," and the twinned and tragic preoccupation with hope *and* failure also characterized his last work of fiction.[54] Melville believed prevailing theories of political authority based in consent and social utility did not provide adequate resources—symbolic, theoretical, and literary—for confronting and navigating the tensions that constitute an aesthetic democracy, and he worked to make up for that deficit in many of his novels, including *Billy Budd*. Rather than resolving or hoping to transcend these tensions, *Billy Budd* put them on tragic display (see my introduction to this volume). The pervasive sense of irresolution in the novel is even stylistically transmitted in Melville's almost compulsive use of double negatives, which, in Sharon Cameron's words, "at once assert and retract assertion, speak and undo speech, . . . establish and nullify."[55] Melville's last will and testament continues to illuminate the practical and irresolute terrain of political authority—its complicated assemblage of soft compulsion and mesmeric assent—still obscured by the dominant paradigms of contemporary democratic theory. It is his own effort to do the work that Vere admires in the essays of Montaigne: to "philosophize on realities." Less a political treatise offering norms than an acute literary examination of an irresolvable political problematic, *Billy Budd* continues to provoke and disturb, captivate and enchant.

Notes

1. Herman Melville, *Billy Budd*, in *Pierre, Israel Potter, The Piazza Tales, The Confidence-Man, Uncollected Prose, Billy Budd* (New York: Library of America, 1984), 1409; hereinafter cited as Melville, *Pierre . . . Billy Budd*. Further references to this work are to this volume and given parenthetically in the text.

2. E. L. Grant Watson, "Melville's Testament of Acceptance," *New England Quarterly* 6, no. 2 (1933): 319–327; Phil Withim, "*Billy Budd:* Testament of Resistance," *Modern Language Quarterly* 20, no. 2 (June 1959): 115–127.

3. Robert Milder, introduction to *Critical Essays on Melville's* Billy Budd, Sailor, ed. Robert Milder (Boston: G. K. Hall, 1989), 1.

4. Hannah Arendt, *On Revolution* (1963; repr., New York: Penguin Books, 1990), 83–87.

5. Michael Paul Rogin, *Subversive Genealogy: The Politics and Art of Herman Melville* (New York: Knopf, 1983), 302.

6. Elizabeth Samet, *Willing Obedience: Citizens, Soldiers, and the Progress of Consent in America, 1776–1898* (Stanford: Stanford University Press, 2004), 207.

7. See especially William V. Spanos, *The Exceptionalist State and the State of Exception: Herman Melville's* Billy Budd, Sailor (Baltimore: Johns Hopkins University Press, 2011).

8. On Burke's aesthetic account of political authority, see Terry Eagleton, "Aesthetics and Politics in Edmund Burke," *History Workshop* 28 (Autumn 1989): 53–62; Jason Frank, "Delightful Horror: Edmund Burke and the Aesthetics of Democratic Revolution," in *The Aesthetic Turn in Political Thought*, ed. Nikolis Kompridis (New York: Continuum, 2013); Daniel O'Neill, "The Sublime, the Beautiful, and the Political in Burke's Work," in *The Science of Sensibility: Read-*

ing Burke's Philosophical Enquiry, ed. Koen Vermeir and Michael Funk Deckard (New York: Springer, 2011), 193–224; Stephen K. White, *Edmund Burke: Modernity, Politics, and Aesthetics* (Thousand Oaks, Calif.: Sage, 1994).

9. H. L. A. Hart, *The Concept of Law* (New York: Oxford University Press, 1961). For a compelling interpretation that emphasizes Melville's dramatic departure from a positivist conception of law, see Jennifer Culbert's contribution to this volume, "Melville's Law."

10. This topic has not been adequately explored by contemporary political theorists, especially in relation to democratic political authority. Works that offer helpful preliminary orientation to this question include Clifford Geertz, *Negara: The Theatre State in Nineteenth-Century Bali* (Princeton: Princeton University Press, 1980); Clifford Geertz, "Centers, Kings, and Charisma: Reflections on the Symbolics of Power," in *Culture and Its Creators*, ed. Joseph Ben-David and Terry Nichols Clark (Chicago: University of Chicago Press, 1977); Roy Strong, *Art and Power: Renaissance Festivals, 1450–1650* (Berkeley: University of California Press, 1984); Ajume H. Wingo, *Veil Politics in Liberal Democratic States* (New York: Cambridge University Press, 2003).

11. Franz Kafka, "Before the Law," in Kafka, *In the Penal Colony* (New York: Schocken, 1961), 148–150.

12. Rogin, *Subversive Genealogy*, 296.

13. Herman Melville, "Shiloh," in *Battle-Pieces and Aspects of the War* (1866; repr., Amherst, N.Y.: Prometheus Books, 2001), 93.

14. Jacques Rancière, *Dis-agreement: Politics and Philosophy*, trans. Julie Rose (Minneapolis: University of Minnesota Press, 1999), 57.

15. Jacques Derrida, "Before the Law," in *Acts of Literature*, ed. Derek Attridge (New York: Routledge, 1991), 181–220.

16. Richard Flathman, *Freedom and Its Conditions: Discipline, Autonomy, and Resistance* (New York: Routledge, 2003), 69.

17. Alan Heimert, "*Moby-Dick* and American Political Symbolism," *American Quarterly* 15, no. 4 (Winter 1963): 498–534.

18. Herman Melville, *Benito Cereno*, in *Pierre . . . Billy Budd*, 676.

19. Mary K. Bercaw Edwards, "Ships, Whaling, and the Sea," in *A Companion to Herman Melville*, ed. Wyn Kelley (Oxford: Blackwell, 2006), 83.

20. Herman Melville, *Moby-Dick* (New York: Library of America, 1991), 197.

21. Samet, *Willing Obedience*, 9.

22. Richard H. Weisberg, "Accepting the Inside Narrator's Challenge: More on the Christ Figure in *Billy Budd, Sailor*," in *Poethics, and Other Strategies of Law and Literature*, ed. Weisberg (New York: Columbia University Press, 1992), 106.

23. On "characterology," see Amanda Anderson, *How We Argue Now: A Study in the Cultures of Theory* (Princeton: Princeton University Press, 2012), 115–133.

24. See Tracy McNulty, *Wrestling with the Angel* (New York: Columbia University Press, forthcoming).

25. Most notably, Eve Kosofsky Sedgwick, *Epistemology of the Closet* (Berkeley: University of California Press, 1990), 91–130.

26. John Rawls, *A Theory of Justice* (Cambridge: Harvard University Press, 1971), 576.

27. Quentin Skinner emphasizes this aspect of republicanism in *Liberty before Liberalism* (New York: Cambridge University Press, 1998).

28. F. O. Matthiessen, *American Renaissance: Art and Expression in the Age of Emerson and Whitman* (New York: Oxford University Press, 1941), 514; Richard H. Weisberg, "Accepting the Inside Narrator's Challenge: *Billy Budd* and the 'Legalistic' Reader," *Cardozo Studies in Law and Literature* 1, no. 1 (Spring 1989): 27–48.

29. Edmund Burke, *Reflections on the Revolution in France*, ed. J. G. A. Pocock (1790; repr., Indianapolis: Hackett, 1987), 67.

30. See the essays compiled in "Symposium on Billy Budd," *Cardozo Studies in Law and Literature* 1, no. 1 (Spring 1989).

31. Rogin, *Subversive Genealogy*, 294–296.

32. James Green, *Death in the Haymarket: A Story of Chicago, the First Labor Movement and the Bombing That Divided Gilded Age America* (New York: Pantheon, 2006).

33. Robert K. Wallace, "*Billy Budd* and the Haymarket Hangings," *American Literature* 47, no. 1 (March 1975): 108–113.

34. Quoted in Green, *Death in the Haymarket*, 214.

35. Quoted ibid., 224.

36. Alan Trachtenberg, *The Incorporation of America: Culture and Society in the Gilded Age* (New York: Hill & Wang, 1982), 203.

37. Bernard Williams, *In the Beginning Was the Deed: Realism and Moralism in Political Argument* (Princeton: Princeton University Press, 2012), 3.

38. Weisberg, "Accepting the Inside Narrator's Challenge."

39. Larry J. Reynolds, "*Billy Budd* and American Labor Unrest: The Case for Striking Back," in *New Essays on* Billy Budd, ed. Donald Yannella (New York: Cambridge University Press, 2002), 21–48. See, however, Roger Berkowitz's account of Melville's troubled commitment to poetic and political form in his contribution to this volume, "Melville's War Poetry and the Human Form."

40. James R. Hurtgen, "Melville: *Billy Budd* and the Context of Political Rule," in *The Artist and Political Vision*, ed. Benjamin Barber (New Brunswick, N.J.: Transaction, 1983), 261.

41. See Harrison Hayford and Merton M. Sealts Jr.'s discussion in their annotated edition of *Billy Budd, Sailor (An Inside Narrative)* (Chicago: University of Chicago Press, 1962), 196.

42. For an insightful literary examination of the role of "murmuring" in Melville's work, see Michael Jonik, "Murmurs, Stutters, Foreign Intonations: Melville's Unreadables," *Oxford Literary Review* 33, no. 1 (2011): 21–44.

43. On the politics of the "infrasensible," see William Connolly, *Neuropolitics: Thinking, Culture, Speed* (Minneapolis: University of Minnesota Press, 2002).

44. Samet, *Willing Obedience*, 205.

45. Hershel Parker, *Herman Melville: A Biography*, vol. 1, *1819–1851* (Baltimore: Johns Hopkins University Press, 1996), 605.

46. Thomas J. Scorza, *In the Time before Steamships:* Billy Budd, *the Limits of Politics, and Modernity* (DeKalb: Northern Illinois University Press, 1979), 173.

47. Burke, *Reflections*, 68; Melville, *Moby-Dick*, 179.

48. Burke, *Reflections*, 68.

49. Thomas Paine, "Rights of Man," in *Political Writings*, ed. Bruce Kuklick (Cambridge: Cambridge University Press, 1989), 86.

50. I develop this reading of *Moby-Dick* in "Pathologies of Freedom in Melville's America," in *Radical Future Pasts: Untimely Essays in Political Theory*, ed. Romand Coles, Mark Reinhardt, and George Shulman (Lexington: University Press of Kentucky, forthcoming).

51. Barbara Johnson, "Melville's Fist: The Execution of *Billy Budd*," in Johnson, *The Critical Difference: Essays in the Contemporary Rhetoric of Reading* (Baltimore: Johns Hopkins University Press, 1980), 79–109.

52. See James C. Scott, *Domination and the Arts of Resistance: Hidden Transcripts* (New Haven: Yale University Press, 1992).

53. Herman Melville, *Israel Potter*, in *Pierre. . . Billy Budd*, dedication.

54. Wilson Carey McWilliams, "Herman Melville: The Pilgrim," in McWilliams, *The Idea of Fraternity in America* (Berkeley: University of California Press, 1973), 328–371.

55. Sharon Cameron, "'Lines of Stones': The Unpersonified Impersonal in Melville's *Billy Budd*," in Cameron, *Impersonality: Seven Essays* (Chicago: University of Chicago Press, 2007), 184.

Melville's Law

Jennifer L. Culbert

When we think about law, how often do we essay a portrait and fail to hit it? As the legal philosopher H. L. A. Hart observes, "Few questions concerning human society have been asked with such persistence and answered by serious thinkers in so many diverse, strange, and even paradoxical ways as the question 'What is law?'"[1] Hart suggests that the difficulty of answering this question once and for all is due to the challenge of addressing issues raised when we think about law, issues like the nature of obligation, the relationship of law to justice, and the meaning of rules.[2] In this essay I suggest that these issues present such a challenge because we conceive of them in terms of a particular philosophical tradition. In this tradition we try to grasp the essence of law.[3] Inspired by the fiction of Herman Melville, I propose we take another tack. Specifically, I propose we consider how all these diverse, strange, and even paradoxical answers to the question "What is law?" may be understood not as unsuccessful attempts to grasp the essence of law but rather as reflections of the experience of law.

When this experience is described in the conventional literature, it is usually represented as an experience of being subject to an external or internal will that uses the promise of physical harm, moral suffering, psychological pain, or social distress to deprive us of the opportunity to achieve or enjoy some desired end. This characterization of law reflects the major premise of legal positivism—that law is what is posited by a will or, rather, "a will empowered so to will" that thereby binds us.[4] When I pay close attention to the experience of law, however, what I observe is not an experience of subjection to or triumph of a will but rather an experience like love.

To describe this experience, I turn to Melville's final, and famously unfinished, novella, *Billy Budd*.[5] *Billy Budd* is a work of fiction that has been interpreted, like Sophocles's *Antigone*, as depicting the tragic consequences of an irresolvable conflict between natural (or ancient or divine) law and positive (or modern or state) law.[6] This conflict is frequently represented as a war of wills: the gods' versus the king's, God's versus man's, the people's versus the state's, the individual's versus society's, the individual's versus itself. On my account of *Billy Budd,* these interpretations do not illuminate key tensions in the text as much as they illustrate the hegemony of legal positivism in the modern world.[7] In this essay I do not comment directly on that claim. Instead, I show how the experience of law in Melville's work is like an experience of love.

With this remark, I do not mean to suggest that law *is* love for Melville—or for anyone else, for that matter—but rather that law is *like* love. This is an important distinction because the analogy collapses or obscures a distance between law and love, a distance that the simile preserves. And it is in this in-between space, I argue, that we may glimpse the possibility of law as something other than a will working through opposition to realize a particular social or political order.[8] Specifically, we may see law not as a willed blow resolving matters but as a touch exposing and unsettling them.

Obviously, this is an unusual way to discuss law. I do so in the spirit of a legal realist who takes seriously the claim that we live in an appearing world, so that when law is defined as "whatever judges or other relevant officials do," it is defined by what is seen to be done.[9] This means that, unlike legal realists such as Jerome Frank, I eschew psychological (and gastronomical) approaches to law in an attempt to attend to what appears or what presents itself.[10] Though these appearances may imply interiorities in the same way that a surface may imply a three-dimensional space, Melville's style of writing bids us to resist the habit of projecting the hidden depths we typically mine for meaning. Or, rather, it constantly tempts us to indulge this habit but abandons us in the pit when we try to come up with something tangible and certain.[11] Thus, I begin to answer the question "What is law?" by reading Melville's story *closely* rather than *deeply,* sticking to the surface to see what *Billy Budd* makes possible for us to think about law.

Law

There are more interpretations of *Billy Budd* than there are readers of Melville's final piece of fiction. The long short story revolves around a handsome sailor with a "vocal defect" named Billy Budd, who is pressed into service as a foretopman on a British warship, the *Bellipotent,* during the Napoleonic Wars and after the Spithead and Nore mutinies. Budd is popular with everyone except for the ship's master-at-arms, John Claggart, who accuses the young sailor of plotting mutiny. Brought before the ship's captain, Captain Edward Vere, to answer the charge, Budd is tongue-tied. Urged by the captain to defend himself, the foretopman suddenly strikes the master-at-arms with his fist, killing the superior officer instantly. To determine what should be done with Budd, Captain Vere convenes a drumhead court, at which he is not only the primary witness to the events in question but also the presiding officer. The captain is clearly sympathetic to the sailor but nevertheless pushes the court to sentence him to death. The next morning, as the ship's crew watches, Budd is hanged. The story concludes with three different endings. One ending is a tale about Captain Vere on his deathbed; his last words are Billy Budd's name. The second tale is an account of events printed in an authorized naval publication, according to which a noble Claggart is stabbed to death by Billy Budd, who is cast as the ringleader of a plot against the *Bellipotent.* The final tale is a ballad in which Billy Budd anticipates his execution, speaking his last words as if already at the bottom of the sea.

It is commonly observed that when Billy Budd is sentenced to hang, his penalty is never completely legally justified.[12] When Captain Vere informs the ship's surgeon of his decision to convene a drumhead court, the doctor is struck by the captain's choice to depart from convention. The surgeon knows the captain could simply have put Billy Budd in confinement, "in a way dictated by usage," and waited until the *Bellipotent* rejoined the squadron to refer the whole matter to the admiral (1406–1407). The surgeon, however, does not question or resist the captain's orders because he realizes that to do so would be mutiny (1407). In other words, he defers not out of respect for custom or tradition but out of fear of punishment under martial law. We might summarize, then, by saying that what is theoretically recognized as law may ultimately be based on "social rules," but it seems that what is actually practiced as law is ultimately based on threats of violence.[13]

The captain, however, seems to worry not so much about the reactions of his officers to his decision as about the response of the crew. Specifically, the captain expresses concern that the crew will interpret the failure to punish a sailor for killing a superior officer as a sign of fear (1416–1417). Putting Billy Budd in confinement would then be "deadly to discipline"

(1417). In other words, Captain Vere determines Billy Budd not only must be put on trial but also must die because the men expect the foretopman to be punished severely, and the captain is concerned that if he violates the crew's expectations he will lose control of the ship. In brief, he worries that waiting to punish Billy Budd will strike the sailors as wrong, and it will strike them as wrong because they have been trained to assume that a certain type of behavior on the *Bellipotent* is normal.[14]

Thus, both despite *and* because of the fact that the men on board the *Bellipotent* have been drilled in military discipline to such a degree that "a sort of impulse whose operation at the official word of command much resembles in its promptitude the effect of an instinct," any violation of convention appears to threaten to undermine the efficacy, and legitimacy, of the captain's orders (1430).[15]

As usage dictates both that Captain Vere wait to try Billy Budd and that he act immediately to put down a threat—a threat that, to complicate matters further, may not even materialize until the captain tries to put it down—it would seem that the law of social rules is really no law at all.[16] At the same time, on its own terms, martial law appears no more "legitimate" than usage because its efficacy depends on circumstances that it does not completely control. Despite his position of authority, Captain Vere cannot simply do as he wishes. In the end, Captain Vere is damned if he acts and damned if he does not. No matter what he decides to do, the "legitimacy" of his decision is compromised, and, consequently, the violence he commands and uses to effect his decision is not completely legal. No coherent philosophy or practice of law authorizes him to condemn Billy Budd to death. When the surgeon comes to examine Claggart's body in Captain Vere's cabin, Captain Vere suddenly exclaims, "Struck dead by an angel of God! Yet the angel must hang!" (1406). As many readers have observed and complained, this "must" is never fully explained.[17] Its source and its force are as mysterious as Claggart's feelings for Billy Budd.[18]

I find two possible explanations of this "must" compelling but problematic. The first explanation casts Captain Vere's decision to execute Billy Budd as an exercise of sovereign power. Melville's story is set in 1797. The British navy is at war with French revolutionary forces. At the same time, mutiny has broken out, not once but twice, threatening the British fleet. The normal rule of law has been suspended and martial law governs the British on the high seas. It is an exceptional moment. Captain Vere reminds the drumhead court of this fact when he observes that the court operates according to a code dictated by "imperial" rather than private conscience (1415). Acknowledging the hesitation of the officers on the drumhead court to condemn Billy Budd, Captain Vere recurs to "the facts": "In wartime at sea a man-of-war's man strikes his superior in grade, and the blow kills. Apart from its effect the blow itself is, according to the Articles of War, a capital crime." The captain then observes, "We proceed under the law of the Mutiny Act. In feature no child can resemble his father more than that Act resembles in spirit the thing from which it derives—War" (1415–1416). As many readers of *Billy Budd* remark, concerns about security seem to trump all others, including justice.[19] When the very existence of the state is at stake, "political" matters appear to outweigh "legal" ones. Interpreted this way, the handsome sailor in the story must hang not because he deserves to die and legally has been found guilty of a capital offense but because his death is necessary for the greater good. In brief, Billy Budd is sacrificed.[20] On this reading, for the benefit of king, country, and crew an innocent sailor is executed in a public ceremony with all the trimmings of a ritual.[21]

This sacrifice may well be a personal one for the captain. When he challenges the officers on the drumhead court to admit that they are reluctant to find Billy Budd guilty of murder because he is "a fellow creature innocent before God," Captain Vere includes himself among those who feel this to be so. He tells them, "Well, I too feel that, the full force of that. It is Nature." He goes on, however: "But do these buttons that we wear attest that our allegiance is to Nature? No, to the King. Though the ocean, which is inviolate Nature primeval, though this be the element where we move and have our being as sailors, yet as the King's officers lies our duty in a sphere correspondingly natural? So little is that true, that in receiving our commissions we in the most important regards ceased to be natural free agents" (1414).

Such passages are used to justify interpretations of *Billy Budd* as tragedy and Captain Vere as a man "trapped in a tragic dilemma, a formalist torn between adherence to the rule of law and his own heart and conscience."[22] But these passages are just as often used as evidence of Captain Vere's limited or flawed character. Robert Cover argues that though the captain may well have struggled with the moral-formal dilemma—parading his helplessness before the law, lamenting harsh results, intimating that in a more perfect world, or at the end of days, a better law would emerge—he ultimately "marched to the music, steeled [himself], and hung Billy Budd."[23]

Yet others argue that Captain Vere was not formalist enough, and that he only claimed to follow the law so as to be able to kill Billy Budd out of an exaggerated desire for order or bitter resentment.[24] To these readers Richard Posner replies, "Vere is in sole command of a major warship in a major war. This is an awesome responsibility. . . . We are not meant to think that he had no choice, but no more are we meant to think that he was acting illegally or out of envy. His bookishness, his 'pedantry,' are intended to make us realize that Vere *knew* he faced a tough choice."[25]

But to the extent that Captain Vere faces a tough choice, his actions are no longer determined by the political concerns manifest in the implementation of military law. As we already observed, there is evidence that martial law does not necessarily require or call for the trial of Billy Budd, let alone his execution. The sovereign decision, then, is not the decision of a distant king but of Captain Vere. Consequently, when Captain Vere exclaims that Billy "must" die, he does not express his sense of obligation to a sovereign but rather exercises the power of sovereignty himself.[26] As Carl Schmitt elaborated, the sovereign is he who decides on the exception.[27] The sovereign is the one who recognizes the unprecedented and unexampled, that which is "not codified in the existing legal order" and "cannot be circumscribed factually and made to conform to a pre-formed law."[28] In *Billy Budd,* when the foretopman strikes the master-at-arms, Captain Vere decides that accepted practice does not apply. Given what he determines to be an exceptional situation, the captain declares that what is most holy, an angel of God, must be treated as a common murderer and hung.

The captain makes this decision from a position designated by a normally valid legal system but one that at the same time stands outside this system, for he exercises a competency that cannot be codified by the system. Thus, Captain Vere's decision of Billy Budd's fate sounds to the surgeon who witnesses it as "mere incoherences" (1406). And yet the surgeon complies with the captain's commands, as do the lieutenants and the captain of the marines, although they are also surprised and concerned by Captain Vere's decision (1407).[29] At the same time, as Schmitt's philosophy insists, the captain continues to operate in a juridical framework. Captain Vere himself makes this clear when he reminds the members of the drumhead court that they do not operate as "natural free agents" (1414). With this reminder, the captain assures the officers of the ship that the circumstances that he determines to be exceptional do not cast them all out of the state and back into a state of nature. He calls for an exception to the social rules and military law by which the ship would be guided in "normal" times, but his "must" nevertheless remains "legal."

As I have already said, I find this interpretation of the experience of law—the force of Captain Vere's "must"—compelling. I also find it problematic, however. One particular difficulty stands out. This interpretation does not account for Captain Vere's insistence that he is somehow obliged to make the decision that he makes. For instance, speaking to the drumhead court, the captain explicitly recognizes that "the case is an exceptional one." But, he goes on, "for us here, acting not as casuists or moralists, it is a case practical, and under martial law practically to be dealt with" (1414). He also reminds the court: "Our vowed responsibility is in this: That however pitilessly that law may operate in any instances, we nevertheless adhere to it and administer it." Again, acknowledging that "the exceptional in the matter" moves the hearts of the members of the court and confessing that it moves his heart as well, Captain Vere tells his officers that they must decide with their heads (1415). Referring once more to their hearts and to the fact that he shares the officers' feelings, however, the captain suggests that even their heads do not rule here, as "in this military necessity so heavy a compulsion is laid" (1417). In brief, the sovereign power ostensibly exercised here shades into its opposite, signaling that in *Billy Budd,* as Philip Loosemore suggests, "Melville . . . grapples with . . . the fundamental blurring of sovereignty and subjection, norm and exception, that it seems to entail, in the security emergency of revolution."[30] Writing before Giorgio Agamben's influential analysis of the security emergency and the institution of the permanent state of exception, Michael Rogin observes how "natural" and "man-made" authority are imbricated in *Billy Budd* to such an extent that the boundary between natural force and human power is dissolved, placing men—officers and bluejackets alike—at the mercy and disposal of forces "beyond human reach."[31] This means Captain Vere's "must" has no special force or significance. In a condition of undecidable ambiguity, the experience of law as such is indistinguishable from any other kind of social, political, moral, or biological compulsion.

The second explanation of the force of Captain Vere's "must" explicitly takes issue with the experience of law as an experience of pure will or sovereign power. This approach to the mystery of the "must" in *Billy Budd* analyzes that mystery as the effect of repression, specifically the repression of eros in law.[32] According to Freud, aggression is only one of the drives that give rise to civilization and the law by which it is sustained.[33] The other drive is eros, which binds communities libidinally. In her reading of *Billy Budd,* Martha Umphrey suggests that, to the extent that legal positivism assumes that law originates in a performative act of violence and denies the libidinal drive that brings people together, legal positivism is characterized by instances of opacity when this unacceptable impulse is blocked.[34] Umphrey draws attention to some of these instances in *Billy Budd* to recover the erotic dimension of law.

Many readers of *Billy Budd* have suggested that the outcome of Billy Budd's trial would have been different if Captain Vere had not explicitly prohibited the members of the drumhead court from consulting their emotions.[35] Umphrey makes a different, more subtle point, however. Following Freud, she claims that emotion can never be ruled out in a legal situation because eros is central to the sustenance of legal authority. Thus, eros can never be completely obscured or denied.[36] She illustrates the point with Billy Budd's execution. Standing with a rope around his neck before all the officers and crew of the *Bellipotent,* Billy speaks his final and only words: "God bless Captain Vere!" (1426). Umphrey claims these words "ratify and transcend the execution that Vere has brought about."[37] Though Captain Vere has gone out of his way to ensure that Billy Budd will be convicted and condemned to death, Billy Budd's final words suggest that he bears no ill will against his captain. On the contrary, his words seem to express approval or thanks for what Captain Vere has done. Alternatively, or simultaneously, his final words suggest that Billy Budd is indifferent to the world in which the captain acts and therefore is indifferent to the consequences of the captain's actions. His only concern is for Captain Vere himself, and so Billy Budd appeals to a higher authority to support the captain. Whatever its significance might be, Billy Budd's utterance has a profound effect on the men summoned to witness his punishment. Instead of rising against an authority that not only can but also will inflict a lethal penalty on a sailor who is presumed to be innocent, without volition and in one voice they echo Billy Budd's "benediction" (1426). As Umphrey points out, Billy Budd's benediction actually reverses the order of authority; he is being hanged as a criminal or a traitor, but he is the one bestowing blessings and leading the ship's populace in a unanimous salute to the ship's captain.[38] In this scene, she claims, eros triumphs over violence.[39]

This reading of *Billy Budd* calls attention to instances when law, understood as the product of a will empowered to posit law by its own efficacy, is revealed to be the product of a will that is efficacious by virtue of its capacity not only to use lethal force but also to bring people together. Thus, this reading demonstrates the limits of an explanation of the legal "must" that focuses only on force or violence by showing how, at the heart of the matter, the will that posits law or empowers the will to posit law deploys eros as well as aggression. This reading also explains the mystery of the "must" of legal experience, as it suggests the force of the "must" is more or less consciously obscured by the story we tell ourselves about law, specifically, that law is nothing other than the monopoly of legitimate violence.

While I find this interpretation of the experience of law particularly suggestive, I nevertheless find it frustrating, too. For instead of facing the widely acknowledged fact that throughout *Billy Budd* the characters' inner thoughts are never revealed—and hence the irony of the story's subtitle, *An Inside Narrative*—the silences of the text are cast in Umphrey's reading as occasions of repression, and hence moments when something, and in particular something mistakenly assumed to be shameful, that is, eros, can be "discovered" and brought out into the light.[40] What is more, this reading implies that through a practice of projection and recuperation, law may be healed, that is to say, restored to its whole self so it will no longer be so inclined to pathological outbursts of violence. Thus, the "true" nature of law is assumed to be something other than what the characters experience as law. A perverted but redeemable law sends Billy Budd to the gallows.

In what follows, I try to avoid thinking so deeply about law. I am not concerned with making law better—that is to say, I am not interested in finding a way to redeem law as a sovereign exercise of power or as the product of a dynamic between two drives, human aggression and eros. Instead, I try to think of law superficially, in a realist manner, after a fashion. Thus, I try to attend to the surface of the matter and what strikes us there.

Love

When we take this superficial approach to *Billy Budd*, what do we see? Some critics complain that we don't see much.[41] Indeed, on one level, for all of the events recorded in Melville's story, not a lot actually happens. There are no personal epiphanies; the characters do not grow or develop. Despite the period in which the story is set, there are no political or more broadly social transformations; no wars are won or lost, no revolutions occur, no man is liberated. What critics who appreciate only narratives of transformation overlook, however, is that Billy Budd's arrival on the *Bellipotent* coincides with a proliferation of body-to-body touches that destroy the self-possession of the men on board.[42]

Observing these touches, I suggest that Melville's novella traces what I call, after Jean-Luc Nancy, the *advent* of love.[43] The advent of love is the arriving or the beginning of love. It is the commencing of love, a commencing that does not cease. Love comes, it happens, it takes place, but, as it does not reach an end or any final destination, it is always suspended in its arrival. That is to say, love comes but it also goes, or, rather, it goes on . . . and on. Cutting across us rather than stopping and realizing or fulfilling the promise its appearance may seem to imply, love, as Nancy would have it, is "a moment of contact between beings, a light, cutting and delicious moment of contact, at once eternal and fleeting."[44] Nancy calls this incessant coming and going "the crossing of love."[45]

In her famous reading of *Billy Budd,* Barbara Johnson calls attention to several such moments of contact and also describes them as crossings.[46] Observing how good and evil, innocence and guilt, criminal and victim, change places in the story, Johnson suggests that Melville sets up his plot in the form of a chiasmus.[47] This chiasmus structure is evident in a passage that describes the moment when Captain Vere recognizes that Billy Budd cannot defend himself against Claggart's charge of mutiny:

> Though at the time Captain Vere was quite ignorant of Billy's liability to vocal impediment, he now immediately divined it. . . . Going close up to the young sailor, and laying a soothing hand on his shoulder, he said, "There is no hurry, my boy. Take your time, take your time." Contrary to the effect intended, these words so fatherly in tone, doubtless touching Billy's heart to the quick, prompted yet more violent efforts at utterance. . . . The next instant, quick as the flame from a discharged cannon at night, his right arm shot out, and Claggart dropped to the deck. Whether intentionally or but owing to the young athlete's superior height, the blow had taken effect full upon the forehead. . . . A gasp or two, and he lay motionless. (1404)

It is Vere's intention to soothe, but the effect of his words is to provoke;

Vere's benevolence touches Billy's heart, but Claggart's forehead suffers the impact of a fist propelled by the captain's kindness. Johnson reads such reversals in parallel terms—ignorance/intelligence ("ignorant"/ "divined"), calm/inflamed ("soothing"/"violent"), words/deeds ("said"/"blow"), heart/head ("heart"/"forehead")—as an indication that Melville is not as preoccupied with "the static opposition between evil and good" as he with "the dynamic opposition . . . [of] man's 'nature' and his acts."[48] What really interests him are the "twisted relations between knowing and doing, speaking and killing, reading and judging, which make political understanding and action so problematic."[49] According to Johnson, Melville's text shows that these relations are so "twisted" because the difference *between* the opposing pairs—intention/appearance, good/evil, Billy/Claggart—is really a difference *within* each one of them.[50] What is more, she observes, "a difference *between* opposing forces presupposes that the entities in conflict be knowable. A difference *within* one of the entities in question is precisely what problematizes the very *idea* of an entity in the first place."[51] Johnson claims that it is *this* difference that prevents us from ever fully realizing the consequences of our actions.[52] The entity to which responsibility would be attributed is never fully present, as it were, either to itself or to others. Thus, we do not know ourselves or what we do. We are not masters of our actions or our fates. We are called to judge and so to determine consequences and assign blame retrospectively. Yet judgment is an act itself, open in its turn to judgment.[53] Consequently, we are never finished.

Against the backdrop of Nancy's remarks about love, I am inclined to read the pairs of oppositions that Melville erects and the devastating effects of the crossings between them in a similar but more ragged fashion. Specifically, I find that Nancy's remarks about love suggest an alternative way of reading the crossings that Johnson identifies. To put that alternative crudely, rather than reading these crossings under the regime of contradiction, we might read them under the regime of exposition. Under the regime of exposition, the bursts, flashes, blows, and cuts that make manifest the moments of contact between ostensibly opposing pairs do not express what has until then been repressed—a difference within—but rather display, in Nancy's words, "the world is a 'with,'" a *Mitwelt* or shared world.[54] In a shared world, being is "being-with." Being-with does not mean that one is beside another, being with by being next to another who is also present. In a shared world, the verb *to be* means "to share existence." In other words, one "is" not; one shares being, one "with others" rather than "is." To put the matter another way, existence does not belong to anyone; no one possesses it. No one possesses being because being is not a *private* property.

On this reading, every interaction in *Billy Budd* exposes human "finitude" or human "inappropriability" rather than the logical inconsistency of a subject's identity. For that which is inappropriable has no property that belongs to it; nor can it acquire or realize any such property in a dialectical relationship with an outside or other. That is because the Hegelian logic that would dictate the process by which the singular being would come to possess itself or know itself as a self through a confrontation with an outside or an other—a process of sublation or *Aufhebung*—is unavailable to that which has no being and therefore is not.[55] As singular being does not possess being, self-contradiction is impossible.

The exchange of properties in *Billy Budd* demonstrates this point insofar as throughout the story we see contact between the characters shattering their ostensible identities, dispossessing them of themselves. Being with others, they change. This is represented by the way they become other than themselves by taking on the properties of the other who has touched them. In a flurry of cuts, glances, blows, and digs, they lose their self-possession, or the appearance of possessing a self.

For instance, when the lieutenant from the *Bellipotent* takes Billy Budd from the merchant ship *The Rights of Man* to serve the king, Billy Budd's former captain explains that he is so distraught about the loss of this sailor because of Billy Budd's effect on the crew. Captain Graveling tells the lieutenant, "Before I shipped that young fellow, my forecastle was a rat-pit of quarrels. . . . But Billy came; and it was like a Catholic priest striking peace in an Irish shindy. Not that he preached to them or said or did anything in particular; but a virtue went out of him, sugaring the sour ones" (1356). Here the apparent reversal that takes place on board *The Rights of Man* is explicitly ascribed to a "striking" arrival. What is more, the change that takes place in the sailors on the ship is described as something that occurs by osmosis rather than opposition. The "sour ones" are not converted but "sugar[ed]." In brief, members of the crew may be touched by Billy Budd but they are not saved by the power of his appearance in any Christian or Hegelian sense of a process of triumphant transformation.[56]

Of course, other instances of the exchange of properties do not appear to occur in so relatively mild a manner. Consider the oft-analyzed relationship between Billy Budd and Claggart. This relationship appears to begin when Billy Budd chances to spill soup across Claggart's path (1380). Before this affair, the narrator insists, Billy has had no "special contact" with Claggart. On this occasion, however, it becomes apparent that "at heart, and not for nothing," Claggart is "down on" Billy Budd (1381).

How Billy Budd has had contact with Claggart is left ambiguous, but *that* Claggart is struck by Billy Budd is already obvious. Even one of the lowliest members of the *Bellipotent*'s crew realizes that Claggart loses his self-possession when Budd comes on board. First, Claggart has this corporal lay traps for the foretopman. Then, when Claggart receives reports from this corporal recounting episodes of Billy Budd's expressions of resentment about being impressed and his ill will toward the officers, the master-at-arms does not suspect their veracity. Claggart's trust in these reports may be due in part to the fact that he knows "how secretly unpopular may become a master-at-arms, at least a master-at-arms of those days" (1386). Nevertheless, as the officer in charge of maintaining order on the *Bellipotent,* Claggart is required to be suspicious of everyone. In this case, however, Claggart's "uncommon prudence" leads him not to verify his faithful understrapper's stories but to impulsively cut himself off from the possibility of "enlightenment or disillusion" about them (1387). In this regard, Claggart becomes like the famously dumb Billy Budd.

Though there is no obvious explanation for Claggart's unusual behavior, eros is a reason often offered for his recklessness. Psychoanalytic readings of Melville's text, in particular ones that emphasize the homoerotic tensions on board the *Bellipotent,* refer to a story told in the narrative to illuminate Claggart's character indirectly, a story about a man who "is a nut not to be cracked by the tap of a lady's fan" (1382). The interpretation of Claggart's feelings for Billy Budd as sexual ones that must be repressed or denied, and then are distorted or perverted by their forceful suppression, is further supported by certain "demonstrations" of Claggart's feelings. It is recorded (although "unobserved") that Claggart's glance would follow Billy Budd "with a settled meditative and melancholy expression" that would sometimes "have in it a touch of soft yearning, as if Claggart could even have loved Billy but for fate and ban" (1394).

Of course, such readings conceive of eros in the familiar terms of a movement beyond the self—a movement through which the self strives to become one with a forbidden other or to become whole. If, as I have suggested, however, love is at play on the *Bellipotent,* an encounter with an other does not redeem or complete anyone, or fail to do so. Instead, such an encounter dispossesses the subject of its being and goes on, ricocheting throughout the ship, leaving the men broken open and marked by the touch of an other or a run-in with "the outside *itself*."[57] In brief, the subject is marked by what cannot be resisted, mastered, or worked through.[58] To see this, we do not look behind what is presented to us, which would require us to project what we find there. Instead, we look to the frontage of things, the surface where these things take place.

With this in mind, recall that Claggart is down on Billy Budd "not for nothing."[59] The formulation "not for nothing" may prompt us to look for something to explain Claggart's hostility. If we resist this impulse, however, we might observe that "not for nothing" may mean "for something" *or* "for something that *is* not." What is more, reading "not for nothing" as "for something that is not" illuminates the cause that is given for Claggart's enmity: "an antipathy spontaneous and profound" (1381). Like "not for nothing," this response is indistinct. Certainly, it does not seem to shed any light on the original question about the matter of Claggart's feelings, for being "down on" a man means nothing more or less than having "antipathy" toward him. Indeed, to identify a spontaneous and profound antipathy as the reason for being down on a man is only to reiterate the mysteriousness of the relationship. That said, in its circular and self-referential structure, the tautological explanation of Claggart's feelings for Billy Budd does indicate something. Specifically, it indicates that Claggart's feelings are without a cause. Yet there is contact. A relationship between Claggart and Billy Budd occurs. This relationship has no source or known origin, however. It appears to come from nowhere, spontaneously emerging to unsettle and break the self-possession of the selves touched. As the narrative states, the relationship between Claggart and Billy Budd partakes in "the mysterious" (1381). No motive or reason explains it. Nevertheless, it takes place, and its effects cannot be denied. One of these effects is that Claggart, once suspicious, becomes naive and innocent; another is that the guileless Billy murders a man and appears to the captain, a man who believes only in history, as an angel of God.

Law Like Love

I turn now from these reflections on love in *Billy Budd* back to my original question, "What is law?" To answer that, I have suggested we address ourselves to the experience of the mysterious "must" in Captain Vere's passionate exclamation over Claggart's body: "Struck dead by an angel of God! Yet the angel must hang!" (1406). To do that I have proposed we think about law in *Billy Budd* not in terms of will or violence but in terms of love. Specifically, I have proposed we think about law in terms of Nancy's thinking about love, for Nancy's definition of love can account for the destructive effects we see in *Billy Budd* and, what is more, it can do so without projecting into the text something to find that we then use to realize and make whole our interpretation. The task at hand now is to see how these reflections on love illuminate law.

Following Melville's example, I undertake this task by indirection. Instead of telling a tale about an aggressive woman with a fan and an appetite, however, I recite a poem. The poem is "Law Like Love" by W. H. Auden.[60] Written during the heyday of legal realism, the poem reflects the realist view that law is a product of human beings and therefore is subject to human foibles and frailties. "Law Like Love" begins by briefly but succinctly and beautifully reviewing different philosophies of law.[61] In a few simple words, Auden introduces a natural law in which nature takes pride of place—

> Law, say the gardeners, is the sun,
> Law is the one
> All gardeners obey
> To-morrow, yesterday, to-day

—and a natural law in which tradition and social institutions that have evolved over time demand respect—

> Law is the wisdom of the old,
> The impotent grandfathers feebly scold.[62]

In this review of different philosophies of law, Auden indicates the many ways in which human beings have conceived of law through time. In addition, the poem suggests, in realist fashion, how our understanding of law is directly related to our position in the world: the young claim law is the senses, whereas the priests say, "Law is the words in my priestly book," and the judges insist, "Law is as I've told you before."[63] Legal scholars offer a different perspective but, just like the other perspectives, it is one that reflects the values and priorities of the speaker. In the case of legal scholars, moral critique is suspended in favor of conclusions based on empirical observation and cautious generalization. All this is communicated in the lines "Law is only crimes / Punished by places and by times."[64]

In her reading of "Law Like Love," Linda Meyer argues that Auden's poem provides a history of jurisprudence as a history of nihilism.[65] Indeed, after the scholars (all good legal positivists) pronounce, "Law is neither wrong nor right," the poem continues:

> Others say, Law is our Fate;
> Others say, Law is our State;
> Others say, others say
> Law is no more,
> Law has gone away.
> And always the loud angry crowd,
> Very angry and very loud,
> Law is We,
> And always the soft idiot softly Me.[66]

Though a whole political and philosophical history may seem skeptically retold in these lines, I think in at least one significant regard Auden's "Law Like Love" is not nihilistic, at least not in any "passive" sense.[67] Specifically, "Law Like Love" does not suppress "The universal wish to guess / Or slip out of our own position / Into an unconcerned condition."[68] In the last few stanzas the narrator self-consciously attempts to offer his own definition of law.

This attempt is complicated, however. It is complicated by the fact that the narrator refuses to say "Law is."[69] The reason for his refusal is ambiguous. According to the narrator, "all agree / Gladly or miserably / That the Law is."[70] To say simply what everyone already knows may, consequently, fail to satisfy the narrator's vanity; he admits to a wish to be able to assume a position in which he does not have to suffer the limits of the human condition, a position from which he would be able to define law once and for all. As we have seen, others' definitions of law betray how embedded they are in their particular place and time. The narrator may want to say something original, universal, and eternal about law, but given that the verb at issue ("to be") is ironically the one we use to convey such qualities, he cannot say something along these lines if he says "Law is."

Alternatively, the narrator may refuse to say "Law is" because he understands that we live in a world of words (rather than things in themselves), and therefore nothing we say can illuminate law qua law. In other words, when we say what "Law is" all we do is "identify Law with some other word."[71] Given that we will never succeed at transcending the web of language, the narrator thinks it "absurd" to try and therefore may prefer to say nothing.[72]

Finally, as Meyer suggests, the narrator may refuse to say "Law is" because he wishes to "release . . . 'Law' from any other words limiting or defining it."[73] The narrator's reticence may then be an expression of concern about the future of law. For by defining law once and for all, we may restrict or deny law's responsiveness, its ability to cognize unforeseen legal events and apply to facts that have not yet taken place and may not yet even be imaginable.

I am inclined to read the narrator's refusal to say "Law is" along these lines as well, but with a slightly different emphasis. I suggest that "some other word" may limit or define law not because a word can provide only a partial and restrictive description of law, but because with or rather through that word we seek to "complete" law. The issue as I see it is not that we risk settling for a less comprehensive or capacious understanding of what law can be, should be, or is, but, rather, that some other word is the first step on a familiar dialectical path that directs us toward the goal of subsuming all loose ends either in overcoming some obstacles we find along the way (eros perhaps) or realizing the essence of law in the struggle to achieve the goal (the story of law as a bildungsroman). In either case, the path leads inward rather than outward. For, rather than answering the question "What is law?" in "an unconcerned condition," we find ourselves once more engaged in a relation with an ostensible mystery that is quickly reduced to an object through which we can better realize ourselves.

This interpretation of the refusal to say "Law is" offers another perspective from which to read the title of Auden's poem and to observe how law appears in the poem itself. In particular, it draws attention to the fact that when the narrator gives in to the universal wish to say something more, he uses a simile. A simile is a figure of speech that compares two dissimilar things. Unlike other figures of speech that do the same thing, however—

metaphors, for instance—similes explicitly preserve the distinctness of the two things being compared. When the narrator in Auden's poem succumbs to the desire to say something about law, what he says does not assume identity between terms. Stating hesitantly "a timid similarity," he says, "like love."[74]

Thus, what the poem says about law emerges out of the space between "law" and "love," a space held open by the simile while it holds the two terms face to face. Like surfaces in a hall of mirrors, the two terms reflect and illuminate one another in an infinite back-and-forth. In this dynamic, law is ascribed qualities. These qualities are not derived from any penetrating analysis but instead come to light when "love" subtly refracts and distorts the image of "law" that it reflects.

> Like love we don't know where or why,
> Like love we can't compel or fly,
> Like love we often weep,
> Like love we seldom keep.[75]

In brief, like love we do not know where law comes from or why it comes to us. If it has a source, this source does not appear to us or explain itself. All we know is that it occurs, and that we do not control it. We are not able to make law do or be what we will. Nor can we escape it, even when it causes us to suffer. But we cannot preserve it, either. We fail it or it eludes us.

When Captain Vere exclaims, "Struck dead by an angel of God! Yet the angel must hang!" Hannah Arendt claims the tragedy of law is revealed, and that tragedy is that law is human.[76] Law does not transcend the human condition of being with others. In her reading of *Billy Budd,* Barbara Johnson reaches a similar conclusion from different premises when she suggests that "law is the forcible transformation of ambiguity into decidability"[77] in a condition in which "every judge is in the impossible position of having to include the effects of his own act of judging within the cognitive context of his decision."[78] The tragedy, the inevitable (illegitimate) violence of law, inheres in the impossibility of finding a position in which the effects of the application of authority are contained.[79] Law is thus a lethal manifestation of our inability, as mortal and contradictory beings, to command our actions, to anticipate and determine their effects.

What I have tried to suggest in this essay is that law qua law is not, in *Billy Budd* at least, necessarily the instrument of a commanding will, one that aspires to realize itself perfectly but always falls short with fatal consequences that we are called to judge again and again. Rather, law qua law is more like an experience, in particular *an experience of that call* to judge. This experience is one of an irresistible provocation, a propelling or compelling force on the occasion of an encounter with an inappropriable other. Moved this way, we are exposed to our condition of sharing the world. On this account, law is not then a tragic experience of repetitively and inevitably *erring*—to use a favorite Melville word—determination. Law is instead known to us as the experience of a force that comes from nowhere and wrecks our self-possession. The grounds of this insight are found, Nancy says, in the middle of the philosophical tradition of thinking about love, for it is there that love is defined as "that which is not self-love"[80]—that is to say, as that which is not love of the self as property, as "the objectivized presence of subjectivity, its realization in the outside world."[81] In brief, and in sum, I timidly suggest that the experience of law is like the experience of an encounter—in a glance, a caress, a jab, a blow—that exposes us to how we share the world, how we "with others," how we "are" not, how we hurt the ones we love.

Notes

Substantial portions of this essay originally appeared in "Shattering Law: Encounters with Love in *Billy Budd*," *Quinnipiac Law Review* 28, no. 1 (2010): 765–780. I am grateful to the Law Review Association of the Quinnipiac University School of Law for allowing me to reprint that material. I must also acknowledge the support of the American Academy in Berlin and the Center for Ethics and Public Affairs in the Murphy Institute at Tulane University. I have benefited greatly from the opportunity to present this material in several venues to different audiences at the Center in Law, Society, and Culture at the University of California, Irvine; the annual meeting of the Association for the Study of Law, Culture, and the Humanities; the conference "A Return to the Senses: Political Theory and the Sensorium," organized by Davide Panagia; the conference "Law and Love," organized by Linda Ross Meyer and Martha Merrill Umphrey; and the American Academy in Berlin. Finally, I owe thanks to Jason Frank, Jane Bennett, and all of the participants in the "Law's Love" seminar (fall 2009).

1. H. L. A. Hart, *The Concept of Law* (Oxford: Oxford University Press, 1961).

2. Ibid., 6–13.

3. Even Hart, who warns that no easy resolution to the definition of law is possible, claims that "it is possible to isolate and characterize a central set of elements which form a common part of the answer to all three [questions that we have identified as underlying the recurrent question 'What is law?']" (ibid., 16).

4. Philippe Nonet, "What Is Positive Law?" *Yale Law Journal* 100, no. 3 (1990): 667.

5. Herman Melville, *Billy Budd, Sailor (An Inside Narrative)*, in *Pierre, Israel Potter, The Piazza Tales, The Confidence-Man, Uncollected Prose, Billy Budd* (New York: Library of America, 1984), 1353–1435. Further references to this volume are cited parenthetically in the text.

6. See Robert M. Cover, *Justice Accused: Antislavery and the Judicial Process* (New Haven: Yale University Press, 1975), 1.

7. Though Stanley Fish does not make this particular claim, he famously argues that interpretations always take place within a set of institutional constraints. See Stanley Fish, "Fish *v.* Fiss," *Stanford Law Review* 36, no. 6 (1984): 1325–1347. Brook Thomas does not take issue with Fish's conclusion but suggests that if we accept it, we then need to ask ourselves why certain institutional constraints are accepted rather than others and why some modes of interpretation are granted authority while others are not. Brook Thomas, "*Billy Budd* and the Untold Story of the Law," *Cardozo Studies in Law and Literature* 1 (Spring 1989): 50. This essay does not directly address itself to that need, but some readers of *Billy Budd* offer interpretations of the story that shed light on the matter, and some critics of legal positivism do as well. See, e.g., William Spanos, *The Exceptional State and the State of Exception: Herman Melville's* Billy Budd, Sailor (Baltimore: Johns Hopkins University Press, 2011), 36–74; Marianne Constable, *Just Silences: The Limits and Possibilities of Modern Law* (Princeton: Princeton University Press, 2005), 31.

8. This focus is inspired in part by Hannah Arendt's reading of *Billy Budd* in *On Revolution* and her claim that it is in "the distance, the worldly space between men where political matters, the whole realm of human affairs are located." Hannah Arendt, *On Revolution* (New York: Viking Press, 1963), 86.

9. My debt on this point is to Hannah Arendt, who claims throughout her work that we live in an appearing world. See Hannah Arendt, *The Human Condition* (Chicago: University of Chicago Press, 1958), and *The Life of the Mind*, 2 vols. (New York: Harcourt Brace Jovanovich, 1978).

10. Jerome Frank is famously claimed to have said that judges' decisions may be influenced, or even determined, by what they had for breakfast. See Jerome Frank, *Courts on Trial: Myth and Reality in American Justice* (Princeton: Princeton University Press, 1949), 161–162. For a discussion of this claim, see Frederick F. Schauer, *Thinking Like a Lawyer: A New Introduction to Legal Reasoning* (Cam-

bridge: Harvard University Press, 2009), 129. For an alternative kind of elaboration of the point Frank is actually making, and one that is potentially compatible with the approach taken here, see Jane Bennett, *Vibrant Matter: A Political Ecology of Things* (Durham: Duke University Press, 2010).

11. Jason Frank makes a similar observation about *Billy Budd* when he argues, "It is not what is hidden that . . . Melville's novella illuminate[s], but the allure of what is enigmatically manifest." Thus, "*Billy Budd* [is] less a 'judge's story' than a phenomenological analytics of authority." See Jason Frank's "The Lyre of Orpheus: Aesthetics and Authority in *Billy Budd*," in this volume.

12. The matter is often treated as an issue pertaining to the justice of Billy Budd's execution and Melville's intention in depicting such a flawed trial. See, among others, Aviam Soifer, "Status, Contract, and Promises Unkept," *Yale Law Journal* 96, no. 8 (1987): 1916–1959; Richard P. Cole, "Orthodoxy and Heresy: The Nineteenth Century History of the Rule of Law Reconsidered," *Indiana Law Review* 32, no. 4 (1999): 1335; Alfred S. Konesky, "The Accidental Legal Historian: Herman Melville and the History of American Law," *Buffalo Law Review* 52, no. 4 (2004): 1179–1276; Daniel J. Solove, "Failure of the Word: Melville's *Billy Budd* and Security in Times of Crisis," *Cardozo Law Review* 26, no. 6 (2005): 2443–2470; Philip Loosemore, "Revolution, Counterrevolution, and Natural Law in *Billy Budd, Sailor*," *Criticism* 51, no. 1 (2011): 99–126.

13. I borrow the language of social rules from H. L. A. Hart, who, in *The Concept of Law*, defines "social rules" as rules in a social situation that make "certain types of behaviour a standard" (83). Taking issue with John Austin's command theory of law, Hart argues that social rules are not present in every social situation (79–84). A person does not have to act in a particular way—that is to say, we do not expect her behavior to meet a particular standard—when she is held up at gunpoint, for instance. While we may say the threat of violence "obliges" her to hand over her wallet, we would not say that she fails to carry out an obligation or breaks a rule if she manages somehow to avoid giving the gunman her money (80–81). According to Hart, "Rules are conceived and spoken of as imposing obligations when the general demand for conformity is insistent and the social pressure brought to bear upon those who deviate or threaten to deviate is great" (84). Of course, how "social pressure" is brought to bear is ambiguous in this statement, and it may entail great violence. See Robert Cover, "Violence and the Word," *Yale Law Journal* 95, no. 8 (1986): 1601–1629.

14. It is possible to interpret Captain Vere's dilemma in terms of what Hart calls the "internal" and "external" aspect of rules. According to Hart, in *The Concept of Law*, "When a social group has certain rules of conduct, this fact affords an opportunity for many closely related yet different kinds of assertion; for it is possible to be concerned with the rules, either merely as an observer who does not

himself accept them, or as a member of the group which accepts and uses them as guides to conduct" (86). From the "internal point of view" individuals "accept and voluntarily co-operate in maintaining the rules, and so see their own and other persons' behaviour in terms of the rules" (88). From the external point of view, the position of observers who merely record "the regularities of observable behaviour in which conformity with the rules partly consists," individuals may "be able to predict with a fair measure of success, and to assess the chances that a deviation from the group's normal behaviour will meet with hostile reaction or punishment" (87). Captain Vere seems to take both the internal and the external point of view. While he is aware that the sense of the moral correctness of the rules of the social group on the *Bellipotent* and the feeling of obligation these rules engender in members of the group do not necessarily mean that the rules correspond in any way to principles of a greater or natural morality or justice, he is in a position to make this observation because he has embraced the assumptions that inform the legal positivists' approach to law and therefore cannot appeal to any "higher" morality or justice to legally legitimate his actions.

15. With this observation, I am suggesting that it is not so easy to distinguish in *Billy Budd* between what Hart calls "primary rules," under which "human beings are required to do or abstain from certain actions, whether they wish to or not," and "secondary rules," rules that "provide that human beings may by doing or saying certain things introduce new rules of the primary type, extinguish or modify old ones, or in various ways determine their incidence or control their operations" (*The Concept of Law*, 78–79). By contrast, Jason Frank suggests that *Billy Budd* is concerned less with primary rules than with secondary rules, and in particular with the secondary "rules of recognition" on which law depends. See Frank, "The Lyre of Orpheus."

16. To the extent that "social rules" are exemplary of positive law, this observation raises a question about the possibility of meaningfully conceiving of law in positivist terms. In particular, it raises the question of the possibility of meaningfully conceiving of law in terms that have distanced or excluded a relationship with justice. H. L. A. Hart and Lon Fuller famously debated this point. See H. L. A. Hart, "Positivism and the Separation of Law and Morals," *Harvard Law Review* 71, no. 4 (1958): 593–629; and Lon Fuller, "Positivism and Fidelity to Law—A Reply to Professor Hart," *Harvard Law Review* 71, no. 4 (1958): 630–672. On this point as it is raised by Melville in his novella, see Loosemore, "Revolution, Counterrevolution, and Natural Law."

17. Though he does not explicitly identify this question as motivating his reading of *Billy Budd*, Brook Thomas claims that *Billy Budd* is ideally suited for the task of exploring the untold story of law, the story that "defines the legal system" ("*Billy Budd* and the Untold Story of the Law," 51). As Robert Cover reminds us, Thomas says, "the persuasiveness of a decision depends upon an implied narrative

that makes its reasoning seem logical" (ibid.). See Robert M. Cover, "*Nomos* and Narrative," *Harvard Law Review* 97, no. 1 (1983): 4–5. Jason Frank supplements this claim when he suggests the implied narrative that makes a decision persuasive is not "narrowly discursive" or primarily concerned with reason but is, rather, "broadly aesthetic." See Frank, "The Lyre of Orpheus."

18. At once calling attention to and deferring an account of the mysteriousness of this "must" in *Billy Budd*, Jason Frank suggests that in the novella authority "spellbinds." See Frank, "The Lyre of Orpheus."

19. See, among others, Harrison Hayford and Merton M. Sealts Jr., introduction to Herman Melville, *Billy Budd, Sailor (An Inside Narrative)*, ed. Harrison Hayford and Merton M. Sealts Jr. (Chicago: University of Chicago Press, 1962), 26; William Domnarski, "Law-Literature Criticism: Charting a Desirable Course with *Billy Budd*," *Journal of Legal Education* 34, no. 4 (1984): 702–713; Laurie Roberston-Lorant, *Melville: A Biography* (1996; repr., Amherst: University of Massachusetts Press, 1998), 594.

20. For variations on the theme of sacrifice, see, e.g., Bernhard Radloff, *Cosmopolis and Truth: Melville's Critique of Modernity* (New York: Peter Lang, 1996); James McBride, "Revisiting a Seminal Text of the Law & Literature Movement: A Girardian Reading of Herman Melville's *Billy Budd, Sailor*," *Margins* 3, no. 2 (2003): 285–332. Edwin M. Yoder makes this observation as well, pointing out in particular the moments in the text when Billy Budd is identified with Christ, as in the saga of the spar from which Billy was hanged: "The spar from which the foretopman was suspended was for some few years kept trace of by the bluejackets. Their knowledges followed it from ship to dockyard and again from dockyard to ship, still pursuing it even when at last reduced to a mere dockyard boom. To them a chip of it was as a piece of the Cross" (1433–1434). See also Edwin M. Yoder Jr., "Melville's *Billy Budd* and the Trials of Captain Vere," *St. Louis University Law Journal* 45, no. 4 (2001): 1119.

21. Solove, "Failure of the Word," 2456.

22. Ibid., 2447. See Charles Reich, "The Tragedy of Justice in *Billy Budd*," in *Twentieth Century Interpretations of* Billy Budd, ed. Howard P. Vincent (Upper Saddle River, N.J.: Prentice-Hall, 1971), 56; Steven Wilf, "The First Republican Revival: Virtue, Judging, and Rhetoric in the Early Republic," *Connecticut Law Review* 32, no. 5 (2000): 1675; Ilana Pardes, *Melville's Bibles* (Berkeley: University of California Press, 2008), 120.

23. Cover, *Justice Accused*, 6.

24. Lawrence Friedman, "Law, Force, and Resistance to Disorder in Herman Melville's *Billy Budd*," *Thomas Jefferson Law Review* 33, no. 1 (2010): 61–80; Robert H. Weisberg, *The Failure of the Word: The Protagonist as Lawyer in Modern Fiction* (New Haven: Yale University Press, 1984).

25. Richard Posner, *Law and Literature: A Misunderstood Relation* (Cambridge: Harvard University Press, 1988), 161; emphasis in original.

26. For a class-based analysis of this decision, see Susan L. Mizruchi, *The Science of Sacrifice: American Literature and Modern Social Theory* (Princeton: Princeton University Press, 1998), 144.

27. Carl Schmitt, *Political Theology: Four Chapters on the Concept of Sovereignty*, trans. George Schwab (Cambridge: MIT Press, 1985), 5.

28. Ibid., 6.

29. The events following the captain's verdict, including Billy Budd's "benediction," make good Captain Vere's decision on the exception. According to Schmitt, the constitution may prescribe that the decision on the exception will be made by the sovereign and that the sovereign will decide the exception. As I have argued elsewhere, however, "even when a decision is legally prescribed in this way, the law does not designate who is capable of taking the decision. Therefore, he who purports to be sovereign must show himself to be sovereign in deciding. Indeed, he proves himself to be sovereign by showing himself to be competent. When the exception is decided as such, he who has decided it is revealed as the sovereign." Jennifer L. Culbert, *Dead Certainty: The Death Penalty and the Problem of Judgment* (Stanford: Stanford University Press, 2008), 148. In other words, despite his official position of authority on board the *Bellipotent*, it is possible that Captain Vere is not competent to be sovereign.

30. Loosemore, "Revolution, Counterrevolution, and Natural Law," 102. Both Solove and Friedman observe the present-day resonances of this argument.

31. Michael Paul Rogin, *Subversive Genealogy: The Politics and Art of Herman Melville* (New York: Knopf, 1983), 315. See Giorgio Agamben, *Homo Sacer: Sovereign Power and Bare Life*, trans. Daniel Heller-Roazen (Stanford: Stanford University Press, 1998). Anticipating perhaps Agamben's figure of bare life, Rogin argues, "Authority repossessed instinct on the *Bellipotent*. Uniforms and rituals naturalized man-made institutions, placing them beyond human reach. Men regained their location in nature. But this was not the rights-granting nature of the Declaration of Independence, but a nature in which they were assimilated to beasts" (*Subversive Genealogy*, 315). William Spanos may thus follow in Rogin's footsteps when Spanos claims that in Melville's tale Billy Budd is reduced to "bare life" (*The Exceptional State*, 118–121).

32. Martha Merrill Umphrey, "Law's Bonds: Eros and Identification in *Billy Budd*," *American Imago* 64, no. 3 (2007): 413–431.

33. Sigmund Freud, *Civilization and Its Discontents* (1930), trans. David McLintock (London: Penguin, 2002).

34. Umphrey, "Law's Bonds," 416.

35. See, for example, Lynne Henderson, "The Dialogue of Heart and Head,"

Cardozo Law Review 10, nos. 1–2 (1988): 123–148; Julius G. Getman, "Colloquy: Human Voices in Legal Discourse," *Texas Law Review* 66, no. 3 (1988): 577–588.

36. Umphrey, "Law's Bonds," 417. Jason Frank explicitly states he is not persuaded by readings of *Billy Budd* that explain Claggart's actions by reference to his repressed homosexual desires, but I find interesting parallels between Umphrey's larger argument about the repression of eros in *Billy Budd* and the role of eros in the efficacy of law and Frank's claim that "an assemblage of mesmeric agency and sensory soft compulsion . . . constitutes and sustains the novel's relations of authority." See Frank, "The Lyre of Orpheus."

37. Umphrey, "Law's Bonds," 427.

38. Ibid., 426–427.

39. Love, though, turns out to be as incapable of being separated from aggression in law as aggression is from love. And so love also does violence in this scene. Specifically, it "does violence to the violence that represses it" (ibid., 427). To demonstrate this point, Umphrey draws attention to the effect of Billy Budd's final words on Captain Vere (ibid., 426). The captain stands "erectly rigid as a musket in the ship-armorer's rack," a stance that is attributed in the narrative to either "stoic self-control or a sort of momentary paralysis induced by emotional shock" (*Billy Budd,* 1426–1427). This description leaves Captain Vere's feelings ambiguous. Nevertheless, the fact that the captain *has* feelings, feelings that make him go stiff, can no longer be denied. In his speech to the drumhead court, Captain Vere acknowledges he has feelings for Billy Budd, but he constantly insists that these feelings be put aside or "ruled out" (*Billy Budd,* 1415). To the extent that Billy Budd's final words of love violently expose the limits of Captain Vere's ability to rule out his feelings and his identification with the pitiless will that empowers martial law, it turns out that Billy Budd is indeed a "fighting peacemaker" (*Billy Budd,* 1357).

40. The repression may be particularly difficult to work through, as it may be compounded in the text. Umphrey reads the narrator's decorous refusal to describe the meeting when Captain Vere tells Billy Budd his fate not only as a gesture intended to protect Captain Vere's fantasy of a pitiless law—a fantasy he shares with the drumhead court when he explains that the only source of law they may consider is an arbitrary and unfeeling code—but also as a repression of the storyteller's own anxiety about the erotic dimensions of law (Umphrey, "Law's Bonds," 425).

41. See, e.g., Kingsley Widmer, "The Perplexed Myths of Melville: *Billy Budd,*" *Novel* 2, no. 1 (1968): 25–35.

42. For a suggestive exception to this rule, see Norman Holmes Pearson, "*Billy Budd:* The King's Yarn," *American Quarterly* 3, no. 2 (1951): 100.

43. Jean-Luc Nancy, "Shattered Love," trans. Lisa Garbus and Simona Sawhney, in Nancy, *The Inoperative Community,* ed. Peter Connor (Minneapolis: University of Minnesota Press, 1991), 97.

44. Ibid., 92.

45. Ibid., 98.

46. Barbara Johnson, "Melville's Fist: The Execution of *Billy Budd*," in Johnson, *The Critical Difference: Essays in the Contemporary Rhetoric of Reading* (Baltimore: Johns Hopkins University Press, 1980), 83.

47. Ibid. A chiasmus is defined in the OED Online as "a grammatical figure by which the order of words in one of two parallel clauses is inverted in the other."

48. Johnson, "Melville's Fist," 83.

49. Ibid., 108.

50. Ibid., 106.

51. Ibid.; emphases in original.

52. Ibid., 108.

53. Ibid.

54. Nancy, "Shattered Love," 103.

55. Ibid., 98.

56. Certainly Captain Graveling does not expect the crew of his ship to remain as they have become after Billy Budd is taken (*Billy Budd*, 1357).

57. Nancy, "Shattered Love," 97.

58. This description resonates with Walter Benjamin's concept of divine violence. See Walter Benjamin, "Critique of Violence," in Benjamin, *Reflections: Essays, Aphorisms, Autobiographical Writings*, trans. Edmund Jephcott, ed. Peter Demetz (1978; repr., New York: Schocken Books, 1986).

59. On double negatives in Melville's text, see Sharon Cameron, "'Lines of Stones': The Unpersonified Impersonal in Melville's *Billy Budd*," in Cameron, *Impersonality: Seven Essays* (Chicago: University of Chicago Press, 2007). I am grateful to Jason Frank for bringing this discussion to my attention.

60. W. H. Auden, "Law Like Love," in Auden, *Collected Poems*, ed. Edward Mendelson (1976; repr., New York: Vintage International, 1991), 262–264.

61. Ibid., 262–263.

62. Ibid.

63. Ibid.

64. Ibid., 263.

65. Linda Ross Meyer, "Law Like Love?" *Law and Literature* 18, no. 3 (2006): 441. In this regard, she claims, the poem is like Nietzsche's short but devastating history of metaphysics in *Twilight of the Idols*. See Friedrich Nietzsche, *Twilight of the Idols* (1889), trans. R. J. Hollingdale (London: Penguin, 1968).

66. Auden, "Law Like Love," 263.

67. On passive nihilism, see Friedrich Nietzsche, *The Will to Power* (1888), trans. Walter Kaufmann and R. J. Hollingdale (New York: Random House, 1967),

§22. On active nihilism see Friedrich Nietzsche, *The Gay Science* (1882), trans. Walter Kaufmann (New York: Vintage, 1974), §347.

68. Auden, "Law Like Love," 263. The following reflections are suggestive also for a reading of another of Herman Melville's short works, "Bartleby, the Scrivener" (1853). See Herman Melville, "Bartleby, the Scrivener: A Story of Wall-Street," in Melville, *The Happy Failure: Stories* (New York: HarperCollins, 2009), 1–49.

69. Auden, "Law Like Love," 264.

70. Ibid., 263.

71. Ibid.

72. Ibid.

73. Meyer, "Law Like Love?" 443.

74. Auden, "Law Like Love," 264.

75. Ibid.

76. Arendt, *On Revolution,* 84. Arendt argues here that *Billy Budd* is a story about the danger of absolutes in the human world. According to Arendt, Billy Budd embodies absolute good and John Claggart represents absolute evil, so when Budd strikes Claggart dead, one absolute is opposed to and negates the other. As human beings are neither absolutely good nor absolutely evil, however, such matters are beyond their ken. Thus, no matter how good and innocent Budd may truly be, all that is apparent to his fellow men is that he has killed a man and poses a threat to the precarious order of human society. Therefore, Budd must be put to death. Arendt claims, "The tragedy is that the law is made for men, and neither for angels nor for devils"; she concludes, "The absolute . . . spells doom to everyone when it is introduced into the political realm" (ibid.).

77. Johnson, "Melville's Fist," 107.

78. Ibid., 108.

79. Christoph Menke analyzes this tragedy and proposes that in response to the question that follows—Is there *another* way of enacting law?—we seek to judge differently. He calls this way of judging "judging without triggering fate." See Christoph Menke, "Law and Violence," *Law and Literature* 22, no. 1 (Spring 2010): 1–17.

80. Nancy, "Shattered Love," 94.

81. Ibid., 95.

Acknowledgments

I owe many thanks to this volume's contributors for writing such provocative and compelling essays on Melville's political thought. I have learned from all of them and also from the many rewarding exchanges we have had over the past two years. A special thanks to Lawrie Balfour and George Shulman for their insightful feedback, encouragement, and friendship. Stephen M. Wrinn, the director of the University Press of Kentucky, has been supportive from the very beginning, and I appreciate the opportunity he has given me to translate my long-standing interest in Melville into something substantial. Those of us working in the fields of American political thought and politics and literature owe much to Steve and Patrick Deneen for bringing this series, Political Companions to Great American Authors, into the world.

Many chapters of this book were originally presented to audiences at the annual meetings of the American Political Science Association and Western Political Science Association. I think I can speak on the contributors' behalf in saying that we are grateful for the thoughtful feedback we received on these occasions. I would also personally like to thank participants in Cornell's American Studies Seminar, Northwestern's Center for Global Culture and Communication, the Democratic Vistas study group, and Duke's Political Theory Workshop for their helpful comments, questions, and suggestions. Thanks also to Kevin Duong for his terrific comments and keen editorial assistance.

Versions of two chapters have already appeared in print. I would like to thank the *Review of Politics* for permission to republish Susan McWilliams's "Ahab, American," and the *Quinnipiac Law Review* for permission to republish Jennifer L. Culbert's "Melville's Law." Where possible, because of quality and accessibility, we have referred to the Library of America editions of Melville's work rather than the Northwestern-Newberry editions.

I first read Melville in the context of a remarkable undergraduate course taught by Jack Schaar at the University of California, Santa Cruz.

Jack's deeply resonant understanding of American politics, and his appreciation of literature's importance to political theory, left a lasting imprint on me and many others fortunate enough to be his students. Jack passed away in December 2011. This book is dedicated to him.

Selected Bibliography

Works by Melville

Battle-Pieces and Aspects of the War. 1866. Reprint, New York: Da Capo Press, 1995.

Billy Budd, Sailor (An Inside Narrative). Edited by Harrison Hayford and Merton M. Sealts Jr. Chicago: University of Chicago Press, 1962.

Clarel: A Poem and Pilgrimage in the Holy Land. Edited by Harrison Hayford, Hershel Parker, and G. Thomas Tanselle. Evanston and Chicago: Northwestern University Press and the Newberry Library, 1991.

The Confidence-Man: His Masquerade. Edited by Harrison Hayford, Hershel Parker, and G. Thomas Tanselle. Evanston and Chicago: Northwestern University Press and the Newberry Library, 1984.

Correspondence. Edited by Lynn Horth. Evanston and Chicago: Northwestern University Press and the Newberry Library, 1993.

Israel Potter: His Fifty Years of Exile. Edited by Harrison Hayford, Hershel Parker, and G. Thomas Tanselle. Evanston and Chicago: Northwestern University Press and the Newberry Library, 1982.

Journals. Edited by Howard C. Horsford and Lynn Horth. Evanston and Chicago: Northwestern University Press and the Newberry Library, 1989.

Mardi: And a Voyage Thither. Edited by Harrison Hayford, Hershel Parker, and G. Thomas Tanselle. Evanston and Chicago: Northwestern University Press and the Newberry Library, 1970.

Moby-Dick. New York: Library of America, 1991.

Moby Dick; or, The Whale. Edited by Harrison Hayford, Hershel Parker, and G. Thomas Tanselle. Evanston and Chicago: Northwestern University Press and the Newberry Library, 1970.

Omoo: A Narrative of Adventures in the South Seas. Edited by Harrison Hayford, Hershel Parker, and G. Thomas Tanselle. Evanston and Chicago: Northwestern University Press and the Newberry Library, 1968.

"The Paradise of Bachelors and the Tartarus of Maids." In *Billy Budd and Other Stories.* New York: Penguin, 1986, 259–286.

The Piazza Tales and Other Prose Pieces, 1839–1860. Edited by Harrison Hayford, Alma A. MacDougall, and G. Thomas Tanselle. Evanston and Chicago: Northwestern University Press and the Newberry Library, 1987.

Pierre, Israel Potter, The Piazza Tales, The Confidence-Man, Uncollected Prose,

Billy Budd. New York: Library of America, 1984.

Pierre; or, The Ambiguities. Edited by Harrison Hayford, Hershel Parker, and G. Thomas Tanselle. Evanston and Chicago: Northwestern University Press and the Newberry Library, 1987.

Redburn: His First Voyage, Being the Sailor-Boy Confessions and Reminiscences of the Son-of-a-Gentleman, in the Merchant Service. Edited by Harrison Hayford, Hershel Parker, and G. Thomas Tanselle. Evanston and Chicago: Northwestern University Press and the Newberry Library, 1969.

Redburn, White-Jacket, Moby-Dick. New York: Library of America, 1983.

Selected Poems of Herman Melville: A Reader's Edition. Edited by Robert Penn Warren. Boston: David R. Godine, 2004.

Typee: A Peep at Polynesian Life. Edited by Harrison Hayford, Hershel Parker, and G. Thomas Tanselle. Evanston and Chicago: Northwestern University Press and the Newberry Library, 1968.

Typee, Omoo, Mardi. New York: Library of America, 1982.

White-Jacket; or, The World in a Man-of-War. Edited by Harrison Hayford, Hershel Parker, and G. Thomas Tanselle. Evanston and Chicago: Northwestern University Press and the Newberry Library, 1970.

Biographies of Melville

Arvin, Newton. *Herman Melville.* 1950. Reprint, Westport, Conn.: Greenwood, 1972.

Delbanco, Andrew. *Melville: His World and Work.* New York: Knopf, 2005.

Garner, Stanton. *The Civil War World of Herman Melville.* Lawrence: University Press of Kansas, 1993.

Leyda, Jay, ed. *The Melville Log: A Documentary Life of Herman Melville, 1819–1891.* 2 vols. 1951. Reprint, New York: Gordian Press, 1969.

Mumford, Lewis. *Herman Melville.* New York: Harcourt, Brace, 1929.

Parker, Hershel. *Herman Melville: A Biography,* vol. 1, *1819–1851.* Baltimore: Johns Hopkins University Press, 1996.

———. *Herman Melville: A Biography,* vol. 2, *1851–1891.* Baltimore: Johns Hopkins University Press, 2002.

Roberston-Lorant, Laurie. *Melville: A Biography.* 1996. Reprint, Amherst: University of Massachusetts Press, 1998.

Works on Melville's Politics

Adamson, Joseph. *Melville, Shame, and the Evil Eye: A Psychoanalytic Reading.* Albany: State University of New York Press, 1997.

Adler, Joyce Sparer. "*Benito Cereno:* Slavery and Violence in the Americas." In *Critical Essays on Herman Melville's* Benito Cereno, edited by Robert E. Burkholder. New York: G. K. Hall, 1992, 76–93.

———. "*Billy Budd* and Melville's Philosophy of War." *PMLA* 91, no. 2 (1976): 266–278.

———. *War in Melville's Imagination.* New York: New York University Press, 1981.

Alvis, John. "*Moby-Dick* and Melville's Quarrel with America." *Interpretation: A Journal of Political Philosophy* 23, no. 2 (1993): 223–247.

Arsi, Branka. *Passive Constitutions: 7½ Times Bartleby.* Stanford: Stanford University Press, 2007.

Barnum, Jill, Wyn Kelley, and Christopher Sten, eds. *"Whole Oceans Away": Melville and the Pacific.* Kent, Ohio: Kent State University Press, 2007.

Berthold, Dennis. "Democracy and Its Discontents." In *A Companion to Herman Melville,* edited by Wyn Kelley. New York: Blackwell, 2006, 149–164.

Bickley, Bruce R., Jr. "'Civilized Barbarity': Melville and the Dark Paradoxes of Waging Modern War." In *War and Words: Horror and Heroism in the Literature of Warfare,* edited by Sarah Munson Deats, Lagretta Tallent Lenker, and Merry G. Perry. Lanham, Md.: Lexington Books, 2004, 125–144.

Buel, Lawrence. "Melville and the Question of American Decolonization." *American Literature* 64 (1992): 215–237.

Busch, Frederick. 1973. "Thoreau and Melville as Cellmates." *Modern Fiction Studies* 23, no. 2 (1973): 239–242.

Clymer, Jeffory. "Property and Selfhood in Herman Melville's *Pierre.*" *Nineteenth-Century Literature* 61, no. 2 (2006): 171–199.

Deleuze, Gilles. "Bartleby; or, The Formula." In *Essays Clinical and Critical,* translated by Daniel W. Smith and Michael A. Greco. Minneapolis: University of Minnesota Press, 1997, 68–90.

Dimock, Wai Chee. *Empire for Liberty: Melville and the Poetics of Individualism.* Princeton: Princeton University Press, 1989.

Domnarski, William. "Law-Literature Criticism: Charting a Desirable Course with *Billy Budd.*" *Journal of Legal Education* 34, no. 4 (1984): 702–713.

Downes, Paul. "Melville's *Benito Cereno* and the Politics of Humanitarian Intervention." *South Atlantic Quarterly* 103, nos. 2/3 (2004): 465–488.

Duban, James. *Melville's Major Fiction: Politics, Theology, and Imagination.* DeKalb: Northern Illinois University Press, 1983.

Fisher, Philip. "Democratic Social Space: Whitman, Melville, and the Promise of American Transparency." *Representations* 24 (1988): 60–101.

Franklin, Bruce H. "Apparent Symbol of Despotic Command: Melville's *Benito Cereno.*" *New England Quarterly* 34, no. 4 (1961): 462–477.

Fredricks, Nancy. *Melville's Art of Democracy.* Athens: University of Georgia Press, 1995.

Friedman, Lawrence. "Law, Force, and Resistance to Disorder in Herman Melville's *Billy Budd.*" *Thomas Jefferson Law Review* 33, no. 1 (2010): 61–80.

Heimert, Alan. "*Moby-Dick* and American Political Symbolism." *American Quarterly* 15, no. 4 (1963): 498–534.

Herbert, Walter T. *Marquesan Encounter: Melville and the Meaning of Civilization* (Cambridge: Harvard University Press, 1980).

Hurtgen, James R. "Melville: Billy Budd and the Context of Political Rule." In *The Artist and Political Vision,* edited by Benjamin Barber. New Brunswick, N.J.: Transaction, 1983, 245–265.

James, C. L. R. *Mariners, Renegades and Castaways: The Story of Herman Melville and the World We Live In.* 1953. Reprint, Hanover, N.H.: Dartmouth College Press, 2001.

Jay, Gregory S. *America the Scrivener: Deconstruction and the Subject of Literary History.* Ithaca: Cornell University Press, 1990.

Johnson, Barbara. "Melville's Fist: The Execution of *Billy Budd.*" In Johnson, *The Critical Difference: Essays in the Contemporary Rhetoric of Reading.* Baltimore: Johns Hopkins University Press, 1980, 79–109.

Kaplan, Amy. "Transnational Melville." *Leviathan: A Journal of Melville Studies* 12, no. 1 (2010): 42–52.

Karcher, Carolyn L. *Shadow over the Promised Land: Slavery, Race, and Violence in Melville's America.* Baton Rouge: Louisiana State University Press, 1980.

Kavanagh, James. "That Hive of Subtlety: *Benito Cereno* and the Liberal Hero." In *Ideology and Classic American Literature,* edited by Sacvan Bercovitch and Myra Jehlen. Cambridge: Cambridge University Press, 1986, 352–383.

Keyssar, Alexander. *Melville's* Israel Potter: *Reflections on the American Dream.* Cambridge: Harvard University Press, 1969.

Kuebrich, David. "Melville's Doctrine of Assumptions: The Hidden Ideology of Capitalist Production in 'Bartleby.'" *New England Quarterly* 69, no. 3 (1996): 381–405.

Lawrence, D. H. *Studies in Classic American Literature.* 1923. Reprint, New York: Penguin, 1990.

Lee, Maurice S. "Melville's Subversive Political Philosophy: *Benito Cereno* and the Fate of Speech." *American Literature* 72, no. 3 (2000): 495–519.

Levine, Robert S., ed. *The Cambridge Companion to Herman Melville.* Cambridge: Cambridge University Press, 1998.

Levine, Robert S., and Samuel Otter, eds. *Frederick Douglass and Herman Melville: Essays in Relation.* Chapel Hill: University of North Carolina Press, 2008.

Maguire, Ian. "'Who Ain't a Slave?' *Moby-Dick* and the Ideology of Free Labor." *Journal of American Studies* 37, no. 2 (2003): 287–305.

Markels, Julian. *Melville and the Politics of Identity: From* King Lear *to* Moby-Dick. Champaign: University of Illinois Press, 1993.

Matterson, Stephen. "Indian-Hating in *The Confidence Man.*" *Arizona Quarterly* 52 (1996): 21–36.

Matthiessen, F. O. *American Renaissance: Art and Expression in the Age of Emerson and Whitman.* New York: Oxford University Press, 1941.

McBride, James. "Revisiting a Seminal Text of the Law & Literature Movement: A Girardian Reading of Herman Melville's *Billy Budd, Sailor.*" *Margins* 3, no. 2 (2003): 285–332.

McLoughlin, Michael. *Dead Letters to the New World: Melville, Emerson and American Transcendentalism.* New York: Routledge, 2003.

McWilliams, Wilson Carey. "Herman Melville: The Pilgrim." In McWilliams, *The Idea of Fraternity in America.* Berkeley: University of California Press, 1973, 328–371.

Milder, Robert. *Exiled Royalties: Melville and the Life We Imagine.* New York: Oxford University Press, 2006.

Morrison, Toni. "Unspeakable Things Unspoken: The Afro-American Presence in American Literature." *Michigan Quarterly Review* 28, no. 1 (1989): 1–34.

Nixon, Nicola. "Compromising Politics and Herman Melville's *Pierre.*" *American Literature* 69, no. 4 (1997): 719–741.

Olson, Charles. *Call Me Ishmael!* 1947. Reprint, Baltimore: Johns Hopkins University Press, 1997.

Otter, Samuel. *Melville's Anatomies: Bodies, Discourse, and Ideology in Antebellum America.* Berkeley: University of California Press, 1999.

Parker, Hershel. "Melville's Satire of Emerson and Thoreau: An Evaluation of the Evidence." *American Transcendental Quarterly* 7, no. 2 (1970): 61–67.

———, ed. *The Recognition of Herman Melville: Selected Criticism since 1846.* Ann Arbor: University of Michigan Press, 1967.

Pearson, Norman Holmes. "*Billy Budd:* The King's Yarn." *American Quarterly* 3, no. 2 (1951): 99–114.

Pease, Donald E. "*Moby Dick* and the Cold War." In *The American Renaissance Reconsidered,* edited by Walter Benn Michaels and Donald E. Pease. Baltimore: Johns Hopkins University Press, 1985, 113–155.

Reich, Charles. "The Tragedy of Justice in *Billy Budd.*" In *Twentieth-Century Interpretations of* Billy Budd, edited by Howard P. Vincent. Upper Saddle River, N.J.: Prentice-Hall, 1971, 56–66.

Reynolds, David. *Beneath the American Renaissance: The Subversive Imagination in the Age of Emerson and Melville.* New York: Knopf, 1988.

Rogin, Michael Paul. *Subversive Genealogy: The Politics and Art of Herman Melville.* New York: Knopf, 1983.

Rowe, John Carlos. "Melville's *Typee:* U.S. Imperialism at Home and Abroad." In Rowe, *Literary Culture and U.S. Imperialism: From the Revolution to World War II.* New York: Oxford University Press, 2000, 77–96.

Sanborn, Geoffrey. *The Sign of the Cannibal: Melville and the Making of a Postcolonial Reader.* Durham: Duke University Press, 1998.

Schaar, John "The Uses of Literature for the Study of Politics: The Case of Melville's *Benito Cereno.*" In Schaar, *Legitimacy in the Modern State.* New Brunswick, N.J.: Transaction, 1981, 53–88.

Scorza, Thomas J. *In the Time before Steamships:* Billy Budd, *the Limits of Politics, and Modernity.* DeKalb: Northern Illinois University Press, 1979.

Sedgwick, William Ellery. *Herman Melville: The Tragedy of Mind.* Cambridge: Harvard University Press, 1945.

Smith, Henry Nash. *Democracy and the Novel: Popular Resistance to Classic American Writers.* New York: Oxford University Press, 1978.

Solove, Daniel J. "Failure of the Word: Melville's *Billy Budd* and Security in Times of Crisis." *Cardozo Law Review* 26, no. 6 (2005): 2443–2470.

Spanos, William V. *The Errant Art of* Moby-Dick: *The Canon, the Cold War, and the Struggle for American Studies.* Durham: Duke University Press, 1995.

———. *The Exceptionalist State and the State of Exception: Herman Melville's* Billy Budd, Sailor. Baltimore: Johns Hopkins University Press, 2011.

———. *Herman Melville and the American Calling: The Fiction after* Moby-Dick, *1851–1857.* Albany: State University of New York Press, 2008.

Stuckey, Sterling, and Joshua Leslie. "The Death of Benito Cereno: A Reading of Herman Melville on Slavery." In Stuckey, *Going through the Storm: The Influence of African American Art in History.* New York: Oxford University Press, 1994, 153–70.

Sundquist, Eric J. "*Benito Cereno* and New World Slavery." In *Reconstructing American Literary History*, edited by Sacvan Bercovitch. Cambridge: Harvard University Press, 1986, 93–122.

Thomas, Brook. "*Billy Budd* and the Untold Story of the Law." *Cardozo Studies in Law and Literature* 1, no. 1 (1989): 49–69.

Umphrey, Martha Merrill. "Law's Bonds: Eros and Identification in *Billy Budd.*" *American Imago* 64, no. 3 (2007): 413–431.

Wallace, Robert K. "*Billy Budd* and the Haymarket Hangings." *American Literature* 47, no. 1 (1975): 108–113.

Warner, Michael. "What Like a Bullet Can Undeceive?" *Public Culture* 15, no. 1 (2003): 41–54.

Watson, Grant E. L. "Melville's Testament of Acceptance." *New England Quarterly* 6, no. 2 (1933): 319–327.

Watters, R. E. "Melville's 'Isolatoes.'" *PMLA* 60, no. 4 (1945): 1138–1148.

———. "Melville's 'Sociality.'" *American Literature* 17, no. 1 (1945): 33–49.

Weisberg, Richard. "Accepting the Inside Narrator's Challenge: *Billy Budd* and the 'Legalistic' Reader." *Cardozo Studies in Law and Literature* 1, no. 1 (1989): 27–48.

Withim, Phil. "*Billy Budd:* Testament of Resistance." *Modern Language Quarterly* 20, no. 2 (1959): 115–127.

Yoder, Edwin M., Jr. "Melville's *Billy Budd* and the Trials of Captain Vere." *St. Louis University Law Journal* 45, no. 4 (2001): 1109–1122.

Zagarell, Sandra A. "Re-envisioning America: Melville's *Benito Cereno.*" *ESQ: A Journal of the American Renaissance* 30 (1984): 245–259.

Zoellner, Robert. *The Salt-Sea Mastodon: A Reading of* Moby-Dick. Berkeley: University of California Press, 1973.

Zuckert, Catherine H. "Leadership—Natural and Conventional—in Melville's *Benito Cereno.*" *Interpretation* 26, no. 2 (1999): 239–255.

Contributors

Kevin Attell is an assistant professor of English at Cornell University. He has translated several works by the Italian political philosopher Giorgio Agamben, including *The Open: Man and Animal* (Stanford University Press, 2004) and *State of Exception* (University of Chicago Press, 2005). He is currently completing a book titled *Agamben and Deconstruction*.

Lawrie Balfour is a professor of politics at the University of Virginia. She is the author of *Democracy's Reconstruction: Thinking Politically with W. E. B. Du Bois* (Oxford University Press, 2011), *The Evidence of Things Not Said: James Baldwin and the Promise of American Democracy* (Cornell University Press, 2001), and several essays on race and democracy. Currently, she is working on a book examining reparations for slavery and Jim Crow.

Roger Berkowitz is an associate professor of political studies and human rights at Bard College, where he also directs the Hannah Arendt Center for Politics and Humanities. He is the author of *The Gift of Science: Leibniz and the Modern Legal Tradition*, an account of how the rise of science has led to the divorce of law and justice (Harvard University Press, 2005), and coeditor of *Thinking in Dark Times: Hannah Arendt on Ethics and Politics* (Fordham University Press, 2010) and *The Intellectual Origins of the Global Financial Crisis* (Fordham University Press, 2012).

Jennifer L. Culbert is an associate professor of political science at Johns Hopkins University. She is the author of *Dead Certainty: The Death Penalty and the Problem of Judgment* (Stanford University Press, 2007) and coeditor of *States of Violence: War, Capital Punishment, and Letting Die* (Cambridge University Press, 2009). She is currently completing a project on the jurisprudence of Hannah Arendt.

Thomas Dumm is the William H. Hastie, Class of '25 Professor of Political Ethics at Amherst College. He is the author of several books, including *A Politics of the Ordinary* (New York University Press, 1999) and *Loneliness* *as a Way of Life* (Harvard University Press, 2008). He is also coeditor of *The Rhetorical Republic: Governing Representations in American Politics* (University of Massachusetts Press, 1993) and author of many articles on American political thought and culture. He is currently completing a book on the politics of home entitled *Coming Home* (Harvard University Press, forthcoming).

Kennan Ferguson teaches political theory at the University of Wisconsin, Milwaukee. He is the author of *All in the Family: On Community and Incommensurability* (Duke University Press, 2012), *William James: Politics in the Pluriverse* (Rowman and Littlefield, 2007), and *The Politics of Judgment: Aesthetics, Identity, and Political Theory* (Lexington Books, 1999).

Jason Frank is an associate professor of government at Cornell University. He is the author of *Constituent Moments: Enacting the People in Postrevolutionary America* (Duke University Press, 2010), and *Publius and Political Imagination* (Rowman and Littlefield, forthcoming). He has published widely on democratic theory and American political thought and is currently working on a project titled *The Democratic Sublime: Political Theory and Aesthetics in the Age of Revolution*.

Roger W. Hecht is an assistant professor of English at SUNY College at Oneonta, where he is director of the International James Fenimore Cooper Conference and Seminar. He is the editor of *The Erie Canal Reader: 1790–1950* (Syracuse University Press, 2004) and the author of articles on Melville, Harriet Beecher Stowe, John Burroughs, and the farmer-poets of the Anti-Rent movement, as well as a poetry collection, *Talking Pictures* (Cervena Barva Press, 2012). He is working on a book about the literary products of the Anti-Rent War.

Michael Jonik is a lecturer at the University of Sussex in the School of English and American Studies. His research and teaching examine seventeenth- through nineteenth-century American and transatlantic literary and intellectual history in relationship to the history of science, politics, religious studies, and philosophy. He has recently published essays on Melville in the *Oxford Literary Review* and *Leviathan* and is completing two books: *A Natural History of the Mind: Science, Form, and Perception* *from Cotton Mather to William James* and *Melville's Uncemented Stones: Character, Impersonality, and the Politics of Singularity*.

Shannon L. Mariotti is an associate professor of political science at Southwestern University. She is the author of *Thoreau's Democratic Withdrawal: Alienation, Participation, and Modernity* (University of Wisconsin Press, 2010) and articles on Thoreau, Emerson, Du Bois, and Adorno in journals such as *Political Theory* and *TELOS*. She is currently writing a book analyzing Theodor Adorno's writings on political culture in the United States titled *Adorno and Democracy in America*.

Susan McWilliams is an associate professor of politics at Pomona College. She has published widely on American political thought and culture, and she is currently working on a book that explores images of travel in the history of Western political thought.

Sophia Mihic is an associate professor of political science at Northeastern Illinois University. She has published works on feminist theory, the philosophy of social science, and the writings of Dorothy Parker.

George Shulman is a professor at New York University's Gallatin School of Individualized Study, where he teaches courses in political theory and American studies. He is the author of *Radicalism and Reverence: Gerrard Winstanley and the English Revolution* (University of California Press, 1989) and *American Prophecy: Race and Redemption in American Political Culture* (University of Minnesota Press, 2008), which recently won the American Political Science Association's David Easton Award. He has published widely on politics and American literature.

Tracy B. Strong is a professor of political science at the University of California, San Diego. He is the author of several books, including *Friedrich Nietzsche and the Politics of Transfiguration* (University of California, 1975), *The Idea of Political Theory: Reflections on the Self in Political Time and Space* (University of Notre Dame Press, 1990), *Jean-Jacques Rousseau and the Politics of the Ordinary* (Sage, 1994), and *Politics without Vision: Thinking without a Banister in the Twentieth Century* (University of Chicago Press, 2012).

Index

Political Companions to Great American Authors

Series Editor
Patrick J. Deneen, University of Notre Dame

Books in the Series

A Political Companion to Saul Bellow
Edited by Gloria L. Cronin and Lee Trepanier

A Political Companion to Herman Melville
Edited by Jason Frank

A Political Companion to Walker Percy
Edited by Peter Augustine Lawler and Brian A. Smith

A Political Companion to Ralph Waldo Emerson
Edited by Alan M. Levine and Daniel S. Malachuk

A Political Companion to Walt Whitman
Edited by John E. Seery

A Political Companion to Henry Adams
Edited by Natalie Fuehrer Taylor

A Political Companion to Henry David Thoreau
Edited by Jack Turner

A Political Companion to John Steinbeck
Edited by Cyrus Ernesto Zirakzadeh and Simon Stow

CPSIA information can be obtained at www.ICGtesting.com
Printed in the USA
BVOW07*1820091113

335553BV00001B/1/P